D1525340

Mark H. McCormack's
EBEL
World of Professional
Golf 1987

Mark H. McCormack's
EBEL
World of Professional
Golf 1987

Photographs by Lawrence Levy

William Morrow and Company, Inc.
New York   1987

Library of Congress ISSN: 0891-9909
ISBN: 0–688–07027–2

Printed in the United States of America

First U.S. Edition

1 2 3 4 5 6 7 8 9 10

Contents

1.   The Year In Retrospect

It is obvious that American golf is no longer number one. It seems to me that those who run the United States PGA Tour are not concerned, but well they should be, because the biggest problem is that our players are complacent. They do not care enough to become champions.

Fred Couples was an inadvertent spokesman for his generation when, at the Western Open, he said he would quit for the year if he won.

Can you imagine, around 1957, Arnold Palmer saying he would quit because he didn't *need* to work beyond August? If Arnold had, he might *need* to work today and so might all professional golfers, because the golf boom could have fizzled at the start.

Twenty years ago, while writing my first *World of Professional Golf* annual, I noted, "The danger that youngsters in alligator shoes may begin to behave as if they had a *right* to make $40,000 a year is a matter that may come to plague U.S. golf. I do not think prosperity has much helped the calibre of U.S. golf. The primary benefit I see in the big money on the U.S. tour is that it is certain to enhance the international aspect of the sport. For 60 years golf was played around the world, but there was no such thing as world golf. In the past decade that has changed, in large part because of the money to be made in the United States."

Golf became an international game of significant proportions, but somewhere along the way the Americans got passed. There are hard numbers to back up my contention. Sony Corporation is sponsoring a worldwide ranking system, sanctioned by the Royal and Ancient Golf Club of St. Andrews. The Sony Ranking is based on a rolling three-year average, and is a computerized refinement of a system which I began publishing in these annuals in 1968. According to Sony, the top four players in the world are foreigners; in 1968, there was one more foreigner in the leading 10, but the Americans were firmly on top. A comparison:

1968 McCormack Ranking	*1987 Sony Ranking*
1. Jack Nicklaus, U.S.	1. Greg Norman, Australia
2. Arnold Palmer, U.S.	2. Bernhard Langer, W. Germany
3. Billy Casper, U.S.	3. Seve Ballesteros, Spain
4. Gary Player, South Africa	4. Tsuneyuki Nakajima, Japan
5. Bob Charles, New Zealand	5. Andy Bean, U.S.
6. Julius Boros, U.S.	6. Bob Tway, U.S.
7. Neil Coles, Britain	7. Hal Sutton, U.S.
8. Peter Thomson, Australia	8. Curtis Strange, U.S.
9. Frank Beard, U.S.	9. Payne Stewart, U.S.
10. Kel Nagle, Australia	10. Mark O'Meara, U.S.

(The complete 1987 Sony Ranking may be found in the appendixes of this annual.)

Palmer, I think, put his finger on why American golf has declined. The American tour, he says, makes it too easy for golfers to earn a living. No longer do they play to win. They play to get a good paycheck.

Several other veterans have been quoted on this, including Jack Nicklaus and Raymond Floyd, both of whom scored major victories in 1986 despite being in their 40s.

Floyd blames the PGA Tour's all-exempt policy in which 125 players have free rides, versus an exempt top-60 in past years, with weekly qualifying to fill the other spots in tournaments. Nicklaus agreed, saying, "I don't think American players are very hungry. They don't have to scrape and fight the way they used to, but the foreign players still do."

Nowadays on the American tour when you ask golfers, "How did you do last week at Greensboro?" they answer, "I finished fifth" as if that was good, something to be proud of. After all, a fifth-place payday might be worth $20,000 at a tour stop like Greensboro.

In the not-so-distant "old days" the great champions cared more about winning and treated the prize money as secondary. Nicklaus says, "You will always have a certain number of golfers who are not going to settle for just being good. We were playing against the history of the game rather than trying to fill our pockets by July and go fishing."

I think foreign golfers have that championship mentality. They are a hardy bunch, as they must be to cope with the various time zones and the strange foods, courses and officials found in their travels in Britain, Europe, Africa, the Far East, Australia and the United States.

Seve Ballesteros helped to provide the confidence that they could win—in the major championships and against Americans on their home ground. Bernhard Langer and Sandy Lyle have also won major events and on the PGA Tour. The last Ryder Cup Matches and the 1986 British Open demonstrated the depth of European talent, which has been further strengthened in the past year by the emerging Swedes.

The best example at present is Greg Norman, who developed his game on his native Australian tour then on the European circuit and for the past year has played better than anyone else on earth. Not to be overlooked is Tsuneyuki (Tommy) Nakajima. He has won 13 tournaments in Japan over the past two years and could have won one of 1986's major titles.

In comparison to these fellows, Americans are complacent. I have a hunch that one reason is the deletion of match play from college golf schedules since the early 1970's. In match play you either win or you lose, and it's that win-lose mindset that makes golf champions. When you've lost in match play, you have no excuses. All you can say is "The other guy beat me." That's a very definitive statement and, to a true competitor, a very painful one.

Look at how college stroke-play tournaments are scored, from the smallest invitationals up to the NCAA Championship. Each team has five players, they knock out the worst score, and the team with the lowest aggregate wins. Coaches have done all they can to diminish the importance of individual titles. They constantly preach "team" and know that having four players in the top 20 or 25 will win the team title, regardless of who the medalist—the real winner in my view—might be. The players carry this philosophy of aiming for top-20 finishes on to the PGA Tour.

Some of the complacency stems from the cushy lifestyle we give our players. They sometimes care more about being comfortable and making a good living from their sport than about winning. (I've been accused of being partly responsible for the increased earnings. True enough. But I'm not responsible for them not wanting to be champions. I have a fairly comfortable life myself, but I still want to be number one at what I do.)

Much of the blame must be attributed to the equalizing policies of the PGA Tour, which is run by the players. Five are legitimate superstars, 15 are would-be superstars, and most of the rest are players who will never make it. But when each player has one vote, the bottom players have clout. So what do they want? They want exemptions and to make sure that 35th-place prize money is sufficient to keep them going (rather than earning a living elsewhere). Through their one-man one-vote system, these players control the exemptions and distribution of money and, not unexpectedly, they do so with considerable self-interest.

I have two problems with this system. One, it's obviously hurting American golf. Two, who said the PGA Tour was supposed to be an equal opportunity employer?

Here's what I would do to get American golf back to its winning ways. I would return to an exempt top-60 and restore weekly qualifying. And I would restructure the distribution of prize money. In a tournament with $1 million in prize money, first place would earn $500,000, second place $200,000, third place $100,000, and fourth place $50,000. I would use the remaining $150,000 to pay down another 12 places. Nobody else gets anything. That way winning would become more important and finishing 10th would be significantly less rewarding.

I'm all for giving everyone a fair shot at winning, but I'm against trying to distribute money *fairly* in a competition where victory, not *fairness*, is the whole point.

"Life is not fair, but golf is ridiculous," said Jim Murray, the *Los Angeles Times* columnist. And how Greg Norman would agree, after his 1986 performance.

Norman gave new meaning to what the British, in their passion for brevity, used to call the Impregnable Quadrilateral—the Grand Slam. Greg led all four championships into the final round and won just one, the British Open. He played himself out of another, the U.S. Open. To deny Norman the other two required one of the best rounds of Jack Nicklaus' life in the Masters and the best shot of Bob Tway's life in the PGA Championship.

It was "The Year of the Shark" nevertheless. Norman became the first golfer to earn over one million dollars in prize money in a single year—$1,146,584 to be exact—and won nine tournaments (10 if you count Australia's victory in the Dunhill Nations Cup). It was arguably the best year anyone has had since Arnold Palmer launched the modern era of professional golf.

Mark McNulty had a nine-victory year, but all except one were on the

South African circuit. Tsuneyuki (Tommy) Nakajima won seven times (all in Japan) and Seve Ballesteros won six (all in Europe) as he was limited by a PGA Tour suspension to four American events.

Norman's earnings were nearly $300,000 over the worldwide record of $860,262 set by Bernhard Langer in 1985. Not included in Norman's figure were $700 in unofficial money from a first-round loss in The International, $6,494 in pro-am winnings, $75,000 bonus for winning both the British Open and Panasonic European Open, and $80,000 bonus for placing seventh on the PGA Tour's Vantage Cup competition (in only 19 U.S. tournaments). That would give Norman a total of $1,308,078 in on-course income, not including appearance fees he receives when playing outside the United States.

His victories were in the Panasonic Las Vegas Invitational and Kemper Open in America; the British Open, Panasonic European Open and Suntory World Match Play Championship in Britain, and the Stefan Queensland Open, National Panasonic New South Wales Open, West End Jubilee South Australia Open, and National Panasonic Western Australia Open. Although the Dunhill Nations Cup was a team competition, you might also count that because Norman had the lowest 72-hole score by three strokes.

Six of Norman's victories were in succession in September and October, when he was being compared to Byron Nelson and Crocodile Dundee, the Australian hero of a popular movie of the time. Nelson won 11 in a row, and 18 for the year, in 1945—an awesome total but not inconceivable when you consider that Ben Hogan followed with 13 wins in 1946 and 11 wins in 1948, and Sam Snead won 10 in 1950. Roberto de Vicenzo is credited with over 230 victories and must have had some impressive yearly totals as well, but nearly all of his wins came in South America and many in what would be considered as club tournaments.

The best comparison in the modern era would be with the 1974 seasons of Gary Player and Johnny Miller. This was a landmark year for the PGA Tour in several respects. Deane Beman became commissioner, and purses began the spiral which saw the total tripled in 12 years. That year, Player won 10 tournaments including the Masters and British Open, one on the PGA Tour, two in Spain, three in South Africa, the Australian Open and the Brazilian Open. Miller won nine tournaments, eight in America and one in Japan, and earned $400,255 worldwide, the most ever to that point. Just as Norman lost U.S. Player of the Year honors to Tway, Miller got the nod in 1974, while Player finished a ridiculous fifth on the list.

The comparison of Norman's 1986 performance with Player's in 1974 is a good one. Each had nine unquestionable victories and one requiring an asterisk; Player's 10th was a 36-hole affair in Spain. And Gary nearly won the Grand Slam. He was virtually eliminated from the U.S. Open in the second round (he tied for eighth) after he hit out of bounds while trying to play safe. He was seventh in the PGA Championship, but I wouldn't have bet against him if he had entered the PGA with the other three titles under his belt.

Norman, a 31-year-old Queenslander, reached golf's pinnacle 10 years after becoming a professional, a decade in which he won 40 tournaments worldwide. Unlike most, who play golf from age five or six, Norman did not

GREG NORMAN'S 1986 PERFORMANCE

TOURNAMENT	POS.	SCORES					TOTAL	MONEY
Spalding	T4	71	69	71	67		278	9,875
Bob Hope	T53	68	73	72	65	72	350	1,370
Phoenix	T5	64	71	66	70		271	19,000
Pebble Beach	Cut	76	77	73			226	
Hawaiian	T39	71	71	72	70		284	2,050
Australian Masters	T8	74	71	74	72		291	4,505
Bay Hill	T38	70	73	70			213	2,150
USF&G	T27	74	72	73	67		286	3,550
TPC	T33	70	71	77	70		288	4,654
Masters	T2	70	72	68	70		280	70,400
Heritage	T2	70	68	69	70		277	33,600
Las Vegas	1	73	63	68	64	65	333	207,000
Memorial	T10	73	67	71	68		279	13,335
Kemper Open	1	72	69	70	66		277	90,000
U.S. Open	T12	71	68	71	75		285	11,870
Atlanta	T3	71	72	66	64		273	24,000
Canadian Open	2	72	76	62	73		283	64,800
British Open	1	74	63	74	69		280	105,000
Western Open	T5	71	74	72	70		287	16,950
PGA Championship	2	65	68	69	76		278	80,000
International	Cut	(Stableford)						
Meyers Challenge		(Team Event)						40,000
World Series	T20	68	71	72	75		286	8,567
European Open	1	67	67	69	66		269	52,500
*Dunhill Cup	1	67	67	70	73		277	100,000
World Match Play	1	(Match Play)						75,000
Queensland Open	1	67	70	70	70		277	11,700
New South Wales	1	65	70	67	73		275	14,625
S. Australian Open	1	75	68	75	65		283	11,700
Australian PGA	2	69	69	66	73		277	12,636
*Nissan Cup	3	68	69	71	68		276	38,625
Australian Open	T7	70	72	72	68		282	5,422
W. Australian Open	1	72	70	66	68		276	11,700

*Denotes team event (Australia)

start the game until he was 16, after caddying for his mother, who then played off a three handicap. A Nicklaus instruction book as his guide, Greg went from a 27 handicap to scratch in two years.

He went full-time on the European Tour in 1979 and decided after 1983, when he won seven events including his second World Match Play (this year's was his third), that the time had come for his assault on the American circuit. His goals for 1984 were two victories and $300,000; he achieved both, along with playoff losses to Fuzzy Zoeller in the U.S. Open and to Tom Watson in the Western Open.

A lingering, baffling physical ailment restricted Norman for 15 months, and he won only two tournaments in 1985, both in Australia. His problem was a brochial disorder that was cured in the spring.

One difference in Norman's game in 1986 was his improved play around the greens, which Greg attributed to his late-blossoming "touch" and explained to journalist/friend Larry Guest, "Take Seve for example. He started when he was four or five, chipping with one club. Your feel for the game becomes much more acute—moving your hands around, feeling a softer grip, a firm grip, things like that. All the guys who started at an early age do have an advantage. It simply takes time to develop feel and touch. I spend more time now working on my short game than anything else, and that's the crucial factor."

Norman makes his home with his wife, Laura, and two children in Orlando, Florida, near Arnold Palmer's Bay Hill Club. He's popular among the members, playing in their daily "shoot-outs" when at home. (In view of Norman's lackluster 1985 play, the Bay Hill regulars named him their "most improved" golfer at a party to celebrate his British Open win.) I also have a residence at Bay Hill, and I remember when Greg came back in March for the Hertz Bay Hill Classic, having won a little over $20,000 in four American starts, including a missed cut at Pebble Beach. Even then, he was confident of having a great year. Late one afternoon, Greg was practicing chip shots and giving tips to several low-handicap amateur pals. Someone remarked that the tour hadn't been very exciting to that point. "I'll create some excitement," Greg said, matter-of-factly.

It was not until the Masters that he did. It's interesting that Norman not only has some of Palmer's flair, but he also has inherited the mainstays of Arnie's Army, a group that's been following Palmer so closely for so long that they're on a first-name basis. Look at Norman's gallery sometime and you'll see the familiar logos of Bay Hill, Latrobe, Wake Forest, etc. on their shirts. Once Palmer missed the Masters' cut, they were out in force with Norman on Saturday when he shot 68 to take the lead, and sweated with him through a difficult Sunday afternoon. Greg was not playing well, and when he hit out of bounds on the 10th, I imagine more than a few turned in the direction of Orlando and other familiar points.

Then, as Nicklaus was also gaining momentum, Norman scored four birdies in a row and came to the 18th needing a par to tie, a birdie to win. If he were to have trouble, I thought, it would be off the tee; when he drove well, I believed a birdie was a good possibility, considering his streak of the moment. He then hit that awful shot right of the green, and everyone except Greg himself conceded the victory to Nicklaus.

The defeat proved a lot. To others, it was a test of Greg's character that he passed with colors; he was the only challenger to stay until after the ceremony to congratulate Nicklaus. As for himself, Norman "discovered that day that my maturity level had reached the point that it must be to win a major championship. When I thought back to Augusta, I was encouraged by my composure over the last five or six holes—even when I bogeyed the last hole. I didn't bogey it out of nervousness. You get excitable about the whole deal and your adrenalin flows. But I never once got nervous or insecure about being in that position. And I have felt that in years past, when I had a chance to win the British Open and the U.S. Open."

He proved as much three months later at Turnberry, but before that came another second-place finish the week after the Masters at the Sea Pines Heritage Classic, his victories at Las Vegas and the Kemper, and his topsy-turvy week at the U.S. Open.

The Open was at Shinnecock Hills, on the eastern edge of Long Island, quite a way from New York City, but near enough to attract boisterous New York spectators, one of whom prodded Norman into an act he regretted. This same summer, New Yorkers tore up the turf at one baseball stadium and threw a knife at a visiting player at another. The phenomenon is not new. More to the point, I remember that in 1967, for the first time in my experience the pro-Palmer, anti-Nicklaus faction exceeded all bounds of good manners in three New York-area tournaments: Westchester, Thunderbird and the U.S. Open at Baltusrol. And when Nicklaus won again at Baltusrol in 1980, they were fanatical to the opposite extreme.

Norman's incident happened at the 14th hole in the third round. On the previous hole, Norman took a double bogey which, combined with Lee Trevino's birdie, erased Greg's three-stroke lead. Then a heckler accused Norman of "choking" and Greg went to the gallery ropes to confront the young man, suggesting that he should hold his comments until after the round, when Norman could do something about it. Norman went on to shoot 71 and led by one stroke, but later said, "I think the only mistake I made all day was going up to that spectator." Norman would be remembered in this championship primarily for that confrontation. He was off his game in the final round and his 75 left him tied for 12th place.

When Norman won the British Open, it was as Norman Mair wrote in *The Open Championship 1986*, "a triumph over course and conditions; a triumph which owed a great deal to a refreshing and determinedly positive attitude." He could have lost it in the gales of the first round or the icily slashing, horizontal rain of the third, but held on for 74s on both days. Between those scores was Norman's brilliant 63 in the second round, equalling the championship record. It could have been 60; Greg needed three-three on the last two holes but scored four-five. He posted a 69 in the fourth round and pulled away for a five-stroke victory, knowing on the last two holes that all he needed was to sign his scorecard correctly.

Norman is endearingly frank and, when he finally had the British Open trophy in his arms, he admitted, "Truth be known, even when I was sitting at the presentation table waiting for them to give me the trophy, I was so scared I had done something wrong with the card. I just knew somebody was going to walk up and say, 'Gee, I'm sorry, Greg, but we can't give you this after all.' I was petrified that I might have signed the card wrong or put down my nine-hole score in the box for the ninth hole."

In the PGA Championship at Inverness in Toledo, Ohio, Norman looked to be the winner nearly all the way—until Tway holed a 25-foot bunker shot on the last hole, the only bunker he was in all week. Norman cruised into the final round and held a four-stroke lead with nine holes to play. Greg lost control of his game; he shot 76, missing seven fairways—four of the last nine—and 11 greens. A double bogey on the 11th halved his lead, Tway tied him after 13 holes and they went stroke-for-stroke after that.

They were still tied on the 18th tee. Both hit one irons, Tway into the right rough and Norman, the fairway. Tway was short of the green with a nine iron and in a bunker. Norman hit a pitching wedge past the flag, but the ball spun back off the green. He seemed sure of making a par. With that in mind, Tway hit his shot out of the sand. It took a couple of bounces and rolled into the hole. Usually unemotional, Tway started jumping and shaking his clinched fists. "It was a dream come true," said Tway, who had a final-round 70. "'That may never happen again in my career. I can't imagine what the odds are. It was just unbelievable . . . I wasn't trying to make the shot. I'm not that good. I was just trying to get it close."

Norman could only look on in disbelief, and said later, "If that doesn't go in the hole, it's 20 feet past." Greg was going to hit a sand wedge and keep his third shot below the hole, but after Tway's birdie, he went with a pitching wedge and knocked the ball eight feet past. He missed the meaningless putt.

There were only two more American tournaments on Norman's schedule. He left the United States after the World Series of Golf with $653,296, a PGA Tour record for yearly earnings, but one which Tway seemed sure to surpass, since he planned nine tournaments after reaching the $600,000 plateau in the PGA Championship. In Australia at the time, Norman got a small measure of revenge when Tway was eliminated by Steve Pate in the second round of the Seiko-Tucson Match Play Championship, concluding his year with $652,780—$516 shy of Norman's total.

"I do not know Steve Pate very well, but when I see him some time in the future on the American tour, I want to buy him the biggest pot of beer he can drink," Norman wrote in an exclusive column for the *Sydney Morning Herald*.

That also was the week Norman's winning streak ended at six tournaments. Mike Harwood shot 64 in the final round to edge Norman by two strokes in the Toshiba Australian PGA. It had begun in the Panasonic European Open—when he took No. 1 in the Sony Ranking in a battle with Ballesteros and Langer, who were also entered—and continued through two more tournaments in Britain and three in Australia.

As Norman and his wife returned to their hotel that evening, Laura told him, "In a way I am glad you lost because now you can carry on like your normal self." Greg wrote in his newspaper column, "I guess she was quite right—wives usually are—because the pressure of continuing this winning roll was starting to get to me."

Although Norman did not defend either his Australian PGA or Open titles (Rodger Davis won the latter), he still had one victory left in his million-dollar year, winning the Western Australia event in Perth in the midst of the America's Cup trials. The ball with which he passed the $1 million mark in the Dunhill Nations Cup was subsequently auctioned by Spalding, with the proceeds to Nancy Reagan's drug abuse program. Interestingly enough, Norman had his great year playing a non-wound golf ball, becoming the first player in the modern era to win a major championship doing so.

The top 10 leaders on the World Money List were:

1.	Greg Norman	$1,146,584
2.	Tsuneyuki Nakajima	789,067
3.	Bob Tway	782,330
4.	Bernhard Langer	745,878
5.	Andy Bean	688,438
6.	Bob Charles	580,753

7. Mark McNulty	565,719
8. Payne Stewart	564,809
9. Masashi Ozaki	552,228
10. Isao Aoki	542,751

A total of 12 golfers—also including Bruce Crampton ($532,515) and Dan Pohl ($514,855)—earned more than $500,000. Twenty-eight (including Ballesteros, No. 19 with $445,448) earned more than $400,000; 54 earned more than $300,000 and 88 earned more than $200,000. The brothers Ozaki—Masashi, Tateo and Naomichi—together earned $1,388,010, or 223 million yen. Charles and Crampton had enormous success in their first year on the U.S. Senior Tour, and Charles earned more than in his entire career on the PGA Tour.

(The complete 1986 World Money List may be found in the appendixes of this annual.)

I cannot imagine any one event in golf that could have excited the public as much as Jack Nicklaus winning the Masters—save Arnold Palmer doing it. Yet I disagree with two of the game's most respected journalists, Herbert Warren Wind and Dan Jenkins, who wrote that Nicklaus' victory was the most important since Bobby Jones won the Grand Slam in 1930. Jack's win was great for golf, great for all of us. We felt younger in the glow of his major triumph at age 46. People who don't even follow golf were talking about it for days. It was *the* sporting highlight in America for 1986. But a lasting impact on the game? Hardly. Events which have had long-term effect, Jones' Grand Slam and Palmer's summer of 1960, for example, were not so easily defined at the time. I may be proven wrong, but I don't think so.

As is often the case, Peter Dobereiner—another journalist in the league with Wind and Jenkins—summarized it best in my opinion: "If the 1986 Masters proves to be Nicklaus' last major title, which is by no means a foregone conclusion in the light of his flippant insistence that he is too dumb to retire, then it will mark a fitting climax to a career that has illuminated with unprecedented brilliance the sporting scene for a quarter of a century."

It may prove to have been a fitting climax to Nicklaus' career—which was beyond most of our imaginations on Sunday morning in Augusta, Georgia. The telephone rang early at the Nicklaus house, where on the refrigerator was taped a newspaper clipping stating that Jack was "done, through, washed-up and finished."

"My son Steve called me," Nicklaus would recount after it was all over, "and he asked me, 'Well, Pop, what's it going to take?' And I said, "Sixty-six will tie and 65 will win.' And he said, 'Well, go ahead and do it.' "

Nicklaus was still even par for the day as he reached the ninth green, having an 11-footer for birdie. There came a roar, and Nicklaus backed off his putt. Then another roar. Tom Kite and Seve Ballesteros had holed consecutive wedges for eagles at No. 8. "Let's see if we can make a roar of our own," Nicklaus told the gallery—and they did as Jack sank the putt. Ballesteros was then one stroke ahead of Greg Norman and six ahead of Nicklaus. For the 65 that Nicklaus thought he needed, he wanted 30 on the last nine, the course record. He did it, playing "probably the finest golf of my career."

Twenty-foot birdies at the 10th and 11th took Nicklaus to five under par, four strokes behind. "Suddenly, somehow," he said, "I was making putts." He overshot the 12th green and bogeyed, then drew the ball tightly around the dogleg at No. 13 with his three wood. "Shots like that are a little too much for my 24-year-old heart," said Jackie, his eldest son and caddy. With a two-putt birdie, Nicklaus was back to five under and then only two behind Ballesteros.

After a one-putt par at No. 14, Nicklaus hit a long drive at the 15th. There were 202 yards to the pin. "Do you think a three (eagle) on this hole would go very far," he asked. "Let's see it," Jackie said. The four-iron shot hit four feet in front of the hole, spun left and stopped 12 feet away. He holed the putt. The crowd erupted. "The noise was deafening. I couldn't hear anything. I mean nothing," Nicklaus said. "All I knew was I was hitting greens and making birdies and I was going to keep doing it." At the 16th, a key hole in other Nicklaus victories, Jack's five iron was five feet right of the hole, kicked left and nearly went in.

Back in the 15th fairway, Ballesteros eyed much the same shot that Nicklaus had earlier. He stroked a vicious hook into the pond and took a bogey-six. Kite was on the green and two-putted for a birdie. Suddenly, there was a three-way tie between Nicklaus, Ballesteros and Kite. Norman reached the turn at seven under but double-bogeyed No. 10. The attention was focused on the others until Greg birdied the 14th and 15th to climb back within one stroke of the leaders.

Nicklaus holed an 11-foot putt for birdie at No. 17, which meant he had played the last five holes in five under. He parred the last hole for a 279 total. Kite parred the 17th. Ballesteros took himself out of the running there with a three-putt bogey. "I played very good," Seve said, "Just one bad shot, that's all." Kite, who has been in the top six at the Masters eight times without winning, had a brave approach to the 18th, 12 feet right of the flag. He hit the putt too weakly and it drifted just below the hole. "I made that putt," he insisted. "It just didn't go in."

Now only Norman was left with a chance. He did better than Nicklaus at the 16th and needed just a two-footer for his third straight birdie. He rolled in a 10-foot birdie at No. 17 to tie Nicklaus. Oh, but for Norman's second shot at the 18th, a four iron into the gallery right of the green. "That shot was the first time I let my ego get the better of me," Norman said. He wanted to hit a high, hard shot that would drop softly next to the hole. "I just made a bad weight shift going back," he said. "Halfway through the swing, I knew I was in trouble." He did well after that to get the ball 15 feet from the hole, but his putt to tie slid by the left side.

So Nicklaus, who was the youngest Masters champion when he won in 1963 at age 23, became the oldest when he won his sixth Masters at age 46.

That launched "The Year of the Oldies"—as it was called at the time, before Norman claimed the year for himself. Raymond Floyd emerged from a last-round mad scramble at Shinnecock Hills to win the U.S. Open at age 43, the oldest winner of that championship ever, and Bob Murphy underlined the theme on the PGA Tour, winning the Canadian Open (Norman was runner-up), also at age 43.

Ten players either held or shared the lead during the last round of the U.S. Open. Norman started with a one-stroke lead and was tied after one hole, when Hal Sutton, with whom he was paired, made a birdie to match that of Lee Trevino in the pairing immediately ahead. There was a three-way deadlock. The competition became infinitely more complicated, but Norman figured in the race only briefly. He bogeyed the third and sixth, then joined a huge tie for first place with a birdie at the seventh. He came apart with three straight bogeys from the ninth, and two more later, along with a single birdie. "I went flat," he said. "When I missed that four-footer and made bogey at the sixth, all the emotion went out of me . . . Nothing would light the fuse."

Lanny Wadkins and Chip Beck rushed in with 65s and 281 totals, as 10 pairings remained on the course. Veteran observers knew that Floyd was one to watch. His intensity then was obvious. "When he's playing well, you can see it in his eyes," said Payne Stewart, who was in Floyd's pairing. "They got real big and he just focused on what he was doing." Stewart collapsed with four bogeys in the last six holes, while Floyd got the smell of victory with his 10-foot birdie at the 16th. That gave Raymond a two-stroke lead, and no one could then produce the miracle needed to catch him. He won with a 66 and 279 total.

When Floyd won at St. Petersburg as a rookie in 1963, he was the fourth youngest winner in PGA Tour history (for a while he was mistakenly considered the youngest). As the oldest U.S. Open winner ever, he had come full circle, and also completed a sweep of the U.S. major titles, following his PGA Championships in 1969 and 1982, and his Masters title in 1976. Strangely, Raymond had seldom before played well in the Open; his best finish in 21 attempts was sixth place back in 1965. "I wish I knew why," Floyd said at Shinnecock Hills. "I analyzed and replayed, and I could find no reason. Believe me, if I could, I would have won it long ago." He had another victory, the 21st of his career, later in the year at the Walt Disney World Oldsmobile Classic and placed ninth on the U.S. money list with $380,508, his top earnings year ever on the circuit.

Bernhard Langer was watching on television in the locker room at San Diego when Bob Tway finished. "Has that guy ever won before?" Bernhard asked. After two playoff holes, the former Masters champion got his answer: Tway had his first PGA Tour win in the Shearson Lehman Brothers Andy Williams Open. By the PGA Championship, Tway had two more victories. He held off Floyd and a group of others to win the Manufacturers Hanover Westchester Classic and overtook Hal Sutton with a 64 in the last round of the Georgia-Pacific Atlanta Classic. He also led the U.S. Open after the first round and tied for eighth among his 13 top-10 finishes for the year, and he needed no introduction to Norman as they set off on the final round at Inverness. His four victories were the most for a second-year player since Nicklaus won five in 1963.

Tway, 27 years old, was a star at Oklahoma State University, was on the All-America team three times and was voted the best college player in the country in 1981. He was a "can't miss" player who did miss—he took three tries, until November, 1984, to earn his PGA Tour card and was forced to play the European, African and Asian circuits. When he finally earned his card, it was despite a double bogey, triple bogey, bogey finish. That left

Tway in 24th place among the qualifiers—and rookies receive places in tour events according to their qualifying positions. He got to play in only six of the first 17 tournaments in 1985. In the second half of the season, he got 19 opportunities and made the most of them, finishing 45th on the money list with $164,023.

Much has been made of Tway's bunker shot to win the PGA Championship on the 72nd hole; virtually forgotten was the course-record 64 on Saturday that put him in contention, and totally ignored was the open-bladed "sand blast" from deep rough on the 71st hole. Tway thought, if anything, that was a better shot than the celebrated one on the next hole. He had to invent a trick shot to save his par, to guess the distance to pop the ball out onto the green and to guess the speed of the roll. As Dan Jenkins said in *Golf Digest*, Tway may never have invented a better one.

Even before the PGA, Tway was being described as "the next superstar." Gary Player recognized as much after playing with Tway in a Tournament Players Series event three years ago. "How do you describe it?" Player said. "It's very seldom you play with a youngster or anyone and are that impressed by them the first time out. But this kid had everything. When I went home that night I told my son Wayne, 'I have just played with the next superstar.' I'm sure now he will go from strength to strength."

Besides Tway, there were nine multiple winners on the American circuit in 1986; Fuzzy Zoeller won three tournaments and eight players won two each, including Ben Crenshaw in a comeback year, Norman, Floyd, Sutton, Calvin Peete, Corey Pavin, Andy Bean and Dan Pohl.

I continue to marvel at the accomplishments of Zoeller, whose career supposedly ended in September, 1984, when he underwent surgery for a back problem. But Fuzzy recovered to win the Hertz Bay Hill Classic in 1985, and added the AT&T Pebble Beach National Pro-Am, Sea Pines Heritage Classic and Anheuser-Busch Classic titles in 1986. The lame-armed Peete also continued to baffle the game's purists with victories in the MONY Tournament of Champions and USF&G (New Orleans) Classic, and led the tour again in driving accuracy.

Bean came off a winless 1985 campaign to capture the Doral Eastern Open and Byron Nelson Classic titles, plus the unofficial Kapalua International, and placed fourth on the money list with $491,938. Pohl's victories in the Colonial National Invitation and the NEC World Series of Golf propelled him to fifth place with $463,630. Those earnings were more than double the previous best for Pohl, who had not won in his eight previous professional seasons.

Sutton took sixth on the money list with $429,434, winning the Phoenix Open and Memorial Tournament, and was fourth in the U.S. Open. Pavin had victories in the Hawaiian Open and Greater Milwaukee Open. It was nearly a great year for the Texas duo that has been linked since childhood, Crenshaw and Tom Kite, who were seventh ($394,164) and eighth ($388,169) respectively. Crenshaw, recovering from a hyperactive thyroid condition that had deprived him of a victory since the 1984 Masters, won the Buick Open and Vantage Championship, and was a top-20 finisher in all four majors. Kite had that heart-breaking miss on the 18th green to tie for second in the Masters, but later won in the Western Open.

Curtis Strange, the 1985 leading money winner, dropped to 32nd with $237,700 and had one U.S. victory, the Houston Open. Other one-time winners of note included Hale Irwin, who won the unofficial Bahamas Classic to start the year but did little else; John Mahaffey, who triumphed in the Tournament Players Championship; 1985 British Open champion Sandy Lyle, who recorded his first American victory at the Greater Greensboro Open; Jim Thorpe, who won his second straight Seiko Tucson Match Play, which was the last playing in that format, and Mike Hulbert, who led the 1985 qualifying tournament graduates with $276,687 for 21st place and won the Federal Express St. Jude (Memphis) Classic.

Prominent non-winners included Payne Stewart, for the third consecutive year, who was third on the money list; Tom Watson, who has not won on the PGA Tour since the 1984 Western Open; Scott Verplank, the former amateur standout who won the 1985 Western Open; Vardon Trophy stroke leader Scott Hoch (who won in Japan), 1985 major champions Bernhard Langer (who won twice in Europe), Andy North and Hubert Green, Craig Stadler, Mark O'Meara (who won in Australia), and U.S. Open runners-up Chip Beck and Lanny Wadkins, who was the 1985 PGA Player of the Year.

Stewart is known for being a strong player in the major championships and his PGA Tour earnings of $535,389 included top-10 finishes in the Masters, U.S. Open and PGA Championship (and he tied for 35th in the British Open). He was runner-up in three Tour events: AT&T Pebble Beach National Pro-Am, Colonial National Invitation and Vantage Championship. Two of those were rain-shortened.

There are some who would bury Watson as a king of the game and erect a memorial by the Road Hole at St. Andrews, dated 22 July 1984, when Watson's bogey cost him that British Open loss to Seve Ballesteros. Watson's only victory since was the Australian Open in the autumn of 1984, but in 1986 there were signs that he might reclaim his former standing. He was third in four tournaments, and was 24th or better in three majors, including a tie for sixth in the Masters.

If anyone on the PGA Tour deserved sympathy, it was Larry Mize, who squandered a four-stroke lead with eight holes to play in the Tournament Players Championship, then led Norman by two strokes with two holes to play in the Kemper Open, only to finish par-bogey to Norman's birdie-par and lose the title on the sixth hole of a playoff when he put two balls into a lake.

Peete (driving accuracy), Mahaffey (greens in regulation) and Joey Sindelar (birdies) repeated as leaders in those statistical categories. Other leaders were Sindelar (eagles), Hoch (scoring), rookie Davis Love III (driving distance), Paul Azinger (sand saves) and Norman (putting and par breakers). Norman was among the top 10 in six of the nine categories.

There were three major controversies during the year, the flap over the former Bing Crosby National Pro-Am and the squabbles of Mac O'Grady and Seve Ballesteros with the PGA Tour.

The official name of the tournament held in late January/February on the Monterey Peninsula was the AT&T Pebble Beach National Pro-Am—but by any name, it was still "The Crosby." Kathryn Crosby, Bing's widow, removed the family name because of objections to commercialism, but sons

Nathaniel and Harry maintained their affiliation. A new "Crosby" was held in June at Bermuda Run, near Winston-Salem, North Carolina. It was an amateur/celebrity charity event, with no professionals, and reportedly had receipts of $300,000 to $500,000—short of an announced goal of $2 million. Nathaniel said that "Crosby" was "like Christmas in June . . . But there is room for two Crosbys. It is a shame to throw 45 years of tradition and nostalgia down the drain."

Despite his off-course battle, O'Grady had his best year, winning $256,344 for 26th place on the money list. O'Grady, who took 17 attempts to qualify for the tour, finally won his first tournament, the Canon Sammy Davis, Jr., Greater Hartford Open. To summarize O'Grady's problems, he was fined $500 after being accused of insulting a tournament volunteer in New Orleans in 1984, and refused to pay the fine, which was deducted from his earnings in the 1985 Bob Hope tournament. O'Grady hired a lawyer and began criticizing Commissioner Deane Beman and some other players in the press. He was fined $5,000 and suspended from the tour for six weeks. O'Grady began litigation, claiming an antitrust violation, but a federal judge firmly denied his request that the tour be prevented from imposing the penalties.

O'Grady served the suspension and paid his fine—then said he would revert to his old practice of not talking to the press in silent protest. He went to Osaka for a vacation with his Japanese wife during the suspension and began practicing *left-handed*. "You know me," O'Grady told *Golf Digest*, "I've got these demons inside me and maybe those left-handed demons are trying to come out . . . No one's ever tried to develop their golf skills on both sides to the same level of performance. I'm bored with it right-handed. So I said to myself, let's do the impossible. At this point I'm about 80 percent there. I won't tell you where and when, but I promise you, I'll be teeing it up somewhere, sometime, left-handed. Maybe when I'm leading a tournament by four or five shots going into the last round."

Welcome back, Mac.

Ballesteros was suspended from the PGA Tour for the year for failing to play the required minimum of 15 events in 1985. He was allowed to play only at New Orleans, as defending champion, and at the three U.S. majors not under PGA Tour jurisdiction. Ballesteros planned to play in several mini-tour events, but entered only one because of the death of his father in the spring. Although Seve was a strong contender at the Masters, he did not fare well in his other American appearances. He tied for 63rd in New Orleans, tied for 24th in the U.S. Open and missed the cut in the PGA Championship. He later was invited by Beman to the World Series, but dismissed the invitation as an "after-thought" and stayed at home.

While Beman apparently had no choice but to enforce the rule, there was much criticism of his decision and pressure for a reversal. Said Crenshaw, "The ruling is bad as it excludes one of the two best players in the world. I think the public around the world has a right to see the best players. That's what the whole tour is for. I think the commissioner ought to work for golf. Let's try to think of the whole scheme of things, not just where the United States and the PGA Tour fits in . . . I think the tour has gone overboard on this thing and the rules should be changed."

The PGA Tour Policy Board announced the new policy in October. There would be three options available to foreign players in 1987:

1. As a tour member, to participate in 15 events and receive unlimited conflicting event releases on their home circuits.

2. Retain tour membership and play in less than 15 events per year, but forfeit the privilege of receiving unlimited conflicting event releases on their home circuits.

3. Foreign players who had not previously joined the tour could elect to participate as non-members (a maximum of five events plus the Masters, U.S. Open, PGA Championship, World Series and Nissan Cup.)

The PGA Tour introduced two programs in 1986 sponsored by R. J. Reynolds/Nabisco, each with $2 million prize funds: the Vantage Cup, a bonus pool for the players, and the Nabisco Challenge, a charity competition with the same points system. Under the Nabisco Challenge, "teams" of professionals competed on behalf of the tournaments, who chose their players in a "draft" similar to those in American team sports. Both the Vantage Cup and Nabisco Challenge were designed to encourage players to play heavy schedules, particularly the late-season events, and RJR/Nabisco also took up sponsorship of the former Texas Open, renaming it the $1 million Vantage Championship. The programs were to be redesigned for 1987, with the Vantage Championship becoming the Nabisco Grand Prix, with the points system keyed to that one event. The Vantage promotion was to be switched to the PGA Senior Tour.

The energetic Beman, age 47, who also found time to devote to his golf game after a dozen years and entered the Irish Open and British Open, continued to push for innovations on the tour. Among the Beman-inspired projects over the years have been Vantage Scoreboards, Stadium Golf, Family Golf Centers, Epson Statistics and MCI Long Distance Competition. In total, the tour now lists 16 licensees: official automobile, hospital, airline, exercise equipment and nutritional products, computer, athletic/fitness shoe, thirst quencher, rental car, truck, golf destination, charge card, camera, aircraft, cruise line, timepiece and hotel.

One of Beman's great successes, the still-expanding PGA Senior Tour, was dominated by first-season players—Bruce Crampton, Chi Chi Rodriguez, Dale Douglass, Gary Player and Bob Charles—and resulted at the year's end in the creation of a "Super Senior" division to accommodate such founding members as Sam Snead and Julius Boros.

Arnold Palmer, whose 50th birthday in 1979 inspired the full-fledged Senior Tour, did not win an official tournament, but got a victory in the unofficial Unionmutual Classic. And Palmer provided the Senior highlight of the year—two consecutive holes-in-one in the Chrysler Cup team event, which drew front-page headlines. The two aces came on the pro-am days, with a five iron on the 187-yard third hole of the Tournament Players Club at Avenel in Potomac, Maryland. "I was awed by the whole thing," said Arnie, who now has 13 holes-in-one for his lifetime.

Crampton was the leading money winner with $454,299 plus $50,000 unofficially and $11,000 from the Mazda Champions with Pat Bradley and a total of $532,515. He won seven official tournaments, including three of the last four, and the unofficial Doug Sanders Celebrity Classic. The Australian, known as "The Ironman" is his younger days, replaced countryman Peter Thomson in the No. 1 position. Thomson was winless after scoring nine victories in 1985. "I've just got a touch of old age," said the 57-year-old Thomson.

Crampton's other victories were the Benson & Hedges Invitational at The Dominion, MONY Syracuse Senior Classic, GTE Northwest Classic, PaineWebber World Seniors Invitational, Pepsi Senior Challenge, Las Vegas Senior Classic and Quadel Senior Classic.

Douglass had four victories including the U.S. Senior Open, while Player and Rodriguez won three times each. Player's total included the PGA Seniors Championship, and Rodriguez won the Senior Tournament Players Championship. Other first-year winners, with one victory each, were Bobby Nichols and Butch Baird. Charles flirted with winning all year, but came away empty-handed until he and Amy Alcott won a playoff in the season-ending Mazda Champions. The $250,000 share boosted Charles' earnings to $580,753.

Leading the old guard was Don January, who won four times including the Liberty Mutual Legends of Golf with Gene Littler, who had two individual victories. Twice the Senior money leader and never lower than fourth, Miller Barber won only the season-opening MONY Tournament of Champions and barely made the top-10 list.

There were 34 events on the 1986 Senior calendar, 31 official plus three unofficial tournaments, for a total payout in excess of $8 million, more than double the total of three years ago. There were 37 tournaments projected for 1987, including a huge boost from Vantage. The "Super Seniors" will have 10 places in 1987 events, playing one pro-am day plus 36 holes of competition for $26,000 purses. The Senior fields were to be expanded from 52 to 72 players and a 36-hole cut instituted for the first time, with the low 48 players plus ties.

A Senior British Open was also announced for 1987, to be held the week following the British Open. The £150,000 event will be sanctioned by the PGA European Tour. The Senior PGA Tour has demonstrated the popularity of the over-50s, and I think the same success can be achieved in Britain.

Finally, I am pleased to note that the flap over Bob Toski came to nothing, despite some counter attempts in the press. Toski was accused of improperly marking his ball on the greens in three tournaments in late 1985—no one who knows Bob would ever believe he would intentionally cheat—and he took a three-month voluntary leave from the tour early in the year.

Seve Ballesteros could play only four tournaments in America, so he concentrated his efforts in Europe. He won six tournaments, including a tie with Bernhard Langer in the Lancome Trophy, marking the third time in four years that he won six. However, Ballesteros' lack of success in the major championships, his fewer appearances, and the generally lower gradings of European tournaments in the Sony Ranking, dropped the Spaniard from No. 1 to third in the world behind Greg Norman and Langer. Of course, Norman's magnificent play had a lot to do with that, but Ballesteros missed his chance to at least temporarily regain No. 1 in the Suntory World Match Play Championship, when he was eliminated in the second round.

Ballesteros was aiming for his third successive World Match Play title and his fifth overall, but Norman emerged the winner. Together, they have won all the World Match Plays of the 1980s.

Ballesteros had only two European finishes outside the top four; he tied for sixth in the British Open and tied for 10th in the German Open. He won four in a row before the British Open—Dunhill British Masters, Carrolls Irish Open, Johnnie Walker Monte Carlo Open and Peugeot French Open—and the tournament immediately following, the KLM Dutch Open. His European earnings were a record £242,208 and he became the first to have more than £1 million in career earnings, closing the year with £1,069,114 in official money.

Langer did not win until the German Open in August, but was in the top three 10 times worldwide to secure his Sony Ranking place. He tied for third in the British Open (the week his first child was born), tied for eighth in the U.S. Open and tied for 16th in the Masters. Sandy Lyle did not win in Europe, but his Greensboro victory and such finishes as runner-up in the World Match Play held his position as the third European in the Sony Ranking.

Spanish rookie Jose-Maria Olazabal, rising from 469th to 43rd in the Sony Ranking, was No. 2 on the European money list with £136,775 and had two victories in the Ebel European Masters/Swiss Open and Sanyo Open. Before becoming a professional, Olazabal was the first ever to win these three championships: British Amateur, Youths and Boys. Olazabal, 20 years old, was quick to make his presence known on the European circuit, placing fourth in the Cespa Madrid Open in his second start. In addition to the two victories, Olazabal had six top-10 placings and was the first rookie ever invited to the World Match Play, where he played Jack Nicklaus, and lost, in the second round.

England's Howard Clark won two of the first five tournaments, the Cespa Madrid Open and Peugeot Spanish Open, and placed third on the European money list with £121,902. Two who played well in the British Open, Ian Woosnam of Wales (£111,798) and Gordon J. Brand of England (£106,314), were also in six figures, along with South Africa's Mark McNulty (£101,327). Woosnam won the Lawrence Batley Tournament Players Championship and McNulty took the Portuguese Open title, to go along with his eight victories on the South African circuit. South Africa's John Bland was also a European winner in the Suze Open and earned £58,306. On the Safari Tour that preceded the European circuit, Brand won the Nigerian Open and the Ivory Coast Open, and Woosnam won the Kenya Open.

It was a great year in Europe for the men from Down Under. Aside from Norman's three individual titles—British Open, Panasonic European Open and World Match Play—the Australian team of Norman, David Graham and Rodger Davis repeated as champions in the Dunhill Nations Cup at St. Andrews. Davis won the Whyte & Mackay PGA Championship and was seventh on the European Tour with £95,428. He tied for second in the Carrolls Irish Open and was second in the German Open. Ian Baker-Finch did not win, but was 11th on the money list with £76,304 and was runner-up in the Peugeot Spanish Open and Bell's Scottish Open. Aussie Peter Senior won the PLM Open in Sweden and New Zealander Greg Turner made his debut a success by winning the Scandinavian Enterprise Open, after earlier claiming the Singapore Open.

The rise of the Swedes has been noted for several years, and in 1986 they made a break-through. Ove Sellberg took the honor of being the first to win a tournament of international scope, with his victory in the Epson Grand Prix. In that match-play event, Sellberg beat countryman Anders Forsbrand in the semi-finals then beat Clark for the title, while Forsbrand placed third. Forsbrand was second or third in three European events and was No. 8 on the money list with £84,706, and Sellberg placed 16th with £64,175. Two other Swedes also had top-five finishes during the year, Magnus Persson and Mats Lanner.

David Feherty and Ronan Rafferty were a successful duo for Northern Ireland. Rafferty was ninth on the money list with £80,355 and Feherty won the Italian Open and Bell's Scottish Open while placing 17th with £72,569. Des Smyth, from the Irish Republic, was 12th with £68,905. Gordon Brand, Jr., led Scotland with £78,639 for 10th place.

England's Nick Faldo and Paul Way and Scotland's Sam Torrance did not win. Faldo was fifth in the British Open and challenged for a half-dozen titles, and Torrance was in the running four times. One to really feel sorry for was Way. The former Ryder Cup player dropped to 125th on the money list, earning only £5,260.

The only Spaniard to win, aside from Ballesteros and Olazabal, was Antonio Garrido. Among the winless were such key golfers as Jose-Maria Canizares, Manuel Pinero and Jose Rivero. And what a controversy there was involving Garrido!

At the Madrid tournament, Way refused to sign Garrido's scorecard for a 68 that would have tied him for the lead. Brand, Jr., supported Way, as they claimed Garrido moved his ball while marking three putts. Official John Paramor ruled that Garrido was sufficiently careless to be disqualified, but that he wasn't cheating. Garrido nevertheless left the course in tears, and talked about quitting, but said he reconsidered after receiving letters of support from across Europe. Five weeks later, Garrido won the London Standard Four Stars National Pro-Celebrity.

The year in Australia and New Zealand started out ordinarily enough, with victories by the likes of Frank Nobilo, Stewart Ginn (who also won in Asia), Ossie Moore, Bob Shearer and Lyndsay Stephen, and by a visiting American, Mark O'Meara, in the most prestigious event of the early circuit, the Australian Masters.

What a difference there was when Greg Norman returned in October, riding a three-tournament winning streak which he extended to six with victories in the Stefan Queensland Open, National Panasonic New South Wales Open and West End Jubilee South Australia Open. The string was broken when Mike Harwood shot 64 in the Toshiba Australian PGA to beat Norman by two strokes. Before returning to his Florida home, Norman concluded his year by winning the National Panasonic Western Australia Open.

Norman brought record crowds to the Australian events and generated interest that was compared to the impact Don Bradman made on Aussie cricket a half-century ago. As usual there was controversy, with Norman himself asking in the *Sydney Morning Herald*, "I want to know when Graham Marsh and Terry Gale are going to show their faces on the Australian golf tour."

Gale was the chairman of the Australian circuit and Marsh, the immediate past chairman, but both were off playing in Japan at the time. As Greg noted, the problem was inherent: "I do not believe an active tournament player can do the job anyway . . .

"They will attack me because I am getting appearance money for my Australian tour. But I am here and playing. They are not. I could go to Japan and probably make more money than I am receiving on the Australian tour, but I believe I should be here. I have a loyalty to Australian tournaments which other people don't seem to have."

Norman was joined by Marsh and Gale for the National Panasonic Australian Open, when Rodger Davis capped a superb year, winning the championship after Ian Baker-Finch faded on the last three holes. Davis earlier won the PGA title in Britain and shared in the Dunhill Nations Cup victory, and wrapped up the year with wins in the Air New Zealand-Shell Open and Nissan-Mobil New Zealand Open.

Tsuneyuki (Tommy) Nakajima won seven tournaments on the Japan Tour and climbed to No. 4 in the Sony Ranking. Clearly Japan's best golfer, the 32-year-old Nakajima has won 37 tournaments in his 11-year career, and 28 tournaments in the past five years. Nakajima had two good placings in major events, sharing eighth in both the Masters and British Open. He had a great opportunity to win the British, trailing Norman by one stroke entering the last round, but then shot 77.

He defended championships in the Japan Open and Kanto PGA, and also won the Japan Match Play, Mitsubishi Galant, Mizuno Open, Golf Digest Open and Nissan Cup. Japan also won the Nissan Cup team title, and was second to Australia in the Dunhill Nations Cup, under Nakajima's leadership.

Nakajima's most memorable day, however, was the semi-final of the World Match Play, when he and Sandy Lyle were engaged in the finest match ever in that championship before Lyle won at the 38th hole. They shot 65s in the morning round and 64s in the afternoon, combining for 27 birdies and four eagles. Lyle sank a 45-foot putt for eagle to continue the match beyond the 36th, and won two holes later, when Nakajima three-putted. If ever a match deserved not to have a loser, this was it.

Two of Japan's older stars, Isao Aoki and Masashi (Jumbo) Ozaki also had outstanding seasons. Aoki, now 43 years old, was the first Japanese to win an important international title when he claimed the 1978 World Match Play, and also won the 1983 Hawaiian Open by holing a 128-yard wedge shot on the 72nd hole. But Aoki had not won since 1983, when he had six titles, and perhaps some were wondering if he would ever win again.

Aoki proved any doubters wrong in a span of 11 tournaments at midseason when he won four: Sapporo Tokyu, Japan PGA, KBC Augusta Classic and Kanto Open. The last two were back-to-back.

Ozaki, age 39, is the eldest of three brothers who are increasingly reminiscent of the South African Hennings a decade ago. Jumbo, who was winless in 1985, won four times and Tateo (Jet) and Naomichi (Joe) together won three. Jet and Joe were teammates with Nakajima in the Dunhill Nations Cup, and Joe went on to the World Match Play, losing in the second round to Norman.

Jumbo won the Fuji Sankei, Nikkei Cup, Maruman Nihonkai Open and Jun Classic; Jet won the Bridgestone International and Daikyo Open, and Joe won the Pepsi Ube Open.

Two victories each were posted by Masahiro Kuramoto, Teruo Sugihara and David Ishii, a Japanese-American from Hawaii. Ishii was in the running for many titles, and the UCLA graduate won the prestigious Chunichi Crowns and Niigata Open. Kuramoto won the ANA Sapporo Open and Tokai Classic, and Sugihara won the Tohoku Classic and Kansai PGA.

Australian Graham Marsh, who as previously noted was under criticism for playing here rather than supporting his home circuit, is the most successful invader ever. He won his 22nd Japanese title in the Suntory Open. Countryman Brian Jones, who won three 1985 Japanese titles, added the Bridgestone Aso crown to his list.

The Americans were shut out until Curtis Strange led them to victory in the Japan/USA team event, and later Bobby Wadkins won the Dunlop Phoenix and Scott Hoch won the Casio World Open. But Yasahiro Funatogawa won the Taiheiyo Club (Pacific) Masters, the third straight victory there by a Japanese golfer after the Americans had won eight of the first 11.

Taiwanese golfers dominated the Asian Tour, but were four weeks into the circuit before winning. Japan's Seiichi Kanai led off by winning the Cathay Pacific Hong Kong Open, followed by Australian Stewart Ginn (Benson & Hedges Malaysian Open) and New Zealander Greg Turner (Singapore Open). Then came Taiwanese Ho Ming Chung (Thailand Open), The Phillipines' Frankie Minoza (Indonesian Open), Taiwanese Lu Hsi Chuen (Charminar Challenge Indian Open and Republic of China Open), Taiwanese Tsao Chin Teng (Korean Open) and Japanese Hideto Shigenobu (Dunlop International).

When Pat Bradley wins a tournament, her mother in Westford, Massachusetts, rings a cow bell from the porch to announce the news (once in the middle of the night to signal a victory in Japan). There must have been a lot of noise coming from the house in 1986, because Bradley dominated the American LPGA circuit. She very nearly took the Grand Slam—failing by only three strokes in the U.S. Open. Among her five victories were major titles in the Nabisco Dinah Shore, LPGA Championship and du Maurier Classic, plus she won the prestigious Nestle World Championship and S&H Golf Classic.

Jane Geddes won the U.S. Open title. But Bradley, with her 1981 Open championship, became the first player to win all four modern LPGA major titles. She has won six major LPGA events and a total of 21 tournaments in her 13-year career. Only Mickey Wright had previously won as many as three in one year.

Her official earnings for 1986 were $492,021 breaking the record held by Nancy Lopez, who missed most of the year while having her second child, a daughter, Errin Shea. (Later in the year in *Shea* Stadium, her husband, Ray Knight of the New York Mets, became Most Valuable Player in baseball's World Series.)

Aside from Bradley, there were seven multiple winners on the LPGA tour, including Geddes, whose U.S. Open victory was the first of her career, and who later also won the Boston Five Classic. Juli Inkster won four times (Women's Kemper Open, McDonald's Championship, Lady Keystone Open, Atlantic City Classic) and Patty Sheehan won three times (Sarasota Classic, Kyocera Inamori Classic and Konica San Jose Classic).

Two-time winners, in addition to Geddes, were Mary Beth Zimmerman (Standard Register, Uniden Invitational), Amy Alcott (Mazda Hall of Fame, National Pro-Am), Betsy King (Henredon Classic, Rail Charity Classic) and Ayako Okamoto (Elizabeth Arden Classic, Cellular One-Ping Championship).

Bradley won about all there was except Rookie of the Year (Jody Rosenthal). She was Rolex Player of the Year, won the Mazda Series, the Vare Trophy for scoring average (71.10) and led in top-10 finishes with 17. King was second in top-10 finishes with 16, and was also runner-up on the money list with $290,195. Completing the top five were Inkster ($285,293), Alcott ($244,410) and Geddes ($221,225).

Before turning to the 1986 season in detail, we recall the passing of . . . Baldomero Ballesteros, patriarch of the Spanish golfing family . . . Eric Brown, 61, winner of 28 titles in Britain and the Open championships of Italy, Switzerland, Ireland and Portugal . . . Ronnie Shade, 47, a longtime factor in British golf . . . Walter Burkemo, 68, winner of the 1953 PGA Championship and one of America's foremost club professionals . . . Alice O. Kirby, 65, the 16th woman to turn professional and a charter member of the LPGA . . . Ellen Griffin, 67, a teacher of many LPGA stars . . .Leo Fraser, 76, an influential figure in the U.S. PGA . . . Jimmy Adams, 75, a four-time member of the British Ryder Cup team . . . Jack Toski, 75, the eldest of four golfing brothers and a respected teacher . . . Johnny Dawson, 83, credited with "inventing" golf in the California desert and declared by Bobby Jones the "uncrowned king of golf" during his playing days.

2. The Masters Tournament

It is a measure of the magic of Jack Nicklaus that his charge to his sixth Masters championship in April still ranked as the American sports highlight of the year in December. Other moments shone briefly, but no other event enthralled so many, sports fans or no, as did Nicklaus' victory. There were too many facets to this diamond, too many ways in which Nicklaus captured—or, more appropriately, recaptured—the light and the imagination of the public.

The drama of the tournament could have stood on its own. There was the return to Augusta of Byron Nelson; the return to the front of the American stage of Seve Ballesteros; the return to good health and good golf by 1984 champion Ben Crenshaw; the Augusta National record round of 63 shot by Nick Price, erasing a mark first set in 1940 (no, not by Nicklaus; he was three months old). There was also the electricity of Sunday, one of the most exciting shootouts of this decade even without the presence of Nicklaus. After all, the champion began the final round five shots back, then played the last 10 holes in seven under par, including a record-tying 30 strokes on the back nine. Then he sat with the rest of the world and watched as first Tom Kite, then Greg Norman, failed to tie him at the 72nd hole. No picture has ever evoked more poignancy than the sight of Kite slumping to a crouch, head bowed, when his 12-foot birdie putt at No. 18 slid below the cup.

And because that champion was Nicklaus, winning his 20th major (six Masters, four U.S. Opens, three British Opens, five PGAs and two U.S. Amateurs), an aura settled about the tournament as soon as Norman took the final stroke. Who would be a more appropriate winner of the 50th Masters, the golden Masters, than the Golden Bear? A decade from now, more people will be able to tell you where they watched Nicklaus hug his son and caddy Jackie behind the 72nd green than, say, where they watched Raymond Floyd win the U.S. Open. No slight is intended to Floyd, another old lion who proved he wasn't biding his time until he qualified for the Senior Tour. Rather, it is a tribute to Nicklaus, who won his first Masters in 1963 at age 23, then won his sixth in 1986 at age 46, or half a lifetime later. So many things had changed. Take his wardrobe. In 1963, Fat Jack wore a 44 long green jacket and a black hat. Augusta National and its galleries belonged to Arnold Palmer. In 1986, Nicklaus wore a 42 regular green jacket and his hat was white. He owned Augusta National, right down to the last pine needle.

It had been an amazing transformation. As Nicklaus rolled on, as he continued in 1965, 1966, 1972 and 1975 to show that no one could perform more skillfully among the azaleas than he, the people flocked to him as though they were sinners and he had the word of God. When Nicklaus completed his 28th Masters with a score of 74–71–69–65—279, nine under par, and received the winner's check of $144,000, the fans responded with a mixture of love, affection, tradition, nostalgia and perhaps gratitude. Maybe they weren't growing old. If Nicklaus had won his first Masters in 1963, this couldn't be 1986. He was young again, as were we all.

The gallery, if so mannered a term could be used, surpassed any of the previous 49 in volume and enthusiasm. The Masters has long prided itself on the decorous behavior of those behind the ropes. As it is written in the Masters Tournament Policies and Customs, beneath the heading of "Patrons":

"The Masters Tournament patrons know their golf and they respect golf gallery etiquette. They expect to see the game at its best and regularly show every courtesy to the players and to one another. They are quiet when silence is required, remain stationary while a shot is being executed and in many ways encourage the efforts of the contestants. They make it the custom not to disturb a player's concentration by accosting him during a Tournament round, even if he is a personal acquaintance. . . ."

The late Clifford Roberts, lord of the Augusta National manor, once banned telecaster Jack Whitaker from working at the Masters because he described a large assemblage of Masters patrons as a "mob." This time around, in view of the Nicklaus charge, that description might have been appropriate. The roar that went up when Ballesteros hit into the water on the 15th hole on Sunday—Nicklaus, standing nearby on the 17th tee, would later describe it as "a funny sound"—rivaled any of those that cheered the Spaniard when he won the Masters in 1980 and 1983. Up to now, all receptions accorded the Masters participant finishing a round have been measured alongside the one given to a 52-year-old Ben Hogan when he shot his 66 in the third round of the 1967 Masters. No longer. When Nicklaus strolled to the final green, the fans 20-deep nearly shook the cathedral of pines off its foundation.

(Judging by the reaction in the weeks following, the rest of the nation felt the same way. CBS-TV received so many inquiries about obtaining a video cassette of the tournament that one went on the market in midsummer. One acquaintance attended a wedding in Pensacola, Florida, where the husband-to-be and his groomsmen nearly missed the ceremony, having sequestered themselves in a hotel room to cheer Nicklaus home.)

The talk of Nicklaus in the days leading up to the tournament centered upon the assumptions of the golf community that the Golden Bear didn't have any more chance of winning the Masters than you or I. He was, perhaps, Gary Cooper in *High Noon,* an aging gunfighter who wouldn't admit what the rest of the world already knew: he had lost his stuff. Nicklaus admitted that his growing business concerns had left him little time to be concerned about golf.

"We used to come out here and we loved it," said a fellow 46-year-old, Lee Trevino. "This week, we forced ourselves. I was talking to Jack about it and he said, 'I feel better at the office now.' It makes it difficult to cope when people think we're as good as we were 10 years ago."

There had been no PGA Tour victories since the 1984 Memorial, a.k.a. The Tournament That Jack Built, and he hadn't won a tournament he hadn't founded since the 1982 Colonial. In 1986, Nicklaus had entered seven events, missed three cuts and withdrawn from a fourth. His high finish had been a tie for 39th at Hawaii. Nicklaus had won $4,404, which placed him 160th on the money list, one spot behind Dan Halldorson.

Kismet fans: note that on Masters Sunday, Halldorson would win the Deposit Guaranty Classic in Hattiesburg, Mississippi.

Nicklaus arrived at Augusta several days after he had missed the Tournament Players Championship cut by three strokes with a score of 74–73—147. Yet he had been encouraged by his play at Ponte Vedra. Before the TPC, he had worked with Jack Grout, the longtime Columbus, Ohio, pro who taught him the game. Grout induced Nicklaus to lessen the role of his hands in his swing. Then Jackie, the 1985 North and South Amateur champion and now a pro, gave him some chipping tips he had received from Chi Chi Rodriguez. They also involved taking the hands out of the swing.

Nicklaus also had a new putter, an oversized black one his MacGregor people had developed to lessen the twist in a putting stroke, and an old tip. "The thing I was really conscious of those last nine holes was keeping my head still and being aggressive with the putter," Nicklaus would tell Sarah Ballard of *Sports Illustrated*. "All week people, including Barbara, had told me I was moving my head when I putted. After the second round my friend Bob Hoag said, 'You always told me to tell you, so I am. You're moving your head.' The next day Tom Weiskopf came up and said, 'Mind if I say something? You're moving your head.' That convinced me. The aggressiveness came a week before at a USGA dinner in Atlanta. They showed me a film of highlights of my four Open wins, including a 22-foot putt I made at Baltusrol in 1967 to break Hogan's record. I took the putter back only four or five inches, but I must have gone through it 18 inches. I really popped the ball. I haven't been doing that in recent years."

After he needed only 13 putts in the final 10 holes, MacGregor received a 10-week backlog of orders for the ZT Response putter. A commemorative version of the putter, called the Nicklaus 20 came out during the summer.

With all this help, Nicklaus began seeing some improvement. "I started hitting shots the way I wanted to and I knew it was coming," he would say. Following his practice on Friday before Masters Week, Nicklaus turned to his wife Barbara and said, "I think I finally found that fellow out there I used to know." However, he said this only to Barbara. The rest of the world would discuss his prospects of winning based on the information it had, which left little room for optimism. What was said wasn't pretty.

On Easter Sunday, the weekend prior to the tournament, Tom McColister of *The Atlanta Constitution* waved a red cape in front of Nicklaus and dared him to charge. McColister doesn't own a poison pen. He's a rumpled, friendly sort of guy, always with a good word and a clasp of the shoulder for old friends. He's also a solid reporter, a veteran of the golf beat. In his story, McColister claimed that Nicklaus was "done, through, washed-up and finished." A business associate placed it on the refrigerator in the home Nicklaus had rented for his stay in Augusta. Every time Nicklaus looked for a snack, he became more determined.

McColister wasn't the only one to think Jack was done, just the first to make his thoughts public. After the tournament, Kite admitted that on the same Sunday McColister's story appeared, he ventured at dinner that "I not only thought Jack couldn't win this tournament but I also said I didn't think that he'd ever win another one. Bright, huh?"

Said CBS-TV analyst Ken Venturi, on Masters Tuesday: "I haven't seen (Nicklaus) play because he hasn't been around to be on the air. Jack's got to start thinking about when it is time (to retire). . . . . He's already said that he's got more things on his mind than golf. Sometimes the things you used to just let happen just don't anymore. I think Jack's trying so hard and saying, 'I've got to do it.' Before, it happened just because of how good he was. Even though he's preparing for the Masters and the other majors, it's not a switch you can turn on and off. He'd like to win again for everybody who said he was down and out but, well, everybody would. The whole world is looking for Babe Ruth to hit another home run and Ben Hogan to shoot a 66."

When Masters Week began, the talk of comebacks centered around not Nicklaus, but Ballesteros, who was considered a co-favorite despite the scarce amount of competitive golf he had played in the first quarter of the year. The two-time Masters champ had become *persona non grata* to U.S. PGA Tour Commissioner Deane Beman, who was the force behind the decision to suspend Ballesteros for not meeting the Tour's 15-tournament minimum in 1985. The disdain Ballesteros had shown for Beman appeared again in Augusta, where he called Beman "a little man trying to be a big man." "Forget Deane Beman," he said before the start of play. "This tournament is more important than Deane Beman." On that the two men could agree, even if Beman didn't accept the invitation to attend the Masters. (Beman's other nemesis, the never-boring Mac O'Grady, remained uncharacteristically quiet during the Masters. He shot 82–70—152 and missed the cut.)

Ballesteros had played in only two tournaments in the States before the Masters, and one of those wasn't even on the PGA Tour. He finished tied for 22nd (worth $1,375) in a satellite event in Lake City, Florida, in late February. He missed the cut in the USF&G Classic in New Orleans, the one tournament Beman allowed him to play (he was defending champion) in late March. In the interim, Ballesteros had rushed home to Spain to be at the bedside of his father, who succumbed to cancer.

In light of all this, how sharp could Seve's game be? He answered, sharply, upon his arrival in Augusta, "This tournament is mine." No doubts there, though he would later recant that statement.

Ballesteros also showed a sharp wit. When asked during a press conference on Wednesday, his 29th birthday, about the effect his lack of competitive golf would have on his chances, Ballesteros replied, "I know this course as good as I know my house." The suggestion was made that his profession didn't allow him to be in that house often. Ballesteros smiled. "It is a small house," he said. "One bathroom, one bedroom. I know it." Someone asked him about the problems caused the foreign golfers by an IRS ruling that anyone in the United States more than 120 days would have their worldwide earnings subjected to American taxes. "I'm not having any problems with taxes," Ballesteros said. "I'm not making any money. I'm $90 up in side bets this week. That's the biggest check I've won all year."

The other co-favorite, defending champion Bernhard Langer of West Germany, was more serious in lamenting the IRS ruling, with good reason. He ranked fifth in money winnings with $160,515, even though he hadn't won a tournament. He had come close in San Diego, where Tway beat him in a sudden-death playoff.

The course Langer would play wasn't the same one on which he won the year before. The greens on the ninth and 18th holes had been tampered with, in order to make them—easier? It's true. The players' annual complaints about the severity of the bent grass greens, installed in the autumn of 1980, finally had been heard. The back edge of both greens was lowered by a foot and a half, and each green was lengthened. "The club came to the conclusion that the pin areas and slopes should be altered for a more fair test of golf," said course superintendent Billy Fuller.

Amid all the comebacks, a tip of the cap to Fuller. With cooperation from the heavens, Fuller brought forth the return of the azaleas, which survived the winter unscathed and emerged their old resplendent selves right on schedule. They could also be seen in bright sunshine every day of the week except Tuesday, when two hard showers put a damper on the practice rounds. The .72 inches of rain left the course a tad vulnerable until Thursday's winds dried it out. All four of the tournament rounds were played in dry, temperate weather, albeit cooler than normal for a Georgia spring. The thermometer didn't often read above 70.

Wednesday's annual par-three contest is the only time all week that staid Augusta National lets down its hair. Anyone may wander in off Washington Avenue and buy a ticket, though lines were so long for both the par-three and the practice rounds that advance sales are being considered. The players concentrate on having a good time and entertaining the audience. Payne Stewart, the walking haberdashery, appeared in black plus fours, a tuxedo shirt and black tie, while former champion Billy Casper wore a purple getup that might have gotten him arrested in an earlier era.

But neither was the best sight of the nine-hole event, nor was Gary Player's ace at No. 7, the first hole-in-one in the par-three since 1983. Player made that one, too. No, the warmest applause was reserved for Byron Nelson, the two-time Masters champion making his first appearance at Augusta National in several years. Nelson had been sidetracked by his wife Louise's long illness, which ended in her death in 1985. Nelson has, thankfully for the rest of us, returned to the public eye. Nelson played in the par-three as part of a threesome with two of his protégés, fellow two-time champion Tom Watson and Scott Verplank, the Texan who was making his first appearance at Augusta as a professional.

As full of folly as the par-three is, the sight of Larry Mize losing the title in a playoff made everyone wince. Mize is a native Augustan, and two weeks before the Masters, he had fumbled away a four-shot lead on the final nine of the TPC and lost to John Mahaffey. This time, he made it to the third hole of sudden death, only to lose to Gary Koch. Mize would make a stab at redemption in the final round of the tournament, when his 65 propelled him to a two-under-286 finish and a tie for 16th, which, of course, qualified him for the 1987 Masters.

Both Mize and Koch had played the nine-hole tournament in four-under 23. Though Koch contended early in the tournament, he continued the tradition of a par-three champion never being victorious on Sunday. The other losing streak, belonging to winners of the annual precursor to the

Masters, the Greater Greensboro Open, would be carried on by Sandy Lyle of Scotland, who nonetheless earned the admiration of all on Sunday. Having been tapped by destiny as the unfortunate who would be paired with Nicklaus, the 1985 British Open champion never allowed his concentration to falter, and responded with a one-under 71.

In what would be a Masters relatively free of controversy, one arose because of the Augusta National's decision not to extend invitations to all the members of the European Ryder Cup team that had so soundly thrashed the Americans at The Belfry. Only those who otherwise qualified—Ballesteros, Langer and Lyle—were in the field of 88. So many professionals had qualified domestically, along with the high number of amateurs (10) that are invited in a post-Walker Cup year, that there had to be a restriction on foreign invitees, said tournament chairman Hord Hardin. "So many of our patrons have to stay as much as 100 to 150 miles away and drive in every day," Hardin said. "We don't want 7 a.m. starting times."

As it was, the honorary starting twosome of Gene Sarazen and Sam Snead were scheduled for 8:15 a.m. Thursday. The morning was so cool—sweaters and blazers were abundant along the veranda—that the two of them teed off several minutes early. Didn't want to stand around too long. Playing on the theme of their print advertisement for Wilson Ultras, Sarazen asked Snead if he was using one of his long balls, which solicited a good chuckle from the early birds stationed around the first tee. Snead responded with a trademark drive down the middle, and Sarazen matched it. Few minded that he did so on a mulligan.

The traditional opening round pairings were made along the same lines as in past years. The amateur champions received royal treatment. The British winner, Garth McGimpsey of Northern Ireland, teed off at 10:01 a.m. with four-time Masters champion Palmer, while U.S. winner Sam Randolph of Southern California played with the defending champion, Langer, beginning at 11:53 a.m. Other pairings of interest included:

11:04 a.m.	Fuzzy Zoeller, Jay Sigel
11:39 a.m.	John Mahaffey, Lee Trevino
11:46 a.m.	Raymond Floyd, Sandy Lyle
12:07 p.m.	Curtis Strange, Tom Kite
12:28 p.m.	Seve Ballesteros, Hal Sutton
1:03 p.m.	Jack Nicklaus, Scott Verplank

The two leaders, however, came from pairings that no one particularly noticed. And they weren't nearly as interesting as their caddies. At 8:37 a.m., in the second group, Bill Kratzert, who qualified for the championship by tying for 14th in the 1985 Masters, went off the first tee with Roger Maltbie, and at 10:15 a.m., Ken Green, the 1985 Buick Open champion, began his round with Bill Glasson. Kratzert's bag was carried by Chuck Hofius, a microwave components salesman from Kratzert's hometown of Fort Wayne, Indiana. Green's caddy was his older sister, Shelley.

Hofius was playing shutterbug Wednesday, awaiting the beginning of Kratzert's practice round, when Kratzert approached him and told him that he had fired his caddy. "I told him, 'Pick up the bag. Let's go,' " Kratzert said. "He was pretty scared. He kept asking me what to do and where to stand." Hofius, who met Kratzert in a Fort Wayne donut shop, said "I was drafted. It was like, 'OK boy, Uncle Bill wants you.' "

Kratzert mentioned how pleasant it had been to have a friend available for in-round bullshooting. It took the edge off the pressure. Green had the same thing in mind when he coaxed his sister away from her bookkeeping job in Florida in 1983. "She has no clue at all when it comes to golf," Ken announced. "I'm just out there for moral support," Shelley said. "He loves to talk. He's a little chatterbox out there." She calls him "Greenie." The Masters put a crimp in their style: the two of them often dress in the same ensemble. Shelley donned the familiar white coveralls, though Masters officials exempted her from the rule that all caddies must change into civilian clothes in their waiting area before leaving tournament grounds and allowed her the privacy of her own hotel room.

As one may imagine, Kratzert and Green, who also share the same guru in teaching pro Peter Kostis, played in relative anonymity. Judging from their rounds, the place to watch them was the first green. Kratzert began his day by rolling in a 60-footer from the front of the green over the rise. Green did the same from 40 feet, and each continued to ride his putters to the top of the leaderboard. Kratzert added a birdie at the par-four 360-yard seventh by landing his approach shot within two feet, then bogeyed the 435-yard par-four ninth to make the turn at one-under 35, as did his partner, Maltbie. The twosome reached the 16th tee at three-under, but Maltbie hit into the water and took a double-bogey five. Kratzert, who had made four on each of the back nine's par-fives, rolled in an eight-footer for birdie at 17 and finished with a 68, three shots ahead of his partner.

Kratzert had completed his third consecutive round below 70 at Augusta National. After being in the first twosome off the tee in last year's third round, Kratzert strung together two 69s. Yet he called this "the best complete 18 holes I've put together at Augusta." Green, about nine holes behind Kratzert, birdied the second hole and bogeyed the third, then he started banging the cup from as far away as he could get. Green sank a 70-footer at the fifth hole to return to two-under, birdied the par-three sixth and made the turn in 33. As Green made the turn, another player began putting up red numbers in a hurry. Koch, an hour ahead of Green, bounced back from three consecutive bogeys through the turn to reel off birdies at 12, 13, 15 and 16, three from 30 feet or longer, and finished at 69. Green kept pace with Koch on the back nine, though consistency wasn't the hallmark of his game. He bogeyed the 10th and 17th holes and birdied the 13th, 16th and 18th, the latter from 40 and 35 feet, respectively, to bring home a 68.

Green had also shared the first-round lead two weeks earlier at the TPC. He wasn't sure what to make of his four-under performance. "What can I say? So I made a few putts, four or five no-brainers," the 27-year-old Connecticut native said. Green also reminded everyone that he was not the reigning PGA champion—"the other day I was playing with Hubert and at the ninth green, a lady asked, 'Why does Hubert Green have two caddys?' "

Shelley was a trendsetter in gender only. Tsuneyuki Nakajima of Japan and Ballesteros also employed their brothers as caddys, and both men broke par (Ballesteros, however, brought Vicente, instead of Manuel, the brother/caddy with whom he had quarreled during the 1985 Masters. "You know us

Spaniards," Seve said. "We have hot blood."). Neither would break 70, however. When three golfers did so in the morning rounds, eyebrows were raised across the course. But then the wind, out of the west, raised a notch, too. The greens dried out quickly, and Augusta National began counter-punching. Receiving those blows were the marquee golfers, who teed off later in order to provide USA Cable watchers with a good show. Johnny Miller, in the back fringe at the par-three 12th, putted down the hill toward the pin and watched as the ball lost its brakes and dove into Rae's Creek. He finished with a 74. Only five players reached the 15th green in two all day. It quickly became apparent that the early leaders weren't going to be challenged until Friday.

Two players from the Far East, Nakajima and Chen Tze-Chung of Taiwan, known in these parts as Tommy and T.C., respectively, came the closest to mastering the afternoon winds. Chen blazed through Amen Corner, making birdies at the 11th through the 14th holes to reach three under. At 18, his 12-foot putt for a share of the lead slid just below the cup. Nakajima bogeyed the first two holes, then settled down with a 15-foot birdie putt at No. 3. Birdies at Nos. 5, 8, 10 and 13 brought him to the 18th tee three under, and he, too, would take a stab at sharing the lead. "I was aiming for a birdie," he said. "I used a six iron when I probably should have used a five." His approach shot flew over the green and he couldn't get up and down for par.

Two other foreigners, Norman of Australia and Dave Barr of Canada, joined Nakajima at 70, along with a trio of domestics: Kite, Tway, who had been relegated to the last twosome of the day, and Watson, who needed nine one-putts to quell his balky irons. This was a change. His putter had been the culprit in his recent fall from grace. "The wind was blowing shots all over the place," he said. "(My putting) was nice to see. I'm putting with a lot of confidence now for the first time in a long time."

Another half-dozen were at one-under 71: Maltbie, Ben Crenshaw, Danny Edwards, Corey Pavin, Hubert Green and Ballesteros. That made for a total of 16 players under, and adding Glasson and Fred Couples at even par, 18 within four shots of the lead. The most popular score of the day was two-over 74, achieved by a dozen competitors, including Langer and Nicklaus. After Nicklaus got up-and-down for par from the back fringe at 18, Pat Summerall intoned, "And he's not out of the picture."

In the next morning's *Los Angeles Times,* Mike Downey wrote, "When athletes in other sports lost whatever edge made them excel, they often retired to a lifetime of golf. What, then, is a Nicklaus to do?"

Shoot a one-under par 71 and reach the halfway point at one-over 145. "Well, it's the best two rounds I've played this year," Nicklaus said Friday. "I've hit the ball very well, and yesterday I had 11 what I call makeable putts, from 15 feet and in, putts I had to make, and I made one of them. Today I had 12 and I made four of them. When I have the ball that close to the hole and I play that well, I've got to make more putts. I think the greens are very, very difficult right now. And I'm amazed the guys are making many putts out there. It's real tough."

Much was made in 1986 of the demise of the American golfer. Though it was hardly news to the cognoscenti, the general public didn't begin to realize the enormity of the change until the Masters. Friday's second round went a long way toward making things perfectly clear. Golf again belonged to the rest of the world.

When play ended, five of the first eight spots belonged to the passport brigade. The leaderboard looked as follows:

Seve Ballesteros	71–68—	139
Bill Kratzert	68–72—	140
Tommy Nakajima	70–71—	141
Danny Edwards	71–71—	142
Ben Crenshaw	71–71—	142
Greg Norman	70–72—	142
T. C. Chen	69–73—	142
Bernhard Langer	74–68—	142

First, the casualties: Ken Green disappeared quickly, taking bogeys on the fourth through seventh holes and shooting 41 on the front side. He finished the round in six-over 78 and, at 146, had fallen seven shots out of the lead. Judging from his puckish behavior in a post-round press conference, he knew it wasn't a question of whether his game would disintegrate, just when. He described his round as "hockey in the trees. It's playoff time for hockey," said the Connecticut Yankee, "and I wanted to get in the mood." Barr and Couples also excused themselves from the frontrunners, each shooting 77 to fall to five- and seven-over par respectively. A Couples drive gone awry struck a patron in the back on the 11th hole, a patron who thought herself versed enough in golf to avoid being struck. Said a bruised Mitzi Edge, on leave from the LPGA Tour, "I didn't think he could hit it that far."

The rest of the field, however, seemed to close ranks. Langer was the first to make a move, shooting 32 on the back side. He gave credit for his 68 to a switch he made to a lighter putter after Thursday's round. "The greens were so fast I felt I couldn't do much with the heavy putter," he said. "Now I can hit through the ball."

Ballesteros, Kratzert, Chen and Watson were tied for the lead at four under as the final twosomes reached the back nine holes. With a birdie at 10, Watson grabbed his share of the lead, replacing Norman, his playing partner, who four-putted the swiftly sloping green and took a double-bogey six. Watson then stumbled through Amen Corner with a bogey and triple bogey at 11 and 12. On the latter hole, the wind knocked his tee shot into Rae's Creek and he followed that with a three-putt. He came home with a two-over 74, even for the championship.

Then Crenshaw reappeared. It seemed as if he had been missing for two years, since that sentimental Sunday when he won his green coat after so many near-misses. He had been through a divorce, and a thyroid condition that caused mood swings and a precipitous loss of weight. He missed 14 of 23 cuts in 1985, winning only $25,814. Crenshaw had nearly matched that amount in 1986 when he came to the Masters, and couldn't have been more pleased now that his life (he's remarried) was coming back into order. "I don't think anyone has had a more up-and-down career than I have," he said after Friday's round. "When you're off your game, you wonder how you ever let it get that bad in the first place. Then you wonder if you'll ever get it back."

He got his round back with an eagle at 13, sinking a 30-foot putt, to move to three under. He would lose a stroke to par with a three-putt at 15, the par putt doing a boomerang act around the cup from three-and-a-half feet.

Ballesteros had lost his share of the lead when he mis-hit a three-wood second shot at 13 out of the right rough and into Rae's Creek. Then he suddenly reasserted himself. Ballesteros had reached the 15th green in two, hitting what was by far the longest drive of the day on the 500-yard par-five, then, from 225 yards out, plopping a three wood 25 feet away from the pin. As the putt rolled toward the hole, he raised his arms high above his head in that familiar triumphant gesture. Suddenly, as it dropped, he was five under, with a two-stroke lead over Crenshaw, Kratzert, Chen and another late charger, Nakajima. Seve's aggressiveness backhanded him on the next hole, when he overruled brother Vicente and hit a five iron off the tee instead of a six. Faced with a downhill shot out of a bunker to a cup on a downslope, Ballesteros took not his sand wedge but his putter. The ploy failed to get him close to the hole, and he two-putted to fall to four under.

As it became clear that Ballesteros would have the second-round lead, a handful of other golfers began watching his score with more than casual interest. The Masters cuts to low 44 and ties, but includes all those within 10 shots of the lead. Ballesteros's bogey at 16 gave hope to two former champions, Craig Stadler (1984) and, in his 29th Masters, 50-year-old Gary Player (1961, 1974, 1978), whose necks were on the guillotine at six-over 150. Player had reached 150 by shooting one-over 73 on Friday, and what he said after the round made my bones creak. "I played just as well as I did when I shot a 64 here," said Player, speaking of the round only eight years before that earned him his third green jacket. "I couldn't play any better." In eight years, he had aged nine strokes.

Ballesteros would cut the two of them off at 18, when he sank a 15-foot putt for a birdie to return to five under. That also broke a tie with Kratzert, who had a two-putt birdie at 13. Kratzert would swap shots with par over the next two holes as well, bogeying 14 but birdieing 15, to finish one shot out of the lead.

Despite the loss of Stadler and Player, a healthy number of 48 players made the cut. Among those who found themselves free for the weekend were Sutton, whose even par 72 couldn't repair the damage done by an opening 80; Hale Irwin, who has finished in the top 10 five times, but put together two rounds of 76; perennial Masters do-gooder Andy Bean (75–76); 1976 champion Floyd (74–78); Palmer (80–76—156); and all of the 10 amateurs except Randolph, who shot 75–73—148. He would add rounds of 72 and 73 to finish at five-over 293.

Friday, as always, was a day for shuffling around, jockeying for position. The moves begin on Saturday. On this particular Saturday, the golfers played a denuded course. The wind, the fangs in Augusta National's teeth, had left the greens crackling, so the decision was made to water, water everywhere. Then the winds disappeared. The third round resembled target practice. "The course was as defenseless as I've ever seen it," Watson said.

"How easy was it?" Nicklaus asked. "I was told there were only two bogeys on 12 and half the field made (scored) two. Does that answer your question?"

With conditions such as these, you would think Ballesteros would have distanced himself from the field. However, the wind allows Seve to show off his accurate touch. On this calm day, no one had a more accurate touch, or had had one in 49 previous Masters, than Zimbabwean-South African-Floridian Nick Price.

He had teed off at 11:56 a.m. Price's unremarkable opening round of 79, complete with six three-putts, had forced him to scramble for a three-under 69 on Friday just to make the cut. "After what Curtis did last year," said Price, referring to Strange's opening two rounds of 80–65, "everyone who shoots 78 or 79 doesn't give up."

His standing in 32nd place meant the early tee time, which, in turn, meant that his round went unseen by most of the world. Price was walking up the 18th green when CBS-TV began televising from Augusta. If you weren't there, you missed some show.

Well, you could have missed the first hole. Price did. He drove into the right fairway bunker, wedged out, hit another wedge 15 feet away from the pin and missed the par putt. One over. He bounced back with a one-putt birdie at the par-five second hole. Still, he reached the fifth tee even for the day, four over for the tournament, having missed two of the first four greens. Then he played the next 14 holes nine under par.

Price hit driver and five iron to 15 feet at the 435-yard fifth and made the putt. He sank a 20-footer from the fringe at the 180-yard par-three sixth, and as he had at No. 2, hit a wedge to six feet at the eighth and birdied the front side's other par five. He made the turn in 33. Beginning at No. 10, Price ran off four consecutive birdies, draining putts of four, 15 and 20 feet for the first three. "I knew I had two par fives left. It's not often that you get through 12 six under. I knew I was going after the record after 12," Price said.

Again, he didn't reach a par five in two. At 13, Price's drive went into the trees on the right side of the fairway. He punched out in front of Rae's Creek, and hit a wedge to six feet. He made that one, too, and stood seven under for the day. He had putted the ball 17 times in 13 holes. Tony Lema once said that the name Amen Corner came into being because when you leave the 13th hole you say "Amen." Price didn't have to say it—the throng that had coalesced at the far end of the Corner was screaming it, and a few "Hallelujahs" as well.

He parred the 14th in routine fashion, and stood on the tee at the top of the rolling 15th hole, the last par five, with the record in mind. One year ago to the day, Strange had stood on this tee seven under, thought of the record, and flailed his drive into the left rough en route to a bogey. Price hit his drive down the right side, laid up in front of the pond with a five iron and then hit a wedge to four feet. When the putt dropped, Price had birdied all four par fives without reaching any of the greens in two.

"The first time he mentioned the record," said Price's caddy, David McNeilly, "was on 15. He leaned over and said, 'The course record is on. Let's go.' Then he hit what I thought was his best shot of the round at 16."

Again with the five iron, Price dropped his tee shot within three feet of the cup. He made the two, his third birdie of a par three, and his 10th birdie in 15 holes. Two to play. He was nine under, and two pars would break the course record set by Lloyd Mangrum in the opening round in 1940, and equaled by Nicklaus (third round, 1965), Maurice Bembridge of England (fourth, 1974), Hale Irwin (fourth, 1975), Player (fourth, 1978) and Miller Barber (second, 1979).

A 15-foot birdie attempt at 17 slid past the cup. "I only hit two poor shots," Price said. "My drives on the opening and closing holes. I wasn't going to back off. I was greedy." From the rough on 18, he hit a four iron to 30 feet away. The thunderous applause rained down upon him as he walked up the 18th fairway. Price studied the putt and, as he promised, he didn't back off. He stroked the ball hard, so hard that it hit the back of the cup, circled the rim and settled on the edge. The tap-in gave him the course record and a five-under 211 score for the tournament. Had that 30-footer fallen, Price would have scored 29 on the back side.

"I think," Price said, "Bobby Jones held up his hand from somewhere and said, 'That's enough, boy.' "

But it wasn't enough, only the biggest of the assaults. It was the kind of day when Donnie Hammond, the quiet Floridian who won the Bob Hope Chrysler tournament to get his first invitation to the Masters, shot a five-under 67 and tied Price at 211. (This was actually Hammond's second Masters. He had worked as a gallery guard at the 13th hole 10 years before). It was the kind of day when Langer would reach five under with a 69 and say, "I just feel it could have two or three shots better."

It was the kind of day when Norman, who, after his four-putt double bogey at the 10th hole on Friday, fought back with birdies at Nos. 15 and 16 to finish two under, blitzed the back nine Saturday in 32 to shoot four-under 68 and take the third-round lead by himself at six-under 210. He got there, Norman said, by being patient. "In the past, I've always been too aggressive here. I've changed my line of thinking," said Norman, giving an inkling of how he had matured into who would be the best golfer of 1986.

It was the kind of day when the two Toms, Watson and Kite, playing together, would each shoot 68 and finish in a tie with a third Tom, Nakajima, at four-under 212. Nakajima played the first 12 holes Saturday poorly, dropping three strokes to par. He stood even for the tournament. But he rallied with birdies at four of the next five holes to thrust himself back into contention. In fact, nearly everyone would have the sort of streak during the third round that Nakajima had. Only 14 players failed to match or break par (though one of them was Kratzert, who shot four-over 76 and faded to even 216). Seventeen players broke 70.

It was that kind of day for nearly all of the contenders, all except Ballesteros. The Spaniard's putter simply wouldn't cooperate. "I had 15 putts inside 20 feet and I didn't make any," Ballesteros said. He had clung doggedly to the lead for the first 16 holes. A birdie at the third hole had pushed him to six under, and then followed a string of 11 consecutive, frustrating pars. He once again mastered the 15th, this time with a birdie-four. He came to the 17th tee seven under, with a one-stroke lead over Norman.

Ballesteros bogeyed the final two holes. A three-putt from 50 feet at No.

17, followed by a wild drive at 18, and Ballesteros fell into a tie with Price, Hammond and Langer at five under, one stroke behind Norman. It also meant that instead of being in the showcase final pairing on Sunday, Ballesteros would play with Kite and Norman would play with Price, a close friend, neighbor and fishing and skiing buddy from Florida. "I like my position, but not the way I finished," Ballesteros said afterward. "I tell my brother that it was no good to have such a nice day."

The winds hadn't been there to spread the field. The contenders were all bunched: One at six under, four at five under and three at four under. Then, in a group of seven at two under, Nicklaus. His 69 had been only his second round below 70 in the last 15 at Augusta National. "I would assume I am close enough to be in the hunt," Nicklaus said. "Anytime you're in Augusta, it's the number of players rather than shots. Certainly where I am is in pretty good shape. I put myself in a position where, if I play a good round Sunday, I've got a good chance to win the golf tournament."

The last five twosomes of Sunday's final round:

1:32 p.m.	Sandy Lyle (214), Jack Nicklaus (214)
1:40 p.m.	Tom Watson (212), Tommy Nakajima (212)
1:48 p.m.	Seve Ballesteros (211), Tom Kite (212)
1:56 p.m.	Donnie Hammond (211), Bernhard Langer (211)
2:04 p.m.	Greg Norman (210), Nick Price (211)

The phone rang at the temporary Nicklaus abode in suburban Augusta early Sunday morning. "My son Steve called me," Jack would recount after it was all over, "and he asked me, 'Well, Pop, what's it going to take?' And I said, 'Sixty-six will tie and 65 will win.' And he said, 'Well, go ahead and do it.'" Just a little conversation between father and son, a chat that would become a symbol of Nicklaus's comeback. Actually, Jack's choice of shirt that day was also a symbol, one in memory of a friend. Craig Smith, the son of the minister of the Nicklauses' church in Florida, had died of cancer a couple of years before at the age of 13. "Craig always liked for me to wear a yellow shirt because he thought it was good luck," Nicklaus said. "I didn't tell anybody about it. But that's the reason I wore the yellow shirt. I saved it for Sunday."

The day came out of a North Georgia travelogue: sunny, temperate but with a breeze. The early finishing scores weren't extraordinary by any means. Only four of them broke 70. Veterans Johnny Miller and David Graham finished at two-over 290 with a 69 and a 68, respectively. Lanny Wadkins's 69 made up in part for his first-round 78, but he completed play at three-over 291. The other below-70 round drew all the attention. Mize never had broken 70 in 11 previous rounds at Augusta National, but his seven-birdie, no-bogey 65 left little doubt that he had put his TPC trauma behind him. He finished tied for 16th at two-under 286, which means he'll be invited back in 1987.

And, to begin with, the leaders did little to distinguish themselves as well. Norman clung to his lead through the first seven holes, saving pars at Nos. 1, 2 and 4. At the same time that Norman birdied the sixth to drop to seven under, Ballesteros made a three at the par-four seventh to remain within a stroke. The legend maintains that the Masters doesn't begin until the 10th tee on Sunday. This one heated up two holes earlier.

Ballesteros and Kite stood in the eighth fairway, six and three under, respectively, each with a short pitch to the green for their third shot. Kite, from 81 yards out, delicately landed a sand wedge close to the pin and watched it roll into the cup for an eagle-three. When the roar subsided, Ballesteros, 40 yards out and right of the mounds that protect the green, lobbed a wedge that stopped rolling when it landed on top of Kite's ball. Dueling eagles. Ballesteros, at eight under, also regained a one-shot lead over Norman.

One hole ahead, Nicklaus stood on the ninth green, now six shots out of first. He had birdied the par-five second hole to drop to three under, but three-putted the treacherous par-three fourth, missing a four-footer for par. He then missed a similar putt for birdie at the sixth. He was still two under. It was on the ninth green that his charge began.

Nicklaus' ball was 11 feet behind the hole. He cocked his ear toward the roar of eagles up the hill at the eighth, turned to the gallery surrounding the ninth green and said, "O.K., let's see if we can get a roar up here." The crowd laughed. Jack and Jackie, player and caddy, looked at the putt, compromised on their read of the green, and Jack sent it home. They got a roar up. Three under.

His tee shot at No. 10 hit a spectator on the right side of the fairway. The patron was unharmed. Nicklaus had a good lie, and hit his four iron 25 feet away. "For some reason," he would tell Ballard of *Sports Illustrated*, "as I looked at the putt it just looked like I was going to make it. I hit the ball. It rolled. I looked at it. It kept going." Four under. Nicklaus was three shots out of the lead, as Ballesteros bogeyed the ninth hole to fall into a tie with Norman, but more important, only six players were ahead of him. Kite, on the 10th tee, stood five under, as did Price and Langer, both of whom were on No. 8, and, because of a 31 on the front side, Jay Haas, who finished fifth in 1985.

A drive and eight iron at No. 11 left Nicklaus 22 feet away from the pin, tucked on the left side of the green behind the pond. Nicklaus, using Lyle's ballmark as a guide, putted inside of it by about an inch and sent it into the heart of the cup. Five under. CBS-TV's Steve Melnyk had to yell into his microphone to be heard above the din. The Augusta National telegraph hearkened everyone on the course to the fact that the Bear was loose. Only two players, Ballesteros and Norman, were in front of him. Kite had missed a six-foot birdie putt at the 10th, one of a series of makeable putts on the backside that just wouldn't fall for him. In the 19th holes and the living rooms of the world, golfers and nongolfers began to wonder whether they could get their hopes up.

The bottleneck of fans at the 11th green and 12th tee resembled Grand Central Station at rush hour, both in bodies and decibels. As Nicklaus told Ballard, "The hardest thing at Augusta is coming to the 12th tee pumped up. It leaves so much room for danger. If you shy off even a shade to the right you're going to catch the bank and go into the water, and if you shade off a little to the left, you can go into the back bunkers."

The hole was 162 yards away, the breeze beginning to kick in its typical late-afternoon dance. Nicklaus chose a seven iron over a six, aimed left to avoid Rae's Creek, and hit it too far left. The ball settled on the back fringe. Nicklaus left a pitch eight feet above the hole, and missed the delicate downhill putt. He dropped to four under, in a tie with Price and Langer, three shots out of the lead. He said afterward that the bogey won the championship for him. "I got aggressive after that," Nicklaus said. "I got determined."

Still, there were only six players ahead of him, though Kite would close the gap on his partner, Ballesteros, and Norman with a birdie at the 11th to go six under. And Norman was in trouble again at the 10th. The hole on which he had a four-putt double bogey on Friday was giving him fits again. His drive clipped a pine on the left side of the fairway, and kicked out into the fairway, but he was 300 yards away from the green on the 485-yard downhill par four. He leaned into a fairway wood, and pushed it into the gallery on the left, short of the green and behind a pine. His chip shot came out hot, skidded across the green and into the bunker, from where he failed to get up and down. Said his wife Laura, at the veranda, "Not the 10th again." Another double bogey, and the Aussie fell out of his share of the lead and into a tie with, among others, his playing partner, Price, who birdied the hole. Everyone agreed that Norman was out of contention. How could he bounce back from a double bogey?

Nicklaus' tee shot at the 13th hugged the trees. He came perilously close to missing the dogleg, and landed so near the edge that he had one of the few level lies available on the sloping fairway. "Shots like that are a little too much for a 24-year-old heart, Dad," Jackie said. But the gamble paid off: he needed only 210 yards to reach the green. He dropped a three iron 30 feet left of the hole and rolled it within tap-in range. Birdie. Five under. Tie with Norman and Price, Haas, who played the back side in a frustrating 36 and was in the clubhouse, and Payne Stewart, in red knickers and cap, and coming off a birdie at the 15th. Stewart would bogey the 17th, however, and finish at 69–284.

"I walked over to the 14th tee, looked up at the leader board and noticed that only Seve and Tom were ahead of me," Nicklaus told Ballard. "There were several guys tied with me, but I didn't even look to see who they were. I knew I was going to keep making birdies—or that I had to keep making birdies. I felt both ways."

Ballesteros and Kite, still seven and six under, came flying out of the tunnel at 13 with magnificent drives. Seve followed with a second shot that landed where Nicklaus's approach had, 30 feet away. Only the ball released, and rolled eight feet away. He made the putt, moved to nine under; Nicklaus was four shots out, and Seve and most of the patrons realized that, PGA Tour experience or no, Ballesteros was still the best in the world. This would be his third Masters. Who could have guessed that he would not play another hole under par?

Kite lost ground with his two-putt birdie at No. 13, though in moving to seven under, he broke a brief tie with Corey Pavin, who had eagled No. 15 from 30 feet. Pavin walked to the 16th tee with a smile on his face, but he had to be thinking about his scores on the par-three hole the previous three days:

bogey, bogey, double bogey. He hit a thin five iron and dumped it into the water. Another double bogey ensued, and he finished the tournament three under. "I think it's self-explanatory that the hole cost me the tournament," Pavin lamented afterward. Those six strokes would have made him nine under.

Nicklaus parred the 14th with a delicate pitch from the back fringe that stopped within lag range. He unleashed a long drive at the 15th, a 298-yarder that surprised even him. Standing at his bag, he turned to Jackie and said, "Think a three would go very far here?" "Let's see it," the son replied to the father. He took out a four iron for the 200-yard shot. "It never left the flag," he would tell Ballard. "It just covered it, and the ball came into the green moving slightly right to left. It landed about 18 inches short of the hole and ran 12 feet by. As I walked down on the green (not via the Sarazen Bridge, but on the right side, where he checked the nearby leaderboard) I knew I had to make the putt if I wanted to have a chance to win. I already knew that Seve had eagled 13."

Ballesteros was on the 14th green, just 20 feet away from a birdie that would for all intent end the tournament. He left it on the high side of the hole, just off the lip. Kite had dropped his approach only 10 feet short of the hole, and ran the ball in. He was seven under, two shots out again, and the two of them walked to the 15th tee. It would be some time before they completed that hole.

Nicklaus addressed his putt, then backed off because of applause at the nearby 16th green. "Even though the pin was not in the same place," he told Ballard, "I remembered the putt I had in 1975 when I left it short. I didn't hit it strong enough and the ball broke off on me. So this time I made sure that I didn't let the ball break off." He was in a tie for third place, with Haas, Watson, who stood out in the fairway watching him, waiting for the opportunity to make his third consecutive birdie, and McCumber, who had eagled the 15th.

He stroked the putt, and as it neared the hole, Jackie crouched, fists clenched. When it fell, he leaped high in the air, and hearts everywhere leaped with him. Seven under, and tied for second with Kite, one shot behind Ballesteros. That twosome heard it all from the tee up the hill. Jack walked to the side of the green, looked skyward and sighed. He looked misty-eyed as he walked to the 16th tee. "I couldn't hear anything," he said. "I mean, nothing!"

With the pin at No. 16 tucked tight on the pond and at the bottom of the green's swell, Nicklaus opted for a five iron on the 170-yard hole. Watson had just hit his second shot at the 15th where Nicklaus had been, so he had one putt to pull within a stroke of Ballesteros. Seve had hit a 302-yard drive, surely the longest of the day to that point, and was walking down the fairway as Nicklaus stood over his tee shot.

Jack didn't like where he had teed the ball, so he moved it to the right. He hit the ball, and as it reached its apex, he reached down and got his tee. For one thing, Nicklaus is too nearsighted to follow the ball in flight, and for another, the pin's location was too low to see where the ball would land. "I could hear the gallery at the green starting to rumble," Nicklaus said, "and I said, 'Oops, I've hit it close.' " The ball landed back of the pin, and backed up within inches of it before settling three feet below it. The roar was again the sound of jet engines. On the 15th green, Nakajima waited to putt until Nicklaus finished walking to the green, and Ballesteros waited a little longer in the fairway.

After Lyle had birdied from eight feet, quite a feat considering the noise and emotion building around his partner, and after Watson, back at 15, missed his eagle putt that some thought he might have rushed because of the impending explosion ahead, Nicklaus calmly rolled in his putt. Eight under. One stroke out. In the few minutes in which Nicklaus had made up the three-shot deficit, Ballesteros had been able to hit only one shot. Mostly he stood and listened and waited. Kite was first up. He hit a three iron 20 feet right of the hole.

"I wasn't under pressure," Ballesteros would say the next day. "It's just that I hit too easy a swing with a four iron. I should have hit a hard five." His shadow stretched behind him, Ballesteros swung and hit a pull hook that wasn't close to clearing the pond. There was a cheer; it was no murmur of disappointment like the one that followed Strange's poorly hit four iron the year before. The "funny sound" to which Nicklaus referred was a brief violation of golf etiquette, the kind rarely heard at Augusta National. Given the occasion, Mr. Roberts may have looked the other way. I'm not sure.

As he had at 10, Nicklaus hit his tee shot at No. 17 into the gallery on the left. "I kept getting tears in my eyes," he said. "I had to say to myself, 'Hey, you've got some golf left to play.' " Nicklaus had a good lie, however, and was only 125 yards away from the green. Three holes back, Norman rolled in a 15-foot putt for birdie to move to six under, two shots behind the leader, plural at least until Ballesteros stroked the eight-foot-par putt he stood over at the 15th. He left it out on the high side, and Nicklaus was suddenly a co-leader. Kite, who had left his eagle putt a distressing five feet short, rolled it in, and there were three leaders.

But not for long. Nicklaus lofted his pitch to 11 feet. "I knew that this putt would give me the lead," he told Ballard, "*if* I could make it. It was a two-break putt. The ball broke right and then turned immediately back to the left and went in, absolutely dead center." Nicklaus waved his putter in a big arc, urging the ball in, and that's the shot that made the magazine covers and front pages. Venturi, the winner of perhaps the most emotional U.S. Open in 1964, told the CBS-TV audience, "This is the most emotional and largest ovation I've ever heard."

At No. 16, Kite had hit the ball through the green into the gallery, and had a tricky downhill pitch to the pin. Ballesteros had an entirely different problem. His ball was only 15 feet short of the pin, but it was perched on the lip of the steep bunker that fronts the green. He stood with his right foot in the sand, his left on the grass and with his hands halfway down the shaft of the putter.

It was a great improvisation from the master of such, and he putted the ball within a foot of the cup. Kite's putt from off the green ran seven feet past the hole, but he made the putt he had to make to stay in contention. Meanwhile, the workers on the large scoreboard behind No. 16, who had been waiting patiently for the players to finish the hole, forwarded the news everyone had been waiting to hear. As Ballesteros and Kite walked off the green, a big red "9" on Nicklaus's row of numbers. The crowd erupted.

Norman, who at No. 15 had hit the longest drive of this or probably any other day, 310 yards, two-putted from 40 feet to move to seven under. "Everybody was following Jack and Seve and there was about 70 people following us," Norman said. "I looked over at Nicky and said, 'Let's just wake these people up and let them know we're still here.' "

The leaders (only four, as Watson's charge had stalled at six under) looked like this:

Jack Nicklaus	Nine under, 17 holes played
Seve Ballesteros	Eight under, 16 holes played
Tom Kite	Eight under, 16 holes played
Greg Norman	Seven under, 15 holes played

Nicklaus hit a textbook drive at the 18th, but failed to hit his second shot onto the upper plateau of the bi-level green. He was 40 feet away, below the hole. He walked up the hill to Hoganesque applause. Then he stood over the ball as long as he ever did, putted it right at the heart of the hole, only to watch it stop a foot short. He allowed Lyle to putt out for his 71–285, then he tapped in. Yet another roar, probably the warmest one, in appreciation from those who realized that, win or lose, he had returned to them in grand fashion.

He wouldn't lose to Ballesteros, who, as he had in the third round, hit a poor approach at the 17th and found himself 50 feet away. Seve knew he was one shot behind, and he knew that birdies at 18 are given, not taken. He decided to roll the dice on this one putt. He wasn't going to be short. When the ball stopped, 10 feet past the hole, he wasn't going to be the champion, either. The heart gone out of him, Ballesteros three-putted, and fell to seven under. After putting out, in realization that his challenge was over, Ballesteros tipped his cap and said, "Thank you" to the cheering crowd.

Kite made his par at the 17th to roars from the hole behind him. Norman had hit his tee shot high and right of the pin at No. 16 and watched the ball trickle down within four feet of the hole. He knocked the ball firmly into the cup, and suddenly *he* was eight under. Kite, however, had finally gotten to the 72nd green with a chance for a playoff. He could ask for no better. From 165 yards, he had dropped an eight iron onto the upper plateau of the green only eight feet from the cup. If he made the putt, it would put him in the best position yet to end the incessant description of Kite as the best current player never to win a major.

He headed right for the pin, right for it, and somehow rode across the lower lip of the cup without falling. He ended the championship one shot out. "I made that putt," Kite said. "It just didn't go in. Honest to God I had hit that exact same putt seven or eight times in practice. I knew where it was going. It never went left. For some reason, it went left that time. Maybe it hit a spike mark. Who knows? When I walked up I said, 'Gosh! I've had this putt before. Nothing to it. Just hit it firm.' It takes a good, solid putt. How it did what it did, I'll never know. It was 10 to 12 feet and in a perfect place below the cup. I can go out there right now and never hit a better putt."

And then there was Norman. He had sprayed his tee shot at No. 17 left, just short of the seventh green and in a divot mark next to a sprinkler. He had two tall pines just in front of him, and he was one shot behind Nicklaus, who watched him on television from the safety of the Bobby Jones cabin aside the 10th tee. Norman dug under the ball, pinched off his follow-through, and lifted the ball over the trees. It bounced in front of the green and rolled up to the green, stopping 12 feet short of the hole. Again, he beelined the ball to the bottom of the cup. Again, for the first time since the 10th hole, he had a share of the lead. A birdie wins it. A par puts a 31-year-old man in a playoff with a 46-year-old man who would have been stiffening for the better part of an hour.

"The last two days I hit a driver," Norman said. "This time I hit a three wood. But I suppose I should have used a driver again." He was 175 yards away from the green. Alongside him stood his caddy, Pete Bender.

"Four?" Norman asked.

"It's the perfect club," Bender replied.

Norman lashed into it. "I think that shot was the first time I let my ego get the better of me," he said. "My style of play is to win—and win as soon as I can. I wanted to try to hit a high shot, but I hit the ball too high and too hard. I didn't get enough weight transferred on my swing and I left the club face open." The ball landed 10 people deep into the gallery on the right side of green, pin high, but above the hole with a bunker in between. The best chance Norman had to save par was to drop the ball on the back of the green and hope it didn't run too far away. He hit an excellent shot, stopping the ball 16 feet behind the hole.

The par putt drifted to the left, four feet past the hole.

Nicklaus had his sixth Masters title.

After the TV ceremony with Hardin, after Langer had held his green jacket for him to slip into, Nicklaus went to the press tent. It was a love-in.

"Where do you want me to start? 1959?" he asked. He was gentle in serving up the crow. The subject of McColister's column arose.

"To be honest, I kind of agreed with it, I'm afraid," Nicklaus said. "But I got to thinking. 'Dead, huh? Washing-up, huh?' And I sizzled for a while. But I said to myself, 'I'm not going to quit now, playing the way I'm playing. I've played too well, too long to let a shorter period of bad golf be my last.

"This was Sunday at the Masters," he continued. "There's a lot of pressure. The other guys feel it, too. They can make mistakes. I knew that if I kept my composure down the stretch, as long as I kept making birdies, I'd be OK. I kept that right at the front of my mind.

"I don't like to win a golf tournament on somebody else's mistakes. I like to win with my own clubs. But I'm tickled pink. Over the last few years, some people have done things, things I have no control over, that kept me from winning golf tournaments. Like what happened at Pebble Beach (when Watson chipped in at the 71st hole to steal the 1982 U.S. Open). This time, a couple of guys were good to me and allowed me to win."

Said a philosophical Kite, "Golf is not like tennis, nor basketball or football, where you can control your opponent. You cannot control your opponent. If Jack misses a couple of putts, I win the tournament. But he didn't did he? We did."

3.   The U.S. Open

It is one of the quirks of big-time golf that only the Masters and the British Open, among the four major competitions, are organized and controlled totally by their sponsoring organizations. The Augusta National Golf Club, which runs the Masters, and the Royal and Ancient Golf Club of St. Andrews, which conducts the British Open Championship, not only run the competitions, they also take care of such ancillary matters as ticket sales, marshals, housing for players and press, parking, and all the other details that go into the conduct of a modern major sports spectacle. Traditionally, however, the PGA of America, which runs the PGA Championship, and the United States Golf Association, the sponsor of the U.S. Open Championship, have been satisfied to run the actual competition and, aside from telling the host club how they want the course set up, turn over the day-to-day work to committees of volunteer members organized by the clubs themselves.

This system has worked successfully for the U.S. Open. The clubs have enjoyed the arrangement because they've earned large amounts of money through the sale of program advertising (the Masters has never had a program), through the sale of tickets (the club gets one third of the money), all the revenue from parking, and a substantial portion of the income from concessions. By the middle 1980s, a club could earn well over $1 million, which certainly helps in holding down assessments and in paying off the enormous tax bills some of them face.

By choosing to take the Open to the Shinnecock Hills Golf Club in 1986, the USGA had to abandon its usual method, however, and take on the overall management of the championship itself, just like Augusta and the R&A, because Shinnecock Hills, near the village of Southampton, on the eastern end of Long Island, has only a small seasonal membership and couldn't provide the volunteers who are so eager to participate at other clubs. The small wooden clubhouse, a relic of the late 19th century, is neither air-conditioned nor heated. It is open only from early May until early November. Then the doors are closed, the electricity turned off, and out on the golf course the flagsticks are taken from the holes. Shinnecock Hills is closed.

With no membership to call on, the USGA relied on staff members, who handled their normal assignments as well as the added burdens of the Open, and some additional temporary personnel.

As if this weren't enough of a handicap, the four-lane divided highway leading from the west funnels into a two-lane county road about a mile from the club's entrance. Everyone assumed traffic would back up and create nightmarish problems. All things considered, the 1986 Open figured to be a disaster.

Instead, it was a triumph. Traffic flowed smoothly; everyone who either wanted or could afford one had a hotel room ($150 a night was an ordinary price that week); and Raymond Floyd played some wonderful golf, shooting

66 in the last round—32 over the last nine holes—finished the 72 holes in 279, and won by two strokes over Lanny Wadkins and Chip Beck.

While Floyd's golf was superb and his victory was popular with both the fans and the other golfers, it was overshadowed to some degree by the golf course, for this was not your normal United States Open course.

Shinnecock Hills reaches back to the roots of golf in the United States. The club was organized and its original course laid out in the early 1890s after a chance meeting between William K. Vanderbilt, Duncan Cryder, and Edward S. Mead, three men of wealth and influence. They were vacationing at the time that Willie Dunn, Jr., a small, neat, Scottish golfer-turned-architect, was laying out a course near Biarritz, a popular French resort on the Bay of Biscay just north of the Spanish border. Dunn had designed the Royal Montreal Golf Club in the 1870s, but he had returned to Europe, believing France had a more promising future in golf than the United States. When the Americans asked him for a demonstration of this new game, Dunn played several shots across a ravine to within a few yards of one of his new holes. Convinced by this demonstration that golf would catch on back home, the Americans persuaded Dunn to come back and build a course on 80 acres of land they had bought for $2,500 about two miles from the Shinnecock Indian Reservation.

When Dunn arrived in March of 1891 he was shown some rolling, sandy ground covered with blackberry bushes and dotted with burial mounds. With about 150 Indians from the reservation as his labor force, Willie had 12 holes ready for play by June. (If not memorable, golf course building and design was at least quick in those days.) Dunn left some of the burial mounds where they stood, scraping away the faces and converting them to bunkers or other obstacles.

Golf caught on better than anyone expected. Soon the original 12 holes became congested, and Dunn added an additional nine holes for the exclusive use of women golfers. The entire complex was abandoned before long, and a new 18-hole course was built. It might have been the first 18-hole course in the United States.

Shinnecock also had the first clubhouse built expressly for a golf club. It was designed by Stanford White, a partner in the celebrated New York firm of McKim, Mead & White. White also designed the original Madison Square Garden and lived in an apartment on the upper floors. In 1906 he was shot and killed in the roof garden cabaret by Henry K. Thaw, the wealthy husband of the showgirl Evelyn Nesbitt, who had become White's mistress. The incident was dramatized in the movie *The Girl In the Red Velvet Swing*.

When the United States Golf Association was formed, in 1894, Shinnecock became one of the five charter members, and in 1896 it became the site of the second U.S. Open and Amateur (they were both played during the same week). H. J. Whigham, an Englishman who had emigrated to the United States and become drama critic of the *Chicago Tribune,* won the Amateur, and James Foulis, a Scottish immigrant, won the Open, only a 36-hole event in those days (it went to 72 holes in 1898).

No black man has ever won the Open, but one came very close at Shinnecock. John Shippen, a young caddy whose father was a Presbyterian minister-teacher at the Indian reservation, entered and played over the protest of some foreign professionals (Theodore Havemeyer, the USGA president, told them Shippen was going to play even if they didn't). A 78 in the first round left Shippen tied for first place with five others, including Foulis. Shippen and Foulis played stroke-for-stroke through the first 12 holes, but after driving into a sand road on the 13th, a short par four, Shippen wasted a number of strokes trying to dig the ball out and eventually made 11. He shot 81 against the 74 of Foulis, and finished fifth, with 159. Foulis shot 152.

Shinnecock Hills had measured only 4,423 yards for the Open, but in the next few years the course was rebuilt, strengthening what the members had perceived as weaknesses exposed by the best players of the day. New tees stretched Shinnecock to more than 5,000 yards (many par-four holes were lengthened to around 400 yards and two par-fives pushed beyond 500 yards), greens were remodeled and made larger, and fairways and greens seeded with finer strains of grass. When the revisions were completed, the members felt they had as fine a course as any.

After the 1896 Open and Amateur and the Women's Amateur of 1900, which was won by Beatrix Hoyt, a club member (her third consecutive championship), the USGA more or less forgot about Shinnecock. Nevertheless, the club became a center of social life in the Hamptons (Southamption, Bridgehampton, East Hampton, all wealthy enclaves of the moneyed class). During the 1920s Shinnecock and the Meadow Club, the tennis counterpart of the golf group, became the hub of weekend partying. Shinnecock held dances on Friday nights and the Meadow Club on Saturdays. Young couples arrived with their hip flasks and spent the evenings dancing the Charleston and the black bottom and listened to the brassy sounds of the Sheik of Araby and the mellow tones of Poor Butterfly, strolled the moonlit dunes, and stayed for an early breakfast of scrambled eggs and sausage. Here was the ambience Jay Gatsby lusted for.

It was nice while it lasted, but times changed, and over the next two decades, Shinnecock Hills changed too. A highway was routed through the property, destroying parts of the old course and forcing the club to rebuild. The expense of the new course, the effects of first the Depression and then the Second World War and the decline of golf during that time, together with social and economic changes, brought Shinnecock close to ruin. It was saved by some longtime members who organized a refinancing in 1948.

To build the new course, Shinnecock called on the organization of Toomey and Flynn, which had originated in Philadelphia but by then had an office in New York. The choice couldn't have been better, for Bill Flynn, who did the design work, was among the most gifted of golf course architects. His organization was responsible for a number of courses where national championships have been played: Cherry Hills, in Denver; nine holes of The Country Club, in Brookline, Massachusetts; the James River course of the Country Club of Virginia, near Richmond; the Kittansett Club, on Buzzard's Bay, in Massachusetts; and the Cascades course of The Homestead, in Hot Springs, Virginia, perhaps the country's finest mountainside course. He also laid out the Spring Mill course of the Philadelphia Country Club, where Byron Nelson won his Open and where Sam Snead took an eight on the last hole to lose, but this is not among his finer works.

Flynn had become interested in golf course design in the early years of the century, when he worked on the construction of the Merion Golf Club, near Philadelphia. Hugh Wilson, a Merion member, was largely responsible for the design, and Flynn was the club's greenkeeper. When the job was finished, the two of them talked about a partnership. Wilson's health was failing, though, and he decided against it. Flynn went ahead, anyhow, and joined with Howard Toomey, a prominent Philadelphia engineer who was a close friend of Wilson's, and formed the architectural concern of Toomey and Flynn (the combination of names had a nice bouncy rhythm). With Flynn handling the design work and Toomey the construction and finance, the firm prospered.

Besides creating some of our finest golf courses, Toomey and Flynn helped develop young designers as well. Dick Wilson and Bill Gordon were among their disciples. Flynn's influence is evident in many of their creations, especially in the serpentine fairway contouring he did so well. Dick Wilson worked on the Shinnecock renovation, walking the course each night, occasionally playing shots to the greens, but more often toward the bunkers, shaping them to gather in the misplayed shots.

Dunn's original course had lain between the clubhouse and the south shore of Long Island. With part of that property gone because of the road, Toomey and Flynn turned away from the Atlantic and built their new course to the north. The land where the old course lay was abandoned, but some of Dunn's work is still there; old caddys who were around before the new course was built can lead you through the scrub and point out abandoned greens and old bunkers carved into the sides of steep hills.

The Toomey and Flynn Shinnecock is among the dozen or so finest golf courses in the United States. It is a superb driving test—the tee shot must be both long and straight—and it demands even more from the medium and short irons.

The course begins on the highest point of the property, near the old clubhouse, which has been expanded over the years with a few additions that have neither changed its character nor added to its comfort, then sweeps downward to lower ground, weaving among the sandy scrub and through forests of pines, set well enough back from the fairways to keep them largely out of play.

Golf at Shinnecock is different from golf nearly anywhere else in the United States. When the game came to North America it moved inland, away from its seaside origins among the lonely tumbling dunes of coastal Scotland. In the move inland the game lost much of its original flavor. The land is more nearly level—perhaps not flat, for heaven knows we have some terribly hilly courses, but then not so rippling as the linksland—and the effect of the wind was lost as well. It raged across those lonely Scottish wastes, but it is not nearly as much a part of the game in America.

Shinnecock is about as close as we have come to matching the game's Scottish origins. With its sand base, the ground has the appearance of linksland, and situated on the narrow eastern end of Long Island, it is exposed to high winds that bluster in from the Atlantic to the south and Long Island Sound to the north. Wind can be a formidable consideration even on a normal day.

Shinnecock has trees, of course (but then so do Carnoustie and Muirfield), but they don't often come into play. Mostly the rolling nature of the ground and the placement of the bunkers, along with a healthy stand of rough grass that sometimes reaches knee height are the major influences. The taller grasses in the rough are quite fine, but beneath them grows a much more sturdy and wiry strain. The faces of the bunkers may seem unkempt, but Shinnecock is not heavily groomed. In some respects it resembles Pine Valley, since most of its fairways are islands, and to reach them the shot must carry across formidable stretches of wilderness. At Shinnecock it is rough; at Pine Valley it is sand.

The course itself is a par 70 that was stretched out to 6,912 yards for the Open with the addition of some new tees. It has just two par-five holes, one of 535 yards and the other of 544, and four par threes, the longest 226 yards and the shortest 158, and 12 par fours. The par threes and par fives offer a good variety, but the strength of Shinnecock, as it is with any truly championship course, is in its par fours. Four of them are under 400 yards, and four others are 450 yards or more. Almost all the short holes play into the fresh sea wind, while the longer holes usually play downwind. The greens on many of the longer holes are wide open, allowing shots to be run onto the greens, as they must be on windy days.

The players had never seen an American course quite like it, and they were both surprised and pleased—perhaps even ecstatic.

Peter Jacobsen said, "This is by far the best course I've ever played the Open on. It reminds me so much of Royal St. George's and the other fine links courses we play in Europe."

Lee Trevino bubbled. "I love this course; it's one of the greatest I've ever played. It doesn't favor one kind of player. You can go high, go low, hook, fade, do what you want. I wish all our courses were like this."

"It's one of the best courses I've ever played," David Graham said. "The design of the greens is absolutely gorgeous. The par-four greens are open in the front; all the trouble is left of the greens and right of the greens. When they built this course they realized that golf is not played by just those people who hit the ball far and high; they realized there was wind, and they gave players who hit the ball low a chance to run it onto the green. This is the finest course I have played in the United States, except possibly for Pine Valley." Then, spreading his arms wide and holding his palms toward heaven, he cried, "It's perfect."

Playing in his first Open, Mac O'Grady had trouble controlling his emotions and his metaphors. "I love the golf course. You can exercise all the colors of your talents. When you play here you have to play every shot in the bag."

Hale Irwin, who said once he'd like to lead an organization devoted to preserving our old courses, said, "Most of us gravitate toward the traditional, and that's certainly what we have here. I'm not saying those newer courses are bad, but it's nice to play a course like this."

Thinking of some of the Tour courses, Lanny Wadkins said, "This is a real special place. The atmosphere is more like a British Open, with the small clubhouse, the wind blowing, the way the course looks. We're not playing through rows of condominiums and large houses. You're just out here to play golf, and that's the way it should be."

"I'll tell you what's great about Shinnecock," Jack Renner said. "No railroad ties and no greens in the middle of lakes," a knock at the Tournament Players Club at Sawgrass.

Regardless of their enthusiasm and the obvious similarities to what they had faced in Britain, no one seemed prepared for what happened in the opening round, for Thursday was no ordinary June day. The wind had come up on Wednesday, the day before the championship began, causing new problems with club selection (Raymond Floyd blistered a drive on sixth where a new tee set it up to play at 471 yards, but he didn't reach the fairway, and on the 16th, a 544-yard par five that played directly into the wind, Bernhard Langer needed two drivers and a five iron to reach the green), but on Thursday the weather was dreadful, and for the most part the scores were terrible.

The wind whipped in from the northeast between 20 and 30 miles an hour with sudden gusts at even greater velocity, the temperature dropped to the high 40s, chilling the players' hands so they had trouble holding onto their clubs, and rain fell through much of the day, once so heavily that play was suspended. No one could remember an Open day like this. Bill Williams, the USGA president, greeted friends by saying, "Welcome to the first playing of the British Open in the United States." Some disagreed, claiming that while they had seen the British Open played in winds as strong or stronger, in rains as hard or harder, and on days as cold or colder, they had never seen such a combination of all three (they would a month later).

The northeast wind had turned Shinnecock into a terror. Of the four longest par fours, the wind helped only on the sixth, where those who managed to find the fairway (the drive is blind; the players aimed at a copse of trees on the far side of the fairway) usually had something less than a six iron left, and some had less. Tom Watson had needed a one iron to reach the green on Wednesday, but with the quartering wind he used only a pitching wedge on Thursday, and Roger Maltbie went from a three wood on Wednesday to a nine iron on Thursday. On the other hand, holes that played into the wind were impossible. While at 409 yards the 10th was at least 50 yards shorter than the sixth (the new back tee was never used), Greg Norman was 40 yards short of the green with a drive and four iron. At 447 yards and with its green set 30 feet or more above the level of the fairway, the ninth was practically unreachable (indeed, of the 155 men who got that far, 120 had bogey or worse), and the 18th (450 yards), which runs parallel to the ninth, was not much easier. Nor was the 12th, playing to 472 yards through a left-to-right crossing wind. Tom Watson tried to explain how the game must be approached in this kind of weather.

"First you have to realize there are a lot of bogeys out there. Second, you try to keep your hands warm and dry. It's simple, really. You just get into the back of your mind that par is a really good score on every hole."

Indeed it was, for scoring was unusually high. Tom Cleaver, a 27-year-old former mini-tour player who was among the first group to play that morning, slipped up quietly beside the starter and said, "This is your last chance to mow the rough." The offer was rejected, and Cleaver shot 77. Of the first 12 starters, only five shot under 80. (Cleaver, by the way, birdied both the tough second and the seventh, a 188-yard par three that is among the finest examples of a redan-type hole in American golf.) Of the 155 men who completed the first round (Jerry Pate withdrew after four holes because of an injured shoulder), 45 shot 80 or higher and only 46 shot 75 or better. The average score was a fraction under 78, and 88 men shot 40 on at least one nine. Twenty-four players were tied at 75, 12 others had 74, three shot 73, six more had 72, Greg Norman came in with 71, and Bob Tway led with 70. It had been 12 years (1974, at Winged Foot) since no one had broken par in the first round.

Few men hit half the greens in regulation. Payne Stewart, who had developed into a fine big occasion player (tied for second in the 1985 Open and second outright in the 1985 British Open), reached 11 greens, and Scott Verplank, who had won the 1985 Western Open as an amateur, hit 10. No one else hit more than nine. Even though he shot 70, Tway hit only eight greens, Norman hit only seven, and both Denis and Tom Watson, who tied at 72, hit only nine.

Tway had begun his round early, teeing off at 8:01, along with Maltbie and Miller Barber. He began the day by holing a four-foot putt to save a par after bunkering his approach to the first hole, then drilling a five-iron approach to 20 feet on the third and holing the putt. After giving up that stroke on the fourth by leaving his approach short, Tway holed saving putts of 10 feet on the fifth and four feet on the seventh. Still even par, he nearly holed his approach to the eighth leaving it only a foot from the hole, but like everyone else, he couldn't reach the ninth green and bogeyed again. Level par for the first nine even though he had hit only four greens, Tway quickly dipped two under by holing birdie putts of 20 feet on the 11th after a superb six iron, and from 25 feet on the long and hard 12th following a stinging five iron.

Tway was two under par then, even though he was struggling against the rising force of the wind and the chilling cold, but he lost those two strokes over the next three holes and had to fight to finish with 70, holing a three-footer on the 17th and a twisting 10-footer on the 18th to save his pars.

It was just about noon when Tway, Barber (80), and Maltbie (76) finished, and the weather was becoming worse. Rain began falling so heavily that play was suspended for 15 minutes at about one o'clock. Scattered over the course, Greg Norman was playing about 20 minutes behind the Tway-Barber-Maltbie group, Bernhard Langer was an hour behind, and Tom Watson, 45 minutes behind. Jack Nicklaus, Lee Trevino, and Seve Ballesteros were to play later in the afternoon. As Maltbie strode into the tiny, cramped old locker room he spotted Ballesteros sitting at a round table near a tray of snacks and staring at the television coverage.

"You play yet?" Maltbie asked. Ballesteros shook his head. "Have fun," Maltbie said.

Kenny Knox sat at a table sipping a soft drink, talking quietly, and savoring his 72. "If you don't hit the fairways, you have no chance to hit the greens."

Looking toward the other end of the room, Maltbie saw Jack Renner talking to a reporter about his round. "What did Jack shoot?" Somebody told him 85. (Renner withdrew.)

Beginning to get ready for his round, Ballesteros poked his head around a corner and asked, "Still raining out?" Everyone nodded.

Out on the course, the great men of golf were struggling. Norman had done remarkably well by hitting six greens on the first nine (official statistics say five, but he was on the fringe of the third and putted), and had gone out in 36, losing one stroke to par. Norman played the second nine in even par 35, but he managed this by one-putting seven of the nine greens, only one of them for a birdie. He holed saving putts of 10 and 12 feet on two holes, along with two from inside one foot and two others from six and four feet. He birdied the 17th, another of Shinnecock's superb par threes, by rolling in an 18-footer.

When it was over, Norman said his 71 was equal to a 67 or 68 on a good day.

Norman had been paired with Craig Stadler and Ben Crenshaw, and although neither one of them scored as well as Norman, they had not played themselves out of the championship just yet, with 74 and 76, respectively. Meantime, both Andy North, the 1985 United States Open champion, and Sandy Lyle, who had won the 1985 British Open, had done just that. North, who had injured his wrist early in the year, shot 79, and Lyle 78.

Tom Watson was laboring. He had never been the same since he lost the 1984 British Open to Ballesteros by hitting his approach to the 17th at St. Andrews into the road, and now he had played the first nine at Shinnecock in 38, three strokes over par. Turning his game around, Watson came back in 34, one of only three nine-hole scores under par (Knox went out in 33, one-putting to save pars on five holes and for birdies on two others, and Michael Malaska, a Californian who was not to begin until after two o'clock, would play the second nine in 33).

Even though it was spectacular, Watson's 34 was not a pretty sight, for he had to birdie three holes to pick up that one stroke, and the birdies were more lucky than skillful. His game seemed to be collapsing as he dropped his tee shot into a greenside bunker at the 11th so deep that from where he stood he couldn't see the surface of the green, but he holed the shot for one birdie, rolled in a 20-footer for another, chipped in for a third, then saved par on the 18th by holing a 12-footer.

Meanwhile, the whole world had been waiting to see Jack Nicklaus, wondering if his amazing victory in the Masters was simply a fluke or if indeed he was to remain a power in the game. As he had done so often in the past, Nicklaus had gone through meticulous preparation. By the time the first round began, he had played seven rounds at Shinnecock and had done a television show exploring the course and explaining how it should be played. By then he had learned as much about it as anyone. He knew it was a left-to-right course that favored the man who could fade his tee shots, as Jack usually does, and he understood that it was difficult, which was good for him, since it left fewer men for him to beat; those with lesser talent would beat themselves. Furthermore, by winning the Masters, he had put himself into the proper frame of mind.

"Winning the Masters makes me believe I can win here," he said during one of his practice rounds. "My chances are probably better than a high percentage of the field because of the type of course Shinnecock is. Strength and length are not tremendous factors here, but I've got to work on driving the ball better. By the time the Open starts, I should be all right."

Great player though Nicklaus is, however, he is not immune from the effects of weather. He arrived a little more than an hour ahead of his 1:30 starting time, chatted briefly with the other players in the locker room, then went to the practice tee to warm up. Instead he spent most of his time huddled under an umbrella. After play was suspended, he strolled back to the locker room, ate a banana and picked up a couple of sandwiches to take to his son Jackie, who caddied for him.

His round finally under way, it was obvious Nicklaus was in for a difficult day, for even though he played the first eight holes in even par, he was not playing the assertive, assured golf he had played in those final dramatic holes at Augusta in April, and he was holding his score together with his work around the greens. He was hitting only an occasional green, but his little chips and pitches, never one of his strengths, often left him with little work to do with his giant putter.

Jack had his first slip on the ninth, for under the conditions of the day, even the greatest player of the age had difficulty with this demanding hole. He was out in 36, not at all a bad score, but then he collapsed on the second nine. Because of a lapse in technique on the 10th (he was late transferring his weight from his right to his left foot coming into the ball) he pushed his ball so far to the right it sailed over the gallery and into heavy underbrush. Gallery, players, and caddys thrashed around in the bushes, and then Nicklaus, believing the five-minute allotment permitted under the rules had expired, walked back to the tee and played another shot. It was a lost ball, the first he could remember in competition. (The ball was found eventually, perhaps inside the five-minute allowance, but no one could be sure). Nicklaus made a double-bogey six, then added two more at the 13th and 18th, where he missed putts of three and four feet, shot 41 coming home, and finished the day with 77. He had hit only four greens, but at the same time he had needed only 26 putts.

Assessing the round, Nicklaus said, "This was the most difficult day I have ever seen in American championship golf."

Because of the suspension of play, the day ended with 18 players still on the course. They came back and finished on Friday morning. At the end of the first 18 holes, then, the leaders looked like this:

Bob Tway	70
Greg Norman	71
Kenny Knox	72
Tom Watson	72
Denis Watson	72
David Frost	72
Rick Fehr	72
Tommy Nakajima	72
Gary Koch	73
Jodie Mudd	73

Other scores of interest:

Bernhard Langer	74
Lanny Wadkins	74
Lee Trevino	74
Scott Verplank	75
Raymond Floyd	75
Fuzzy Zoeller	75
Seve Ballesteros	75
Ben Crenshaw	76
Curtis Strange	76
Jack Nicklaus	77

The wind had swung around to the southwest overnight and had lost much of its strength, but it was still chilly and overcast Friday morning, and the early starters played in sweaters. Gradually through the day the clouds grew thin and wispy, and by early afternoon they had disappeared. The sun grew warm, the sky turned bright blue, and the golfers not only shed their sweaters, they seemed to solve Shinnecock's mysteries. Whereas no one had broken par on Thursday, eight men were under 70 on Friday. One man shot 66, four others 68, and three shot 69.

It had become the general wisdom that to score well at Shinnecock, the birdies had to be made on the first nine, for the home nine can be savage. It was news to Joey Sindelar, a 28-year-old professional from the town of Horseheads, in upstate New York, who had come out of nowhere to win two tournaments in 1985. Sindelar had been baffled by Shinnecock's first nine on Thursday, shooting 43, but he had come back in 38 to salvage an 81. Beginning his second round shortly after noon, he matched par going out, then sped home in 31, birdieing four straight holes beginning at the 12th. After a big drive, he dropped a seven iron to five feet on the 12th, rolled in a pair of 15-footers on the 13th and 14th, and wedged to two feet on the 15th.

Sindelar had shot 66, a competitive course record, but it had no effect on the championship except to indicate that Shinnecock would yield to first-class golf. Playing two groups behind him, Danny Edwards played the second nine in 30, matching the Open record for nine holes, and of more significance, Greg Norman, in the group behind Edwards, raced around the first nine in 31.

Norman combined good golf with good luck. After a birdie on the first, he bunkered his tee shot on the fierce second but came out to two and a half feet and saved par, and after a routine par four on the third, he pitched to a foot on the fourth and within 12 feet on the fifth and birdied both. He was two under par for 22 holes then and leading the tournament.

With the change in wind direction, the sixth was playing as long as it had on Wednesday, and even after a satisfactory drive, Norman needed a two iron to reach the green. His ball carried well on, but the green falls away toward the rear and Greg's ball rolled off the back and into the rough. A timid chip failed to reach the crest of the rise and rolled back off the green, stopping against the higher grass of the rough. Now Norman drew out his sand wedge and played a shot that has become standard on the pro tour.

Laying the face of the club well back, he hit the ball with the blade of the club. It skidded up the slope, began a gentle run downward toward the hole, hit the flagstick and dropped. A par four.

He was not out of trouble just yet. After a solid par three on the seventh, he drove into a fairway bunker on the eighth, and with his ball lying close to a fairly steep front wall, played a spectacular nine iron that rose quickly, cleared the bunker's face with little to spare, carried to the green, and stopped within five feet of the cup. He holed the putt and dipped to four under for the day and three under for the tournament. A bunker shot to two feet saved his par on the ninth.

Norman had passed Tway long ago and climbed into first place, for unlike nearly everyone else, Tway was scoring worse in the second round than he had in the first and was on his way to a 73. Lee Trevino was closest to him, but he was five strokes back. Greg was turning the Open into a rout.

Suddenly, just as he was pulling away from the field, his game lost its edge. He stopped making birdies, missed his pars on the 10th and 13th, struggled home in 37, and had to be content with 68.

By the time Norman finished, Trevino and Raymond Floyd had already posted their 68s, and Payne Stewart was coming in with another close behind him. Trevino and Floyd had started together at 8:19 in the morning after barely surviving the first round with scores of 74 and 75, and Stewart had been even shakier, with 76, but with the change in the weather they were able to pull their games together and begin to climb.

Trevino had been working seriously on his game. Unable to pound practice balls by the hour, Trevino had spent a week at the Wethersfield Country Club, near Hartford, Connecticut, where his father-in-law is the club professional, playing every night until dark, then had gone off to England for the Dunhill Masters. While he had lost some distance over the years and some confidence in his old soft fade—he was hitting the ball with a more upright swing to relieve the pressure on his back and couldn't work the ball as he had—Trevino was still a formidable competitor. He had won the PGA Championship in 1984, when he was 44, and even though he was 46 in 1986, and had missed the cut in four of the last five Opens, he still had confidence.

Trevino played a rather erratic round on Friday; every time he birdied, he seemed to follow with a bogey. He was still even par after the 15th hole, but then he rolled in birdie putts from 20 feet on the 16th and from 20 feet on the closing hole. As the last putt dropped, Lee's face split in a wide grin, and he raised his fist.

Floyd's 68 was much neater. He did not have a bogey, although he had to hole putts of 20 feet, eight feet, and seven feet to save some pars, and where he had hit only six fairways and six greens on Thursday, he hit 11 of 14 fairways and 13 greens on Friday. An 18-foot putt fell on the fourth hole and a 20-footer on the 17th, and he finished the round with 16 pars and two birdies.

Even though he had lost strokes to the field over the last nine holes, Norman was the only man under par after 36 holes, with 139, and at the end of the day he held a solid three-stroke lead over Trevino and Denis Watson, who had added 70 to his opening 72. Tway, meanwhile, had fallen into a tie for fourth place, at 143, with Floyd and Tom Watson, who had 71.

Because 16 men had tied at the cutoff score of 150, 70 men survived for the last two rounds, more than usual (conditions call for the field to be cut to the low 60 and ties for the last two rounds). Among those who barely made it were Jack Nicklaus, whose putter was keeping him alive. Where he had used only 26 putts in shooting 77 in the first round he had 29 in the second-round 72. He was in with a stroke to spare, at 149.

The leaders at the end of 36 holes:

Greg Norman	71–68—139
Lee Trevino	74–68—142
Denis Watson	72–70—142
Tom Watson	72–71—141
Bob Tway	70–73—143
Raymond Floyd	75–68—143
Tommy Nakajima	72–72—144
Mac O'Grady	75–69—144
Bobby Wadkins	75–69—144
David Frost	72–72—144
Bernhard Langer	74–70—144
Lanny Wadkins	74–70—144
Payne Stewart	76–68—144

Other scores of interest:

Ben Crenshaw	76–69—145
Craig Stadler	74–71—145
Hal Sutton	75–70—145
Seve Ballesteros	75–73—148
Kenny Knox	72–76—148
Sandy Lyle	78–71—149
Jack Nicklaus	77–72—149
Andy North	79–71—150

Missed the cut:

Hale Irwin	77–74—151
Bob Murphy	79–71—151
Bill Rogers	75–76—151
Curtis Strange	76–79—155
George Burns	83–72—155

As the third round began, the bad weather was gone and Saturday promised to be another lovely spring day. The sun had gathered strength, the sky was bright and blue, the air was clean and clear, and the light wind was coming out of the southwest once again at five or 10 miles an hour, bringing with it the smell of the sea.

The high scorers started early in the day and the leaders brought up the rear. Norman and Tway were to tee off at 2:30 in the afternoon, just after

Floyd and Denis Watson, at 2:21, and Tway and Tom Watson, at 2:12. Nicklaus, meanwhile, was off at the unaccustomed hour of 10:45, paired with David Ogrin, a tradition-minded young man who in observance of Shinnecock's ambience showed up the next day dressed in a white button-down shirt and four-in-hand tie.

With his hopes for a fifth Open growing dim after burning so brightly at the beginning of the week, Nicklaus reminded us once again that he was the most dangerous late-round player of his time by speeding around in 67 and beginning a remarkable climb. While he was never a contender, he played an exceptional Open, nevertheless, added 68 the next day, and finished with a final score of 284, only five strokes out of first place. His 135 for the last 36 holes was beaten only by Chip Beck, who played them in 133, one stroke above the record 132 set three years earlier by Larry Nelson.

As Nicklaus was beginning his move, so was Seve Ballesteros. For all his talent, Ballesteros had never been at his best in the Open, although he had opportunities. He had gone into the fourth round at Oakmont in 1983 sharing first place, at 212, with Tom Watson, but as he was shooting 36 on the first nine, Watson was shooting 31, and Ballesteros dropped from the race. Again in 1985 at Oakland Hills he was closing in on the leaders after 15 holes of the third round, but he played the last three poorly, dropping two strokes to par, and shot a dull 71 the next day when two or three strokes under par would have won. Now, starting out nearly three hours ahead of the leaders after a 75–73 start, he began playing his best golf, and he was making up ground quickly. A stinging two iron to the difficult sixth bit and stopped within four feet of the cup, and he rolled it in for his third birdie of the day. Another good iron to the wonderful seventh trickled off the green, but he made his par, and then he drove to the edge of the eighth fairway and pitched to within 20 feet of the cup.

Ballesteros took his time lining up the putt, and when it dropped, he squared his shoulders, his face took on a pleased, tight-lipped self-satisfied expression, and as the gallery's applause went on, he flashed a brief smug smile. He was four under par for the round by then, and who knows what he might shoot, for Ballesteros is capable of wonderful bursts of scoring. But that was as far as he was to go. Out in 31, he began missing fairways and greens, shot 37 coming in, finished with 68, shot 73 the next day when once again he needed a sub-par score, and finished 10 strokes out of first place.

As Ballesteros was cooling off, Ben Crenshaw and Hal Sutton were getting hot. Off an hour before Norman and Trevino, Crenshaw birdied three of the first five holes, running in two 10-footers and a 20-footer, lost a stroke on the 10th where he overshot the green, and then eagled the 14th by holing a full six iron. Ben was four under for the round now, but then he threw away three strokes. An erratic driver throughout his career, Crenshaw drove under a tree on the 15th, costing him a double bogey, and into a bunker on the 16th, losing another stroke. He came back in 37 for his second 69, which left him four over par for the 54 holes, at 214.

After Crenshaw had ripped through the first nine, Hal Sutton, in the group behind him, had come to life on the second nine. Sutton had worked into contention with a 70 on Friday after opening with 75 and had played the first nine in 35, even though he had missed three greens. Like Crenshaw he missed the 10th, but where Ben had bogeyed, Hal chipped in for a birdie and followed by dropping a lovely iron within three feet of the cup on the 11th for another, wedged to eight feet on the 15th for a third, and played a six iron to 12 feet on the 17th for his fourth birdie of the second nine. He had come back in 31 and shot 66. He had 211, one stroke over par, the best 54-hole score so far.

At the same time, Tway had recovered his poise after Friday's disappointing round and had played a steady 69. He stood at 212, a stroke ahead of Mike Reid, Raymond Floyd, Denis Watson, Payne Stewart, and Mark McCumber. The scoring pace had picked up. Both Sutton and Reid had shot 66, Scott Verplank, Lennie Clements, and Jack Nicklaus had 67, five others had 68, and six more 69.

None of this seemed to matter just then, because Norman had the Open in hand. After playing several rounds with him in practice, Nicklaus had said Greg was playing as well as anyone he'd ever seen. Indeed, he had been sensational throughout the year, winning two tournaments and coming within one stroke of tying Jack at Augusta. He seemed ready to win a significant event, and after nine holes of the third round, it looked as if the Open would be the one, for he had gone out in 33 and stood three under par after 45 holes. He had taken a three-stroke lead into the third round, and even though he had overshot the 10th and bogeyed, he was still three strokes ahead after the 12th.

As he climbed the gentle grade to the 13th tee, Norman stood two strokes under par while Trevino, who was paired with him, was one stroke over par, and up ahead, at various other points on the course, Sutton, Tway, McCumber, and Denis Watson were two over. Norman was looking good.

While the 13th is far from the most difficult hole at Shinnecock, it has some problems. It had been playing slightly into the wind the last two days, its narrow fairway is set at a right-to-left angle to the line of flight, and the ground tilts to the left in the landing zone, kicking shots into the left rough. Since the hole is so short—only 377 yards—and the tee shot so demanding, hardly anyone used his driver. Norman chose to play a fairway wood.

Unlike most first-class players, who tend to hit their bad shots to the left, Norman tends to hit them to the right. He pushed his drive far into the deepest rough and carried his second shot over the green into tangled grass and underbrush bordering a parking lot. He was in trouble. He would have like to play a high lob that would drop softly onto the back edge of the green and roll toward the hole, possibly saving his four, but a shot like that calls for a full backswing, and Norman didn't have enough room. Instead, he punched his ball low, trying to bounce it off the rear bank of the green where it rose above the surrounding ground so it would hop onto the green. It didn't work; his sharp downward blow carried the ball over the bank, across the green, and into the rough on the other side. From there he played a timid chip four feet short of the hole and missed the putt. A six.

Trevino had begun the day only three strokes behind Norman, but he had been playing solid stuff, and his old fade was working its wonders. He was hitting fairway after fairway and green after green, missing those he missed only narrowly. Nevertheless, he was losing ground. When Greg had turned for home in 33, Lee was five strokes back, but he picked up one of those with a par at the 10th where Norman bogeyed and another on the dangerous 11th, where he covered the flag with a seven iron and coaxed in a touchy 15-foot downhiller for a birdie two. Three strokes behind once again.

They were still three strokes apart as they began the 13th, but while Norman had driven into the rough, Trevino had played a safe iron into the fairway and then went for the flag with a seven iron. He nearly holed it; the ball hit only inches from the cup and braked itself two feet away. He dropped his putt for the birdie three, and when Norman holed out in six, Trevino had made up five strokes in four holes.

It is easy to see when Trevino is in a businesslike mood. He keeps his attention focused on the job before him, walks with a quick, determined stride, looks straight ahead, and seldom clowns with the gallery. He was in just such a mood now, for all at once the complexion of the Open had changed, and the old warrior was in the hunt once again. But so it seemed was half the field. Four strokes off the lead only minutes earlier, Sutton was within one stroke of Norman now; Tway was back in contention, and so were Crenshaw, McCumber, Stewart, Reid, the Watsons, Verplank, and Floyd. This was no time for jokes.

The pace of play had slackened somewhat over the last few holes, and after Trevino and Norman had driven into the 14th fairway, they had to stand and wait while Floyd and Denis Watson putted out. Throughout the day the gallery had grown noisy and restless, charging about as one player after another made a move. As Norman stood near the gallery ropes staring straight ahead at the green with his arms folded across his chest, a voice rose above the hum of the crowd and called out, "Norman, you're choking."

With his lips in a tight line and curled slightly upward at the corners as if he were amused, Norman turned his head slowly to the right and looked into the crowd. He watched for only a moment, then turned back and looked ahead once again. As Watson and Floyd walked off, Norman drew an iron and drilled a shot onto the heart of the green.

Then an extraordinary thing happened. Instead of heading toward the hole, Norman turned to his right, walked into the gallery, and pointing his finger at a spectator who seemed to be in his late 20s or early 30s snapped, "If you want to say something to me, say it to me after this round when I can do something about it."

It seemed a foolish thing to do, particularly after Norman had had such a bad hole and should have been concentrating on the job at hand, but perhaps it had a sort of therapeutic effect, giving him the opportunity to work off some of the anger he must have felt over his double-bogey, because he settled down and played errorless golf the rest of the way, finishing with 71 and 210.

Trevino, meanwhile, played stroke-for-stroke with him until the long and trying 18th, where his drive faded a little more than he had planned and jumped into the rough. Gambling with a wooden club, Lee dug his ball out of the grass, but it caught a crossing bunker cutting into the left side of the fairway a few yards short of the green, and he took three more strokes to get down. With a bogey five, he shot 69 for the day and fell a stroke behind Norman, tied with Sutton at 211.

The leaders with 18 holes to play:

Greg Norman	71–68–71—210
Hal Sutton	75–70–66—211
Lee Trevino	64–68–69—211
Bob Tway	70–73–69—212
Mike Reid	74–73–66—213
Mark McCumber	74–71–68—213
Payne Stewart	76–68–69—213
Raymond Floyd	75–68–70—213
Denis Watson	72–70–71—213
Tom Watson	72–71–71—214
Bernhard Langer	74–70–70—214
Lennie Clements	75–72–67—214
Scott Verplank	75–72–67—214
Ben Crenshaw	76–69–69—214

Other scores of interest:

Jack Nicklaus	72–72–67—216
Chip Beck	75–73–68—216
Lanny Wadkins	74–70–72—216

With one round to play, 14 men stood within four strokes of one another, another was five behind, and six more lay six strokes off the lead. From a runaway, the Open had turned into a tight scramble that would become even tighter as the last day wore on.

Anticipating a close, intense battle for the championship, a few eager spectators began crossing the footbridge spanning the road and entering the gate before seven o'clock, heading for the grandstands behind the practice tee or else finding choice locations at some of the key holes.

Sunday was another clear day. A soft wind was coming out of the south, barely strong enough to ripple the coves and inlets off the Atlantic, which lay calm and glassy at dawn, but by early afternoon it was backing to the southwest and picking up strength. By the time Norman and Sutton teed off, at 2:40 in the afternoon, it was whipping in at more than 20 miles an hour, and as it gathered force, Lee Trevino began looking better, since he is such a fine wind player. As if to prove it, he dropped a nice little pitch onto the first green, hole high 12 to 15 feet to the left of the cup and holed the putt for a birdie three, which dropped him to even par for 55 holes and tied him with Norman, who had just driven.

Minutes later Norman made his par, but Sutton, who was paired with him, matched Trevino's birdie, and now Norman, Sutton, and Trevino were all even par and tied for the lead.

It went on like this through much of the day, as first one man, then another moved ahead and then fell back. Starting 50 minutes ahead of Norman and Sutton, Crenshaw ran off four straight birdies beginning at the third, dropped to even par, and suddenly had the lead to himself, for Trevino, Sutton, and Norman had stumbled briefly and lost strokes. Then Mark McCumber, three groups behind Crenshaw, birdied three of the first five and assumed the lead at even par, for by then Crenshaw had bogeyed the difficult redan seventh. Moments later McCumber, too, bogeyed the seventh.

By then it was impossible to tell how anyone stood. Tway moved ahead with a couple of birdies that brought him back to even par, then lost a stroke, and out on the course, the scoreboard attendants were trying desperately to keep up with a constantly changing situation, for up ahead, playing an hour and a half ahead of the 54-hole leaders, Lanny Wadkins and Chip Beck had gone wild. Both men had begun the day six strokes behind Norman, and now Wadkins had gone out in 34 and was roaring home with a string of birdies. He made two at the frightening 11th, hitting an eight iron to 12 feet, and then, playing superb irons, ran off three more birdies beginning at the 14th. He dropped a seven iron to three feet on the 14th, a wedge to two feet on the 15th, and a sand wedge to 15 feet on the 16th. By the time he was through the 16th hole, he was back to one over par.

Beck, meanwhile, had played the first nine in a steady 35, but then his putter turned hot and he birdied five of the next six holes, rolling in two 30-footers and a 25-footer. With three holes to play, he had caught Wadkins.

At 4:10, an hour and a half after the last pair had left the first tee, the scoreboard showed nine men tied at one stroke over par:

Norman	through 7
Sutton	through 7
Trevino	through 8
Tway	through 8
Stewart	through 8
McCumber	through 8
Crenshaw	through 10
Wadkins	through 16
Beck	through 15

Twenty minutes later Stewart and Sutton had birdied, and now the scoreboard showed:

Stewart	even par through 10
Sutton	even par through 9
Wadkins	one over through 17
Beck	one over through 15
McCumber	one over through 10
Tway	one over through 9
Crenshaw	two over through 12
Trevino	two over through 9
Norman	two over through 9
Floyd	two over through 10

One over par for 71 holes, Beck played two superb shots to the 18th, dropping his approach to four feet, but with a chance for his sixth birdie on the second nine, which would have given him 29 for the round and dropped him to even par for 72 holes, he missed. 281.

While others were making up ground, Norman was falling back. He was not the aggressive, confident player he had been through the first three rounds, and, indeed, had been shaky from the beginning. He had played a tentative approach to the first green that barely reached the front of the green, charged his first putt on the third hole but saved his par by holing a three-footer coming back, tried to punch a low shot into the fourth green but played it poorly, pulling it onto the collar of the green yards from the hole, and then three-putted. Next, with the fifth green reachable in two shots because of a following wind, he pulled his drive into the rough, losing a chance to go for the green, and from a good lie in the sixth fairway left his approach short and bogeyed. He pulled his game together briefly, making a birdie on the tough seventh, but he bogeyed five of the next eight holes and fell out of the race. He had lost his game.

Payne Stewart, meanwhile, began looking like the man to beat. He had dropped to even par and had held the lead briefly after playing the first five holes in three under par. Turning for home in 33, he had birdied the scary 11th, and after pushing his drive on the 12th into deep rough, he had played a wonderful iron to five feet for another. He was one under par for 66 holes, but with so much going on all over the course, he couldn't be sure if he was one stroke ahead, two ahead, or if indeed he was ahead at all.

Stewart was playing the last nine with Floyd, who had been pretty much ignored, partly because he had done nothing to attract much attention this week and partly because no one expected much of him in the Open, judging not only from his past record in the championship but also from what he had done in the previous tournament. Especially dangerous when he was ahead, Floyd had led the field going into the last round of the Westchester Classic, but instead of pulling away, he shot 77, allowing Tway to win his third tournament of the season.

The drive from Westchester to Shinnecock takes approximately three hours; during the trip he had a long discussion with his wife, Maria, a slender, dark-haired, strong-willed beauty. Evidently it helped.

While Floyd had become one of the most successful professional golfers of the previous decade—a dangerous player capable of scorching bursts of scoring when it mattered most—he had not done well in previous Opens. The 1986 championship was his 22nd. In the previous 21 he had been among the low 10 scorers only twice; he was sixth in 1965 and eighth in 1971, and had six other finishes ranging from 12th to 16th.

Even when he had finished relatively high, he usually had one bad round. As a young man he had gone into the last two rounds of the 1964 Open one stroke behind Ken Venturi, but while Venturi shot 66–70 the final day, Floyd finished with 72–77. He shot 76 in the third round the next year and was beaten by six strokes by Gary Player and Kel Nagle (Player won a playoff); began with 79 in 1969 and lost by six to Orville Moody; began with 143 in 1974 and finished with 78–76; opened with 76 the next year and finished four strokes behind Lou Graham and John Mahaffey (Graham won that playoff); and opened with 75 and 76 in 1978 and lost by six strokes to Andy North.

In a career that had spanned 23 years, Floyd had been among the more durable of all golfers and had won tournaments in three decades. In 1961, when he was just six months past his 20th birthday, he had won the St.

Petersburg Open, in Florida, becoming one of the youngest players ever to win a tour tournament, and in the years since he had won 19 more, including the 1969 PGA and the 1976 Masters. He was overpowering at Augusta, shooting 271 and matching the record score Jack Nicklaus had set in 1965.

Born in North Carolina, the son of a former army man who had become a golf professional after leaving the military service, Floyd earned a reputation as a swinger in his early years on the tour. His reputation reached a peak of sorts when he sponsored a topless all-girl band. At times he seemed to believe the best way to make an early morning starting time was to stay up all night. He was overweight, strutting along the fairways with his belt line bulging from 20 or so excess pounds, but he was young enough to manage it for a while. He was 27 when he won the PGA and three other tournaments in 1969, but then he began playing badly, sank to 70th on the money-winning list in 1972 and then to 77th the following year. Once his game began its skid, there seemed to be no end to how far he could fall. He hadn't won a tournament since 1969, and it looked as if he might never win again.

Then he met Maria Fraietta. They were married, he settled down, gave up his bon vivant image, lost weight, began raising a family, and transformed himself into a power in golf again. While he was still bulky in 1986, he carried it well.

Nothing could be done with his swing, though; it is not one a beginner would want to copy. Floyd stands up to the ball very straight, takes the club back on a flat plane with an even, measured pace, his left wrist supinated rather more than normal, then lashes into the ball with good power. It is an unorthodox style that causes other professionals to snicker. Not among the more accurate players on the tour, he hit on an average two of three greens— 12 in a round—according to statistics gathered at each tournament, but he is a remarkably good putter. He stands up to the ball straight and stiff-backed, places his mallet-headed putter behind the ball with tedious care to assure the face is lined up precisely to the line he wants the ball to take, sets himself with equal care, and taps the ball with a firm legato stroke. He seldom misses when he has the ball within holing range.

His life put in order, Floyd began making progress with his game once again. He won the Kemper Open in 1975, his first victory in six years, and the following spring he dominated the Masters from the first day, shooting 65, 66, 70 and 70 and winning by eight strokes over Ben Crenshaw.

That had been 10 years earlier. During that decade Floyd had become one of the more successful professionals of the time. As the 1986 championship began, though, it looked as if he would have another of his indifferent Opens. He began with 75, which really wasn't bad considering the conditions. Because of the wind and the cold, he said he simply had no feel and had survived because he had putted so well (he had 25 putts). He had improved his position with 68 on Friday, and then shot 70 on Saturday. He had gone into the last round at 213, three strokes over par, and played the first nine in 34, picking up another stroke on par.

After a par on the 10th, Floyd had played a lovely seven iron into the 11th green and had coaxed that delicate downhill 18-footer into the cup. One over par now, and suddenly, almost without warning, Floyd was in the thick of the battle. It seemed for a moment that he hadn't even been in the tournament until this moment, and no one was quite ready to deal with him, for when Floyd is on his game he can be intimidating.

He was still a stroke behind Stewart, since Payne had also birdied the 11th, but just as he had thrust himself into contention, it looked as if he had played himself out of it by driving into a fairway bunker on the 12th hole. Stewart was only a little better off, though, since he had driven worse than Floyd, but from a fairly clean lie in the rough, he played a superb iron onto the green perhaps five feet left of the cup. Floyd, meantime, had no choice; he played a safe pitch onto the fairway, then dropped a sand wedge about 20 feet past the cup.

Floyd seemed certain to lose two strokes to Stewart there, which could put him out of reach, but he holed the putt for a par four and lost only one. He was still one over par, but, nevertheless, he had fallen two strokes behind Stewart, for Payne had holed his putt. Now the 13th was to play a key role once again.

Driving with a one iron after Stewart had hit a wooden club, Floyd placed his ball in perfect position in center fairway. Before the round began he had determined to play conservatively, but with the holes running out he played the kind of shot the great players execute when it counts most—a daring six iron fired directly at the flagstick, which was set on a narrow tongue of the green, about 24 feet beyond one of the deep bunkers protecting the right front, and about 20 feet from the edge. His ball bit and stopped within four feet of the cup.

Stewart's ball, meanwhile, played with no less daring, seemed to have little on it and rolled into some scruffy rough beyond the collar. Using his putter, Stewart put too much snap into his sharp, descending blow; the ball shot toward the pins, caught a corner of the cup, and slipped four or five feet past. He missed coming back, and when Floyd holed, he had caught up.

While Floyd was picking up strokes, everyone else seemed to be throwing them away. Norman had fallen apart and was on his way to 75, Crenshaw began scattering shots, bogeyed three holes on the second nine after his wonderful 32 and finished with 69 and 283; McCumber bogeyed the 13th and lost two strokes on the 16th; after a superb birdie on the ninth, Sutton lost two strokes coming in and shot 71 and 282; Trevino was two over after the ninth and never recovered; and Tway took seven at the 16th and matched Trevino's 282. Stewart overshot the 14th and bogeyed, and he was finished too.

The Open belonged to Floyd, if he could hold on. Like Stewart he overshot the 14th with his seven iron (his caddy wanted him to play a six iron), but he holed a four-footer to save par, played a three wood and pitching wedge to six feet on the 15th but missed the birdie opportunity, and then he won the championship with an attacking eight iron into the 16th green, punched low to fight the wind. His ball skidded dead 10 feet from the cup, he holed the putt, and for the first time in those four days dipped under par. It was all he needed. Wadkins and Beck had finished with their 281s by then, each breaking the course record with blistering 65s (matched that day by Mark Calcavecchia, who finished with 287), and everyone else had crumbled. No one on the course was closer than three strokes behind him. If he could par the last two holes, he would shoot 279 and win by two strokes.

After another daring shot into the left corner of the 17th within 15 feet of the cup, Floyd strung a drive to the center of the 18th fairway, then played a careful four iron to the front of the green. Two putts and he had turned the final nine holes in 32 and the last 18 in 66, a stunning score under the tension of the Open. Floyd had played the last 54 holes in 204 strokes and had not bogeyed a hole in either the second or fourth rounds. No one had ever done better, although Jack Nicklaus had shot 204 over the last three rounds at Baltusrol in 1967, when he had won the second of his four Opens.

The final putt holed and his 279 safely in hand, Floyd climbed the steep hill leading from the home green to the sanctuary of the scorer's tent, dropped into a chair, took a deep breath and said, "I finally won me an Open."

At 43 years, nine months, and 11 days, Floyd had become the oldest man who had ever won the championship. Although both Ted Ray and Julius Boros were 43 when they won—Ray in 1920 and Boros in 1963—they were a few months younger than Floyd.

Throughout the championship, his putting had been superb. He had needed only 25 in the first round, 29 in each of the next two, and 28 in the fourth, a total of 111. While statistics of this kind are difficult to accumulate, it is probably a record. Billy Casper had only 115 in the 1959 Open, which was believed to be a record at the time. On the other hand, Floyd's tee-to-green work was only ordinary. He hit only 45 of the 72 greens in regulation and 38 of the 56 fairways on driving holes, which is about average for all his competitive rounds. Nevertheless, he was as high as par 70 in only one of the last three rounds, and until he won, no one had succeeded in winning the Open after having failed so many times in the past.

In the early morning light half a day after Floyd had won, a thick fog lay over eastern Long Island. Looking outward from the porch of the old clubhouse that has stood for nearly a century atop the lofty hill, the golf course that had teemed with more than 16,000 spectators less than 12 hours earlier was lost in the mist. The ninth green sat high above the layer of fog close by the clubhouse, but nothing else could be seen. The yellow flagstick that had stood defiant at the crest of the long hill leading upward to the green had been removed before the evening dusk, and the Shinnecock Hills flag no longer snapped in the smart southwesterly breeze. As the crowd had drifted away Sunday evening and the grounds crew had gathered the flagsticks from the cups, romantics had taken a final look at Shinnecock and wondered if they'd ever see an Open at this grand old course again. It had been played there 90 years earlier, and now, as it lay lost under a milky shroud, it was as if, like Brigadoon, Shinnecock Hills had gone back in sleep for another century.

4. The British Open

They have a saying in the Ayrshire area, along the western coast of Scotland: "If you can't see Ailsa Craig, it's raining. If you can, it's going to rain." Ailsa Craig is that huge dome of granite rising out of the chill sea about 11 miles off the coast. If your timing is right—that is, just after the rain has stopped and before it starts again—you can see it out there, dominating the horizon. The view is particularly good if you climb the 105 wide steps to graceful, red-roofed Turnberry Hotel stretching across the top of the hill. From the hotel windows, you can look down over Turnberry's famed Ailsa Course and out across the sea. On a calm day, the sea is glassy and the coastline quiet. But those days are rare. They were rarer still in mid-July, 1986, when the 115th British Open returned to Turnberry and was born of two storms—one from off the sea, the other from the golfers.

The 1986 Open will go down as one of the most turbulent in history. The complaints ranged far and wide: from the width of the fairway to the height of the rough to the prices at the hotel to—and no one had ever heard this one before—the thickness of the paint in the cups. The Royal and Ancient Golf Club of St. Andrews, which was bringing the Open to Turnberry for only the second time, eventually conceded some points. Whether the complaints were valid will be argued as long as the Open is discussed. But everything finally became too much for Jack Nicklaus, even though he failed in his try for a fourth championship. "The people you hear doing so much complaining," Nicklaus said, "are the ones with the highest scores."

When both storms at last had blown over, Greg Norman, the big stark-blond Australian, had won his first major title and had finally, as he put it, "got the monkey off my back." There was a lot of emotion hidden in that calm statement, that final Sunday afternoon. Earlier in the season, Norman had led both the Masters and the U.S. Open going into the final round, and saw his hopes drain away. As memories, these were heavy loads to carry.

The 1986 Open didn't need any extra added attractions. It could stand on its own for any number of reasons long before the first ball was hit. To begin with, it was the British Open, the world's oldest golf competition. It is also one of the world's richest golf events, with a purse of £602,750 and a first prize of £70,000. And it had its customary field of the world's greatest players.

Another kind of electricity was also surging through the Open. Golf's "oldtimers," always respected and feared but not given much of a real chance these days, now could not be discounted out of hand. The most prominent among them, Nicklaus, Raymond Floyd, and Lee Trevino, 46, were very much in the picture with the game's new leaders, such as five-time winner Tom Watson, two-time winner Severiano Ballesteros, defending champion Sandy Lyle, former Masters champion Bernhard Langer, who by the way had more than golf on his mind. His wife, Vicki, was back home in Germany awaiting the arrival of their first child any minute. Langer at first was going to bypass the Open, but finally entered at his wife's urging. Langer was to insist throughout the Open that the impending birth was not weighing on his mind. Of course, he could hardly forget it. The subject would occupy the entire Open as a kind of sub-plot. And then there was Norman. His near-misses at the Masters and U.S. Open had raised many eyebrows. Some observers were beginning to question whether Norman could hold a lead under pressure, and Norman was willing to fire back at his critics.

There was also a grim shadow hanging over this Open. These were the times of political terrorism in many parts of the world—bombs planted and detonated in crowded places, kidnappings and murders, airplane and boat hijackings. Some of these activities were linked to Libyans. In April, President Ronald Reagan ordered a retaliatory bombing of Tripoli, and Libyan leader Muammar Qaddafi threatened retaliation against the United States. Thus many Americans were afraid to travel overseas. The impact on tourism was heavy. Britain and Ireland alone suffered a drop of at least 30 percent over previous years. In addition, numerous American athletes expressed fears about competing in Europe, and some golfers hinted they might not play in the British Open. But when tee time arrived on Thursday morning for the first round, one of the largest American contingents ever was ready—41 of them. This was an encouraging sign. In 1985, there were fewer fears of international travel, but for a variety of other reasons, only nine of the top 20 American money-winners played in the Open at Royal St. George's. This time, only four prominent Americans were absent.

Arnold Palmer, who had an exemption into the Open, wired to Michael Bonallack, secretary of the Royal and Ancient: "My game simply has not come around to a caliber that would make it appropriate for me to compete in this year's Open Championship." The other three were Hal Sutton and Calvin Peete, for personal reasons, and Lanny Wadkins, who missed his flight and could not make other arrangements. Japan's Tateo Ozaki, who also was exempt, withdrew because of back trouble.

This Open was special for yet another reason, and in it lay the potential for a kind of friction rarely if ever seen on a golf course. One of the most powerful men in the game, Deane Beman, commissioner of the U.S. PGA Tour, had resumed playing and had entered the Open. Beman, now 47, was dead serious, and his efforts were praised by most observers. Beman had been a crack golfer years ago. In his brilliant amateur career he won two U.S. Amateurs and one British Amateur, and as a pro he went on to win four times on the American tour before becoming its commissioner in 1974. He hadn't played competitively since then. That's an absence of some 12 years from the demands and the pressures of big time golf. He began working on his game early in the year, announcing his intention to come out again on a limited basis, but not on the U.S. tour. He proved to be good enough to make the halfway cut in the Irish Open at tough Portmarnock. He got no special consideration from the R&A for the British Open. He came in through a qualifier, scoring 70–70—140 at Western Gailes. With Beman in the Open, the stage was set for possible fireworks.

Earlier in the year, when Beman announced his intention to enter the Open, Bonallack was asked by a number of reporters in high humor whether he would pair him with Ballesteros and Mac O'Grady. "It's a possibility," Bonallack responded, with an impish smile. Everyone knew what that meant. The two golfers and Beman had been feuding all year. These were two complex cases that boiled down to this: Beman had suspended Balles-teros from the U.S. PGA Tour for 1986 since he did not play in the required 15 tournaments in 1985. Ballesteros could not play in the U.S., except at New Orleans, where he was the defending champion, and in the Masters, U.S. Open, and PGA Championship, which are not Tour events. Beman suspended and fined O'Grady in a case stemming from O'Grady's alleged insult to a volunteer at a tournament. O'Grady publicly railed against Beman, and his penalty escalated from the initial $500 fine to a $5,000 fine and a six-tournament suspension. He sued Beman in the U.S. courts. The case had not been resolved as the season wore into the summer. So there was at least the possibility that sparks would fly.

"How would you feel," Beman was asked, "if you were paired with Mac and Seve?"

"It wouldn't bother me," Beman said evenly.

But Bonallack did not group the three. In fact, the draw for the first two rounds seemed to be designed to keep them far apart. As it turned out, that possible meeting was about the only fireworks Turnberry lacked. There seemed to be a bit of everything else. Turnberry withstood it well, though. As a former air base, it had known sterner times than golf competitions.

Turnberry's Ailsa Course was laid out before World War I as a recrea-tional course for well-to-do visitors at the hotel up on the hill. It was a testing course, though, not a championship course. At the time of World War I, it was requisitioned by the government as an airfield. A monument to those who died there stands near No. 12 green. The course was hardly back in golf, it seems, when it was requisitioned again as an airfield for World War II. Deep concrete runways replaced the rolling fairways. Turnberry seemed lost forever. But somehow, between 1946 and 1954, it was reborn as a golf course, and by common consent, one of the finest tests in the world. What history took away with one hand, it gave with another. Turnberry lacks the rich patina of such Open venues as St. Andrews, Muirfield and Royal Birkdale. It held only one Open previously. But that one in 1977 may be the most famous of all—the mighty Tom Watson versus Jack Nicklaus duel. Many observers rate this one the greatest match in the history of golf. If it is not that, then it certainly is among them. Watson and Nicklaus had gone off into another world. They matched each other through three incredible rounds, each posting 68–70–65. There was only one fitting way for this to end, and that would be on the final hole. And that's where it did end. Nicklaus holed a putt of over 30 feet for his birdie and a 66, and Watson turned and dropped a two-footer for a 65 and the victory by one stroke. And that was what everyone talked about at Turnberry, 1986—until the various storms broke.

By about 3 p.m. of the first round, a joke was circulating:

"They've suspended play."

"Why?"

"The sun came out and the wind stopped."

Everyone longed for just a taste of the weather on Monday, when it was about 85 degrees, and calm and blue. From Turnberry Hotel on the hill, you could see not only Ailsa Craig, but all the way to Northern Ireland as well. Then Tuesday was merely cool and overcast. On Wednesday, the weather turned foul. Then on Thursday, savage. That might be the best way to describe the day that greeted the players for the start of the 115th British Open Championship. It was a raw, cold day, with relentless, knifing winds of about 35 miles an hour. Turnberry is tough enough under the best of circumstances. But now it was almost scary. It was not the worst blow ever to hit golf at Turnberry. The distinction remains with the gale that struck during the 1973 John Player Classic. That one blew down the tented village. But this one would certainly do. Even Michael Bonallack paid it a dark compliment. He said it was the toughest day he had witnessed through more than 30 years' association with the Open.

Thursday's wind had changed direction, rendering the practice in Wednesday's wind all but useless. The par-three sixth, 222 yards, for example, couldn't be reached with a driver on Wednesday, but was a six-iron shot now. At the 411-yard 14th, golfers teeing off with two irons and three irons were catching a fairway bunker fully 280 yards away. And then there was this other testimony to the force of the wind: Australian Vaughan Somers, who shot 73, needed only an 18-inch putt for a bogey-five at No. 8. At the instant he was about to tap in, a gust of wind blew the leg of his rain trousers and it snared his putter. He took a six.

Turnberry offered adventures of all descriptions. There was the ninth hole, for example—a 455-yard par-four across a bit of the ocean and a stand of jagged coastal rocks to a fairway whose sides fall away from a hogback middle. It left Jack Nicklaus, after a 78 start, muttering, "Did anyone hit the ninth fairway today? In fact, is there a fairway there?" Apparently there was, but barely. Some 10 players out of the starting field of 153 had hit it. Nicklaus salvaged a bogey there, but he needed a miracle finish to escape catastrophe. After careening crazily down the back nine—starting at No. 10, he made four straight bogeys and a double bogey—he eagled No. 17 with a drive, six iron, and 15-foot putt, and birdied No. 18 from 25 feet. He had two double bogeys on the back. The first was at No. 14. Of all of Turnberry's horrors, No. 14 was the Count Dracula of the first round.

No. 14 is a 440-yard, par-four straightaway toward the sea, with a green protected by bunkers on the left, right, and front. Throw a stiff wind into the golfer's face, and there sits enough test for anyone. In this case, too much. For the day, it inflicted 43 double bogeys, and it played to an average of 5.14 strokes, the toughest hole in the first round. No. 14 was perhaps best seen through the eyes of two players, Bernhard Langer and Ian Woosnam.

Langer said simply, "No. 14 was impossible today. I could have hit the two best drives of my career and could not have reached the green." Bernhard is known as a long and powerful hitter. He bogeyed the hole. A birdie at the 16th and an eagle at the 17th brought him in at a comfortable two-over 72.

Woosnam, on the other hand, not only reached No. 14, he birdied it. He was quite simply the only player to birdie it in the first round. He did it with a 20-foot putt after a big drive and a one iron some 210 yards. "The best one iron I have ever hit, and into the wind," he said. He got no arguments.

If No. 14 was a horror story of a hole, one Andrew Broadway, 25-year-old Englishman, turned in a horror story of a round. Most of a round, anyway. For people who enjoy dark humor, Broadway was the star of the day.

Broadway, complaining of a sore back, played in the morning when the weather—if it varied much at all—was at its most fierce. At the par-five seventh, he took four swings in the thick rough just 40 yards from the green, and moved the ball only about a foot. He took a 10 on the hole. His best score on the front was a bogey, of which he made seven. He went out in 49. At the par-four 10th, he made an eight. It was then he decided, that this was not his day or his Open. He was already 18 over par. He quit keeping score, but he completed the round.

Among the victims was Craig Stadler, the former Masters champion, whose power is obvious in his stocky body and thick arms and wrists. But these weren't quite enough. Trying to get his ball out of the rough, he hurt his left wrist. "I damned near broke my wrist," he said, "and I doubt whether I moved the ball an inch. Essentially, I was playing one-handed after that, and I don't have any feeling here." He was rubbing the top of his left thumb. Asked what kept him plugging away, Stadler said that if he had got into the heavy rough again, he might have quit and walked in rather than risk permanent injury. He left Turnberry that afternoon saying that he intended to play on Friday, despite having a slim chance of making the 36-hole cut. "But it all depends on how my wrist feels," he said. On Friday morning, he withdrew.

Australian Ian Baker-Finch, the surprise of the 1984 Open at St. Andrews, where he led much of the way, suffered a surprise of a different kind this time. He was moving well at only one over par through five holes, and his name was on the leaderboard. "Suddenly, almost the next thing I knew, I was 14 over par," Baker-Finch said. "I actually lost three balls, something that's never happened before. And on three different holes, too." He finished with a crushing 86. The strong 69 he was to post the next day would not be enough to get him through the 36-hole cut, but it did get him a dubious consolation—a share of the Open record for the widest variations in rounds. His 17-stroke swing matched that of Nicklaus (83–66) in the 1981 Open at Sandwich.

If the Open brings out the worst in players, it also sometimes brings out the best. Take, for example, Richard Masters, 29, a club pro from a nine-hole course in Yorkshire making his first Open appearance after seven or eight tries (he wasn't sure which). He had to survive a playoff to get through the Open regional qualifier, then he posted 70–67 in the final qualifier to make the Open with authority. He returned 73 for his first Open round, a figure which doesn't tell the whole story. He had 11 one-putt greens. "I was nervous to start with," Masters said. "But holing a 30-foot putt for a birdie on the first hole made me feel better." Four of his one-putts were for birdies, and four of them salvaged bogeys—a 10-footer and three 12-footers. (The dream ended the next day. An 81 took him out of the Open.)

Most eyes were on Raymond Floyd. No one had won the U.S. and British Opens in the same year since Lee Trevino in 1971. Could Floyd pull it off? The answer, almost immediately, was no. Floyd took himself out of the running quickly at Turnberry. He struggled to a first-round 78, and in the process suffered a fate like that of Peter Jacobsen in the 1985 Open at Royal St. George's—an overabundance of lost golf balls and none of them his own.

At No. 14, Floyd had driven into the bushes to the right. "A really deep bushy area," he said. "I thought of hitting a provisional, but I was told my ball had been found. Well, they found four balls while we were there, but none of them was mine." Floyd went back to the tee and this time hit the ball to the left, and at length, after taking two putts from 15 feet, he left No. 14 with a disastrous quadruple-bogey eight. Until then, he was a respectable five over. But the 78 left him with too much ground to make up.

Sandy Lyle's chances of repeating as the Open champion dimmed decidedly after he returned a 78. He had an outward half of 42. That, plus a three-putt double bogey at the 14th and a three-putt bogey five at the 16th left him saying, "I would have been happy with a 75, but 78 leaves me with an awful lot to do."

Seve Ballesteros' Spanish temper burst out briefly, providing some heat for the chilling day; but his caddy, American Nick DePaul, was the only one who felt it. Ballesteros stunned the gallery at the third green when he lashed out at DePaul, saying, "You underclubbed me. Do that again and I fire you. Get out!" Ballesteros had ended up 45 feet from the hole and three-putted for a bogey five, on his way to a 76. Ballesteros later tried to make light of the episode. "I shout loud because he no hear so good," he said. He did not make light, however, of the slow play. He needed about five and a half hours to get around. "That is too much," he said. "When it's as cold and windy as it was and you have to wait, it is almost impossible. We waited half an hour on the sixth tee. I don't know why people have to take so long." Ballesteros said at the 10th he complained to an official about the slow pace. "They are watching others make their shots when they should be deciding what they are going to do themselves," he said. But he put most of the blame on himself, for mental lapses. "There is still a long way to go," he said. "And if we get three more days like this, maybe 320 shots is going to win this tournament." His was an odd round. He took double-bogey sixes at both the eighth and the 14th, and he eagled No. 17 from 12 feet.

DePaul's discomfort was nothing compared to that of John Thomas, good friend of Welsh golfer Philip Parkin. Parkin, on his way to a 78, pushed his drive at the third hole, and the ball caught Thomas flush on the head and knocked him out. Thomas was treated at a nearby hospital.

Ian Woosnam, the son of a Welsh farmer, stands 5 feet, 4½ inches tall and weighs about 150 pounds, and is known as the "Welsh terrier" for his gritty game. He wasn't so surprised at his 70 as he was that he could even play. His chronic sore back had gotten worse over the previous six months. A visit to a doctor left him feeling somewhat better, he said. At any rate, no sore back was going to keep him out of the Open. "I would have played on one leg, if necessary," he said. Woosnam had won the 1986 Kenya Open and his best showing to date on the European Tour was a third in the Cepsa Madrid Open the second week of the season. He missed the cut in two straight appearances before the British Open. "That made me more determined," he said. "But I did not expect to finish with a 70. I was only thinking of trying to keep my concentration." He shook off a front-side 39 that included a double-bogey six at No. 8, then came in with a 31, his "best nine holes in a major event," he said. "Today, it was like picking up 10 shots." It was a bogeyless back nine—birdies at the 10th (from 12 feet), the memorable one at No. 14, and an eagle-three at No. 17 on a 12-foot putt. The 70 left him one stroke ahead of Nick Faldo, Gordon Brand, and Robert Lee, all Britons, and Anders Forsbrand, a Swede. Faldo put on a furious stretch drive, scoring birdies at the last three holes for his 71. He holed from eight feet at No. 16, got down in two putts from 35 feet for a four at No. 17, and dropped an 18-footer at No. 18. "Anything up to a 76 was very good today," Faldo said. "Every par you made was great, and a birdie—you felt fantastic." Forsbrand played the back nine in two-under 33, with four birdies and two bogeys, giving him a 71. Earlier in the year, Ove Sellberg won the Epson Grand Prix, becoming the first Swede ever to win on the European Tour. That plus Forsbrand's play in the Open were merely the latest indications that golf is on the rise in Sweden. And there was an indication that public interest in golf is also on the rise. Nine Swedish journalists came to Turnberry. There was only one in 1985 at Royal St. George's.

Norman, meanwhile, was posting up 74 that was unimpressive, considering his hot start. He birdie the second and fourth to stand at two under after four holes. That edge was wiped out in an instant by a double-bogey six at the fifth, where he went from left rough to right rough and finally three-putted from 18 feet. After making the turn in level par, he gave no indication that he had brought a championship game with him. He came home in 39 that included a three-putt double-bogey six at No. 12, three single bogeys, and just one birdie, a four at No. 17. "It was extremely tough today," he said. "Some of the players are being humiliated. You're hacking away for a 74, and it feels like a 64. At the 12th, the ball was going into the right side of the hole and the wind moved it an inch and a half. Today was just the kind of day when you walk off with a headache, from the concentration and just fighting the wind," he said.

At day's end, the leaderboard looked strange. It was not long ago that a British Open leaderboard looked like a U.S. Open leaderboard, for all of the American names. But this time, the Americans were in scarce supply, even with 41 of them in the field. And those on the leaderboard were unfamiliar figures—Sam Rudolph and Ron Commans, both sharing fifth place on 72. Commans was playing the European Tour with little success, and Randolph was a new professional fresh from a strong amateur career. Nicklaus had posted a 76. Tom Watson complained of bad driving, a bad short game, and misjudging his club selection. "All together, though," he said, "it wasn't that bad a day. I did after all finish with a 77." Perhaps that comment as well as any spoke of what kind of day it was. Think of it: a golfer of Watson's caliber not completely upset with a 77.

The most prominent American names in sight were a curious mix—the veteran Andy Bean at 74; Bob Tway, the hottest player on the U.S. tour, also at 74, and of all people, Deane Beman, the U.S. tour commissioner, at 75.

If Woosman was a surprise leader, Beman was a surprise survivor. It escaped no one's notice that Beman, returning to competitive golf after a 12-year layoff, had just finished in front of the two players he was feuding with. Beman shot 75, one better than Ballesteros and O'Grady. Informed of this later, Ballesteros just grinned weakly and lowered his head into his hand. "Good for him," Ballesteros said. "He wins off the golf course and he wins on the golf course." But it was not a personal issue with Beman. At Turnberry, he was a golfer, not a commissioner. "I was just trying to survive," he said. "I putted as badly as you can putt for 14 holes." He came to life in time, however. He birdied the last three holes on putts of 15 feet, three inches, and 25 feet.

Had not Woosnam returned that 70, this would have been the first British Open to have an over-par score leading after the first round since Bill Melhorn's 71 at Sandwich in 1928. (Walter Hagen won that one with a 292. In those days, they used the expression "level fours" instead of "par." The last ledger above "level fours" was Cyril Tolley in 1924 at Hoylake, where Hagen won with 301.)

Raw figures are one thing, comparisons are another. It wasn't until the entire field finished that one could appreciate what an accomplishment Woosnam's par 70 was. It meant, of course, that no one broke par. But a look at the whole picture made that 70 a jewel in a rough setting. A statistics buff totaled things up and discovered that the cumulative score for the 152 who completed the round was 1,233 over par, which averages to 8.1 over par per player. Woosnam was 25 strokes ahead of the tailenders, and 43 players returned 80 or more. This Open was shaping up as one for the books.

The first-round leaders:

Ian Woosnam	70
Nick Faldo	71
Gordon Brand	71
Robert Lee	71
Anders Forsbrand	71
Ian Stanley	72
Andrew Brooks	72
Sam Randolph	72
Bernhard Langer	72
Ron Commans	72
Derrick Cooper	72

The weather improved for the second round, but not all that much. Friday was much like Thursday, but a bit less severe. It was still cold and gray and windy, but the wind had abated somewhat. It was still a golfing problem, but it wasn't quite as punishing as Thursday's. And of course, the rough was still there and the fairway still narrow.

While no one could break Turnberry's par 70 in the first round, 14 did in the second. It was this kind of day: Tommy Nakajima had 12 one-putt greens, and even more incredibly, nine in a row, and he improved by seven strokes with a three-under-par 67. He gained not one stroke on the leader. That was because Greg Norman, taking over from Ian Woosnam, shot a seven-under 63, tying the record low for a major championship. Except for some excessive boldness at the wrong time, Norman might have had a 62 or even less.

Perhaps the most amazing thing about Norman's 63 is that it included *three* bogeys. Unfortunately, with a record within reach, he three-putted No. 18 from 28 feet. "I was trying not to leave that putt short," Norman explained. "I totally misjudged the speed. I was not trying to lag up, I was trying to make it. When I saw at No. 17 how close I was, I thought I could shoot 60 today. At 17, I was too aggressive (he was trying for an eagle-three and had to settle for a birdie) and at 18 I misjudged the speed." Norman said he had no idea that he was within reach of the record. In fact, he didn't even know what the record was. "That's the type of person I am—I always want to shoot the lowest score I can," he said.

For the record, Norman's 63 went this way:

No. 1 —par four, two putts from 18 feet.
No. 2 —birdie three, 18-footer.
No. 3 —birdie three, five-footer.
No. 4 —birdie two, four-footer.
No. 5 —bogey five, three putts, 60 feet.
No. 6 —par three, two putts, 40 feet.
No. 7 —eagle three, 20-foot putt.
No. 8 —bogey five, two putts, 18 feet.
No. 9 —par four, three-footer.
No. 10—birdie three, five-footer.
No. 11—birdie, one-footer.
No. 12—par four, two putts, 18 feet.
No. 13—par four, two putts, 18 feet.
No. 14—birdie three, three-footer.
No. 15—par three, two putts, 18 feet.
No. 16—birdie three, eight-footer.
No. 17—birdie four, two putts, 18 feet.
No. 18—bogey five, three putts, 28 feet.

"When I went out," Norman said, "I just said to myself that we are not going to let the wind of yesterday affect the rhythm and swing—just make sure that the tempo destroyed in the wind yesterday was not affected today." He credited the crowd with spurring him on. "At No. 13 and especially at No. 14," he said. "And after that, there seemed to be 15-16,000 people who kept me going. Basically, I had to keep my emotions under control. When I got to No. 17, it was so quiet, so deadly quiet, that it felt eerie. But I don't want people to think the score I shot today makes the course easy. It still played tough."

Norman would get no argument from the players chasing him. Ballesteros, for one, found nothing to like in his game. "Nothing right," he said. "Driving, irons, chipping, putting—nothing right." And so his 75 left him teetering on the cut until day's end, when he was finally spared at 151. Woosnam, the first-round leader, took a double-bogey at No. 8, the big damage in a 74 that carried him back to sixth place, seven off the lead. Nick Faldo, spurred by an eagle-three at No. 17, returned a 70 that left him only one over and four off the lead, a joint third with Nakajima. As if Norman's 63 and Nakajima's putting weren't surprises enough for one day, along came Gordon J. Brand, a two-time winner on the 1986 Safari Tour in Africa. A former cornet player in a Yorkshire sauce-works band, Brand began using his middle initial in an attempt to differentiate himself from a fellow European Tour golfer, Scotland's Gordon Brand. They are continually mistaken for father and son. But to his dismay, he said, some people then thought the "J." stood for "junior." This time, the difference was pronounced—20 strokes, to be exact. The "other" Gordon Brand came in with a 79 for a 159 total and missed the cut. Gordon J. Brand was shooting 68 for a 139 total to hold second place, just two strokes behind Norman. It was a solid round of two bogeys and four birdies. "I simply played every shot as it came," he said. "If there was one shot in the round I liked, it was the two-iron tee shot at the sixth." It put him to six feet, and he jumped on the opportunity and made his birdie.

The 63 put Norman into choice company. Only nine others have made a 63 in a major event: Johnny Miller, 1973 U.S. Open; Bruce Crampton, 1975 U.S. PGA Championship; Mark Hayes, 1977 British Open; Jack Nicklaus and Tom Weiskopf, 1980 U.S. Open; Isao Aoki, 1980 British Open; Ray Floyd, 1982 U.S. PGA Championship; Gary Player, 1984 U.S. PGA Championship; and Nick Price, 1986 Masters. The performance eventually gave Norman a share of second place for the widest variation of rounds by a champion, 11 strokes (74–63). Jack White, in 1904, went from 80 to 69. The record is held by Henry Cotton, 14 strokes (65–79) in 1934. Norman now also shares course records of two Open sites. Mark Hayes posted a 63 at Turnberry in the 1977 Open. Norman had a 65 at St. Andrews in the 1985 Dunhill Nations Cup, matching the score there of Neil Coles in the 1970 Open and Nick Faldo in the 1979 British PGA.

It was generally assumed that Norman's 63 was more impressive than Hayes' 63 in the 1977 Open because Turnberry was, by acclamation of those who played it both times, a more difficult course this time. Perhaps a comparison of figures might be useful:

1977, average score, second round—74.29
1986, average score, second round—74.07

1977, average score for those making 36-hole cut—71.79
1986, average score for those making 36-hole cut—71.89

1977, average score for those missing 36-hole cut—77.54
1986, average score for those missing 36-hole cut—76.34

There are some possible conclusions to be drawn from all this. First, Turnberry might have been easier in 1977, but not that much so. Second, perhaps the field for the 1986 Open was that much stronger, overall. And third, discounting the phenomenal scores shot by Tom Watson (268) and Jack Nicklaus (269) in their duel, only Hubert Green scored better in 1977 (279) than Norman did this time (280).

Nakajima's 67 gave him the lead early in the second round. "I'm very pleased to be leading," he said through an interpreter, "but the day is not finished yet." He would not remain in the lead, but he would always own one of the most remarkable performances in the Open. It was marred only by a three-putt, but that was from 65 feet and cost him a bogey at No. 3. Nakajima, who needed only 25 putts in the round, began his binge of 12 one-putts on the first two holes. He parred No. 1 from 10 feet and No. 2 from three. He birdied No. 4 from 16, and then went into a series of four two-putt greens. His nine straight one-putts, good for five birdies and four pars, began at No. 9, where he dropped a three-footer for a par. Another three-footer got him a par at No. 10. Then came two birdies, from 10 and 22 feet; then two pars from 10 and two feet, then three more birdies beginning at No. 15, from 20, 10, and 15 feet. He had taken the back nine in 30, his best nine ever in a major championship, he said.

With a large international press corps on hand for the Open, it was of academic interest that the Sony Ranking was receiving its first widespread examination. As the Open wore along, it would be interesting to see whether the golfers would justify their ratings. And they did. Coming in to the Open, Ballesteros was ranked No. 1, Langer No. 2, Norman No. 3, and Nakajima No. 4. By the end of the second round, Ballesteros was the only one of the four not crowding the top of the leaderboard.

Tom Watson seemed to have something going at last when he went two under over the first six holes (three birdies, one bogey). Then he missed an opportunity for another birdie when he bunkered a shot at the long seventh. That seemed to summon trouble. At No. 9, he drove into deep rough below the lighthouse and bogeyed. At No. 10, where he had driven into deep rough again, his hunger to make up ground overwhelmed his golf sense. His playing companion, Mark McNulty, was content to chop back onto the fairway and he saved his par four. But Watson elected to go for the green. The try failed badly. He left the ball so deeply snarled in rough that it took a small army of spectators to find it. The hole cost him a double-bogey six. Still, he managed to finish with a one-over 71. Sandy Lyle, meanwhile, clearly was not headed for a second Open title. The question was, would he even make the cut? He managed a birdie at No. 1 after a weak tee shot, but as the course became less forgiving, his work became more difficult. Starting at No. 12, he dropped three strokes over the next four holes. He pulled himself together for birdies at the 16th and 17th, then put himself into an awkward situation at No. 18. There was no shot in his bag that would get him to the green from where his tee shot had finished, close to a bunker. So he invented a bail-out shot on the spot. He hit his putter left-handed, advancing the ball about 100 yards. A bogey left him with a well-scrambled 73, and he retired to what he called the "sweat box"—the long wait to see whether he would make the cut. And he did, right on 151, along with Jack Nicklaus (73) among others.

Jose-Maria Olazabal, a youngster in his first professional year, came on to remind the spectators that Ballesteros isn't the only Spaniard who can play this game. Olazabal, 20, opened with a 78 and improved by nine strokes, becoming the first in this Open to break Turnberry's par 70. His 69 gave him a 147 total that left him 10 strokes off the lead. Unlike the young Ballesteros, Olazabal took nobody by surprise. He had a spectacular amateur record that included winning the British Boys, the Amateur, and the Youths Championships, and he was low amateur in the 1985 Open—all before turning 20. The R&A presented him with a silver cup at Turnberry in tribute to his accomplishments. He came into this Open already 12th on the PGA European Tour Order of Merit with £32,173. His best finishes were a second in the London

Standard Four Stars Pro-Celebrity, and fourth in both the Cepsa Madrid Open and Carrolls Irish Open.

Before the Open began, Deane Beman was asked whether he would be playing to make the cut. The question was well-intended. Beman was, after all, 48, and until the Irish Open a few weeks earlier, he hadn't played competitively in 12 years. The questioner, however, was not familiar with the Beman spirit. Beman was gentle and polite, but quite firm. "I never play just to make the cut," Beman replied. "When I play, I play to be the best." It was, of course, a statement of intent, not a prediction. Beman was and is too deep into golf not to be a realist. So one of the more interesting aspects of this Open came to an end, when Beman came in with a 78 for the second round. With an opening 75, Beman had a 153 total, and only 151 and better—precisely 70 players—could continue into the final two rounds (the R&A having done away with the 54-hole cut). Beman's undoing came at the par-four second, where he made a six, and at the par-four fifth, where he made a seven. Another questioner approached, and in what amounted to a compliment under the circumstances, asked Beman if he was pleased with his "accomplishment." Beman again was gentle, but oh-so-firm. "I don't consider missing the cut an accomplishment," he said. With that, he was soon on his way back to the United States, leaving the realities of competitive golf and returning to the realities of being a commissioner—which in this year had become more complicated than ever before. Two of the principal complications, Ballesteros and O'Grady, posted 75s and just made the cut at 151.

About the same time, the year became even more complicated for Beman. Word came from San Diego that O'Grady, through his attorney there, had just filed a $12 million lawsuit against Beman in U.S. District Court. O'Grady's suit alleged, among other things, that Beman and the PGA Tour had conspired against him, had intentionally inflicted emotional distress on him, and had denied him his rights of free speech.

Perhaps it was a sign of the times, or maybe the course was simply out of their class, but all five amateurs who entered the Open—four Britons and an Irishman—failed to make the 36-hole cut. The closest was England's Mark Davis, with 78–78—156, five strokes over the limit. The others were Andrew Cotton, 79–79—158; Ireland's Garth McGimpsey, 85–76—161; Jeremy Robinson, 84–79—162, and David Curry, 85–80—165.

The effect of Norman's 63 on the field might be viewed this way: Nakajima improved his own score by seven strokes, from 74 to 67, yet gained nothing on the lead. Brand improved by three (71–68), but fell one further back. Tom Watson improved by fully six (77–71), but slipped four more behind the lead—from seven to 11. Guy McQuitty, on the other hand, improved by eight strokes, only to fall 20 strokes further astern. If this Open needed a mix of dark humor, light humor, and good nature, McQuitty provided it. "Thank God my fiancée wasn't here to see my horror show," he said.

McQuitty, 23, a club assistant from Exeter, England, was playing in his first Open. His club sent him £500, and some clothing manufacturers in the tented village outfitted him. He posted a 95 in the first round, which was 25 over par. Hoping to fashion a respectable showing before leaving after the cut, he plunged into the second round. It wasn't going much better. Mortified, he begged for other forces to rescue him. "I said to myself, halfway through the round, 'Beam me up, Scotty,' " McQuitty said, taking a line from *Star Trek,* the popular American science-fiction television show. But no help was forthcoming, extraterrestrial or otherwise, so in the best traditions of the game, he swallowed his medicine and stuck with it. He finished with an 87. That gave him a total of 182. "I really wished I wasn't here," McQuitty said. "It got so bad I was actually scared to stand over the ball." He retired saying that it was his worst performance anywhere, that he enjoyed the Open despite it, and that he intended to work on his game and come back a better player in 1987. He also revealed a streak of character that was summarized by at least one golf writer: "There is no quit in McQuitty."

The second-round leaders:

Greg Norman	74–63—	137
Gordon J. Brand	71–68—	139
Tommy Nakajima	74–67—	141
Nick Faldo	71–70—	141
Bernhard Langer	72–70—	142
Ian Woosnam	70–74—	144
Anders Forsbrand	71–73—	144
Greg Turner	73–71—	144
Jose-Maria Canizares	76–68—	144

On Saturday, it rained. The joke about not being able to see Ailsa Craig underestimated this storm. It hit late in the afternoon, and was so heavy and fierce that the golfers could barely see down the fairway they were playing. These included leader Greg Norman and challengers Gordon J. Brand and Tommy Nakajima. "It was horizontal, and it stung my eyes," said Norman, who staggered down the stretch. Nakajima, who wears glasses, said they were certainly no advantage, and even television viewers could vouch for that. Rain splattered against camera lenses, giving the audience the same blurred view Nakajima had. Norman began the round leading Brand by two strokes and Nakajima and Nick Faldo by four. He had stretched his advantage to five at one point. Then came the staggers. When it was over, Norman had a 74 and a precarious one-stroke lead on Nakajima, who had shot 71. Brand shot 75 and slipped to a joint third, three strokes behind with Ian Woosnam, whose 70 lifted him back into contention.

Only one golfer was able to break par, returning a 69, and he was not even within shouting distance of the leaders. It was Taiwan's Ho Ming Chung, the Bangkok Open champion, playing in his first British Open, and in fact making his first visit to the United Kingdom. Ho's case was a dramatic example of how difficult the day was. He began the round at the tail end of the field, one of 15 players tied for 63rd place. The 69 carried him all the way to a joint 16th for the final round. The pleasure he took in the round, however, was offset by his first exposure to Scottish seaside weather. "It was very cold and miserable out there," he said. "Club selection was very difficult because of the wind." (He would finish the Open with a 77 for 297, a joint 43rd.) After Ho, the next best scores were par 70s turned in by Woosnam, David Graham, Manuel Pinero, Danny Edwards, and Sandy Lyle. At the other end of the scale were 82s by Britain's Tommy Horton and American Kristen Moe.

The weather had not relented, and neither had the complaints. Ballesteros, after a 73 left him at 224, 13 strokes off the lead, was particularly sharp. "This course is far too 'American,' " he said. "It doesn't make it fair for the European players or the spectators. The rough is too tight and the fairways are too narrow. It's ridiculous in the sort of weather we've been having. The Americans can get away with it because their weather is constant, but when you add British weather, it just becomes crazy." Ballesteros didn't know it, but he had an unexpected ally in Scotland's Sam Torrance, who hauled himself to within seven of the lead with a strong 71 for 218. "In calm conditions, the course would be in perfect shape," Torrance said. "But with the wind it's just a bit too difficult. The back nine today, frankly, were impossible." But impossible was a relative term to Torrance. Under the circumstances, he manhandled the back nine for a two-under 33. He put a nine iron to within six feet at the 10th, and after squandering that birdie opportunity, he birdie the next three. He hit the flagstick with a seven iron at No. 11, put a two iron to six feet at No. 12, and holed a 20-footer at No. 13. He dropped a shot at the 14th and solved the last four holes in level par.

The back nine was where Norman came to grief. He had played the front in one-under 34, despite a double-bogey at the short sixth and a bogey at No. 9, and was comfortably in the lead coming home. He was four under par for the championship at the turn and holding a four-stroke lead on Nakajima, who had pulled to level par with an outward 34, and a five-stroke lead on Brand, whose outward 37 put him at one over. Norman and Brand were the final twosome, and Nakajima and Nick Faldo were the pair just ahead of them. Coming home, they battled a southwesterly wind and the torrential downpour much of the way.

It was then that the erratic play the critics point to cropped up in Norman's game. He had an odd back nine—no birdies, and bogeys on every other hole, starting with No. 10. He two-putted from close range there, and two-putted the 12th from five feet, and his lead was melting away. He was his old self at No. 13, where he covered fully 60 feet in only two putts to save his par. Two possible obstacles had removed themselves just up ahead. Faldo and Langer, neither of whom could find a birdie, were working on 76s. Brand was plugging away in pars after bogeys at the 10th and 11th, and a bogey on the last hole would move him further out of the way. But Nakajima was coming on. He made a stunningly brilliant save at No. 12. His four-iron approach got away from him, ending up in the thick grass on the slope of a steep hill to the right of the green. The problem was that the hill stood between him and the green, and it towered about 30 feet above him. He was faced with a completely blind shot out of rough so dense he could barely get his club through it. Hanging on the slope, his left foot well above his right, Nakajima took a mighty swing. The ball soared over the crest of the hill and disappeared from his view. The thunder from the gallery told him the story.

The ball had come down about 16 feet from the flag. He holed the putt for his par four, and when Norman bogeyed the 12th behind him, only two strokes separated them.

Then Nakajima seemed to take himself out of the picture with a double-bogey six at No. 16, where he put his two-iron second shot into the water in front of the green. But he shook it off and immediately got one stroke of that back with a birdie at No. 17, on a 25-foot putt. A five-footer at No. 18 gave him a par and a 71. "I feel comfortable now, but during the round I was very excited," he said. Then soaked by the rain and beaten by the wind, he gratefully retired for the day. "I have never played a round in major golf in worse conditions than these," he said.

Observers have said that Norman has a tendency to push his shots—hit them on a line to the right—when the pressure builds. He did it on the final hole of the 1984 U.S. Open at Winged Foot, putting his approach shot into the grandstand. But he made a miraculous recovery for his par to tie Fuzzy Zoeller. He did it again on the final hole of the 1986 Masters, his approach coming down in the gallery to the right of the green. The resulting bogey cost him a chance to catch Nicklaus, who had made a spectacular charge to win. Now he came to Turnberry's final hole clinging to a two-stroke lead, and this time he put his drive into the umbrellas of the gallery in the right rough. Next came what some considered a tactical error. He elected to use his driver out of the rough. "I used the driver to keep it under the wind," he explained later. "If I had used the three-wood, up in the air, it could finish in the stands or in the pro shop or anywhere." The driver out of heavy grass, however, came down short. Finally, he had to hole a five-foot putt to salvage a bogey-five. He had come home in a five-over 40 for a 74, and his lead was down to one stroke over Nakajima, and three over Woosnam and Brand.

Norman rejected any notion that the pressure had got to him. "I was not as smooth with the putter in the wind, and I did not putt as solidly as I could and that is all I am putting it down to," he said. Then there was the weather. "The difficulty of the rain was that you could not see," he said. "The rain was coming down horizontally, and every time I looked up to see where I was going, it hit me in the face and stung." He said the rain also made it difficult to hold the clubs, and that on a number of occasions—at the 12th and the 14th, notably—the club slipped in his hands. "It was a question of survival, sometimes sheer hanging on in this weather," he said. "I hope we don't have to put up with this weather tomorrow. It is impossible to shoot three, four, or five under in conditions like these. I got the worst of the conditions on the first day and today, but that's how it goes. That's the luck of the draw."

It was a combination of bad weather and a bad experience that created a small disaster for the popular American, D. A. Weibring. The downpour swept in as he reached No. 14. He managed to par it, and his only real damage thereafter was a bogey at No. 15—until he came to No. 18. "I wanted to play it well, because I was probably too conscious of what happened last year," Weibring said. That's when he remembered the 1985 Open at Royal St. George's, where a five-six finish on the final two holes cost him perhaps a chance at a playoff with winner Sandy Lyle. He remembered that as he stood on Turnberry's No. 18 tee. He hit a good drive. But then he pulled his two-iron approach into the left rough. "Terrible lie," he said. "I hit a sand wedge and the ball went deeper. I tried to hit it as hard as I could with my next, and the ball moved one inch, no more. Then I shanked the next one out. I can't describe it any other way." He finally got on the green, then two-putted. He had made an eight. Of the 70 players who completed the last two rounds, it was the biggest score at No. 18. Weibring came into the second round in fairly good shape at 145, and he was three over for the day until that eight. It left him with a 76 for a 221 total.

Perhaps the only truly happy player to come out of the miserable day was Scotland's Martin Gray, but it had nothing to do with his score. He was happy because he finally got to play with his idol, Jack Nicklaus, whom he has admired for many years. "It was a wonderful experience," Gray said. "My only disappointment was that he did not play as well as he can." Nicklaus, in fact, shot 76, the same as Gray, and they finished tied at 227, 16 strokes off the lead.

Tsuneyuki Nakajima, whose first name has been transliterated into "Tommy" for the sake of the English-speaking golf world, was having a splendid career in Japan and had earned his spot among the top players in the game. He learned the game as a youth principally on a pitch-and-putt area complete with a bunker his father, Iwao, built behind their home. He won the Amateur Public Links at age 18 and the Japan Amateur at 19. He turned professional in 1976, at age 21, and his first victory was in the 1977 Japan PGA. He has won the Japan PGA and the Japan Match Play three times each. But he probably is best known in the West for one failure rather than all his successes—because that failure was spectacular. It came at the 1978 Open at St. Andrews, in the third round. Nakajima was among the contenders, then took a nine at No. 17, the Road Hole. It took him four strokes to escape from the Road Bunker, which St. Andrews caddys now call "The Sands of Nakajima." He is also famed for the 13 he took at the par-five 13th in the 1978 Masters. In 1985, Nakajima won six tournaments, tying Ballesteros and Langer for the most wins by any golfer in the world. Coming into this Open, he had won four tournaments—the Japan Match Play, the Mizuno, the Mitsubishi Galant, and the Kanto PGA.

No Japanese has ever won one of golf's four major titles—the U.S. and British Opens, the U.S. PGA, and the Masters. Nakajima suddenly found himself faced with the very real possibility of being the first. "I am now one shot behind Greg," he said, "and I know it will not be easy to beat him. I have met him many times in Japan. All I can say is that I will do my best. To be the first Japanese to win a major championship would be one of the greatest things, and one I would have thought might never happen. All I can say is I am going to give it everything I've got."

Later Saturday evening, one golfer was the happiest man at Turnberry, but it had nothing to do with golf. He was Bernhard Langer. The big moment finally had arrived. His wife, Vikki, called him during the night to inform him that at about 8:30 p.m., their daughter was born. Langer's response was, "You're kidding." Jackie Carol Langer weighed nine pounds.

The third-round leaders:

Greg Norman   74–63–74—211

Tommy Nakajima	74–67–71—212
Ian Woosnam	70–74–70—214
Gordon J. Brand	71–68–75—214
Gary Koch	73–72–72—217
Jose-Maria Canizares	76–68–73—217
Nick Faldo	71–70–76—217
David Graham	75–73–70—218
Sam Torrance	78–69–71—218
Raymond Floyd	78–67–73—218
Bernhard Langer	72–70–76—218

On that Sunday morning back in June at Shinnecock Hills, Greg Norman came out for the final round of the U.S. Open leading by one stroke and "feeling flat," as he put it. He said he simply couldn't stir himself, and he gradually drifted back, leaving behind him the Open that had been his to win. This time, with the British Open nearly in hand, whatever problems awaited him, being flat wouldn't be one of them. He forced himself to fret over the coming final round, reminding himself of how other majors had slipped away. "My wife, Laura, kept asking me how I felt, and I told her I felt fine," Norman was to say later, with a grin. "I didn't want her to know I was nervous as hell." He couldn't even finish his breakfast. In this high state, he went off to see whether he could hold the lead and win his first major title, and fulfill the promise everyone had seen in him.

Of course, there was the "question." Norman knew he would have to face it sooner or later. It first rose in the 1984 U.S. Open, when he put on an incredible finish to catch Fuzzy Zoeller over the closing holes. But it was remembered that on the final hole of regulation play, needing a birdie to win, Norman hit his approach wildly to the right. Only a miraculous 45-foot, downhill-sidehill putt saved him the tie. Then he faded badly in the playoff the next day, posting a 75 and losing to Zoeller by eight strokes. Earlier in the 1986 season, he led both the Masters and the U.S. Open by one stroke going into the last round, and both titles slipped from his grasp. Now he was leading the British Open by one going into the last round. The question was a disturbing one. No matter how it was phrased, it came to this: Could he stand up under the pressure? The question actually came up on Saturday after he had struggled down the back nine of the third round and his commanding lead shrank to one stroke. Norman answered the question politely, but with a noticeable edge to his voice: The misfortunes of the Masters and the U.S. Open would have no bearing on how he played now. He simply would do the best he could.

It is said you can get all four seasons in one British Open, and as if on cue, balmy summer arrived on Sunday for the final round. This was the best weather of the Open. The sun finally broke through. The sky, so leaden and forbidding earlier, now was blue with brushed-in clouds. There was still enough wind to make the players think, but by afternoon the flags atop the grandstand at No. 18 were barely stirring. If Norman was to get a challenge, it wouldn't be from the weather.

But it didn't come from the golfers, either. Bernhard Langer, who closed with a rush for his best round, a 68, said it for everybody at the end of the day: "Nobody made it difficult for Greg."

If Norman needed any inspiration beyond his own self-induced case of nerves, he had got it the night before from some fellow golfers shortly after dinner at the Turnberry Hotel, where many of the players were staying. First there were the urgings of Fuzzy Zoeller, Hubert Green, and John Mahaffey, who owned two U.S. Opens, two U.S. PGAs, and a Masters among them. But most of all there were the words from Jack Nicklaus. Norman recalled the conversation: "He told me, 'Nobody in the world wants you to win this championship more than I do,' " Norman said. "And when the greatest golfer the world has ever known tells you something like that, it makes you feel really special." All Norman had to do now was go out and win it.

British Opens of the recent past were marked by electrifying last acts. There was, for example, Seve Ballesteros's careening finish in 1979; and in 1982 the collapse of Bobby Clampett and then Nick Price, leaving Tom Watson the winner; and Ballesteros's breathtaking rush over a faltering Watson in 1984, and Sandy Lyle's gritty battle in 1985. This Open, on the other hand, was a complete departure. To all intents and purposes, it ended the moment it started—on the first hole of the final round. Nakajima was trailing Norman by only one stroke when they teed off in the final twosome at 2:40 p.m. About 10 minutes later, Nakajima three-putted No. 1 from less than six feet—his next-to-last from about one foot—and took a double-bogey six. Norman parred. In the group ahead, Gordon J. Brand and Ian Woosnam, who had started three strokes behind, also had parred No. 1. Thus Norman had a three-stroke lead on his three nearest competitors. He had only to nurse his game home and leave it to the others to challenge the mighty Turnberry, and the championship was his. Of course, Norman does not nurse his game anywhere. He played Turnberry as though he were in the first round. He came home like a champion, with a one-under 69. Others closed strong, but they had too much ground to make up. Five others posted 69, and two bettered it—Ballesteros with a 64 and Bernhard Langer with a 68. Norman finished level-par 280 and became the first Australian to win the Open since Peter Thomson took the last of his five championships at Royal Birkdale in 1965. Norman won by five over Brand, the largest margin since Johnny Miller's six-stroke victory at Royal Birkdale in 1976. He was six ahead of Langer and Ian Woosnam. And only some later fireworks—an eagle by Brand and two birdies by Woosnam—made it even that close. Nakajima staggered to a 77 that included bogeys on the final three holes, and finished a joint eighth at 289.

Norman himself figured it was over by the eighth hole: "When I hit that four-iron in there, I said, 'All right, guys, that's it. I've shut the gate.' " He put that shot five feet from the flag and holed the putt for one of his three birdies. His challengers couldn't close the gap. His margin jumped to five at No. 3, where he holed a 75-foot bunker shot for a birdie-three. It slipped back to three when he bogeyed No. 5 and Nakajima and Woosnam both birdied No. 7. Then it climbed. Norman birdied No. 14 to go to level par, and when Nakajima bogeyed No. 16, the gap was an awesome seven strokes.

Brand had high hopes. His best finish on the European Tour to that point of the season was a fifth in the Carrolls Irish Open just a few weeks earlier. His best previous finish in the British Open was 19th at Sandwich in 1981. Now he had a chance to win. A slim one, but a chance. But he played himself out of contention with a 39 on the front nine that included a double-bogey six at No. 5 and a hit spectator at No. 7, where he took a bogey six. "I couldn't believe the way I played the front nine," he said later. "I was just hoping to hit the fairways. But after nine holes, I knew the Open was not going to be mine." At that point, he was eight behind Norman, and three behind Woosnam and Nakajima. He kept plugging, though. He finally found a fairway at the 12th, and he birdied. He eagled No. 17 in his bogey-free back nine for an inward three under 32 and the 71 that gave him a 285 total, sole possession of second place, and the biggest paycheck of his career, £50,000.

Woosnam's hopes were as slim as Brand's. He also started the day at four-over 214, and he played himself out almost as quickly. He offset bogeys at the second and third with birdies at the fifth and seventh, then bogeyed the eighth to turn in one-over 36, at which point he trailed Norman by five. Then he took himself out of it with three rapid-fire bogeys beginning at No. 10. "I three-putted No. 11 from so close it was ridiculous," he said. "Dropping those three shots was too much." Birdies at No. 14 and No. 17 helped ease his disappointment and gave him a two-over 72 and a 286 total, and a share of third with the onrushing Langer.

Langer had insisted all week that waiting for news from the hospital back home in West Germany was not affecting his play. "I was trying to block everything out so I could concentrate," he said. He returned scores of 72, 70, and 76 in the first three rounds. But the day after Jackie Carol arrived— "Afterwards, my thoughts were with them," he said—as he posted his best round, the two-under 68. This at least suggested the easing of what must have been a heavy concern. Langer went out in 36 but came home in 32 with four birdies and one bogey for the 286 that tied him for third place with Woosnam.

Nick Faldo added to an Open record that is among the best in history for a non-winner. He closed with a 70 for 287 and fifth place. He credited a quick telephone tip from his coach, Dave Leadbetter, who had spotted a posture problem while watching him play on television. "That put me right," Faldo said. "But unfortunately, my putting was off. I played like Tarzan but scored like Jane." Aside from his joint 54th in 1985, Faldo's highest finish over the past eight years was a joint 19th in 1979. He had two others in the top 15, and five in the top 10, including the fifth in this one. He shares an Open record with Jack Nicklaus, Lee Trevino, and Phil Rodgers for having three rounds in the 60s without winning. Faldo did it in 1984 at St. Andrews, when he posted 69–68–76–69 and finished joint sixth on 282.

The real Seve Ballesteros arrived about three days too late. He posted a six-under 64 for the final round, just one stroke from the Open record Norman had matched two days earlier. It gave him an eight-over 288 total and briefly left him the leader in the clubhouse. The weather had improved immensely, but it's doubtful that good weather was the answer. He has played well under poor conditions in the past. Perhaps it was as simple as putting. Earlier, he had complained of not being able to make a putt. This time he reaped a bumper crop. He holed from 35 feet at No. 2, from 40 at

No. 10, and from 15 at both the 14th and 16th—all for birdies. His patented scrambling also was back. At No. 17, he drove into the left rough, then hit his second almost out of bounds when his club got tangled in the thick grass. After a free drop from near a fence, he put his third to four feet and holed for the birdie. This was a happier Ballesteros but not a mollified one. "No, I don't change my opinion," he said. "It's a good golf course, but its setup is too severe. They shouldn't set up a course the way they do in the U.S. Open." Ballesteros was informed that Tom Watson intended to write a letter of complaint to the R&A, and was asked whether he would, also. "I believe they can read English," Ballesteros quipped. "They will see it in the papers." With that, he retired from the 115th British Open as the early leader. Could he win? "I hope the weather gets terrible," he said, grinning. "Then maybe I have a chance to win."

The sudden slip of the Americans in the British Open might be worth a study of some kind. Americans had enjoyed near domination of the Open since Arnold Palmer's first victory in 1961. The leaderboard generally looked as if it belonged at an American tour stop. Going back only 10 years, to the 1977 Open, Tom Watson won and nine of the top 10 finishers were Americans. The view begins to change, slightly at first, starting with 1980. Watson won, and Americans held seven of the top 10 places. In 1981, Bill Rogers won, and there were four Americans in the top 10. In 1982, Watson won again, and again there were four Americans in the top 10. In 1983, it was Watson again, and the top 10 included five Americans. Then came Ballesteros in 1984 and Sandy Lyle in 1985, and four of the top 10 were Americans each time. With Norman's victory, the Americans were kept away from the old trophy for the third year in a row—the first time this had happened since Arnold Palmer led the Americans back to the Open in 1960. And there were only two Americans in the top 10—Gary Koch a joint sixth at 288 and Fuzzy Zoeller a joint eighth at 289. For the first time since Tony Jacklin's victory in 1969, there was not an American to be found in the top five.

Perhaps it was only fitting that an Open born in controversy should not end completely at peace, no matter the serene blue skies that marked the final day. There was one more angry voice to be heard, and the complaint might go down as the strangest in Open history. It came from Mac O'Grady, who closed with his best round, a 70 for a 298 and a joint 46th (with Nicklaus, among others), and then he made this complaint to the R&A Championship Committee: That the white paint had been applied too thickly on the inside of the cups, and this caused putts to lip out. Alistair Low, chairman of the Championship Committee, said O'Grady's views had been noted, but that the committee was disappointed that the complaint had not been brought to their attention sooner if it was felt to have been a problem earlier in the week.

But in the end, it was the "Norman Conquest" (the newspapers again could not resist the temptation) that occupied everyone's attention. As in so many Opens, the firm hand of a caddy was felt, and Norman was quick to praise his, Pete Bender. It happened at No. 7. "I tried to force my tee shot and hit a quick, low hook," Norman said. "As I went down the fairway, Peter said 'I can see you are walking very fast. Now I want you to walk at the same speed I am.' " The calming effect was noticeable immediately.

Norman, who had birdied No. 3 and bogeyed No. 5, now "shut the gate" with that four iron to five feet at No. 8. At No. 9, he got a par he really didn't expect to get. He hit his approach through the green and into the bleachers, and received a free drop. Suddenly, Nakajima, whose knowledge of English is slim, was raising a question about a possible rules violation. Norman had taken his drop closer to the hole. He also was disturbed. An interpreter eventually straightened out the matter. "A new rule said you must drop in a drop area, irrespective of whether it's closer to the hole," Norman said. "Actually, I got an easier shot. But I never heard of a rule in golf where you can drop the ball closer to the hole." He pitched on, then, and holed a six-foot putt for his par to make the turn in one under and stay even for the Open. He still led Nakajima and Woosnam by five. Two putts from 12 feet cost him a bogey at No. 11, and then it seemed a new surge of inspiration hit him. At the 14th, he lashed a seven-iron out of the rough that hit the flagstick, and a three-foot putt gave him his final birdie of the day and a six-stroke lead with four holes to play. He might have had another at No. 17, but a strange thing happened. Norman drove into the rough, came out with a sand wedge, then put a six-iron shot only five feet from the hole. Then he turned to his caddy. "Pete," he said, "I can't even see the hole. My mind has gone dead. Tell me what the line is and how hard to hit it." Even the resourceful Bender was of no use here. Norman banged the short putt about four feet past the cup, and had to hole that one coming back for his par five. But the rest of his game was at peak level. "I hit some iron shots on the back nine that impressed even me," Norman said.

All that was left now was that inspiring walk up the 18th fairway, through the thunder of the gallery lining both fairways and packed into the grandstands around the green. Norman hit his approach on, then was all but lost in the ceremonial swarm of the spectators. He knew only one uneasy moment. A guard trying to keep the people back fell and disappeared under the stampede. He reappeared unharmed. Norman found his ball some 60 feet from the hole, and this time his mind was not blank. He two-putted for his par four, the 69, the 280 total, and his first major championship. All the near misses in the world didn't matter now.

5.   The PGA Championship

It ended with one of the greatest shots in golf history, but to call the 1986 PGA Championship a classic confrontation would be a misnomer. It was Greg Norman's to win until Bob Tway snatched it away at the 72nd hole with a bunker shot into the hole.

Norman led until he bogeyed the 14th hole in the final round at the Inverness Club in Toledo, Ohio, and they were tied when they teed off at the 354-yard No. 18. The final hole at Inverness doesn't seem very difficult, but looks are deceiving. "It's the hardest easy hole I ever played," said Jack Nicklaus. From an elevated tee, it's a drive to a fairway that doglegs right toward a small plateau green. Miss the drive to the right and your ball winds up in a downhill lie in the rough; hit it too hard and it runs through the fairway into the rough to the left. Except when the wind blows toward the tee, it calls for an iron or a fairway wood off the tee.

Norman and Tway tried to cut the dogleg as much as they could. Norman's drive hit the right rough and trickled into the fairway; Tway's stayed in the deep grass. Tway's nine iron from 130 yards was not quite enough, his ball falling into the bunker that guards the right front of the green. "I didn't have a good lie. I was just trying to get it on the green," Tway said. "My first thought was that it was buried in the bunker." Norman hit a pitching wedge and went for the flag. He probably puts more backspin on his iron shots than most players, and this time that ability proved costly. His ball hit the green, took one bounce toward the hole and backed up, rolled down and stopped a foot or so in the deep collar around the green. "I thought I hit a good shot; I was surprised it was in the deep grass," Greg said. "I hit a good shot with a bad result."

The advantage was still with Norman. He had a short chip and appeared to have a par in hand. Tway was facing a shot that needed to be hit perfectly for a chance at par. Hit it too easy and Tway faced a curling downhill putt; hit it too hard and the ball could roll off the green. "He was below the hole and I knew if I got it up and down and he didn't make it, there would be a playoff," Tway said. "I wasn't trying to make it, I was just trying to get close. When the shot went in, I was so excited—if I had jumped that high in school I probably would have made the basketball team."

Tway's shot hit the green softly and rolled toward the hole like a rabbit to its warren—all of 20 feet. Norman still had a chance to tie, but emotionally he was drained. "I changed my mind. I had a sand wedge in my hand, I was going to get the shot up the hill and play for a four," Greg said. "But I relined my thinking; I figured I can't leave it short, I've got to go for it." He hit a pitching wedge, the ball came out too swiftly and never had a chance. He two-putted for a meaningless bogey—with a two-stroke lead on Peter Jacobsen, he was virtually assured second place.

Tway had a 70 for 276, an eight-under-par score that marked the first time anyone had broken par in a major tournament at Inverness. Norman had a 76 for 278 and visions of a season that might have been. He led the Masters until Nicklaus overtook him in the final round. He led the U.S. Open until the fire went out in the last round and Raymond Floyd came out of a throng to win. He won the British Open with a dominating performance. And he led the PGA Championship until Tway caught him with a sensational final nine and won with a shot that marked the first time the PGA had been decided by a birdie at the final hole.

Norman arrived at Inverness as one of the favorites, at the conclusion of one of the greatest seasons in PGA Tour history. He had won the Panasonic-Las Vegas Invitational and the Kemper Open, in addition to the British Open, and was the leading money winner with a record $564,729. Tway had won the Andy Williams Open, the Manufacturers Hanover Westchester Classic and the Georgia-Pacific Atlanta Classic and was the No. 2 money winner with $460,005. But Tway received little mention from those who handicap tournaments. The feeling seemed to be that as a 27-year-old pro in his second year on the tour, Tway lacked the experience to win a major tournament. The prognosticators apparently chose to ignore Tway's showing in the earlier majors of 1986. He tied for eighth place in the Masters. He led the U.S. Open after the first round and ultimately tied for eighth place. Troubled by the winds at Turnberry, Bob tied for 46th in the British Open, then missed the cut in his next two tournaments as he tried to recover his swing.

So it was that when reporters wrote of likely winners they mentioned Norman, Severiano Ballesteros, Andy Bean, Hal Sutton, Fuzzy Zoeller, Tom Kite, Calvin Peete, Floyd and Nicklaus, veterans all.

At 6,982 yards, Inverness was not an overly long course with a par of 35–36—71. The tree near the No. 8 tee that stirred such controversy in the 1979 U.S. Open was no longer a subject of discussion. It will be recalled that in the 1979 U.S. Open Lon Hinkle figured the 528-yard dogleg-left hole could be shortened by hitting a drive down the adjacent No. 17 fairway, then hitting an iron over the trees to the green. Some tried it and succeeded; some tried and failed. Nevertheless, it caused the U.S. Golf Association to have a full-grown fir planted in the opening between the No. 8 tee and No. 17 fairway after the first round to prevent the shortcut. The tree did little good; players had already realized the risk wasn't worth the potential cost. Seven years later, the tree still stood, but no one attempted to hit a drive over or around it to the 17th fairway.

The Hinkle tree and Tway's fabulous bunker shot added a couple of chapters to a club that was deep in golf history, a regular stopping place for the U.S. Open. Ted Ray won his only U.S. Open there in 1920 with a score of 295. In 1931, Billie Burke defeated George Von Elm in a 144-hole playoff after they had tied at 292. In another playoff, Dick Mayer beat Cary Middlecoff after they tied at 282 (par was 70 then). Hale Irwin, desperately trying to keep his game together on the final nine, won with a 284 in 1979.

Inverness was founded in 1903, but Donald Ross didn't build the present course until 1919. The next year, the U.S. Open was held there. The first course was nine holes and originally was eight holes. The architect left one hole out, then rectified his error by inserting a par-three. When Ross was commissioned 16 years later, he rebuilt the original nine and added another nine. Because of alterations made for each tournament, the course has played to different pars—70 in 1957, 72 in 1920 and 71 the other years.

Although this was the first PGA Championship at Inverness, it was not the first professional tournament on the course. The Inverness Four Ball was played from 1935 to 1953 and attracted 16 of the best touring pros to compete in a round-robin format. Ben Hogan and Jimmy Demaret won four times, and Sam Snead won four times with different partners. Byron Nelson was the club's pro from 1940–44, leaving in 1945, the year he won 18 tournaments, including 11 in a row.

Nicklaus was 17 years old when he made his U.S. Open debut at Inverness in 1957. "I hit a three wood, seven iron and made a 35-foot putt for birdie at the first hole," Jack recalled. "I parred the next two holes and I was leading the Open at 17. Then I choked. I double-bogeyed the fourth hole and shot two rounds of 80." Nicklaus returned as a pro in 1979 and again he missed the cut, with 74–77—151. The PGA at Inverness was a milestone. When Nicklaus teed off in the first round it marked his 100th start in a major, his 25th in the PGA. He and Walter Hagen, with five victories apiece, share the record for the most PGA titles. Nicklaus was 46, but after his astounding triumph in the Masters five months earlier, no one was saying he couldn't win again.

The hottest player going into the PGA was Ballesteros. He had won five of his last six tournaments in Europe, the exception being the British Open, where he closed with a 64. Ballesteros still was at odds with PGA Tour Commissioner Deane Beman, so when Beman extended an invitation to the World Series of Golf, Ballesteros declined, saying he had other commitments. What, he was asked. "I'll be home . . . reading the newspapers," he said.

The Opens that were played at Inverness were held in June, when the rough is thick and deep. That was probably a reason that par had never been broken. But the PGA was staged in August, when the rough was thinned by hot weather. The weather had another effect on the course: the greens were bumpy, not in their normally smooth condition, but still fast.

A heavy thunderstorm struck the course late Wednesday afternoon. It smoothed and softened the greens, and almost guaranteed that the winning score would be under par.

The course record fell in the first round. The record for the old course was 62 by Byron Nelson; the low for the new course was a 67 by Irwin in 1979. Norman crept up on the record, playing the front nine in one under par, his birdie coming on a 2½-foot putt at the fourth hole after a great six iron. Then Greg mugged the course on the back nine for a 31 and 65. He birdied No. 11 with an 18-foot putt, No. 12 with a seven-footer and chipped to within a foot for a tap-in at the par-five No. 13. After saving par with a fine chip at 14, Norman birdied 15 from 10 feet and 16 from five feet. It was a near-perfect round. The only shots that marred it were a five-iron tee shot at the sixth hole that went into a bunker and a sand wedge approach at the eighth hole that came up a woeful 45 feet short. But Norman rectified the mistakes by blasting to within a foot at No. 6 and sinking the putt at No. 8.

"The rain made the golf course play that much easier," Greg said. "You could hit a driver. It would not run as far, but you could get it closer with a short iron to the green. The course played four shots easier than in the practice rounds. The only problem is it throws out your game plan. After practicing on a hard, fast course, you don't know how to play when it's soft. The only change was that you couldn't hit a driver at 16.

"I wasn't hitting the driver well until the 16th hole. I was trying to play the driver left to right, I was fighting to cut the ball instead of just letting it happen. No. 8 was the only hole in a long time that I underclubbed. The shot I enjoyed the most was the six iron to the fourth hole. The ball did exactly what I wanted. I visualized the shot. The eight iron to 12 was a good shot, the five iron to 15, too. Everything I visualized went where I wanted it to go. I didn't attack at all. The golf course just lent itself to a good round."

Norman, 31, was in his fourth year on the American tour, but he had spent many more years on the international circuits. The age and experience, he said, were primary factors in his outstanding year. "It's maturity. I'm playing about the same, maybe I'm playing a little better and I'm putting a little better, but the older I get, the less I am affected by mistakes. And I've learned how to handle pressure. The harder you work, the more it pays off in the long run. I always wanted to win a major and now that I've won one I can adjust my sights a little bit. I'm having great fun. I'm having a good year now, but if everything goes the way I want, I'll have a great year."

Nicklaus was very much in contention with a 70 that should have been better. He bogeyed the 16th and 17th holes. He birdied Nos. 1, 8, 9 and 10 on putts of 15, three, 12 and eight feet and bogeyed No. 2 when he missed a two-footer. Jack was satisfied with his round. "In the first three majors, I had scores of 74, 77 and 78 in the first round," he said. "I knew if I had any chance of winning here, I had to get off to a decent start. It's a decent score; the only thing is I had a 67 or 68 looking at me."

Craig Stadler and Phil Blackmar were the closest to Norman with four-under-par 67s. Stadler made six birdies, including putts of 30 feet at the second hole and 25-footers at the ninth and 18th holes. His mistakes came at the eighth hole, where he had to take a drop away from a fence, and at the 17th green, which he three-putted. "The first nine I kind of escaped," Stadler said. "I made some good long putts and I missed some short putts. This is a fun golf course if you're hitting your irons well—you've got to hit the greens."

Stadler was fresh off the Scandinavian Open, which he lost in a playoff after bogeying the last three holes. "I feel like there's something in my subconscious keeping me from scoring well," he said. "There have been weeks where I felt good and wanted to play and I played awful and there were weeks where I felt bad and I played well. It's been in my head, not my game. I've got to find something to get me fired up, to get me going again. In the Scandinavian I shot 66, 66, 66 and then boom! boom! boom! three bogeys. When I flew home, I was wondering what happened."

Blackmar, at 6-7 and 250 pounds, the biggest man on the tour, was a surprise contender. "I haven't played in a month and when I do that I never know what's going to happen," he said. "I needed the weeks off to regroup. I relaxed and spent the time with my family. I hadn't had more than a week off since February and my game kept getting worse and worse. In the Open, I hit only 22 fairways—that's five and a half a day."

Blackmar didn't know what to expect. He birdied Nos. 3 and 4 with putts of six and 40 feet, then gave those strokes back with bogeys at the next two holes. At the 528-yard No. 8, his sand wedge to the green took one bounce and backed into the hole for an eagle-three. "That turned my round around and put it in a positive direction," Blackmar said. He birdied 10, 12, 13 and 16 and bogeyed 14, and was so pumped up at the prospect of a 66 that he hit a flyer out of the rough at 18 and over the green and bogeyed.

Gary Koch also had been having a fine year in the major tournaments. He tied for 16th in the Masters, tied for 15th in the U.S. Open and was sixth in the British Open. He had the experience and the savvy to win at Inverness. So when Koch opened with 68, he had to be regarded as a contender. After his birdies at the first three holes, he settled in for a succession of pars until the back nine, which he began birdie-par-birdie, putting him five under. He missed the green at the 14th hole and bogeyed and three-putted from 35 feet at 17, missing his second putt from four feet.

"I hit 14 greens and I drove it out of the fairway only three times," Koch said. "Those first three birdies set the tone of the round and let me go out and enjoy it. I made a silly mistake at 17. I never saw anything that indicated the ball was not rolling well on the greens. The switch (from fast to slower greens) is easier than going from soft to very fast. I prefer practicing knowing the course is not going to get any tougher than this.

"I've finally come to the realization that the majors are just another tournament. In the past I put too much emphasis on them and I put pressure on myself because I wanted to do well. Basically, I came here with the attitude that I would play as well as I could. My key in all the majors this year is to play the golf course and stick to that. There's no reason to vary from your game plan when you get a good start."

Koch was tied at 68 with Australian Wayne Grady, Wayne Levi, Ronnie Black and Jacobsen. Jacobsen was in an unfamiliar position. For three months he had struggled without realizing he had an infection in his stomach and intestines. "I took it lightly," Peter said, "but it knocked me on my can physically; I lost strength. Now I'm 100 percent. I saw a doctor last week and he put me on medication. I think I drank some bad water. It's nothing a win couldn't take care of."

Jacobsen birdied the first and third holes, but offset them with bogeys at five and 10. Then he birdied Nos. 11, 12 and 15 with some good irons. "The good start put me in a better frame of mind for the middle holes," he said. "Now that the greens are soft, they're holding a shot from the fairway if the ball is struck properly, but not from the rough. I like the PGA, the way it sets up courses. You can get a club on the ball in the rough; the rough is not up to your knees. I seem to play well in the PGA—I made a run at it in 1983—I get pumped up." Jacobsen was in the race to stay, but he couldn't keep in step with Tway and Norman.

Grady, in his second year on the American tour, is from Brisbane, the same city that spawned Norman. "He was playing when I was just starting," Grady said. "He was always a great player. He had an idea where he was going and he's done it." With a little more than $25,000 in winnings, Grady was having a year the opposite of Norman's. "I feel like my game is coming around, although it had a couple of hiccups through the round," Grady said. "It's been a frustrating year, but I feel I can make a decent year of it. The biggest effect was not being patient. I started getting fast and I haven't given myself a chance; I've been forcing it, doing it the wrong way. I've been going through three and four things every day, trying to do this and that, always experimenting, not working on one thing."

A two-iron shot against a tree—"The only shot I missed."—cost Grady a double bogey at the seventh hole, nullifying a birdie at the third hold, but he settled down after that. He played the back nine in 32, finishing with birdies at the last two holes—blading a sand wedge from the fringe at the final green and sinking a 40-foot par putt at the 15th.

Some people let outstanding rounds get away; others made good rounds out of potentially bad ones. Levi played the first 13 holes in five under par, then double-bogeyed No. 14 and bogeyed 15. Lietzke played erratically, yet managed a 69 that tied him with Larry Mize, Bob Gilder, Bobby Wadkins, Gene Sauers, Fred Couples, Mike Hulbert and Jay Haas. "It was a scrambling round, but it could have been three shots lower if I had driven in the fairway," Lietzke said.

Lietzke made only one bogey and his short game was superb as he made three birdies and saved par at the last two holes, sinking a 25-foot putt at No. 17 and holing a five-footer after blasting from a bunker at 18. "I was close," Lietzke said. "I missed six or seven fairways and the rule of thumb at Inverness is you have to hit the fairways. I broke that rule. But the rough is not as severe. The last two years it was more severe than I've seen it in the PGA. It wasn't very penalizing."

Gilder was a replacement for Jack Renner, who withdrew on Monday because of illness. "Ronnie Black had to par the 72nd hole (in the Western Open) and he nudged me out (from an automatic berth)," Gilder said. "I thought I should have been here. I was playing well, which is another reason I wanted to be here." Gilder played a near flawless round, a drive into the trees at the 15th hole causing the only blot. Mize, who had suffered several heartbreaking losses earlier in the year, said he played a "really solid round," but mixed six birdies with four bogeys and four pars through the first 14 holes before parring in. "It could have been a little better with the way I played on the back," he said. Mize started the back nine with three birdies and then "I got the fats going three holes in a row."

Inverness had never been subjected to the abuse suffered in the first round: 25 players broke par; one broke the course record, two others tied the old mark; 16 players broke 70 and nine others shot 70. After one round, here's the way the leaders stacked up:

Greg Norman	65
Craig Stadler	67
Phil Blackmar	67
Gary Koch	68
Wayne Grady	68
Peter Jacobsen	68

Wayne Levi	68
Ronnie Black	68
Larry Mize	69
Bob Gilder	69
Bruce Lietzke	69
Bobby Wadkins	69
Gene Sauers	69
Fred Couples	69
Mike Hulbert	69
Jay Haas	69

The second round was delayed for half an hour by fog, leaving the early starters champing at their bits. Inverness had been proved vulnerable and now everyone wanted a shot at it . . . and at overtaking Norman. But the course was starting to dry out and the greens were getting harder. Hulbert, who teed off three hours before Norman, tied for the lead with birdies at the eighth, ninth and 10th holes, but that was before Norman had stepped to the first tee. There were some good rounds shot—Payne Stewart, Jim Thorpe and Mark Wiebe tied the previous course record—but at the end of the day Norman was still on top, and by twice as many strokes.

Hulbert seemed like the most out-of-place player among the contenders at the end of the round, a prime candidate to wither and die when the heat came on. But Hulbert had displayed amazing staying power in a few earlier tournaments and he showed that a major championship makes no difference. He wears tinted glasses, talks slowly, looks like a collegian, but when his game is on, the course doesn't matter. He had tied for third, a shot behind Tway and Bernhard Langer, in the Andy Williams Open in La Jolla, California, and had tied with Raymond Floyd, a stroke behind Dan Forsman, in the rain-abbreviated Hertz Bay Hill Classic in Orlando, Florida.

In the Williams and Bay Hill tournaments, the television announcers had called him Hurlbert. "They can pronounce it right now. I hope they'll remember me," Hulbert said after his second-round 68 pulled him into a second-place tie with Stewart.

Two under par after one round, Hulbert began the second round with a bogey and those who had begun to follow him in idle curiosity started to drift away. But Hulbert dropped putts of five and 18 feet at the next two holes and he was off on one of the best 16-hole stretches in the tournament. He made birdie putts of seven, 12, and eight feet at Nos. 8, 9 and 10 and that put him at six under for the tournament, in a tie with Norman. "I didn't notice the leaderboard until those three birdies," Hulbert said. "I was trying to catch Norman, that's what I was trying to do. I played with Norman once, I think it was in the third round of the Memorial, and it was fun. It will be fun again."

Although having opportunities on the next seven holes, Hulbert couldn't get his name above Norman's on the leaderboard. For the second day, he missed the fairway at the 18th hole and the bogey took some of the luster off the 68 that tied him at 137 with Stewart, who finished in the preceding threesome with a 67.

Stewart always seems to be in contention in majors. He tied for eighth in the Masters and for sixth in the U.S. Open. After Shinnecock Hills, his game went downhill. "My game has been nonexistent for a month," he said after the second round at Inverness. "After the Open, my attitude was bad. I kept playing but I didn't enjoy it. I went to see Harvie Ward and he got me interested again. We prepared for this tournament. At Canada, I probably had the worst attitude, I couldn't have cared less. I guess you could call it burnout. The Open might have had something to do with it, leading the tournament and not winning."

The session with Ward, his tutor, paid off. Stewart, who had opened with a 70, reached the 398-yard first hole with an eight iron and then sank an eight-foot putt for birdie, touching off what was to be a near flawless round. He made birdie putts of 10 feet at the seventh hole and 20 feet at the 11th and holed an 18-foot chip shot from the fringe above the hole at the final green. He saved a few pars, most notably with a chip to within a foot of the hole at 13 and with a 15-foot putt at 17.

"I did exactly what I wanted to do," Stewart said. "I'd take the pars when I did not have makeable birdie putts. Pars are good here. I wanted to give myself the opportunity to make birdie putts." At most of the par-four holes Stewart used a one iron off the tee instead of a driver. "Why hit a driver and a wedge when you can hit a driver and an eight iron?" he said. "The idea is to get the ball on the green. I'm accustomed to playing well in majors. You have to hit a lot of different shots and I love fast greens. I get more intense to play in a major than to play in a regular event. I find my concentration level is better, my game is usually more fine-tuned and I enjoy it much more."

Thorpe, like Hulbert, also was a surprise contender, but for a different reason. Thorpe had won twice in 1985, likes the difficult conditions of major tournaments and has been a contender several times, but his recent performance had shown that something was not right. "I won $100,000 by the TPC (he actually had won a little more than $88,000) and I now still have $100,000," Thorpe said, fingering the bandage wrapped tightly around his left wrist. "I've had tendinitis in my left wrist for three years. It doesn't hurt me as badly as it did. I have been wearing a wrist band and it seems to help. It (the ailment) cuts down on my ability to practice. This is my fourth tournament in 17 weeks. Tendinitis is treated with rest. I'm probably hitting the ball better now, but I'm not hitting it quite as hard. I use a seven iron or eight iron instead of a nine iron."

Thorpe, who takes a short swing that relies on much wrist action, didn't seem to be bothered by his tendinitis in the second round. He chipped in from 20 feet for a birdie at the second hole, saved par with a chip to within two feet at the fourth hole, birdied Nos. 10 and 11 with putts of six and eight feet and reached the 523-yard 13th in two with a two iron and two-putted for birdie before finally giving a stroke back at the 15th hole. "I was driving well, but I was not taking a lot of chances," he said. "I like tough golf courses. I'm strong; I don't mind playing from the rough. Normally, in a major you don't find the greens holding, but you can muscle it from the rough and bounce the ball on the green. . . . At this point, Norman is the man to beat. Anybody can get hot. On this type of course, you can shoot five or six under and win."

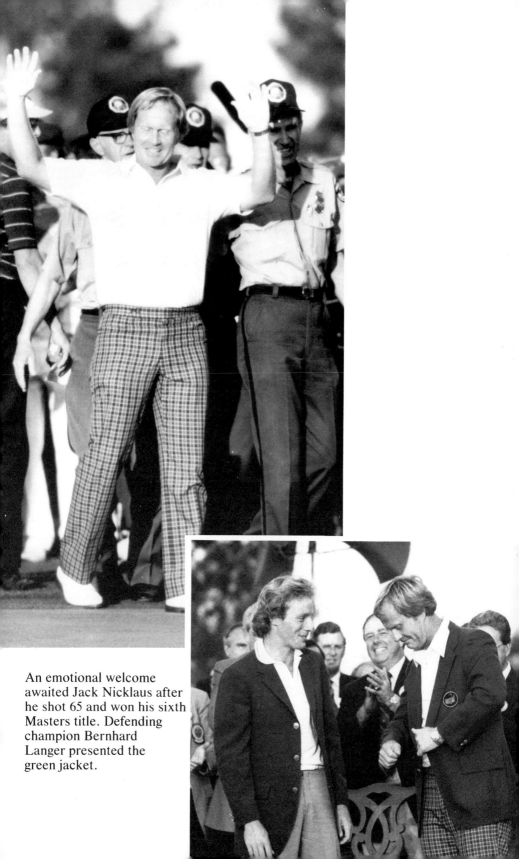

An emotional welcome
awaited Jack Nicklaus after
he shot 65 and won his sixth
Masters title. Defending
champion Bernhard
Langer presented the
green jacket.

Jack Nicklaus was four strokes behind entering the final round.

Tom Kite missed this eight-foot putt
and a chance for a playoff.

Needing a birdie to win or a par to
tie, Greg Norman made a
bogey after this approach shot
right of the 18th green.

Seve Ballesteros hit into the water at No. 15, ruining his Masters chances.

A 63 in the third round by Nick Price broke the Masters scoring record. He finished fifth.

A 74 in the second round left Tom Watson (above) in a tie for sixth with Jay Haas.

Japan's Tsuneyuki (Tommy) Nakajima shared eighth place.

Raymond Floyd
charged in to win the
U.S. Open with a last-
round 66. He was
congratulated on the
18th green by Payne
Stewart.

Joining Raymond Floyd for the presentation were daughter
Christina and wife Maria.

After his Masters victory,
Jack Nicklaus (left) was again
a favorite, but he took 77
in the rainy first round.

Greg Norman led after the second and third rounds, then shot 75
and tied for 12th. Large crowds attended at Shinnecock Hills,
and a few rowdy spectators upset Norman in the third round.

For the second straight year, Lanny Wadkins lost the U.S. Open by two strokes with a 281 score.

Chip Beck tied Wadkins for second place after missing this putt at No. 18.

Hal Sutton (above) and Lee
Trevino entered the final
round of the U.S. Open
one stroke behind, but their
71s left them tied for
fourth place.

Payne Stewart (left) and Ben Crenshaw tied for sixth place.

Greg Norman (left) ran into difficulty just when it seemed the PGA Championship was his.

Bob Tway holed a bunker shot on the 18th to claim the PGA Championship as his fourth win of the year.

Peter Jacobsen placed third in the PGA Championship.

Payne Stewart (left) and Bruce Lietzke tied for fifth place.

So Hulbert, Stewart and Thorpe were enjoying their position. The only question was how close they would be to Norman when the day expired. Greg kept them guessing for 14 holes, then manhandled the last four holes for a 68 and 133 that left him four strokes ahead of Hulbert and Stewart and five in front of Thorpe, Jacobsen and Nicklaus. Norman's round began more slowly than the day before, but he kept going further under par. A seven-foot birdie putt following an eight-iron approach at the 401-yard fifth hole got him to seven under for the tournament. He went to eight under with a seven-foot putt following another eight iron at the 420-yard ninth hole. At the 11th, he three-putted for bogey. "I laughed at myself. I didn't want to have any bogeys," he said. "That threw me off the rails a little bit and I lost my concentration and the edge I had maintained for 28 holes. At Kapalua, I won with only two bogeys. I'm dying for the day I can play 72 holes without a bogey. When I got that bogey I went off at a tangent. Hell, if I don't have any more bogeys from here on in, two bogeys is not bad . . . even with two bogeys, it was a good round because I brought it back."

Norman missed the green at the 14th hole and bogeyed, putting him even-par for the round and lifting the hopes of those in the clubhouse. Then his touch returned. At the 15th hole, his ball was off the back edge of the green, above the hole. Using a sand wedge like a putter, he holed the 20-foot shot for birdie. After saving par with a chip to within a foot of the cup at No. 16, he sank a 20-foot birdie putt at 17 and hit pitching wedge and seven-foot putt for birdie at 18. That gave him the 68 and doubled his lead to four strokes. Some thought he might be unstoppable. "Now that we've eliminated a lot of the field, everybody is in position to set himself off," Norman said. "But with the course getting harder, it's going to be harder for somebody to shoot a 62 or a 63 and come out of the pack and beat you." How wrong was Norman.

Greg was feeling good about his chances. "I hit it very solid again, except for a couple of loose shots. I'm more relaxed about it, one because I finally won a major and two, because one of my goals came. But I want to win more." Norman was even able to shrug off the presence of Nicklaus, who snatched the Masters title away from him in April. "I gave it to him at Augusta; I don't want to give him the PGA Championship. I don't want to take anything away from him, he played well at Augusta, but I had my chances and I made it easier for him. I'm aware that everybody's behind me and I hope to keep it that way, too."

"I'm obviously in very good position," said Nicklaus, who turned in a 68—138 before Norman began his round. "Even if Greg shoots another 65, there won't be many in front of me." There weren't, although there might have been two strokes fewer between them. At the 18th hole, Nicklaus' nine iron hit near the pin, but the backspin pulled the ball 30 feet downhill. He three-putted for a bogey.

"I did a little scratching with my driving on the front nine, but I got that straightened out on the back," Nicklaus said. A seven-foot birdie putt at the fourth hole offset a bogey at the second and "got the round turned around." He birdied the fifth hole from 10 feet, saved par with an 80-foot pitch-and-run to within a foot at the eighth, giving him a 34 going out. Then Nicklaus began doing tricks with his seven iron. He hit it 141 yards at the 363-yard

No. 10 hole, setting up a four-foot birdie putt. At the 167-yard No. 12, he came up three yards short and in a bunker with it and saved par with a 14-foot putt. At the 458-yard No. 15, he reached the green with a 167-yard seven iron. At the 405-yard No. 16, he hit the seven iron 141 yards and dropped a 20-foot putt for birdie and at the 431-yard No. 17 he hit a 173-yard seven iron to the green. "The wind conditions caused a variety of shots," Jack said. "Two seven irons were into the wind, one was with a crosswind and two were downwind."

Jacobsen followed a game plan that paid off with a 70 that included two birdies—a 20-footer at the eighth hole and a 50-foot pitch-and-run from the front fringe at the 14th—and a bogey at the 18th that came off a missed green. "I'm following a game plan," Jacobsen said. "I'm just putting the ball on the putting surface. The greens are so small, you play for the center of them and work the ball one way or the other. One of the things I'm trying to do is keep the ball short of the hole. The bogey at 18 doesn't take anything away. This is a major and whether you bogey the first hole or the last, it doesn't matter. Once you get on the course, everybody is concerned with himself. The time to look at the leaderboard is at the 72nd hole; that's when you know whether you have a chance to win or not."

Some saw their chances were slim; some saw their chances were nil. Stadler took a 74. Blackmar played the first seven holes in three over par and began a backward march with a 73. Koch went more quickly with a 77. Raymond Floyd fell one stroke short of the cut with 76–71—147. Among the others who missed the cut were Ballesteros (74–76), John Mahaffey (71–78) and Arnold Palmer, who once again missed in a try for the only major he has never won with a 75–77. "My putting book is selling well. I'm going to go back and read it. That (putting) is why my score is a 77, not a 66," Palmer said. Tom Watson, also needing a PGA title to fill his major portfolio, hit 17 greens and managed a 69, which left him in relatively good position at 141.

The scoring in the second round almost matched that of the first: 14 players turned in scores below 70, 23 were under par and 35 had rounds of par or better. The field averaged 73.98 strokes a man in the first round, 73.60 in the second. Here's the way they stood after 36 holes:

Greg Norman	65–68—	133
Mike Hulbert	69–68—	137
Payne Stewart	70–67—	137
Peter Jacobsen	68–70—	138
Jim Thorpe	71–67—	138
Jack Nicklaus	70–68—	138
Ronnie Black	68–71—	139
Bruce Lietzke	69–71—	140
Phil Blackmar	67–73—	140
Scott Simpson	70–70—	140

Norman came out of the third round still clutching a four-stroke lead, but he got a hint of what was to come. Tway broke his course record with a seven-under 64, and gained second place with a 206 total. "I'm extremely happy. I kind of got myself back in the golf tournament, that's what I did," Tway said.

Lee Trevino had pointed Tway out as "the next superstar" at the U.S. Open after Bob had battled through atrocious weather to take the first-round lead at Shinnecock Hills. Many young pros have been tabbed "the next Jack Nicklaus" or "the next Arnold Palmer" over the years without ever justifying that label, but Tway was making Trevino look good. Especially in the third round at Inverness. He birdied eight holes, four on each nine, bogeyed one—the ninth with three putts from 30 feet—and missed only one green.

After opening with 72–70, Tway trailed Norman by nine strokes at the start of the round and teed off five groups ahead of him. His charge was fueled by birdies from eight and 10 feet at the second and third holes. Tway missed a six-foot birdie at the fifth hole, but dropped putts from 20 and 15 feet at the seventh and eighth, putting him four under par for the round and the tournament. He had made a little headway; Norman was one under for the day, his lone birdie on the front nine a chip-in from 25 feet at the fourth hole.

The three-putt at nine slowed Tway, but only temporarily. He birdied No. 11 from 10 feet, No. 13 with two putts from 25 feet, No. 15 with a 30-foot putt and No. 17 with a 25-footer. The birdie at the 15th moved him within four strokes of Norman and the one at the 17th cut the difference to three. Norman made it four strokes again with a 20-foot birdie putt at No. 16.

At the 523-yard No. 13, Norman made perhaps the best par of the tournament. He pushed his drive into the right rough, which was not too bad. The hole doglegs left and the best way to approach the green is from the right. But Greg's ball was near the lip of a fairway bunker. In order to hit the ball, Norman had to stand with his left foot in the sand and his right in the rough above the bunker. He pulled out a six iron and attempted to hit the ball, with no thought of reaching the green. His pulled shot cleared the small stream at the bottom of the hill, jumped into the left rough and stopped under a large fir tree. He couldn't hit it swinging right-handed. So . . . "I turned a sand wedge upside down and hit it lefty," Norman said. "I moved it about six feet." He was still in the rough, but at least he could hit the ball conventionally. "I had 73 yards to the front of the green, but I didn't have much of a backswing. I chipped it about 10 yards short of the green. I was so mad at myself, I said, 'I'm going to chip this SOB in, make five and get out of here.' " And that's just what he did. "It was one of those deals where being positive paid off."

His third-round 69 seemed to have shaken off everyone except Tway, Jacobsen, Donnie Hammond and Stewart—and the last three were living on hope. "I didn't play as crisply as I did the first two days. I didn't have the touch with my putter; I either hit it too hard or too soft," Norman said. "I hung in with my chipping, especially at two holes. I didn't want anybody to get close. The third round is crucial and you can use it as a springboard. Tway's 64 was an exceptional score. People don't appreciate how good it is. You can't get frustrated. If you get frustrated, you try too hard, and if you try too hard, you have the tendency to make bogeys. Last year I played well and nothing happened and this year I'm playing well and everything's happening."

Norman said a man watching the tournament on televion called the Rules Committee and said Norman had broken a rule when he broke a branch on his backswing in his little adventure under the fir. "That was my father," said the quick-witted Jacobsen. The committee found Norman not guilty.

Tway said he was "extremely happy" with his round, but it was difficult to tell. He appears to be one of the most unemotional players on the tour. He never let the realization that this was his day creep into his mind. "I try not to do that. If you do that, you make double bogey. I just try to plug along. You can't get complacent. This is not my lowest round, but it's one of the best because of the magnitude.

"I don't think Greg is going to back up. Then again, he can. I think I'm going to have to shoot two or three under tomorrow. In order for me to have a chance, I have to play very well, but then again if he starts making bogeys and I birdie, who knows?"

"Greg is playing so well right now, it's hard to think of anything happening," Jacobsen said.

"There's going to be pressure and tension in the air, it's going to be like nothing else out there," Norman said of the final round.

Jacobsen, the Tour's top mimic, gave an outstanding impression of Apollo Creed baiting Rocky when he shouted "I want you! I want you!" to Norman as the Australian entered the press interview area. It was mostly for laughs. Jacobsen wanted Norman, but he figured he couldn't get him. "This could be his worst round of the week," Jacobsen said. "Somebody's going to have to challenge Greg. He has reached a level with McEnroe and Navratilova. It's kind of intimidating to see a guy play so well. Greg is tough mentally. The harder the course, the better his chances are. Norman grew up on the European Tour, and when you play the European Tour, you go through the school of hard knocks."

Jacobsen, who said he was still not completely recovered from his stomach problem, lost a stroke to Norman with a one-under 70 but that gave him third place to himself at 208, six strokes behind. He had four birdies and all of them were on the sensational side—20-footers at Nos. 1, 6 and 12 and a 50-footer at 14. He hit his tee shot into the lake at the par-three third hole, but he came out of it with no worse than a bogey when he sank a 15-foot putt. He missed the greens at Nos. 6 and 15 and bogeyed, but he was happy with the way he played.

If the drama now had three leading characters—Norman, Tway and Jacobsen—the third round was not strictly a three-man-show. Hammond, who began the back nine with three straight birdies, shot a 68 that vaulted him into a tie for fourth place with Stewart, who settled down for a 72 after a stumbling start. Nicklaus stayed within hoping distance with a 72 that left him in a deadlock at 210 with Lieztke, who started the back nine birdie-birdie-bogey-birdie en route to a 70. Tony Sills broke the nine-hole record for a major tournament at Inverness, and Ben Crenshaw got off the worst shot of the tournament . . . or at least the most painful.

At the 18th hole, Crenshaw hit a nine iron about 30 feet above the hole, leaving himself with a delicate downhill putt. "I felt like it was the 40th iron shot I hit past the hole and at Inverness you can't do that," Crenshaw said. In exasperation, he threw his iron into the air, then forgot to duck. The club hit him on the back of his head. "It was embarrassing, believe me," Ben said. He didn't realize he had hurt himself until he felt the blood trickling down the back of his neck as he walked down the fairway. Crenshaw neatly holed the putt, then went to a hospital, where he received three stitches to close the wound after posting a 72 for 217. The incident made him the target of some good-natured kidding before he teed off in the final round: TV announcer Dave Marr wore a hard hat as he introduced Crenshaw at the first tee and Trevino stuck a plastic can over his head as Crenshaw reported to the practice range. The incident also elicited perhaps the best line of the tournament. "The difference between us and pros," wrote Jack O'Leary of the *Boston Herald*, "is that we skull wedges and they wedge skulls."

Sills played the front nine in 30 and got to four under for the tournament. Then disaster struck. No. 10 is a relatively easy par-four. It's 363 yards long and the approach is a wedge or nine iron to a green that is downhill behind a small stream. Sills hit his tee shot into the right rough. His approach cleared the stream but fell into a hazard. He got his ball on the green, about 30 feet from the hole . . . then four-putted for a triple-bogey seven. "Oh, it hurt, sure it hurt," he said, "because it easily could have been no more than a bogey." The triple bogey didn't shatter Sills. He birdied the next hole and came in with a 69.

Thorpe self-destructed in the middle of the front nine en route to a 73 and Nicklaus' putter deserted him in a 72 that almost assured he would not win another major championship in 1986. Hulbert never got anything going as he struggled to a 74 and Watson saw his bid for his first PGA title all but vanish when he played the last eight holes in three over par after playing the first 10 in two under.

There were several signs indicating this would be Norman's victory, not the least being his four-stroke lead. His 202 was two strokes off the 54-hole record and his five-stroke lead was one shy of the 54-hole mark. He needed only a 68 in the final round to break the 72-hole record of 271 set by Bobby Nichols in 1964. And the last time a 54-hole leader didn't win was in 1979, when Rex Caldwell stepped aside as Crenshaw and David Graham met in a playoff, won by Graham. So here's how it looked after three rounds:

Greg Norman	65–68–69—	202
Bob Tway	72–70–64—	206
Peter Jacobsen	68–70–70—	208
Donnie Hammond	70–71–68—	209
Payne Stewart	70–67–72—	209
Jack Nicklaus	70–68–72—	210
Bruce Lietzke	69–71–70—	210
D. A. Weibring	71–72–68—	211
Jim Thorpe	71–67–73—	211
David Frost	70–73–68—	211
Mike Hulbert	69–68–74—	211

On Sunday, a heavy downpour struck the course at 2:31 p.m. and, as the greens and bunkers filled with water, the chances of completing the round on time diminished. After a two-hour delay, play was called for the day. "It's not a washout," said PGA president Mickey Powell. "Every shot counts. We're trying to make the championship the best we can make it, but the conditions are not good. And the weather forecast (for the rest of the day) is not good." The final round was scheduled to resume at 1:15 on Monday. "It's not just for TV," Powell said. "Tom Walker (the superintendent at Inverness) needs more time to prepare the course."

Thirteen players had completed their round when play was halted. One had turned in an under-par score, Irwin with a 68. Norman, Tway and Jacobsen, in the final threesome, had just teed off at the second hole when the sirens blew. Norman had a scrambling par on the first hole. "I don't think it's going to affect me at all," Norman said. "It's just disappointing that we can't finish on the day we'd like to—for everybody. Some players had checked out of their motels and had their cars packed, and there are plane reservations that have to be changed. But basically the course was unplayable. I was supposed to appear on the CBS morning show. Now I can sleep in. But the next tournament (The International) starts Wednesday, depending on the draw, so that means many players will get only one practice round on the course."

Three tournaments had been reduced from 72 holes to 54 holes because of rain earlier in the year and ominously Tway had fared better than Norman after a washout. At Pebble Beach, Norman shot 77–73 and Tway 73–69. At Bay Hill, Tway shot a 69 and Norman a 70. Norman did not play at San Diego but Tway won with a final-round 69.

Tway also parred the first hole before the halt, but Jacobsen bogeyed, dropping him seven strokes behind.

"I marked my ball with a tee because I got it for free on the first tee. Norman marked his with a 100-dollar bill," Jacobsen said on ABC-TV. "I hope they change the policy about every shot counting because I bogeyed the first hole and I'm in the rough on the second. But now I have a chance to catch Greg. The greens will be soft and you can hit irons close to the hole. I've been hitting my irons well all week. Now if I can get it out of the rough at No. 2 and make par there . . . ."

Tway hit his drive into the left rough at the first hole, hit his second six yards short of the green, then sank a six-foot putt for par. Like Norman, he found the middle of the fairway at the second hole before the deluge stopped play. "I never really worry about what he (Norman) is doing. I don't have control over him," Tway said. "I just know I have to shoot a good round under par. He'll be tough to catch. But I want to be there if he doesn't play well. I might have to shoot three or four under. If he shoots well, it doesn't matter; I might have to shoot a lot lower just to be in it." As it turned out, Tway didn't need a super round to win, just a super shot.

The wet weather had departed by Monday morning—actually by late Sunday afternoon—leaving the course in the same condition as for the first round. Norman had talked about how difficult it was for someone to come out of the pack with a low round on a hard, fast course; a condition that would have suited him in the final round. A soft, yielding course was another matter. A leader could play well and someone could hole everything, as Johnny Miller did at Oakmont in the 1973 U.S. Open. On the other hand, a man who had played as smoothly as Norman had for three days was not expected to score much over par. But Greg did.

D. A. Weibring, in a group at two under at the start of the round, played erratically over the first seven holes, then settled down to play the last 11 holes in two under and take fourth place with a 69 for 280. The shot that gave him fourth place by himself was a chip-in at the 15th hole. Lietzke played the front nine in one over, then the back nine in one under for a 71 that tied for fifth place with Stewart, who had a 72, at 281.

Thorpe, his aching left wrist constantly getting him in trouble, shot a 39 on the front nine that effectively eliminated him. Then Thorpe acted as if he would birdie every hole on the back nine, six of the first seven, before flopping in with two bogeys for a 71. Crenshaw and David Graham played nearly flawlessly, but, of course, it was too late for them. It was too late for everyone except Tway, Norman and Jacobsen, as they gave no indications they were about to back up.

At the 185-yard third hole, Norman hit a six iron over the green and bogeyed. Tway hit the green with a six iron and sank a 12-foot putt for birdie. Just like that, Norman's lead had been reduced by half, from four strokes to two. Jacobsen birdied the fourth hole, but still trailed by five. Tway missed the fairway at the fifth, and saved par with a 35-foot putt.

Tway and Norman both bogeyed the seventh. The hole was cut into a ridge on the green, making it very difficult to stop a ball from going downhill. Both Tway and Norman hit above the ridge and both hit their balls off the green. Tway missed the fairway with his tee shot at the ninth hole, failed to make the green and took a bogey. When Norman hit the green with a six iron and dropped an 18-foot putt for birdie, the margin again was four strokes. "I felt comfortable with my lead," Norman said. "Four shots ahead with nine holes to go, nine out of 10 times, you're going to hold it."

Jacobsen also bogeyed the seventh, and when he kept in step with Norman and Tway with a 36 on the front nine he seemed to be just an interested spectator of history.

"I didn't have a chance to win until Greg double-bogeyed the 11th hole," Peter said. "I hung in there and had a lot of fun." Jacobsen didn't realize at the turn how close he would come to getting his foot in the door.

At the 11th hole, Norman hit his tee shot down the fairway—onto a sand-covered divot. It's the rub of the green, of course, but it was a rub that hurt. He hit his next shot into a buried lie in a bunker about 30 yards short of the green, and his chip came up 15 feet short. He two-putted for the double-bogey six. When Tway parred, the difference was two strokes. The momentum changed there. Through the first 54 holes, Norman had made only two bogeys. On the front nine of the final round, he had doubled his total. And now, after two holes of the final nine, he was two over par.

Both parred No. 12, then for a fleeting second it looked as if they would be tied. Tway reached the 523-yard No. 13 with a two iron and had a 15-foot putt for an eagle-three. His putt rolled to the hole then turned left. But his birdie and Norman's par left Greg with a mere one-stroke lead. At No. 14, Tway hit his drive into the right rough, but walloped a seven iron onto the green and parred from 20 feet. Norman went for the green with a nine iron and missed. He nearly holed his wedge shot on the fly, but the ball rolled 15 feet past the hole. He missed the putt and bogeyed. Now they were tied. It was only the second time in the tournament that Norman did not lead by himself. Meanwhile, Jacobsen parred the first four holes on the back nine, and when he dropped a 10-foot putt for birdie at 14, he was only two strokes back. With four holes to play, Norman and Tway were tied at seven under, Jacobsen was five under and Lietzke, who had birdied Nos. 12 and 13, was four under.

Norman didn't lose the tournament; Tway won it. Bob did it with a magnificent repertoire of shots over the final four holes. At No. 15, Tway hit his drive into the rough, then followed with a shot into the gallery, right of the green. He had a chip from a downslope. Norman also missed the green, but had a straight-in shot and chipped to seven feet below the hole. Tway's shot hit the green and rolled to the vicinity of Norman's. Both made their putts for par. Jacobsen also missed the green, but was not so fortunate. He came up short with a chip and bogeyed. That eliminated him. Three strokes back with three holes to play is too much.

Tway and Norman both parred 16. At No. 17, Tway hit his approach into the deep rough to the right of the green. His problem was not to get the ball close, but just to get it on the green. He could barely see the ball, but he chipped it three feet from the hole and matched Norman's par. "That shot was harder than the one at 18," Tway said. "It's a shot I practice, a lob shot. But you don't know how it's going to come out. It came out soft. That gave me a chance; I was still in a tie."

Then came the fateful 18th. "I didn't have a good lie, but I was able to get my club on the ball," Tway said of his shot from the rough. "I was just trying to get it on the green. When it came down, my first thought was that it might be buried. It was much better in the bunker than in the rough."

When Norman's approach spun back off the green, Tway was thinking of a playoff. So was Norman. "I thought I hit a good shot," Norman said. "I was surprised it was in the deep grass. I hit a good shot with a bad result. He hit a great bunker shot. He thought I was going to make four. I'm sad I lost the tournament. With a 76, I obviously didn't play very well. But you can't control what other people are doing. There are no ifs, ands or buts in this game. You have to take what happens. You have to swallow the pill now and then. After the ninth hole, I said to my caddy, 'Pete, we still have a long way to go. Let's put in a solid nine holes.' I felt comfortable with the lead I had. I had a chance to win the tournament, and I didn't."

Jacobsen birdied the 18th hole for a 71 that gave him third place and a ringside seat on history being made. "It's a helluva lot better to have been there and tried than never to have been there at all," Jacobsen said of Norman's showing in the four majors. "It's a hell of an accomplishment to lead all four majors. Greg Norman is a great guy, to be able to smile after he was beaten by an unbelievable shot. I got such a rush when that happened. The thing that stands out about Bob is his relaxed attitude. I was impressed with his putt at the seventh hole. I was impressed with his poise. He showed a lot of moxie under the gun. At 15, and especially at 17, when he got it up and down I thought he was going to win the tournament. And I'll never forget that shot (at 18)."

6. The Dunhill Nations Cup

It takes longer than two years to establish a tradition, but the Dunhill Nations Cup has progressed further in that span than any tournament in my experience, with the possible exception of the World Match Play, which took an immediate foothold when we started that championship at Wentworth in the autumn of 1964.

The venue of the Old Course at St. Andrews, Scotland, has proven to be an incalculable advantage for the Dunhill Nations Cup. It's a stirring experience to see the flags and golfing representatives of 16 nations on a crisp autumn day over those hallowed links which are regarded as the birthplace of the game. Whether you are a Scot, American or Zambian, that must create a special feeling indeed. The announcement that the tournament would return to St. Andrews in 1987 was welcome news for all concerned.

The year had already been labeled "The Year of the Shark" before we reached the Dunhill final in late September, but little did we realize then that Greg Norman was about to also take the "Mr. October" tag once held by American baseball player Reggie Jackson for his playoff exploits. When Norman led Australia to a repeat victory in the Dunhill Nations Cup, it was the second of his six consecutive victories that raised his total for the year to nine, including four in four appearances in Britain, the most notable of which was, of course, the Open Championship.

On the Australian team with Norman were David Graham and, replacing Graham Marsh from the 1985 team, Rodger Davis. They were second-seeded behind the United States team consisting of Raymond Floyd, Mark O'Meara and Lanny Wadkins. Seve Ballesteros and his Spanish teammates were also highly regarded. Completing the field were seeded teams from England, Scotland, Wales, Japan and Canada; regional qualifying teams from Ireland, New Zealand, Italy, Indonesia, Sweden and South Korea; and two teams, Zambia and Argentina, chosen to represent the continents of Africa and South America.

The start was eagerly awaited, every hotel room in the ancient university town was booked, and spectators were planning daily trips from Edinburgh, Dundee, Glasgow and beyond. The contestants were also anticipating the tournament, especially two who had been engaged all year in a battle for global honors.

Norman had taken first place from Ballesteros in the Sony Ranking with his recent win in the Panasonic European Open, and Ballesteros said then he hoped to play Norman in the final of the World Match Play. Norman responded that "I want to play you in the semifinal of the Dunhill Cup—and I want to drill you." It was nothing meant to be taken harshly—just a good-natured rivalry—but, sadly, they never met, not at St. Andrews or at Wentworth a week later.

Spain lost to Ireland 2–1 in one of two first-round surprises, the other being Argentina's 2–1 win over England. The other matches were 3–0 decisions by the favored teams, except for Canada's 2–1 margin over Sweden.

The Australians began their defense against Italy, as Davis led off with a seven-birdie, no-bogey 65 to equal the Old Course record set by Neil Coles in 1970 and tied by Nick Faldo in 1979 and by Norman in last year's Dunhill. Winner of the Wythe & Mackay PGA Championship, Davis scored his birdies on holes Nos. 3, 7, 9, 10, 14, 16 and 18 to win by five strokes over Costantino Rocca's fine 70. Rocca's countrymen couldn't come close to that standard. Norman won 67 to 77 over Guiseppe Cali and Graham won 68 to 79 over Baldovino Dassu. The only bogeys the Australians made were on the second hole, by both Graham and Norman. Greg scored an eagle-three on the fifth and a rare birdie on the 17th.

From the moment that Ballesteros put his opening drive into the Swilken burn, it was clear that this was not Spain's day. He did not feel well and coughed throughout, while Ronan Rafferty was at ease in posting a no-bogey 67 to Ballesteros' 74. "I had nothing to lose," Rafferty said. "All I hoped to do was enjoy myself."

Spain's premature exit for the second year came on Des Smyth's 71 to 73 win over Jose-Maria Olazabal, after Jose Rivero had gone past David Feherty 71 to 73. Rivero scored four birdies in five holes starting at the 10th. That surge enabled Rivero to win despite two double bogeys, at the sixth and 17th. The crucial hole in the Smyth-Olazabal game was the 14th, when Olazabal drove out-of-bounds, enabling Smyth to gain one stroke and lead by two. There might still have been a tight finish, had the Irishman not holed from 30 feet for his four, "not the easiest thing to do when your hands are shaking," Smyth said.

It was widely noted that Argentina's 2–1 margin over England was the same score as when the two countries met earlier in the World Cup soccer competition, when Argentine Diego Maradona was accused of scoring a goal with his hand. Responding to a jovial query from the press, Vicente Fernandez said, "Yes, I used my hand, but only to pick the ball out of the hole." Fernandez, who won the 1979 PGA Championship on the Old Course, was out in 33, three strokes ahead of Howard Clark, and won with 67 to Clark's 70. England's Nick Faldo took care of Armando Saavedra 69 to 72, and the crucial point was decided between Argentina's Adan Sowa and Gordon J. Brand.

Consecutive birdies on the 13th and 14th enabled Brand to go ahead, then everything went disastrously wrong for England at the 16th. Sowa hit a fine approach to about 10 feet, and Brand followed with a second shot that rolled down into a little gully behind the green. Brand chipped within four feet of the hole. Sowa put the pressure on by holing the 10-footer; Brand missed his putt, creating a two-stroke swing. Both bogeyed the 17th and parred the 18th, for Sowa's 69 to Brand's 70.

The United States had its predictably easy match against Zambia, with Wadkins and O'Meara returning 70s and Floyd, 72. The Zambians' best score was Paul Tembo's 79; Peter Sinyama shot 81 and Samiel Mwanza, 83. "For them to have beaten us," Floyd said, "they would have had to have their best rounds, and us to have our worst." Zambia made a game of it for a while, and was tied when the final pair had completed three holes and the lead-off pair was through five. And Mwanza scored a birdie-three on the notorious 17th hole, one of only six during the tournament, with a majestic five-iron approach to within two feet of the hole.

Dr. Kenneth Kaunda, the Zambian president, had sent the players a good-luck telegram and had urged them to represent their country well. He could be proud of their performance. Their scores indicated they would have been a good match for Indonesia, which was 26 over par to Zambia's 27 over.

Another measure of Zambia's participation may come later because the three, club professionals all, surely returned to tell the others of their experiences and perhaps to inspire young players in their country to take the game seriously. Golf, they had learned, offered unheard-of opportunities. "It is a fortune," Sinyama said of the $7,500 guarantee for first-round losers. "I could never save it in my life." The prize money was enough for Sinyama to buy a new house, which he said he planned to do.

As noted earlier, Indonesia was another thrown against the giants of the game, and Scotland won easily with rounds of 68 by Sam Torrance, 69 by Sandy Lyle and 71 by Gordon J. Brand. Wales had all three players under 70 to beat New Zealand. Mark Mouland returned 69 to beat Greg Turner (77) in a pairing of this year's European Tour winners, Ian Woosnam shot 66 to beat Frank Nobilo (71) and Philip Parkin's 69 ousted Bob Charles (73).

While little was known of South Korea, much was expected of Japan, whose Tsuneyuki (Tommy) Nakajima was ranked No. 4 in the world. He was joined by the brothers Tateo (Jet) and Naomichi (Joe) of the famous Ozaki golfing family. All were under par—Joe Ozaki (67), Nakajima (68) and Jet Ozaki (71)—while Cho Ho-Sang's 74 was South Korea's best score. Choi Youn-Soo returned 78 and Cho Sang-Ho, 79.

The match of Canada versus Sweden offered potential for an upset because no country has made greater strides in golf than Sweden in recent years. Anders Forsbrand was ninth on the European Order of Merit and Ove Sellberg, who won the Epson Match Play event earlier in the year, was 18th. The third Swede, Mats Lanner, was ranked 42nd in Europe.

The Canadians countered with three U.S. PGA Tour regulars. Sellberg secured Sweden's point by beating Richard Zokol 72 to 75, and Forsbrand was about to take another point until three-putting the 12th, 13th and 14th holes. Dan Halldorson needed no further invitation and won 69 to 71. Dave Barr got Canada's final point with 69 to Lanner's 74.

The Canadians went against the United States in the second round and, in a reversal of roles from the previous day, were on line for a surprising victory until Zokol took a quadruple-bogey eight on the 17th, the infamous Road Hole, in a 74 to 76 loss to O'Meara. Barr had the day's best round, 66, and won by two strokes over Wadkins, then Floyd sank a birdie putt at No. 18 in a tense match to defeat Halldorson 69 to 70 and provide the United States with a 2–1 decision. Japan beat Argentina, also by 2–1, to advance against the Americans, while in the other half of the draw Australia beat Wales and Scotland beat Ireland, both by 3–0 margins.

Seldom has there been a tournament at St. Andrews without the Road Hole figuring prominently in the result. In recent years, Tom Watson met disaster there in the fourth round of the 1984 British Open, and in the inaugural Dunhill Nations Cup, Graham hit a magnificent five-iron shot for a birdie to guide Australia into the final. There were only six birdies at No. 17 in 1986, all in the first two rounds, and Zokol's eight was the high for the tournament in which the Road Hole played to a 4.51 average against its par of four.

At one point the Canadians were ahead in every match on this gray, damp afternoon and the Americans first saw a glimmer of hope in Zokol's misfortune. Playing first, and trailing by one stroke, O'Meara hit his approach shot into the Road Hole bunker and Zokol followed him in. O'Meara played out safely to the right, then Zokol took four strokes to remove his ball, resulting in scores on the hole of five and eight, respectively, and giving the Americans a two-stroke advantage with one hole remaining.

"In hindsight, it's easy to talk about," said Zokol, "but looking at the situation, I knew that if I got out the first time, I would win the match, because O'Meara was never going to make par. I felt I could do it, and I wanted to take a two-stroke lead down to the last hole. I gambled, and I lost."

Wadkins made four consecutive birdies, only to have Barr match every one. Lanny hit a wedge two feet from the cup at No. 7, and Barr holed from 25 feet. Wadkins hit his putt from 12 feet at the eighth, and Barr, from eight feet. Both holed eight-footers at the ninth, and Barr made a 24-footer at No. 10, forcing Wadkins to sink a 12-footer. The Canadian made a 30-footer at the 12th to be one ahead, but Wadkins drew level again with a 12-footer at No. 15. Barr's par-birdie finish provided the difference, as Wadkins missed the 17th green then Barr holed a 12-footer to close him out.

That left it to Floyd, and what better man for the situation than that steely-nerved veteran who had shown in the U.S. Open that even at age 43, he was still very much the competitor he had always been. Both had putts of about 15 feet on the 18th, though Halldorson was the closer by inches. Raymond made his, then Halldorson missed. Afterwards, Floyd admitted that he had been breathing heavily. "I still don't have my breath back," he said. "I don't think I have ever had more pressure than this, down the last five or six holes. I guess it's the format, it's playing along with two other guys on your team, and it's playing for your country.

"I always felt I calmed in a pressure situation, but I didn't calm today. I just feel relief."

Floyd was two strokes down after 11 holes, with Halldorson then three under par. "Dan played well," he said, "and I made the putts the last five or six holes that counted." Raymond made three birdies in four holes from the 11th to draw level, and at the 14th he made a six-foot birdie before Halldorson missed a three-footer. The Canadian three-putted No. 15 to fall behind, and missed a grand opportunity at the next hole. Floyd had chipped well past the hole, about 30 feet, while Halldorson had an eight-footer for birdie. But Floyd sank the putt and Halldorson did not. Raymond missed the 17th green and took a bogey to be tied as they played the last hole.

Halldorson had the first shot into the 18th green, his wedge finishing just behind the flag, then Floyd matched that stroke before holing the left-to-right breaking putt. Halldorson's try broke too much before the hole and was out. "I had a good picture of the break, I had some putts from there in practice," Raymond said afterwards. "It does not break as much to the right as you think. I had it right on the line and knew it was good half way to the hole. I knew it was there. Dan was almost on the same line. He didn't hit his putt hard enough, it didn't have enough pace.

"I've never had much success on the 18th, for all the times I've played it," said Floyd, recounting three British Opens, one PGA and now two Dunhill Nations Cups. "As I came off, I thought it might have been the first putt of any length I have ever made on that green."

The late rushes of Fernandez and Sowa were not enough to carry Argentina past Japan. The one Argentine point was by Saavedra, who beat Jet Ozaki 69 to 72 in the last game. Fernandez birdied the last three holes but still lost to Nakajima, who had two birdies of his own to win 67 to 68. Both birdied the 16th, Fernandez had a remarkable four iron to five feet at No. 17, then Nakajima virtually secured the point for Japan with a wedge to three feet on the 18th. Fernandez made a nine-footer then Nakajima settled the match with his birdie.

Sowa was four strokes down with two holes left, then it became more interesting at the 17th when Joe Ozaki hit his second shot over the green to the road, eventually taking a bogey, while Sowa holed from 20 feet for birdie—which meant successive birdies there for the Argentines. Ozaki put his approach shot to No. 18 within 15 feet of the hole, five feet inside Sowa's, and that pretty much settled it. Both took pars, and Ozaki won 69 to 71.

When Australia was seeded second to the United States, rather than first as the defending champion might be, that probably was because Davis was perceived as untested, and perhaps there were also some questions about Graham's game at the time. The Aussies made a decision about the order of play that was proving to be very wise by the second round, and was an important factor in their victory. They sent Davis off first and, as the higher seeded team in all their matches, Australia could allow Davis to choose his individual opponent. (In this competition, the higher seeded team nominates the first match, and the lower-seeded team, the next two matches).

"Rodger is going to be the most relaxed, and that is the key to the whole thing," Norman confirmed after Australia swept Wales. Davis defeated Mouland 71 to 73, Norman beat Woosnam 67 to 71 and Graham beat Parkin 68 to 69.

Davis and Mouland recorded pars through the first 11 holes, then Davis went ahead with birdies on Nos. 12 and 13. Mouland bogeyed the 12th, was three down, and dropped another shot at No. 15. Mouland birdied the 17th and Davis bogeyed, his first of the tournament, but by that stage the margin was too great for Mouland to overcome.

Norman posted a six-birdie, no-bogey score in easily winning his game, and Graham's game was not as close for most of the time as the one-stroke difference would indicate. Davis was seven under par, with seven birdies, after 15 holes but double-bogeyed No. 16 and bogeyed No. 17 before settling down to par the final hole.

Scotland defeated Ireland by two strokes in each game in the last of the second-round matches. Brand beat Rafferty 68 to 70, Torrance beat Smyth 70 to 72, and Lyle beat Feherty 70 to 72. All six players had 35s on the first nine; the 14th was a pivotal hole. Brand made a 15-foot birdie putt there to go ahead of Rafferty, who then bogeyed No. 16 to fall two strokes behind after hitting into the Principal's Nose bunker. Torrance also birdied the 14th to move two strokes clear of Smyth. The Irishman birdied the next two holes, then drove out of bounds and took double bogey at No. 17. Feherty was one ahead of Lyle after birdieing the 14th, but bogeyed both the 16th and 17th to decide that game.

Only Lyle was up to standard in Saturday's semifinal, however, as Australia won 2–1 to advance along with Japan, which defeated the United States by that same score. Lyle's 68 was good for a two-stroke win over Graham—the only game the Australias were to lose all week—but Davis beat Brand 72 to 74 and Norman beat Torrance 70 to 72.

In the lead-off pairing, Davis got a break when Brand's tee shot at No. 14 hit a television cable and bounced over a fence, out of bounds. Brand took a double-bogey seven and was then five strokes behind. He made two birdies after that, but to no avail.

Lyle and Graham were tied going to the 17th. The Australian took two strokes to get out of the Road Hole bunker and that was the difference. Lyle had to make a comeback after being three strokes down with his level-par 36 on the first nine. Sandy did it with two birdies and an eagle. He chipped to three feet for a birdie at No. 10, holed a 12-foot putt for another birdie at No. 13 and chipped in from 28 yards for eagle-three at No. 14.

The Norman-Torrance game, which was in doubt until the final hole, started weakly as both hit their approach shots into the burn at No. 1. Torrance made six there and Norman, five. Through nine holes Norman was two strokes ahead, and went in front by three with his birdie at the 14th.

Like Graham ahead of him, Norman took two strokes from the Road Bunker and his double bogey brought Torrance within one shot. "This format is unbelievable. I never had so much pressure on me coming down the last hole," marveled Norman, who admitted that he couldn't bear to even look at his teammates beside the 18th green until he had won.

Torrance coaxed a chip shot to No. 18 within six feet of the cup, then Norman struck a marvelous wedge over the Valley of Sin that came a foot inside of Torrance's ball. "That was probably one of my best—48 yards to the pin and not much room to work it," Greg said. "Originally, I thought of a bump-and-run shot, but when I saw Sam's close, I thought the best chance was to get it close with a loft shot, and at worst be 10 or 12 feet away. It was one of the best 48-yard pitch shots I have ever made."

Graham was glowing over the shot as well. "Certainly the best 48-yard pitch shot I have ever seen," David told the press. "Given the situation, it was wonderful."

Norman still needed to hole the putt, which he did, then Torrance missed his and, as happened the previous year, Sam was a forlorn figure as his disappointed countrymen departed the railings along the 18th hole.

There was not much drama in Japan's victory over the Americans. O'Meara scored the lone United States point, beating Jet Ozaki 70 to 77; Joe Ozaki trimmed Wadkins 69 to 74, and Nakajima defeated Floyd in the final pairing, 69 to 76.

Joe Ozaki was six under par after 11 holes and won easily despite a bogey at No. 16 and a double bogey at No. 17. Nakajima hit into the burn and double-bogeyed the first hole, but was ahead of Floyd by the fifth. "I took 36 putts, two-putted every green," said the U.S. Open champion. "I played better than my score and did not get a break, and Tommy played well. As far as our team is concerned, well, we have been beaten, we're not happy, but we have to congratulate the other side."

Nakajima, who admitted he was "not confident we could win" against the United States, was surprisingly bold in wanting a final pairing against Norman, who beat him in the British Open. By helping Japan with the Dunhill Nations Cup, Nakajima said, he would feel a sense of revenge.

The Nakajima-Norman match was easily arranged, since the Australians had the first choice and elected to again start with Davis, against Jet Ozaki. The Japanese chose the other two pairings, Joe Ozaki against Graham and finally Nakajima against Norman.

On a very difficult afternoon—the winds averaged over 30 and gusted to 50 miles an hour—the Australians swept all three games although only Norman was even close to par. The results were Davis over Jet Ozaki 76 to 81, Graham over Joe Ozaki 81 to 82, and Norman over Nakajima 73 to 76.

In the third-place match, Scotland played better than that, and won 2–1 over the United States when Brand beat O'Meara 75 to 78, Floyd beat Torrance 73 to 78, and Lyle provided the conclusive point in beating Wadkins 73 to 78. "It was a bit difficult to pick ourselves up (after losing to Australia)," Lyle said, "but the chance of beating the Americans kept us going, and we all played well, even when conditions were almost impossible."

The Australians received $100,000 each from the $1 million purse, and Norman's share lifted him over $1 million for the year—the first golfer ever to achieve that figure in prize money. Japan got $50,000 per player; Scotland, $36,666; and the United States, $26,666.

The most telling figures were these: whereas Australia was 30 under par for the three previous, calm days, in the final they were 14 over par. The Japanese scores soared from 19 under to 23 over. It was as a local member of the Royal and Ancient Golf Club had warned over his pre-lunch pink gin before they went out to play, "These chaps have got to learn how to play golf out there."

Putting was particularly difficult on the already-slick greens. Nakajima was the only player who did not have a three-putt green. Norman had two. The pairing of Graham and Joe Ozaki produced 11 three-putts and one four-putt; the pairing of Davis and Jet Ozaki, seven three-putts.

Davis and Jet Ozaki had a fairly close game for 13 holes, with Davis then at three over par and leading by two strokes. Ozaki double-bogeyed both the 14th and 15th, then bogeyed the 16th. Even a par-birdie finish could not prevent him from going above 80. "Rodger deserves a pat," Norman said afterwards. "He was our lead man and won every match. It meant David and I had only to win 50 percent. The lead is the most important position."

As Davis was bringing his game to a quick conclusion, Graham was still very much in a struggle with Joe Ozaki, which in the face of mounting scores was not decided until Ozaki took two strokes from the Road Hole bunker for a double bogey. "I think having an experienced caddy helped me," said

Graham, who employed Bruce Edwards, Tom Watson's regular caddy. "He encouraged me out there, and said things like he didn't care if I shot 90, so long as the other man shot 91.

"The problem was that he was playing badly, and so was I. He would make a mistake, then I would, and so it would go on. Neither of us was playing well and neither could do anything about it."

Norman concurred with Graham that it was "a matter of hanging in there and keeping patient." The last four holes spelled the difference for Norman, as Nakajima's bogeys on the 15th and 17th holes provided his margin.

"It is good for the team to have won for the second year, good for Australia, and good for golf in general," Norman said at the post-match press conference. "It has been a successful week and the format has proved itself. Dunhill should be happy."

7. The World Match Play Championship

In many respects the Suntory World Match Play Championship at Wentworth was the best there had been in years. The south of England was bathed in the loveliest Indian summer sunshine, Jack Nicklaus was back for the first time since 1971, the crowds came in unprecedented numbers and there was one match, the quarter-final between Sandy Lyle and Tsuneyuki (Tommy) Nakajima, that surpassed anything that had taken place in the previous 23 years of an event that concludes the golfing year in Britain. It was also, ultimately, the most controversial as Greg Norman, by then without a shadow of doubt the No. 1 golfer of 1986, greeted his third victory in six years with the bombshell that he would not be coming back to defend. Deeply resentful of what he claimed were hostile galleries, who jeered and mocked him as he defeated Lyle by 2 and 1 in the final, Norman said that "the line had to be drawn somewhere and this was it."

A stunned British press scribbled frantically into their notebooks, Lyle blinked in disbelief and overnight a nation became divided as the correspondence columns in the national newspapers, backed up by leading articles, reflected the "fors and againsts." Norman, never one to mince his words, was unrepentant. It was his assertion that 90 percent of the gallery that final day was against him and that they were doing their utmost to break his concentration. "I don't feel as if I have won a golf tournament out there but more a battle," he said in his post-match interview.

Norman fumed, "I am very disappointed in the attitude of the crowd. There is absolutely no need to make a noise in the middle of my backswing or clap when I hit a poor shot. I just had to win it after that, but it is a pity that I have to go out on a bad note. Certainly I will play golf in Britain again, but not here. I have played in plenty of English and Scottish events, but it has never been as bad as today. People were banging the metal railings on one hole when I was about to play and moving around all the time.

"After eight holes I said to my caddy, Jackie Lee, 'I just hope I win this one because I won't be here next year.' It really has taken the edge off my victory. When I played Jack Nicklaus in the semi-finals there was more support for him but that was understandable. He is a great favorite and had been away a long time. But today's attitude by the spectators was just too blatant. I'm not saying the crowd was as bad as the football hooligans we read about but let's get the sport back to where it should be, with every spectator appreciating the game and giving both players a fair deal."

It was not the first time Norman had been involved in spectator trouble. Earlier in the year during the U.S. Open Championship at Shinnecock Hills, a spectator called out during the third round that he was "choking" after taking six at the 13th. This was a cruel reference to the wild second shot he had played at the last hole in the Masters at Augusta National when he needed a birdie to win and a par to tie Nicklaus. The five he took meant defeat, while the shot itself was reminiscent of another he had played when he tied Fuzzy Zoeller for the 1984 American Open. Incensed, Norman had walked over and had "words" with the spectator, later intimating that in future he would steer clear of the New York area when playing golf.

There had also been a less publicized and probably rather minor incident the week before the World Match Play in the Dunhill Nations Cup at St. Andrews. Then there had been much support for Scotsman Sam Torrance in his match against Norman, to such an extent that Torrance told the more biased spectators to "back off." They did. "It was up to Lyle to do something similar today," Norman said at Wentworth. "But he did not. That's his decision. At times I felt like saying something myself but I told myself to zip up my mouth. If I had spoken it might have made things worse."

Lyle, something of an innocent when emotions become highly charged, did his best to put everything into perspective. "I thought the crowds were reasonable," he said. "It was natural for them to be on my side. I am the local boy (he lives on the Wentworth estate), I'm British and no Briton has ever won this tournament.

"There were a few idiots out there clapping at missed putts but it is only the sort of thing I would expect if I was playing Greg in Australia. In any case I had enough problems of my own to pay much attention to the crowds." Those problems were real enough, because Lyle had been six down after 14 holes in the morning.

The margin had been reduced to three at lunch and the crowd understandably warmed to him as he reduced it to only one hole with two to play. This was the sort of finish everybody had been hoping for; but it ended in anticlimax. At the 17th in going for the big drive round the corner of the dogleg, Lyle overdid it a fraction, went out of bounds and conceded the match before either man putted. Norman's prize was £50,000, which brought his earnings in Europe to £275,000. Though Greg played only four times, he won them all: the Open Championship at Turnberry, the Panasonic European Open at Sunningdale, the Dunhill Nations Cup at St. Andrews (with David Graham and Rodger Davis) and now the Suntory. That was quite a haul, to say nothing of all he did in the United States and Australia.

In some quarters Norman was accused of bad grace after his Wentworth outburst. It must, however, be viewed in the context of other incidents that have been cropping up from time to time in Britain. Previously the most notorious was in the 1983 World Match Play, when Nick Faldo was playing against Graham Marsh, also an Australian. On the 16th hole, Faldo hit his second shot through the green and into the gallery on the crest of a steep slope. The ball seemed certain to end up in a very difficult place when suddenly it popped onto the green, having either been kicked or thrown back. It was the turning point in a match Faldo went on to win.

Since then no spectators have been allowed to stand at that particular spot while the PGA European Tour, whose officials referee at the World Match Play, also sends out spotters with all matches to make sure the same sort of thing does not happen again. Nor has it, though the more difficult problem to grasp is that of partisanship by the spectators. There have been several instances of this, not only in the World Match Play.

In the 1985 Open Championship at Royal St. George's, David Graham came to the last hole needing a birdie to tie Lyle. The sun was in Graham's eyes and though he struck the shot well, he could not see his ball finish. But he did hear a cheer and he interpreted that as meaning that it was on the green. In fact it meant that it was in the bunker, which made Lyle's victory all the more certain.

Then in the Ryder Cup at The Belfry later that same summer, there was much American comment about the biased attitude of the spectators, perhaps a little bit too hungry for the first European victory since 1957, though in those distant days it was still a purely Great Britain and Ireland team and not one that could call on the services of the European countries. Holes won by the Europeans were greeted with ecstatic cheering, only slightly moderated when it was earned by an American missing a putt. Sometimes it even went beyond that, as when Andy North drove into the water at the 18th against Torrance, more or less assuring Europe of the winning point.

Though Lee Trevino, the American captain, subsequently described some of this American team as "a lot of crybabies," there was some British discomfort at the lack of sportsmanship, generated as it has become by golf now being a game for the masses rather than a pastime for the few. Even that most orderly of events, the U.S. Masters, carries on its daily pairings sheet a reminder from the late Bobby Jones on the game's first rule, which covers etiquette.

Even that did not prevent spectators from cheering Seve Ballesteros' mistake on the 15th hole that assisted Nicklaus' victory in April of this year.

And no such reminder was on display at the everyday American tournaments of the 1960s when an overweight, crew-cut Nicklaus first came along to threaten the throne occupied by Arnold Palmer. Many were the cheers that echoed in Nicklaus' ears as his odd misplay found a bunker. But he weathered it. The excellence of his golf spoke more than words. He changed his appearance, too, and it was not long before, as the new king, he was forgiven.

While there were many who admired Norman for speaking his mind, there were also those whose respect he lost. Match play is a peculiar beast, for it is natural for the spectators to take sides, certainly more than in stroke play. They were also keen for a close game, which it had hardly looked like being when Norman stood six up so early. It was this that probably prompted the occasional clap when the Australian missed a putt for the half. The same thing happens at Wimbledon, that most British of all the sporting institutions, when a player muffs an easy volley and has his or her lead cut to 6–0, 2–1. Most people have a favorite and the underdogs always get the sympathy.

Nor should it be forgotten that Wentworth is hardly the easiest course for spectators. There are few short cuts from one vantage point to the next and the fairways are tightly lined with trees. Spectators have to sprint ahead for the occasional glimpse of play and many of them carry stepladders and even milk crates on which they perch for a better view. Inevitably there must be some crowd movement when someone plays a shot, because half of them are probably not even aware that it is being played. With movement there is also noise. It is not deliberate. It simply cannot be avoided.

Large and enthusiastic crowds are also a direct result of the appeal of tournament golf. It must be more uplifting that playing before a sparse gallery showing little interest. It also encourages sponsors, and the more that happens, the bigger the purses become and the richer the players get. There must be some rough to go with the smooth, as the British say, and I sincerely hope that Norman will reconsider his comments made in the heat of the moment and return to Wentworth.

The first hint of trouble had come on the first day of the tournament. Again it was Lyle who was involved as, in what could be termed the preliminary round, he beat his fellow Briton, Howard Clark, by 2 to 1. Afterwards Clark, who is seldom afraid to speak his mind, declared, "There is now in golf an unruly element who boo, jeer and hiss at crucial moments as they deliberately try to antagonize players. We've all seen this sort of thing in other sports in Britain and now it's happening in golf.

"They were at me right from the start of my match with Sandy. I don't know whether they had a few 'bob' on Lyle, but they did their best to upset me and sometimes they succeeded. There must have been a bus load of them out there and they all seemed to be called Jimmy. There has always been partisan behavior here because it is match play, but I'm not just talking about Wentworth because it is happening in all the tournaments. I would like to see something done about it but I don't know what the solution is."

Clark's temperament has nevertheless always had a slight question mark against it and, particularly toward the end of an always close match, there was no doubt that he was feeling the tension. Sweat-plastered lank hair fell to his forehead and a succession of cigarettes followed one another rapidly. Nevertheless the Yorkshireman held the lead for much of the time once he had broken the deadlock at the eighth hole in the morning, where Lyle needed three putts. This lead was immediately lost via a bunker at the ninth, but Clark regained it with a two at the 10th and when his opponent missed the green at the 11th, he went two ahead.

Again Lyle came back with a birdie at the long 12th, though with the course running fast all week, the hole hardly rated a par five. This was still the difference between them at lunch, birdies having been exchanged at the 16th and 17th, Clark scoring 72 to Lyle's 73. Weak putting as much as anything was at the root of Lyle's rather lackluster play but, over lunch, he reverted to the overlapping grip rather than the two-hander he had been using.

It worked at once. At the first in the afternoon Lyle holed from five feet after bunkering his second shot to avoid going two down and then sank a confident putt for a two at the second to draw level again. The tide was beginning to turn, though Clark did briefly get ahead once more at the seventh where Lyle drove too far and into the ditch that crosses the fairway. Clark's lead was lost at the ninth, where he conceded and Lyle drew ahead with a birdie at the 11th, and took the 14th and 15th as well, the latter with a birdie. It was noticeable that Clark looked very hard at the gallery after he had pushed his tee shot to the 14th, though he was certainly happier when he came back with birdies at the 16th and 17th to be only one down. He was given no further chance. At the 18th Lyle was comfortably home with a one iron and two iron, and putted safely dead for his birdie-four and the match.

Lyle's inward half of 32 was the first indication that he might be running into form after an otherwise lean season, but in many ways a more captivating match was that in which Jose Maria Olazabal, a young Spaniard making his first appearance, defeated the vastly more experienced American, Lanny Wadkins, to earn a quarter-final match against Jack Nicklaus. No rookie had ever before been invited to play in the tournament but Olazabal, a very cool customer, gave every appearance of someone who had been there many times. He was around the West Course in 66 in the morning and four up.

He was ahead right from the start, winning the first hole with a par four, and two up after three. By the sixth Wadkins had drawn level only to lose the next two holes and then run into an avalanche of brilliant strokes from the audacious young Spaniard down the home stretch. Olazabal was back in 31, culminating in a birdie, eagle finish as a drive, three iron and his 45-foot putt found its mark down the 18th.

Wadkins had meanwhile played the back nine in 33, four under par, only to lose ground rather than gain. Nor was there any change to the turn in the afternoon, as Olazabal played those nine holes in 35. However, Wadkins still had something left, winning the 12th with an eagle and 13th with a par. Now nerve was needed as much as anything, and Olazabal had it. Despite birdies from Wadkins at both the 16th and 17th, the Spaniard matched them both and was safely through.

Olazabal was eight under par for his 35 holes and, calmly munching a piece of ice afterwards, claimed not to have been at all nervous. Nor did he expect to be the following day against Nicklaus. It was, he claimed, "just another match against just another golfer." Such an attitude had, earlier in his career, helped him to become the first to complete the hat trick of the British Amateur, Youths and Boys championships. His earnings in his first season on the European Tour were already well in excess of £100,000, his first win having come in the Ebel European Masters Swiss Open with another later to follow in the Sanyo. Seve Ballesteros beware!

Significantly, Olazabal also had Ballesteros' caddy, Nick DePaul, carrying his bag. So wise a head did make a difference. At the 17th in the afternoon, with Wadkins in strong pursuit, Olazabal had been on the point of taking a wood for his second shot. But DePaul urged him to play safe with a four iron and then rely on a pitch and single putt. It worked.

The landslide of this first day was the 7 and 6 defeat of Ben Crenshaw by Naomichi (Joe) Ozaki, of that prolific Japanese golfing family. It had by no means always looked like it. Crenshaw was ahead for much of the first nine holes, which he completed in 33, and two up after 12, where he had another birdie. But from then on he was overwhelmed, as Ozaki played the last six holes of the morning round in four under par with birdies at the 13th, 14th, 17th and 18th. Furthermore, he won five in a row from the 13th, being held to a half only at the 18th. So Ozaki was three up at lunch and there was no relaxing afterwards.

Ozaki resumed birdie, par, bogey, eagle, birdie, birdie and was six up. There was absolutely nothing Crenshaw could do to stem the tide and he was closed out by a birdie, eagle finish at the 11th and 12th. The American had not brought his game with him and he knew enough of Ozaki's golf to know that he would be up against it. Even so, Crenshaw had not envisioned so devastating a defeat.

In the fourth match Rodger Davis, making his first appearance, came back from two down at lunch to defeat Nick Price of South Africa by 2 and 1. Davis had been in good form ever since he had a spell in America in August, where he benefited from long sessions on excellent practice grounds.

The Australian, who always plays in plus twos, had won the Whyte and Mackay PGA Championship at Wentworth earlier in the year and may have been disconcerted when he went around in 69 in the morning only to be two down. Nor was he ever in front, as Price went out in 34 and then came home in 34.

But there was a dramatic shift afterward, as Price lost the first three holes, only one of them to a birdie. Once ahead, there was no stopping Davis as he advanced to two up at the turn with an outward half of 33. A birdie by Crenshaw at the 11th might have begun a recovery, but Davis matched it and immediately drove the knife home with an eagle at the 12th. From then on he was able to relax, though Crenshaw did summon one last burst with birdies at the 15th, 16th and 17th. The first two of these cut his deficit to two holes but Davis matched his four at the 17th and that was it.

So there it was: in the order of play, Davis was through to meet the defending champion, Seve Ballesteros; Lyle was due to meet Tommy Nakajima of Japan; Olazabal had a potentially magical confrontation with Jack Nicklaus and Ozaki faced Norman. And how it whetted the appetites of the golfing public. From an early hour all roads seemed to lead to Wentworth in a steady stream of traffic. There was not a spare parking space to be had and, with the sun slowly penetrating the early morning mist, the atmosphere was quite electric with anticipation.

The Burma Road, as Wentworth's West Course is sometimes called, has seldom looked better, but ultimately one match was to eclipse all others. The history books had to be rewritten as, in an utterly enthralling clash of the most brilliant golf on either side, Lyle defeated Nakajima at the 38th hole. The barest bones of it were that they shot 65s in the morning and were tied. If that seemed an impossible act to follow, the two of them then surpassed it in the afternoon as they shot 64s and were still level. It took another two holes for these two warriors to settle it, and if ever a match deserved not to have a loser, this was it.

Between them Lyle and Nakajima had a staggering 27 birdies and four eagles in 36 holes, which they both completed in 129 shots, 15 under par. This beat by four the record against par, held by Bob Charles in 1969, Nicklaus in 1966 and Nakajima himself in 1985, all being 11 under par when they won, though in those instances the distances were 29, 31 and 31 holes. A further example of the quality of the play was that the better ball of Lyle and Nakajima was 117 for the 36 holes, 60 in the morning and 57 in the afternoon.

It was not only the brilliance of the scoring but also the ingredients of the match itself that had the crowd breathless. Having been so evenly matched before lunch, the score being tied for 12 of the 18 holes, Lyle was four up after the seventh in the afternoon only to find himself two down with five holes to play. There were all the ingredients of attack, counterattack and then dramatic recovery with time fast running out.

Lyle came out of the starting gate quicker. Nakajima was bunkered at the first and then lost the second as well, this time to a birdie-two. Recovery was instant. At the third the Japanese chipped in for a birdie-three, holed from five yards for an eagle at the next and then single-putted the fifth for a two. His lead was equally brief, Lyle answering with a birdie at the sixth and they were tied again. But the standard had been set, both out in 32 but Nakajima not drawing ahead again until the 12th, though it took him an eagle-three to do it. The putt was all of 50 feet, but Lyle got one in himself from 18 feet at the next for a birdie and with a three at the 16th led once more. However a slight error cost Lyle the 17th, where Nakajima was safely on in two and it was all even as they began the afternoon round.

Lyle came out of his corner like a man possessed. He played six holes between the second and seventh in seven under par with five birdies and one eagle. Even if Sandy missed a green, it did not matter; he still holed, as at the third with his putter and at the seventh with his wedge. Then there was the 50-foot putt that found the bull's-eye at the fifth and, not least, another of 24 feet for an eagle at the fourth.

Nakajima must have wondered what had hit him. At least he managed to halve the fifth in two and the seventh in three and, when Lyle erred with second shots to the eighth and ninth, each time to take five, the Japanese won them both, first with a par and then with a birdie. So Lyle was back to two up, out in 30 to Nakajima's 32. At once the tables turn. Nakajima started with a two at the 10th, a three at the 11th and they were all square. Briefly Lyle stood his ground with a matching birdie at the 12th but he took three putts from a long way at the 13th and then lost the 14th as well, Nakajima holing up the slope from some distance for a two. Now two down, Lyle was deep in trouble.

Again there was a twist to the remarkable tale. Still two up with two holes to play, Nakajima missed the green at the 17th while Lyle got down in two for his birdie. There was just a hole between them now, and Lyle summoned one final effort. On the green in two at the 18th, he bolted a 45-foot putt for an eagle-three, leaving his opponent to pick his ball up when, to all intents and purposes, he thought he was going to face a relatively short putt for the match.

So down they went into extra holes and Lyle prevailed with a five at the second, the 17th. Nakajima had missed the green right, overhit his pitch and took three putts. It was a sad end to a wonderful match. "The last time I played golf as exciting as this was when I lost in the final here against Ballesteros in 1982," said Lyle. "I feel as if I shot the lights out today, but even when I was two down with two to play, I did not give up."

It was not, on the other hand, Ballesteros' day. All week he had been suffering from a heavy cold and he was not so much beaten as trampled into the ground, as Davis crushed him by 7 and 6. Lackluster, Ballesteros never recovered from a disastrous start, going to the turn in 37 in the morning and standing three down as Davis won the sixth, seventh and ninth, two of them with pars.

There were signs of a recovery when Ballesteros came back in 32 to cut the margin to two holes, but his hopes died as he played a loose four iron to the fourth in the afternoon and went three down again. Davis needed no further bidding. Two more birdies in the next four holes made the difference between them six holes while a run of three, three, four from the ninth brought the shutters down.

Not until the last putt was holed did Davis let slip a sigh of relief. He had not trusted Ballesteros for one moment, even when the Spaniard was four, five and six down. So the Australian resolved from the outset to pretend that Ballesteros was not even there. "Seve has the charisma to dominate you," he explained. "When he walks onto the course, he looks as if he owns the place. And when he holes a good putt, he makes you think he is unstoppable.

"So I decided not to watch him. I looked at the trees, the spectators, the planes flying in and out of Heathrow, anywhere but at Seve. It enabled me to concentrate on my own game and it paid off." He was 10 under par for the 30 holes. Ballesteros made no excuses, saying, "When you play badly there are so many good players around these days that you can easily get beaten." Even so it was a famous scalp for Davis who, only five years earlier, had largely given up golf and instead went into the hotel industry in his native Australia. That had proved even more unsuccessful and his decision to give the game another try is not so far one he has regretted. Nor is he likely to.

All around it was not a happy day for the Spanish. Olazabal duly got his dismisal notice, as Nicklaus beat him by 5 and 4. Nor was the result ever in much doubt, though that hardly mattered to the vast crowd that swarmed after them. It was enough to see Nicklaus playing again on a stage he had graced 22 years earlier in the very first World Match Play Championship. That he came back at all was due to commitments in the field of golf architecture that had taken him to both Austria and St. Mellion in Devon. That done, he arrived "to play a bit of golf."

And play a bit of golf he did. This was the Nicklaus everyone likes to remember: drive after drive piercing fairway after fairway, iron shot after iron shot dropping like shot partridges over distant flagsticks. Olazabal is not the sort of young man who gets easily overawed, but for once his lethal short game was not quite so lethal and it made all the difference. He held on through the first four holes, but when Nicklaus holed the marginally shorter putt for a two at the fifth, he took a lead he was never to relinquish.

Another birdie followed an exquisite pitch to the sixth; he was presented with the eighth when Olazabal hit his second into the right-hand bunker and then Nicklaus took the ninth as well with a six iron close to the flag. Out in 32 the U.S. Masters champion was four up. When Olazabal at last holed a good putt—30 feet or so—to take the 11th, there was speculation that this might be the spur. But Nicklaus was in no mood to relent. He was totally solid down the home stretch, picking up the birdies that are always in the offering at the par fives. Olazabal halved only one of them, the 12th, for at the 17th and 18th he made two crucial mistakes. At the 17th he pitched well, no more than three feet from the flag, but missed the putt. Then at the 18th he pushed his second into a bush, had to take a penalty drop and lost that as well. Five down.

Nicklaus had shot 66 and that really was like old times. It would have taken a mammoth recovery by Olazabal to get back into the match, and though the Spaniard played the outward half after lunch in 33, he won only two holes, the third and ninth, and had previously lost the first. That was pretty well it, Nicklaus raising one more mighty cheer when he eagled the 12th. Two holes later it was all over.

Afterwards Nicklaus refuted reports in some newspapers that he was on the point of retirement. "I did not come all the way to London to say I was quitting," he pointed out forcefully. "What I did say was that I am cutting down on my tournament play, but then I have been doing that for some time. I will still compete in the majors and though I am not the force I was once, I will still take them very seriously and might even win one. Nobody expected me to win the Masters this year, but I did."

The least eventful of the four quarter-finals was that in which Norman defeated Ozaki by 4 and 2, and that suited most people, since it meant Norman would play Nicklaus with the opportunity of exacting some revenge for what had happened in the Masters. The Australian was by no means at his best, and it was his good fortune that Ozaki failed to recapture his form of the day before. Norman's 34 to the turn was unexceptional, but it still left him five up. Such a position dulled his senses.

However, Norman was soon forced to wake himself up, because Ozaki suddenly came back. He got his first birdie at the 11th, another at the 13th and when Norman bunkered his tee shot to the 14th, the margin was back to one hole. It was something of a crisis for Norman, though not for long. He won the 16th with a three and then unleashed two fine shots to the 18th to take that hole as well, Ozaki failing to get up in two.

Even so, the Japanese refused to lie down. Though he lost the first in the afternoon to go four down, he came back with two birdies right away, that at the third being very rare. He made the top tier of the green with a four iron and stroked the putt safely home. At two down and 15 to play, anything could yet happen. It was not to be. Ozaki was in trouble at the fourth and sixth and lost both to pars. Next it was Norman who made the mistakes, losing the seventh and 10th. Only two up once again, but the Australian's eagle-three at the 12th—astonishingly the first eagle he had ever had in the World Match Play—was the sure signal of the end being in sight. It came at the 16th.

Norman was understandably not happy with his play. He was not much better than even par for the 34 holes and blamed complacency and lack of concentration. Perhaps his mind was on other things, like his forthcoming confrontation with Nicklaus. It was a match both of them wanted, Nicklaus admitting that "Greg will start as the favorite. He's taken a lot of money off me in practice this season because we often fix up a game together before tournaments." Norman was not to be deceived. "I think by saying that I am favorite, Jack's using a bit of reverse psychology," he grinned. "The old dog still has a few tricks up his sleeve."

However, the man of the moment was Lyle, carrying once again the hopes of the British public, still denied in all these years a home winner. One could only speculate at the time how much that match with Nakajima would have taken out of him. Lyle spent a quiet evening. He flopped in a chair and slept.

Far from suffering a reaction, Lyle resumed against Davis in much the same manner as he had finished against Nakajima, swinging into an early lead of two up after only three holes and never once allowing his opponent to get any closer. He shot 67 in the morning—which meant successive rounds of 65, 64, 67—and led by four up. The margin of victory was a more modest 2 and 1.

It meant that Lyle was in the final for the third time, the others being in 1980 and 1982, and this was to be a repeat of 1980 since, in the other semifinal, Norman had a closer win, by one hole over Nicklaus. Neither was quite at the top of his game, but Nicklaus, having trailed for much of the day, put on a late spurt and actually led with four holes to play. In the end he was to be denied, but the big crowd certainly had its money's worth.

Their biggest difficulty was in deciding which match to watch; on the one hand, Lyle, the remaining Briton, and on the other, Nicklaus who, at 46, was almost certainly making his last appearance in World Match Play. Again the fairways were lit by gentle autumn sunshine, though an early morning mist was still about when Lyle set off against Davis. His concentration was quickly tested.

Just as he was about to putt on the first green, having splashed out from the greenside bunker to around three feet, a camera clicked. Normally Lyle would have taken little notice, backing briefly away for perhaps just one more quick look. This time he went through the whole rigmarole again, examining the short putt from all sides before rolling the ball home dead center. Many a match has in its time turned at the first hole and this extra care by Lyle ensured that he did not at once fall behind. He got his half and by the time he left for the fifth tee he was two up.

A nine iron to five feet at the second brought a birdie-two and he got up-and-down from off the green at the fourth for his four. David Musgrove, his perceptive caddy, oberved, "Sandy may not know it himself, but this is one of the two or three most determined weeks he plays all year." The determination was self-evident.

A third birdie at the sixth put Lyle three up and, though Davis stirred himself with a three at the seventh, Lyle was out in 32. Perhaps Davis had taken too much out of himself in beating Ballesteros. There was a lethargic look about him as if he were battle weary. At the 12th, for instance, he took three putts from not very far to go three down and then he missed the next green to take five and go four down. His chip ought to have saved him the half, but his putter let him down again.

There the difference stayed until lunch, Davis winning the 14th but losing the 16th. He could have been five down but managed to get up-and-down from a bunker at the 18th. A revival was possible still, particularly when, immediately after lunch, Davis won the first hole and then halved the next two.

The next two holes reflected the command Lyle held and the lethargy Davis could not break. Lyle had to hit the ball only twice, once on each hole and won them both to go five up. The circumstances were unusual. Davis, driving first at the fourth with a one iron, pushed it quite alarmingly. Lyle was down the middle.

Off they trudged, but when Davis reached the area into which he had driven, he was told, "Your ball is over the ditch and that is out-of-bounds." The Australian's retort was, "It's a pity you hadn't said so five minutes earlier while I was on the tee." He at once conceded the hole. Later Davis pointed out that there were plenty of officials and spotters, some with radios, and it ought to have been possible to get word back to him. "Anyway, there was no way I was going to walk all the way back up the hill again and so I gave Sandy the hole," said Davis.

Lyle had just as little work to do at the fifth. Having hit a seven iron to eight feet, he was able to stand back and watch Davis find a bunker with his tee shot, come out to 10 feet, miss the putt and concede again. It was almost like a little holiday for Lyle.

Then, right out of the blue, Davis made four consecutive birdies from the 11th and won three of them. It was a match again. He hit a sand wedge to three feet at the 11th, halved the 12th in birdie fours, sank a longish putt for a three at the 13th and followed it with a four iron stone-dead at the short 14th. Now the Australian tide was running strong, and Lyle needed a bit of luck to stem the flood.

Carving his drive into the trees, Lyle could only chip out sideways. He still needed a three iron for his third and he missed the green. He has played better chips in his time, as well, but an important putt from around 12 feet found its mark and that was good enough for a half in five. Davis, from a good drive, had missed the green as well with a four iron, but it took him three more to get down. How typical it all was of match play. But Lyle had his breath back, and was still two up when it might so easily have been one, and a short while later was through to his third final.

A feature of the Norman–Nicklaus match was how much longer the Australian now is off the tee. This was evident right from the start when Greg needed only an eight iron for his second shot to the first against a two iron from Nicklaus. There was frequently a three- and four-club difference between them and that does tell in the long run. Nicklaus's ally was experience and the knowledge that if he could get his blow in first by landing his shot close to the flag, the pressure would be on his opponent.

But that eight iron and two putts on the first hole of the day was sufficient to put Norman ahead right away, since Nicklaus did not find the green with his two iron and took five. After that, there was instant deadlock, the next nine holes being halved in par figures, with the exception of the fourth, which they halved in birdie fours, Norman via a bunker. It was Nicklaus' turn to scramble a half at the ninth, but he could not match the Australian's birdie three at the 11th and fell two behind.

The next two holes were exchanged. Norman drove into the trees at the 12th and had no chance of a shot at the green. Nicklaus, on the other hand, was comfortably home with a drive and mid-iron. However it was the American who made the mistake at the 13th, missing the green with, for once, the shorter club—a seven iron against Norman's six. So that made it down again and in fact it took a bit of luck to give Nicklaus the lift he needed.

More than once he had chided himself with the exclamation "Aw, Jack" as he struck the odd drive not exactly where intended and another escaped his lips at the 15th which, in his early days here used to be a par five but is now a much better par four. This drive was tugged left but rebounded off a tree and back into play. It is at moments like this that a player must make the most of his luck, and Nicklaus seized the opportunity to put the pressure on Norman by finding the green with a two iron. Greg, on the other hand, put a three iron into the right-hand bunker and lost the hole.

This was great encouragement to Nicklaus who promptly rammed in a 24-foot putt for a birdie at the 16th and the match was tied, a position that did not change down the 17th and 18th, both of which were halved in birdie fours. Nicklaus nevertheless had to single-putt both, their disparity in length being particularly evident at the 17th where he needed two drivers and a wedge to reach the green against a driver and three wood from Norman. Still, all square at lunch was exactly how everybody wanted it, with the old master still able to hold his head up against the player who is currently the best in the world. Both were around in 69.

It was not long after lunch before Norman regained the lead against his boyhood hero, one whose books he had read avidly in the early days of his career. He went ahead with a two at the second and should have gone even farther clear at the fifth, only to miss from three feet after both had hit their tee shots wide of the green. Norman's putting was not particularly sharp around this time, but he did get one in for a three at the seventh and at two up with nine to play, all was going according to his plan.

And then suddenly it all changed. Nicklaus won three holes in a row to be one up with five and then only four holes to play. At the 11th his pitch was deadly, a nine iron to less than three feet, and at once Norman fouled up his drive at the 12th, as indeed he had done in the morning. This time there was even less of an escape route, and Nicklaus was able to walk on to the 13th tee without being asked to play his second shot. His spirits soaring, Nicklaus, though using a three iron against a six by Norman, hit the better second shot to the 13th, holed the putt for a birdie and a buzz of anticipation swept like a wave through the crowds.

Could Nicklaus, having got to the front for the first time at so crucial a stage, find the impetus to keep him there? He could not. Though the 14th was halved and Nicklaus pierced the 15th fairway with his drive, he knew at once that he had mis-hit his four iron to the green. Though it eluded the left-hand bunker, he was faced with an awkward little chip, feet slightly below the ball.

In fact Nicklaus played it pretty well, to around four feet, but his putter, or more accurately his stroke, let him down and the match was tied once more. Now, with the two big par fives to come, the advantage was back with Norman. They halved the 16th, but at the 17th the reigning Open champion unleashed two mighty strokes with his driver and found the right side of the green, 60 feet from the flag. Nicklaus, short in two, chipped well enough to look as if he might well get his four, but Norman trumped him by holing his putt for an eagle-three. "It was a bit of a freak, he had the honesty to admit later. "I was just hoping to get down in two but the hole got in the way."

Now one down with just the 18th to come, Nicklaus summoned one last massive effort. To a massive roar he hit a drive and three iron to 10 feet while Norman, with the same club, ran through the green and had to chip back. He did it well enough, to around three feet and, in a wonderful but typical act of generosity, Nicklaus gave him the putt. How the mind went back to that tied Ryder Cup match at Royal Birkdale in 1969, when Nicklaus did the same thing against Tony Jacklin in the deciding match before sinking his own for a half, not only between themselves but between the teams as well.

At least Nicklaus now knew what he had to do. It was a do-or-die putt for an eagle-three, slightly downhill, right to left. It was never in from the moment he hit it, but perhaps the finest golfer of all time had gone down honorably and the salute he got at the end was well-deserved. Norman even felt a tinge of disappointment that Nicklaus had not holed for a three. "I was having so much fun out there," he said later, "that I wanted to go down the 37th. I didn't want the sun to set today."

Though no one knew it at the time, he was also to make one other remark that may have tempted fate. Asked about the possibility of a partisan crowd for the final against Lyle, Norman said, "Everybody will be hoping for Sandy to win but I don't expect any problems from the fans. They have always been very fair to me." Within 24 hours he would be whistling a very different tune.

The day of the final was oddly forbidding from the start. Much thicker mist clung among the trees, footmarks traced their way across the dew-laden grass and water dripped from dying leaves. It put an immediate damper on everything and spirits were by no means lifted when Norman shot into an immediate and seemingly invincible lead, three up in the first five holes, five up after nine and six up after 11. "I felt as if I had got out of bed on the wrong side," reflected Lyle subsequently. His wife, Christine, once a professional golfer herself and now the mother of two small boys, thought it was more delayed reaction. Her husband had been less affected by that tumultuous quarter-final match against Nakajima two days earlier than had been feared. He had played in much the same vein against Davis in the semi-finals, but now the machinery refused to function. He was at odds with himself.

This was fatal against Norman, who had had the easier route to the final and was therefore more fresh. He did not so much as have to win the holes as stand back and let Lyle make the mistakes. Lyle's first nine holes of 39 was not very good at all, and it was only to be expected that Norman would make the most of it.

Having got away with a four at the first via a bunker, the Australian hit an eight iron to 20 feet at the second and holed the putt for a two. One up. At the third, which neither played particularly well, Lyle made the bigger mess of it and Norman took the hole with a five. Two up. They halved the fourth in more respectable birdie-fours, Norman again coming out of a bunker before single-putting, while at the fifth Lyle took three putts. Norman was three up now and the slowly swelling gallery was as down as Lyle was also feeling. There was no hiding place. He missed the seventh fairway and lost the hole to a four and was all over the course at the ninth before losing that to a par as well. Norman was five up and he had not yet had to move out of third gear.

At the 11th the margin between them became an even more embarrassing six holes, as Norman played a drive and wedge to 20 feet and holed the putt for his third birdie. Then Lyle at last stirred himself with a four on the long 12th, which got him a half, followed by another birdie at the 13th with a drive and six iron to two feet. He had won a hole at last, though the respite was short-lived. At the short 14th, up the hill to the two-tiered green, Norman hit a five iron to some six yards and holed the putt for a two. Six up again.

At this rate the final would be all over soon after lunch and the crowd's relief was understandable when Norman found a bunker with his second to the 15th, took five and lost a hole. At the next he was marginally strong with his approach and when he chipped a shade strong, someone cheered. Norman missed the putt, heard a clap and glared at the gallery. So Greg was back to four up and support for Lyle continued to grow at the 17th, which he took with a birdie four. That was three holes in a row now and it looked for all the world as if it would become four in succession when at the 18th the 1985 Open champion came out of a bunker at the last to not much more than three feet. Two down at lunch would not only have been a great recovery, but it would have made a real match of it in the afternoon. The putt slid by, and Lyle whacked his thigh in disappointment.

Still, the situation was not as bad as it might have been and, when Lyle hit the first green after lunch while Norman found the bunker on the right, there was some chance of the gap between them again being narrowed. Instead, Norman played a marvelous shot which ran straight into the hole for a birdie-three and he was back to four up again. But Lyle clung on and soon got a hole back at the third, where Norman took three putts from off the green. When the second of them for the half missed, there was again the thinnest of cheers and a look of thunder returned to Norman's face. It was not enough to get so fussed about.

The next two holes were halved, but at the sixth Lyle played a fine pitch from the left side of the fairway to five feet, holed the putt for a birdie and was at last back to only two down. Any momentum was not immediately sustained. Norman came back with a birdie at the seventh, lost the eighth but won the ninth, pars in each case being good enough.

In hindsight it was the ninth which was almost certainly the critical hole. Lyle, caught at the very top of his backswing by a clatter against a railing, hooked his drive into trees on the left. Norman, following, sent his into trees on the other side of the fairway. Both could only chip out sideways but Lyle, playing first to the green, dropped his third shot only six feet or so from the flag. That raised quite a cheer but Norman, following him, played just as good a shot and by a matter of inches was closer to the hole. However, Lyle would be putting first and if only he could get it in, the pressure would be very much on Norman. To a groan, Lyle missed, Norman holed and that was three up again when it might so easily have been only one. Both were out in 34.

Down the back nine, Lyle's practice was to rely more on his one iron from the tee, Norman keeping faith with his driver. On the face of it this may have appeared to give the advantage to the Australian. In fact it made little difference. The 11th, 12th and 13th holes were all halved conventionally, as had been the two short holes, the 10th and 14th. With only four holes left and Norman still three up, the match was coming to a predictable and quiet conclusion.

But suddenly Lyle landed two punches that rocked Norman back on his heels. A one iron and six iron to five feet at the 15th brought a birdie after

Norman had missed from not much farther away. Immediately Lyle struck again. This time it was a one iron and wedge to 12 feet and when that putt went in as well, Norman was clearly unsettled. He was a couple of feet closer to the hole, but when he missed the putt, his position was much more perilous than it had looked 20 minutes earlier.

One of the best things about Wentworth is that the 17th and 18th are such make-or-break holes. Both are par fives but it is birdies and often eagles that are invariably needed. This very knowledge was Lyle's whole undoing. Going for the big drive down the left-hand side, he got it wrong by possibly as little as two degrees. Indeed, when he hit the shot, he did not immediately think his ball was out of bounds. It was a heartbreaking moment when he learned that it was. Equally, a huge surge of relief swept over Norman, who nevertheless took the opportunity to find the green with a drive and one iron. That was enough for Lyle to concede the match.

8. The U.S. Tour

There's no doubt the two golfers who dominated the 1986 U.S. PGA Tour were Greg Norman and Bob Tway. The only puzzle was that Tway, playing for 10 weeks after Norman left for the overseas circuits, failed to overtake the Australian for the money-winning title.

Norman called it a year in America after the World Series of Golf in late August, having won the Panasonic Las Vegas Invitational and Kemper Open, with record earnings of $653,296. It didn't seem that the record would last, because at that stage Tway had earned $622,805. Instead of gaining steam, Tway ran out of petrol. He finished with $652,780—$516 shy of Norman's total.

Tway, whom Lee Trevino has called the next superstar, snatched the PGA Championship away from Norman by holing a bunker shot on the 72nd hole, after having earlier won three tournaments, the Shearson Lehman Brothers Andy Williams Open, Westchester Classic and Georgia-Pacific Atlanta Classic. After failing on his first three attempts in the PGA Tour school, Tway qualified in 1985 and won $164,023, which was indicative of the potential of the 27-year-old former All-America from Oklahoma State University.

Threaded between the winners and losers of 1986 was an ongoing feud between Mac O'Grady and Deane Beman, commissioner of the PGA Tour. It began at the 1985 New Orleans tournament, when O'Grady was fined $1,000 for allegedly insulting a volunteer. O'Grady appealed and the fine was reduced to $500, which he still refused to pay, and the amount was deducted from his earnings. The episode didn't end there. O'Grady became abusive in the press, hired a lawyer and made various threats. The penalty was increased to a $5,000 fine and six-week suspension. O'Grady ultimately had to pay, but not before he won the first tournament of his 14-year career.

If anyone looked to blossom in 1986, it was not Tway but Payne Stewart. For the third straight year, Stewart did not win a tournament, but was in contention so often that he placed third among the money winners with $535,389, a record for non-winners. A total of 19 players earned more than $300,000 and 83 won $100,000 or more. Among the $100,000 winners were Davis Love III and Brian Claar, the 14th and 15th rookies to earn that much. It took $61,980 for a player to retain his card.

Among those who came up short was Hale Irwin, whose streak of $100,000 seasons ended at 14 when he placed 128th with $59,983. But Irwin retained his exempt status as a two-time U.S. Open champion. Tom Watson struggled through his second consecutive season without a victory, but had earnings of $278,338, the 10th straight year he has won over $200,000.

It was a very good year for some veterans. Jack Nicklaus won the Masters for the sixth time at age 46, and Raymond Floyd became the oldest U.S. Open winner ever at age 43. Bob Murphy, also 43, won the Canadian Open. At 31, Ben Crenshaw wasn't in their age bracket, but he made a pleasing recovery in winning the Buick Open and Vantage Championship, his first triumphs since the 1984 Masters.

Several newcomers made an impact. Kenny Knox and Fred Wadsworth came out of the qualifiers to win tournaments, the latter in his hometown at the Southern Open. It had been six years since a Monday qualifier had won. Three graduates of the 1985 PGA Tour school won—Mike Hulbert, Rick Fehr and Ernie Gonzalez.

Ten players won more than one tournament, led by Tway's four victories. Other multiple winners were Norman, Floyd, Crenshaw, Fuzzy Zoeller, Calvin Peete, Hal Sutton, Dan Pohl, Corey Pavin and Andy Bean.

Bahamas Classic—$300,000
Winner: Hale Irwin

The Bahamas Classic at the Paradise Island Golf Club near Nassau was not an official PGA Tour event. But it was coordinated by the PGA Tour and the money was of PGA Tour proportions.

Davis Love III, fresh from the tour qualifying school, and Bob Tway and Bob Lohr, coming off their freshman year on the circuit, got the attention at the start. But it was Hale Irwin, 40, readying for his 19th year on the tour, who grabbed the $72,000 first prize. Irwin shot a course record-tying eight-under-par 64 in the third round and followed that with a 67 for a 19-under 269 that beat runner-up Donnie Hammond by six strokes.

The Bahamas Classic was the first PGA event in the Bahamas since the Bahamas National Open concluded the schedule in 1971. The Paradise Island course is 6,976 yards and has plenty of water and trees to torment those who hit shots off line. It was the penalties of the course as well as relative inexperience that was to catch up with Love, Tway and Lohr. Love, a long-hitting son of a pro, began his first professional tournament with a 65 'that left him one stroke behind Lohr. Love followed with a 68 and Lohr a 69, tying them for the 36-hole lead.

Then Irwin went to work. He made an eagle, five birdies and two pars for a 29 on the back nine and a 64 in the third round that pulled him into a first-place tie with Scott Hoch. Hoch played steady golf for three rounds, then collapsed. Irwin began the final round by hitting his drive into the edge of a lake, but he was able to play it out and save par. Then he went into the lead by himself on the fourth hole and won going away with a 67. Love placed third and Hoch fourth.

MONY Tournament of Champions—$500,000
Winner: Calvin Peete

There were a lot of changes in the Tournament of Champions at LaCosta in Carlsbad, California: (a) Instead of being scheduled in March, when the season was well under way, the tournament for the tour winners of the year before was moved up to January and became the 1986 opener; (b) because of the competition of pro football on television, the tournament began on a

Wednesday and ended on a Saturday; (c) an amateur, Scott Verplank, was entered for the first time; (d) Calvin Peete won.

It will be recalled that in the 1985 T of C Peete became so upset about a putt he missed at the fifth green that he stickhandled it so often he lost count and was disqualified. This time Peete bogeyed the fifth hole in the first two rounds, two of the three bogeys he made in the tournament. Otherwise he played nearly flawless golf as he produced a 21-under-par 68–67–64–68— 267. Mark O'Meara tied the old tournament record for LaCosta of 273 and lost by six strokes. Phil Blackmar was third, another four strokes behind O'Meara.

Peete, 42, said he had set a goal of being both player of the year and leading money winner. To help attain it, he had lost five pounds in an effort to relieve some of the pressure on his ailing back. The $90,000 he earned gave him a big step in the right direction. But for the bogey at the fifth hole, Peete would have had the outright lead after the first round. As it was, his 68 gave him a share of first place with Mark McCumber.

Tom Kite shot a bogey-free 66 in the second round that he called "one of the best I've played in a long time." That put him into a tie for first place with Peete, who birdied the last three holes for a 67—an unlikely performance later in the spring when the wind is in the golfer's face—and O'Meara, who had a 65, at 135. Verplank, a 21-year-old senior at Oklahoma State University, made his presence felt with a 67 that left him four strokes behind.

The third round belonged to Peete even though a number of players turned in low rounds. He birdied five of six holes in the middle of the round for a 64 that tied the course record and gave him a 54-hole total of 199 that equaled the course mark for three rounds. Peete one-putted 11 greens. O'Meara turned in a creditable 67, but now he trailed by three strokes. Verplank moved into third place with a 68 but he, too, lost ground to the leader. The final round was merely a formality for Peete. He methodically shot a 68 and only two players—Corey Pavin and Hal Sutton, neither contenders—beat that score.

Verplank, meanwhile, shot a 72 that tied him for fourth place at 279 with Danny Edwards and Bernhard Langer. Had he been a pro, Verplank would have won $23,667. When he won the 1985 Western Open he couldn't accept the $90,000 winner's share because he was an amateur.

Bob Hope Chrysler Classic—$600,000
Winner: Donnie Hammond

The 90-hole Bob Hope Chrysler Classic was both an indication of the present state of the PGA Tour and a peek at the future. The players who took the first four spots—Donnie Hammond, John Cook, Jodie Mudd and Hal Sutton—are all under 30 years of age. They'll be heard from for years to come. And, oh, can they play.

Sutton and Cook have been heard from before as winners of tournaments, Sutton the PGA Championship in 1983. Hammond, 28, had shown steady progress in three years on the tour; his playoff victory over Cook at

Bermuda Dunes was no great surprise. And the day will come for Mudd, a tragic figure in the final round of the 1984 Masters.

"The first one who goes 30 under wins," said Gary McCord halfway through the Hope, alluding to the way the field was playing the four courses on which the Hope is played. He wasn't far off. It took seven under par to make the cut. And Hammond and Cook tied at 25 under—335. Hammond won the playoff with a 12-foot birdie putt at the first hole, making him 26 under for 91 holes. Mudd placed third, two strokes behind, and Sutton was fourth, another stroke back.

Hammond, who won the 1982 PGA Tour qualifier by an amazing 14 strokes, said he had a premonition he would win. "I finished second to Hale Irwin in the Bahamas Classic (two weeks earlier). The tournament in Nassau gave me a lot of confidence." And his hobby as an astronomer helped calm him for the final round. The night before he and a friend drove to a hill high above Palm Springs and Hammond said he pointed out some of the constellations. "That and talking about golf helped me. I told myself, 'I don't care if I shoot 76, I'm going to try to shoot 66 and win.' "

He did exactly that, although the 66 actually put him in position to win. Mudd, off a 68 at LaQuinta, held a one-stroke lead over Cook, Hammond and Sutton going into the final 18 holes and probably wishing the tournament ended after four rounds. But Mudd and Sutton, even though they shot 69s, had enough putting problems in the final round to let Cook and Hammond make it a two-man battle coming down the stretch. Cook went out in 32 and Hammond in 34 and when Cook sank a 15-foot birdie putt at the 12th hole he led Hammond by three strokes.

Then the momentum swung toward Hammond. He birdied 13, 14 and 15, tying Cook, then fell a stroke behind with a bogey at 16. "But I was still confident," he said. And he proved that with a two-iron at the 205-yard No. 17 that set up a five-foot birdie putt. A 230-yard three-wood at the 505-yard 18th hole followed by a good chip produced another birdie. Cook, playing in the threesome behind him, reached the 18th in two, but his 20-foot putt for eagle stopped eight inches short. In the playoff, Cook's approach rolled over the green and he hit a great chip to within inches of the hole for a cinch par, but Hammond calmly rolled in a 12-foot birdie putt for his first victory.

Hammond stayed in the hunt throughout the week. Sutton and Bob Tway led the first round with 65s and in the second round it was Craig Stadler and Larry Mize who took over at 132. Mudd, who rebounded from an opening 72 to a 65 in the second round, stayed hot with a record-tying 63 at Bermuda Dunes on Friday that tied him for the lead with Cook. A 68 on Saturday gave Mudd the lead to himself, but after 72 holes the tournament wasn't over.

Phoenix Open—$500,000
Winner: Hal Sutton

Hal Sutton's life had undergone a few changes between the end of the 1985 season and the beginning of the 1986 Tour. He married the former Denee Miller, who had a three-year-old daughter by a previous marriage, thus picking up instant responsibility. And he changed his swing. Nothing drastic. Just enough to give him extra yardage. The combination showed quick results: In the Tournament of Champions he tied for seventh and in the Bob Hope he placed fourth. And in the Phoenix Open he rode a 54-hole cushion to his sixth victory in less than five years on the tour.

The tournament was to be the last at Phoenix Country Club, one of the oldest sites on the PGA Tour. The tournament was to be moved to the Tom Weiskopf-designed Tournament Players Club in North Scottsdale, Arizona, in 1987. Whether it was for old times' sake or just to bask in the fine weather, the tournament lured most of the big-name players, including Jack Nicklaus, who hadn't played in Phoenix since 1968, and Tom Watson, whose last visit there was in 1976. Nicklaus finished far back and Watson missed the cut.

Sutton, who had been in contention in the Hope the week before, maintained his touch at the tight, tree-lined course. He opened with 64–64 and when he tacked on a 68 in the third round he had a four-stroke lead with 18 holes to go. Then the greens, hardened by constant wind, took some fire out of Sutton's game and he had a struggle to hold off Tony Sills and defending champion Calvin Peete in the final round.

Sills, 30, a Californian who tried six times before winning his playing card and has an intestinal problem, was just one of those jockeying for second place until he came to the seventh hole. Then he reached the green in two at the 542-yard hole with a four-wood and sank a 12-foot putt for eagle. "I didn't give a thought to winning until then," he said. When Sutton stepped to the tee at the 204-yard 15th hole he led Sills by one stroke. Three years earlier, Sutton led by two strokes when he came to the tee, hit his ball into the lake to the right and lost the tournament. This time he hit a high three-iron that left him with a 22-foot downhill putt. He sank the birdie putt and when Sills bogeyed the hole Sutton's lead was once again three.

Sills wasn't finished. When Sutton hit his ball into a bunker behind the green at the 420-yard No. 17, then missed a five-foot par putt, it looked as if there would be a two-stroke swing. Sills was only three and one-half feet from a birdie, on the same line as Sutton's putt. Sutton had played for a break and the ball had gone straight. So Sills played straight for the hole . . . and the ball broke. That did it. Sills missed an eagle putt of six feet at the 18th hole, but Sutton had a two-putt birdie himself at the easy par-five. Sutton finished with a 71 for 267 and a two-stroke edge on Sills and Peete, who both shot 68 for 269.

AT&T Pebble Beach National Pro-Am—$600,000
Winner: Fuzzy Zoeller

The AT&T National Pro-Am was born in controversy, was played in controversy and was marked by controversy at the end of its inaugural showing. It used to be called the Bing Crosby National Pro-Am, but when AT&T wanted to add its name to the sponsorship, Bing's widow, Kathryn, refused to allow the Crosby name to be attached to it and pulled out in favor of an amateur-celebrity tournament in North Carolina in the summer.

But it was still the Crosby. The celebrities and the weather saw to that. The Crosby has long been noted for its weather—rain, cold, snow, wind, you name it—although some years the weather has been unusually nice. This time it wasn't nice. Bing would have loved it. The weather was so bad that for the third time in 12 years the tournament concluded after 54 holes instead of 72.

After a one-hour delay because of a downpour, the first round was played in sunshine and wind that at times seemed as if it might scour the three courses off the Monterey Peninsula and deposit them in the Pacific Ocean. Fuzzy Zoeller shot a remarkable 69 at Spyglass Hill and when they had finished sifting through the scores they found Zoeller was a stroke behind Willie Wood and Kikuo Arai. But the real tournament had hardly begun.

Rain washed out the second round, setting up a Monday conclusion of the tournament. When play resumed on Saturday, officials said the lift-and-clean rule was in effect because of the wet condition of the courses. The decision did not sit well with Zoeller, who wondered why those who played Spyglass Hill, the toughest of the three courses, could use winter rules when he couldn't in the first round, when the course was just as wet. Zoeller, of course, lost his protest, but his anger diminished when he shot a six-under-par 66 at Pebble Beach, giving him the lead for keeps. On Sunday, the gale-force wind returned and Zoeller shot a 70 at Cypress Point, giving him a five-stroke lead over Payne Stewart.

None of those watching the tournament on national television ever got a glimpse of Zoeller. The cameras were parked at Pebble Beach, the customary course for the final round, on Sunday. All TV viewers saw were Jack Nicklaus struggling—he failed to make the cut—and a number of movie stars, among them Clint Eastwood, James Garner and Jack Lemmon, the last named making a succession of poor shots in probably his longest TV airing as a golfer.

Rain once again interfered on Monday, making Pebble Beach unplayable. So officials decided the tournament would conclude on Tuesday, much to the surprise and dismay of many contestants. An hour later, the decision was changed. The tournament was over and the pros would be paid as if it were a 72-hole tournament. Which meant Zoeller earned $108,000 even though he had played only 54 holes. It wasn't the Crosby, but it sure seemed like the Crosby.

Shearson Lehman Brothers Andy Williams Open—$450,000
Winner: Bob Tway

Bernhard Langer indicated he knew little of Bob Tway after he lost to Tway in the Shearson Lehman Brothers Andy Williams Open in San Diego, California. But many others certainly had. A brilliant amateur career had preceded Tway's debut on the PGA Tour in 1985—three-time college All-America, numerous amateur victories and college player of the year in 1981. And in his first year as a professional he placed 45th among the money winners with $164,023.

It's a moot point whether Tway would have won at San Diego had the tournament gone its scheduled 72 holes because of the jam at the finish—15 players finished within four strokes of Tway and Langer. But Tway and Langer played well enough—Tway with 67, 68 and 69 and Langer, making his first appearance in San Diego, with 70, 66 and 68.

The tournament is played on two courses at the Torrey Pines municipal complex, the North and South. The South is about 350 yards longer and is customarily used in the final two rounds, after the field has been cut. This time it was used for only one round after the cut. A heavy rain that poured an inch and a half of rain on the course on Saturday washed out the third round and set up a 54-hole event. It was the first rainout of a tour stop in San Diego in 35 years and the second week in a row a tournament was reduced to 54 holes.

As usual, the North course produced the lowest scores in the first round, six 66s. Of the six, Larry Rinker was the only one who finished near the top, in a tie at 206. The weather returned to normal the second day and Larry Mize took the lead by tacking a 68 onto his opening 66. But Mize vanished with a 75 two days later, after sitting out the day of rain. It is noteworthy to mention that Tony Sills was among those who trailed by two strokes after a 66, giving him 14 rounds in 1986 at par or under. Sills' streak ended on Sunday with a 73. Two putts he made might have been a tipoff of what was to come—he sank a putt of more than 100 feet for birdie at the third hole and a 40-footer for par at the seventh. Nobody makes those kinds of putts every day.

In the final round, about half the field took a shot at the lead. At one point, there were 16 players within two shots of the lead. Paul Azinger finally emerged as the leader at 13 under par. But at the par-three 16th, Azinger hooked his tee shot over the green and into a canyon and took a double bogey. He tied with Mike Hulbert and Mark Lye at 205, one stroke behind Tway and Langer.

Langer completed his 68 half an hour before Tway and awaited his fate as Tway moved into the lead following Azinger's misfortune. His fate was a playoff (he is now 1–1 on the U.S. tour) as Tway bogeyed the 17th hole. Undisturbed by losing a chance to win in regulation, Tway won on the second hole with an unerring birdie putt.

Hawaiian Open—$500,000
Winner: Corey Pavin

Tom Watson hadn't won since the 1984 Western Open. But after the third round, there he was, leading the Hawaiian Open and apparently on his way to ending his drought. And after the final round there was Corey Pavin, savoring his two-stroke victory after a scintillating six-under-par 66 that gave him a 72-hole total of 272. Watson, so solid through the first three rounds, scraped out a 73 that tied him for third place with Bernhard Langer—the loser in a playoff at San Diego a week earlier—and two strokes behind Paul Azinger. A week earlier, Azinger had tied for third, one stroke behind Bob Tway and Langer.

Mac O'Grady made as many headlines—maybe more—with his talk as Pavin and Watson did with their golf clubs. O'Grady finally revealed why he wouldn't talk to the news media in 1985—he was angry at Commissioner Deane Beman for extracting a $500 fine from him for remarks he allegedly made to a woman volunteer at the 1984 USF&G Classic. O'Grady said he sought to embarrass Beman by not talking to newsmen. He still wouldn't talk to American writers, although he did talk to Japanese writers in Hawaii. O'Grady called Beman "a little man, Mr. Thief with a capital T," and said "the President of the United States doesn't even have the right to go into my account."

George Burns, a pro who gained a measure of fame for his critical remarks aimed at the U.S. Golf Association, shot to the front with a nine-under-par 63 in the first round, his first under-70 round of the year. "I just happened to make them all in one round," he said. He didn't break par in the next three rounds. O'Grady took over after 36 holes (with scores of 64–69, followed by 74–73), then unleashed his blast at Beman in the Honolulu *Star-Bulletin* and repeated them in a TV interview with Lee Trevino. Pavin and Watson quietly moved into position for a run at the championship, Pavin with 67–67 and Watson with 68–69.

Watson made his move in the gusty third round, starting at the 513-yard ninth hole, which he reached in two with an eight-iron after a 338-yard drive downwind. He sank a two-foot putt for eagle and the charge was on. He birdied No. 13 and finished with six-foot birdie putts at the last two holes for a 66 that gave him a one-stroke lead over Azinger.

"That's the best I've played in a long time," Watson said. Then somebody mentioned to him that 13 years earlier, before he had won his first tournament, Watson led the Hawaiian Open by one stroke after three rounds, then shot a 75 and placed third. "I wish you hadn't mentioned that," he said.

Watson took two bogeys early in the final round and his bogey-bogey finish relegated him to a 73 and a tie for third place. Pavin was three strokes behind at the start of the final round and quickly took command with birdies at the second, fourth and sixth holes as Watson slipped. Pavin missed a six-foot eagle putt at the ninth hole, but the resultant birdie gave him a 31 on the front nine and a two-stroke lead.

Watson cut the difference to one stroke going to No. 13, a par-five easily reachable in two because of the tail wind. Both did reach it in two, but Pavin sank an eagle putt from three feet after a perfect five-iron approach and Watson managed only a two-putt birdie. Then Watson three-putted the next hole, his fire dead. But the pressure was not yet off Pavin. Azinger was still in the chase. And when Pavin three-putted the 17th hole, the difference between them was two strokes. But Pavin sank a return putt of a little more than six feet at the final green for a par and pressure became elation.

Los Angeles Open—$450,000
Winner: Doug Tewell

The last time Doug Tewell surfaced was in the 1985 PGA Championship at Cherry Hills Country Club. He had just broken Arnold Palmer's course record with a 64 in the first round and some people seemed to expect him to apologize. Palmer had set the old mark of 65 in the final round of the 1960 U.S. Open and there was a segment who thought if the tournament record was to fall, it should have been to a player of more renown.

Maybe Tewell isn't one of the bigger names on the PGA Tour, but 1986 was his 12th year on the tour, which is somewhat remarkable considering he nearly decided to leave it after the 1979 season and he made the PGA Championship his final tournament of 1985 to rest a persistently ailing back that caused him even more pain than it had in previous years. He figured a long rest would let him avoid undergoing a back operation. And he had won twice, both victories coming in 1980. Plus, nobody just scrapes it around Cherry Hills and comes out with a 64.

Apparently the rest did wonders for his back. He won the Los Angeles Open at Riviera Country Club and he did it convincingly—by seven strokes with 69-72-66-63—270. The 63 was just a stroke off the course record and Tewell said it was helped along by Lanny Wadkins, his playing companion in the final round. "I ran like a scared rabbit. Lanny had me petrified," he said. In the third round, Tewell was paired with Wadkins and Willie Wood and they had a combined best ball of 15 under par as Tewell shot a 66 and the others 67s as Tewell came from five behind to take the lead away from controversial Mac O'Grady. But in the final round Wadkins, with a 72, and Wood, with a 70, were left in the dust. For that matter, everybody was.

Before Tewell started shooting lights out, O'Grady grabbed the attention, with his mouth as well as with his clubs. O'Grady, still feuding with Commissioner Deane Beman, opened with 68-68 and stirred up another controversy. After his second round, O'Grady avoided the press by running from the 18th green to the locker room and when he was cornered there he refused to talk. But afterward he called Shav Glick of the *Los Angeles Times* and said Riviera "is like a cheap public course. Riviera was once great, but today it would make a good runway for LAX (Los Angeles airport)." Los Angeles had been hit by a three-inch deluge just before the start of the tournament and the greens marked up easily. But nobody seemed to agree with O'Grady's assessment. "I don't know what course he was playing, but I was playing Riviera, a great course," said Wadkins.

O'Grady's complaints seemed to work their way into his golf swing. He shot 75 in the third round, then slipped far out of contention with a 73 the final day. Among those who flew by him was Clarence Rose, who shot 66-68 the last two days and took second place with 277, one stroke ahead of Wood. And that's all the final day was, a battle for second place.

Tewell went out in 31, then started the back nine birdie-birdie. When he teed off at the 18th hole only the formality of signing his scorecard remained. One final flourish: A five-iron to the 18th green that stopped eight feet from the flag. "After I hit that, I started getting goose bumps," Tewell said. "The roar was deafening. I guess that's what everybody dreams about. I always said I wanted to win one in the right way."

Honda Classic—$500,000
Winner: Kenny Knox

The victory by Kenny Knox in the Honda Classic at the Tournament Players Club at Eagle Trace in Coral Springs, Florida, is the stuff of fantasy. It's the kind of triumph that makes an uncounted number of dreamers think "it can happen to me."

Consider: Knox, 29, a native of Tallahassee, Florida, had earned his place in the field by grabbing off one of the four spots in the 140-man qualifier the Monday of tournament week; he had unsuccessfully tried to earn his PGA Tour card seven times and lost it three times, he had never placed in the top 10 in the few tournaments he had played in three years; his career winnings were a paltry $49,492; the Honda was the first tournament he qualified for in 1986 . . . and he shot an 80 in the second round. Yet he won by one stroke over Jodie Mudd, Clarence Rose, John Mahaffey and Andy Bean with a one-under-par 287, the highest winning score in the 15-year history of the tournament. He was the first Monday qualifier to win a tournament since Jeff Mitchell captured the Phoenix Open in 1980.

"I lived in Georgia the first 16 years of my life, but I swore I'd never go to Augusta National until I was able to play in the Masters," Knox said, naming one of the first ancillary rewards of his Honda victory. "I told him not to give up until he was absolutely sure he had accomplished everything he wanted to," said Karen Knox, who had caddied for her husband from the 1984 U.S. Open through the 1985 season.

Given Knox's background, few took him as a serious contender when he opened with a six-under-par 66 that gave him the first-round lead by two strokes. Five times he saved par with his chipping and that eventually catches up with a player. He had to scramble again in the second round and watched Bean, who had a second 69, go past him. But birdies at the last two holes gave Knox a 71 and a 36-hole total of 137 and he led Bean by a stroke.

On Saturday, Knox turned in an 80, a score that ordinarily would have dissolved his dreams of winning. But Saturday was not an ordinary day. The wind blew at 30 miles an hour, sometimes up to 45 mph, and just about everybody had a difficult time keeping his golf ball on the course. Even-par was the best anybody could do—Tom Weiskopf shot an 86 after a 68 the day before—one by Rose, who tied Bean (77) for the lead at 215. The field averaged 79.21. Knox's 80 did little damage; he trailed by only two strokes.

The wind subsided in the final round and Knox, who was expected to be out of it, came charging back. A 40-foot chip-in for birdie at the third hole dissolved the two-stroke difference as Bean and Rose bogeyed the hole. Two more birdies put Knox ahead for keeps. The hole that really won it for him, however, was No. 7, which he bogeyed. Knox said he had been hitting a four-iron to the green, "but the wind was blowing, so I decided to hit the three-iron." As he hit it, the wind died and his ball buried in a bunker behind the green. The green was downhill toward a lake and he had to dig the ball out of the sand. He got it out, but it rolled across the green and into the water.

Now he had to decide whether to take a drop on the other side of the lake about 100 yards from the green or drop another ball into the bunker and hope for a good lie. He dropped. "When I was taking my stance, I kept saying to myself, 'Make it, make it,' and it trickled in as pretty as you please." Knox had changed a potential triple bogey into a bogey and it did wonders for his confidence. He parred the next seven holes and when he sank a two-footer at 15 his lead was two strokes.

But the tournament wasn't over. Knox three-putted 18 for a 70 and 287, giving Bean and Rose a chance to set up a playoff. But Bean's approach stopped on the front of the green and Rose missed a downhill 15-foot putt for birdie. "I'd already made up my mind I'd won the tournament," said Knox. "If I was forced into a playoff, I'd just go out and win it again."

Doral Eastern Open—$500,000
Winner: Andy Bean

Hubert Green fumbled away victory in the Doral Eastern Open and he admitted it. "I was humbled today," he told *Miami Herald* sports editor Edwin Pope. "I blew it. But it is just a game, a game called golf. . . . Sports are just sports. It's not life and death. Too many people in sports think the world owes them a living. It doesn't. . . . We need to be put in our place. I was. I should have won this and I didn't. I blew it."

Perhaps Green was being a little hard on himself, but the fact is he led Bean by five strokes and Tom Kite by three with nine holes to go and he led them by two and three, respectively, with four holes remaining and he didn't win. As it was, he had to sink a 15-foot bogey putt at the final green just to tie Bean and force a sudden-death playoff as they tied at 276, 12 under par. Bean won it on the fourth hole with a birdie-three. It made him the first three-time winner of the tournament. He also won in 1977 and 1982.

Green shot a 70 and Bean a 71, putting them in the middle of the pack as Doral's Blue Monster took a beating amid perfect weather in the first round. And at the outset it looked as if lightning was about to strike for the second straight week as Mark Calcavecchia grabbed the lead with a 66. Kenny Knox came out of the pre-tournament qualifier to win the Honda Classic the week before and Calcavecchia had to qualify to get into the Doral. At the Honda, Calcavecchia caddied for Ken Green. Calcavecchia followed with three consecutive par 72s at Doral, which left him tied for eighth place at 281, but this week the weather was too good to let seven under win.

Kite, who had opened with a 66, came back with a 67 and led by three strokes. The cut came at one-under 143, the lowest ever for the tournament. It figured it was going to take a super score to get in position for a run at the championship, so Green came up with one in the third round, matching the tournament record with a 64 for 204. En route, he equaled the front-nine record with a seven-under 29. That gave him a two-stroke lead on Kite and a three-stroke edge on Bean going into the final round. And the margins had grown to five and three as they made the final turn toward the clubhouse.

Bean figured the game was just beginning. "I was happy when I saw which way the wind was blowing when we started (the final round). That meant we would be playing the last four holes into the wind, which would be to my advantage." It was in the playoff, but first he had to catch Green, who led him by two strokes with four holes to go. "At that point, the only way I could lose was to give it away, and that's what I did," Green said.

Green and Bean both bogeyed the 15th hole, then Green had his lead cut in half when he missed the fairway and bogeyed 16. Green's drive at 18 went into the lake that borders the left side of the fairway and he had to work to get the tying bogey. Kite, with a chance to make it a three-man playoff, hit into a hazard near the lake and also bogeyed, leaving him one stroke short, in a tie at 277 with Mark O'Meara, who closed with a 66.

The wind was blowing into the face of the golfers in the playoff and the longer-hitting Bean capitalized on that at the 16th hole. He walloped a 290-yard tee shot, then hit a 60-yard wedge to within five feet for an easy birdie. "I felt I was going to win last week (in the Honda, in which he placed second), but I was trying so hard, maybe too hard, instead of just letting it happen, and I made some mistakes that cost me," Bean said. "This week I made some mistakes, too, but I was able to keep coming back. There is a lot of satisfaction in that for me."

Hertz Bay Hill Classic—$500,000
Winner: Dan Forsman

They will long remember the 1986 Hertz Bay Hill Classic as the Year of Wind and Rain, but Dan Forsman will recall it as the Weekend of the Big Chill, as in goose bumps. Forsman called his second PGA Tour triumph "an unbelievable experience," and nobody doubted his feelings.

Playing head-to-head with Raymond Floyd, a man with 24 years of experience on the Tour to four for Forsman, in the final two rounds, Forsman won by one stroke with 67–67 to Floyd's 69–66. And Mike Hulbert threatened to spoil their party with a final-round 64 that tied Floyd for second place.

It was an exciting finish to a tournament that got under way in a storm—climatic and verbal. It began with PGA Commissioner Deane Beman announcing he planned to penalize Mac O'Grady for his actions and his remarks as he protested a fine imposed by Beman a year earlier, and why Seve Ballesteros was not eligible to play the Tour (he didn't play the mandatory 15 tournaments in 1985). It also began with a 25 mph wind that made the par-71, 7,100-yard Bay Hill course even more difficult, followed by rain and tornado warnings that made the players sit idle for two days and set up a 36-hole final day for a 54-hole tournament.

Only 15 players broke par in the first round, led by Bob Tway with a five-under 66. He had a two-stroke lead over Forsman, Floyd, Tom Kite and Dan Pohl. He retained the lead for two days as the miserable weather conditions made the course unplayable. When the Saturday round was called off, NBC came up with a live and greatly acclaimed interview show featuring Vin Scully, host Arnold Palmer and Lee Trevino. Defending champion Fuzzy Zoeller, Mark O'Meara, Corey Pavin and Floyd appeared on it, but Tway turned down an invitation, saying, "I felt I could spend my time more wisely." Probably a bad decision, in terms of public relations, and the extra practice didn't seem to do him much good.

Tway's decline began in the middle of the front nine Sunday morning as Forsman and Floyd got their head-to-head battle under way. Forsman's 67 gave him a two-stroke lead on Floyd, Wayne Levi and Scott Simpson as Tway watched the field pass by with a 72. Forsman was very aware that Floyd was his biggest threat. "He seems to thrive on one-on-one situations. I could feel my heart coming out of my chest," he said. "I've watched him many years on television, and there we were, fighting it out."

With nine holes left, Forsman was hanging onto a one-stroke lead. At the 15th hole, Forsman sank an 18-foot birdie putt and Floyd missed a birdie from eight feet, doubling Forsman's lead to two strokes. Minutes later, Forsman's lead was back to two strokes as Floyd chipped in for birdie at 16. And his one-stroke advantage wasn't just on Floyd. Hulbert birdied 15, 16 and 17, putting him in a deadlock with Floyd.

Forsman and Floyd parred 17 and Hulbert parred 18. When he stepped to the tee at the 18th hole, Forsman said he recalled the way he had won his first tournament, the Quad Cities a year earlier, by sinking a 10-foot bogey putt. This time, he vowed, he wouldn't put such pressure on himself.

But four-foot par putts to win can often be as excruciating as 10-footers. Forsman hit the green and was faced with the need to two-putt from 20 feet to win. His first putt was off by four feet. But Forsman made it, then had the final word on O'Grady: "He gave me the inspiration when I needed it. He helped me when I was down and I'll never forget that."

USF&G Classic—$500,000
Winner: Calvin Peete

As a late starter on the PGA Tour—he joined it in 1975, when he was nearly 32—Calvin Peete was making up for lost time. Now, in his 43rd year, he was on a roll that looks as if it will carry him into his PGA Senior Tour career. Peete's runaway victory in the USF&G Classic at Lakewood Country Club in New Orleans, Louisiana, was his 11th in five years, his 12th including his first victory in 1979. It also was his second triumph of the year (the other came in the Tournament of Champions).

Just as at the Bay Hill tournament the week before, the USF&G was troubled by rain. Play on Wednesday and Thursday was washed out, setting up a 36-hole final on Sunday. And just as at Bay Hill, Commissioner Deane Beman, Seve Ballesteros and Mac O'Grady were involved in discussion without settling matters. As defending champion, Ballesteros was permitted to play at New Orleans. But Ballesteros' presence was short-lived. He missed the cut by a stroke with 75–72. Two other "name" players also were absent from the 36-hole windup. Masters champion Bernhard Langer missed the cut with 78–76 and Jack Nicklaus pulled out after the first round because of the death of his mother-in-law.

In the wake of the rain came a wind and a drop in temperature that made the opening 68s by Peete and Nick Faldo seem like much lower than four under par. Pat McGowan was the only other player to break 70 and he was near the top to stay.

Dick Mast, a refugee from the mini-tours, had a five-hole run of birdies and an eagle as he carved out a 64 in the second round, but Peete pitched in for an eagle at the 16th hole and when the day ended he led Mast by a stroke with a 67–135. Nobody knew it, but the tournament was over. Peete was on his stick and he has proved to be one of the game's better front-runners.

Peete shot a 66 in the morning round on Sunday, giving him a five-stroke lead on McGowan, who had moved into second place with a 68. "What are the chances of somebody catching you?" someone asked Peete. "They're not worth a plugged nickel," he replied. He was correct. A birdie by Peete and a bogey by McGowan at the first hole in the afternoon improved Peete's lead to seven strokes and he breezed in from there with a 68 for 269 and a five-stroke margin on runner-up McGowan. Peete's $90,000 payday gave him the money lead with $230,598 and moved him a step closer to his season goal. "I want to be player of the year," he said.

Tournament Players Championship—$900,000
Winner: John Mahaffey

John Mahaffey could empathize with Larry Mize after Mahaffey's victory in the Tournament Players Championship at the TPC Sawgrass course near Jacksonville, Florida. Mize had let victory slip away on the final round, just as Mahaffey had seen U.S. Open victories get away from him at Medinah in 1975 and at Atlanta in 1976. "I know how Larry feels, because I've been there. It's only a matter of time and experience for him," Mahaffey said.

Time and experience earned Mahaffey the PGA Championship in a dramatic playoff with Jerry Pate and Tom Watson at Oakmont in 1978. And the latter gave him the TPC title when the still-maturing Mize fell apart on the finishing holes. Measured monetarily, it was a costly collapse—Mahaffey won $162,000, Mize $97,200. Psychologically, victory could have been a tremendous boost for Mize, who had stumbled after leading in the Heritage and the Kemper Open a year earlier.

"Choke is a word a lot of us don't like," Mize said, "but I guess I did. But they say every time you get in this position you gain something, you learn something. I just know I'm tired of losing." And lose is what Mize did. He took a four-stroke lead on Mahaffey into the final round and lost by one stroke, shooting a final-round 76 for 276 as Mahaffey turned in a 71 for 275. Only one player, Tom Kite, intruded on their private battle in the final round, but Kite faded and tied for fourth place.

The TPC course hardly resembled the dreaded Pete Dye layout that drew such critical complaints when it was opened in 1982. Numerous changes, especially to the greens, had softened it and in the fall of 1985 the greens were changed from Bermuda grass to bent grass. The weather was perfect for all four rounds and the course took a beating. It took a score of 144—even par—to make the cut. And some big names failed to survive it, among them Curtis Strange, the 1985 leading money winner; tournament favorite Calvin Peete and three major tournament winners of the year before—Andy North (U.S. Open), Hubert Green (PGA) and Sandy Lyle (British Open).

As the big names foundered, the little ones stepped forward. Jim Gallagher and Brad Fabel scored the first holes-in-one at the course in the first round, but at the end of the day the leaders at 66 were Ken Green, Bob Tway, Keith Fergus, Tony Sills and Mize. Mize added a 68 in the second round and Bob Murphy, a 43-year-old veteran, tacked a 65 onto his opening 69, deadlocking them for the lead at 134, a 36-hole record for the tournament. One shot back was Dave Rummells, a first-year tourist who tied the record with a 65–135. Rummells, who had broken 70 in only three of his previous 23 Tour rounds, birdied six holes in a row, starting at the 16th (he began his round on the back nine), equaling Tom Watson's tournament record. But Rummells followed that feat with a disastrous 79.

Mize stayed on course in the third round with a 66 for 200, beating the 54-hole record by six strokes. Almost unnoticed, Mahaffey blasted out a 65 that put him in second place, four strokes back. And at the outset of the final round it looked as if Mahaffey would back up and leave the road free for Mize. Mahaffey had to scramble for pars on the first two holes and when Mize birdied the sixth hole the difference was five strokes. Bogeys at the seventh and eighth holes cut Mize's lead to two as Mahaffey birdied No. 8. But Mize birdied the long ninth and when Mahaffey bogeyed the 10th Mize's lead was back up to four strokes.

But Mahaffey is nothing if not patient. He birdied 11. As they went to the 14th tee, Mize still led by three strokes. And that's where he began to unravel. With the pin on the right of the green, he missed on the right and was left with a sure bogey. At 15, he hit a bunker on the wrong side of the green and when he exploded across the green he had another bogey. Meanwhile, Mahaffey was having problems, too. He three-putted the 14th green and missed a six-foot birdie putt at 15. So he still trailed by two strokes at the 16th tee. That's where the big turnaround came. Mize drove into the rough at the 497-yard par-five, hit his approach over the green and bogeyed. Mahaffey ran a four-iron onto the green and two-putted for birdie. Now they were deadlocked. If Mize was choking, it didn't look it as he belted an eight-iron to within six feet of the hole at the island 17th. But he pulled the putt. At the 18th, Mahaffey hit the green, 20 feet short of the hole, and Mize missed on the right. Mize chipped to five feet. Mahaffey putted to within four feet. With a chance to send the tournament into sudden death, or maybe win, Mize missed his putt. Mahaffey unerringly sank the winner.

The victory, his ninth in his 16 years on the tour, marked another milestone in the rebirth of John Mahaffey. His career has been marked by physical problems, marital troubles, a drinking problem and major disappointments. He changed his swing in 1983 in an effort to get more length and with the change came a reversal in attitude. "I had reached a point where I decided that if I was ever going to be competitive again I had to turn my life around," he said. "We don't ever reach our full potential, but we can sure darn try. I want to be the best player I can be."

Greater Greensboro Open—$500,000
Winner: Sandy Lyle

Sandy Lyle has played in, and won, tournaments all over the world, including the 1985 British Open championship. His next ambition, as he headed for the Masters, was to win a tournament on the U.S. PGA Tour. He finally did it before the noisy crowd that makes the Greater Greensboro Open one big party, winning by two strokes over menacing Andy Bean. "He's finally gotten it into his head he can play over here and that's important," Bean said.

Lyle, who played at Greensboro under a sponsor's exemption, had never finished in the top 10 in any of the few tournaments he had played in the U.S. His best finish was a tie for 13th place in the 1986 Tournament of Champions. But charged up by the vociferous fans at Greensboro, he turned in a 68–64–73–70—275 and turned back a challenge by Bean to crack the American tour barrier. "There are 140 guys each week who can win here. In Europe, there might be 25 capable of winning each week. That's a big difference," he said, explaining why his first victory in the U.S. had come with such difficulty.

Because it falls the week before the Masters, the Greensboro, or GGO as it is called, does not attract many of the big-name players, who use the week to prepare for the first major of the year. But there were enough to keep the fans happy and they quickly found a hero in Lyle. The Scotsman is a long hitter, which was to his advantage on the 6,984-yard Forest Oaks Country Club course. The course was playing short because of recent dry weather and for only the second time since 1967, the tournament went four days without rain.

Leonard Thompson came out of the gate for a 66 that gave him a one-stroke lead over David Edwards. But Lyle, with a 68, was just getting warmed up. In the second round he carved out an eight-birdie, no-bogey 64 that tied the course record and gave him a five-stroke lead. A 73 in the third round reduced his lead to three strokes over Tom Purtzer, but Lyle had his wits around him. "All I had to do was keep it under 72 and let the others fire at me," he said afterward.

He kept it under 72 with a 70 and the others fired. But the only one who came close to catching him was Bean, who finished with a 67. When Lyle missed a four-foot birdie putt at the 15th hole after Bean birdied it, the margin between them was one stroke. And that's the way they stood as Bean, playing in a group in front of Lyle, teed off at 18. Bean hit a super shot to the green, 12 feet from the hole. But he left his birdie putt short. Lyle, who used a three-wood at most of the par-fours, cut the dogleg at the 426-yard hole, leaving himself with a three-quarter wedge to the green. He hit his approach 15 feet from the cup. He needed two putts to win. He made it in one.

Deposit Guaranty Classic—$200,000
Winner: Dan Halldorson

Since he teamed with David Barr to win the 1985 World Cup for Canada, Dan Halldorson's game had been in a slump. At Hattiesburg, Mississippi, in the Deposit Guaranty Classic, he finally came out of it, a week too early for Paul Azinger. In what amounted to a 36-hole shootout on the final day, Halldorson and Azinger both shot 66–66 and Halldorson won by two strokes with a 263.

"I finally started playing well. I've been playing so badly, but I finally started making some shots and looked like a golfer," Halldorson said.

Rookie Rocco Mediate, with a 65–66, and Halldorson, with 64–67, led after two rounds, but when the third round was postponed because of rain and a 36-hole windup was scheduled, Azinger was the happiest man. "I love it. You're playing more holes and it gives you a chance to get it going," he said. And get it going, he did. His only problem was Halldorson kept in step with him through the Sunday double round. Halldorson figured Azinger and Scott Hoch were the ones he had to beat and he was correct. Hoch placed third at 268.

Halldorson maintained his two-stroke edge on Azinger after the third round and even though Azinger strung together three birdies in the middle of the final round, he still trailed by a stroke. Azinger finally got his chance at the 17th hole and he blew it. The 17th is a par-five and Azinger hit a three-iron to the green, giving him a putt of less than five feet for an eagle three. But as Halldorson watched from the fairway, Azinger's putt lipped out. Halldorson then reached the green with a three-wood and two-putted for birdie, keeping his slim lead. Azinger's fight was ended.

He three-putted the 18th green and Halldorson parred for a two-stroke decision.

Sea Pines Heritage Classic—$450,000
Winner: Fuzzy Zoeller

South Carolina claims it gave birth to golf in the United States and at the Sea Pines Heritage Classic the bicentennial of that founding was celebrated. Natives and visitors partied every night and boats docked in the Hilton Head Island Harbour constantly blew their foghorns as if it were New Year's Eve.

But the person who had the best reason for celebration was Fuzzy Zoeller, who won a tense duel on the final green for his ninth PGA Tour victory, his second of the year and his second in the Heritage. He also won in 1983. Zoeller went to the 72nd green tied with Greg Norman, Roger Maltbie and Chip Beck and avoided a four-man sudden-death playoff—it was nearly a five-man match—by holing a 12-foot birdie putt for a 71 and 276. Maltbie (69), Norman (70) and Beck (70) tied for second at 277 and Jay Haas (71) just missed making it a five-man tie for second when he failed to sink a six-foot as the foghorns honked.

After earlier rounds of 68, 68, 69, Zoeller went into the final round with a two-stroke lead on Norman, Beck and Haas. That advantage quickly vanished when Zoeller double-bogeyed after a wild drive at the first hole. But he was unperturbed. He had double-bogeyed twice before in the tournament and recovered. But when Zoeller bogeyed the fourth hole and Maltbie went out in 33, Zoeller trailed by three strokes and Norman, Beck and Haas were between him and Maltbie. It was time to get started and Zoeller did by sinking a 30-footer at the 11th hole for his first birdie of the day. At the par-three 14th, Maltbie, playing in the group in front of Zoeller, hit his tee shot over the green and bogeyed. Zoeller nearly sank his seven-iron tee shot, the resultant birdie tying him for the lead. Beck also birdied 14, joining Zoeller, Norman and Maltbie atop the leaderboard with Haas a stroke behind. Beck bogeyed 15 and as they went to the final hole Zoeller, Norman and Maltbie were deadlocked for the lead and Beck and Haas were one stroke behind.

Maltbie's approach was 40 feet away from the hole and he settled for par. Norman had a 15-footer for birdie and missed. Beck hit his iron to within 15 feet, almost on the same spot where Norman had been, Zoeller was three feet closer and Haas was half the distance from the hole that Zoeller was. Beck sank his putt for birdie. If Zoeller missed his and Haas made his, there would be a gang on the tee of the first playoff hole. Zoeller ended it by making his putt. "I got an awful good read from Chip's putt," he said. Haas' miss cost him a few thousand dollars, but nobody seemed to notice.

Dan Halldorson, who had won the Deposit Guaranty Classic the week before, remained on his hot streak for the first two rounds at Harbour Town, taking a one-stroke lead with an opening 66 and maintaining that edge with a 68 on the second round. Then Halldorson's magic ran out. At the same time, Bernhard Langer, the defending champion, had his magic return—briefly. Langer came within a stroke of the course record with a 64 in the third round that pulled him to within five strokes of Zoeller after he barely made the cut. Then he slipped badly with a 75.

Zoeller took charge with a 69 in the third round. The charge ran out at the start of the final round, but somehow he found a way to get it started again just in time to win.

Houston Open—$500,000
Winner: Curtis Strange

In the first round of the Houston Open, when 45 players broke par, Curtis Strange broke his putter. He rapped his putter on the bridge at the island green of the Tournament Players Course at The Woodlands and the head snapped off and plopped into the water. He putted the rest of the way with a sand wedge and that might have cost him a stroke or two.

Spotting Calvin Peete a five-stroke lead also is the wrong thing to do, but Strange was able to surmount the handicap as he ultimately beat Peete head-to-head for his second Houston Open victory. Strange defeated Peete with a birdie putt of a little more than 20 feet at the third playoff hole—No. 18 on the course—after they had tied at 274, which is 14 under par. In 1980, Strange won at Houston by defeating Lee Trevino on the first hole of sudden death.

There probably were many who discarded Strange as a likely champion after his opening 72. And not just because he had to break in a new putter. In front of him were Peete, Tom Watson and Jay Haas, all playing well, and the majority of the best field in the history of the tournament. The shift to The Woodlands attracted some top players who had been absent from the tournament for years.

Peete's 70 in the second round gave him a two-stroke lead and put him five ahead of Strange, who came back with a 68. Mike Sullivan, just trying to make the cut, set the course record with a 63 in the second round, with birdies at seven of his last nine holes. But Sullivan's outburst was a one-shot thing.

The third round quickly developed into a three-man race with Peete, Watson and Haas deadlocked at 11-under 205 at the end of the day. It was Watson's day until the finishing holes. He birdied five of his first six holes before being slowed by a bogey. At the par-five 13, Watson tried to go for the green in two and his ball joined Strange's putterhead. So he took a drop— then hit a sand wedge approach into the cup for a birdie. Watson also birdied 15, putting him 13 under for the tournament. But he bogeyed the difficult 17 and 18. "I had a chance to break away from the pack," he lamented after his 68.

Meanwhile, Haas, who had four birdies and an eagle, bogeyed 17 after hitting a wild tee shot and settled for a 67. Peete birdied 11 and 12 and parred in, a performance he was to repeat in the final round with tragic consequences. Strange, almost unnoticed, had a 68 and trailed by three strokes.

Watson, with a 71, and Haas, with a 74, slowly dropped back in the final round as the battle became one between Peete and Strange. And for a while it looked as if it were only Peete. At the fateful 13th, Peete bounced his second shot onto the green and two-putted for a birdie, putting him 14 under. He got no lower. Strange stayed on his heels with birdies at 10 and 11 and got to within one stroke with a birdie at 15. As Peete marched in place, Strange caught him with a 15-foot birdie putt at 17. Not about to let his grasp of the lead slip away, Strange scrambled out of deep rough to save par at 18, then had to watch as Peete's attempt at a winning birdie putt from 15 feet failed to drop. Strange had a 66, Peete a 69.

The first hole of sudden death, No. 16, was a repeat of the final hole, Strange saving par, Peete missing a birdie putt. At the second hole, both missed birdie putts from 15 feet. At the third hole, both had putts of a little more than 20 feet for birdie. Strange's putt just made it to the hole. "It kind of fell in drunk," he said. Peete, who had led or shared the lead from the outset of the tournament, missed by an inch in his bid to send it to a fourth hole.

Panasonic Las Vegas Invitational—$1,140,000
Winner: Greg Norman

The Panasonic Las Vegas Invitational is a five-day, 90-hole pro-am played over three different courses—Las Vegas Country Club, Desert Inn Country Club and Spanish Trail Golf and Country Club. The final two rounds, everybody plays at Las Vegas CC.

Given the format, the change of courses and the long rounds (about six-hour average), Greg Norman's first victory of the year was remarkable indeed. After opening with a 73, Norman played the final 72 holes in 260 as he tied the PGA record for 90 holes with a 333 that had a touch of disappointment. The blond Australian wanted to break the record, but he three-putted the last two greens.

By the time his putter broke down, Norman's conquest was well assured. He won by seven strokes over Dan Pohl, who hung on to take second-place money of $124,200, by far his biggest paycheck. Norman collected $207,000, putting him atop the money leaders.

However, the man who could have benefited most was Donnie Hammond, one of the little-known players who took center stage in the early rounds at Las Vegas. Panasonic had offered a $250,000 bonus to anybody who could win the Pebble Beach AT&T or Bob Hope and the Las Vegas Invitational. Fuzzy Zoeller won at Pebble Beach, but after three rounds at Las Vegas he was eight strokes behind, just barely in the tournament. Hammond, on the other hand, was tied for the lead after 54 holes. He had won the Hope in a playoff and now he could collect $457,000 with a victory in the desert. Norman quickly squelched that dream as he strode through the last two rounds like an Internal Revenue Service agent at tax time, taking the biggest chunk out of the million-dollar-plus purse.

Until Norman got in gear, it was a tournament for the have-nots and the little-knowns. Perhaps they felt more comfortable playing in a prolonged pro-am with a change in venue each day. Paul Azinger and Jeff Grygiel, with 64s, led the first round, then retreated. Up stepped Bob Lohr with a 65 for 132 and the second-round lead by two strokes over Ken Knox and Mike Hulburt. Norman bounced back from his opening 73 for a 63. He trailed by four, but his charge was just beginning.

Lohr shot a 70 and Hammond a second straight 66 in the third round for a 202, but the field was so tightly bunched it looked as if even the man in last place could win. The field was cut after 54 holes and it took a score of five under to survive it. One of those who just did was Tom Watson. Two under with 10 holes to go. Watson made successive eagles, then made three birdies on the back nine to pull to within five strokes of the leaders. Norman, meanwhile, turned in a 68 and lurked two shots off the pace.

The final two rounds are played at Las Vegas CC, which was equivalent to a jackpot for Norman. He blasted out a 64 that gave him a three-stroke lead over Pohl, who had a 66. Watson made a short-lived charge at the outset of the final round, but Norman kept turning out the birdies and pars until he bogeyed 17. By then, his lead had swelled from six to seven strokes to eight strokes, the only battle remaining the one for second place. Pohl had a two-stroke lead over Larry Nelson and Steve Pate when he teed off at the final hole. Then came the only real excitement of the final round. The difference between second place and a tie for second place is about $40,000. Pohl hit a six-iron into the water in front of the 18th green. But he managed to get it up and down for a bogey and claim second place by himself.

Byron Nelson Classic—$600,000
Winner: Andy Bean

Everybody seemed to have a different opinion about the new Tournament Players Course at the Las Colinas Sports Club in Irving, Texas. Some liked it, some disliked it. And everybody had a different idea about how to play it.

Andy Bean's idea turned out to be the best—keep the ball in play, preferably on the fairway. The TPC layout was only 6,767 yards, one of the shortest of the stadium courses, and was tight and doglegged with small greens. It demanded accuracy. According to the PGA statistics, Bean and Mark Wiebe tied for 32nd in the percentage of fairways hit (.696), but figures can be misleading. Bean beat Wiebe by one stroke with 66–68–67–68—269 for his second victory of the year.

"The trick here was getting the ball in the fairway. I did that throughout the tournament and that's why I'm very pleased," said Bean after he survived a tense final hole. After Wiebe birdied the 17th hole, Bean hit a four-iron into the bunker guarding the 217-yard hole and bogeyed. Suddenly, what had been at one time a four-stroke lead had diminished to one stroke. Wiebe nearly holed a 20-foot chip shot at 18, then waited for Bean as Payne Stewart, his playing companion, told him "strange things happen at this hole." A year earlier, bunker troubles cost Stewart a two-stroke lead at the final green and he lost to Bob Eastwood in a playoff. However, Bean avoided the sand and two-putted for a winning par.

Second place wasn't a total disappointment for Wiebe. In the previous three tournaments he had failed to make the cut. But in the Nelson he was in the hunt all the way. Mark Hayes jumped out to a 64 in a first round that was marked by treacherous Texas winds and Bean stepped into a tie for second with his 66. Hayes and the wind let up in the second round and Bean went on top by one stroke over Wiebe (69–66) with a 68.

Three inches of rain hit the course Friday night and Saturday morning, delaying play for two hours and 16 minutes. A lift-and-clean rule was invoked when play began and, naturally, par took a beating. Bean's 67 gave him a two-stroke lead over Wiebe, Stewart, Craig Stadler, Bobby Wadkins and George Burns after 54 holes and Bean figured he would need another 67 the next day to win. But nobody came up with a big round and when Bean birdied seven, eight, nine and 11 and Wiebe bogeyed 15, Bean had a comfortable four-stroke lead. Well, seemingly comfortable. His bogeys at 15 and 17 and Wiebe's birdie at 17 prevented him from just strolling in.

Colonial National Invitation—$500,000
Winner: Dan Pohl

For his first eight years on the PGA Tour, Dan Pohl was known for his prodigious driving and his ability to come close without winning. He led the PGA Tour in average driving distance in 1980 and 1981 and was second for the period 1980–85. But his best finish was second, including a playoff loss to Craig Stadler in the 1982 Masters—a defeat that was not upsetting—and a playoff defeat by Phil Blackmar in the 1985 Hartford Open.

But Pohl learned from his experiences and it all paid off with a victory in the Colonial National Inviation at Colonial Country Club in Fort Worth, Texas, as Pohl beat another hard-luck player, Payne Stewart, with a birdie on the first hole of a sudden-death playoff. It was the third loss in three playoffs for Stewart—all in Texas. "Texas owes me one at least," said Stewart, who played his college golf at Southern Methodist University in Dallas. "But if I let these second-place finishes bother me, my banker would hate me."

Pohl said he went from drive-for-show to putt-for-dough when he began tempering his power about 1983. He went to a stiff shaft and began hitting his drives with a cut instead of a hook. "The combination of that with the maturity of having been in these circumstances has made me a better player," Pohl said. "It's a hard lesson to learn when everybody wants to see you hit it a long way."

Pohl shot 68–69 in the first two rounds, leaving him one stroke behind the co-leaders, Howard Twitty and Dave Edwards, and two strokes in front of Stewart. Then everybody sat down for a day as a thunderstorm wiped out the third round and reduced the tournament to 54 holes. Tom Watson made the biggest move in the final round with an eight-under-par 64, but he was too far back at the start of the round to put any real pressure on the leaders, ultimately tying for third place with Bill Rogers and Bernhard Langer.

Twitty and Edwards quickly backed up in the final round and the race became a three-man affair involving Pohl, Stewart and Gene Sauers, who led the first round with a 66. Sauers ran out of petrol on the final nine. Now it was Pohl and Stewart and Pohl slipped with a bogey at 15. But he quickly recovered for a birdie at 16. Still, he had to sink a 10-foot putt at the 18th green to force the playoff. Pohl finished with a 68 and Stewart with a 66 for 205.

Two strokes by Pohl later, the tournament was over. The playoff began at the par-three 16th hole. Stewart hit his tee shot over the green; Pohl rapped a three iron to within 12 feet of the hole. Stewart chipped to within two feet. Pohl sank his 12-footer.

Pohl finished the tournament far behind the leaders in average driving distance, but he led in greens hit in par, and that's one statistic that paid off.

Memorial Tournament—$577,730
Winner: Hal Sutton

Off his scintillating victory in the Masters, golf fans had to think Jack Nicklaus could win any tournament when he's within distance of the lead. At Muirfield Village Golf Club in Dublin, Ohio, they know he can. Even the players figure Nicklaus is not out of it until the last putt is sunk.

It was that premise that helped Hal Sutton win the Memorial Tournament with a score of 271, nine strokes under the tournament record for one of the most difficult courses on the tour. "I made up my mind that Jack was probably going to get hot. I just wanted to answer whatever he dished out," Sutton said, explaining the final-round 68 that left him with a four-stroke margin over Don Pooley and six over Nicklaus, who tied for fifth place.

It was the second victory of the year for Sutton and it was earned under trying circumstances. He was in the middle of obtaining a divorce from his second wife, Denee, whom he married in October of 1985. That was at least part of the reason he had missed the cut in four of seven tournaments, including the Masters. Then there was the Muirfield Village course and the imposing figure of the course's designer, Nicklaus. A pre-tournament rain had softened the course and it never did dry out, which is why the scoring was so low. Twelve others beside Sutton broke the former 72-hole record. But the greens remained fast, hitting a 12 on the Stimpmeter in the third round.

Nicklaus, with a tip from his teachers, Jack Grout and Phil Rodgers, that changed his hip position, came flying out of the gate with a six-under-par 66 that put him a stroke behind Dan Halldorson and the race was on. Halldorson won the Deposit Guaranty Classic the same weekend that Nicklaus won the Masters. Halldorson would have tied the Muirfield Village record of 64 had he not missed a 14-inch putt at the first hole. Sutton was one of the many who broke 70 with a 68.

Nicklaus came back with a 70 and Halldorson a 71, tying them with Doug Tewell, who had a 70, and Pooley, 67, for the halfway lead at 136. Sutton, with a 69, was one of six who lurked a stroke behind. Saturday was moving day and Sutton moved, eagling the 15th hole and birdieing 16 and 17 en route to a 66 that put him three strokes in front of Tewell, Pooley and Halldorson. Nicklaus, with a 72, was five strokes back and said, "If I shoot a good round it will be exciting." He said something similar after the third round of the Masters. The words were not lost on his fans . . . nor Sutton.

The fans around Muirfield Village on Sunday expected a charge from Nicklaus and cheered every good shot he hit. But Nicklaus didn't manage enough good ones as he shot a 69. It was Sutton and Mark O'Meara who caused the loudest cheers. O'Meara shot a 66 that tied him for third place with Johnny Miller, five strokes behind Sutton.

Sutton learned what it was like to be stalked by Nicklaus when he won the PGA Championship at Riviera in 1983 with Nicklaus dogging his every step. And when he three-putted the fifth green at Muirfield Village, if looked as if he might be in for another tense showdown. But he didn't let it happen. After the bogey he made two straight birdies and made four birdies on the back nine as Nicklaus' charge died for a 68.

Kemper Open—$500,000
Winner: Greg Norman

"I don't feel snakebit, but I do feel dejected. But something's wrong if you lose and you're not upset," said Larry Mize after the Kemper Open at the Congressional Country Club in Bethesda, Maryland. Maybe he didn't feel snakebit, but he sure looked as if he had fang marks on his psyche. And rightfully so. For the second year in a row in the Kemper and the third time in a year, Mize let victory slip away from him. This time it took a little longer.

Greg Norman caught Mize with a six-under-par 66 in the final round, then beat him on the sixth hole of a sudden-death playoff as Mize met a watery demise. On the sixth extra hole—the third time they played the 18th hole the final day—Norman won with a routine par when an eight iron out of the rough by Mize went over the green and into three inches of water on the other. A drop, a pitch into water on the other side of the green and Mize had a double bogey six and another second place. "It was a little sad to win the tournament the way we finished up the 78th hole. You'd rather fight it out to the death than basically have the hole given to you," Norman said.

Perhaps, in the end, the hole was given to Norman, but he did come from three strokes behind in the final round and he did shoot a 66 for 277 and he did sink a nine-foot putt for birdie at the 71st hole, a critical birdie as Mize missed the fairway with his drive at 18, hit his second into a difficult lie in a bunker, then failed to get it up and down for par. A year earlier, Mize held a four-stroke lead with nine holes to play and Bill Glasson won with a 45-foot birdie putt at the final green. And in the Tournament Players Championship earlier in the year he also failed to hold a lead on the final nine.

The players said adieu to Congressional as plans called for a move to the new TPC course at Avenel in Potomac, Maryland, in 1987. The six-hole playoff made it a memorable goodbye, but there was some memorable—and not so memorable—golf played before the final round. Long-hitting Fred Couples, whose first tour victory came in the Kemper in 1983, tied the course record with an eight-under 30–34—64 in the first round and took a three-stroke lead. The next day he plunged to a 77, the dam bursting with a quadruple seven at the 211-yard No. 16.

As Couples retreated, on came Charles Bolling to take the lead at the halfway point with a 70 for 137, giving him a one-stroke lead over, among others, Bobby Clampett, who tied the record with a 64. Bolling began the third round by four-putting the first green and as Couples had done a day earlier, he took a disastrous 77.

Meanwhile, Norman and Mize were playing steady golf, Mize with 67–71 and Norman with 72–69. Both shot 70s in the third round, giving Mize a one-stroke lead over Mike Reid and a three-stroke advantage on Norman. Mize shook off Reid with birdies at the 15th and 16th holes in the final round and briefly had a two-stroke lead on Norman. But Norman, playing in the group immediately ahead of Mize, birdied the 17th hole, cutting Mize's lead to a solitary stroke. Norman barely managed to avoid the water at the 18th hole and parred. And when Mize bogeyed, they were off on the longest playoff since John Cook beat Johnny Miller in the 1983 Canadian Open.

Norman saved par with a 12-foot putt at the first playoff hole and Mize got his par from about the same distance at the second. Then came the fateful third trip to No. 18, giving Norman his second victory of the year and pushing his earnings to an almost unbelievable $447,109 halfway through the season.

Manufacturers Hanover Westchester Classic—$600,000
Winner: Bob Tway

Bob Tway's victory in the Westchester Classic at Westchester Country Club in Rye, New York, was a masterful performance, especially considering he was only in his second year on the tour. Unruffled by an opening 73 that left him on the brink of elimination, Tway fought back into contention, shrugged off the specter of the veteran Raymond Floyd in the final round and when the heat was on, Tway made the shots he needed to score his second victory of the year.

Going into the final round, much of the attention was centered on Floyd and Mike Reid, who were tied with Tway at 205, eight under par. The third round was played in a rain that at times became a downpour, conditions that delighted Reid, whose 68 was low round of the day. Much was made of Floyd's experience and how it would make a difference. Even Floyd acknowledged that: "I've been there many times before. I know what it is to win and what you have to do to win."

But Tway was not shaken. "I don't care how many times he's been there. I've got as good a chance to win as anybody," he said. And, indeed, it was Tway, the second-year man, who handled the pressure best in the final round. Reid shot a 72 and his fifth-place winnings pushed his 10-year earnings past $1 million, the first man to reach that plateau without winning a tournament. And Floyd stumbled to a 77 that left him doubting his game on the eve of the U.S. Open.

And Tway? With Willie Wood, a former teammate at Oklahoma State University, and Scott Simpson applying the pressure, he overcame a few errant drives to save par at the 16th and 17th holes. Faced with the prospect of a playoff after Wood had birdied the par-five 18th hole, Tway shook off another drive that flew right and hit a 110-yard sand wedge to within three feet of the hole for the birdie that wrapped it up. Tway's closing 67 gave him a 72-hole total of 272; Wood finished 66–273.

Tway's opening 73 left him eight strokes behind Jay Haas, who had nine birdies, and Tom Sieckmann. Wood and Tway both shot eight-under-par 63s in the second round, Wood moving into a first-place tie with Brett Upper (66) and Sieckmann (69) and Tway vaulting to within two strokes of the lead. Sieckmann and Upper failed to break par in the final two rounds. Floyd, who added a 67 to his opening 68, trailed by a stroke, but he would have been tied for the lead if not for a penalty stroke he called on himself when his ball moved slightly on the third green.

The third round was punctuated by rain and the under-par rounds dropped considerably. Tway, who had hit all of Westchester's small greens in his 63 in the second round, played nearly as well for a 69 in the third round, putting himself in position to win. Wood, who had a 73 in the third round, and Simpson, the 1984 Westchester winner, put the heat on Tway, Simpson getting into the chase with six consecutive birdies starting at the fifth hole. But Tway was up to the challenge.

Provident Classic—$300,000
Winner: Brad Faxon

If Brad Faxon had had his druthers, he would have been in Southampton, New York, instead of Hixson, Tennessee, in the second week in June. Southampton is where they played the U.S. Open, and Faxon was there until the afternoon before the first round as first alternate, hoping he would get a call to tee it up. No one dropped out, so at midnight on Wednesday he was in Hixson, an entry in the Provident Classic that was to be played over a course he had never seen.

It turned out to be a nice turn of events for Faxon. "Fortunately, my caddy was from Chattanooga. He turned me in the right direction and that's where I went," said Faxon, who won by one stroke over Scott Hoch with a 19-under-par 67–62–69–63—261 and collected his best paycheck ever, $54,000.

The Provident Classic was played at Valleybrook Golf and Country Club near Chattanooga and it's the kind of course on which a sick game can get well quickly. But it's also a course on which a player can lose ground with a 67 or 68. Faxon's opening 67 left him three strokes behind, but his seven-birdie, one-eagle 62 in the second round gave him the lead at 129. Hoch shot a 66 and Clarence Rose a 65 in the third round and Faxon slipped two strokes back with a 69 and Rose predicted a shootout in the final round.

It certainly was, and at the finish Faxon was the only one left standing. He birdied six holes from No. 4 through No. 11 and suddenly he was three strokes ahead of Hoch and six in front of Rose. Hoch refused to give up as he carved out a 66 that fell one stroke short as Faxon played out a brilliant 63.

Georgia-Pacific Atlanta Classic—$500,000
Winner: Bob Tway

Bob Tway had been in contention until the final, fateful holes of the U.S. Open and would have been excused had he had a letdown the following week. After all, he had won at Westchester the week before the Open. But Tway refused to get down from his high. "After the Open, I told Tammie (his wife) 'I think I can win in Atlanta.' I knew the course and I was playing well."

Tway was born in Marietta, Georgia, just five miles away from Atlanta Country Club, and his legion of fans grew with every shot that moved him closer to his third triumph of the year. And they had plenty to cheer as Tway strode to an eight-under-par 64 in the final round and won by two strokes over Hal Sutton with a 269. The $90,000 he won gave him $446,119 for the year, the most money won by a second-year player.

Sutton, who, like Tway, had a shot at winning the Open the week before, was nearly shattered by his second-place finish. He was certain he was going to win after his third-round 67 gave him a two-stroke lead going into the final round. "I'm going to make a lot of birdies and they're going to have to come after me," he said. And he did make a lot of birdies—five—in the final round, but a balky putter cost him three bogeys and several possible birdies as he watched Tway race past him. "I thought I'd have to shoot 64 or 65 to win," said Tway and he made it easy with seven birdies ranging from a few inches to 10 feet en route to a 64.

Some of the starring cast from the Open was at Atlanta, including champion Ray Floyd and third-round leader Greg Norman. But Atlanta Country Club was nowhere as difficult as Shinnecock Hills. It seemed as if everybody broke par in the first two rounds, Sutton and Rick Fehr taking the first-round lead with 66s and Doug Tewell moving one stroke ahead with a 64–132 in the second round. Tway trailed by a stroke after two rounds, but when he shot a 71 and Sutton turned in a 67 in the third round, Tway was four back and Sutton seemingly was in control.

In the final round, Sutton's first challenge came from Mark O'Meara, who exchanged the lead with him until Sutton birdied the sixth and seventh holes and O'Meara bogeyed the ninth. O'Meara also bogeyed 11 and 12 and became a non-factor. Scott Hoch rallied for birdies at the 14th and 15th holes and Norman came storming in with a 64 as they tied O'Meara and Willie Wood for third place at 273.

Meanwhile, Tway, who trailed by three strokes with nine holes to go, made his move on the back nine. At holes 10, 11 and 12, Sutton went par-par-bogey and Tway par-birdie-birdie and the three-stroke swing moved Tway into a share of the lead. Sutton went one up with a birdie at 13, but Tway countered with a birdie at 14 and when Tway birdied 15 and Sutton bogeyed the hole, Tway was two strokes ahead. And just to make certain Sutton, playing two groups behind him, would have no shot at a playoff, Tway birdied the 18th hole, too. "I'm not out here for the money; I'm out here to win championships. And I'm not happy with my play today," said Sutton.

Canadian Open—$487,500
Winner: Bob Murphy

He's paunchy, he has a bad back, he wears glasses, he's 43, his last victory was in 1975 and most weekends he's doing color commentary when a tournament is on the CBS network. His name is Bob Murphy and he added another chapter to the Over-the-Hill Gang Strikes Again when he won the Canadian Open in Oakville, Ontario.

"Last year I told my wife I was going out for a six-week stretch and if I didn't play better, I'd quit. I finished fourth and then second and that told me I could win," Murphy said after the fifth victory of a pro career that began in 1968. Murphy shot 71–70–68–71—280, eight under par on the demanding Glen Abbey course and won by three strokes over Greg Norman. The $108,000 he collected was more than he earned in any year since he finished with $127,471 in 1975, his best year.

No Canadian has won the Canadian Open since 1954, but the country's chances were improved when Commissioner Deane Beman allowed the field to be increased from 144 to 153 players by adding Canadians. As a result, 32

Canadians, the highest number in modern times, were entered. Two of them, Dave Barr and Dan Halldorson, raised national hopes until the final round. Hale Irwin, playing nearly flawless golf, took the first-round lead with a 68 and Halldorson was one of six who trailed him by a stroke.

Andy Bean's second straight 69 gave him the second-round lead at 138. Barr, with a 71, was tied with Murphy, Irwin, Bob Tway and Mac O'Grady at 141. O'Grady was awaiting the decision on his appeal of a $5,000 fine and a six-tournament suspension handed down by Beman, but that didn't seem to bother his game. The cut came at 149 and caught Norman packing his bags after a 72–76.

Granted a reprieve, Norman told PGA Tour officials "I'm going to shoot a 66 today," before he teed off in the third round. He did even better than that, tying the course record with a 62 with nine birdies and an eagle. After bogeying the second hole, Norman said, "What the heck, let's just go out and have an enjoyable day". He played the front nine in 30 and a lipped eagle putt at No. 18 prevented him from breaking the course record. But suddenly he was in a tie for second place at 210 with O'Grady and Davis Love III, who both birdied the 18th hole, and one stroke behind Murphy, who also finished with a birdie at the downwind 18th.

The field was bunched behind them. Barr was two strokes back and Halldorson, three. It appeared that Murphy, unused to the rigors of playing under pressure, would have more than he could handle. But it was the others who folded. "I used my experience. I knew patience would be the big thing today," Murphy said. Norman kept hitting poor drives at the wrong time, but nevertheless held on for a 73 and second place. O'Grady had taken the lead in the middle of the front nine and was hitting his ball prodigiously (tournament statistics showed he averaged 323.5 yards with his driver) before a storm caused a suspension of play with Murphy on the 12th tee. Because he was hitting the ball so far, O'Grady attempted to go for the green with his second shot at a par-five hole after play resumed and came up short, hitting a stone wall and landing in a creek. O'Grady went double-bogey, bogey and Murphy was in front to stay.

Canon Sammy Davis Jr. Greater Hartford Open—$600,000
Winner: Mac O'Grady

For more than a year, Mac O'Grady had been the center of a storm. Accused of insulting a volunteer at the 1984 New Orleans Tournament, O'Grady had been fined $500 by Commissioner Deane Beman, an action that unloosed charges by O'Grady against Beman that ultimately resulted in O'Grady's being fined $5,000 and suspended for six tournaments. O'Grady and his attorney fought the suspension, knowing it might cost O'Grady tens of thousands of dollars in winnings. The Tour season was building to a peak with the big-money tournaments.

O'Grady was still awaiting the result of his final appeal (it was denied) the week of the Greater Hartford Open, but that was secondary. He was a last-minute entry at Hartford and he almost didn't come out for the last round because his wife was suffering severe stomach pains. O'Grady is amazing. Despite the lengthy controversy, his golf game seemed to improve every week. And at Hartford, it hit an apex. O'Grady turned in one of the finest final rounds ever as he shot a 62 and finally scored his first victory when Roger Maltbie missed a three-foot putt on the first hole of sudden death.

"This game will be kind to you at times and the game will crucify you at times," O'Grady said. "Today was my day to celebrate. There are moments when you spread your wings and the molecules take over. This was the day for me. God Bless America. This is amazing that I can give thanks to my United Nations of friends on Fourth of July weekend."

O'Grady shot 71–69–67–62—269 and Maltbie 66–67–70–66—269 at the Tournament Players Club in Cromwell, Connecticut, but for three rounds O'Grady was just a face in the crowd knowing he could soon have an unscheduled vacation. The last time he had won was in the Mission Viejo Amateur in 1971, before his 17 attempts to obtain a PGA Tour card.

Tim Simpson, mired in a season-long slump, had taken the week off for a vacation before the Hartford and it seemed to pay off. He opened with a 64 that was interrupted by a 65-minute thunderstorm, then came back with a 66 that gave him a record for the new TPC course and a two-stroke lead on Tom Watson.

Saturday was Watson's day . . . almost. He sank birdie putts of 50, 12 and four feet on the second, third and fourth holes to take the lead. At the seventh hole, Watson knocked an iron to within four feet of the cup. He missed the birdie putt by eight inches . . . then missed the backhander coming back, a careless action that cost him the outright lead after 54 holes. Watson bogeyed the 18th hole for a 70 that left him in a tie with Kenny Knox at 202. O'Grady trailed by five strokes and Maltbie, by one.

After getting the word from his wife that she would be all right, O'Grady went to the practice green prior to the start of the final round and made a change that was to prove amazing. "When I started out I figured I had tried 8,492 different putting strokes during my life. Before the round, I must have thought about using 30 or 40 more different strokes, but, lo and behold, I made a birdie putt at the second hole and it started snowballing."

O'Grady sank a 15-footer at the second hole and followed with birdie putts of 24, 14 and 27 feet on the next three and the charge was ignited. He birdied No. 7 from 13 feet and sank a 90-foot chip shot for an eagle three at the ninth hole as he made the turn in 30. He birdied Nos. 10, 13 and 17 with putts ranging from eight to 32 feet and sank par putts of 10 and four feet at the last two holes. Then he had to sit and wait for Maltbie, playing 70 minutes behind him.

Maltbie acted as if he were going to avoid extra holes. At the 17th hole, he hit a seven iron to within three inches of the hole for a tap-in birdie. A birdie at No. 18 would give him the victory. But Maltbie's six-iron approach stopped 25 feet below the hole and he left his birdie putt 18 inches short. "You want to give yourself a chance, but you don't want to do something crazy," Maltbie said of the first putt.

The first playoff hole was the 172-yard No. 16. O'Grady's seven iron hit the right fringe and bounced to within seven feet of the hole; Maltbie's six iron came up 45 feet short. Maltbie lipped out his first putt, the ball going three feet past the hole. O'Grady two-putted. It looked as if they would play another hole. But Maltbie, who had scored two of his five victories in sudden death, missed the tying putt.

O'Grady, who said he cried for 30 minutes after blowing up in the final round of the Canadian Open a week earlier, had tears in his eyes again, this time of joy.

Anheuser-Busch Classic—$500,000
Winner: Fuzzy Zoeller

For those who watched the final round of the Anheuser-Busch Classic on television, it was just a tournament for second place. Fuzzy Zoeller had wrapped up the championship when the show came on. The only man with a valid chance of catching Zoeller was Jodie Mudd. It quickly became apparent that Mudd's real battle was to hang on to second.

Zoeller trailed Richard Zokol by five strokes at the start of the hot and steamy day. The weather was perfect for Zoeller's chronic back problem. He picked up 15 strokes on Zokol with a 64 and had his third victory of the year with a 10-under-par 274. Mudd had a 69 for 276, and the $54,000 he collected was $20,000 more than Joey Sindelar earned for placing third.

Zoeller just bided his time through the first three rounds, let others strut their way across the stage. But he birdied three of the first five holes, saved par after hitting into the water at the third hole and went out with 33, putting him six under with nine holes to play. "I figured I had a chance, since no one else was making a move," Zoeller said. He birdied Nos. 11, 12, 14 and 15.

"I looked at the leaderboard and saw Fuzzy was 10 under. I knew I had my work cut out for me, but I thought I could make a few birdies," Mudd said. Zoeller had run out of birdies, but not the ability to make some near-impossible pars. At the par-four 16, Zoeller heeled his drive into the trees. He had 205 yards to the green and he got there with a four iron. He parred, and behind him everyone except Mudd backed up. But Mudd wasn't going forward either. He bogeyed 13, but although he regained the stroke at the 15th, he failed to birdie the par-five 16, missing a six-footer, and that proved costly.

Mudd was a leading character until Zoeller went into his final act. Mudd and Adrian Stills, a rookie who had missed the cut eight times in 12 previous tournaments, tied for the first-round lead with 65s. Tony Sills, whose personal and family medical history could fill a book, had a 65 in the second round, putting him in a deadlock for first place with Mudd, who had a 70.

(A comic aside: Bill Kratzert hit a ball into the water at the first and third holes and hit his drive out-of-bounds at the seventh hole. At which point he learned there were no more balls in his bag—his caddie had taken most of them out to reduce the weight—and he withdrew.)

The heat seemed to get to everybody in the third round and Zokol took over the lead at eight-under 205 with a 67. Sills had a 75. Stills a 73. Kenny Knox, who was tied with Mudd for second place, two strokes behind Zokol, had a 77. Gene Sauers and Hal Sutton, tied for fourth, stumbled to 79 and 76, respectively. And the battle-hardened Zoeller came flying home with his beat-the-telecast game.

Hardee's Classic—$400,000
Winner: Mark Wiebe

There were two winners in the Hardee's Classic at Oakwood Country club in Coal Valley, Illinois, and it was difficult to decide who was the happier. Mark Wiebe won the tournament with a 69–65–66–68—268 for his second victory in three years on the tour, and obviously he was delighted. Curt Byrum finished in second place, a stroke behind Wiebe, and the $43,200 he collected felt like a victory to him. Byrum lost his tour card after the 1985 season and was trying to eke out a living by playing in mini-tour events and getting in whatever regular tournaments he could. He got his chance in the Hardee's Classic and made the most of it. Byrum's $43,200 second-place check earning him an exemption for the rest of the year and putting him in position to regain his card in 1987.

Byrum had a chance to win until the 71st hole. He went to the fateful par-three 17th with a one-stroke lead on Wiebe. Suddenly, he was a stroke behind as he bogeyed and Wiebe sank a 13-foot birdie putt. That's the way they finished, with Byrum two strokes ahead of third-place Pat Lindsey.

Wiebe never was far out of contention. Byrum was up and down. Byrum opened with a 64 that left him a stroke behind Bob Lohr. A 70 in the second round gave Byrum a share of second with Wiebe and three others, a stroke behind Russ Cochran (66–67), and Byrum took the lead by himself with another 64 in the third round. Wiebe's 66 put him two strokes behind going into the final round. Wiebe started the round birdie-birdie and grabbed the lead, but three bogeys at the end of the front nine dropped him a stroke behind and caused him to think he had lost the tournament. It was a thought that lingered until the 17th hole.

Buick Open—$500,000
Winner: Ben Crenshaw

The opinions about Ben Crenshaw flew after he finished the 1985 season with only $25,814 the year after he had won the Masters. Even Crenshaw, who had lost 18 pounds, didn't know what his problem was.

He made a video tape on putting and when he viewed it, he noticed his hands and knees shook. He was hitting three irons where he'd formerly hit five irons. Finally, he saw a doctor, at the insistence of his new wife, Julie, and his father. The diagnosis: a hyperactive thyroid gland. He was prescribed an iodine solution and his weight and golf game began to come back. He tied for sixth in the U.S. Open and played well in the British Open. He went directly from Turnberry to Warwick Hills Country Club in Grand Blanc, Michigan, and it all came back in the Buick Open.

Playing like the Crenshaw of old, scrambling out of trouble, putting well and turning in the low scores in a tournament where low scoring was a necessity, Crenshaw won his first tournament since Augusta, beating J.C. Snead and Doug Tewell by one stroke with 69–67–66–68—270. Crenshaw found only one hole from which he couldn't extricate himself, hitting his drive out-of-bounds at the fourth hole in the second round. That triple bogey was the only time he slipped over par on a hole in the tournament.

Warwick Hills was 7,014 yards, but its immaculate condition and a light rain that fell late in the first round made it a tournament for the birdie-shooters. It took 141, three under par, to make the cut and many got their birdies in strings of three, four or more. Crenshaw followed his triple bogey with four straight birdies.

Rookie Davis Love III and Billy Pierot, who finally earned a tour card after "seven or eight" misses, led the first round with seven-under-par 65s. The long-hitting Love added a 67 in the second round, giving him a three-stroke lead. Crenshaw trailed by four. Love's driving got shaky in the third round and a 70 dropped him into a tie for first place with Crenshaw, Tom Purtzer (66) and Steve Pate (65). Love kept going backwards in the final round, his 71 leaving him in a tie for fifth place with Bobby Wadkins, three strokes behind Crenshaw.

The final round became a battle among Crenshaw, Tewell and Snead. Tewell couldn't get his putts to drop, four times on the last five holes flirting with the cup without hitting the bottom. Snead birdied the last hole to tie Tewell, but seemed to be bothered by the noisy crowd that obviously was rooting for Crenshaw.

Crenshaw gave the fans their money's worth, three times avoiding possible disaster. Although Crenshaw made two birdies on the front nine, he temporarily gave the lead to Tewell, playing two groups in front. In the second round, Crenshaw's threesome was warned about playing too slowly, and at the 10th fairway in the final round Crenshaw, Purtzer and Pate were given another slow-play warning. "I lost my rhythm. The next three holes were a blur," said Crenshaw.

His vision cleared just in time. At the 13th hole, Crenshaw hit a four-iron approach under a spruce, about 60 feet to the left of the flag. He couldn't hit it right-handed. So he turned his nine iron upside down, hit it left-handed and pulled off one of the greatest shots of the 1986 season, the ball rolling onto the green and stopping six feet away from the hole. He birdied and made birdie at the next hole, too.

Maybe those were the shots that won the tournament for Crenshaw, but he wasn't finished yet. Leading by one stroke, he hit his drive into a clump of trees and the ball stopped in deep trouble: six inches behind a tree root, with a tree six feet in front of him and trees on either side. "I had to miss the tree in front of me by eight inches," Crenshaw said afterward. He did just that, knocking the ball onto the green and parring. Crenshaw called an eight-foot putt for par at 17 "desperate," and maybe it would have been for the Crenshaw of 1985. But this was the new Crenshaw—"Dave Marr kids me I'm on my 21st comeback"—and the putt was routine.

Western Open—$500,000
Winner: Tom Kite

The Western Open is a throwback. It is the only tournament that supplies caddys for the players. It is one of the traditional tournaments on the tour—if anyone had thought about the professional Grand Slam 40 years ago, the Western Open would have been included.

The Western Open has declined in stature over the years, but it's still a favorite tournament played on one of the tour's more difficult courses, Butler National. And it was appropriate that the 1986 Western was won by a traditionalist, Tom Kite.

It wasn't easy.

Kite had to come from seven strokes behind on the final day, then win on the first hole of sudden death.

Butler National was in superb condition and that was reflected in the scoring in the first round. Ten players, led by Loren Roberts, Bob Gilder and Gary Hallberg with 68s, broke 70 and 26 others were under par 72, an unusual number of par-breakers at Butler National. Fred Couples shot a 68 in the second round and Bobby Wadkins turned in his second straight 69, tying them for the lead at 138. The two leading characters in the Western Open of 1985—winner Scott Verplank and Jim Thorpe—both missed the cut.

The wind kicked up on Saturday and suddenly the fun went out of the game. The 84 survivors averaged almost 75 and Couples, with a 73, and David Frost, with a 71, were co-leaders at 211. Kite, with 70–75–73, was seven strokes back and seemingly out of it. Nick Price was at 215 and Greg Norman was at 217. These were to be the principals in the final round.

Couples and Frost staggered through the front nine in the last round, yet with nine holes to go they were in a tie for the lead with Wadkins, Tom Byrum and George Burns. Up ahead, Norman was putting together a charge. He went out in 35 and when he birdied Nos. 10 and 14, he trailed by only one stroke. But Norman bogeyed 16 and that was to be the difference as Kite made his sixth birdie at the 18th for a 68 and 286. Norman had a 70 for 287. Kite had a long wait to see whether his score would hold up. On most courses, two under par would have no chance, but this was Butler National.

When Kite had completed his round, the leaders were just getting into the back nine. Byrum took the lead with a birdie at the 12th hole, then hit his ball into the water at No. 14 and took a double bogey and crashed. No one else took over. Frost birdied the 72nd hole for a 75, Couples birdied the 71st and managed a 75 and Price carved out a 71, and they were tied at 286 with Kite.

It appeared Kite would be at a disadvantage in the playoff because the others were still hot while he had to sit around for more than an hour, some of that time sitting in the booth discussing the tournament on television. But Kite ended it quickly. A drive down the middle of the fairway and a wedge to within four feet at No. 16, the first hole of the playoff, set him up for a birdie as the other three scattered their approaches. Kite was unerring on the putt as he picked up the ninth victory of his 14-year career.

The International—$1,002,300
Winner: Ken Green

In response to the complaint that the PGA Tour lacked variety, we had The International, a new tournament with a new format. Offering a purse of more than $1 million, The International was sandwiched between the PGA Championship and the World Series of Golf. Although the scoring system drew some criticism, with a few alterations The International may find a long-term place on the tour.

The International used a form of the Stableford System, rarely played in the United States. It wasn't so much a five-day tournament as four rounds of qualifiers followed by a final. Half of the 162-man field played on Wednesday and the other half on Thursday, reducing the field to 78 players for the second round on Friday. That number was further reduced for Saturday's round, and the top 12 scorers then competed in Sunday's final, which paid $180,000 to the winner, $113,000 for second place and down to $28,000 for 12th place.

Under the altered Stableford System, a double eagle earned 10 points, an eagle five points, a birdie two points and a par nothing. A bogey was minus one point and a double bogey or higher was minus three points. Scoring was not on a cumulative basis; the points from one day were not carried over to the next, which was the crux of some of the criticism. Jack Nicklaus, for one, called it "stupid."

People paid attention when Nicklaus spoke because he designed the Castle Pines Golf Club course in the Denver suburb of Castle Rock, Colorado. The course measured more than 7,500 yards, but because of the high altitude it played to less than 7,000 yards. Even so, it was not a course that gave up birdies easily. An outstanding score was plus 14 points—seven birdies—and in the first round a plus three qualified on Wednesday and plus two on Thursday. As the field was reduced, the qualifying scores went up, but not by much. A golfer who led the scoring one day could be eliminated the next day, as happened to Raymond Floyd and Jim Gallagher.

Ken Green had his best day on Sunday, which was the best day. He made three birdies on the front nine for six points. He continued playing flawless golf on the back nine and added three more birdies for a plus 12 and through much of the back nine the battle was simply for second place. Bernhard Langer shook off J.C. Snead and Joey Sindelar to claim that with plus nine. Snead and Sindelar tied for third with plus eight. Green, whose sister Shelley serves as his caddy, had not been having a very good year, but when he placed among the final 12, he relaxed. "The worst I can do is 12th place for $28,000 and that's a lot of money for me," he said before the round began.

The scoring system called for some familiarization, both with the players and the spectators. It quickly became apparent to the players that they did not have to gamble for birdies on every hole (although some thought that's the way it should be) because a large number was not needed to qualify for the next round. And the spectators soon learned that the greatest attraction was those on "the bubble," the term used for those near the cutoff score. Sudden-death playoffs were used every day to get the rquired number of players for the next round. Floyd, one of the higher scorers in the first round, left after the second round. So did Lanny Wadkins, one of the tournament favorites. Gallagher, who led the second round, failed in the third round, along with Nicklaus, PGA champion Bob Tway and Tom Watson. Greg Norman, runner-up in the PGA Championship, didn't last through the first round.

The final 12 were Green, Langer, Snead, Sindelar, Nick Price, Howard Twitty, Ken Knox, Bruce Lietzke, Andy Dillard, Tom Kite, Donnie Hammond and T.C. Chen. If there was a favorite among them, it probably was Sindelar because of his propensity for making birdies. Sindelar made a run for it, but when Green grabbed the lead, he refused to let go.

World Series of Golf—$700,000
Winner: Dan Pohl

Dan Pohl's career on the tour, beginning in 1978, showed a steady improvement. But until Pohl won the 1986 Colonial National Invitation, he was known primarily for losing to Craig Stadler in a sudden-death playoff for the 1982 Masters and for his ability to hit a golf ball out of sight. The first two years of the statistics, Pohl led the tour in average driving distance.

"I finally realized I'm not out here to hit the ball 350 yards. I'm here to score well. It took me a while to back off," Pohl said. And then he became a player. How well was demonstrated as he won the World Series of Golf at Firestone Country Club in Akron, Ohio. Pohl and Lanny Wadkins scattered their tee shots around the countryside in the final round, but somehow Pohl kept coming out of trouble, and his final round score of one-over-par 71 and 277 total beat Wadkins by one stroke. It earned Pohl $126,000, and just as important, it earned him a 10-year exemption.

"Normally, I'm a guy who hits 14 or 15 greens, shoots 71 or 72, then wonders why he's not winning," Pohl said. "I wasn't comfortable with the driver all week and today it showed," particularly on the final nine holes, on which Pohl, Wadkins and Donnie Hammond played as if they were in a death struggle for the U.S. Open. It was hit the drive, then walk into the woods, the rough or a bunker and hit the next shot. Pohl and Wadkins survived; Hammond bogeyed five of the last seven holes and tied for fifth place, four strokes behind.

Pohl's wife was at home in Mt. Pleasant, Michigan, awaiting the birth of their third child and Dan joked afterward that watching him on television might cause her to go into labor. "I had a bit of Houdini in me today," he said. Pohl began the round in a tie with Wadkins and quickly took the lead for himself by hitting his approach close to the hole for an easy birdie at No. 1. When he birdied the seventh hole, he was four strokes in front. At the ninth tee, he seemed to realize the importance of his position and lost control of his driver.

Wadkins tried to close in, but he, too, couldn't keep his drives on the fairway and both put on a scrambling exhibition down the stretch. Pohl came out of the sand at the 12th, 13th and 15th holes to save par and cut his way through the rough at the 16th hole to make par. No. 16, Firestone's 625-yard monster, proved to be Wadkins' end. Lanny hit the green in regulation and had a 10-foot birdie putt that would have cut Pohl's lead to one stroke, but he missed. After they both parred 17, Pohl took a two-stroke lead to the 18th tee and even though he bogeyed the hole, the cushion proved enough as Wadkins failed to birdie on a chip shot from the left fringe.

The select field of tournament winners and foreign qualifiers found a course somewhat different from the Firestone of the previous year. The greens had been torn up and rebuilt after the 1985 tournament. Superintendent Brian Babie said it was because of a "bacterial decline" that had infected the grass roots. Maybe so, but many of the greens were recontoured, especially Nos. 5 and 17, where severe slopes were formed, and many complained about changing a well-known and respected course.

Nevertheless, the changes were not reflected by higher scoring. Hammond, Mark Wiebe and Raymond Floyd shared the first-round lead with four-under 66s and Hammond came back with a 68 to lead at the halfway point with 134. Pohl (69–66) was a stroke behind and Wadkins (68–68) trailed by two. Bob Tway and Greg Norman, the 1–2 finishers in the PGA Championship, were expected to be top contenders. Norman trailed by five strokes after 36 holes and went 72–75 the last two days. Although Tway shot a 66—aided by a hole-in-one at the 189-yard No. 5 hole—in the third round, his 74–72 start put him in a hole. Masters champion Jack Nicklaus was in position, three strokes behind, at the start of the final round, but he bogeyed four holes in succession, three by three-putting, on the front nine and couldn't recover.

St. Jude Memphis Classic—$500,000
Winner: Mike Hulbert

At the PGA Championship, Mike Hulbert talked about his friendship with Joey Sindelar and his desire to win a tournament. At Memphis, Tennessee, both came together as Hulbert scored his first triumph and beat his best friend in the St. Jude Memphis Classic.

Hulbert and Sindelar had grown up in Horseheads, New York. They went to different schools, but often met in matches, Sindelar usually winning. Sindelar received many college scholarship offers and accepted one from Ohio State University. Hulbert went to East Tennessee State. Sindelar quickly won a tour card; it took Hulbert four tries. But one thing Hulbert had shown in his first year on the tour was the ability to stay in contention once he got there. He finished one stroke behind in San Diego and Bay Hill and tied for seventh in the PGA.

Colonial Country Club was playing long and difficult. In the first two rounds, there were only seven scores under 70, all on the second day. Howard Twitty opened with 71–67 and Sindelar and Hulbert stayed close behind with 71–71 and 71–72, respectively. A 68 in the third round put Hulbert in a tie for the lead with Twitty, Larry Mize and Gary Koch, with Larry Nelson two strokes back.

Hulbert quickly grabbed the lead for himself in the final round with birdies at the second and fifth holes, then retreated with bogeys at Nos. 6 and 7. Koch held the lead until Hulbert caught him with a birdie at the 10th. Hulbert put his nose in front again when Koch bogeyed No. 11. Nelson tied him with a birdie at 13, but Nelson three-putted 15 for a bogey and was out of it. Meanwhile, Sindelar chipped in for birdie at No. 15 and added birdies at 16 and 17 to take a one-stroke lead. It lasted until Hulbert birdied 16 from 13 feet, setting up the final-hole dramatics.

Sindelar, with a final-round 68, was already in with 281 when Hulbert teed off at No. 18, a par-five bordered by a lake whose green can be reached in two with a good drive. Koch went for it and came up short for a double bogey. Hulbert's drive stopped in the right rough and he laid up with a nine iron. Hulbert had sunk two shots from the same distance—once at the 18th hole—during the tournament and when you do that "you start to think that this might be your week," he said. Fearing he might be too pumped up for a nine iron, Hulbert swung his pitching wedge. The ball hit to the right of the hole, took a bounce, then spun back to within a foot of the cup for a cinch birdie and the victory. And Sindelar was almost as happy as Hulbert that his buddy had won.

"I can't believe it. I don't know when it will hit me. Maybe I'll find a place and go and cry," Hulbert said. He was the seventh PGA Tour golfer to win his first tournament in 1986.

B.C. Open—$400,000
Winner: Rick Fehr

If Rick Fehr had taken his putter and sand wedge home, had them gold-plated and mounted after the B.C. Open, everyone would have understood. Fehr, who had to requalify for a Tour card after placing 133rd on the money list in 1985, used his putter and sand wedge to perfection to win at Endicott, New York, for his first tour victory. He shook off everyone but Larry Mize in the first three rounds, then turned back several challenges by Mize in the final round.

Fehr, 24, wasn't hitting his driver solidly, yet he ate up the par-five holes. "I was laying up. I did my scoring with my sand wedge," he said. Fehr shot 65–66–67 in the first three rounds, putting him 15 under par. Mize was in second place, three strokes behind, and everyone else was hoping for a miracle.

It was up to Mize to put the heat on Fehr in the fourth round, and he did. But Fehr refused to fold. Mize birdied the second hole with a 25-foot putt; Fehr matched it with a five-footer. Mize birdied the par-three No. 4 and Fehr bogeyed, cutting Fehr's lead to one stroke. But Fehr wedged close for a tap-in birdie at the par-five No. 5. Mize chipped in for birdie at No. 6; Fehr matched it with a 25-foot birdie putt. "I said to myself, 'Now I've responded to his surge,' and at that point I felt I was going to be the champ," Fehr said.

But Fehr wasn't champion yet. He birdied the ninth hole to build his lead to three strokes, but that was his last birdie. Mize missed birdie putts at Nos. 10 and 12 and bogeyed 13, a vital mistake in retrospect. Mize birdied 14 and

Fehr bogeyed 15, reducing Fehr's lead to two strokes. Mize thought if he could birdie the last three holes he could win. He got his first chance when his 18-foot putt at 16 was on the same line as Fehr's 25-foot putt. But Mize missed on the left. The end came when Fehr split the fairway at the 18th hole, a hole so difficult from the tee that many players hit irons just to keep their drive out of the trees on the right or the lake on the left.

Bank of Boston Classic—$400,000
Winner: Gene Sauers

It's questionable whether Gene Sauers won the Bank of Boston Classic or Blaine McCallister lost it. "He had so many opportunities. He gave it to me," Sauers said.

McCallister could have won at the 72nd hole, but missed a five-foot birdie putt. Sauers sent them to extra holes with a bogey six. McCallister had another chance at the first hole of the playoff and failed to cash in, but no one blamed him. Sauers' tee shot at the par-three hole spun back into a yawning bunker and his blast just managed to get the ball to the hill at the top of the bunker. In the meantime, McCallister's seven-iron tee shot stopped eight feet from the hole.

"I just said, 'I've got to chip it in,' " said Sauers, and he did. McCallister still had a relatively short putt to win. He missed. "He's off the green and he has a harder shot than he had in the sand," McCallister said. "I was thinking win and when he chipped in my balloon sank."

McCallister got another chance to win at the next hole. Sauers' approach again went into a bunker; McCallister's stopped on the fringe, 35 feet above the hole. Sauers' recovery came to rest 10 feet below the hole; McCallister putted to within two feet. Sauers missed; so did McCallister. "That's where I handed it to him," McCallister said. Sauers slammed the door shut on the third playoff hole with a 15-foot birdie putt for his first victory in three years on the tour. "People say it's hard to draw it back under pressure. I know what they mean now," said Sauers, who shot 70–71–64–69—274 to McCallister's 72–68–67–67—274 at Pleasant Valley Country Club.

Wayne Grady and Brian Claar, with 66s, took the first-round lead and Curtis Strange surged into a tie for the lead at 138 with Mark O'Meara at the halfway point. Strange had a 65 and O'Meara, 67. Sauers' 64 gave him a one-stroke lead over Strange after 54 holes, but McCallister was just two behind.

The final six holes were all Sauers-McCallister and they alternated between nervousness and brilliance. A birdie at 13 got McCallister to within a stroke of Sauers. But Sauers birdied 14 from 15 feet, and McCallister missed a matching birdie from 10 feet, giving Sauers a two-stroke lead. After both birdied 15, McCallister climbed to within a stroke of Sauers with a five-foot birdie putt at 16 on the strength of a marvelous four iron. They went to the 18th tee with Sauers leading by a stroke and he immediately put that advantage in jeopardy by pushing his drive into the trees. Eventually, Sauers was lying four after a nine-iron shot rolled 60 feet past the hole and McCallister was lying three after a neat pitch to within five feet of the cup. The door was open, but McCallister tripped on the rug.

Greater Milwaukee Open—$400,000
Winner: Corey Pavin

At 25, Corey Pavin was one of the up-and-coming players on the tour. In two years, he had won more than $628,000 and had won a tournament each year. He began 1986 by scoring his third victory, in the Hawaiian Open. Like most of the players, he has goals (a major victory, leading money winner, etc.) and one was to win at least two tournaments in one year. He finally cleared the hurdle in the Greater Milwaukee Open, overcoming Dave Barr's bid for his first victory in five years.

The tournament, played at Tuckaway Country Club in Franklin, Wisconsin, a suburb of Milwaukee, was troubled by inclement weather, which made playing uncomfortable but scoring easier. And for the second week in a row, the champion was decided by playoff after Pavin and Barr deadlocked at 272, Pavin picking up three strokes on Barr with a final-round 67. The playoff went four holes, Pavin winning it with a 10-foot birdie putt after they had parred the first three holes.

The par of 71 took a beating on the first day, Tom Byrum and Jay Delsing leading the way with 65s. Delsing's round was helped by successive eagles. Pavin was a stroke behind and Barr was four back. But Barr followed with a 64, helped by an afternoon starting time that avoided most of the rain and fog, giving him a two-stroke lead after 36 holes. Pavin's 72 left him five back. Pavin picked up two strokes with a 67 in the third round, but Barr continued to lead, his 69 leaving him one stroke in front of David Frost. Frost got a boost with a hole-in-one at the 197-yard eighth hole with a four iron. But there were nine players within four strokes of the lead, including Pavin.

The final round was delayed for 40 minutes by rain and fog, but that didn't seem to bother Pavin. Five birdies by Pavin, and an eagle and eight pars by Barr erased the difference between them on the front nine. Pavin bogeyed the 10th hole, but he birdied No. 16 and when Buddy Gardner also birdied 16, there was a three-way tie for the lead. Gardner folded with bogeys at the last two holes. Barr had a chance to win but missed a short birdie putt at the last hole.

Southwest Golf Classic—$400,000
Winner: Mark Calcavecchia

When the Southwest Classic ended at Fairway Oaks in Abilene, Texas, the person perhaps most surprised that Mark Calcavecchia had won was Calcavecchia himself. "Winning a PGA Tour event was the furthest thing from my mind," he said.

Calcavecchia shot 68–70–66–71—275 and won by three strokes over Tom Byrum. He won by pulling away in the stretch. "If anyone had told me I would birdie three of the last five holes to win, I would have told them they were crazy. I didn't think I had it in me," said Calcavecchia, who had not won in five years on the circuit.

Calcavecchia had top-10 finishes in his two previous tournaments. When he opened with a 68 at Fairway Oaks, he seemed headed toward another good payday. He may have won the tournament midway through the second round. He had double bogeyed the eighth hole and bogeyed the ninth. His nerves were jangling. At Fairway Oaks, the distance between the ninth green and 10th tee is about 100 yards. Many players cover it in a cart. Calcavecchia decided to walk. "That was a perfect time for me to fly off the handle. But I took that walk and regrouped, so to speak," he said.

It seemed to work, as Calcavecchia shot 70 and tied Paul Azinger for the lead at 138, six under par. Calcavecchia's 66 in the third round gave him a five-stroke lead over Byrum, who had 67. Azinger took a double bogey at the fifth hole and crashed to a 74. "This thing is a long ways from over," Calcavecchia said, knowing his game had yet to be tested under pressure.

His game began to show signs of deterioration in the final round. Calcavecchia missed four putts of five feet or less on the first seven holes, and he trailed Byrum by a stroke. Once again, he had a talk with himself. "You wouldn't believe the garbage that went through my head," he said. And once again, the talk helped. He birdied the ninth hole after blasting to within three feet of the hole with a difficult bunker shot and that put him in a tie for the lead.

At that time, Craig Stadler was signing for a tournament-record 63 that left him at 279. Calcavecchia said he wasn't worried about Stadler until he got to the 10th tee and saw that Stadler had finished at nine under par. Gathering his strength, Calcavecchia birdied the 10th hole. When he bogeyed No. 13, he had another pursuer in D. A. Weibring, whose birdie at 13 moved him to within two strokes of the lead. But Weibring failed to birdie the par-five No. 14, and a par at No. 15 ended his hopes. Calcavecchia and Byrum both birdied No. 14, and when Byrum birdied 15 and Calcavecchia parred, they were tied with three holes to play. At No. 16, a par three, Byrum hit his tee shot to within 10 feet of the hole. Calcavecchia swung a six iron and played the wind perfectly, as the ball stopped three feet from the cup. Calcavecchia birdied after Byrum parred, and widened his winning margin with a birdie at 17, where Byrum bogeyed.

Southern Open—$350,000
Winner: Fred Wadsworth

If Mark Calcavecchia's victory in the Southwest Classic was in the neighborhood of unbelievable, Fred Wadsworth's triumph was a fairy tale. The Southern Open is played in Columbus, Georgia, Wadsworth's hometown, and even a soap opera writer might find having the hometown boy score his first PGA Tour victory before the local fans too much to use as a plot, let alone that the hometown boy was making only his second tour appearance.

But that's the way it was, as Wadsworth won with a 67-67-68-67—269 at Green Island Country Club. Fred had made a name for himself as an amateur, the 1984 Eastern Amateur among his conquests. He then played the minitours. He got into the Southern Open the hard way, gaining one of the four berths available in the Monday prequalifier. (Kenny Knox took the same route to his victory in the Honda Classic earlier.)

Wadsworth trailed Jim Thorpe by two strokes after the first round and was a stroke behind Payne Stewart (66–67) after 36 holes. Thrope, who had a 71 in the second round, came back with 64 on Saturday, putting him a stroke in front of Stewart and Larry Nelson, and two ahead of Wadsworth.

The cheers of the home crowd felt good, but Wadsworth was just playing for a big payday, maybe enough money to win a tour card. When he birdied the ninth hole, his first birdie of the last round, he raised his sights. Winning had been out of the question, but now it wasn't. A birdie at the 10th hole gave him a share of the lead with Stewart. He pulled away with birdies at Nos. 12 and 17, winning by two strokes over John Cook, who closed with a 65; Tim Simpson, who had a 66; George Archer, who had a 69, and Thorpe, who had a 71.

And after he collected the $63,000 check, Wadsworth headed for a telephone to call his University of South Carolina sweetheart, Juli Medlin, to set a wedding date. "We had decided not to get married until we could afford it or I got on the tour. There are no excuses now," he said.

Pensacola Open—$300,000
Winner: Ernie Gonzalez

If Ernie Gonzalez develops into a PGA Tour star with his own line of clothing, it would be appropriate if he had a logo consisting of a gray cloud and a raindrop. That combination brought his first victory in the Pensacola Open at the Perdido Bay Country Club in Pensacola, Florida.

The tournament went only 36 holes because of persistent rain and Gonzalez was on top with 65–63—128. The purse was cut by one fourth, giving Gonzalez $40,500, about $10,000 more than he had earned in 1986 to that point. He received all the other perks that go with winning—an invitation to the Masters, Tournament of Champions, World Series of Golf and a two-year exemption.

Only half the field finished the first round on Thursday. One of those was Gonzalez, whose 65 tied for the lead with Curt Byrum and Jeff Sluman. Phil Blackmar, who played only two holes on Thursday, played the back nine in 30 on Friday for a 64. The second round was scheduled for Saturday and a 36-hole windup was marked down for Sunday. Joey Sindelar shot a course-record 62 for a 36-hole total of 129. Gonzalez nearly matched Sindelar with his 63, bogeying the last hole as the rain once again began to fall.

Gonzalez didn't know it, but his first victory was in the bag. The third round was rained out early Sunday morning. Four hours later, play was re-scheduled for Monday, when it rained again, causing the fifth rain-shortened tournament of the year, and the first that didn't go past the second round.

Gonzalez, 25, is a native of San Diego, who lost his tour card after one season in 1985 and won it back by placing 50th—and last—in the qualifying school. He is a lefthander, the first to win a PGA Tour event since Bob Charles in the 1974 Greater Greensboro Open.

Walt Disney World/Oldsmobile Classic—$400,000
Winner: Raymond Floyd

Ray Floyd has played professional golf long enough to know that a tournament isn't over until the last putt has dropped. Payne Stewart and Lon Hinkle have been around long enough to know that one mistake can lead to a defeat. So it was in the Walt Disney World/Oldsmobile Classic in Orlando, Florida. Floyd won because of his perseverence, and Hinkle and Stewart didn't win because they made that one error.

With rounds of 65, 66 and 71, Stewart led (or shared the lead) through three rounds and seemed headed toward his first victory since 1983. He never got there. Payne shot 74 and tied for fourth place. It was his 15th top-10 finish and the $20,666 prize boosted his earnings for the year to $427,389, the most ever won on the PGA Tour without a victory.

Hinkle, who hadn't won since 1979, led Floyd by two strokes with two holes to play. Even Floyd admitted, "It looked like I didn't have a chance." Hinkle gave him that chance with a bogey at the 17th hole, which left Floyd, Stewart and Mike Sullivan within a stroke of the lead. "I felt I needed to birdie the last three holes," said Sullivan, who birdied No. 16, parred 17 and sank an 18-foot birdie putt at No. 18 for a 71 and 275 total.

Sullivan then was tied for the lead with Hinkle, who was in the final threesome with Floyd and Stewart. Floyd and Stewart had to birdie and Hinkle needed a par to send the tournament into a playoff.

Stewart failed on a 25-footer for birdie, and Hinkle missed his par putt from a slightly shorter distance. Floyd had a 20-footer for birdie—and he sent it unerringly on its way, setting up a three-man playoff with Sullivan and Hinkle. The playoff began at the 203-yard No. 15. Sullivan missed the green and Hinkle and Floyd knocked their tee shots into a bunker. Sullivan had to chip over a mound, and his ball rolled 10 feet past the hole. Floyd blasted out to within six feet, and Hinkle made a marvelous shot, putting his to within a yard of the hole.

It looked as if the playoff would go another hole. Quickly it was over. Sullivan hit a weak putt that stopped short. Floyd dropped his six-footer, and said he figured, "At least you're still in the playoff." But Hinkle didn't hit his putt hard enough and it broke, caught the edge of the cup and spun out. Floyd had his second victory of the year, and at 43 had his fourth $350,000-plus season in six years. Another big winner was PGA champion Bob Tway. When Andy Bean tied for 19th place, Tway clinched the Vantage Cup championship, which paid a $500,000 bonus. Combined with the $647,780 he had collected in regular winnings, it capped a very lucrative season for him.

Vantage Championship—$1,000,000
Winner: Ben Crenshaw

There were two big winners in the Vantage Championship at Oak Hills Country Club in San Antonio, Texas: Ben Crenshaw and Payne Stewart.

Crenshaw earned his second victory of the year and the $180,000 first-place check. Stewart turned in his third second-place finish of 1986, but walked off with a check for $408,000—$108,000 plus a $300,000 bonus for placing second in the Vantage Cup race, which was won a week earlier by Bob Tway.

The tournament was troubled by fog and rain from the outset and ultimately was halted after the third round Sunday morning, when lightning and a heavy rain delayed play so long that officials decided the fourth round could not be completed before darkness. The decision not to complete the tournament on Monday was not accepted by many players. One of the most vociferous complaints came from another Texan, Tom Kite, who said he would file a letter of complaint with Commissioner Deane Beman. Kite trailed Crenshaw by six strokes and Stewart by five when the tournament ended.

Crenshaw opened with a 65 on Thursday and held the lead until Chip Beck, Ken Brown and Bernhard Langer completed their first round on Friday. Fog and rain interrupted the round and led to the dismissal of two of the bigger names—Tom Watson and Lee Trevino.

Watson played 14 holes on Thursday and when he returned to his motel room, he tried out the numerous putters he had brought along with him. When he found one he liked, he put it in his bag. On Friday, as he prepared to putt at the 15th green, his caddy noted Watson was not using the putter he had in the first round and an embarrassed Watson disqualified himself. A player is not permitted to change clubs during a round and Watson was still playing his first round. It was the first time he had ever been disqualified. Trevino was watching the tournament on television after his round and saw he was credited with shooting a 68. He knew he had a 69 and informed tournament headquarters of the mistake, thus disqualifying himself.

Stewart shot a 65 and Crenshaw a 67 on Saturday, putting them in a tie for the lead at 132. Stewart's round was much more solid than that of Crenshaw, who said, "My rhythm wasn't quite together today." A 36-hole windup was scheduled for Sunday, an arduous day that might have been too much for Crenshaw earlier in the year, when he suffered with a hyperactive thyroid. "That's of no concern now," he said.

Obviously, it wasn't. Sunday morning was clear and sunny and Crenshaw shot a 64 for a 196 total after 54 holes to a 65 and 197 for Stewart. They began the round on the back nine and both birdied their first hole. Stewart took the lead for himself with a 15-foot birdie at the 367-yard 17th hole, then immediately gave it away . . . for keeps. At the 198-yard No. 18 (their ninth hole) Stewart hit a five iron into a bunker near the green. He failed to extricate the ball on his first blast and ultimately took a double-bogey five as Crenshaw parred. They both birdied four holes on the final nine, Crenshaw's best a 15-foot putt at the eighth green.

The weather had turned nasty again, and an hour after Crenshaw and Stewart had completed their third rounds, they found themselves winner and runnerup, respectively. "I never thought the weather would be a factor," Crenshaw said. It was not only Stewart's third second-place finish of the year—he was winless in 1986—but also the fourth time he had placed second in Texas tournaments.

Seiko-Tucson Match Play Championship—$700,000
Winner: Jim Thorpe

The PGA Tour experiment with match play came to an end, as Jim Thorpe won the Seiko-Tucson Match Play Championship for the second straight year at Randolph Park Golf Club in Tucson, Arizona. The tournament was to return in 1987 with a standard 72-hole format, a new sponsor and venue, StarPass in suburban Tucson.

Most people agree there should be some variety on the tour, but apparently match play wasn't the answer in Tucson. Too many top players decided not to enter and too many of those who did play were eliminated early. The result was that spectators stayed away in droves. (Too bad they don't come to England sometime and see a *genuine* match play event.)

The tournament lasted three years and nobody enjoyed it more than Thorpe, who seems to thrive on head-to-head competition, although the Tucson event was not match play, but a stroke-match combination.

Some of the early matches were outstanding. One of the best was a first-rounder between Rick Fehr and Gene Sauers. They shot 64s and Sauers won with a birdie on the first extra hole. None of the first-round winners shot a lower round than Fehr, but he was gone.

Thorpe beat Brad Faxon, 68–70, in the first round and got past Dan Forsman with a par on the 19th hole after they had tied with 70s. That set up a pivotal match with Ben Crenshaw, who won the Vantage tournament the week before. Ben won the "shootout" at Randolph on Tuesday and led his team to victory with the low pro score in the pro-am. Crenshaw had shot 66 and 72 in erasing Fred Couples and Hubert Green. He turned in a 67 against Thorpe . . . and lost by four strokes, as Thorpe shot 63, the low round of the tournament.

Bob Tway, who had looked like a shoo-in to take the money-winning championship after Greg Norman had ended his year in the United States in August, was expected to reach that pinnacle at Tucson. All he had to do was win two matches, assuring himself at least the $12,500 that went to third-round losers. But Steve Pate beat Tway, 69–73, leaving him still shy of Norman and contemplating what one fewer stroke somewhere during the year might have meant.

While Thorpe was working his way to the final, Scott Simpson, almost unnoticed, was heading toward a showdown with him. Simpson, disgusted with his poor year, had not played for 11 weeks, but after the birth of a son three weeks earlier, he decided to return at Tucson. He defeated Dan Pohl with a birdie on the first extra hole after they tied at 72, then got past Danny

Edwards, 70–74, in the second round. Suddenly, his game returned. He shot 66, 65 and 69 in eliminating Gary Koch, Lanny Wadkins and Ken Green in the next three rounds.

Meanwhile, Thorpe beat Tim Simpson, 69–71, and Phil Blackmar, 68–71, after disposing of Crenshaw. The final was nip-and-tuck, with Thorpe leading by a stroke when they teed off at the par-three 15th. Simpson three-putted from 50 feet, giving Thorpe a two-stroke lead and the margin was doubled when Simpson bogeyed the 17th hole and Thorpe birdied. The third-place match was not nearly as close, with Green beating Blackmar, 67–74.

Tallahassee Open—$200,000
Winner: Mark Hayes

The last official tournament of the year is always interesting because of the sidelights. Everybody wants to win the first-place check, of course, but there always are a number who would settle for just placing in the first 10 because of the effect it would have on their future. A few thousand dollars can mean the difference between a passport to the next year's tour or enduring the rigors of trying to requalify for a card.

So the winners at Tallahassee, Florida, were Mark Hayes, with his first tournament victory since 1977; Tom Sieckmann and Antonio Cerda. Sieckmann came from far back in the money race to take the 125th spot by winning $10,400 for finishing in a third-place tie with Danny Briggs and Jim Gallagher Jr. at 275, two strokes behind Hayes and one behind Russ Cochran. Sieckmann did it by shooting a 66 in the final round. Cerda won only $1,132 and placed 126th on the money list, but he too gained a 1987 exemption because the money Bobby Cole won in the World Series of Golf was listed as unofficial because he got in with a foreign exemption.

While all this was going on, Hayes was working towards the fourth title of his 13-year career on rounds of 68, 67, 68 and 70 for a 273 total. Hayes had been retailoring his swing and his mental approach to golf for more than two years and they came together at Tallahassee. For the mental part, he contacted Dr. Bob Rotella of the University of Virginia, "who taught me to relax, even if not playing well."

Isuzu Kapalua Invitational—$600,000
Winner: Andy Bean

The Isuzu Kapalua Invitational at Maui, Hawaii, is not part of the PGA Tour, but has grown into one of the most attractive events for the pros. There is a luau every night, there is no 36-hole cut, the last-place finisher among the 44 contestants is guaranteed $2,000, and first place from the $600,000 purse is $150,000.

Andy Bean won by two strokes over rookie Davis Love III. It might be more correct to say that Love lost. Bean played a bogey-free 70 in the final round, and Love slipped behind him as his putting stroke sputtered. Bean finished with a 278 total, and Love, with a 73 for 280. Paul Azinger took third with 73 and 283.

The tournament was Love's to win or lose through the first three rounds. Love, perhaps the longest driver on the tour, awed the spectators with his tee shots, but in the end it was the short game that won it for Bean. "All week my chipping left me with good putting opportunities," Bean said. For two rounds, at least, few noticed. Love and Nick Faldo took the first-round lead with 68s, and Bean trailed by four. Bean fell to five back with a 68 in the second round, as Azinger went in front with a remarkable 65 for 135.

Love's putting problems developed at the sixth hole of the third round. The sixth is a 532-yard par-five that played into the wind. Love hit his tee shot into a fairway bunker and his second went only about 100 yards. He was short of the green with his third, then chipped about 10 feet past the cup. His first putt was eight inches from the hole, and he carelessly tapped the ball and missed for a double bogey. Bean, playing in the group in front of Love, holed a bunker shot for an eagle-three at the sixth—a pickup of four strokes that put Bean into the lead.

Love birdied the seventh hole and took a one-stroke lead after 54 holes with an eagle-three at the 18th. Love's drive at the par-five traveled about 350 yards, leaving him about 200 yards to the green. He placed a six-iron shot into the middle of the green, then sank a 50-foot putt for a 70 to Bean's 68.

But the sixth hole had uncorked a mean streak in Love's putter. He three-putted the first, fifth and 17th holes in the final round and kept losing ground for an eventual 73, as Bean kept chipping and putting his way to a 70. Azinger, who had virtually slipped out of contention with a 75 in the third round, grabbed third place with a 73.

J. C. Penney Classic—$650,000
Winners: Juli Inkster and Tom Purtzer

Tom Purtzer accomplished in the J. C. Penney Classic what he failed to do on the PGA Tour in 1986. Although earning over $218,000, Purtzer had not won a tournament, but he and partner Juli Inkster combined for a 23-under-par 265 total to defeat Val Skinner and Mike Hulbert by two strokes in the J. C. Penney Classic. It was the fifth victory of the year for Inkster, who won four events and over $285,000 on the LPGA circuit.

Purtzer and Inkster were winging in the first round with an 11-under-par 61 at the Bardmoor Country Club in Largo, Florida. Their 69 in the second round reduced the lead from four strokes to one over Skinner and Hulbert, who shot 65–66. They improved the margin to four strokes again in the third with 66. Craig Stadler and Lori Garbacz were then second, as Hulbert and Skinner slipped to third place with 71.

Hulbert and Skinner made a good run with 65 in the final round, but Inkster and Purtzer withstood the challenge, and had a chance to match or break the tournament record. They tied the record, 24 under par, with one hole remaining. But Purtzer missed a six-foot par putt and they closed with 69. Each of the winners collected $65,000.

Chrysler Team Invitational—$550,000
Winners: Gary Hallberg and Scott Hoch

Gary Hallberg and Scott Hoch, former college teammates at Wake Forest, finally entered the winner's circle in the Chrysler Team Invitational after placing second for the past two years. They had a tournament-record 251 total, 37 under par at the Boca West Country Club in Boca Raton, Florida, to win by one stroke over Bob Tway and Mike Hulbert, who was second the previous week with another partner, Val Skinner.

Much attention was centered on the Nicklaus team—Jack and sons Jackie, Steve and Gary. In the pro-am, Jack and Jackie were the pros, and Steve and Gary were the amateurs. They missed the cut, but in the better-ball competition, Jack and Jackie shot 256 and tied for fourth place.

Tway and Hulbert opened with a 13-under 59, leading by one stroke over Dick Mast and David Peoples. Tied for third place with 61s were the teams of Hoch and Hallberg, and Russ Cochran and Ernie Gonzalez. In the second round, Tway and Hulbert shot 62 to lead by two strokes over Danny Briggs and Larry Rinker. At that stage, Hoch and Hallberg trailed by three.

Brad Faxon and Denny Hepler climbed into contention with 61 in the third round, moving within one stroke of Tway and Hulbert, with 64. Hoch and Hallberg also shot 64 and were two strokes behind. The eventual winners shot 63 on the last day, starting a sensational drive at the 14th hole, when Hoch birdied from 30 feet. Hallberg birdied the 15th from 12 feet, and Hoch sank a 12-footer for another birdie at No. 16. Then, at the par-five 17th, Hallberg rammed in a 20-foot putt for an eagle that clinched the title.

9.   The U.S. Senior Tour

In the parlance of card players, it could be said that the Senior PGA Tour followed suit in 1986. The non-American domination of golf on the regular tours of the world, especially in the person of Australian Greg Norman and, to a lesser extent, Spaniard Seve Ballesteros, carried over into the seniors realm with the banner being flashed by another Australian resident of the United States. That man, Bruce Crampton, arrived on the over-50 scene with a bang, virtually duplicating what yet another Australian, Peter Thomson, did in 1985.

Even though he had been out of golf entirely for nearly eight years before launching a competitive tuneup during his 49th year, Crampton had been expected to join the winners' ranks quickly and frequently in senior golf. But few anticipated that he would become so monopolistic in his first season. He didn't win until April in the unofficial Doug Sanders Celebrity Classic, but followed with seven victories during the next seven months in regular Senior PGA Tour official events, including three of the last four at season's end. Crampton had a remarkable scoring average of 69.8 as he fell just one short of Thomson's nine victories in 1985. Bruce banked $532,515 from regular tournament competition, official and unofficial, a record $454,299 in official Senior PGA Tour events.

Playing in all but one of the 31 tournaments on the regular 1986 Senior Tour schedule in a reprise of his "Ironman" role of years gone by—he was not eligible for the Senior Tournament of Champions in January—Crampton put together his outstanding year of golf as follows:

TOURNAMENT	POSITION	SCORE	MONEY
Treasure Coast	T13	213	$4,725
PGA Seniors	T10	295	6,250
Senior Roundup	10	208	5,500
Vintage	12	285	6,277.50
Mathis/Los Angeles	3	207	18,750
*Sanders Celebrity	1	202	25,000
**Legends of Golf	8	263	8,000
Sunwest/Pride	T20	217	3,218.75
Dominion/San Antonio	1	202	37,500
United Hospitals/Phila.	4	208	12,500
Denver Post Champions	T3	211	17,187.50
Senior Reunion/Dallas	T6	211	5,906.25
Senior TPC	2	208	27,000
USGA Senior Open	T4	283	10,165
Greenbrier	T6	211	7,250
Grand Rapids	T8	207	7,500
Syracuse	1	206	30,000
Commemorative/New York	T9	207	6,387.50

Digital/Massachusetts	T4	206	10,000
Northwest/Seattle	1	210	37,500
**Showdown/Jeremy Ranch	T9	257	6,468.75
Bank One/Lexington	T6	207	6,500
United Virginia Bank	4	207	18,750
World Invitational	1	279	30,021
Barnett/Suntree	T4	210	6,197.92
Hilton Head	T12	221	4,212.50
Pepsi Challenge/Atlanta	1	136	37,500
Tucson Match Play	3	—	30,000
Las Vegas	1	206	37,500
Shearson-Lehman/Florida	1	200	30,000
**Mazda Champions	6	195	11,000
	Total Earnings		**$532,515.67**

*Non-Tour event. **Unofficial team events.

It makes for an interesting comparison. A 15-tournament career winner on the regular PGA Tour and the fifth man to become a winnings millionaire (behind Palmer, Casper, Nicklaus and Trevino, in that order), Bruce had his best season in 1973, when he won four times and finished second on the money list behind Nicklaus. His winnings: $274,266.

If anybody had been expected to do what Crampton did in 1986, it was Gary Player. The South African superstar had won the first time out as a senior in late 1985 and quickly added the PGA Seniors Championship in mid-February. Not playing a full schedule like Crampton and most others, though, Player settled for spring victories in Philadelphia and Denver and fifth place on the official money list of the Senior Tour.

The 1986 circuit had 12 other winners, three of them in unofficial tournaments. Of that trio, Bob Charles, another first-year senior, ended a frustrating season on an extremely-high note. The New Zealand left-hander, who had win after win slip away from him during the year, teamed with Amy Alcott to capture the climactic Mazda Champions tournament in Jamaica just before Christmas. The prize-money present of $250,000 in the unofficial event made Charles the tour's overall money leader with $580,753. Arnold Palmer picked up his only victory in the non-tour Unionmutual Classic in Maine at the end of September and Bobby Nichols, also a circuit freshman, joined with Curt Byrum to win the Showdown Classic at Jeremy Ranch in Utah.

Of the remaining nine victors, six won more than once. Dale Douglass, yet another newcomer, scored four victories, including the USGA Senior Open and the Vintage; Chi Chi Rodriguez, also among the seven first-season winners, picked up three, as did Don January, who, in addition, teamed with Gene Littler to take the Legends of Golf, the inspiration of the Senior Tour. January now has 23 individual seniors titles on his record. Littler, Lee Elder and Charles Owens each took a pair of individual victories.

The other rookie winner was Butch Baird, the victor at Hilton Head. Jim Ferree finally won on the senior circuit after a batch of near misses, taking the Grand Rapids title in a playoff. Like Palmer, Miller Barber had a disappointing season. The holder of 21 individual titles in his first five seasons on the Senior PGA Tour, Barber captured the season-opening Tournament of Champions, but that was it. Perhaps most surprising, though, was Thomson's inability to score a single victory in 1986 after his phenomenal 1985 season. He dropped back to 15th on the money list.

The Chrysler Cup, a variation on the venerable international Ryder Cup Matches, made a successful debut in senior golf in September of 1986 at the new TPC at Avenel development in suburban Washington, D. C. Palmer and Littler led the U.S. team to a decisive victory in the inaugural. The 1987 renewal and subsequent Chrysler Cups are to be played in the early season at the TPC at Prestancia in Sarasota, Florida.

The dominance of the first-year players—19 individual, the Showdown and the Mazda titles among the 35 tournaments—and the anticipation of more strong players coming onto the circuit in the next few years prompted the creation of an over-60 division and separate competition within the tournaments for the 1987 season. However, the bigger change for 1987 was the expansion of the fields in the standard tour events from 54 to 72 players with a cut to 48 after the Saturday round. The pro-ams were to be played on Wednesdays and Thursdays so that the 54 holes of the tournament proper on Fridays, Saturdays and Sundays would be pro-only rounds. Also coming into the picture in 1987 was the heavy involvement of RJR/Nabisco through its Vantage cigarette division with a $1 million tournament in the autumn at Winston-Salem, North Carolina, and other monetary participation during the season.

Senior Tournament of Champions—$100,000
Winner: Miller Barber

Nine times during his fine career on the regular PGA Tour, Miller Barber qualified for the exclusive Tournament of Champions, the annual meeting of the previous year's winners only, and never even came close to a title. His best was a tie for sixth in 1965, nine shots behind winner Arnold Palmer. When LaCosta added the seniors to the cast in 1984, Barber finished dead last and in 1985 he was seven strokes behind Peter Thomson at the end.

How the tables turned in 1986! Considering his 20 seniors victories, it was appropriate that Barber added the Tournament of Champions crown—they literally stuck one on his head—to his fine record. He did it in solid style, leading from second round to finish and winding up five strokes in front of runner-up Palmer with a six-under-par 282. His booty was $30,000 in the season's opener on the Senior PGA Tour in early January.

A faltering finish in Wednesday's opening round prevented Barber from scoring a wire-to-wire victory. He bogeyed three of the last four holes for 70, yielding first place to Lee Elder, who played the same stretch in one under for 69. Another 70 on Thursday shot Miller three strokes into the lead as Elder managed just a 74 over the 6,911 yards of the LaCosta course north of San Diego. Palmer was then five back.

With his putter bailing him out of some driving problems Friday, Barber fired his third straight 70 for 210 and a five-stroke lead over Palmer, who also shot 70 after double-hitting a short putt on the eighth hole to blunt an apparent charge. Although Barber settled for a par 72 Saturday, it created no tension. Neither Palmer nor Elder could mount a challenge and also had 72s, Palmer's birdie at the 17th preserving his one-shot edge over Elder at the finish.

Because of the multiplicity of wins on the part of several players during the 1985 season, only eight players qualified for the T of C on the senior side and Gary Player declined his invitation, electing to wait until February to resume his senior campaigning.

Treasure Coast Classic—$225,000
Winner: Charles Owens

The earlier career of Charles Owens could be charitably described as undistinguished. Lack of earnings drove him off the regular PGA Tour in the late 1970s with only a "second-tour" win and some $15,000 to show for eight seasons of effort. Even that was commendable, though, because Owens, the son of a Central Florida course superintendent, plays the game with a left leg fused at the knee and a cross-handed grip.

His poor fortunes continued when he had occasional opportunities to play on the Senior PGA Tour until he rigged up a 50-inch putter with a split grip that seemed to solve his past problems on the greens. It helped him to several high finishes and a $78,158 season in 1985 that made him an exempt player for 1986. With that pressure off, Owens quickly became a winner on the Senior Tour when play resumed in February in his native Florida with the Treasure Coast Classic at Fort Pierce. Leading from the opening round, the 56-year-old Owens scored a three-stroke victory at the Tournament Players Club at Monte Carlo with his 14-under-par 202, collecting a $33,750 check.

Owens, whose bad leg came as the result of a parachuting accident while in the Army, dazzled the Treasure Coast field in the first round. During the "very exciting day," the soft-spoken black pro ran in five birdie putts and eagled the par-five 16th hole with a 40-yard chip for a 65 and a one-shot lead over Harold Henning and Paul Harney. Charley's second round wasn't as spectacular but was equally solid. He again played without a bogey, birdied two of the last three holes and posted a 69 for 134. That gave him a two-shot advantage over Harney (70) and Walt Zembriski (69) at 136. Don January, who had opened with 72, jumped into the picture at 138 with a 66 that Saturday.

Owens permitted little room for challenge Sunday, the major ones coming from Lee Elder early with a six-birdie streak that eventually led to a 64 and January later on. Charley made his only bogey of the tournament when he overshot the 13th green into a bunker to open the door a crack. Undaunted, he made a tough birdie at the par-three 15th from 20 feet to re-establish a three-stroke lead only to have January birdie the 16th and 17th and cut the margin to one. However, January hooked his tee shot into the water at the 18th, took a double-bogey and 67. Owens parred the last three holes for 68 and a three-stroke margin over January and Elder.

General Foods PGA Seniors Championship—$250,000
Winner: Gary Player

Florida proved a sound launching pad for Gary Player's new golf career as a senior. Less than a month after turning 50, Player captured the Quadel Seniors at Boca Grove, Florida, in late November of 1985. Three months later, the South African Hall-of-Famer added his first major seniors title just up the Florida coast at Palm Beach Gardens, getting his first full season on the Senior PGA Tour off to an impressive start.

Player never trailed on his way to victory in the General Foods PGA Seniors Championship over the Champions course at PGA National Golf Club in Palm Beach Gardens. At the end, he had only to hold off Lee Elder, his only challenger after 36 holes, and did so by two strokes. He finished with a seven-under-par 281, the best score since the PGA Seniors was installed on the Champions course in 1983.

An opening-round 68 on a brisk Thursday morning put Player into a tie for the first-round lead with Miller Barber, the 1981 PGA Seniors champion, as only two other players—Elder (70) and Fred Hawkins (69)—broke par. As the winds continued to blow, Player matched his opening round and spurted into a seven-stroke lead over Elder. Gary protested that he didn't have a "safe lead" at that point and events Saturday tended to prove that. Just as Arnold Palmer saw an eight-shot 36-hole lead nearly disappear on the same course in 1984, Player had his healthy margin reduced to three as Elder made up five strokes on the last five holes Saturday, shooting 69 to Player's 73.

With nobody else in sight, all eyes were on Player and Elder Sunday. Gary widened the margin to five on the front nine as Lee took three bogeys. However, Elder mustered another challenge with a birdie-bogey swing at No. 10 and his fourth birdie on the back nine at No. 17 pulled him within two of Player. Gary allowed him no closer, finishing with a par-72 to Lee's 71. Charles Owens, the Treasure Coast winner the week before, and Jim King tied for third, seven shots behind Elder.

Peter Thomson, the defending champion, who launched his brilliant season with his PGA Seniors victory in 1985, did not return and two-time winner Palmer withdrew at the last minute with a back problem.

Senior PGA Roundup—$200,000
Winner: Charles Owens

The impressive score of 202 again served Charles Owens well when the Senior PGA Tour resumed action after a month's hiatus with a series of events in the West. Owens, who had scored his first circuit victory with that score in early February in Florida, mustered another 54-hole total of 202 at

Sun City West near Phoenix. That time, though, it merely put him into a playoff with Dale Douglass, the Senior Tour's newest 50-year-old, and it took two extra holes before Owens claimed his second victory and the top spot on the money list.

Owens started slowly over the 6,672 yards of the Hillcrest Golf Club course, opening with a one-under-par 71 that left him five strokes off the pace of Peter Thomson, the star of the 1985 circuit who was making his first start of the season, and Joe Jimenez, a longtime Midwestern club pro on leave from Jefferson City (Missouri) Country Club for his year's shot at the senior tour after gaining exempt status for 1986 by finishing second in national qualifying. They had just a shot on Douglass, Miller Barber, Doug Sanders, Jerry Barber and Bruce Crampton.

Another 67 advanced Douglass into the lead Saturday at 134, but Owens made the big noise. He shot a tournament-record 64—nine birdies and a bogey—to climb into a second-place tie with Thomson (69) and Sanders (68) at 135. Chi Chi Rodriguez missed joining them when he hit a tree on the final hole.

Fortunes waxed and waned Sunday. Sanders held the lead for four holes after birdieing the 11th from 20 feet, then yielded it to Douglass at the 15th when he bogeyed from the sand and Dale holed a 15-footer for a birdie. Owens joined Douglass in the lead with a 20-foot birdie putt at No. 16, they both birdied the 17th and matched pars at the 18th to force the playoff, Owens with 67 and Douglass with 68. Owens recovered from an errant second shot on the first extra hole and sank a 12-footer to stay alive with Douglass sitting two feet from the cup. They both missed the 17th green, the next hole, but Owens almost sank his pitch and got the victory when Dale came up short with his approach and missed a six-foot par putt.

Vintage Invitational—$300,000
Winner: Dale Douglass

Better than most of the tournament players during his long run on the PGA Tour, Dale Douglass still had never achieved top-echelon status. With three victories in a nine-month stretch gaining him some recognition and two of them in 1969 pushing him to a spot on the Ryder Cup team that year, the genial, soft-spoken Coloradan was generally considered a journeyman pro. He and wife, Joyce, have lived comfortably over the years. Nobody, though, tabbed Dale for stardom in 1986 when he passed the 50-year-old mark and switched from the regular to the Senior Tour.

His initial start in the Senior Roundup surprised many, his second event stunned even more. All of the Senior Tour's leading players were on hand for the rich and prestigious Vintage Invitational in desert Southern California and Douglass handled them all with relative ease. He put together rounds of 67, 70, 69 and 66 over the two fine courses of the Vintage Club at Indian Wells and his 272 was just a stroke off the tournament record set by Gene Littler in the first Vintage in 1981. Nobody had broken 280 since, although the next four finishers to Douglass did—Gary Player at 276, Jim Ferree and

Chi Chi Rodriguez at 278 and Lee Elder at 279. The $40,500 first prize shoved Douglass into the money-winning lead.

Never out of the lead at the end of any round, Douglass got off to a wildly strong start Thursday. In the course of shooting 67 on the tougher, par-72 Mountain course, on which every man played three rounds, Dale started with a double bogey, but had an eagle and a hole-in-one before making the turn. Arnold Palmer, coming off a back injury, opened with 68 on the par-71 Desert course, recording an eagle, five birdies and three bogeys on the back nine alone. George Lanning also shot 68. Douglass followed with the 70 Friday and shared the lead at 137 with Howie Johnson, who holed a 42-yard wedge shot at the last hole for his 68. The 69 on Saturday put Douglass a stroke ahead of Palmer, Bill Casper and Jim Ferree at 207 and he let nobody challenge Sunday. By the time he birdied the rugged 16th hole, he had a three-stroke lead. The 66 produced a four-shot victory. How often does the third-round leader of a tournament shoot the best score the last day?

Johnny Mathis Seniors Classic—$251,250
Winner: Dale Douglass

Dale Douglass took his hot hand west from Palm Springs to Los Angeles and joined Charles Owens as a double winner. Again, Douglass took the doubt out of the outcome with a flashing 66 finish that put off the pursuers in the second Johnny Mathis Seniors Classic at Mountain Gate Country Club. For the second week in a row, Douglass was never out of first place and the victory boosted his earnings for his first three weeks as a Senior PGA Tour player to $96,000, some $5,000 more than he won in 1969, his best season ever on the regular tour.

Douglass accomplished the victory in the Johnny Mathis in a different fashion from his Vintage win in some ways, though. Rather than put himself in the hole as he did at Indian Wells with an opening double-bogey, Dale birdied four of the first five holes and went out in 32. His 67 put him a stroke in front of an unlikely duo—Ben Smith and Mike Souchak—with the more-dangerous Bruce Crampton and Peter Thomson, the defender, next at 69. However, the story of the day was the hole-in-one of Charley Sifford that didn't produce the briefly-promised reward of $100,000 in cash to go with a new car. A sign was inadvertently posted proclaiming both and was up until after some four groups had played that par-three 15th hole. It was hastily removed when discovered before Sifford holed his five-iron tee shot. The sponsors had been unable to get insurance on the $100,000.

"I never knew how much fun it was to be 50," said Douglass the Saturday after his ninth straight sub-par round as a senior—69—staked him to a two-stroke lead after 36 holes. Crampton birdied the last hole for a second 69 and 138 and Chi Chi Rodriguez, yet another 50-year-old, also shot 69 to join Smith and Mike Fetchick at 139. Souchak fell back with 76. Douglass had three birdies, no bogeys.

Rodriguez was the only real challenger Sunday, but couldn't dent the resolve of Douglass, who closed with a brilliant 66, the product of eight birdies and two bogeys, to cancel out a similar effort by the Puerto Rican. Dale's total was 202 and he won by three over Rodriguez, five over Crampton, who finished with a 69.

Doug Sanders Celebrity Classic—$140,000
Winner: Bruce Crampton

In 1957, a 21-year-old Australian named Bruce Crampton, virtually unknown to American golf followers, picked up his first check on the PGA Tour—$693.75—when he tied for 13th in the Houston Open at Memorial Park Golf Course. Nearly 30 years later, Crampton was back at Memorial Park, playing for the first time as a senior 50-year-old in the Doug Sanders Celebrity Classic. At week's end, he pocketed $25,000 and his first title, albeit "unofficial," on the Senior PGA Tour.

Crampton, who had come out of a lengthy retirement to join the Senior Tour when he turned 50 in the fall of 1985, ran in a 10-foot birdie putt on the 54th hole to break a four-way deadlock and capture the title in the "fun" event staged by Sanders during an open week on the regular schedule, attracting most of the leading pros and many of Doug's celebrity friends. Bruce's scores were 66, 67 and 69 for a 14-under-par 202, the winning total for a fourth time in 1986.

Orville Moody opened the tournament on top with a 65, a shot ahead of Crampton and Gay Brewer. Then, Bruce and Peter Thomson edged a stroke in front of Charles Owens and Dale Douglass Saturday, Crampton with his 67 and Thomson with 68–65 for his 133. Owens and Douglass had pairs of 67s. It was anybody's game Sunday, as the tournament went its scheduled 54 holes for the first time in four years, escaping the usual heavy spring rains of April in Texas.

Finally, as Crampton and his group played the final hole, he and three others—Owens, Thomson and Howie Johnson—were all 13 under par. Crampton's decisive birdie gave him his first victory in a pro tour event since 1975. That spring, two years before he quit the tour to go into the oil business, he won his 15th and last victory on his way to golfing millionaire status. Ironically, it, too, came in a Houston Open, played that year at the Woodlands.

Liberty Mutual Legends of Golf—$500,000
Winners: Don January and Gene Littler

Nothing new at Onion Creek in 1986. Well, that's not quite so. Fred Raphael, who devised and "sold" the Legends of Golf to television back in 1978 and thereby, as it turned out, launched the Senior Tour, added some of the new 50-year-olds and juggled some of the twosomes of the previous year. But, he left intact the defending team—Don January and Gene Littler—and they calmly played their way to a repeat victory, this time by a record 255, which is 25 under par at the Onion Creek course in Austin, Texas.

Actually, it was the third victory in the Legends for both of them. Littler teamed with Bob Rosburg to win in 1981 and January joined forces with Sam Snead and finished on top the following year. Gene and Don merged talents in 1985, January explaining: "He's been beating me for 45 years, so I decided to join him."

Before they took charge, the tournament offered two early surprises. The first-round leaders, with a 61, were Paul Harney, who was coming off a 1985 injury seige, and 63-year-old Jack Burke, who rarely plays any other senior events. Perhaps as astonishing was the 70 shot by Arnold Palmer and Gary Player, who was making his Legends debut. Many had considered those two senior members of golf's famous Big Three of the 1960s odds-on favorites as a Legends team. But, the 70 put them too far behind the eight ball, their subsequent 64–64–63 only getting them up into a fourth-place tie, six strokes behind the winners.

Littler and January took charge Friday with a 61 for 126 and a two-stroke lead over Lee Elder and Chi Chi Rodriguez, another Legends newcomer. Littler did most of the damage that round, rapping in eight birdie putts. It was January's turn Saturday as the team shot 65 for 191 ("I just played lousy," said Littler.) That moved them four strokes in front of four other groups—Peter Thomson/Harold Henning, Jim Ferree/Charley Sifford, Bob Toski/Mike Fetchick and Elder/Rodriguez. The strongest challenges to the winners Sunday came early from Rodriguez and Elder, who caught up at 21 under par before Littler birdied the ninth, 11th and 12th. They reached 25 under when, with January "in the pocket," Gene dropped a 20-footer for the final birdie. The surprising Ferree/Sifford team was still alive at the 72nd hole, but could make only a par, which Littler and January matched to secure a two-stroke victory with their 64. Sifford and Ferree finished second with 62 and 257, a shot ahead of Rodriguez and Elder, who closed with 63 for their 258.

Sunwest Bank/Charley Pride Senior Classic—$250,000
Winner: Gene Littler

It wasn't the Skins Game, but "carry-overs" were in vogue the first week of May in Albuquerque, New Mexico. Gene Littler and Don January, coming off their commanding victory the week before in the Legends of Golf, maintained their sharpness at the next stop on the Senior PGA Tour, finishing 1–2, respectively, in the Sunwest Bank/Charley Pride Senior Classic. Littler in particular.

Gene the Machine, who hadn't scored an individual victory on the Senior Tour since the first event of 1984, raced to a wire-to-wire victory over the 6,744 yards of Four Hills Country Club's course at Albuquerque, finishing with the familiar 1986 total of 202 and a two-stroke victory over January. He was six in front of third-place Bob Charles.

Actually, when play ended prematurely in Friday's first round, Al Balding had the lead with 67. But a rain delay had prevented Littler and 17 others from finishing their rounds. When they did the next morning, Gene birdied two of his three remaining holes for 65 and a two-shot lead over Balding, the veteran Canadian still seeking his first win on the senior circuit. Littler followed that three-hole finish Saturday with a 66 in the regular round—eight under par for his 21 holes that day—and spurted five strokes in front of January, who put a 67 with his starting 69 for 136. Charles and Chi Chi Rodriguez were at 137.

So, on Sunday, off went Littler and January, the Legends winners but this time opponents for the Charley Pride title. Littler started strongly with birdies at the first and fourth holes and played without error until a bogey at the 15th dropped his margin over the consistent January to three strokes. Gene bogeyed again at the 17th and put his approach at the 18th on the fringe with January on the green 20 feet below the cup. But Littler got down easily in two, making January's birdie chance meaningless. He missed, anyway, and took a 68 to Gene's 71 for his runner-up 204. The prize for Littler was $37,500, considerably less than he collected in that early 1984 victory in the Tucson Match Play Championship—$100,000—just before he broke an arm in a garage accident and missed much of the season.

Benson & Hedges Invitational at the Dominion—$225,000
Winner: Bruce Crampton

That 202 was the magic number yet again on the Senior PGA Tour when the elder statesmen of the game returned to Texas for the Benson & Hedges Invitational at the Dominion, the plush new club at San Antonio. The 202 total was the winning score on the 1986 senior circuit for a sixth time at the Dominion and was the same score shot by Bruce Crampton when he won the unofficial Doug Sanders Celebrity Classic the month before up the road at Houston. The 202 at the Dominion put the first-year senior onto the official winners' list and lined his pocket with $37,500.

Rain and insects plagued the early rounds of the tournament. Rain and a flash flood Friday prevented half the field from finishing. Crampton got in with a 67 before the weather ended play, but Dale Douglass posted a 66 and Bob Charles matched the 67 when the rest of the players completed their first rounds the next morning. Charles flashed some of his old putting wizardry that day, following the 67 with a 65 that afternoon for 132 and a two-stroke lead over Crampton, who had another 67. Douglass was another shot back after a 69. It had been a slow round for many of the players as fire ants emerged on the greens after the heavy rains and many of the players, especially Crampton, spent a lot of time brushing the putting lines clear of the pesky bugs.

The final round turned into a duel between the New Zealander and the Aussie. Charles lost his putting touch, though, and three-putted three of the first 10 greens. Crampton finally overtook him on the back nine and took the lead at the 16th with a routine par as Charles missed the green, chipped poorly and bogeyed. In effect, it ended at the par-three 17th where Bruce holed a 27-foot birdie putt as Bob was suffering a bogey after trapping his tee shot behind the green. Crampton finished with 68 for his 202, while Charles took a 72 for 204 and the runner-up slot by three ahead of Douglass, Gary Player and Doug Sanders.

A reminiscence by the 1–2 finishers from Down Under: The two had finished 1–2 in reverse order in the 1954 New Zealand Open when both were 18 years old.

United Hospitals Senior Championship—$200,000
Winner: Gary Player

By mid-May, Gary Player had settled comfortably into his expected prominent spot on the Senior PGA Tour. He scored his third victory on the circuit that week in the United Hospitals Championship just outside Philadelphia and since joining the circuit in late 1985 had finished in the top five eight times. No more beating his head against the young men on the regular tours of the world except in the major championships and some of the events on the tour in his native South Africa.

His experience and talent showed vividly at Philadelphia. Facing 6,406 yards through stands of old trees on the hilly Chester Valley Country Club course at Malvern in the western suburbs, Player usually kept his driver in the bag and the ball in the fairway, a strategy reminiscent of that which he used to win his first PGA Championship 24 years earlier not far away at Aronomink. As a result, Gary led from start to finish and won by a shot over Bob Charles and Lee Elder. He was four under par at 206.

Player opened with a four-under 66, making six birdies with putts ranging from four to 30 feet. He led Gordon Jones by two, Charles, Miller Barber, Gardner Dickinson and Walt Zembriski by three. Bruce Crampton mounted a serious charge for a second straight win Saturday when he produced a tournament-record 65. At day's end he was in second place at 137, just a stroke behind Player, who bogeyed three of the last four holes for 70 and 136. Also in range after 36 holes were Dale Douglass at 139 and at 140 Charles, Elder and Arnold Palmer, who bounced back from a 74 with 66, the day's best round.

It remained tight to the end. Charles grabbed the lead when he birdied the 11th as Player was bogeying the ninth. However, Gary birdied the 11th and 12th to regain the lead and held it to the finish. He had a scare at the final green, though. Leading by just a stroke, his approach bounded over the putting surface into a tough lie. But, the longtime master of the short game deftly pitched to five feet and sank the par putt for 70 and the one-stroke victory. Charles and Elder had 67s for their 207s.

Coca Cola Grand Slam Championship—$230,000
Winner: Lee Elder

Lee Elder should have a hard time turning down any invitations to go to Japan to play in a golf tournament off his track record in senior competition. Only two months after passing the 50-year mark, Elder scored his first senior victory by seven strokes in the unofficial Coca Cola Grand Slam near Tokyo in September of 1984. Less than two years later, Lee did it again, this time winning by six in the Grand Slam at Narita's Oak Hills Country Club. The victory came at the end of May, Elder's first of 1986 after his four-win season in 1985 although he had remained a frequent challenger and one of the leading money-winners.

Elder took charge from the start, opening with a 65 to take a two-stroke lead over George Lanning and widening the gap the second day with a 66 for 131. At that point, he led Miller Barber, the defending champion, by seven, Gene Littler, Mike Fetchick and Masao Hara of Japan by eight. On a day of generally high scores, Elder maintained his edge over Barber as both players shot 71s Saturday when the 70s of Billy Casper and Bob Charles were the lows in the third round.

Lee wrapped up the convincing victory with another 71, a steady round of 17 pars and a one-foot birdie putt at the par-three 11th hole. Barber made six birdies, but four offsetting bogeys blunted any chances he had to take a run at the winner. He shot 70 for 279, finishing six strokes off the record pace of Elder, who picked up a $50,000 check at the closing ceremony. Littler and Don January tied for third at 281.

Denver Post Champions of Golf—$250,000
Winner: Gary Player

Roberto de Vicenzo, the globe-trotting Argentinian, made one of his infrequent visits to the Senior PGA Tour at the end of May and, at age 63, nearly picked off the title of the Denver Post Champions of Golf. Instead, the victory went to another of the game's fabled international winners, Gary Player, who was continuing his commanding play on the Senior Tour. It took the South African, 13 years the junior of de Vicenzo, four overtime holes to vanquish the Argentinian over the 6,700 yards of the new TPC course at Plum Creek in Castle Rock, a Denver suburb.

Consider this statistic: Player has 131 documented victories on his record in all parts of the world and the Senior Tour media guide credits Roberto with more than 100 international titles and 230 victories in his career.

The remarkable de Vicenzo jumped off in front that Friday, putting together an eagle, five birdies and a bogey for 66 and a three-stroke advantage over Chi Chi Rodriguez, Mike Fetchick and Bob Erickson. Rodriguez came up with one of Saturday's three 67s and moved into the lead at 136, a shot in front of de Vicenzo (71) and Player (67). That set up an international, final-round grouping of the American from Puerto Rico, the Argentinian and the South African, but the final round quickly turned into a duel between Roberto and Gary as Chi Chi's "best golf of my life" Saturday deserted him and he staggered to an 81 and a 10th-place finish.

Meanwhile, Player and de Vizenzo were working their ways to matching 71s and 208s, setting up the playoff. After going three holes without a decision in the season's second playoff, Player's fourth straight par ended the duel as de Vicenzo chipped poorly and bogeyed. It was just Gary's fourth playoff victory in 15 tries in America over the years and only the second in sudden death. The win was Player's third on the 1986 circuit and fourth since reaching his 50th birthday in November of 1985. The $37,500 first-place check established him as the circuit's No. 1 money-winner.

Senior Players Reunion Pro-Am—$200,000
Winner: Don January

Home was more than where his heart was, Don January discovered the first week of June. It was where his golf game was. "It was like a yo-yo," said January of his performance level in the weeks before the Senior Players Reunion Pro-Am in his hometown of Dallas. But, his usually solid game returned during the week he took off prior to the tournament, thanks to the advice of old pro friend George Alexander that he return to his reliable upright stance. The result was Don's first individual victory of the year, in fact, since he won his 20th individual senior title 11 months earlier at the Greenbrier.

The victory did not come easily. January, who had won the Legends of Golf with partner Gene Littler in April, birdied the last two holes for a 69, 203 and a two-stroke triumph over Chi Chi Rodriguez, with whom he traded the lead six times and shared it on three other occasions during the final round of the Crosby-style tournament at Bent Tree Country Club and its 6,804-yard course. Rodriguez, frustrated for a second week in a row in his search for his first victory on the Senior PGA Tour, finished with a 70 for 205, one better than Walt Zembriski, who closed fast but too late with 68 for his 206.

The two final-round protagonists dominated the tournament from the start. They opened with 66s that Friday, leading Al Chandler by a shot, Bruce Crampton, Bobby Nichols and Bill Casper by two. On Saturday, January holed a 30-foot birdie putt on the last green for 68—134 and a one-stroke lead over Rodriguez. Defending champion Peter Thomson made his bid for contention, firing a 65 for 137, tying with Chandler and Casper. Both January and Rodriguez carded a flock of birdies and bogeys and were never more than a stroke apart until the very end. Chi Chi had the lead for the last time at the 15th hole, then bogeyed the par-five 16th to drop back into a final tie before January's closing birdies—a five-footer off a five-iron tee shot at the par-three 17th and an eight-footer off a six-iron approach at the par-four 18th. Interestingly, January had won his first PGA Tour event in Dallas in 1956 and nothing in his hometown since.

Senior Tournament Players Championship—$300,000
Winner: Chi Chi Rodriguez

After Chi Chi Rodriguez had come up just short once again the week before in Dallas in his quest for his first Senior PGA Tour victory, he philosophized: "I guess I was not destined to win. But I forget the failures of the past and look to the opportunities of the future." Rodriguez made the most of it when the next opportunity came along seven days later in Cleveland, nailing down the sought-after icebreaker in one of the circuit's most prestigious events— the Senior Tournament Players Championship at the highly reputable Canterbury Country Club, scene of the playing of several of golf's most important events over the years.

In shaking off the earlier failures as promised and winning his first tour event at any level since the 1979 Tallahassee Open, Rodriguez seized the lead in the rain-delayed second round Saturday and clung tenaciously to it Sunday, fending off challenges from Gay Brewer and Bruce Crampton to score a two-stroke victory with a 10-under-par 206, the first time in its four-year history that the event was shortened to 54 holes. The Thursday round was washed out and canceled.

A pair of 68s by Gary Player and Brewer accounted for the first-round lead when play resumed Friday, Player's abetted by an eagle-deuce and Brewer's salvaged by eight par saves. Rodriguez, along with Lee Elder and Howie Johnson, was next at 69. Chi Chi took over first place Saturday with a solid 67 for 136, three shots in front of Brewer and four ahead of Elder, Don January and Peter Thomson. He hit every green and carded five birdies in setting a new TPC record for 36 holes.

Brewer closed the gap to a stroke three times Sunday before fading badly on the back nine. One time was at the eighth hole, where a Chi Chi bogey after seven pars, "woke me up," Rodriguez noted later. He birdied the next two par-fives—No. 9 and No. 13—and led by two as the final groups played the last holes. Then, Crampton stated his case, holing a 25-foot birdie putt on the final green for 67 and 208 as Chi Chi watched from the fairway, knowing his lead was down to one again. He promptly fired a perfect eight-iron approach litle more than three feet from the cup, rolled in the putt and saluted the victory with a final brandished sword/putter performance. Arnold Palmer, who had won the Senior TPC the previous two years, closed with a 67 to tie Lee Elder and Don January for third place at 210.

USGA Senior Open—$275,000
Winner: Dale Douglass

The rather surprisingly brilliant debut of Dale Douglass in senior golf reached its highest point in Columbus, Ohio in late June. Never a serious contender for any major championship in his long career on the regular PGA Tour, the 50-year-old Douglass captured the Senior PGA Tour's equivalent of the U.S. Open—the USGA Senior Open—in impressive fashion, holding off the menacing threat of a Gary Player charge in the final going when his own game was faltering. He edged Player by a stroke with his five-under-par 279 over the USGA-stiffened 6,709 yards of the fine Scioto Country Club course in the Ohio capital city. It was a Senior Open record.

Just as he did in his two earlier victories in his four-month Senior Tour career, Douglass put the bit in his mouth in the first round and never trailed thereafter. His best round was the first. He shot a Senior Open record score of 66 that Thursday—seven birdies and two bogeys on the par-71 course—and took a two-strokc lead on Lee Elder. Eight other players broke par, but most of the "name" players were farther back. A 72 on Friday was good enough for Douglass to open his lead to three strokes over Ken Still and Jim Ferree (both with 69–72—141). Host pro Walker Inman, inserted into the tournament as a replacement when Sam Snead withdrew, shot the day's best score—67—to join three others at 142.

Player staked his claim Saturday with a five-under-par 66 to possess second place, but Douglass actually enhanced his position that day. His 68 and the fading of his closest pursuers put him at 206, four strokes ahead of Player and six in front of Ferree and Harold Henning. Player closed in on the early holes, making birdies at the eighth and 11th after Dale had bogeyed the seventh.

The margin remained at one until the 15th, probably the most critical hole. After saving par from three feet at the 14th, Dale recovered from a plugged lie in another greenside bunker at the 15th to five feet and, after Player had three-putted, sank the putt to open a two-stroke margin. Another bogey by Gary from a bunker at the 16th gave Douglass all the cushion he needed, even after Player birdied the 17th. Dale played the 18th carefully and took a bogey for 73. Henning shot 69 to finish third, a shot behind Player. With the $42,500 check, Douglass increased his Senior Tour earnings close to $200,000 in little more than three months.

Greenbrier American Express Championship—$200,000
Winner: Don January

Don January surely has joined the many persons who wouldn't miss their annual visits to The Greenbrier, the venerable resort in the mountains of southern West Virginia. He could hardly enjoy his sojourns there more. Twice January has gone to White Sulphur Springs for the tournament and twice has left the famous establishments with the title of the Greenbrier American Express tournament in hand.

The veteran had a tougher go of it in 1986 before capturing his second individual title of the year and his 22nd in senior golf. A two-stroke winner in 1985, the 56-year-old Texan had to work overtime to win at Greenbrier again when Jim Ferree shot a brilliant 66 in the Sunday round with the help of a hole-in-one at No. 4 to catch him. January's par on the first extra hole secured the victory, frustrating Ferree once again in his bid for a win on the Senior PGA Tour.

Charles Owens, with an eagle-four birdie spurt at one point, shared the first-round lead with Bruce Crampton at 68 as January opened with a two-under-par 70 over the 6,709-yard Greenbrier course. It was Don's turn for a streak of birdies Saturday. He birdied four of the last five holes for 66 and his 136 gave him a two-stroke lead over Crampton, who had a 70 that day as co-leader Owens stumbled with a 78. Little noticed was the 67 of Ferree, who had opened the tournament with 74 and so was still five strokes off January's pace.

Because Don couldn't get anything going early in Sunday's round, it was anybody's game after the front nine. Then, a three-putt double-bogey cost January sole possession of the lead at the 13th. He came back with a birdie at the 14th, matching one by Ferree, and the two were tied for the lead as Ferree recovered from a poor second shot at the par-five 18th and parred. January could do no better after trapping his second and they returned to the first hole for the playoff. Both drove into a fairway bunker and Ferree's "best ever" sand shot was too good, running over the green into heavy rough. He did well to get within 15 feet, but missed the putt and January's par brought him another American Express Greenbrier title. He didn't want to leave White Sulphur Springs without it.

Grand Rapids Classic—$251,250
Winner: Jim Ferree

How often pro golfers win when they are not supposed to. Such was the case for Jim Ferree when the Senior PGA Tour made its first stop in Grand Rapids, Michigan, in mid-July. The articulate Ferree, who had let several earlier chances for his first senior victory slip by, had just suffered another near-miss the past Sunday with his playoff loss to Don January in West Virginia. In addition, he was nursing a tennis elbow that required pain medication and was trusting his normal woes on the greens to an elongated, pendulum-style putter designed by Charles Owens to compensate for his fused leg.

It was playoff time again for Ferree at Grand Rapids' Elks Country Club, but this time he emerged the winner, defeating Gene Littler and Chi Chi Rodriguez on the first extra hole when he birdied from eight feet with the strange-looking putter. The three had finished the 54-hole event with nine-under-par 204s. Ben Smith, another non-winner, missed the playoff by a stroke after his Sunday 68.

Owens himself was the first-round leader as he had been the week before at Greenbrier. This time, he opened with 67, one stroke better than Ferree, Littler, Rodriguez, Smith and Bruce Crampton. Low scores abounded the second day as 22 players had rounds in the 60s. Ferree's 66 was the best, though, and it enabled him to grab the lead at 134 by a stroke over Owens, his putter benefactor; Crampton, who had birdied four of the first five holes, and Littler, who had five birdies on the first six holes of the back nine. Rodriguez (68–68) was among three at 136.

Littler opened the door for the playoff Sunday. Leading Ferree (70) and Rodriguez (68) by a stroke coming to the final green, Gene three-putted for his 69 and the three-way tie. It was his only bogey of the day. All hit the green on the first extra hole, but Ferree picked up the $37,500 first prize when he sank the eight-footer after the other two had two-putted for pars.

MONY Syracuse Classic—$200,000
Winner: Bruce Crampton

The first-year seniors regained command of the circuit when it made its annual stand in Syracuse. Bruce Crampton, in the midst of his excellent initial full season back in action, scored his third 1986 victory in the MONY Syracuse Classic, finishing strongly to squeeze out a one-stroke victory with his seven-under-par 207 at Lafayette Country Club in Jamesville, New York.

A second-round 65 was the key to the success of Crampton, who had won twice in Texas in the spring at San Antonio and in Doug Sanders' unofficial celebrity event in Houston. It enabled him to take the lead and gave him enough of a cushion to withstand late runs by Chi Chi Rodriguez, Roberto de Vicenzo and Orville Moody on Sunday.

Journeyman Bob Erickson took the first-round lead with a four-under-par 67, one stroke better than Moody and Rodriguez, as Crampton opened with 70. Bruce crafted most of the 65 on the front nine Saturday. He had four birdies and an eagle for an outgoing 30, bogeyed the 10th, then picked up two more birdies on the way home. The 135 put him a stroke in front of Moody, another player toying with the Charles Owens putting stick, and three ahead of Erickson (71), Ben Smith and Butch Baird, another veteran of the regular tour making his first Senior PGA Tour start.

Moody, the 53-year-old one-time U.S. Open champion, who had been Crampton's partner earlier in the year in the Legends, wrested the lead away from Bruce during the rainy Sunday round. After 13 holes, he led by two shots as Crampton slipped one over par for the damp day. After 15, Moody and de Vicenzo, enroute to a 67, led by one, but Crampton birdied the par-five 16th to catch those two and Rodriguez, who had just finished with 66 for his 207 to match de Vicenzo. Crampton birdied again at the par-five 17th and was ahead by one after Moody, finally betrayed by the new putter, three-putted from the collar. Bruce's solid two-putt par at the 18th clinched the $30,000 victory.

The Commemorative—$200,000
Winner: Lee Elder

A certain sameness remained with the Commemorative when it was moved in 1986 from historic Newport, Rhode Island to suburban New York. The winner, Lee Elder had scored one of his four 1985 victories on the Senior PGA Tour when the Golf Digest and Merrill Lynch folks staged their final Commemorative tournament at Newport. Sleepy Hollow, one of the respected clubs in metropolitan New York, became the new home for the tournament in early August of 1986 and Elder handled the 6,545 yards of its course equally well.

With a second-round 64, one of three such scores posted that week at Sleepy Hollow, Elder took charge and he went on to a two-stroke victory with his 199, the first sub-200 winning score of the season. It was his first official victory of the year, but his second senior win of 1986. Lee had run away with the title in the Coca-Cola Grand Slam in Japan in May.

Chi Chi Rodriguez scored the week's first 64 in Friday's first round after rain had washed out Thursday's pro-amateur start. Rodriguez ran off seven birdies and took a bogey on the par-70 course, jumping off to a two-stroke lead over Dale Douglass as Elder and four others began with 67s. Elder was devastating Saturday. Working out six birdies in the middle of his round, Lee parlayed his 64 into a four-stroke lead over Rodriguez (71) and Gene Littler (68).

Elder's 68 Sunday was more than enough, although Rodriguez and Littler hung tough. Chi Chi shot 66 for 201, closing the final margin to two strokes, and Littler finished another shot back after a 67. Elder's 199, worth $37,500, was a tournament record. For the second day in a row, Lee avoided bogeys, clicking off birdies at the sixth and 11th holes in putting together the 68. Remarkably consistent, Elder added another top-10 finish for 1986, an area he had missed only twice all season. Buck Adams had the other 64 Sunday over the par-70 course at Scarborough and it jumped him into a sixth-place finish.

Digital Classic—$200,000
Winner: Chi Chi Rodriguez

Little wonder Chi Chi Rodriguez had claimed the No. 1 position on the Senior PGA Tour halfway through his first full season on the circuit. When he scored his second victory in the Digital Classic at Nashawtuc Country Club in Concord, Massachusetts, Rodriguez extended to 17 his consecutive string of finishes in the top 10, all except three of those fifth or better.

In fact, he went to Massachusetts after finishing second or tied for second in his three previous starts, one the playoff loss to Jim Ferree at Grand Rapids. So, the flamboyant Puerto Rican went one step further at Nashawtuc, coming from three strokes off the pace in the final round with a 66 to land the title in New England's only stop on the Senior Tour. He secured the one-stroke victory over Gary Player, 203 to 204, with a birdie on the final hole from a lie in heavy grass that prompted him to claim that "even Clark Kent would have had trouble making birdie from where I did."

Bob Charles and Gay Brewer shot 65s for the lead on a rain-interrupted first day over the par-72 course, both putting brilliantly. Charles took just 29 putts and Brewer, racing darkness, birdied five holes in a row, starting at No. 13, to overtake the New Zealander. Charles, a frequent contender but still seeking his first Senior PGA Tour victory, moved into sole possession of first place Saturday, his 69 for 134 a tournament record. He birdied two of the last three holes to take a two-stroke lead over Player and Bruce Crampton.

Rodriguez shot 67 Saturday to move within three of the top. He closed in on Charles on the front nine Sunday, then took charge when he birdied the 10th, 11th and 12th holes. By then, his main adversary was Player. Chi Chi sank a 35-footer at the 16th "that went through three time zones" and Gary missed birdie putts from eight and 15 feet on the last two holes. Still, Rodriguez needed the five-footer he holed after his splendid trouble shot at

Greg Norman was congratulated by caddy Pete Bender after
winning the British Open.

Greg Norman shakes hands with third-place finisher Bernhard Langer as Michael Bonallack carries the British Open trophy to the ceremony.

After the second round, Greg Norman was posing with a record-equaling scorecard. At the end, he and wife Laura were holding the British Open trophy.

Gordon J. Brand, aided by
68 in the second round,
was the runner-up in the
British Open.

Bernhard Langer had 68
in the fourth round—the day
after the birth of his
first child.

Ian Woosnam's 70 led the first round. He shared third place with Langer at the finish.

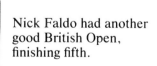

Nick Faldo had another good British Open, finishing fifth.

Seve Ballesteros didn't get on track in the British Open until the fourth round, when he posted 64 to tie for sixth.

U.S. PGA Tour Commissioner Deane Beman, Ballesteros' nemesis for 1986, played well but missed the 36-hole cut.

Gary Koch led the U.S. players, finishing tied for sixth.

Tom Watson, trying for a record-equaling sixth British Open title, was 16 strokes off the pace.

Japan's Tsuneyuki (Tommy) Nakajima entered the last round of the British Open one stroke behind, but then shot 77 and finished nine behind.

115th OPEN GOLF CHAMPIONSHIP
LEADER BOARD
Burroughs
COMPUTERS

6.40 ROLEX

HOLES	+PAR−	PLAYER	SCORE
72	E	NORMAN ★	280
72	+ 5	BRAND GJ	285
72	+ 6	LANGER	286
72	+ 6	WOOSNAM	286
72	+ 7	FALDO	287
72	+ 8	BALLESTEROS	288
72	+ 8	KOCH	288
72	+ 9	NAKAJIMA	289
72	+ 9	MARCHBANK	289
72	+ 9	ZOELLER	289

POSITION AFTER 71 HOLES

PLAYER   SCOR FOR ROUP

WELL DONE
GREG

SEE YOU
AT
MUIRFIELD

The leaderboard said it all—Well Done, Greg.

Severe winds and the notorious Road Hole were twin terrors in the Dunhill Nations Cup at St. Andrews.

Australia repeated as the Dunhill Nations Cup champion with Rodger Davis (left) joining Greg Norman and David Graham.

RAF jets passed over the Royal & Ancient Club House during the opening ceremony.

Japan's Tommy Nakajima (above) and Spain's Seve Ballesteros
hit into the burn on the first hole at St. Andrews.

Scotland's Sam Torrance (left) and America's Lanny Wadkins came up short in the Dunhill Nations Cup.

The semi-final duel of Jack Nicklaus (left) and Greg Norman was a highlight of the Suntory World Match Play Championship.

Norman defeated Sandy Lyle in the Suntory final, then was critical of the partisan Wentworth spectators.

Michio Torii of Suntory presented the championship cup to Greg Norman, along with children Morgan Leigh and John Gregory.

the 18th green to take the one-shot victory. Charles shot 71 and finished third.

GTE Northwest Classic—$250,000
Winner: Bruce Crampton

The pattern of yesteryear was working again for Bruce Crampton. Known as "The Ironman" in his days on the PGA Tour because he rarely missed a tournament, Crampton found that paying off with 15 victories over a 14-year span. Bruce saw no reason to do things differently when he returned to action in senior golf. He didn't skip a single tournament for which he was eligible in late 1985 and well into 1986 and it paid off with four victories.

The third on the regular Senior PGA Tour came in mid-August at the new GTE Northwest Classic, staged at the Sahalee Country Club near Seattle. Crampton posted rounds of 67, 71 and 72 for a six-under-par 210 and defeated Don January and George Lanning by two for the title, picking up a $37,500 check.

Bruce was never out of the lead at the course in Redmond, Washington. The opening 67, spurred by an eagle, tied Walt Zembriski for the lead, a shot ahead of Miller Barber. January holed from the sand at the 18th hole Saturday for 67 and a share of the lead with Crampton at 138. Zembriski was at 139 and played with the two regular tour veterans in the final group Sunday.

Crampton took the lead for keeps at the par-three fifth when he holed a 30-foot birdie putt and widened the gap with another birdie at the 10th as January double-bogeyed and Zembriski fell into a bogey streak. Even when Bruce knocked his second shot out of bounds at the 12th and double-bogeyed himself, he still had a three-shot lead over Billy Casper and Miller Barber and par in did the job. January rallied with birdies at the 13th and 15th hole and lost a playoff opportunity when he missed short birdie putts on the last two greens. Lanning, one of the few successful club pros on the Senior PGA Tour, birdied the last hole for 70 and a share of second place with January at 212. The showing delighted Lanning's friends from his home area nearby in Tacoma.

The Showdown Classic—$700,000
Winners: Bobby Nichols and Curt Byrum

Curt Byrum couldn't have found a better way to curry favor with his girlfriend's father than he did in the Showdown Classic (the former Jeremy Ranch Shootout.) The 25-year-old South Dakotan played outstanding golf for the first three rounds, then turned matters over to his senior partner, Bobby Nichols, whose daughter Leslie he had been dating, to apply the coup de grace on the final Sunday of the team event at Salt Lake City.

The result was a record-breaking performance and firsts for both pros— Nichols' first since turning 50 in April and Byrum's first in a PGA Tour event. They shot a startling 39-under-par 249 over the 6,947 rolling yards of the Arnold Palmer-designed Jeremy Ranch course in the mountain highlands outside of Utah's capital city. The remarkable score, fashioned with rounds of 61, 65, 61 again and 62, bettered by a stroke the record winning score of Don January and Mike Sullivan in 1984.

Nichols, a standout on the regular tour in the 1960s and early 1970s who had not won since the 1974 Canadian Open, professed embarrassment that he was not helping his young partner more in the early going, but Byrum needed little aid except to have Bobby's ball regularly in play while he was making birdies and eagles. The new partnership seized the first-round lead with the first 61, heading Gary Player and his pro son, Wayne, by a stroke and three other teams by two. On day two, January and his new partner, Brian Claar, a last-minute substitute for Sullivan, who was enduring back trouble, roared into the lead with a 60 for 124 as Nichols/Byrum took a 65 and the Players a 64 for 126s, joined there by Bob Goalby and nephew Jay Haas (64–62).

Byrum was steaming Saturday. He made seven birdies and two eagles himself to form the 61 that jumped them back into the lead, a stroke ahead of January/Claar. Then, it was Nichols' turn. With half a dozen teams threatening, Nichols came up with five birdies and an eagle, the major share of the effort that produced the finishing 62 and a two-stroke victory over Harold Henning and Denis Watson, who closed with 60–61 to edge the Players and Goalby-Haas by a shot for second place. January and Claar had a 68, falling to eighth place.

Bank One Senior Classic—$200,000
Winner: Gene Littler

For the second time in six weeks, Gene Littler found himself in a three-man playoff on the Senior PGA Tour and again it was pretty much of his own doing. At Grand Rapids in July, Littler three-putted at the 72nd hole to force that playoff, which he and Chi Chi Rodriguez lost to Jim Ferree. At Lexington, Kentucky, on the last day of August, Gene missed a five-foot birdie putt at the 72nd hole. Another playoff, this time with Miller Barber and Bob Goalby.

Littler reversed the outcome, outlasting the other two in overtime. Goalby dropped out at the first extra hole with a bogey, Barber failed to get up and down from a bunker two holes later and Gene had his third win of the season with the victory in the Bank One Classic at Griffin Gate Golf Club. It was the 13th, including three team wins in the Legends of Golf, in senior competition for the 56-year-old Californian.

Others occupied first place after the first two rounds. Bob Erickson and Jimmy Powell overshadowed the better-known pros the first day with 65s, then Bob Charles started with an eagle and shot a 65 in Saturday's round for 132 and a one-stroke lead over Barber, two over Littler, Goalby and Powell. Both Barber and Littler blistered Griffin Gate with eight-under-par 63s over its 6,640 yards.

Sunday appeared to be Barber's day in the early going. Miller birdied three of the first four holes, then the seventh for an outgoing 32 and a four-shot edge over Littler and Goalby as Charles faded toward a 71 and 203. However, Barber unknowingly had run out of birdies. Littler birdied the 11th, 13th and 15th while Goalby holed his eight-iron tee shot at the 13th and birdied the 15th. Both one back. Then, Barber three-putted the 16th green and it was all even. All three parred in for 201s to force the playoff.

The Chrysler Cup—$600,000
Winner: United States

Arnold Palmer, the American captain, sounded a warning after his United States team had taken rather full measure of its International opponents in the inaugural Chrysler Cup, a senior version slightly removed from the venerable Ryder Cup Matches, which made its debut in competitive golf the first week of September at the new TPC at Avenel in suburban Washington, D.C. "Don't come to any long-term conclusions based on just this week," cautioned Palmer after he had literally led his eight-man team to a 68½-to-31½ victory. "Our side played exceptionally well, and frankly, the International team didn't play as well as I thought it would."

The Americans led from the first day with Palmer scoring points for his team in every round after exciting the golfing world with holes-in-one at the par-three No. 3 on consecutive days of the pro-amateur. He and Gene Littler edged Gary Player, the International captain, and Bob Charles, 1 up, in the opening four-ball competition in which the first 16 points were up for grabs. Lee Elder and Billy Casper also picked up four points with their 2-and-1 victory over Bruce Crampton and Roberto de Vicenzo, while Peter Thomson and Harold Henning scored the only International triumph, 1 up over Chi Chi Rodriguez and Dale Douglass. Christy O'Connor and Al Balding almost sprung an upset, but had to settle for a tie with Don January and Miller Barber when O'Connor three-putted at the 18th with his partner out of the hole.

Depth told the story during the next two days of singles duels. In match play Friday, Rodriguez, Douglass, Barber, Littler, January and Palmer were victors, Crampton and Thomson getting the only wins for their team. That moved the U.S. further ahead, 28 to 12, and the score went to 44½ to 19½ Saturday as Rodriguez, Douglass, January and Palmer won again in medal matches, Casper rebounded from a Friday trouncing and defeated Player, Littler halved with Charles, Crampton won again and O'Connor surprised with a win over Barber.

The final round was straight stroke play with points allotted to the first eight places. The U.S. claimed 24 of the available 36 points as Palmer and Littler shot 69s to capture 15 of them off the top. Rodriguez took five more, tying Charles for third at 70. January, Player and Crampton got three points each with their 72s and Balding and Casper half points for their 73s.

Some adjustments in the tournament format were planned in an attempt to keep the issue more in doubt entering the final rounds of the future. That future includes the second staging of the annual event the first week of April in 1987 at the new TPC at Prestancia at Sarasota, Florida, an intended change that is not a negative reflection at all on Avenel or the spectator and corporate interest in Washington. Instead, Avenel becomes the new venue for the Kemper Open on the regular PGA Tour.

United Virginia Bank Seniors—$300,000
Winner: Chi Chi Rodriguez

Chi Chi Rodriguez took a firm grip on the lead in the money-winning race on the Senior PGA Tour when he scored the third victory of his "freshman" year on that circuit in the United Virginia Bank Seniors, one of the richer seniors events. He pocketed $45,000 of the $300,000 purse with a sparkling 67–66 finish at Hermitage Country Club outside of Richmond, Virginia, his 202 total, 14 under par, giving him a three-stroke victory.

Bob Charles took the first-round lead with a five-under 67, a stroke ahead of Billy Casper and two in front of eight other players, including Rodriguez and Gary Player, who were to battle it out later that weekend. Two putts were particular factors in Chi Chi's 67 Saturday. He "woke up" after missing a three-footer for a bogey at the 10th hole and he took a one-shot lead over Player when he sank a seven-footer on the 18th green. Jimmy Powell was at 138 after a pair of 69s, followed by Don January and Peter Thomson at 139.

Rodriguez was playing so well Sunday that he was never threatened. The 202 was a tournament record by five strokes. Even though he also shot 66, January finished three strokes behind Chi Chi in second place, Player slipping to third with his 69. Another stroke back was Bruce Crampton at 207, followed by Powell, Charles and Thomson at 210.

The record score in the fourth playing of the UVB over the 6,640 yards of the Hermitage course followed a 211 in the inaugural by Miller Barber and 207s the next two years by Dan Sikes and Thomson.

PaineWebber World Seniors Invitational—$200,000
Winner: Bruce Crampton

Apropos of the top caliber of the field and the known difficulty of the course, Bruce Crampton found his fifth victory of 1986 the toughest of them all to achieve. It came down to a 13-foot putt on the final green, the difference between the win and a three-way playoff, and the implacable Australian rolled it in for his 70 and the one-stroke triumph in the PaineWebber World Seniors Invitational at Quail Hollow Country Club in Charlotte, North Carolina.

It was a struggle all the way for Crampton before he notched his fourth official title on the 1986 Senior PGA Tour. (The unofficial Doug Sanders Celebrity was the other—and the first.) Right off the bat, Peter Thomson, the 1984 World Seniors victor, blistered the course with a tournament-record, seven-under-par 65, spurting to a three-shot opening lead Thursday. The 57-year-old Thomson, star of the 1985 Senior Tour, ran off four birdies in a row in the stretch in establishing his early margin over Crampton. Jimmy Powell was the only other player in the 60s.

Crampton, making his first appearance at Quail Hollow in 10 years, climbed into a first-place tie with fellow Aussie Thomson Friday. An eagle-three at the 10th hole helped Crampton offset three bogeys on his way to a 69 and his 137. Meanwhile, Thomson found his putting less productive and shot 72 for his 137. They were then four shots ahead of the rest of the field with Chi Chi Rodriguez closest at 141.

Lee Elder joined Crampton and Thomson at the top Saturday when he matched Thomson's record 65 and came from seven shots off the lead to catch the Australians, who had par 72s. In fact, Elder had par at the 18th for 64, but bogeyed the hole for the 65 and 209. Thomson had three birdies, three bogeys on the hot day, while the par-five 10th, an eagle hole Friday, extracted a bogey from Crampton, who spent his first three shots in the woods and struggled for the par round.

In the Sunday finish, Rodriguez was in the group in front of the tri-leaders, starting the day at 212. He was eight-under after 16 holes, then failed to convert relatively short birdie putts on the last two greens and settled for 68 and 280. When Crampton bogeyed and Elder double-bogeyed at the 12th hole, Bruce had a one-stroke lead and he maintained it with pars to the finish and the winning 279. Elder shot 71 for 280 to tie Rodriguez as Thomson slipped to 73 for 282. Bruce's toughest par was the last one. He was in two traps on the par-four 18th before sinking the deciding putt.

Unionmutual Classic—$165,000
Winner: Arnold Palmer

The season was running out and Arnold Palmer found himself in a unique position not to his liking. In his first six years of senior golf, Palmer always had mustered at least one victory somewhere along the line. Now, in the final week of September of 1986, his record was devoid of wins. He had floundered about in the second 10 of the Senior PGA Tour money list for most of the season, rarely a serious threat.

Arnold filled the void that week in Portland, Maine, where he led from start to finish in the Unionmutual Classic to score the 91st victory of his remarkable professional career. The title and the money—$38,000—were fine, but the win at the Purpoodock Club at Cape Elizabeth had one drawback. The tournament was not a part of the Senior PGA Tour, so the victory, among other things, did not affect his money-list position nor qualify him for the Senior Tournament of Champions. But, Palmer was philosophic about it. "You need to win once in a while. When you don't, getting back on the winning track is difficult."

He got away strongly over the 6,401 yards of Purpoodock that Friday with a six-under-par 65 that gave him a two-stroke lead over defending champion Billy Casper. Highlight of Arnie's best round in three years was his first of three consecutive eagles on the 501-yard 16th hole. Both Palmer and Casper shot 67s Saturday, nobody else got frisky and the situation at the top was unchanged. A second 68 put Gary Player in third place, four shots off the lead.

In Sunday's final round, Arnold started fast with birdies on the first two holes, the latter with a drive over a stand of trees onto the green. Subsequent birdies at the fourth and eighth distanced Palmer from the rest of the field. However, he took four bogeys with a single birdie on the next six holes, giving the charging Don January a chance until the third eagle at the par-five 16th reestablished a four-shot lead. Palmer finished with 68 for 200, while January shot 66 with birdies at the last two holes for 203 and second place. Casper was third at 207, Player tied for fourth with Dale Douglass at 208.

Fairfield Barnett Classic—$175,000
Winner: Dale Douglass

Dale Douglass added another gem to his sparkling rookie season on the Senior PGA Tour with his victory in the circuit's oldest regular event—the renamed Fairfield Barnett Classic at Suntree Country Club in Melbourne, Florida in early October. The surprising Douglass, whose three earlier wins in his first year of senior golf included the prestigious U.S. Senior Open and the Vintage, captured No. 4 in a virtual head-to-head duel with Miller Barber, the 1981 and 1982 winner at Suntree, his 13-under-par 203 edging Barber by a stroke.

Four players, including Douglass and Barber, opened with 68s over the 6,533-yard course at Melbourne that Friday. The others were leading money-winner Chi Chi Rodriguez, who eventually finished third, and Bob Erickson, who faded out of the top 10 by week's end. Douglass birdied three of the first four holes Saturday, put together a 67 for 135 and finished the day a stroke ahead of Barber (68) and two in front of Rodriguez (69). He had six birdies and a bogey in all. The bogey came at the fifth hole and it was his last one of the tournament.

Dale began Sunday's final round with his third straight birdie at the 505-yard first hole, but Barber matched it and it was back and forth between the two the rest of the day. Miller climbed into a tie with a birdie at the seventh, but Dale countered with birdies at the 11th and 13th as Barber missed a four-footer at the 12th. However, Miller birdied the 14th and 15th and flubbed his chance to take the lead when his four-foot birdie putt at the 17th failed to drop. Then at the 18th, where Douglass played a solid par, Barber nearly drove into the water with a three-wood tee shot, caught a bad lie, barely got the ball across the hazard and bogeyed the hole. Both shot 68s in that closing round, while Rodriguez had a 71 for 208, nipping Jim Barber by a shot.

Cuyahoga Seniors International—$200,000
Winner: Butch Baird

Because he had just begun campaigning on the Senior PGA Tour in July after turning 50 but without exemption-qualifying credentials, Butch Baird did not automatically make the fields of all of the tournaments. In fact, the three-time winner on the regular tour over a long career had resigned himself to sitting out the Cuyahoga International at Hilton Head, South Carolina, when the circuit reached there in mid-October.

However, Baird learned that Monday that he had the spot vacated by the withdrawal of Mason Rudolph, whose two-season efforts on the Senior Tour had been futile. By Sunday, Baird had become the circuit's third rookie winner of 1986 and its fourth first-time victor, rolling to a four-stroke triumph with a three-under-par 210 over the demanding Harbour Town Golf Links, longtime site of the Heritage Classic on the regular tour.

Before the rounds began counting, Butch scored a hole-in-one in the Thursday pro-amateur. He started his title run in earnest Friday, opening his ninth Senior Tour start with a 70 to tie Arnold Palmer and Walt Zembriski, who had a back-nine 32, for the lead. Gusty winds troubled the players Saturday and Baird's 71 was good enough to move him a shot ahead of Zembriski as Miller Barber took third place with a 74–70—144 and Palmer double-bogeyed the last hole for 75 and 145.

Baird, whose last national victory had been in the Texas Open 10 years earlier, plugged along at even par Sunday before getting the break he needed, the break that Chi Chi Rodriguez, in hot pursuit, termed "destiny . . . it's his turn." He drove into trouble and was six yards short of the green after his three-iron recovery shot. He chipped in for birdie and had things well in hand. He birdied the 14th, bogeyed the par-five 15th when he shanked a pitch into a trap at the green, came back with an approach to two feet and another birdie at the 16th, then parred in. He had a 69 and finished four in front of Rodriguez, whose 67 for 214 was the week's best round. Joe Jimenez climbed into third place with 70—217.

After joining Bruce Crampton and Dale Douglass as rookie winners of 1986 and Jim Ferree as first-time victors of the year, Baird reflected on his entry into the tournament. "Maybe I should send Mason some roses."

Pepsi Challenge—$250,000
Winner: Bruce Crampton

The sponsors of the new Pepsi Senior Challenge at Atlanta got a rude welcome to the world of tournament golf, finding out how weather can ruin the best-laid plans, or at least spoil them. The first-time event at Horseshoe Bend Country Club in suburban Roswell encountered a stretch of wet weather that forced the shortening of the event to 36 holes and almost converted it to a one-rounder that would have been an unofficial tournament on the books.

A two-inch downpour flooded out Saturday's round and made the prospects for a Sunday finale a bit dim. However, the small size of the Senior Tour fields gave the grounds crew plenty of time to work on Horseshoe Bend's 6,760 yards Sunday morning, making the course fit for Bruce Crampton to score his fifth official and sixth overall victory of 1986.

Before the rains came, Crampton jumped off strongly with a seven-under-par 65 that tied the course record set in 1983 by Scott Hoch in a U.S. Open qualifier there. It gave him a two-stroke lead on Gary Player, who was out in 32 but settled for 67. Jim Ferree was the only other player in the 60s. He birdied the last two holes for 68 and a two-shot margin over Butch Baird, coming off his victory at Hilton Head.

The three players at the top of the standings Friday finished in that same order Sunday after the Saturday layoff. Crampton shot 71 for 136, holding off Player by a stroke and Ferree by two over the soggy course. "All 36 holes were important," noted Crampton afterward. "The way things turned out, I couldn't afford to miss any. I played good, steady golf, more or less an error-free round." Baird, Bob Charles and Art Wall finished three back of Ferree at 141.

Seiko-Tucson Senior Match Play Championship—$300,000
Winner: Don January

Though always susceptible to an unexpected flare of a hot player, steady golf usually rewards its practitioner over the long haul of match-play competition. Such was the result for Don January in the senior division of the Seiko-Tucson Match Play Championship, played for the final time over the Randolph Park Golf Course in the southern Arizona city. The Tucson sponsors have elected to drop the seniors and revert to stroke play on the regular PGA Tour in 1987.

January, who had won two standard events and the Legends of Golf with partner Gene Littler earlier in the season, had a four-under-par 66, a 69, two 70s and a 71 in the match/medal events on his way to the victory, getting some help from opponent Bob Charles in the title match on the first Sunday of November. Charles, a frequent contender and early-round leader during his first senior season, led January by a shot after 16 holes. However, he three-putted the 17th green—an unheard-of occurrence for him in his younger days when he was often called the best putter in golf—and bogeyed the last hole after missing the green. That gave January the championship, 70 to 71, and the $75,000 first prize.

After bumping off Howie Johnson in the first round, 70–73, the Texan came up with the 66 against Miller Barber, who shot 70 in the losing effort Friday. Don took out Gay Brewer Saturday, 69–73, to advance to the semifinals against Bruce Crampton Sunday morning. Charles reached the other semifinal match against surprising Ben Smith by beating Mike Fetchick, 74–78; Bob Brue, 74–75 and defending champion Harold Henning, 70–73. Scores of 71 gave January and Charles their semifinal victories, as Crampton shot 73 and Smith 74 to set up the finals and consolation match for third place, won by Crampton that afternoon, 70–72.

In the title match, January opened with a bang, holing a 60-foot birdie putt on the first green, and held the lead until Charles birdied the seventh. Then, when January bogeyed the 10th, the left-hander moved a stroke ahead and maintained that margin until his disastrous finish. "I just couldn't get it close to the hole and Bob had me. He played well, but turned me loose on the last two holes," January observed.

Las Vegas Classic—$250,000
Winner: Bruce Crampton

The beat went on for Bruce Crampton in Las Vegas. With the Senior PGA Tour back to stroke play at the Desert Inn Country Club, Crampton surged from two shots off the pace after 36 holes and rolled to a two-stroke victory at the site where most of the players in the field had contested in the Tournament of Champions. It was his seventh victory of a remarkable season, as his $37,500 check made him the first senior with single-year earnings in excess of $400,000.

Crampton gave a signal of things to come when he fired a startling 65 in gale-force winds in the pro-amateur, but started modestly with 71 in much-improved conditions. Bob Charles, again to fail to win from early lead position, started with a 66 Friday, jumping off to a two-shot lead over Dale Douglass, with Miller Barber, Lee Elder, Jack Fleck and Joe Jimenez at 69 and Arnold Palmer and Gary Player at 70 with George Lanning.

Don January, coming off his match-play championship performance in Tucson, carded a 65 Saturday and slipped a stroke ahead of Charles, 136 to 137, as Crampton moved into third place with his 71–67—138. The Australian broke the backs of his opponents early in Sunday's final round when he holed a 45-foot birdie putt at No. 3, a 25-footer at No. 5 and a 35-footer at No. 7. He subsequently added two birdies and absorbed a single bogey, finishing with 68 for 206, 10 under par for the distance.

Douglass closed with 69 to take second place at 208, a stroke in front of Elder and Charles. January could manage just 74 Sunday and dropped into a fifth-place tie with Chi Chi Rodriguez, whose $10,937.50 check insured that he, too, would exceed Peter Thomson's single-season money-winning record of $386,724 in the final official event in Florida two weeks later.

Shearson-Lehman Brothers Classic—$250,000
Winner: Bruce Crampton

When the tournament was played down the road at Boca Grove, it had the great fortune of having as the winner the first three years Arnold Palmer, Arnold Palmer again and Gary Player. In 1986, the Quadel Classic became the Shearson-Lehman Brothers Classic and was moved some 10 miles north to Gleneagles Country Club at Delray Beach, Florida. Neither Palmer nor Player was there, being otherwise occupied in an invitational tournament in

Taiwan that week, but the roster of champions got a worthy addition at week's end in late November.

Bruce Crampton capped the regular season of the Senior PGA Tour at Gleneagles with his seventh circuit victory and eighth overall senior triumph in a performance that typified his record-breaking year. The streaking Australian put together the best 1986 score on a par-72 course and rolled to a four-stroke victory with his 16-under-par 200 over the 6,750-yard course that is home base for four Senior Tour regulars—Billy Casper, Sam Snead, Gay Brewer and Doug Ford. Only Lee Elder's 199 that took the Commemorative at the par-70 Sleepy Hollow course in New York was a lower total during the season.

Nothing would deter Crampton at Gleneagles. He opened with a seven-under-par 65, barely fazed by freak bounce that brought an out-of-bounds and double-bogey at the 10th hole. That gave him a one-stroke lead over Dale Douglass. He had five more birdies Saturday in a 67 that widened his margin to four strokes with the 132. Butch Baird, shooting his second 68, moved into second place as Douglass slumped to 74. Chi Chi Rodriguez, making what was to prove a vain effort to catch Crampton on the money list, was then tied for third at 138 with Casper and Bob Toski. Baird made a front-nine challenge to Crampton Sunday, going out in 32 to close the gap to two strokes. But Bruce reestablished what was to be his final margin when he followed a Baird bogey at No. 10 with a birdie at No. 11. He went on to a 68 for the 200 and the four-shot victory over Baird, who had his third straight 68. Jim Ferree closed with 67 and jumped into a third-place tie at 206 with Rodriguez.

Mazda Champions—$720,000
Winners: Bob Charles and Amy Alcott

Bob Charles chose an excellent time to shake off last-round doldrums and Amy Alcott picked the right moment for a final birdie in the Mazda Champions tournament, the year-ending special event teaming the leading players of the season on the Senior PGA and LPGA Tours. Charles, the most successful left-handed tournament pro in the game's history, had compiled a flock of high finishes, including four seconds, during his initial season on the Senior Tour, but failed to nail a victory, on several occasions frittering away his chances in the final round.

At Jamaica's Tryall Golf and Beach Club in the Mazda, Bob finished strongly with five of the team's seven birdies during the regulation 18 holes Sunday, then turned matters over to partner Alcott in the three-team playoff. Amy dropped a 10-foot birdie putt on the first extra hole to secure the victory and its lucrative rewards—$250,000 checks for each of them.

The tournament, with its 12 players off each of the two circuits, was expanded to 54 holes for its second staging in 1986. The first day, Bruce Crampton and Pat Bradley, the dominant figures on their respected tours in 1986, lived up to expectations as a team, shooting 63 to share the lead with Miller Barber and Judy Dickinson. The best scoring, though, came on

Saturday. Billy Casper and Jan Stephenson produced a 62 for 127 and moved into a one-shot lead over four teams, including Bradley/Crampton and Charles Owens/Jane Geddes, who fired a record 61. Casper and Stephenson retained the lead Sunday until taking consecutive bogeys at the 11th and 12th holes. Meanwhile, Charles had made four of his birdies on the front nine to get his team into contention. Alcott added two on the back nine before Bob two-putted the par-five 17th for another to get them seven under for the day. Amy missed from 18 feet at the last green, but the 64 gave them the lead among the finishers, their total 193.

They watched as Jim Ferree and Ayako Okamoto finished with the same total after each missed long birdie putts on the 18th green. Casper/Stephenson made it a three-team playoff after Bill's 18-foot birdie putt for the win failed to drop. The teams of Arnold Palmer/Chris Johnson and Gene Littler/Becky Pearson missed the playoff by a stroke. Crampton/Bradley could manage just a 67 Sunday for 195.

10. The European Tour

It seems that being mortal is not a luxury permitted Seve Ballesteros. He is very much a victim of his own success. Let any other golfer tail off in the final round and miss a chance to win, and observers only cluck sympathetically. Let Ballesteros do it, though, and they say his game is gone and his spirit crushed, and so forth. That was pretty much the story on Ballesteros early in the 1986 season. In defense of these observers, they had more than a little cause to wonder about him.

The doomsayers were clucking about Ballesteros from the outset. There was his celebrated misfire in the U.S. Masters in April, where victory slipped through his hands in the final round when he smacked a terrible approach into the water at the 15th and followed that up with a bogey at No. 17. Both were critical errors, especially the watered shot at No. 15. But for perspective it should be remembered that Jack Nicklaus was on a rampage after a long dormancy. Nicklaus shot 65 in that final round and outran not only Ballesteros, but Greg Norman and Tom Kite as well for his first victory of any kind since 1984, and his first in a major since 1980.

Ballesteros then opened the PGA European Tour with a series of near-misses—in the Suze Open at Cannes, Cepsa Madrid Open, and Italian Open. It may have been a question not so much of Ballesteros's failures as the expectations others have of him. It is his curse that he is expected to win every time he tees it up. Only history will finally answer the question, but Northern Ireland's David Feherty put things into balance shortly after he outlasted Ballesteros and won the Italian Open.

"People keep saying Seve is not the player he was," Feherty said. "But how can they, when he finishes fourth, second, second, and fourth in the U.S. Masters, Cannes, Madrid and Italian Opens in four weeks?"

Indeed, that would have been a near-spectacular showing for any other golfer. But for Ballesteros' followers, it spelled nothing less than failure and a flawed game. If Ballesteros wasn't the golfer he used to be, he had more than enough reason. There was the death of his father in the spring. Then there was his trouble with the U.S. PGA Tour. In 1985, Ballesteros failed to play in 15 American tournaments, as required by the accommodation reached for him. And so Deane Beman, commissioner of the tour, suspended him from tour events 1986. He was able to play in only one, the USF&G Classic, as the defending champion. He also played in events that are not tour events—the Masters, as a former champion, and the U.S. Open and the PGA Championship under special invitations. He was also invited to the World Series of Golf, but declined to play.

Meanwhile, back to the early part of the season: Just when everyone had written Ballesteros off, he exploded into one of the great performances in PGA European Tour history. He won Dunhill British Masters, and after taking a week off to play in the U.S. Open, he won three straight tournaments in three different countries—Carrolls Irish Open, Johnnie Walker Monte Carlo Open, and Peugeot French Open. Three weeks later he added the KLM Dutch Open, his fourth victory in eight weeks on the schedule, and became the first European Tour player to go over £1 million in career winnings. Later, in what was believed to be unprecedented, he finished a co-champion with Bernhard Langer in the Lancome Trophy. They agreed to share the title when it became too dark for them to continue their playoff. That gave him six (or five and a half) victories for the season. He thus topped the money list for a fourth time, and did it with a record £242,208 in winnings.

For all of Ballesteros's fireworks, it was another Spaniard who captured the fans' imagination. This was young Jose-Maria Olazabal, 20, a mere rookie. Olazabal was no stranger to European fans. He had a spectacular amateur record, having won not only important events in Spain and Italy, but the three top events in Britain—the British Boys, Youths and Amateur. Experts figured that with a little seasoning, he could become a force on the professional tour. They were thinking in terms of years, however, not tournaments. Olazabal turned in some strong showings early in 1986, then broke through late in the season to win the Ebel European Masters-Swiss Open and Sanyo Open. All told, he had eight top-10 finishes, was in the money in 18 of 19 events, and had a stroke average of 70.62. He finished second only to Ballesteros on the Order of Merit, with £136,775. Not surprisingly, he was a unanimous winner as the Henry Cotton Rookie of the Year award.

It was a year of ups and downs for others. For Howard Clark, it was up. He won the Cepsa Madrid Open and Peugeot Spanish Open, both with Ballesteros in hot pursuit, and finished third on the Order of Merit with £121,902, his best in 13 seasons on the tour. It was up also for Ian Woosnam, whose victory in the Lawrence Batley Tournament Players Championship helped lift him to fourth on the money list at £111,798. Woosnam also was the author of perhaps the weirdest hole of the season. In the Peugeot French Open, he needed only a four-foot putt for his par three, and took a 16.

As if underlining the rising quality of golf throughout Europe, 1986 was also an up year for the Swedes. Match play returned to the tour with the Epson Grand Prix, and the winner was Ove Sellberg, the first Swede ever to win a European Tour event. He finished No. 16 on the Order of Merit with £64,175, while countryman Anders Forsbrand, though without a victory, was eighth at £84,706. Langer, who spent most of the season on the American circuit, won the German Open for the fourth time in six years and later shared the Lancome with Ballesteros, and Greg Norman stopped by to take the British Open, Panasonic European Open, Suntory World Match Play Championship and Dunhill Nations Cup for Australia.

It was a surprisingly down year for some others. Sam Torrance failed to win for the first time in six years. Nick Faldo, although winning £65,418, which put him No. 15 on the Order of Merit, went through his second successive winless season.

Sandy Lyle, the 1985 British Open champion, won the Greater Greensboro Open in the United States but came up empty in Europe. He finished

24th on the money list at £48,639, a drop of 23 places and more than £150,000 from his No. 1 finish of 1985. It seemed Lyle couldn't quite get a grip on things. His frustrations perhaps reached their peak in one peculiar round of the Dunhill British Masters, when he returned one of the oddest 70s ever seen. He had to struggle to get home in 41 after going out in 29. At that, Lyle's case was not the most mysterious.

That dark distinction was left to Paul Way. Way, who joined the European Tour in 1981, had an excellent year in 1985—a victory in the Whyte & Mackay PGA, No. 10 on the Order of Merit with £76,140, a berth on the winning European Ryder Cup team, and runnerup (with Howard Clark) in the World Cup. Then he fell out of sight in 1986, dropping to 125th on the money list with £5,260.

Of the seven first-time winners in 1986, perhaps the most appealing was England's John Morgan. He had his best year ever, No. 35 on the money list with £33,568. Morgan was 42, and this was his first victory in 18 years on the European Tour. Fans knew exactly what he meant when he said, ". . . winning was much more important to me than the money."

Suze Open—£102,040
Winner: John Bland

"I can't believe," South African John Bland was saying, "that I gave the best player in the world a two-stroke start and beat him by four." But it was the truth, as raw figures go. Bland returned a 67 in the fourth round for a 12-under-par 276 total as the 1986 PGA European Tour got under way with the Suze Open at Cannes-Mougins. The man to whom he was referring, Seve Ballesteros, had 70–69–68 in the first three rounds. Then, uncharacteristically, Ballesteros contributed to his own defeat with a final-round 73. Coming on the heels of his failed attempt at the U.S. Masters the week before, some saw this as a symptom that something was missing from his mighty game. Ballesteros seemed about to win the Masters when he dumped an approach shot into the water at No. 15 in the final round. He also bogeyed No. 17, opening the door to a resurrected Jack Nicklaus, whose sensational charge to a closing 65 overran not only Ballesteros, but Greg Norman and Tom Kite as well. Whether this slip in the Suze was indeed symptomatic, only time would tell. The season was brand-new.

Ballesteros sent the Cannes galleries into raptures with one of golf's most spectacular recoveries in the second round for a 69 that carried him into a share of the halfway lead with Bland on five-under-par 139. He had staggered to four over par for the second round with a double-bogey six at No. 6. He gave his brother Vicente, who was his caddy, the famous "Lord, why me?" look. Vicente didn't bother with sympathy. "Keep going," he said. "There are 12 holes left." Ballesteros then launched his counterattack—five birdies and an eagle over the next 10 holes. Bland one-putted the last three greens, twice for birdies, to stick with Ballesteros. Ballesteros took the lead with a 68 in the third round, but his magic would end in the final round and Bland's would not.

"Neil Coles came up to me before the off," Bland said, "and asked what I'd give for his 67. I thought that if Neil could do that at the age of 50, so could I at 40." Bland birdied the fourth from 30 feet to get one shot back, then pulled level with another at the seventh. He went two ahead with a birdie four at No. 8, then profited from his own good luck and Ballesteros' bad luck. At No. 9, Ballesteros' ball ended up in a hole beside the green. And at No. 10, Bland pitched over the green, but his ball hit someone in the gallery and bounced back, from where he holed a 30-footer for a birdie. It clearly was Bland's day, and in short order he wrapped up his 14th career victory.

Cepsa Madrid Open—£120,000
Winner: Howard Clark

Howard Clark is very definitely English, but he must count Madrid as his second home, or at least the Cepsa Madrid Open. He took his third Madrid Open convincingly with a 14-under-par 274 and won ⌐n event that was notable for two other reasons: yet another slip by Seve Ballesteros, and the disqualification of Antonio Garrido for incorrectly marking his ball on the greens. Garrido, protesting his innocence, left the Puerta de Hierro course in tears.

Garrido, 42, winner of the 1977 Madrid Open and three other European tournaments, was said to have moved his ball a quarter-inch on three different putts in the second round. Paul Way, his playing partner, refused to sign Garrido's card for what would have been a 68 that would have given Garrido a 136 and a tie with Ballesteros for the 36-hole lead. Gordon Brand, Jr., the third member of the group, who shot 70–139, supported Way. Both called on John Paramor, director of tour operations, for a ruling while they were on No. 9 green, their last of the day. In Paramor's opinion, Garrido was not so much cheating as he was careless. Even so, Paramor considered the acts a serious breach of Rule 20–7 (b), and had no option but to disqualify Garrido. Way was not in contention at the time. He shot 75–77—152 and failed to qualify for the last two rounds.

Clark, who won the Madrid Open in 1978 and 1984, survived a taunting putter for a second-round 68 for a 138 that left him two behind Ballesteros after 36 holes. In the final round, Ballesteros seemed on the verge of taking his first victory of the year when he still led by two at the 12th, a testy par four. It was here that the scales tipped toward Clark. Ballesteros hooked his tee shot and found himself blocked out by a tree. He couldn't get home from there, but he was able to draw his second around the tree. Then he fluffed his pitch, leaving it so short that he three-putted for a double-bogey six. Clark, meanwhile, holed a 25-foot putt from just off the green for a birdie. The three-shot swing took him from two behind to one ahead. Clark, taking deep breaths and exercising his neck and shoulders to stay relaxed, held steady against the Spaniard's ever-present threat.

After both birdied the 15th, Ballesteros gained a stroke with a birdie at No. 16. He kept the pressure on with a fine tee shot just behind the flat at

No. 17. But Clark responded by hitting even closer, to six feet, and holed the putt for a birdie two. Clark now led by two, and he was the winner by one when Ballesteros made four to his comfortable five at No. 18. Ian Woosnam was a distant third at 71–279, and Jose-Maria Olazabal, the promising young Spanish rookie, broke par for the last three rounds and took fourth at 280. The Swedes, who are improving rapidly, were represented by Ove Sellberg, who led the first round with a 67 and finished a solo fifth with 281.

Italian Open—£99,535
Winner: David Feherty

The word heading into the Italian Open was that Spain's Seve Ballesteros would have to forget his recent series of disappointments and get back on track. So it was to be a tournament of surprises, in this order: Briton Mark James was the first-round leader; then Andrew Stubbs, a third-year player on the European Tour, shocked even himself by taking the 36-hole lead; and then, after Ballesteros missed his chance for the fourth straight week, Northern Ireland's David Feherty, 27, finally broke through with a sudden-death playoff victory over fellow countryman Ronan Rafferty. The European Tour was only three weeks old, and already it was a sea of exciting instability.

James held the first-round lead with a dazzling 65 at Albarella, near Venice. Then came Stubbs, 24, who turned professional after Walker Cup selectors ignored him in 1983. Stubbs, the runner-up in the 1981 English Championship and in the 1982 British Championship, was not the man they were looking for to come to the front in this Italian Open. "They were looking for powerful, long hitters," Stubbs said, "and I was simply short and straight." That proved to be the solution in warm, calm conditions on the Adriatic vacation island. He added a 68 to his opening 67 for a 135 total and a one-stroke lead on James and Feherty. But Stubbs was soon to leave the stage.

Drama, however, was to come from a different source. In the fourth round, Rafferty shot the back nine in 30 and tied the course record of 64 to catch Feherty and force the playoff. But it was discovered that a five at No. 1 on Rafferty's card had been altered to a four. He faced disqualification for having signed for a lower score than he made. But officials established that Rafferty had signed the card—including the five—before his marker had mistakenly altered it to a four. So he and Feherty went into the playoff. Feherty ended it with a 12-foot birdie putt on the second hole to collect his first European victory. Ballesteros, who had bogeyed No. 4 to fall three behind, finished with a 71 and a joint fourth at 273.

Feherty joined the European Tour in 1979, and his only previous victory was in the South African ICL in 1984. He sought to correct his problems by going to Surrey sports psychologist Alan Fine, who told him he was "hanging on to (his) anxiety as if it were a family heirloom." Fine made Feherty write a check for £1,000 to an animal charity, to be forfeited if he didn't win. Having won, Feherty decided to donate the money to the charity anyway.

Epson Grand Prix of Europe—£127,000
Winner: Ove Sellberg

After the European victory over the United States in the 1985 Ryder Cup match, Tony Jacklin, European team captain, predicted a Swede could be named to the 1987 squad. Ove Sellberg, 26, a five-year veteran of the PGA European Tour from Stockholm, could be that man. Sellberg staked Sweden's claim early in the 1986 season with a victory in the inaugural Epson Grand Prix of Europe Championship. Not only was he the first Swede ever to win a major European event, his victory was the crowning "upset" in a tournament of upsets at the St. Pierre course at Chepstow, Wales. Match play had thus returned to the European circuit after an absence of seven years. The field of 32 was drawn from the leaders of the 1985 Order of Merit.

A victory by any Swede can be considered an upset and a great tribute to their skill and persistence only because they are comparatively young at golf, and because of the shorter playing season and a lack of national interest in the game in Sweden. "We do well at tennis and skiing, and we are so used to good sportsmen that we are expected to win at golf as well," Sellberg said after his Epson victory. "But they don't know much about it over there yet."

Whatever the obstacles to becoming an outstanding golfer in Sweden, none of them showed in Sellberg at Chepstow. He not only won, he won convincingly, beating Howard Clark, who won the Madrid Open two weeks earlier, three and two in the final. That gave Sellberg the first prize of £25,500, some £13,000 short of his entire winnings in all of 1985, his best season to that point.

Another Swede, Anders Forsbrand, added to the upsets and helped make it a disappointing tournament for 1985 British Open champion Sandy Lyle. Forsbrand beat Lyle on the 19th hole in a playoff for third place. Earlier, Lyle was beaten on the last green by Clark in the semifinal. Then, in the final, Clark lost his touch on the greens, missing from only three feet at the eighth and from four feet at the ninth. "Perhaps it was a bit of a mental letdown after beating Sandy earlier in the day," Clark said, puzzling over his poor putting.

Clark's hopes died when he went two-down after Sellberg's fine birdie at the 12th and missed opportunities at the 14th and 15th. Clark was beaten, finally, when his drive at No. 16 clipped a tree and left him with no chance of making par.

Sellberg, in his semifinal, beat countryman Forsbrand, 3 and 2. Forsbrand then won the third-place playoff match when Lyle took a six at the first extra hole.

Sellberg was a member of the Swedish team which was runner-up to the United States in the 1982 Eisenhower Trophy. His victory in the Epson put Sweden ahead of his own prediction in professional golf. "I did not think we would make it (get a winner) until next year," Sellberg said.

Peugeot Spanish Open—£150,000
Winner: Howard Clark

Seve Ballesteros added another role to his growing presence in golf when he linked up with Camcorp, an Irish sports firm, to promote the £115,000 Spanish Open. Peugeot, the French auto manufacturer, stepped forward with a three-year commitment, replacing the previous sponsor, Benson & Hedges. So when the curtain went up at La Moraleja, near Madrid, Ballesteros had more than just wedge shots on his mind. With Bernhard Langer playing in the United States and Sandy Lyle and Nick Faldo bypassing the event, Howard Clark became the leading candidate to hold the frustrated Ballesteros at bay.

Ballesteros, who had suffered four near-misses in five weeks, saddled himself with too much work with an opening 74, so this Spanish Open became a duel between Clark and the tall Australian, Ian Baker-Finch.

Clark tied for the first-round lead at 68 with Scotland's Ross Drummond and little-known Spaniard Mariano Aparicio. Baker-Finch snatched the halfway lead from Clark with a burst of birdies over the final three holes, offsetting Clark's own birdie-birdie finish. That gave Baker-Finch 68–137 and a two-stroke lead over Clark (71–139). Ballesteros, meanwhile, was not exactly sleepwalking. He put on a furious charge, getting birdies at the 13th and 16th, then chipping in for an eagle at the 18th, finishing 3-4-3-3-3-3. His 66 left him tied for third at 140. His debut as player-promoter ended with him a solo third at 276, four behind Clark.

Clark would borrow a page from Ballesteros' own book of heroics to pluck victory away from Baker-Finch. But first they turned the final round in a rousing duel. They started off tied for the lead at 11 under par. Clark birdied two of the first three holes, then Baker-Finch caught him with a pair of birdies of his own. Clark edged ahead on a 20-foot birdie putt at the 11th, then Baker-Finch barged into the lead with two quick birdies, holing from 10 feet at the 14th and five feet at the short 15th. Clark responded with a birdie at the 16th from five feet, then slipped behind with a three-putt bogey at No. 17. Baker-Finch seemed set to win, then, when he was facing at least a par after putting his third shot at the par-five 18th to within 20 feet while Clark lay two in the rough about 30 feet from the hole.

But Clark is a wizard with the wedge. He had chipped in against Ballesteros in the final round of the Madrid Open just weeks earlier, he had chipped in to beat Sandy Lyle in a playoff for the 1985 Glasgow Open, and he chipped in in the Ryder Cup. He used a pitching wedge those three times. This time he used a sand wedge. He holed it for an eagle and nipped Baker-Finch by one, 67–272, 16 under, to 68–273. The victory was worth £25,000 and lifted him to £64,565 on the Order of Merit, nearly £20,000 above the second-place Ballesteros. Asked to describe his amazing start to the new season, Clark needed only one word for his answer: "Unbelievable!"

Whyte & Mackay PGA Championship—£210,000
Winner: Rodger Davis

The Whyte & Mackay PGA Championship figured to be a battle royal for a number of reasons. Among them: Howard Clark was on a rampage, British Open champion Sandy Lyle had two scores to settle, and the field at Wentworth's West Course was nearly at full strength.

First Clark: The hottest man on the tour, he was fresh from a dramatic victory in the Peugeot Spanish Open and owned two victories and a second out of four tournaments. Clark won the 1984 PGA Championship, setting a course-record 64 in the process. Then Lyle: Two weeks earlier, he was beaten by Clark in the semifinals of the Epson Match Play, and a year ago he was beaten in a playoff for the PGA by Paul Way. And the field: Except for Seve Ballesteros and Bernhard Langer, it was bristling. It included Nick Faldo and Ken Brown, and two talented newcomers, Spain's Jose-Maria Olazabal and New Zealand's Greg Turner.

Faldo, a new member at Wentworth, and Italy's Baldovino Dassu matched 68s to share the first-round lead. Lyle tied for second at 69, and Clark had a so-so 71 that included an eagle three at No. 4 but three fives at the par fours. But the finish did not match the promise.

It came down to Australian Rodger Davis, 35, a tour member since 1977, and Ireland's Des Smyth, 33, a member since 1974. Smyth charged from two strokes behind with three birdies over the last five holes. And so Davis, who entered the final round with a two-stroke lead, seemed doomed to finish second for the 31st time in seven years when he came to the final hole trailing Smyth by one stroke. But he dropped a devilish downhill 25-foot birdie putt for a 70 to tie Smyth (68) at seven-under-par 281. They went off into a playoff that became something of a comedy.

They halved the first playoff hole, No. 15, in bogey fives, and the second in par threes. At the third, No. 17, Smyth seemingly handed the title over by hooking his tee shot out of bounds. All Davis needed now was a par five, and he tried to nurse it home. Trying to play safe, he hit a one-iron off the tee, but into the right rough. Then he put his three-iron second under some trees. And his fourth ran through the green. But he chipped on and dropped his putt for a bogey six to Smyth's seven, and the title and £35,000 first prize were his. It was Davis's seventh career victory, and his first European title since 1981.

Clark, meanwhile, had cooled down. He shot 71-71-73-73—288 and tied for sixth.

Four Stars National Pro-Celebrity—£138,500
Winner: Antonio Garrido

The rising stars had their moment, one a young Frenchman, the other a young Spaniard. But in the end it was experience that paid off when Spanish veteran Antonio Garrido, who had angrily considered retiring from golf, broke through late in the final round to win the £150,000 London Standard

Four Stars National Pro-Celebrity at Moor Park, Hertfordshire. Garrido won by a stroke, but it could be a sign of things to come that one of the men he nipped with a birdie at the 17th in the fourth round was Jose Maria-Olazabal, 20, the fellow Spaniard who only a few years earlier had won the British Boys, Juniors, and Amateur.

It took a change of heart to get Garrido into the tournament. He spoke of quitting the game after being disqualified from the Madrid Open five weeks earlier for improperly marking his ball on three greens. The officials' finding at the time was that he was being careless, not cheating, when he gained about a quarter-inch each time. Garrido, who had vehemently denied mismarking, said he changed his mind about retiring after getting hundreds of letters from supporters in Spain, France, and Italy. But he remained angry with Paul Way, the fellow pro who had raised the complaint. "I will never speak to Paul Way again," Garrido insisted. "What he said was ridiculous, incredible!"

The Four Stars opened on a young note when France's Emmanuel Dussart, 22, took the first-round lead with a 67, and Olazabal tied for second at 68. Both turned professional in 1984 and had not yet won on the PGA European Tour. Dussart, who had failed in two attempts at winning his tour card, was making his British tournament debut as a special invitee. Olazabal, who led the tour qualifying school in 1985, might have had a commanding lead except for four missed putts inside five feet.

It was age's turn next. South African Hugh Baiocchi, 39, shot a 65, and Garrido, 42, a 67 to join Olazabal (68) in a tie for the halfway lead at 136. Olazabal kept pace with one-putt birdies on the last two holes. Northern Ireland's Ronan Rafferty rushed to the front in the third round. His 68 gave him a 206 total and the lead by one over Garrido and two over Olazabal.

Olazabal staged another putting exhibition in the final round in a powerful bid for his first professional victory. Beginning at the 14th, he ran off three straight birdies on putts of six, eight, and 12 feet. His undoing came at the 17th, where he drove behind a tree. Garrido passed Rafferty with birdies on three of the first four holes. Rafferty charged back and caught Garrido twice, but he also three-putted twice for bogeys. Rafferty closed with a 70 and Olazabal with a 68 to tie for second at 276. Garrido, former Ryder Cup and World Cup player, wrapped up the victory and the £21,660 first prize with a clutch six-foot birdie four at the 17th. It was his fifth tour victory and his first since the 1982 Tunisian Open. Garrido departed a happy man for another reason. He was informed a week earlier that the PGA Tournament Committee had decided to take no further action against him over the ball-marking infraction. So the Madrid Open incident seemed to be closed.

Dunhill British Masters—£200,000
Winner: Seve Ballesteros

Lee Trevino returned to defend his Dunhill British Masters title at the Duke's Course, Woburn, bringing his special lightness to the proceedings. He was the guest of the Marquess and Marchioness of Tavistock at Woburn

Abbey, now the privilege of defending Masters champions. "I must go," Trevino said at a pre-tournament press interview. "The butler will shortly be serving afternoon tea." But even Trevino's presence couldn't lighten the first day. Manuel Pinero, one of the heroes of Europe's winning Ryder Cup team in 1985, was disqualified for violating the rule against improving one's lie.

Pinero was seen on television moving, with his foot, some long grass behind his ball in the rough on the 17th fairway. Said television commentator Peter Alliss, "That looks like a nimble bit of footwork, which is not exactly kosher. But who am I to say?" After an inquiry by Tony Gray, a PGA European Tour official, Pinero was disqualified. Pinero said he did not think he was violating any rule. Gray said that Pinero had not intended to cheat. It was the second disqualification this season. A few weeks earlier, Antonio Garrido was disqualified from the Madrid Open for incorrectly replacing his ball on the greens.

Meanwhile, Rick Hartmann, 27, an American playing the European Tour, jumped into the lead with a 66 on some superb putting. He had three twos in an outward 32, and birdied the last three holes coming in. He rolled in putts ranging from 20 to 40 feet. Ballesteros, who had his doubters after a series of near-misses beginning with the U.S. Masters, found an old friend in his putter and turned in a strong 67. He credited Brazil's Jaime Gonzalez, who advised him to move the ball a little farther back in his stance. Result: Ballesteros needed only 28 putts, including a 40-footer at the 14th. Ballesteros said he could not remember the last time he made a putt that long. He also saved some pars, including a vintage Ballesteros scramble at the 18th. He pushed his drive into the rough, put his second into a bunker, his third into another bunker, and exploded just past the flag. British Open champion Sandy Lyle was busy turning on one of the oddest 70s yet seen—29–41—en route to a 286 total, 11 strokes off the lead.

Ballesteros broke through in the final round with a solid 70 for a 13-under-par 275 and a two-stroke victory over late-charging Gordon Brand. Brand sprinted from back in the pack with three birdies over the last six holes for his 67–277. Ballesteros had his hands full with Robert Lee, who fought all the way before settling for 71–278 and a share of third with Bernhard Langer. Over the first nine holes, Lee one-putted seven times, and got birdies on three of them. Lee surprised even Ballesteros with his second birdie, that at No. 4. Lee pushed his drive, and it hit a spectator and bounced back into play. Lee asked Ballesteros whether he could still reach the green in two. "Only if you are a superman," Ballesteros said. Lee proceeded to power a shot that almost reached, then he pitched on and made the putt.

At No. 10, Lee just missed an eagle-three that would have tied him with Ballesteros. Then he bogeyed the 11th to fall to three behind when Ballesteros birdied. Lee stayed afloat with a scrambling four at No. 12, then birdied the 13th with a pitch from 70 yards. Ballesteros bogeyed No. 14 and found himself only one stroke ahead. From this point, Ballesteros' great talent for turning sure bogeys into pars—he needed just 29 putts in his 70— got him through.

Jersey Open—£80,000
Winner: John Morgan

This week, while Raymond Floyd became the oldest ever to win the U.S. Open at age 43, England's John Morgan won the Jersey Open, his first victory in his 18 years on the European Tour at age 42.

"What a great year it has been for the over-forties!" Morgan said. "Now that I've won, I want to win again next week and the week after that. I still dream of winning the Open." The triumph was a long-awaited reward for the much-traveled Morgan, who had won three times on Africa's Safari Circuit and placed second and third in British events. And the victory came hard—a sudden-death playoff victory over Australian Peter Fowler. Perhaps it came as a surprise, too, for Morgan posted a 65 in the first round and wasn't even the leader.

That distinction went to Gordon Brand, who eagled all four par fives and put up a record 62. But he was doomed to fade on the greens. "The way I putted in the first round was a dream," Brand said. "After that, it was a nightmare." He suffered a 75 in the third round and finished a joint third with Howard Clark at 277. Clark closed with a 66, but his victory hopes lay back in the third round, where an out-of-bounds seven at the 16th helped him to a 75. His £4,500 prize, however, lifted his total European winnings to £75,857 and back atop the money list over Seve Ballesteros, who was among the European hopefuls at the U.S. Open this week. In the second round, Morgan moved to within one, 132–133, with a 68 to Brand's 70.

The second round produced as bizarre an 11 as anyone might want. It happened at the 188-yard third, when Scotland's Billy McColl fluffed a chip shot that plugged in a bunker. He barely moved it with his next shot, and the next left it under the lip. He hacked at it. It bounced back and struck his foot, costing him a two-stroke penalty, then fell to the bottom of his own footprint, nine inches deep. He finally got it out, knocked it onto the green, and two-putted. Heroically, he played the remaining holes in par for an 80–152. When it comes to horror stories, South Africa's Hugh Baiocchi had one of his own. He started the final round only a stroke behind Morgan, then three-putted three times en route to a 75 and a share of fifth place.

It was putting that saved the day for Morgan. Not his, but Fowler's. Morgan was leading by two strokes with two holes to play. He lost one stroke of that lead at the 17th when Fowler holed from 15 feet for his sixth birdie of the day. He lost the other at No. 18. Morgan, who had four-putted the 18th in the third round, this time bogeyed it after driving into the rough. Morgan shot 71, Fowler 69, to tie at 274. On the first hole of the playoff, Morgan's 15-foot try for a birdie hung on the lip. But Fowler, former Australian Open champion, three-putted. Morgan had his first title, and a £13,330 prize.

"I love this game," Morgan said, "and winning was much more important to me than the money."

Carrolls Irish Open—£190,275
Winner: Seve Ballesteros

There was more than the usual amount of interest in this Carrolls Irish Open at Portmarnock. It was the debut—or the re-debut—of Deane Beman, commissioner of the U.S. PGA Tour, as a professional golfer. At age 47, and 12 years after he left the circuit to become its chief, he was returning to competition. It would be on a limited basis, and not on the U.S. tour. He had received an exemption into the Irish Open in April, some months after announcing his intention to return to action. The U.S. Open a week earlier was also a target, but back problems kept him from trying to qualify. He also hoped to play in the British Open.

Beman became commissioner of the U.S. tour in 1974, after an outstanding playing career that included two U.S. Amateur championships, one British Amateur, four Walker Cup appearances, and four professional titles on the U.S. tour. His appearance in this Irish Open took on added significance with the presence of Severiano Ballesteros, the defending champion, whom he'd suspended from the U.S. tour for not playing the 15 tournaments required of him in 1985. Those with a waspish sense of humor wondered whether Beman and Ballesteros would be paired together. They were not. Beman made the cut by one at 74–79—153, and finished well back.

Robert Lee, who had a good outing in the Dunhill British Masters just two weeks earlier, forged into the first-round lead on a long putt at No. 18. It was his sixth birdie of an inward 31, and a 66 for the day. That put him one ahead of Australia's Wayne Riley. Ballesteros, who made the British Masters his first title of the season, posted a 68 and was a joint third. After starting on the 10th hole, he caught fire and played a four-hole stretch beginning at No. 13 in five under par—three birdies and an eagle. He moved into the lead in the second round, returning a 75 for 143 in the teeth of near gale winds that whipsawed the flagsticks. American Bob Smith was the only player to break par that day, posting a one-under 71. In the morning, when the wind was its stiffest, 42 of the first 75 players to finish failed to break 80. Said Bernhard Langer (76), "Not only was my ball moving on the greens, but I was, too."

A 68 in strong winds on Saturday, when no one else broke 70, was the key to Ballesteros' victory, for the magic left him in the fourth round. He missed nine fairways and 10 greens. But he had enough game left to post a closing 74 for a three-under-par 285 to win by two over Australia's Rodger Davis (69) and South African Mark McNulty (70), who shared second on 287. It was his second victory in two starts on the European Tour. In six European tournaments, then, he finished second, second, equal fourth, third, first, and first. His total winnings topped £100,000.

Johnnie Walker Monte Carlo Open—£158,215
Winner: Seve Ballesteros

The year of 1986 was fast shaping up as the year of second place on the PGA European Tour. First place, it seemed, had been reserved for Seve Ballesteros.

He did it again in the Johnnie Walker Monte Carlo Open at the par-69 Mont Agel course. He returned a pair of 64s in the closing rounds and made up five strokes on third-round leading Ron Commans of the United States to take his second victory in two weeks and his third in three starts. "My final round was one of the best I've ever played," Ballesteros said. "It could easily have been 60 or better. I feel physically very strong this year, maybe because I exercised so much in the winter."

It seemed as though someone else might have a chance in this one. Both Ballesteros and Sandy Lyle saw potentially sub-60 scores evaporate in the first round. Lyle shared first place on a 65, but for a while was within reach of 59 or less. Lyle was six under par through the first 11 holes. But he missed on four birdie chances of between six feet and 15 feet, and he dropped two strokes to par after missing greens. Poor tee shots would help push him back into the field in the second round. Ballesteros also seemed headed for the 50s, after shooting 31 on the front nine. A triple-bogey seven at No. 11 chilled him. He bunkered his second shot, then slashed his next over the green and into a woman spectator's handbag. He finished eagle-birdie for a 66. His problems were nothing compared to those of Albert Pelissier, 68, former Belgian Open champion and now a driving range professional from Nice. Pelissier posted a 97 and explained he had not competed seriously "since I lost my putting in Mexico in 1953."

Commans, 27, a former Walker Cupper, raced into the halfway lead with a 63—129. Two birdies on the last four holes would have given him a 59, but he got two bogeys instead. Commans, who borrowed $800 from his father to travel to Europe after losing his American tour card in 1985, bogeyed the 11th, then put on a dazzling display. He played the next five holes in 13 strokes, including an eagle-two on an 80-yard wedge shot at No. 15. Commans held the lead through the third round with 67—196. Ballesteros' 64 left him a joint ninth at 201.

While Commans was in the process of drifting back with a 74 in the final round, Ballesteros was getting up steam. If he was slightly disappointed in his 64, it was more than enough to get him a two-stroke victory over South African Mark McNulty, at 11-under-par 265. He became the first to win three in a row since Nick Faldo did it in 1983. His overall figures were staggering. The £26,365 first prize lifted his winnings in seven European outings to over £130,000. And he was an astonishing 67 under par for his 28 rounds. The victory left him within about £60,000 of becoming the first to reach career winnings of £1 million on the European Tour.

Peugeot French Open—£121,600
Winner: Seve Ballesteros

The first three rounds of the Peugeot French Open were played in a heat wave, the final on a gray, damp day. Seve Ballesteros never seemed to notice. Except for an inconsiderate photographer and some slow play, nothing seemed to bother him. He won almost with ease, and left golf to wonder how long he could keep this up. He thus had won the last four European events he had entered—a record—and the last three in successive weeks.

Ballesteros was also at La Boulie to defend the French title he won in 1985 at St. Germain. By all indications, the coast seemed clear enough. Bernhard Langer, Ballesteros' chief competitor of late, would seem to be occupied with thoughts other than golf. He and his wife, Vicki, were expecting the arrival of their first child at any moment. Nick Faldo was still trying to get some swing changes to behave. If Ballesteros was weary from a long run of competition, it hadn't shown yet. He made a 61 in the pro-am. "That was quite special," he said.

Ballesteros' opening 65 gave him a one-stroke lead over Faldo, who four-putted No. 18 (his ninth hole of the day), and South African Mark Wiltshire. Only the supporting cast changed for the second round. Ballesteros' 66–131 put him three ahead of Argentina's Vicente Fernandez (65) and Canada's Ray Stewart (66).

Two golfers blew up in this round, but in different ways. Ballesteros was repeatedly disturbed by cameramen and the Parisian crowd. At the ninth hole, after missing a birdie putt, he threw his ball at a photographer. "I was really mad," Ballesteros said. "It was the second time it happened. Perhaps it was not a good thing to do, but I had to vent my feelings." Ian Woosnam vented his feelings in another way, and it cost him dearly. At No. 3, a par-three, Ian Woosnam missed his par try from four feet. Clearly upset, he began tapping his ball this way and that, even while it was moving. It took quite some time, but his playing partners, Fernandez and Mark James, finally decided that Woosnam had taken six putts and incurred eight penalty strokes. He finished the hole with a 16. It reminded golf fans of the 15 Brian Barnes put up in the 1968 French Open at Saint Cloud, and was well short of the reputed world professional record, the 23 by Tommy Armour in the 1927 Shawnee Open. Remarkably, Woosnam made only an 81 with that 16 on his card. A bogey on the third would have given him a 69.

Ballesteros knew few delicate moments in this French Open, his 48th career victory worldwide. Fernandez made the most serious threat, drawing even briefly in the third round. Ballesteros wrapped it up with a 19-under-par 65–66–69–69—269, which gave him the title and the £20,181 by two over Fernandez. For 32 rounds in Europe, Ballesteros was now 86 under par and held a stroke average of 68.68. He also won more than £150,000.

Car Care Plan International—£110,000
Winner: Mark Mouland

Seve Ballesteros, after four straight victories, sat this one out to prepare for the British Open the following week. His presence might not have mattered. Someone else's time had come.

It was common sense and not a complete lack of confidence that had Welshman Mark Mouland setting his sights on something other than winning the Car Care Plan. That was a real logjam of a finish. Fully 13 players stood within two strokes of one another going into the final day at Moortown. Mouland, 25, former British Boys champion, had had no victories and only £21,565 in winnings since joining the pro tour in 1982. Thus he had no real reason to expect that he would come rushing out of this pack to score his first victory. His real goal, as he stood on the first tee, was to gain one of the five exempt places still available for the next week's British Open at Turnberry. The result surprised even him.

"I can't believe it," Mouland said. "I didn't know I was capable. I had never been in that position before. I had no idea whether I could handle it."

He erased that doubt for himself and all others with a course record-tying 64 and a 272 total that nipped Sweden's Anders Forsbrand (66) by one. Mouland, who had never finished higher than eighth in his five years on tour, played some spectacular golf. At the downhill, par-five 10th, he put his second shot deep into some bushes. He somehow reached the green with his third, and holed the putt for a birdie. At No. 16, a pushed drive left him with a blind second shot. He hit a five iron over the trees, and birdied again.

Mouland, son of Sid Mouland, former Welsh World Cup player, wasn't the only big surprise. Nick Faldo was another, but for a different reason. Faldo made his big move in the third round, just as Australian Lyndsey Stephen, who led through the first two, collapsed to a 76. Faldo, whose last victory was in the Car Care two years ago, posted a strong 67 and leaped 10 places to tie for the lead with Graham Marsh, Vaughan Somers, and American Bill Malley, at one-under-par 206. Mouland, who had posted 72–71–65, was unnoticed in a group two strokes behind.

Faldo, who has been trying to rebuild his swing for several years, seemingly had the tournament won when he started the final round with an eagle three and pulled two strokes ahead of the field. But he fell away almost immediately, taking sixes at both the third and the fifth. His 73 left him a joint 14th at 279.

Mouland, meanwhile, was playing his heart out. Fresh from the great save at No. 16, he went boldly for the flag at No. 17, lying just beyond a bunker, then holed the putt for his three. He won £18,330, almost as much as he had won in his career to date. And thus he created a true tale for evenings at the fireside—of how he stalked a berth in the British Open and bagged his first championship as well.

KLM Dutch Open—£140,000
Winner: Seve Ballesteros

Seve Ballesteros returned to the PGA European Tour, hung out his shingle, and it was business as usual.

He had been gone for two weeks—a week off followed by the British Open, in which he suffered his worst finish of the season to date, a joint sixth. He celebrated his return by making history. In running off with the KLM Dutch Open at Noordwijk by eight strokes, he became the first European Tour player to go over £1 million in career prize winnings. Ironically, Ballesteros, now 29, began his meteoric rise with another Dutch Open title, that in 1976. It was the first of his 48 worldwide victories.

This one was his fifth victory in his last six outings, and the £23,330 first prize lifted his season winnings to over £195,000, and his career winnings to £1,005,838. He has his sights set on topping that figure across the Atlantic, too. "I think it's a great record," he said, "to be the first man in the history of the game to win £1 million in Europe and $1 million in America."

Ballesteros opened with a 69 and trailed leader Vicente Fernandez by one. Then he took command, but under odd circumstances. Protestors of South Africa's apartheid (racial segregation) policy dug holes in the third, seventh, and eleventh greens. Their targets were South Africa-based golfers in the field—Hugh Baiocchi, Mark McNulty, Tony Johnstone, Teddy Webber, and Phil Simmons. The seventh green was restored to play, but the other two were so badly damaged that the second round was reduced to 16 holes. Despite high winds and a violent rainstorm, Ballesteros went out in 30, and finished with a 63 that was one under par for the shortened course. That left him at four under overall with a 132, and the leader by two strokes.

A 71 in the third round gave Ballesteros a four-stroke cushion going into the final round. Never one to coast, he birdied the second from 40 feet and the fourth from 25, and made the turn in 35. That put him six ahead of his nearest rival, the young Welshman, Philip Parkin. Ballesteros kept the pressure on coming home, making three birdies over the next five holes. He finished with a 68 for a nine-under-par total of 271. Second place went to Spain's Jose Rivero, Ballesteros' Ryder Cup teammate, who dropped three straight strokes and turned in 38, then scored an eagle-three at No. 11. Rivero's closing 72 left him at one-under 279.

When it was over, everyone could breathe easier for a while. Ballesteros announced he was taking the next week off, then going to America to try for the U.S. PGA Championship.

Scandinavian Open—£153,250
Winner: Greg Turner

A harsh bit of history repeated itself for Craig Stadler. It was the same event, the Scandinavian Open; and the same course, the picturesque Ullna course outside Stockholm. In 1983, victory was almost in his powerful hands, but he overshot the final green and lost to Scotland's Sam Torrance. This time he led by three strokes with three holes to play, and ended up losing in a sudden-death playoff to Greg Turner, 23, a New Zealander in his first season on the PGA European Tour.

Turner, the 1986 Singapore Open champion, sank a 30-foot putt for a birdie three on the first extra hole to take the £25,500 first prize. Not that he didn't do his share to earn it. In the second round, he returned a dazzling record 62 for a 13-under-par 131 to go ahead by one over Stadler and Australian Ian Baker-Finch at the halfway point. Turner made eight birdies and an eagle in that record round. He holed two 40-foot putts and six others from between 10 and 15 feet, and needed just 24 putts in all.

Baker-Finch, the defending champion, took the first-round lead on 65, a stroke up on Stadler and Mark James. Turner jumped into the 36-hole lead on that 62, and then Stadler ran off his third consecutive 66 for 198 to take the lead by two over Turner going into the final round. In 54 holes, Stadler dropped only one stroke to par. He had fully returned, it seemed, to the form that won him the U.S. Masters in 1982. He seemed unbeatable, in fact, standing 21 under par and three strokes ahead with three holes to play.

"I was in complete command with three holes to play," the disappointed Stadler said, "and had proved to myself I could handle my nerves by getting up and down from a bunker at both 13 and 14." Then the fates of golf struck. He mis-clubbed himself at the short 16th and was plugged in a bunker. There went one stroke of his lead. "I hit poor tee shots on the next two holes, and bad approaches as well, and I three-putted No. 18," he said. "It's very disheartening to throw away a tournament like that. But I didn't choke. My mind just seemed to wander." That gave Stadler a 72, and Turner's 70 was enough to catch him at 270.

Turner found his inspiration in a scolding from his older brother, Glenn, the former New Zealand cricket captain. Greg had finished 35th in the British Open after a closing 77, and took a week's rest. "I went to Lord's to watch the Test match and got a ticking off from Glenn for being a lazy so-and-so," he said. "But it was just the tonic I needed."

PLM Open—£117,075
Winner: Peter Senior

Australian Peter Senior had been casting about, looking for some self-confidence. He found at least £19,500 worth when he held the lead through the final two rounds and won the PLM Open at Falsterbo Golf Club, a flat links course jutting into the Baltic Sea on Sweden's southern tip. It was a double first—the debut of the tournament and Senior's first PGA European Tour victory.

The victory couldn't have come at a better time for Senior, 27, a three-time winner in Australia. He revealed he had been fined about £3,000 by the U.S. PGA Tour for exceeding his allotted five releases to play on the European Tour. Senior gained his American tour card in the autumn of 1985, but won less than £2,000 in 12 events through the first five months of 1986.

He made only two 36-hole cuts. Hoping for a change in luck and a confidence boost, he decided to try the European Tour.

"It was a calculated risk," Senior said. "I had to get back my self-belief and I've done it. Now I can comfortably afford the hefty penalty when I do go back to the States." Helped by a third place in the Monte Carlo Open six weeks earlier, Senior left the PLM with some £40,000 in winnings in eight weeks in Europe.

Senior was not a factor when the PLM got under way. England's Barry Lane, 26, 72nd on the European Order of Merit, fought off high winds for a course-record 65 and the first-round lead by three. New Zealand's Greg Turner, winner of the Scandinavian Open the week before, aiming for a Swedish double, stood a joint second on 68. Senior was four off the pace at 69.

Turner strengthened his bid with a second-round 66, moving into the halfway lead at eight-under-par 134. That put him two ahead of Britain's David Russell. Senior slipped another two strokes off the lead, his 72 leaving him seven back at 141. But he broke through in the third round, shooting 66 to forge into the lead by one. The final round demonstrated two things: that Senior could hold on under pressure, and that Swedish golf is getting stronger fast.

Ove Sellberg, Sweden's first-ever European Tour winner when he took the Epson Grand Prix in May, caught Senior briefly at eight under. Senior responded with three straight birdies, beginning at the par-three eleventh. He sank a 20-foot putt for his birdie-four at No. 13. Sellberg closed with a fine 66, but his opening 76 was too much to overcome and he finished third at 276. But another Swede stepped forward. Mats Lanner came in with a 67, but Senior kept him at bay with birdie-threes from 20 feet at No. 16 and 12 feet at No. 17. Senior's six at No. 18 left him with a 68 for an 11-under 273 and a two-stroke victory.

Benson & Hedges International—£180,000
Winner: Mark James

Mark James missed one of the brightest moments of his golfing life. His eyes were closed when the 15-foot putt dropped, giving him the title and the £30,000 first prize in the Benson & Hedges International on the first hole of a three-way playoff. James, known as a quiet man on the course, burst into a leap and flung his cap into the air. The galleries at Fulford understood. Not only was it his first victory on the European Tour in 15 months, he had just survived against two tough players in crisis that need not have been.

James knew better than anyone that it shouldn't even have come down to a playoff. Only his curious lapse on the final hole of regulation play allowed Lee Trevino and Hugh Baiocchi to tie him. The tournament was all for James' taking. Trevino's approach to No. 18 hit a spectator, and Baiocchi could not get down in two from short of the green. All James needed was to hole a three-foot putt and the victory was his in regulation.

"I should have wrapped it up earlier," James said. "I played a great pitch on the 18th, and not a bad putt. But I just misread it, and I had to go out again." That little three-footer just lipped out, leaving James with a 70 to the 68s returned by Trevino and Baiocchi. The trio had tied at 14-under-par 274, and went out to the playoff.

The finish, however, was not nearly so unusual as the start. James and Gordon Brand, Jr. posted seven-under-par 65s to share the first-round lead, but first they had to survive swarms of flying, biting ants. Play was held up as officials drove off the insects with insecticide sprays. It may have been a first in golf: Play suspended due to ants. "They got inside my shirt and were biting like fury," said Baiocchi, who was in a group with Trevino at 66. "When I pulled off my shirt, there were red weals all over me. We have wild animals on some courses back home (South Africa), but I've seen nothing like this."

The invaders repulsed, the second round proceeded without incident. James slipped to a 70 and back into third place, and Brand held the halfway lead with a 67–132, a stroke better than Trevino (66–67). Trevino put on an awesome show on the greens. Beginning at No. 2, he holed putts of 35, 30, and 18 feet for successive birdies. He got up and down three times for pars, then holed a 40-footer at No. 15 for the first of three more birdies. Aside from that, the big news this time was strictly golf: Sam Torrance and Sandy Lyle, the last two winners of the Benson & Hedges, failed to make the halfway cut.

It came down, ultimately, to the first hole of the playoff. James needed a 15-footer for a winning birdie. He tapped the ball and refused to watch. "I thought the putt would stop short," he said. "I don't think I dared look, and when it dropped in, I had my eyes shut." The missed three-footer on the final hole of regulation was forgotten. "I'm just glad to win," James said.

Bell's Scottish Open—£130,000
Winner: David Feherty

It was the second extra hole of a playoff, and it all came down to two putts, neither of them within real birdie range. North Ireland's David Feherty was about 45 feet from the hole, and Christy O'Connor, Jr. about half that distance, both lying two. Given the length of these two putts, a third extra hole seemed a certainty. But Feherty ignored the length and the pressure of the moment and rolled his in. Then O'Connor missed, and Feherty had wrapped up the playoff victory and the £21,600 first prize in the Bell's Scottish Open at Haggs Castle, Glasgow.

It had started out as a three-way playoff. The third party was Australia's Ian Baker-Finch, who began the fourth round with a four-stroke lead off three straight 66s. He faded to a final-round 72 while Feherty put up a 67 and O'Connor a 68 to create a logjam at 270. At the first hole, a short par-five of only 483 yards and a clear birdie chance, all three played safe by fading their tee shots, left to right. All three came down in the fairway within a few feet of each other. All three hit woods for their second shots. Feherty's shot was on line but short, Baker-Finch's hit the green but bounced into a bunker, and

O'Connor hooked his into the rough and pitched on to about 12 feet beyond the flag. Baker-Finch left his ball in the bunker with his next shot, but he was granted a reprieve when both Feherty and O'Connor missed their putts. But the lanky Aussie, who became instantly popular when he challenged almost to the very end in the 1984 British Open, put himself out when he missed from five feet. That set up the two-man duel at the second playoff hole at No. 18.

It was a sad finish for Baker-Finch. In the first round, he returned a 66 and was one behind New Zealander Frank Nobilo, who took advantage of good conditions early in the day and shot a 65 that stood up as the first-round lead. A heavy rain hit later in the day. Nobilo had five birdies and an eagle, and just one bogey. Baker-Finch charged home from the 13th in the first round, making birdies on four of the last five holes. Nobilo was not to last. In the second round, he soared to a 76, 11 strokes over his start, for a halfway total of 141. That put him nine strokes behind Baker-Finch's 132.

The tournament opened on a strange note. As Howard Clark put it, "I am here to defend a tournament that does not exist any more." The Bell's Scottish Open replaced the Glasgow Open, the 1985 edition of which Clark had won by chipping in for a birdie three at the second extra hole in a playoff against Sandy Lyle. This one would be an unrewarding tournament for Clark. With his best round a 69, he never was in contention and he finished at 284, 14 strokes off the lead. But he had come in good spirits to defend that non-existent title. "I have passed up an invitation to play in the World Series to do so," Clark said, "and hopefully to return something to Glasgow for what they have done for me."

German Open—£164,750
Winner: Bernhard Langer

Bernhard Langer, who fittingly enough practically owns the German Open, broke an eight-month victory drought with his triumph in this one at Hubelrath, Dusseldorf—his fourth German Open title in six years. He did it in a stirring playoff against Australia's Rodger Davis, with a birdie on the fifth extra hole. But Langer's show was almost stolen by Britain's Peter Baker, who had started making a name for himself. Just 18 and a professional for barely a month, he was playing in only his fourth tournament as a pro. He had made his first check, £650, as a joint 48th in the Scottish Open just the week before. And there he was, challenging.

Baker returned a 67 in the first round to share a one-stroke lead with Dennis Durnian and Mark McNulty. He barged into that tie with birdies on the last three holes, and he might have been the lone leader but for three misses from six feet or less on the first five holes. Langer, meanwhile, was hardly in sight. His last victory was in the Million Dollar Challenge at Sun City in December, 1985, and if a victory slump wasn't bad enough, he was also forced to play with strange clubs. His regular clubs were lost in transit as he was returning from the World Series of Golf, and he had to dig out a set he hadn't used and which he didn't like. Langer, the first and only West

German golfer of note and a big local hero, gave his fans little to cheer about with an opening 75 that left him eight strokes off the lead.

The real Langer, now with his regular clubs, showed up in the second round. He announced his arrival with a 65 that carried him over some 40 golfers to a share of ninth place on 140. He credited his iron play with saving him some eight strokes. Ballesteros, who hadn't played in two weeks, was playing well (69–69) but couldn't get enough out of his game for his sixth European victory of the season. He eventually tied for 10th on 279. Young Baker showed no signs of being affected by the pressure until the home stretch. He bogeyed the last three holes for his worst round of the Open, a 72 that left him a joint 10th.

This one came down to a rousing finish. At one point, only one stroke separated the first nine players. But Davis was not to be denied—almost. He closed with a course-record 64, but a huge error cost him an outright victory. Leading by a stroke, he three-putted the last hole and fell back into a tie with Langer at 15-under-par 273, two strokes ahead of the field. They battled through the playoff, including halving a hole in birdies, before Langer sank the decisive birdie putt on the fifth extra hole.

Ebel European Masters/Swiss Open—£263,160
Winner: Jose-Maria Olazabal

The young Spaniard some have called "the next Seve Ballesteros" quickly began establishing an identity of his own in the Ebel European Masters Swiss Open, and if the experts are correct in their forecasts, this marked the start of a dazzling career. Spain's Jose-Maria Olazabal, only 20 and just barely removed from one of the outstanding records in British amateur golf, rolled to this victory as though his time had come.

Just a rookie on the European Tour, Olazabal began the Masters with a 64, but all that got him was a share of the lead with Northern Ireland's Ronan Rafferty and Britain's Derrick Cooper. Then he overran the field with three straight 66s for his first professional victory. His 262 total was 26 under par and good for a three-stroke victory over Anders Forsbrand.

It was the kind of victory that had been expected of Olazabal. Greatness had been predicted for the slight young man from San Sebastian, on Spain's northern coast, but few expected his first pro victory to come so soon.

A comparison with Ballesteros is interesting but has little foundation. Ballesteros, who also comes from Spain's northern coast—in fact, perhaps just 100 miles east of Olazabal's hometown—was a pro for two years before he scored his first victory. But then, he was only 19 at the time. And then he won twice, and led the Order of Merit that year, 1976. Olazabal's victory lifted his season winnings to over £90,000.

Olazabal, the only golfer to have won the British Boys, Youths and Amateur championships, depended on deadly irons and putting. He is not among the longer hitters, so he did not have the advantage so many did in the thin air at Crans-sur-Sierre, some 5,000 feet above the Rhone Valley. Many could reach the par-five holes in two strokes, but in the first round he was home in two only once, yet birdied all four of them. It took a score of under par 72 for anyone to have any chance at all. A total 83 golfers beat par in the first round. Cooper was flirting with a sub-60 round for a while. He went out in 29, and had a chance for an eagle at the 10th. But he missed that putt and could do no better than 35 coming in for his 64.

Olazabal and Rafferty shared the second-round lead with matching 66s. Added pressure came from the veteran Manuel Pinero, whose 67 left him two behind. And Australia's Ian Baker-Finch forced his way into contention with a 63 for a share of fourth. But Olazabal shook off all pressure and made short work of things in the final round.

He was practically untroubled under the hot sun for the finale. He had only two bad moments. At the fourth, he drove under a tree and pitched through the green and took a six. Then he three-putted the seventh. The two errors were to keep him from breaking the European record of 260 for 72 holes, a possibility that would have been within reach when he ran off five straight birdies starting at the 12th. Ironically, Olazabal almost didn't get the chance to perform these heroics. He almost didn't get into the tournament. The entry was especially heavy, and Olazabal did not know until the Friday of the preceding week that he had a place.

Panasonic European Open—£210,000
Winner: Greg Norman

The press was calling the Panasonic European Open one of golf's rare summit meetings. When the classy field assembled at the Old Course at Sunningdale, it was only the second time of the season (aside from the four major championships) that an event contained the world's three best players—Greg Norman, Seve Ballesteros, and Bernhard Langer. But there were those who would not let this flagship event of the PGA European Tour be written off as a three-man tournament.

First, there was Nick Faldo, who had been struggling for some two years. Faldo thrust himself into the picture with a course-record 62 in the first round. It equalled his career-best, but even so it was an odd 62. He went out in a healthy but hardly spectacular 33, thanks to some adept scrambling and an eagle-two at the ninth, which he drove. Then he came home in a sizzling 29. Ballesteros hung close with a 64, Norman was some distance back at 67, and Langer further back with a 68.

In the second round, Faldo then skied a full 10 strokes, to 72, to fall one stroke astern at the halfway point. There, the leaders were Bernard Gallacher and Peter Fowler, each with 68–133. While Norman was posting his second 67 for a share of third on 134, Ballesteros slipped with a 72 and Langer made up two strokes with a 68. But it was the young Spaniard, Jose-Maria Olazabal, who was drawing attention. Some spectacular play had got him to 68–67—135, two strokes off the halfway lead.

At the end, there was a half-surprise. Not unexpectedly, there was Norman. And his challenger was not Ballesteros or Langer, but Ken Brown, who had been playing steady and excellent golf, but almost unnoticed. Yet suddenly there he was, leading Norman by one, 202–203, going into the final round. Norman almost broke free later in the round, but Brown holed two big putts for birdies at the 14th and 15th to draw even going down the stretch. Langer also was closing strong, but a missed green at No. 18 cost him the chance for the birdie he needed to tie. Brown got down in two from a bunker at the final hole for his 67 to tie with Norman (66) at 269, and off they went into the playoff.

At the first extra hole, Brown was short of the green, chipped to five feet, but his putt for a tying four was short. So Norman, who already had his four, was the winner of the £35,000 first prize and the £50,000 bonus the sponsors had put up for the double of the British and European Opens. It was Norman's fourth victory of the year (he had won the Kemper Open and the Las Vegas International on the American tour), and it lifted him over Ballesteros and Langer, to the top of the Sony Ranking. Langer (68) finished third, and tied at fourth were Ballesteros (65), Faldo (68), and Olazabal (66). One wondered whether this might be the look of leaderboards for years to come.

Lawrence Batley Tournament Players' Championship—£130,000
Winner: Ian Woosnam

The Belfry had stood as a baffling problem for British members of the PGA. It is the Midlands headquarters of the PGA, the Britons' club as much as anybody's—until tournament time. Then it treated the Britons like outsiders. No Briton member could win there. It was left for Ian Woosnam, the gritty little Welshman, to break down that barrier, and he did it with authority in the Lawrence Batley Tournament Players' Championship. After staying close to the top in the first two rounds, he rushed home for a seven-stroke victory.

Ken Brown and Jose-Maria Canizares shared that distant second place. If there was any consolation to them, it was that, led by Woosnam, the first three finishers were members of the 1985 European Ryder Cup team that had enjoyed such wild success over the Americans at this very course almost a year earlier.

Fittingly enough, that Ryder Cup victory is what helped Woosnam this time. Troubled by golf problems, he watched video tapes of himself playing in the Ryder Cup to try to get back on track. It seems he found what he was looking for. He also tried a new putting approach. He would line up the putter blade behind the ball and steady it, then move into address. It worked. "That was the best I have putted all year," Woosnam said. "I felt a different man on the greens, and all I had to do was play steadily and make sure I did nothing silly."

The hot scoring of the previous two weeks on the tour cooled quickly with the start of the TPC. Only South African Jeff Hawkes and New Zealander Greg Turner, the Scandinavian Open winner in his first European season, could break 70, both returning 69 to share the first-round lead. It was not an encouraging start for the eight Ryder Cup players who entered. Canizares and Jose Rivero managed 70s, but Paul Way and Sam Torrance posted 79s.

Woosnam shot a 71 and was a joint sixth, two strokes off the lead.

In the second round, two bright young players moved into contention. Ronan Rafferty, with a 67, shared the halfway lead on 140, and Philip Parkin, also with a 67, was in a group with fellow-Welshman Woosnam at 141. That help set up what looked for a while like an all-Welsh finish.

Parkin posed the only real threat early in the fourth round. He got to within one stroke of the lead when Woosnam took five at the first hole. Parkin played steadily for the first five holes, then came to grief. At the sixth, he tried to play safe with an iron off the tee and instead hit into the right rough. His recovery shot hit a thin tree and very nearly hit him on the rebound. He finally took six on the hole, then ran from trouble to trouble and overall dropped six strokes over a four-hole span. He finished with an 82 that carried him to 15 behind, at 292. Not that it mattered to Woosnam. He was rolling smoothly after the first hole and pulled comfortably away for a 69 to break the Belfry Jinx with plenty to spare. His 277 for 72 holes was the lowest ever recorded there.

Sanyo Open—£175,000
Winner: Jose-Maria Olazabal

Seve Ballesteros, the defending champion, came into the £175,000 Sanyo Open at El Prat, near Barcelona, with five victories behind him and his sights set firmly on No. 6, and on matching Norman von Nida's record of seven victories in a European season. But Ballesteros was the victim of unfortunate timing and wry irony. The timing: Ballesteros was trying to do it in 1986, when European golf—indeed, golf throughout the world—was a far different thing than von Nida knew when he won his seven in 1947. And the irony: Ballesteros, perhaps the best golfer in the world, was certainly the finest Spanish golfer ever. But he had been on the scene for only some 10 years, and already he had a budding challenger. This was Jose-Maria Olazabal, a mere 20, a rookie professional, and also practically a neighbor from Spain's northern coast. Olazabal had already scored his first pro victory, taking the Ebel European Masters in September. A month later, he had his second, the Sanyo Open, and the £29,000 first prize lifted his season's winnings to £130,000.

Ballesteros quickly seemed on his way to that sixth victory. He returned a 67 in the first round and shared the lead, and Olazabal was two behind. With another 67, Ballesteros took a three-stroke lead on 134 at the halfway point, and Olazabal was a joint second. But in the third round, apparently, feeling the weakening effects of a month-long chest cold, Ballesteros posted a 73, and it eventually proved his undoing. Olazabal shot a 69 and Sweden's Ove Sellberg a 65 to move into a joint lead on 206, one stroke ahead of Ballesteros. Olazabal, like Ballesteros, is hardly one to sit on a lead. He opened the final round with two fine birdie threes, and there was no catching him. But it was not an easy time for Olazabal and many others. They had to play through swarms of mosquitoes, and they finished covered by bites.

Olazabal returned a 67 in the final round for a 15-under-par 273 total and a comfortable three-stroke victory over Howard Clark. Ian Mosey finished third on 69–277, and sharing fourth at 278 were Sellberg (72), Ian Woosnam (70), and Ballesteros (71). It was another in a line of recent frustrations for Ballesteros. He had lost by seven strokes to Ronan Rafferty in the Dunhill Nations Cup, and by a huge 7 and 6 to Rodger Davis in the Suntory World Match Play just a week earlier. His chances of matching von Nida were fading fast.

Lancome Trophy—£165,775
Winners: Seve Ballesteros, Bernhard Langer (tie)

This one will require an asterisk in the record books. Seve Ballesteros and Bernhard Langer, Europe's two finest golfers, were locked in a sudden-death playoff for the Lancome Trophy when darkness descended on them at St. Nom la Breteche near Paris. Still locked in a tie, they had barely enough daylight left to complete the fourth hole in pars. Then they appealed to PGA officials. With both players having previous commitments and unable to return the next day, the tie was declared. PGA officials said it was the first in the history of the European Tour. "It was really too dark to continue playing, and I believe that this was the fairest possible decision," Langer said. Each player received £22,000, and each added a victory to his European season record.

There were some outbursts here and there, principally Sam Torrance's passing Ballesteros with a second-round 64 and a one-stroke lead on 135 at the halfway point. But it was really a Ballesteros-Langer show all the way. Langer opened with a 73, but moved into position with 66s in the second and third rounds. Ballesteros then seemed bent on closing the season much as he had opened it, by letting the lead slip away.

It was an odd finish for a tournament that Ballesteros had all but locked up. He led Langer by one and five others by two going into the final round. He had an imposing four-stroke lead after the sixth hole. Then Langer began to close the gap with an eagle three at 504-yard seventh, when he holed from 25 feet after a three-iron approach. Ballesteros birdied, and saw his lead trimmed to three. Ballesteros took three putts from the edge of the green at No. 8. At the ninth he made a fine save with a delicate shot from a bunker, but Langer picked up a stroke when he dropped a 10-foot putt for his birdie two. Ballesteros led by one going into the back nine, and both had to labor under a heavy rain that hit them six holes from the finish. Langer missed an opportunity to catch him when his short birdie putt at No. 17 lipped out, but he didn't miss at No. 18. He holed from six feet for a birdie and a three-under-par 69 to Ballesteros's 70, and they finished in a tie at 14-under 274.

In the playoff, under wet, murky conditions, both birdied the first extra hole. At the second, Langer missed the winner from 16 feet. Both birdied again at the third, and then groped their way through the fast-fading light to pars at the fourth. Then unable to play on and unable to return the next day, they settled for the tie.

The Lancome also had opened on something of a historic note. It was the European professional debut of Jack Nicklaus II, now 25, His first round was an awkward 74—awkward because he was three under and in hot pursuit of Ballesteros when he put three balls into the water and took a nine at the par-three ninth. "It was really embarrassing," the tall, lanky Nicklaus said. For the history book, his first European tournament as a pro ended 74–77–79–78—308, and 34 strokes behind the leaders.

Portuguese Open—£100,000
Winner: Mark McNulty

The Portuguese Open was the final event on the PGA European Tour's 1986 schedule, and it began on a wry note—a shortage of golf balls, of all things. Then it ended on something of a somber one when Zimbabwean Mark McNulty, winning in Europe for the first time since the 1980 German Open, announced he was dedicating his victory to a friend lying in a hospital. McNulty, who won £16,000, closed with a sparkling 66 for an 18-under-par total 270 and a four-stroke victory over Ian Mosey. McNulty was a subdued winner, however. His thoughts turned to his friend, golf writer Adrian Frederick, who was badly injured in a traffic accident in Johannesburg a few weeks earlier. "It's going to take a miracle for him to recover fully," said McNulty, who himself narrowly escaped serious injury in a car crash in 1981.

It was a hungry and well-tested McNulty who came to the Portuguese Open at Quinta do Lago. He began the year with five victories in South Africa, then made a strong showing in Europe, finishing second behind Seve Ballesteros in the Monte Carlo and Irish Opens, and third behind Bernhard Langer in the German Open. Once the golf ball shortage was solved by an emergency shipment being flown in, McNulty helped get the tournament off to a rousing start. He and the slumping Sandy Lyle, who was still seeking his first European victory of the year, shared the first-round lead with six-under-par 66s. They were a stroke ahead of Mark Johnson and John Bland. Lyle's 66 was an explosive one. He was one under after 10 holes, then birdied five of the last eight.

McNulty faded slightly in the second round. His 69 left him two strokes behind Lyle (67) and a determined John Bland (66), who shared first place and a two-stroke lead at the halfway point at 11-under-par 133. Bland was hoping to end the season the way he began it—with a victory. "I came from two behind Seve Ballesteros to beat him by four shots in Cannes, so I don't see why I shouldn't beat Sandy," Bland said. He was playing confidently. He was 21 under par for his last four tournament rounds. Lyle seemed to be enjoying a late-season flourish. This was his second straight round without a bogey.

The picture was not cleared up in the third round. McNulty returned a 69, and Bland and Lyle each slipped to 71. This left all three tied for the lead at 204 going into the final day. If a battle royal seemed to be shaping up, McNulty stopped it short. He rammed home birdies on the first two holes, from 40 feet at No. 1 and 20 feet at No. 2, and just that suddenly he was two strokes clear. He was on his way to a 66 and a four-stroke victory. Bland closed with a 72 and finished a joint third at 276, and Lyle with 73–277.

11. The African Tours

Mark McNulty's performance in the past season raises an interesting question: What might he do if he could stay healthy?

The 1986 season was a healthy one for McNulty, and he made the best of it. It was his time, and the Sunshine Circuit became his personal territory. Others need not apply, thank you. All the Zimbabwe-born McNulty did was win five out of its 11 tournaments—the Safmarine South African Masters to kick off the circuit late in 1985, followed early in 1986 by the Wild Coast Sun Classic, the Barclays Bank Classic, and (back-to-back) the Swazi Sun International and the Trust Bank Tournament of Champions. And when he wasn't winning, he was finishing second or third or thereabouts, and he topped the Order of Merit for the fourth time in six years.

Now, that was just on the 1985–86 circuit. When he had tidied things up there, he dropped in on the European Tour and picked off the Portuguese Open. Then he went back to Africa and plucked the richest plum of all, the Sun City Million Dollar Challenge, plus the Helix Wild Coast Classic (again), Germiston Centenary and Safmarine South African Masters (again)—four in a row, and five straight including the Portuguese Open. "I'm a bit lost for words," he said at Sun City. It was a fitting observation for the entire year, in which he won nine times.

This was the same Mark McNulty who just a few years ago lost his card on the American PGA Tour when he had to have knee cartilage surgery. He had to miss six months to recover. And just before that, there was a car crash in South Africa. He barely escaped with his life.

Not that McNulty ruled the Sunshine Circuit unchallenged, however. Two golfers in particular—Fulton Allem and David Frost—kept getting in his way.

Allem, 28-year-old South African pro, came into the season without ever having won on the Sunshine tour. He served notice immediately, finishing fifth in the Goodyear Classic and sharing second with David Frost behind McNulty in the South African Masters in December. Allem tied for third in the ICL and was a solo third in the Lexington South African PGA. He finally broke through for his first-ever Sunshine victory in the AECI Classic, and in the process touched off one of the hottest running battles ever seen in the Sunshine, or perhaps anywhere else. For weeks it seemed that McNulty and Allem were the only two players in the field. Allem edged McNulty in the AEIC, then McNulty beat him the following week in the Barclay's. Allem won the Palabora the next week, and the week after that was second to McNulty in the Swazi Sun. Thus over a five-tournament span, one or the other won, and in four of those one was the runnerup.

Frost was hardly sitting idly by. He won the South African Open and finished second five other times before heading for his second year on the American tour.

After these three were done—eight victories among them—there were only three tournaments to account for. Denis Watson, a veteran from the American tour, won the Goodyear Classic in December, then Gavin Levenson celebrated the New Year with a win in the ICL, and veteran Bobby Cole re-surfaced, turning back pressure from both Frost and McNulty to take the South African PGA, his first victory in years.

The Safari Circuit also was marked by a dominating personality. Britain's Gordon J. Brand ran off with the first two events, taking the Nigerian Open by eight strokes and the Ivory Coast Open by two, both in intense heat. Next came Ian Woosnam, the diminutive Welshman, who took the Kenya Open in a sudden-death playoff against Bill Longmuir.

The Safari closed with successes by two little-known golfers. Garry Cullen, a Briton based in Kenya, scored his first pro victory in the Zambian Open. And then came perhaps the most difficult victory of them all. Stephen Bennett, also a Briton, had to fight rain, lightning, and darkness to win the Zimbabwe Open, the second victory of his career.

Safmarine South African Masters—R100,000
Winner: Mark McNulty

Unbelievable—that might be the only word that fits. All other adjectives seem pale in describing the way Zimbabwe-born Mark McNulty won the Safmarine South African Masters at Milnerton Golf Club, Cape Town. How can anyone believe a 12-stroke swing in only nine holes? And in a howling gale, at that. McNulty leaped ahead of the collapsing David Frost for a four-stroke victory.

The leaderboard changed rapidly. Fulton Allem and Robbie Stewart shared the first-round lead with 66s. Britain's Warren Humphreys, in his first outing since winning the Portuguese Open the month before, saw his bid for a share fail down the stretch. "What really annoyed me," he said, "was that I needed three to get down from nowhere on the last hole." His 70 left him four behind the leaders. In the second round, Allem leaped dramatically into the lead with an eagle on the final hole for a 67 and an 11-under-par total of 133. That put him one ahead of David Frost, who posted a second straight 66. Stewart shot 71 and drifted back. McNulty, meanwhile, added a workmanlike 71 to his opening 69 for a 140 that left him seven behind.

Frost, playing in his first Sunshine Circuit tournament in two years, seemed to have the event solidly in hand when he shot a 68 for a 14-under-par total of 202 and a three-stroke lead through the third round. Then Frost seemed to have it all but wrapped up in the final round, and certainly McNulty was not the likely candidate to overhaul him. McNulty, standing on the eighth tee, was fully seven strokes behind Frost. When McNulty left the 16th green, he was leading by five—a swing of 12 strokes. Frost had three-putted the ninth, then three-putted the 10th, where he missed his second putt from only 10 inches. McNulty gained ground with birdies at the 13th and 15th, while Frost made a double-bogey five at the 15th. Frost, two behind at the 16th, gambled from the right rough and paid for it with an eight while McNulty made a par five on the hole. McNulty finished with a 70 and a 278 total. Allem (77), Frost (80), and Canada's Frank Edmonds (74), tied for second place four strokes behind, at 282.

Goodyear Classic—R100,000
Winner: Denis Watson

When Denis Watson finally nailed down the Goodyear Classic at Humewood, Port Elizabeth, it was almost an anticlimax. Fighting might be commonplace on many other playing fields, but it is all but unknown on the golf course. Yet a fight is what the spectators almost got in the second round, and that's what held their attention. Almost no one noticed that Fulton Allem had forged into the lead, adding a 70 to his opening 69 for a 139 total and a two-stroke lead through two rounds. Even Allem thought that taking the lead was practically secondary. He said he felt more like a boxing referee when Watson and Tony Johnstone, his playing partners, nearly came to blows after signing their scorecards.

Watson and Johnstone exchanged insults after Watson took nearly 15 minutes to play his approach shot to the 18th green. Watson had been denied line-of-sight relief from an advertising sign, and he also delayed play when putting. Johnstone later claimed that Watson had insulted him. And Watson said it was "a labor to play with Johnstone. He has the reputation for the worst manners on tour." Allem managed to calm them down.

The tournament also had a real storm. Winds gusted to nearly 60 miles an hour during the first round. David Frost, who had taken an 80 in the wind the week before in the South African Masters, solved them this time for a 68 and the first-round lead. Allem, who shared second with Frost in the South African Masters, was alone at 69. Nick Price held third with a 70 off an amazingly steady round in the gale—17 pars and a birdie. Allem faded to a 77 in the third round and eventually finished fifth at 286. Watson, despite a sprained wrist, closed with a 69 for a 282 total and a one-stroke victory. It was the second Sunshine Circuit victory of his career.

ICL International—R100,000
Winner: Gavin Levenson

South Africa's Gavin Levenson was knocking at the door of the ICL International for the third straight year. It opened this time when the fortunes of golf took David Frost and an assortment of others out of the picture. Frost held a two-stroke lead with five holes to play, and let it slip away. Levenson's closing effort, a strong 67, was enough to carry him to a one-stroke victory over Frost at the Zwartkops Country Club, Pretoria. The victory was all the sweeter for Levenson because it was such a long time coming. He was the runner-up in the past two ICLs.

Simon Hobday, the ICL champion five years earlier, staked a powerful claim in the first round, collecting five birdies and an eagle for a seven-under-par 65 and a one-stroke lead. Levenson was well back, at 71. In the second round, Mark McNulty slipped into the lead when he added a 67 to his opening 66 for a 133 total and a one-stroke lead over Hobday (69). The second round was also the occasion for some odd fireworks by Portuguese Open champion Warren Humphreys, who manufactured a 65 that didn't impress him. "It wasn't exactly a steady round of golf," he said. At the 10th, he dropped a 50-foot putt for an eagle-three. He also holed from 30 feet at No. 11 and 40 feet at No. 12. But he hurt his chances in the third round, when he three-putted from 25 feet at No. 18. The closing bogey cooled any hopes he had of gaining ground on McNulty, the leader on 69—202. Humphreys chances went completely dead in the fourth round, when he dropped shots on the first three holes.

Levenson, meanwhile, made his move in the third round. He put up a 65 that pulled him to within one of McNulty. But McNulty faltered in the final round, shooting a 72 and leaving the field to Levenson and Frost. Frost was two ahead with five to play, but Levenson caught him with a salvaged par at the 14th and a birdie at the 16th. The end was effective but routine. Levenson missed a six-foot birdie putt on the final hole, and his par left him at 67—270. Then he found himself with an ICL championship when Frost missed a tying par putt from closer and finished with 68—271.

Lexington South African PGA—R110,000
Winner: Bobby Cole

Bobby Cole, 37, the slight South African who resides in the United States, lost his American tour card in 1984. Practically nothing had been heard from his game since he won the 1980 South African Open. So he was pretty much a surprise when he leaped into the thick of things with a 66 and a tie for the lead in the first round of the Lexington South African PGA Championship at The Wanderers in Johannesburg. Cole was in a crowd at the top, sharing the lead with Teddy Webber, Hugh Biaocchi, Ian Mosey, and Mark McNulty. It was reasonable to assume that Cole wouldn't be in that company for long.

Cole quickly proved otherwise. After a 65 in the second round, he posted another 66. He stood at a tournament record 13-under-par 197 for three rounds, two strokes better than the mark by Dale Hayes, that had stood for 10 years. Cole led by three over Webber, who only a few weeks earlier had won his European card at the tour school in Spain. Webber shot a 64 for a 200 total, and stood one stroke better than David Frost, who tied the official course record of 63.

Anyone waiting for Cole to fold was to be disappointed. He shot a 68 in the final round for a 265 total and a five-stroke victory over Frost (69) and Webber (70), and perhaps a ticket to a new future. Cole said he hoped that by winning the Lexington PGA, he would get invited to the World Series of Golf at Akron, Ohio, in August. He said that with a good finish in the World Series and in the five or six U.S. tournaments he expected to play, he might earn enough to regain his playing card and make a comeback. Time would tell.

Wild Coast Sun Classic—R100,000
Winner: Mark McNulty

Few golfers drew any attention away from South Africa's Mark McNulty in his solitary drive to tame the Wild Coast Sun tournament. There was, for example, Tony Johnstone of Zimbabwe. Johnstone spent much of 1985 in Europe hunting for his putting touch. It pretty well eluded him until 1986. He had it in good measure in setting a Wild Coast course record 64 in the second round, an effort boosted considerably by an eagle-two at No. 18, where he sank a five-iron approach shot from a fairway bunker. Johnstone would be hardy enough to finish third at 276, nine strokes off. And David Frost would finish second at 273, six strokes back. This was Mark McNulty's tournament.

McNulty, 32, simply ran off with it. His 66–66—132 for 36 holes was a record by two strokes under Hugh Baiocchi's record of only a year earlier. It left McNulty three strokes ahead of Johnstone and Rick Hartman, an American again campaigning in Europe. McNulty set another record, this after three rounds, with a 71 that left him at seven-under 203. David Frost, a South African in his second year on the U.S. tour, shot 69 and moved to within two strokes, at 203. He was about to get a lot closer, but only briefly.

They were in a match-play battle briefly in the fourth round, after Frost birdied the first three holes to draw even with McNulty. But McNulty went on to match Johnstone's fresh record with a 64 to become the first player on the circuit to break 270. His 13-under-par 267 gave him a six-stroke victory over Frost (68–273).

Southern Sun South African Open—R100,000
Winner: David Frost

After five runner-up finishes on the Sunshine Circuit, there was only one thing left for South African David Frost to do before he packed up and headed back to the U.S. tour. And that was to win. And that's what he did, with authority, taking his first Southern Sun South African Open by three strokes over Zimbabwe's Tony Johnstone at Royal Johannesburg.

Frost, who was returning for a second season on the U.S. tour, left behind an astounding stretch on the Sunshine Circuit—a victory and five seconds in six events. In his 24 rounds, he averaged 68.9 strokes per round, a stunning figure when one considers that he shot an 80 in the final round of the Masters in December and that three of the tournaments were whipped by strong winds.

Johnstone was the early force in this championship. His 68–67 put him at 135 at the halfway point. He led South African Robbie Stewart by three, and Frost was well back in the pack, in fifteenth place on 72–70—142. Heavy weather hit in the third round. A powerful thunderstorm caught nine golfers still out on the course, including Johnstone, who was seven under and on the sixteenth green facing a 12-foot putt to save his par. The nine would return to finish the round the next day, and Frost gave them an intimidating number to shoot at. Before the storm hit, he wrapped up a nine-birdie 66 that included a double-bogey six at the short 17th. It gave him a three-round total of 208.

Frost would not be denied a victory in his last outing before heading for America. In the final round, Johnstone pressed to within a shot, but Frost turned him back with a burst of birdies over the last three holes, including a 40-foot chip-in at No. 17. Frost finished with a 67 for a 13-under total of 275.

AECI Charity Classic—R100,000
Winner: Fulton Allem

Fulton Allem simply had become tired of knocking and not getting an answer. "Instead of knocking again," he said, in unrepressed delight, "I just kicked the door in."

And so went the AECI Charity Classic at Rand Park. Allem dramatically kicked in the door and picked up his first-ever Sunshine Circuit victory. Allem, 28-year-old Viljoenskroon pro, forgot to mention the guard at that door: All he had to do was get past Mark McNulty. Their head-to-head battle, one of the most stirring in years, didn't end until the last hole. Allem holed out for a 67 and a 22-under-par total of 266 to win by a stroke when McNulty missed a 10-foot putt and his bid for a 66. They were so far ahead it seemed the rest of the field was playing a different tournament. Mark Hartness "won" that one at 275.

"I can't describe the feeling," Allem said later. "My body went into another state when I holed the winning putt." Allem had suffered a number of disappointments. He had had eight top five finishes.

Allem's sheet read 70–63–66–67 against McNulty's 69–67–64–67. The 63 tied the course record and gave Allem a one-stroke lead over Nigel Burch at the halfway point. It's almost frightening to think of what Allem might have scored had he not, as he put it, "putted like a dog." He made seven birdies and an eagle in his 30–33, but he missed five putts of less than six feet on the bumpy greens, and his two-footer for a 62 on the final green never touched the hole.

It ended up as match play between Allem and McNulty. Allem started the final round one stroke ahead. McNulty caught him immediately with a birdie on the first hole. Allem seemed doomed again when McNulty pulled two ahead with birdies at No. 4 and No. 5. Then Allem fired back with birdies at the eighth and ninth. But he seemed lost at No. 10, where he three-putted. "I thought I may have thrown it away at that stage," he said. And so they hammered away at each other. It came down to the last hole, a par five.

McNulty hit his tee shot down the first fairway, from where it opens the 18th green to the second shot. Allem chose the conventional path. McNulty's second fell short of the green, Allem's into a bunker. McNulty left his chip about 10 feet short, and Allem's blast from the bunker finished outside that. Allem was putting first.

"I don't know where I was as I stood over the putt," Allem said. "I knew it would move from the left. When my hands stopped shaking, I just hit the ball." The ball dropped, McNulty missed, and Allem stepped through the door and into the champion's room for the first time.

Barclays Bank Classic—$100,000
Winner: Mark McNulty

It started out with a surprise leader but ended up with a familiar winner, and a runaway winner at that—Mark McNulty. It was little-known Bobby Lincoln who set the early pace for the Barclays Classic at Gary Player Country Club in Sun City, Bophuthatswana. Lincoln holed his nine-iron approach shot for an eagle-two at the 440-yard 13th, and added four birdies along the way for a 68 and a one-stroke lead through the first round. But Lincoln faded quickly, setting the stage for another McNulty performance.

McNulty, coming from five strokes off the pace, moved into a share of the 36-hole lead with Fulton Allem, at five-under-par 139. But it took an error at No. 18 to keep McNulty in check. He three-putted the final hole and settled for a 66 to go with his opening 73. Just two strokes behind them at 141 (75–l66), was the promising rookie Trevor Dodds. But it ended up McNulty's show the rest of the way. It was shaping up as an interesting battle. Allem had beaten McNulty by a shot in the AECI Charity Classic the week before.

After a third-round 71, McNulty charged to the front in the fourth round. He pulled four shots ahead of Allem by one-putting the first six greens for two birdies and four pars. By the time his game began to falter, it didn't matter. He bogeyed the final hole to finish with 69–279. The bogey merely kept him from matching the 10-under-par 278 Bernhard Langer shot on the same course in the Million Dollar Challenge two months earlier, in December. It left McNulty with six-stroke victory over Allem (73–285).

Palabora Classic—R120,000
Winner: Fulton Allem

It was one of those tournaments a golfer would like to have bronzed and put into his personal trophy case: only one bogey in four rounds of golf. With that kind of game going, it needed only a theatrical finish to become a classic. And Fulton Allem, riding a three-week hot streak, provided it with a brilliant 65 for a come-from-behind victory in the Palabora Classic at the Hans Merensky Club in Phalaborwa. It was Allem's second victory in three weeks. He had won the AECI Classic two weeks earlier, and the week before finished second in the Barclays Classic at Sun City. Allem made a five-shot swing on the final round in this one. He won by three over Hugh Baiochi after opening the day two strokes behind third-round leader Jay Townsend, a young American.

The tournament was ripe for a blanket finish. Townsend, 25, who spends most of his time playing the European Tour, surged into a one-shot lead with third-round 67, his third straight round in the 60s. His 203 total left him a stroke ahead of Don Robertson, another American, and Allen Henning of South Africa. Allem was one of four players at 205, which meant that six were crowded within two strokes of the lead entering the final round. Townsend lifted above the 60s for the only time, but then with a creditable 71. It was enough to take him out of the race, however.

Baiocchi himself played well enough to win, closing with a 68 for 273. But he had the misfortune of being in the way of a man on a tear. Allem suffered his only bogey of the tournament at No. 10 in the second round, where he missed a nine-inch putt. But he made 19 birdies through the other 71 holes, and finished with a tournament record 270, 18 under par. He left Phalaborwa hoping his performance would attract some invitations to European Tour events. He had missed his European Tour card in Spain the previous November.

Swazi Sun International—R100,000
Winner: Mark McNulty

The Swazi Sun International dawned with some unexpected heat—the reaction to David Feherty's earlier criticism of the South African tour. Feherty, of Northern Ireland, had leveled some criticism at the Sunshine Circuit, and he arrived at the Royal Swazi Golf Club to find himself the object of controversy and a little hate mail. Oddly enough, his criticism could result in larger purses in 1987, according to the response from PGA Executive Director Jimmy Hemphill. But whether the exercise was of immediate help or harm to Feherty was a moot point. He was playing good, solid golf. The problem was, others were playing brilliantly. Feherty finished well up the track at 281, 18 strokes behind the winner, Mark McNulty. It was McNulty's fourth title of the circuit.

The Swazi was another chapter in what had become a running battle between McNulty and Fulton Allem. This one ended up in a sudden-death playoff. McNulty won it on the first extra hole. He put his tee shot 15 feet from the hole. Allem put his into a greenside bunker. He came out too strong, and two-putted for a four. McNulty then had the luxury of two-putting from 15 feet for a par and the victory, which he did.

But how they got to the playoff was a story in itself. They were dueling all the way. McNulty had opened with an eight-under-par 64, and led Gavin Levenson by one and Allem by three. McNulty posted a dazzling 66 in the second round—and found himself standing still. Allem had come in with a 63 to catch him. They were tied at 14-under 130 after 36 holes. McNulty actually trailed Allem by one shot after the third round, but made up the deficit by shooting the front nine in 30 to Allem's 31. McNulty shot a final-round 65, and Allem a 66, to tie in regulation with Sunshine Circuit record aggregates of 25-under 263.

Trust Bank Tournament of Champions—R115,000
Winner: Mark McNulty

When Mark McNulty said, "I'm glad it's over," he was echoing what a lot of others must have been thinking, although for a different reason. McNulty was talking about a stretch of nine straight weeks of competition. The others had to be thinking of the Sunshine Circuit itself—thanks to McNulty. He had practically turned it into the McNulty Member-Guest Circuit, with himself as *the* member.

His runaway six-stroke victory in the Trust Bank Tournament of Champions at Kensington wrapped up the most successful season ever by a Sunshine professional. It was his fifth title in 11 starts. Simple arithmetic tells us that a large number of other golfers were left to battle over the other six.

McNulty posted 70–68–68–66—272, six ahead of Tony Johnstone and American Jack Ferenz. He won R20,000, raising his official earnings to R113,526, some R46,000 over his previous record. About the only other race left, once McNulty got up to speed, was that for Rookie of the Year. The honor went to Justin Hobday (69–280) by only R400 over Mark Wiltshire after Bobby Cole hit into the water on the final hole and dropped back to share sixth with Hobday. Wiltshire was well back at 68–286.

McNulty's opening 70 left him somewhere back in the pack. Bobby Lincoln had 64, and Bobby Cole 66, and there were enough high-60s that a mere 70 seemed pretty distant. The futility of being in the same field with McNulty these days, however, became clear again in the final round. Curiously enough, it was a dropped shot that spurred him. Bobby Cole had scored five birdies going out, and when McNulty had to scramble to save a bogey-five at No. 7, they were tied.

McNulty immediately charged ahead. Two big shots set up a birdie at No. 8, which put him ahead to stay. Then he locked it up at No. 11, where he hit the flag with his approach and Cole bogeyed. "I started easing back from there on," McNulty said. "It was very much plain sailing." His idea of "cruising" might be someone else's idea of a charge. He birdied three of the last seven holes.

Nigerian Open—£100,650
Winner: Gordon J. Brand

This Nigerian Open, at the Ikoyi Club at Lagos, was all but over after the second round. Gordon J. Brand, 30, was in that kind of mood. He shared 11th place on 70 after the first round, moved in front by one stroke with 67 in the second, pretty well locked it up with a 65 in the third, and strolled home with a 70 in the finale. It was his second Nigerian Open victory in four years. His 12-under-par total of 272 gave him the £16,400 first prize on a whopping eight-stroke victory over Malcolm Mackenzie, who posted four straight 70s for a 280.

It took a kind of international incident to put some heat—aside from the 90-plus temperatures—into the event. The incident occurred late in the first round. Alan Evans, 26, of Wales, had requested relief after his drive at No. 17 landed behind the 18th tee. After being refused, he pursued his case through two other officials, and lost, and was accused of making insulting remarks. When Evans finished his round—he made a 76—Everisto Armah, chairman of the championship committee approached him. He asked whether Evans had insulted one of the officials. Said Mr. Armah, "In front of the British High Commissioner, he told me to go away. It was probably youthful exuberance, and no doubt he will grow up. But we could not allow him to continue in the Open." And thus Evans was disqualified before the second round.

Brand broke through in the second round. He moved to six under par, but was short with his approach shots at two of the last three holes and dropped a stroke at each. Paul Kent, 23, posted a 70 for 138 and closed on Brand. But aside from Kent, the field was starting to spread out. First-round leaders Garry Cullen and Neil Hansen, on 67s, each slipped to 75 and drifted far back, and defending champion Bill Longmuir suffered a 79 for 148, after taking eight at the 15th.

Brand, a Ryder Cup international and winner of the Ivory Coast in 1981 and the Nigerian Open in 1983, birdied the second hole from three feet, then ambled home from there.

Ivory Coast Open—£58,425
Winner: Gordon J. Brand

This was the Ivory Coast Open, but those of a poetic bent might have preferred to call it the "Dante's Inferno Open." Fans sometimes say a golfer "survives" certain events. That was almost literally the case with Gordon J. Brand in the Ivory Coast Open at Yamoussoukro. Not that he didn't play well enough to win. He did, with a closing 69 for a come-from-behind victory and a West African double. Just the week before he had won the Nigerian Open, the first stop on the Safari Circuit. But the heat got almost equal billing in this one. The temperature hit 108 degrees in the shade in the first day, and forced Britain's David Russell to withdraw before he completed the first hole. "I felt absolutely drained, physically," Russell explained.

Scotland's Brian Marchbank went coolly about his business, however, when the thermometer hit a reported 140 in the second round. While the heat was melting many challengers, Marchbank rushed home in 31 for a 67 and a nine-under-par 135 total, which gave him a three-stroke lead. His back-nine sprint began with an eagle-three at the 10th, where he holed from 10 feet. He birdied the final hole from 20 feet.

Brand, however, refused to melt, and a spirited duel was on. He trailed Marchbank by one entering the final round. He was behind by three after only three holes when Marchbank pitched and putted his way to a birdie-four at No. 1 and a par-three at No. 2. Brand mounted his charge at No. 5, making three birdies in four holes. His birdie at No. 8 coupled with Marchbank's watered tee shot left them level. Brand then moved ahead when Marchbank three-putted the ninth. Brand finished with 69–273 and a two-stroke victory over Marchbank, and the question was whether he could sweep all five Safari Circuit events. "Winning the next three as well is going to be difficult because the fields are of higher quality," he said.

Kenya Open—£56,750
Winner: Ian Woosnam

The favorite for the Kenya Open was not well known but he was easy to spot. He was the man with the course-record, 11-under-par 60 in the pro-am, a slender Briton named Neil Hansen. Hansen, 24, had to borrow £2,500 to finance him on the tour. He more than made it back with a joint third in the Nigerian Open and a joint 15th in the Ivory Coast Open, good for a total of £5,908. He picked up £750 for his pro-am romp, nine birdies and an eagle, but was not in the picture when the final and real curtain fell at Nairobi's Muthaiga Club.

That drama was left to Ian Woosnam, the diminutive Welshman, and the pleasant Bill Longmuir. They ended up in a sudden-death playoff, which was literally that to Longmuir's game. Woosnam won on the third extra hole almost without a struggle. Longmuir three-putted the par-three hole for a bogey four, and Woosnam walked off with the top prize. That was an unfortunate finish to Longmuir, who had shot a brilliant closing 66 and make up five strokes to catch Woosnam in regulation. They tied at 273, 11 under par.

Oddly enough, it was a wild putter that prevented Woosnam from winning outright. Woosnam, after opening the final round with a five-stroke lead, three-putted twice for bogeys. Longmuir, the 1980 Kenya Open runner-up, seemed to be a dead challenger when he took a double-bogey six at No. 8. But he birdied the next two holes, then went on to finish birdie-birdie for a back-nine 31.

Zambian Open—£55,000
Winner: Garry Cullen

It had been a long time coming for Garry Cullen, and so was all the sweeter. Cullen, 31, a Briton based in Kenya and a professional since 1971, finally scored that first victory. And he did it, at Lusaka, through an odd turn of events that involved a popular Irish veteran and some unwitting help from two former European Ryder Cuppers.

Cullen had come so close before. In the 1982 Sanyo Open, for example, he was a strong second, having posted two rounds of 64. And for fully three rounds of this Zambian Open, there was no reason to believe the fates would be any kinder. After the first round, he stood one stroke behind Richard Boxall, young English pro, who turned in a 69. Cullen made 70 and was tied with tall Paul Thomas, second-year tour pro from England and Henry Cotton's Rookie of the Year for 1985. Cullen added a 69 in the second round, and still trailed by one stroke, this time behind Thomas and Welshman Ian Woosnam, one of the Ryder Cuppers who was to figure so prominently two days later. Thomas posted a 68 and Woosnam a 67 to share the lead at 138. Cullen was one back. (The unfortunate Boxall took himself out of the picture with a 75. He was to finish on 288, a joint 12th.)

A third-round 75 seemed to erase Cullen. Enter the other Ryder Cupper,

Gordon J. Brand. Brand posted a 66 and pulled even with Woosnam (74) at 212. Now there were two battle-tested pros to contend with. Woosnam had won the Kenya Open just the week before, and Brand won the Nigerian and Ivory Coast Opens two weeks before that, and was the leader of the Safari Tour money list. Cullen stood at 214, two strokes behind and tied with the Irishman, Eamonn Darcy, who posted a 73. The fortunes of golf might get either Woosnam or Brand out of the way in the final round, but it would take the work of a fiction writer to remove both of them. But gone they were.

Woosnam exited on a 73. Brand was a different matter. He was now poised to win. But he bogeyed the par-five 14th and the par-four-15th. He righted himself at No. 16, where he chipped in from 30 yards for a birdie two. Moments later, No. 18 became the decisive hole.

Cullen and Darcy had already finished. Both made 69 and were tied at nine-under-par 283. Their fate now rested in Brand's hands. At No. 18, Brand needed a birdie four for an outright victory, a par five for a tie. The chance for a birdie evaporated when he hit behind a tree. But after a fine recovery, he was just two feet from a par five and the tie. He missed the putt.

That sent Cullen and Darcy out into a playoff. And Cullen squeezed home on the first hole—a champion at last.

Zimbabwe Open—£54,585
Winner: Stephen Bennett

In the first round, there was too little light. Night was falling. In the last, there was too much—in the form of lightning. But Britain's Stephen Bennett made the best of both and won the Zimbabwe Open at Harare's Chapman's Club. It was the second victory of his seven-year professional career—he won the 1985 Tunisian Open—and it has to go down as one of the more unusual victories in golf. The start was merely the tip-off. Bennett, 26, must be one of the few champions ever to make a birdie by veranda light. Perhaps the only one. It happened late in the first round.

A heavy overnight rain forced a 90-minute delay in the start of the first round the next day. Bennett was battling against time in the failing light. He dropped a shot at the 15th, and then needed a birdie at No. 18 to tie for the lead. "I could see the ball, but the ground was a blur," Bennett said. "I had almost decided (to stop), having been offered the option to mark and return in the morning to finish. But the lights of the clubhouse veranda came on, and I could just see enough to chip close for my birdie four." that gave him a 68 and a one-fifth share of the first-round lead.

Bennett scrambled to a 69–137 in the second round, holding off challenges by Ireland's Philip Walton and Welshman David Llewellyn, who shared second at 138. He missed only one fairway, twice had to get up and down to salvage pars, and dropped three putts of between 15 and 30 feet for birdies. Late in the final round, Bennett felt a little like Lee Trevino, golf's best-known lightning victim. A storm struck as Bennett was playing the short 17th, and he wisely opted to take shelter until it eased up. "I was absolutely petrified by the lightning," Bennett said. "I was once sheltering in a storm at the Orkney Club, near Johannesburg, when lightning struck a tree nearby. The shock waves almost bowled me over." With the lightning gone, Bennett went out into the torrential rain and two-putted for his par at No. 17, then parred No. 18 to finish 11 under par with a 69–277. He won by two over New Zealand's Stuart Reese.

Helix Wild Coast Classic—R100,000
Winner: Mark McNulty

Mark McNulty's first victory of 1986 was the Wild Coast Sun Classic. The Wild Coast Country Club was also the venue of his sixth win, as McNulty returned to South Africa from the European Tour, fresh off winning the Portuguese Open, to start the 1986–87 Sunshine Circuit with a triumph in the now Helix-sponsored Wild Coast Classic.

The first time around, McNulty won by six strokes with a 267 total. This time, Mark needed a six-under-par 64 on the final day for a 279 total to defeat John Bland by two strokes. He was four shots behind Bland after starting with rounds of 66, 74 and 75.

Vincent Tshabalala, the black South African and former French Open champion, led the first day with 65 before fading to 23rd place. Bland came on with rounds of 70, 67 and 74 for the 54-hole lead, which he could not hold, despite an even-par 70 in the fourth round.

Germiston Centenary—R100,000
Winner: Mark McNulty

A third consecutive victory, and seventh of the year, by Mark McNulty was an all-too-familiar result for Fulton Allem. The 28-year-old Allem, who achieved the first two victories of his career on the 1985–86 Sunshine Circuit, might have won two more but for McNulty. And the same thing was happening as the South African tour started its 1986–87 run—Allem was second by one stroke to McNulty in the Germiston Centenary tournament.

A 70 is not a bad score, particularly for the first round, but that eventually cost Allem the title. McNulty and Hugh Baiocchi started with 64s, a stroke in front of Ian Mosey and two ahead of David Frost, who eventually placed third. McNulty's second-round 69 and 133 total placed him one shot ahead of Mosey and Frost, while Baiocchi slipped with 72 for a 136 total. Allem was one stroke further behind with his 67.

In the third round, Allem came alive with a 63, but still was two shots behind McNulty, who fired a 65 for a 198 total. Frost was at 202, following a 68, and Mosey shot 72 for 206. McNulty came through with 68 in the final round for a 266 total, while Allem gained only one stroke with his 67 for 267. Frost was three strokes further behind with 68 and 270.

Sun City Million Dollar Challenge—U.S. $1,000,000
Winner: Mark McNulty

It was raining hard when Mark McNulty was about to leave the press room at Sun City early in December. Someone offered him an umbrella, and he grinned and turned it down. Someone offered him a ride in a car, and he said no to that, too. And away he went, walking happily in the downpour. "I have every right," he said, "to go singing in the rain."

He sure did. He had just scored the biggest victory of his nine-year career. His come-from-behind win in the Sun City Million Dollar Challenge was worth $300,000 plus an additional $50,000 bonus for the best final round, a 68. It was the first victory by a South African in the six years of the Sun City event.

History had already marked this Sun City tournament in a different way. I deal with this at some length here because this tournament, perhaps more than any other, was buffeted by forces that had nothing to do with golf. Which underlines the fact that golf—despite its international appeal and its civil nature—does not exist in a vacuum.

Sun City did not escape the furious international political storm that tore at South Africa throughout 1986, although in southern Africa it is contended that Sun City is not in South Africa but the independent and racially integrated state of Bophuthatswana.

Country after country called for an end to South Africa's apartheid policy and the nation was becoming increasingly shunned, in many ways, by the rest of the world. In some cases, business giants—among them General Motors and the International Business Machines Corp.—divested themselves of their South African subsidiaries. It was not surprising, then, that golfers, like figures in many sports, were encouraged to spurn invitations to compete there. Some listened, some did not.

England's Howard Clark, for example, received a hurried invitation by telephone as promoters scrambled to fill vacancies left by unaccepted invitations. Clark accepted, but only after first seeking and receiving the approval of the PGA European Tour.

The American tour, on the other hand, cited the negative reaction of the U.S. State Department. Apparently all American invitees but one heeded the message. Lanny Wadkins entered. West Germany's Bernhard Langer, the defending champion, who plays on both the American and European tours, was said not to be aware of the U.S. PGA Tour's position. David Graham, an Australian who lives in the United States and plays the American tour, accepted his invitation on the grounds that he is a golfer and not an instrument of politics. Lee Trevino was a late withdrawal, and Seve Ballesteros did not play because of illness. Both had played in the previous five Sun City events.

There was speculation that a number of players turned down their invitations because of anti-apartheid pressure. Sun City ended up with a nine-man field, but not one of the four major championship winners—Jack Nicklaus (Masters), Raymond Floyd (U.S. Open), Greg Norman (British Open), and Bob Tway (American PGA Championship). Whether they were invited was not revealed. The Sun City field consisted of McNulty and two other South Africans, David Frost and Gary Player; T. C. Chen of Taiwan; Clark and fellow-Briton (Wales) Ian Woosnam, and Langer, Wadkins, and Graham.

The tournament also had its share of friction. Graham threatened to walk out after a two-stroke penalty turned his first-round 71 into a 73. Graham had picked up and then dropped a ball embedded in the semi-rough at the sixth hole, apparently under the impresion that American tour rules were in effect. Graham had not called for a ruling, but merely had asked his playing partner, Frost, another player accustomed to American rules. Frost agreed that Graham could drop. Graham did, and took a five on the hole. It wasn't until he finished the round that he was informed of his penalty. Meanwhile, Clark, making his first Sun City appearance, played the last 15 holes in 11 pars and four birdies, including a tap-in three after a six-iron second to the final hole for a 69. That tied him with Wadkins for the first-round lead. McNulty, with a 74, was in sixth place after the first day.

Clark maintained the pace in the second round, returning a 69 that included a 35-foot putt for an eagle at No. 9. Langer came home in 32 for a 68 to share the halfway lead with Clark on 138. Wadkins slipped back to second on 72–141, and McNulty improved by four strokes to a 70, but moved up just one position, to fifth, on 144. McNulty actually never was in solid contention until the final round, when he leaped to his opportunity as the leaders faltered. Clark and Langer both were two strokes ahead of him entering the final round. Langer tripped first, taking a double-bogey seven at the second hole after hitting his second shot from the rough into a lake. He finished third with a 74 for 286. Clark slipped even further. He began to drift at the ninth hole, where he needed a birdie to catch McNulty, who birdied the first two holes. But he took five there after driving into the rough, then stumbled to a 40 coming home for a 76–288.

It was left to the gritty Wadkins, who almost withdrew because of illness during the third round, to mount the big threat. Wadkins pulled to within a stroke of McNulty with a birdie at No. 8. From there, they dueled shot-for-shot until the decisive 17th, where McNulty holed from 30 feet for his birdie-three and Wadkins three-putted from about the same distance. McNulty's closing 68 gave him a six-under total of 282—the highest winning total in Sun City's six playings—and a three-stroke victory over Wadkins (70–285), who won $150,000 for his runnerup effort.

The victory left McNulty in position for a $1 million prize, which Sol Kerzner, chairman of Sun International, which promotes the tournament, said would be offered in 1987.

Safmarine South African Masters—R110,000
Winner: Mark McNulty

If Mark McNulty was feeling invincible after winning the Sun City Million Dollar Challenge, Fulton Allem would not have disagreed. In the Safmarine South African Masters the following week, the outcome was almost predictable: McNulty won again, and for the fourth time this year, Allem was the runner-up.

This tournament was where it all began for McNulty in December, 1985 (and Allem was one of three runners-up). He continued the pace, winning five of 11 tournaments on the 1985–86 Sunshine Circuit, closing the European Tour with a win in Portugal then winning the first four events played on the 1986–87 Sunshine tour, including the rich invitation-only affair at Sun City.

McNulty had a four-stroke margin, just as he had the year before, with a 270 total on rounds of 70, 65, 67 and 68. Simon Hobday was the first-round leader with a 65. Allem put together a pair of 67s to tie Hobday after 36 holes, then Hobday dropped back in the third round with a 72. McNulty and Allem were tied at 202 entering the final round, but Allem shot 72 for his 274 total, while McNulty breezed in with his 68.

Goodyear Classic—R100,000
Winner: Tony Johnstone

Despite an encouraging start, Mark McNulty's effort to win a sixth consecutive tournament and to sweep the entire 1986 portion of the 1986–87 Sunshine Circuit fell short in the Goodyear Classic at Humewood Country Club in Port Elizabeth. The winner was 30-year-old Tony Johnstone, whose three previous Sunshine victories were all on the 1984–85 tour.

The Zimbabwe-born Johnstone, who also won the 1984 Portuguese Open, triumphed by one stroke over—not again—Fulton Allem, who placed second for a fifth time. McNulty started with a 66, one stroke off the lead, but drifted back to a seventh-place tie with rounds of 71, 71 and 74 for a 282 total. Johnstone's 275 total was formed on rounds of 69, 67, 70 and 69.

Bobby Lincoln and Joe Dlamini were the early leaders with identical rounds of 65–66—131. Denis Watson gained a share of the lead after 54 holes, shooting 66 to tie Lincoln at 202, with Dlamini holding third at 204. Johnstone was at 206 and Allem, 207. Both shot 69s in the final round, while Lincoln finished with 76. Lincoln and Dlamini tied for third at 278 and Watson was fifth at 279 after a closing 77.

12. The Australasian Tour

It has been a long time since Australasia has had two players matching the 1986 performances of Greg Norman and Rodger Davis. There have been other great players, other great seasons, but to have both these eye-catching players in such magnificent form was a bonus.

This was Norman's year. On a world-wide basis, his performances were astonishing, and he did it with a style which, in Australia, caught the attention of young people and brought them flocking to the sport. Davis' season was a mixture of astonishing comeback and fairytale achievement. Beset by putting woes and almost beaten financially by a business venture which went wrong, Davis relied on determination and hard work, and had his best-ever year.

Davis did not take the Player of the Year title from the Great White Shark—that would have been impossible given Norman's superb performances—but he won the admiration of all who watched his Whyte & Mackay (British) PGA triumph, the Dunhill Nations Cup, where he played for the first time for Australia, the Australian Open and back-to-back victories in New Zealand. It was a wonderful effort.

Norman's six-tournament victory streak ended in the Australian PGA, when Mike Harwood came in with a last-round 64. There was, however, no real charge from any of the younger players, although Ossie Moore, who is always steady and often brilliant, finished third in the Order of Merit behind Norman and Davis after last year heading the list. Bob Shearer, who has now settled back in Australia, began to play well when the circuit reached Melbourne on his favourite sand-belt courses and Shearer, Ian Stanley, Ian Baker-Finch and Harwood were within A$3,000 of each other on the Order of Merit.

Baker-Finch had the Open for the taking but double-bogeyed at a critical time, and he was often threatening to win but was never quite able to finish it. Wayne Smith won his first professional tournament and then went on to lead the European Tour qualifying rounds at La Manga, Spain. He is a late-maturing player and has a real chance to carve a career for himself in Australasia and Europe. Brett Ogle did well to finish 10th on the Order of Merit but, in general, the younger players were disappointing in their standings. They seemed in awe of Norman and Davis once that pair got cracking, and Norman was quick to admonish them for accepting a secondary role, rather than thinking only of victory.

New Zealand found a rising star in Greg Turner, who learned his golf on an American campus (University of Oklahoma), and now is honing it on the circuits of Australasia, Europe and Asia. He is the best golfer to come out of New Zealand since Bob Charles.

Nissan-Mobil New Zealand PGA Championship—NZ$75,000
Winner: Frank Nobilo

New Zealand golfer Frank Nobilo, runner-up in last year's event, won the Nissan-Mobil New Zealand PGA Championship by a two-shot margin over Brett Ogle, Australia's highly talented newcomer, with veteran Bob Charles a stroke further back in third place. Played at the delightful Mount Maunganui course at Tauranga, in front of large holiday crowds during the Christmas-New Year period, it was for the Kiwi a good start to the circuit.

Charles led the field on the opening day with a five-under-par 67, two strokes ahead of Mike Harwood and three ahead of a group of players that included Ogle. Nobilo had a steady par 72 but it was his turn to fire 67 on the second day. Heavy rain halted play for an hour and a half in the morning but Charles, 67–70, was two strokes ahead of Nobilo at the finish of the round. At four under par were Ogle, who had another 70, Harwood and Peter Jones.

Nobilo, with a two-under-par 70, took the lead on the third day by a shot from Harwood, while Charles slipped back to third spot with 74 to be at 211, two strokes off the pace. Ogle's one-over-par 73 tied him for sixth at 213 but he remained very much in contention going into the fourth day. The 21-year-old Ogle gave Nobilo a tough fight over the last 18 holes and finished with 69 to Nobilo's 71. The New Zealander won by two strokes, with Ogle losing his chance with a bogey at the 16th. Nobilo birdied the same hole and the double swing clinched the title. Only two other players bettered par on the final day. Peter Hamblett, who finished equal ninth, and John Lister, equal 13th, both shot 71s. Charles finished in third place with a par 72 for a total of 283 and Harwood was a stroke further away in fourth position, with Fowler fifth on 285.

This was a splendid victory for Nobilo and a superb effort from young Ogle whose check for NZ$8,000 easily covered the prize money needed to retain his tour player's card for the 1987 season. Ogle admitted he had not expected to do so well, "but I knew I was playing solidly when I came over to New Zealand and to get so close to winning made the trip well worthwhile."

Foster's Tasmanian Open—A$50,000
Winner: Stewart Ginn

Stewart Ginn achieved his victory in the Foster's Tasmanian Open at Royal Hobart playing with a 50-year-old forged head hickory shaft putter which had cost him a mere two dollars. It was his fourth win in this event and he defeated young Swedish star Magnus Persson at the second hole of a sudden-death playoff.

The week began disastrously for the local administrators when 85 players had to play their qualifying rounds for a second time because of a blunder by an official who started half the field from the white markers. Later another official correctly instructed the remainder of the field to hit from the championship tees.

Nineteen-year-old Jason Deep, the youngest player in the tournament, was the leading qualifier off the front markers and then, at the second attempt at the Kingston Beach course, he shot a five-under-par 68 to share the qualifying lead and take his place in the field on the opening day. Deep, however, failed by one shot to make the halfway cut after a disastrous 81 in near gale-force winds on the first day, but he was not the only one to suffer. Defending champion Ian Roberts shot 76, as did Ian Baker-Finch and Rodger Davis, with Ove Sellberg and Bob Shearer 77 and Mike Clayton 79. Only eight players returned sub-par scores in the first round, and Jeff Senior, troubled for months with tendinitis in his right wrist, fired a splendid four-under-par 68 in the difficult conditions. One shot back were Peter Fowler and Wayne Riley, with Ginn, Lyndsay Stephen and Bill Dunk a further stroke away. Senior, 71, increased his lead to two strokes on the second day from Stephen, Ginn and Fowler, and Persson and Terry Gale, both with rounds of 73–69, were with a group of players three behind the leader.

A record-equaling round of 65 on the third day by Persson gave him a three-stroke advantage and a 207 total. He had birdies at the third, fourth, fifth, seventh, eighth, 15th and 16th holes in his round and needed only 27 putts. Behind him, at 210, were Ginn (69) and Senior (71), with Fowler two strokes back.

At one stage on the final day, Persson had a five-stroke lead, but Ginn caught the 20-year-old Swede when he birdied the 11th and they finished tied at 281. Ginn's four-foot sidehill putt on the second playoff hole clinched the win and he gave full credit to his putter which he had bought as a present for his son, Stewart Junior, who turned up his nose at it because it was so old. "But I think it's a beauty," said the delighted Ginn who had last won the Tasmanian Open in 1980.

Robert Boyd Transport Victorian Open—A$100,000
Winner: Ossie Moore

Ossie Moore broke through for his first professional victory when he birdied two of the last three holes in the Robert Boyd Transport Victorian Open at the Yarra Yarra course in Melbourne. His 280 total edged out fellow-Queenslander Vaughan Somers and New Zealander Greg Turner by one stroke. "Many doubters thought I wouldn't do it," Moore said. "I must admit it has taken a long time but the victory has wiped out years of frustration." Moore had topped the Australasian Order of Merit in 1985 without a victory.

The youngsters made the headlines on the first day. Craig Parry, 20, playing in only his second professional tournament, headed the field with 66. He was three over par after seven holes then fired five birdies and two eagles over the remaining 11 holes to lead by a shot over Rob McNaughton and Sweden's Magnus Persson. One stroke behind them, with 68s, were rookie Brett Ogle, Jeff Senior, Somers and 18-year-old English amateur Peter Baker.

Somers carded seven birdies over the last 12 holes in the second round for a scorching 66 and a 134 total, 10 under par. He had been one over after three holes on each of the first two days but the Queenslander was delighted with his play. "I've improved technically and I'm stronger. It's a nice feeling to believe in yourself and to prove to yourself that you're a very good player," Somers said. McNaughton, 67–70, was second, three strokes off the pace, with Moore, 71–67, one shot further back and Persson and first-round leader Parry at 139. Ian Baker-Finch fired 68 to put himself in contention at 143, but Ogle and Baker, after their first-round 68s, dropped well down the field.

Somers, 72, and Moore, 70, totaling 206 and 208 respectively, fought hard on the third day in Melbourne's notorious hot northerly wind, and an eagle by Somers at the 16th momentarily gave him a firm grip on the tournament. Moore then finished birdie-birdie-eagle to stay close, and Peter Fowler, 211, was only three strokes behind Moore. The wind played havoc with the scores, and Persson dropped seven strokes on three holes between the second and fourth to put himself out of the running.

Somers and Moore had a tense struggle through the final round, in near perfect conditions. Both had birdies at the first hole, but Somers bogeyed the second and third to enable Moore to catch him. From then on the lead fluctuated and Somers birdied No. 16 to tie again. Moore birdied No. 17 but his putt for birdie on the 18th lipped out to leave Somers with a chance. Needing a birdie to tie, Somers drove into a fairway bunker, recovered well from the sand and his approach to the green left him a 15-foot putt for birdie. The ball swung agonizingly past the cup and Somers fell back to share the runner-up spot with Turner, whose final-round 66 was easily the best of the day.

It was exactly the confidence-booster Moore needed, and he said the $18,000 check would enable him to buy some furniture for his new home on Queensland's Gold Coast. "My wife, Mandy, and I have been sleeping on the floor," Moore said. "Hopefully this breakthrough is just the beginning of a great year."

Robert Boyd Transport Australian Match Play Championship—A$60,000
Winner: Peter Fowler

Match play is almost a forgotten art in Australian professional golf circles; amateurs play, but the pros are more inclined to watch it on television, when the Suntory World Match Play Championship is held each year in England. In 1986, match play returned to Australia, although it was not a totally professional tournament. The Australian Golf Union insisted that one amateur be included in the 16-player field. The amateur was from Thailand, Bunchoo Ruangkit, who later pulled out because of a neck injury. His replacement, Brad King from Perth, lost in the opening round to Ossie Moore, 3 and 2.

In 1983, Peter Fowler won the Australian Open on the same Kingston Heath course, but he was not listed among the favorites. The odds-makers were wrong, because Fowler defeated Graham Marsh, Stewart Ginn and

Anders Forsbrand before demolishing Bob Shearer 6 and 5 in the final. The lanky New South Welshman gave a marvellous exhibition of shotmaking, but drew criticism for his slow play. When Fowler beat Marsh and Ginn on the opening day, he was warned three times but was not penalized. Officials spoke to him midway through his semi-final with Forsbrand, but again there was no penalty.

The general standard of play was excellent. Shearer defeated Ian Baker-Finch and Rodger Davis so conclusively that he was 11 under par in the two matches and did not register a five on his card in either match. Ginn was under par in losing to Fowler, then Mike Clayton and Shearer staged a tremendous tussle in the second semi-final.

Australian Masters—A$275,000
Winner: Mark O'Meara

Eagles at the 10th and 14th holes on the final day enabled Mark O'Meara to secure a one-stroke victory over David Graham in the Australian Masters at Huntingdale. This prestigious event, run with such flair by David Inglis and Frank Williams, sported the strongest field seen in Australia for many years, including defending champion Bernhard Langer, European Ryder Cup players Sam Torrance, Paul Way, Ian Woosnam, Philip Parkin and Manuel Pinero, as well as O'Meara Graham and the Taiwanese brothers Chen, Tze Chung (T.C.) and Tze Ming (T.M.). Greg Norman, Graham Marsh and Bruce Crampton also returned to Australia to play in the event, in addition to the local favorite, Ossie Moore, fresh from his Victorian Open win two weeks previously, Ian Baker-Finch, Ian Stanley, Terry Gale and Peter Fowler.

The Masters had its share of controversy—Stanley's putt, Gale's two-stroke penalty—and there was doubt whether Norman would be fit to take his place in the field. Norman, Langer, O'Meara and T.C. Chen were late arriving from Honolulu for the pro-am but played late in the day, and Norman fired a four-under 69, despite a viral infection. The following day, still far from well, Norman teed up with Graham, Peter Thomson and Ian Baker-Finch in an exhibition match at Metropolitan to raise money for the family of the late Guy Wolstenholme. Then it was back to concentrate on the main event.

Graham, with a four-under-par 69, shared the first-round lead with the brilliant young New Zealander, Greg Turner, who was Australasian Rookie of the Year in 1985, and lanky New South Welshman Noel Ratcliffe. They were one stroke ahead of a group of five which included Fowler, Stanley and Baker-Finch, while tournament favorite Langer had a one-under 72, despite bogeys at the last two holes, and O'Meara and Norman both shot disappointing 74s. Graham hurt his left thigh when wrestling with thick scrub at the 560-yard sixth hole and he slid to the ground while preparing to chop a left-handed shot. Somehow he extracted the ball with an overturned nine iron and the ball reached the front of the green. He made his par-five but struggled painfully for the remainder of the round. The sixth hole claimed a number of other casualties, notably Rodger Davis, who took nine, and O'Meara and Langer who had double-bogeys apiece. O'Meara also had his share of trouble in reading the greens.

The most controversial incident came with Stanley, who made the head-lines on the second day when he joined Graham and O'Meara in the lead at six under par. He survived suggestions that he missed the ball while attempting to backhand it into the cup on the third hole. "My conscience is clear. Ian Baker-Finch and my marker, Peter Fowler, are satisfied," Stanley said. Television commentators, and later several players, felt he attempted some kind of a stroke but missed the ball. The tape was replayed on air—and off—many times but Stanley claimed the controversy was "nonsense. If I had a guilty conscience I would hardly have made five birdies over the next six holes."

O'Meara took a share of the lead in the second round with 66, a score matched by Sam Torrance who was a shot behind the leading trio with T.C. Chen. "I have to confess I had two good bounces—one out of trees on the 10th and the other on the front nine when I hit a truck," O'Meara said. "It's the best putting round I've had in a long, long time." Graham played solid golf for his two-under 71 although his right thigh muscle was still troubling him, despite packing the leg in ice overnight and taking anti-inflammatory pills.

O'Meara, Graham and Stanley, all with 71s, still held the lead after three rounds by two strokes over Gale, with Baker-Finch and Wayne Riley a further shot behind. For Graham the day began with a double-bogey on the first hole and Stanley birdied the second to give him a three-stroke lead. O'Meara, after bogeying the first, then challenged with birdies at the third and fourth. Turner and T.C. Chen were four strokes off the pace at 215 and Langer, at 216, was by no means out of the running, but Norman's third-round 74 left him eight shots off the lead and he remained well out of contention despite his final-round 72.

More controversy on that fourth day came from Gale, whose chance of victory disappeared with an incorrect drop and a two-stroke penalty which pushed him from third to sixth place and cost him almost $6,000.

O'Meara's round included a four-putt green on the second hole and he was looking anything but the likely winner when he made the turn in 40 strokes. "I gave myself a pep talk," O'Meara said. "I asked myself 'What would Tom Watson do in this situation?' Well, I knew Watson would just grind away and that's what I did." The eagles on the 10th and 14th were decisive and his 73 edged out Graham, 74, by one shot. Stanley led for much of the afternoon but faltered in the later stages to finish third, with Baker-Finch and Langer tied for fourth. The genial O'Meara knew he needed a perfect drive as he stood on the 18th tee, "and I nailed one right up the middle. It was a great feeling. Now it's the U.S. Masters. I believe my swing has reached a stage where it can stand up to the pressure of that."

Rich River Classic—A$70,000
Winner: Bob Shearer

Bob Shearer ran away with the Rich River Classic at Moama on the New South Wales-Victoria border with a 17-under-par total of 267, eight strokes ahead of his nearest rival, Ian Stanley. It was Shearer's first win since taking the South Australian Open in 1984 and his course-record 64 on the first day, which he followed with rounds of 68–66–69, set the scene for his remarkable victory.

The tournament was played alongside the Australian PGA Seniors Championship, which Orville Moody won by one stroke over Peter Thomson. They finished 10 and nine strokes respectively ahead of the rest of the field. Thomson's 66 and 69 opened up a five-stroke lead over Moody but then a pair of 71s were not quite enough to edge out Moody, who shot 69–71–68–68.

Temperatures were over the 100 mark on the first day but neither Shearer nor Thomson, the leaders, seemed worried by the intense heat. Glenn Vines shot 66 and four players, including Vaughan Somers and Steve Elkington, had 67s. Shearer admitted to "a touch of summer madness" after shooting 68 in the searing heat on the second day. "There were moments of absolute brilliance and others of total rubbish," he said as he took a three-stroke lead over Mike Clayton, 69–66, and Rodger Davis, 70–65. He began his round with a par and then exploded with three birdies and an eagle on successive holes. Max Stevens, a 22-year-old from Emerald—a nine-hole course in central Queensland—equaled Shearer's course-record 64 on the second day and improved his first-round score by 10 shots.

Shearer increased his lead to seven with his third-round 66 while Davis, 70–65–70, and Mike Colandro, 70–67–68, were sharing second place on 205. "They'll have to shoot 60 to beat me," Shearer confidently predicted. "But I intend to attack the course."

On the final day, Shearer never looked like being challenged and was so far ahead that much of the attention was focused on the battle between Moody and Thomson. It was Moody, using an extraordinary looking putter which he designed himself, who finally had the last say. The putter had been lengthened by ramming a two-iron shaft inside the original shaft to finish with a club which Moody is able to balance by pressing the top of the shaft against his chest, not unlike the putter Johnny Miller uses these days.

Shearer meanwhile coasted to his eight-stroke win. His last-round 65 put Ian Stanley into second place at 275, with Colandro at 276 and the trio of Rob McNaughton, Davis and Clayton at 277.

Halls Head Estates-Nissan Nedlands Masters—A$50,000
Winner: Lyndsay Stephen

Western Australian Lyndsay Stephen swept to a nine-stroke victory with a 16-under-par total of 272 in the Halls Head Estates-Nissan Nedlands Masters in Perth. He came from one stroke behind Peter Jones with a six-under-par 66. Ian Stanley finished second, edging out Jones, who had a final-round 77.

Jones led from start almost to finish. His four-under 68 on the first day was one ahead of Stanley and local amateur Jon Evans, with Graham Marsh, Stephen, Roger Mackay and Darrell Brown at two under par. Terry Gale, an eight-time winner of the event, started as firm favorite but described his par

72 as "very ordinary." Gale's playing partners, Bob Shearer and Brad King, were penalized two strokes for driving from the wrong tee. Nedlands is a nine-hole course and the players use the forward tees the first time around and the back markers for the second nine.

Jones, 68–67, increased his lead to four strokes on the second day and Shearer fought back for 66 to share second place with Marsh, 70–69. One shot back, at 140, were Stephen, Stanley and Robert Stephens. Jones' round contained seven birdies, including three in a row at the sixth, seventh and eighth, and the only blemishes came on the ninth green, which he bogeyed both times.

Jones still held the lead at the end of the third round, but Stephen closed the gap to a single stroke, carding 66 for a 10-under-par total of 206. Stephen eagled the first hole on the final day and no one could stop him as he blazed home with another 66 to take the title by nine shots. Stanley's 69 gave him second place over Jones and put him into first place in the Order of Merit at the half-way stage of the year. It was Jones' highest finish in his career and Mike Cahill, with 68 and a four-round total of 283, took the fourth spot.

Fourex Queensland PGA—A$100,000
Winner: Ossie Moore

Greg Norman was in England winning the Suntory World Match Play Championship when Ossie Moore won the Queensland PGA at In-dooroopilly. Moore said at the presentation ceremony that Norman was not invincible and there were young golfers in Australia hoping to catch up with him in the next few weeks.

Moore won by 10 shots, coasting in ahead of Brett Ogle, who had an attack of the putting blues, and Peter Senior. Moore gradually asserted his authority after being one stroke behind on the opening day with an excellent 69. In front of him were Ogle, Wayne Riley and Wayne Smith, the latter playing in his first tournament in months.

Smith had spent the previous two months in America, under the eye of David Leadbetter, sorting out his swing problems. He had only been back in Australia a week and, though keen to play a tournament, was understandably short of competition. His 68 was a good effort but, like the other players, he was at times confused by the grainy greens. Hard luck stories abounded.

Moore tied Ogle for the lead in the second round, a day when swirling thunderstorms and lightning brought suspension of play for 30 minutes. The rain was needed, because the greens were so very hard. Few players broke par, and that was also true on the third day, when Moore made his charge. His six-under-par 66 was a wonderful exhibition of accurate driving and precise approach work which left him with makeable putts on every hole.

Only eight players broke par on the third day and only five managed it over the final 18 holes. Moore had to settle for a par-72. None of his challengers got near him, however, and his seven-stroke lead at the start was never threatened.

Stefan Queensland Open—A$100,000
Winner: Greg Norman

Greg Norman's arrival in Australia was one of the media extravaganzas of the year, with everyone anxious to see if he could win one more tournament, the Queensland Open at Coolangatta-Tweed Heads. "Everyone is waiting to see the Shark! You can't get a room anywhere on the coast and we have reports of spectators traveling long distances for this event," tournament organizers said on the eve of pro-am.

The pro-am did nothing to ease the minds of the players about to meet Norman in the tournament. He fired a casual 67 and said he had "just been having a little fun." That "fun" extended to another 67 on the opening day, but Norman found himself three strokes behind the leader, 24-year-old Robert Stephens.

The crowds on the first day were, as predicted, the biggest ever seen for a Queensland tournament and the players were forced at times to do some of their own marshalling. Norman's 67 was ominous, because he didn't make a putt all day. The greens were firm and promised to become even firmer as the tournament progressed, a disquieting feature for some of the pros who could see Norman's experience as a daunting factor.

Brett Ogle fired 66 to take a two-shot advantage in the second round. Ogle's round was a magnificent exhibition, with a superb iron to three feet for a birdie on the opening hole and a nine iron into the hole for an eagle at the next. There was no stopping him, and birdies at Nos. 14, 15 and 16 provided a delightful finishing touch although, like Norman, he had no luck on the greens, missing birdie putts from within 10 feet four times. Ogle slipped back on the third day with a 73, and Jeff Woodland burst through for a two-stroke lead with a 68.

That set Woodland up for the soul-searching last day, when he was right on the firing line of Norman's bid to win a fourth consecutive tournament. Woodland's bid effectively ended on the 14th hole, where Norman shook his playing partners and roused the gallery with a massive drive which cut the trees on the corner, a superb five-iron pin high and a splendid 30-foot putt for an eagle.

Norman's winning margin was six shots, with Woodland and Peter Senior tied for second place, but for much of the day it was closer than that. However, the Shark added to the impressive list of victories in his astonishing year, with rounds of 67, 70, 70, 70 for his 277 total.

National Panasonic New South Wales Open—A$125,000
Winner: Greg Norman

This time it was Greg Norman on the first day, Norman on the second, and Norman on the third and final days. Another victory for the Great White Shark, but without the problems of having to come from behind. It was clear after 10 holes, barring an accident of massive proportions, that Norman was going to be extraordinarily difficult to defeat. He began sluggishly and was one over par after four holes, then had three birdies and an eagle over the next six—and was on his way. Two more birdies on the back nine gave him a six-under-par 65 and a three-stroke advantage over a very good field of Australian golfers.

There were 10,000 fans on the Concord course for the first round; more than that number for the second. This time, Peter Senior, Ossie Moore and Frank Nobilo provided a challenge, while Norman had a 70 to hold a one-stroke lead. Norman returned a blistering 67 to increase his lead in the third round to five strokes over Nobilo, who had three 69s.

Two massive drives in the final round and Norman's day was set up. He had two birdies. The challengers were in trouble before they had done anything wrong. The round became nothing more than a battle for the second place, which eventually went to Lyndsay Stephen by a stroke over Steve Elkington. Norman, with a two-over-par 73, coasted home and there was no doubt that his concentration was shot to pieces by the lack of competition.

The thousands who thronged the course didn't seem to mind—they simply cheered the booming drives, the deft touches around and on the greens, and the presentation where Greg, wife Laura and daughter Morgan Leigh, age four, held center stage.

West End Jubilee South Australian Open—A$100,000
Winner: Greg Norman

Few golfers have won tournaments with two rounds of 75 included, but Greg Norman managed that in the South Australian Open where, once again, he beat off the challengers on the final day and finished three strokes clear of the field.

This was Grand Prix week in Australia. Norman's liking for fast cars is well known, and his red Ferrari is a splendid sight on Florida roads, even when he is adhering to a 55 mph speed limit. The Formula One racing drivers were engaged in the last event of the year, and Norman had the chance to drive in a celebrity event which had been arranged for the day after the golf tournament. He also could take a practice drive the afternoon the golf tournament concluded, providing he could hurry.

At one stage it seemed that David Graham was going to provide a stumbling block. Graham started three shots ahead of Norman, and normally, you would not bet on anyone to defeat Graham from that position, such is his reputation under pressure. This time, the pressure was not really noticeable until the last nine holes. Norman began with a birdie and a bogey, and was still three behind when he reached the ninth tee.

The ninth hole swung the tournament to Norman, in the same way a par-five hole at Coolangatta two weeks earlier killed off the opposition. Norman hit a booming drive well over the fairway bunkers and a three iron 225 yards to within a yard of the pin. He said later it was one of the best three irons he had hit in years. It certainly knocked the stuffing out of the challengers. After Norman came home in 31 for a 65 and 283 total, Graham said, "Nobody can beat that on this course in these tough conditions."

There were many contrasts between the earlier tournaments and this one at Kooyonga, none more so than the weather. The players had sunshine and tropical conditions in Queensland but, from the moment they arrived in Adelaide, they wore two sweaters and waterproofs. The opening day was foul, bitterly cold, and the players said later the wind-chill factor meant they had real problems in holding the club. The second and third days, with rain added to the intense cold, made life really miserable.

Toshiba Australian PGA Championship—A$180,000
Winner: Mike Harwood

"In one way, it's a relief," Greg Norman said after losing to a course-record 64 by Mike Harwood in the Australian PGA event at Castle Hill. "Although I always dislike losing, at least I'll be able to sit down in a restaurant now and avoid being interrupted in the middle of the meal by well-wishers wanting me to win 12 tournaments in a row. It was nice, and I appreciated it, but it was becoming a bit of a strain."

Harwood fired 67 on the last day of the South Australian Open. At Castle Hill, Harwood started with 69 and was three strokes behind Mike Colandro. Sharing ninth place with Harwood was Norman. It was the same story on the second day. Norman and Harwood once again shot 69s, and were only one off the pace. When Norman reeled off a 66 on the third day, it seemed once more to be all over. Not so, because Harwood held together his game and his temperament, and the Shark's great run was ended.

Another challenger was Graham Marsh, who played well enough, with rounds of 68, 69 and 70, to be within three shots of Norman starting the last day. Rodger Davis was positioned between Norman and Marsh, and then there was Greg Turner, the young New Zealand pro, who fired 65 on the third day, and Ian Baker-Finch, who though not happy with his putting, was a model of consistency and was poised to challenge.

All paled before Harwood's 64, for a 275 total, setting the target for Norman. Harwood was seven shots behind on the final afternoon, and had decided that at least 67 was the score he needed to put some pressure on Norman and the others ahead of him. His round was unusual in several ways, notably that he told himself never once to look at the leaderboards and to instantly halt anyone trying to tell him the scores. It was to be total dedication to playing only the course, with complete disregard for what anyone else was doing.

Certainly it worked and, when he signed his card for 64, it included nine birdies and a solitary bogey at the 12th which he immediately remedied with birdies at Nos. 13, 15, 16 and 18. Norman's double bogey from under the lip of a bunker on No. 14 was the clincher, and not even this great player could snatch back the birdies he needed on the last four holes. He finished with a 73, two strokes behind Harwood.

Victorian PGA Championship—A$100,000
Winner: Wayne Smith

It is always a great moment when a former amateur champion wins his first professional event. The change from playing as a hobby to playing to balance a budget has many times been the undoing of amateur stars. But Wayne Smith, the 25-year-old winner of the Victorian PGA at Warrnambool, successfully made the transition. "This feels great, awesome," Smith said.

Greg Norman wasn't there, nor were David Graham, Graham Marsh, Ian Baker-Finch or defending champion Rodger Davis, all of whom were playing in the Nissan Cup in Japan. Mike Harwood was there, as were Ossie Moore, Terry Gale, and many good Australian pros in an event which had been dramatically upgraded from previous years.

There were many hard-luck stories. Ossie Moore started with a 65 and was playing well on the front nine on the second day. On the par-three 11th hole, however, a wayward one iron was blown by the wind into a corner of the course—literally a corner formed by a fence and the gatepost at the front of the course. With room for a one-inch backswing, he completely missed the ball the first time, just made contact with his next but still needed a chip and two putts before he could make his way to the next tee. He was shaken by this, and more so on the 12th hole, when he arrived where his five iron second shot had finished, to find it buried in the sand. Two to get out and two more putts looked like a disaster, yet he fought back well to finish with a one-over-par 73.

That kept Moore close to leader Smith, who had added a 68 to his first-day 67, and suddenly found himself three strokes ahead of the field, only a few weeks after having gone through an extensive swing change under David Leadbetter. Smith was stroking the ball with a great deal of confidence, although he was disappointed at not having won in the three years since taking the Australian Amateur title.

Smith held his game together on the last day, shooting a steady 70 in windy conditions, with the important moment coming on the par-three 15th, when he told his caddy he could wrap up the event if he could make birdie.

His father, Norm, a 16-handicapper, who had taken off to caddy for his son, read the putt perfectly and Smith holed the 10-footer for his two to make it the good luck story of the week.

National Panasonic Australian Open Championship—A$275,000
Winner: Rodger Davis

Rodger Davis capped a great year with a victory in the National Panasonic Australian Open at the Metropolitan Club in Melbourne. There could be no more contrast between this win and the slump in fortunes which sent him into retirement and almost to bankruptcy two and a half years earlier. A combination of the onset of putting "yips" and a disastrous business venture in a golf course/motel complex had provided a chilling double setback for one of the most popular golfers in Australia. That he was able to come back and have such a tremendous year was a tribute to his determination, as well as his skill.

Davis had an agonizing 15-minute wait at 10 under par to see whether Ian Baker-Finch, Bob Shearer or Magnus Persson, playing in the final group, could birdie the 72nd hole and force a playoff. Baker-Finch had a three-shot lead starting the fourth day, and Davis thought he was out of contention when faced with his final six-inch putt. "Then I looked up at the leaderboard and saw Baker-Finch drop to nine under with a double bogey on 17. I couldn't believe it. It was real dream-time stuff."

Baker-Finch, looking more confident and seemingly with a more positive attitude than for some time, led the tournament on the first three days with rounds of 66, 69 and 69. "I've been saying too many negative things to myself this year, knocking myself down instead of building myself up," Baker-Finch said after his first round. "I've suddenly realized you don't have to knock yourself down. There are a lot of guys out there prepared to do it for you. So I've become more positive to give myself a bit of a boost."

On a tense final day, Baker-Finch led almost the whole way, but it was a fascinating five-way duel to the finish. Graham Marsh joined Baker-Finch in the lead at 11 under par, when Baker-Finch dropped a shot at the 16th, but then finished bogey, bogey to end his chances. Marsh was the favorite for much of the day. His experience around the world in tight situations was evident as others fell away, and when he came to the 17th tee, he was the one exerting the pressure on Baker-Finch, 10 years his junior. Like Baker-Finch, though, Marsh found sand, this time with his second shot, and the ball was lying awkwardly in the greenside bunker. Marsh's bogey was unfortunate but not disastrous, because Baker-Finch caught a fairway bunker with his drive at No. 17 and took double bogey.

Marsh now had a real chance, but a sliced drive cost him any hope of a par. He finished with a three-under 69 to underline how solid his game had been until those two finishing holes. Shearer slipped at the ninth hole when he missed a birdie putt of less than two feet after a supporter yelled at him in mid-putting stroke, "Sink it Bob." Who needs enemies with supporters like that? And Persson's chances ended on the 72nd hole when he bogeyed to slip to fifth place.

The 17th was Baker-Finch's final undoing, following a bogey on 16. "I hit a good drive. It just ballooned a little in the breeze and caught the edge of the trap," Baker-Finch said. "I then hit a good five iron safely out, but I suppose I should have chipped it closer. I never felt like it was slipping away from me. It was just unfortunate I took a six on that hole. If I'd two-putted there, I'd have only needed a par at the last to tie it. Even walking up the last fairway I thought I had a good chance."

National Panasonic Western Australian Open—A$100,000
Winner: Greg Norman

Motivation is the name of the game in these hectic sporting times and Greg Norman needed loads of it when he came to the last challenge of his Australian tour. The shotmaking skill was there, but the putts were just a fraction off line, and other aspects of his short game were not quite razor sharp. He had every reason to be tired and he showed it in the first two rounds of the Western Australian Open, although his scores of 72, 70 would have been more than satisfactory for the average professional. And he had aggravated an old injury to his right wrist on the opening day at Lake Karrinyup, and was tending not to go through with his iron shots.

On his second night in Perth, Greg phoned his wife, Laura, who was staying in Brisbane, and said, "I'm almost gone. Find me some motivation." The answer, quick as a flash, was, "No one has ever topped the U.S. and Australian money lists in the one year. Go for it."

That was all Norman needed. He walked on to the first tee the next day and played golf the likes of which Western Australian fans had not seen in a long time, firing a marvellous 66 and being able to say later that, with an ounce of luck, it could have been a 63. It also took him to within two shots of local hero Terry Gale, whose 68, 70, 68 had his fans ecstatic at the thought of a sixth Western Australian Open win.

It turned into a magnificent shoot-out. Gale refused to give in, and was left with a long putt on the 18th green for a tieing birdie. The tension was maintained until that final stroke, and the lead-up to that moment contained some brilliant golf. Norman made eagle on the seventh hole and birdied the 11th to take a one-stroke lead. Then, despite a pre-shot warning from both player and caddy, a spectator's clicking camera shutter on the 14th produced a drive into a bush and a fruitless chase after the culprit by Norman's caddy.

Now Gale was within a shot of the lead, but he missed a difficult 10-footer on No. 17 as news filtered back that Norman had an almost unplayable lie alongside a tree just off the 18th fairway. All Norman could do was move the ball a few yards, still in the rough. Then came the fruits of motivation. Greg had 154 yards uphill to the flag, and a stiff cross wind was blowing from left to right. From where he was, he had no right to expect to be able to check the ball on the slick putting surface. The ball bounced once, checked, and Norman said later this shot, and the difficult downhill, sidehill 12-foot putt which followed, were two of the finest strokes he played throughout his year.

Air New Zealand-Shell Open—NZ$150,000
Winner: Rodger Davis

Rodger Davis ended the Australian portion of the tour on a high note with his win in the Open, and moved on to New Zealand full of confidence. "If anyone can find more tournaments to play in 1986, please tell me. I don't want this year to end," Davis said after winning the Air New Zealand-Shell Open by three strokes over Bob Shearer and Curtis Strange.

Davis' seven-under-par 63 on the opening day set the pace for his first win in New Zealand. Craig Parry was one stroke back with 64, and Noel Ratcliffe, Peter Senior and Maurice Bembridge, with 65s each, were one ahead of defending champion D. A. Weibring, while Strange and a group of others had 67s.

Strange fired another 67 on the second day, and was tied for fourth with Weibring (66, 68), but still they were six strokes behind Davis who added a 65. Senior was in second place, four shots behind, with Ian Stanley a further stroke away.

With a perfect six-iron shot, Strange aced the 176-yard 14th hole in the third round and picked up $100,000 from American Express. Seven birdies gave Strange a 63 and 13-under-par 197 total, but Davis, with a 67, was still ahead by two shots. Weibring, with a third-round 65, was at 199.

Rain, which started falling just as the last groups were teeing off, and a stiff breeze, made low scoring difficult over the final 18 holes, and Davis had some problems on the front nine. He and Strange were even at the turn, with Weibring three shots back. Weibring's chances disappeared on the 13th with a double-bogey six. Strange slipped back with five bogeys between the 11th and 17th holes, while Davis had seven straight pars before a bogey on 17 put him back to 13 under par.

A par at the 72nd hole gave Davis the victory by three shots. Shearer's 66 tied him with Strange in second place, and Senior, 68, moved up to share fourth place with Weibring. The top New Zealand finisher was Simon Owen, a further shot away at 274 with Vaughan Somers.

Nissan-Mobil New Zealand Open—NZ$120,000
Winner: Rodger Davis

Any golfer whose worst round is 68 has a very good chance of opening the champagne at the end of the fourth day. That is exactly what Rodger Davis managed and, if the previous week he didn't want the year to end, how much better did he feel after another victory?

The Nissan-Mobil New Zealand Open field included defending champion Corey Pavin and the young Spanish star, Jose-Maria Olazabal. Davis won by eight shots with a record 262 total and the second man, Bob Shearer, was never over par on any day. Nor was third place-finisher, Ian Baker-Finch, yet he was 13 shots behind Davis, whose storybook finish to the Australasian tour provided him with his best year ever.

An amateur, Michael Barltrop, led the first day with a 65, while Davis shot 67. Davis then posted a 62 to smash the course record, treating the crowd to a marvellous exhibition. "It was just one of those days," he said. "I had the feeling that no matter what the distance might be on the greens, I had the line right, and I had nothing but good positive thoughts. I can understand better now how the great players manage to keep their game going on a high; how, when you watch them, they never seem to get out of the groove."

That "high" continued in the third round with a 65. On the last day, Davis merely needed to play steadily to take the title, but he did better than that. He shot a 68, and his eight-stroke margin was a fair reflection of his play through the four rounds. It was the climax to a fairytale year of golf for Davis and one of the more remarkable comebacks in Australian sports history.

13. The Asia/Japan Tour

The top stars of Japanese golf operated nearly a closed corporation on their tour in 1986, admitting only a smattering of other winners in the early season and late in the year. That Tsuneyuki Nakajima led the pack surprised nobody, but the sparkling performances of three of his predecessor superstars in Japanese golf and several of his standout contemporaries played a big part in putting the 1986 circuit titles in the hands of a few.

Even though he played an international schedule and seemed to run out of gas at the very end of the year, Nakajima rolled up seven victories during the season, including the Japan Open for a second straight year and the Japan Match Play for a second time. He led Japan to victory in the prestigious Nissan Cup international matches and posted his other wins in the Mitsubishi Galant, Mizuno, Kanto PGA and Polaroid Cup Golf Digest tournaments. He led in money-winnings with official earnings of ¥90,202,066—$563,763 in U.S. equivalent—some ¥11,000,000 short of his record 1985 season.

Sharing the attention of Japanese golf fans were Masashi (Jumbo) Ozaki, Isao Aoki and the timeless Teruo Sugihara, all three of whom enjoyed their best seasons in recent years. Ozaki, who finished only ¥10,000,000 behind Nakajima on the money list, won four times in 1986, the first time he had done that since 1977. The titles: Fuji Sankei, Jun Classic and the Nikkei Cup and Maruman Nihonkai back to back. Aoki had been off top form for a much shorter time and credited a healed elbow injury for his impressive play from June, when he won the Sapporo Tokyu, through the rest of the year when he added the Japan PGA Championship, KBC Augusta and Kanto Open and finished third on the money list with ¥78,341,666. Thus, Ozaki and Aoki remained dead even in career victories with 49 apiece, Aoki with two of his most important overseas in the World Match Play and Hawaiian Open on the U.S. tour. Yet, those two stars failed to catch the remarkable Sugihara, who at age 49 ran his victory total to 50 with triumphs in the Tohoku Classic and Kansai PGA and was in the thick of several other titles battles.

Also contributing to the monopoly of the Japanese stars were the double victories of Masahiro Kuramoto (ANA Sapporo and Tokai), Toru Nakamura (Hiroshima and Japan Series) and Tateo Ozaki (Bridgestone and Daikyo) and single victories of the third Ozaki brother, Naomichi, (Pepsi Ube), and Graham Marsh, the Australian who has been a frequent player in Japan over the years (Suntory), his 22nd win on that circuit. Those nine players collected 25 victories on the 1986 tour. The following chart indicates the importance of age and winning experience as exemplified by those nine players:

	AGE	VICTORIES IN 1986	VICTORIES IN CAREER
Teruo Sugihara	49	2	50
Isao Aoki	43	4	49
Graham Marsh	42	1	22*
Masashi Ozaki	39	4	49
Toru Nakamura	37	2	23
Tsuneyuki Nakajima	31	7	37
Tateo Ozaki	31	2	10
Masahiro Kuramoto	30	2	18
Naomichi Ozaki	30	1	5

(*on Japanese Tour only.)

The only other multiple winners in 1986 were David Ishii, the 30-year-old Japanese-American from Hawaii who won the rich Chunichi Crowns and the Niigata Open, and Hajime Meshiai, who took the Pocari Sweat Open and the ACOM Doubles with Satoshi Higashi. Just three men broke through the domination of the stars with their initial tour victories—the veteran Koichi Suzuki, who used his Yomiuri Sapporo Beer Open win as a springboard to a ¥29,000,000 season; touted college-trained player Akiyoshi Omachi, who took the season-opening Shizuoka Open, and Yoshiyuki Isomura, the Kansai Open champion.

It wasn't total glory for the Japanese, however. Besides the Ishii wins and the Bridgestone Aso triumph of Australian Brian Jones, Americans picked off three of the lucrative late-season titles. Bobby Wadkins, whose only previous Japan Tour victory was in the Dunlop Phoenix, won that richest Japanese event again. Scott Hoch landed his third title in the country in the form of the Casio World Open for a second time. Curtis Strange took the individual victory and led his team to the championship of the ABC U.S. vs Japan Matches.

The Asia Circuit sprung few surprises in 1986. Taiwanese pros again were the most dominant as Lu Hsi Chuen made a comeback of sorts. The 32-year-old Lu, who had won seven Asia Circuit tournaments in his first three seasons, had added just one more title in the 1982–1985 period. But, he was the 1986 season's only multiple victor, winning in India and Taiwan, and captured the overall Asia Circuit championship for the fourth time to go with his consecutive titles in 1979–80–81. Countryman Ho Ming Chung (Thailand) and Tsao Chien Teng (Korea) were the other Taiwanese winners, Tsao for the first time. Lu Chien Soon and Hsieh Yu Shu, though non-winners, had strong seasons and were frequent contenders.

Japanese were champions at the start and finish of the nine-event season. Seiichi Kanai took the Hong Kong crown and Hideto Shigenobu finished in front in the Dunlop International. Although neither had won before in Asia Circuit events, they have multiple victories to their credit in Japan. The other Asia titles went to Stewart Ginn of Australia in the Malaysian Open, Greg Turner of New Zealand in the Singapore Open and Frankie Minoza of the Philippines in the Indonesian Open, Turner and Minoza for the first time.

Players from the usual sizeable American contingent were shut out, something that hadn't happened since 1976. However, John Jacobs save the

U.S. a little face. The 1984 Asia Circuit champion from California won the Rolex Masters in Singapore, where some of the tour's regulars play rather than going to India that week. The venerable Philippine Open again was played with a depleted field and non-circuit status and the title went to home country pro Mario Manubay. The year's richest event in Asia (outside of Japan) came in late November with the staging of the Chiang Kai Shek Centennial at Taiwan Golf and Country Club at Tamsui, where a $300,000 purse and some guarantees beefed up the field with the likes of Arnold Palmer, Gary Player, Bernhard Langer and Hale Irwin. However, the Taiwanese pros handled four miserable days of rain best and veteran Kuo Chi Hsiung, a 12-tournament winner in Asia and Japan, nosed out Lai Tsung Hui for the title with a six-over-par 294 and home players occupied the next four spots.

Cathay Pacific Hong Kong Open—US$150,000
Winner: Seiichi Kanai

Veteran Seiichi Kanai ended a long Japanese drought when he captured the Cathay Pacific Hong Kong Open, the opening stop on the 1986 Asia Circuit. Not since Teruo Sugihara and Isao Katsumata won back-to-back victories at Royal Hong Kong Golf Club in 1969 and 1970 had a Japanese player taken a title at one of the original ports of call of the Far East tour.

The 45-year-old Kanai, who had scored three of his 13 wins on the Japanese Tour in 1985, finished birdie-birdie at Royal Hong to edge Australian Ian Baker-Finch with a one-over-par 285 at the conclusion of a weather-beaten tournament week and land his first Asia Circuit title.

Kanai didn't enter the picture until the third round. Only eight sub-par rounds were posted during Thursday's play which began in raw, rainy weather. New Zealand's Greg Turner and Canada's Jim Rutledge took the lead with 68s, Turner, who had begun the 1985 Hong Kong Open with a 67, nailed his 68 this time with four birdies and a bogey, while Rutledge was helped toward his three-under-par start by a 40-foot eagle putt at the 12th hole. Mitch Adcock and Scott Taylor spiced the day when they aced the 191-yard eighth hole within 45 minutes of each other, though neither capitalized on them.

The Hong Kong Open's "coldest weather ever" greeted the field Friday and only five pros broke par. Turner and Rutledge retained their shares of the lead with 72s in near-freezing temperatures and Taiwan's Hsieh Yu Shu joined them at 140 with a 71. The next four contenders were at 143, but Baker-Finch posted a startling 68 for 144 after missing three short birdie putts early. Kanai jumped into a four-way tie for the lead in somewhat more moderate climes Saturday. His 70, after rounds of 72 and 73, and a 71 by Baker-Finch moved them into the deadlock with Hsieh and Rutledge, who both had 75s. Hsieh absorbed a two-stroke penalty when he lost a ball in the woods at No. 9 and Rutledge endured two double-bogeys, one at his last hole.

Both faded early in Sunday's round, as the Japanese pro aced the fifth hole and the Aussie took the lead with an outgoing 32. Ian was stunned by a double bogey at No. 12, but still was in front until Kanai wedged to two feet at No. 17 for a tying birdie and sank a 20-footer for the winning birdie on the 18th green.

Benson and Hedges Malaysian Open—US$150,000
Winner: Stewart Ginn

Stewart Ginn's decision to return to the Asia Circuit in 1986 after a three-year absence was rewarded at a likely spot—the Benson and Hedges Malaysian Open. The 35-year-old Australian from Tasmania, who had concentrated on home and family in 1983–85, went back to Asia in 1986 and was victorious in his second start, winning at Kuala Lumpur's Royal Selangor Golf Club, where he had scored his only other Asia win nine years earlier.

Malaysia and Royal Selangor have long been favorite places for Australian golfers, ever since Frank Phillips won the first Malaysian Open in 1962. Aussies have won eight times since then and they were one-two in 1986 as Ginn, with his 276 total, edged compatriot Brian Jones, the 1978 Malaysian champion, by a stroke. Ginn had rounds of 70, 69, 67 and 70, eight under par for the distance over the 6,824-yard Royal Selangor course.

Sam Torrance, the European Ryder Cupper, staked a one-stroke lead the first day with his four-under-par 67, the product of six birdies and two bogeys. It gave him a one-stroke lead over Jones, Hidendri Nakajima of Japan and Lu Chien Soon of Taiwan, the 1984 winner. Ginn was among 15 players at 70. Torrance slipped a shot off the pace Friday, when Lu Hsi Chuen and Canadian Ray Stewart, with 69–68s for 137s, took over first place. At that point, Ginn and Jones were two shots off the pace in a large group at 139.

Chen Tze Chung, the 1985 runnerup who has established a good international reputation, staked his bid Saturday and joined Ginn and Jones at the top. Chen shot 68, the Aussies a pair of 67s to take the lead at 206, with Liao Kuo Chih at 208 and Stewart and Lu among four players next at 210. The three leaders hung together through the front nine, then Chen fell back. Jones birdied the 13th to go a shot ahead of Ginn, then dropped back with a bogey at the 15th. The decisive stroke came on the next green when Ginn sank a five-foot birdie putt to take the one-shot lead that he held with two closing pars for the victory, his second of the year. Stewart had won the Tasmanian Open back home in February.

Singapore Open—US$125,000
Winner: Greg Turner

Greg Turner accomplished what only one other New Zealand pro had ever done—win on the Asia Circuit—when he stormed to a record victory in the Singapore Open in mid March. New Zealand doesn't exactly teem with touring golf pros, but only Walter Godfrey, in the 1972 Hong Kong Open, laid claim to a title on the circuit before the 23-year-old Turner came along.

Greg's victory was not surprising, however. Even though just in his second year as a professional, Turner had strong credentials. The younger brother of two field hockey stars in New Zealand honed his golf game on the collegiate circuit as a member of the University of Oklahoma golf team. He had won twice—in New Zealand and Fiji—and in his rookie tour of Asia had tied Chen Tze Ming in the 1985 tournament at Singapore Island Country Club's Bukit Course and lost to the Chinese veteran in the subsequent playoff. He had been a strong contender at Hong Kong and tied for eighth in Malaysia in the two events preceding Singapore.

Turner left little to chance at Singapore. Twice he shot six-under-par 65s enroute to a 13-under-par total of 271, which bested by two strokes the tournament record, held jointly by Kesahiko Uchida (1976) and Mya Aye (1981). The first 65 came Thursday and gave him a two-stroke opening lead over 1983 Singapore winner Lu Chien Soon, three over American Curt Byrum. Canadian Tony Grimes nosed into contention Friday with a 66 for 135 that moved him into a tie with Turner, who shot 70. Byrum's second 68 left him a shot off the pace.

The second 65 virtually settled matters Saturday. It opened a five-stroke lead for the New Zealander at 200 as Grimes took a 70 and Byrum a 71. Between Grimes at 205 and Byrum at 207 were Canadians Ray Stewart and Steve Anderson-Chapman. With the pressure off, young Turner mustered only a par 71 Sunday for the 271, but still finished four strokes in front of runnersup Grimes and American Duffy Waldorf, a recent collegiate star at UCLA in California, who finished 69–67. Chen Tze Chung had three rounds in the 60s after a 71 start and took fourth place with 277, a shot ahead of Byrum.

Thailand Open—US$100,000
Winner: Ho Ming Chung

Another nation was heard from at the Thailand Open. After the Asia Circuit produced 1986 winners from Japan, Australia and New Zealand at its first three stops, it turned matters over to Taiwan when the circuit reached Bangphra. Ho Ming Chung, the veteran Chinese player with three previous tour victories to his credit, stamped out four successive par rounds to capture the 22nd Thailand Open by one stroke with the 288.

Had Ho faltered, two of his countrymen were close by. Lu Chien Soon, who had won there in 1984, was the runnerup at 289 and Lu Hsi Chuen, the 1980 Thailand Open victor, finished in a three-way tie for third with Canadian Ray Stewart and Australian Peter Fowler at 290.

Several lesser-known players were in the limelight earlier in the tournament. Kim Young Il gave Korean golf a moment in the sun Thursday. The 31-year-old Kim, a nine-year professional, opened with a three-under-par 69 and took a one-stroke lead over Japan's Katsuyoshi Tomori, Taiwan's Lai Chun Jen and Saneh Saengsui, an unsung Thailand pro. Tomori's 72 Friday nudged him into the lead with 142, a shot in front of Lai (73), Saengsui (73) and Fowler (72), as Kim shot 76. Ho's steadiness rewarded him with the lead Saturday. The third 72 and 216 advanced him to the top, a shot in front of the surprising Saengsui and Lu Hsi Chuen, two ahead of Lu Chien Soon and Fowler. Lai and Tomori blew themselves out of contention with 80 and 79 respectively.

Thailand fans, whose long-time national star Sukree Onsham had come close but never won during his long Asia Circuit career, stirred Sunday when Saengsui continued his strong play and seized a one-stroke lead after a birdie at No. 10 and an eagle at No. 13. However, Saneh succumbed to the pressure, bogeyed the next four holes and finished in a four-way tie for sixth at 291. Bogeys at 12, 14 and 16 did in Lu Hsi Chuen's title bid and Ho grabbed the lead with birdies at No. 10 and No. 13. He parred in for the victory as Lu Chien Soon missed a tying birdie putt on the last green.

Indonesian Open—US$100,000
Winner: Frankie Minoza

Frankie Minoza joined the ranks of Philippine winners on the Asia Circuit at Indonesia, where he had experienced one of his several near-misses the year before as he sought the elusive first victory in his fourth professional season after a distinguished amateur career in Asia. Minoza followed in the footsteps of two of his noted golfing countrymen as an Indonesian Open champion, Ben Arda having won the inaugural event in 1974 and Eleuterio Nival the 1982 tournament at Jakarta. Minoza had finished second to Lu Chien Soon by a stroke at Pondok Indah Golf Club in 1985.

Minoza stayed close throughout the tournament and rallied from three strokes off the lead Sunday to annex the victory. He was four back after the first round, when Hsieh Yu Shu, Peter Fowler of Australia and Ho Ming Chung, who had just won at Thailand, opened with 65s. Hsieh moved three shots ahead Friday, adding a 67 for 132 as Fowler had a 70 and Ho a 71. Minoza's 68—137 put him in fourth place at that point and he continued to pare off strokes Saturday. Still, with his 67 and 204, the Philippines pro was three shots off the pace and had five players in front of him. Ho, Hsieh and Stewart Ginn, the Malaysian Open winner, shared the lead at nine-under-par 201, Ho and Ginn having shot 65s and Hsieh a 69. Lin Chai was at 202 and Fowler at 203.

Minoza put together a solid 66 Sunday—four birdies, no bogeys—as he rolled into the lead and captured the title with his 270. Yu Shu shot 70 and finished second at 271, a stroke in front of Ginn (71), Ho (71) and Lin Chia (70).

Charminar Challenge Indian Open—US$100,000
Winner: Lu Hsi Chuen

A field of 156 golfers teed off in the first round of the Charminar Challenge Indian Open in Calcutta, but 154 of them may as well have been spectators so far as the winning of the championship was concerned. That matter was in the hands of the other two players—Taiwan stars Lu Hsi Chuen and Lu Chien Soon—all week. Hsi Chuen eventually prevailed in the four-day duel, beating Chien Soon by two strokes in an exciting finish at Royal Calcutta Golf Club.

Chien Soon fashioned a 67, six under par over the 7,285 yards of the par-

73 Royal Calcutta course, and grabbed a two-stroke lead the first day. Hsi Chuen was among five players in the 69 group. The leader bogeyed his first hole of the day before gathering seven birdies on the remaining 17. The other Lu turned the tables Friday. The three-time circuit champion shot a flawless, five-birdie 68 and moved two strokes in front of Chien Soon, who managed only a 72 despite an eagle at the 15th hole. Two shots farther back as the unlikely contender next in line was little-known Thai Somsak Sri-Sanga, who ultimately finished in that position but eight strokes behind the winner.

Chien Soon regained the lead Saturday with his second 67 for 206 as Hsi Chuen shot 70 for 207 with an eagle at No. 15 on his card. It was clearly between these two players then with Sweden's Per Arne Brostedt a distant third at 213. The situation between the two Lus was unchanged after nine holes Sunday with both men one over par for the round. Chien Soon appeared victory bound when he moved three strokes ahead after Hsi Chuen bodied the 14th. But, the latter rebounded immediately with an eagle at the 15th to cut the margin to one. Then, disaster befell Chien Soon at the 17th, where he overshot the green and wound up with a double-bogey. Now, Hsi Chuen had the lead back and he finished with the two-stroke margin when the shaken Chien Soon bogied the last hole.

The win was Lu Hsi Chuen's ninth on the Asia Circuit, but his first since 1983 at Manila. He also had two victories on the Japanese Tour on his fine record.

Republic of China Open—US$120,000
Winner: Lu Hsi Chuen

While his victory in the Indian Open after a three-year drought on the Asia Circuit had to be quite gratifying to Lu Hsi Chuen, it couldn't possibly have compared to his follow-up victory the next Sunday. That one came in front of the home folks in the Republic of China Open, a tournament he had been striving to win back through his eight pro seasons and his brief amateur career.

As frequently happens to the tournament in Taiwan, rain hampered play and washed out the Friday round, so the event was a 54-hole one for the second time in three years. Lu, whose famous uncle, Lu Liang Huan, was defending champion and a four-time winner, sandwiched an opening 67 and closing 69 around a 76 on a day of generally-high scores Saturday for his winning 212, four under par at the Chang Gung Country Club's 7,015-yard course near Taipeh. It was the 18th time in 22 China Opens that a Taiwanese player took the victory.

Lu's 67 in the first round gave him a share of the lead with Lu Chin Han, a shot in front of Wayne Smith and Mike Cunning, two ahead of Lu Chien Soon and Wong Teh Chong. When play resumed Saturday, Lu Chin Han took sole possession of first place with 72 and 139. The 76 dropped Lu Hsi Chuen behind him, Curt Byrum at 141 and Lu Chien Soon and Smith at 142.

Chin Han fell out of contention early in Sunday's final round with bogeys on four of the first five holes, yielding the lead to Byrum. Hsi Chuen closed the gap, catching the American with birdies at the 12th and 15th holes. Then, the talented Taiwanese pro took final command at the next hole—a 530-yarder—with a drive and three-wood onto the green and a two-putt birdie. Byrum finished with 72 for 213 and was joined in that runnerup spot by John Jacobs, the 1984 China Open winner and Asia Circuit champion who, like Lu Hsi Chuen, was coming off a victory the previous Sunday. Californian Jacobs, who won the Rolex Masters at Singapore, had a 67 finish for his 213. Shen Chung Shyan and Lu Chien Soon were next at 214.

Korean Open—US$130,000
Winner: Tsao Chin Teng

Victory was a long time in coming for Tsao Chin Teng, the latest in a long list of Asia Circuit winners from Taiwan. Tsao was 30 before he even launched his professional career and the victory—in the Korean Open, eighth stop on the 1986 tour—came in his seventh season on the circuit, ending a long period of frustration for him but adding to the exasperation of fellow Taiwanese Hsieh Yu Shu.

Hsieh led after the first round, was just a shot behind Tsao after three rounds and bogeyed the 72nd hole to miss a tie and a playoff chance at victory. Twice earlier in the season, Hsieh failed to win from co-third round leadership positions, finishing second at Indonesia and third at Hong Kong. With the final-hole bogey at Nam Seoul Country Club, Hsieh turned over the Korea title to Tsao, who also shot 71 in the final round to preserve his one-stroke margin. His 280 was eight under par for the distance at the 6,861-yard course in Seoul.

Hsieh was the only player in the 60s Thursday, taking a two-stroke lead with his 68 as Chin Teng began his title quest with 71. The 37-year-old pro shot 67 Friday and took a one-stroke lead over Australian Peter Fowler, who rebounded from an opening 73 with 66 for 139. Hsieh took 73 Friday for 141, leading Stewart Ginn, Lu Hsi Chuen and former winners Shen Chung Shyan and Chen Tze Chung by a stroke. Hsieh came back Saturday with 69 and trailed Tsao (71—209) by a shot after 54 holes with Fowler at 212 and Lu and Chen menacing at 213.

However, the latter two had 75s and were never in the picture Sunday. Oh Jong Man, an unknown Korean pro, jumped into third place in the final standings at 282 with a closing 67. Lu and Chen tied with Koichi Suzuki and Cho Chul Sang of Korea for fourth at 288, three strokes behind Fowler, who had 73 Sunday.

Dunlop International—¥50,000,000
Winner: Hideto Shigenobu

The Dunlop International annually concludes the Asia Circuit season with its staging at the Ibaraki Golf Club near Tokyo, but this year it seemed more like the stop on the Japanese Tour that it really also is. The regulars on the Asia Circuit played second fiddle to the stay-at-home pros who play almost exclusively on their own tour. The eventual Dunlop winner was Hideto

Shigenobu, a journeyman who had won four times earlier in his seven years on the Japanese Tour, and the other strong contenders throughout the event were fellow travelers on that circuit.

Masahiro Kuramoto, one of Japan's finest, led for the first two rounds. He opened with a dazzling, eight-under-par 64, two better than his nearest pursuer, Hisao Inoue. Though shooting only a 70 Friday, Kuramoto widened his lead to three strokes over Noburo Sugai (67–70) and Masashi Ozaki (70–67). Inoue, with 72, was at 138 with Naomichi Ozaki (70–68). Kuramoto had four birdies, two on the opening holes putting him 10 under for his first 20 holes, and two bogeys.

The veterans Jumbo Ozaki and Inoue moved in front Saturday. Ozaki, 39, winner of 45 events in Japan during his long career but winless in important tour events for three years, shot 70 with four birdies and Inoue 69 for his 207 as Kuramoto slipped to a 75 and fell behind Sugai and Wayne Smith of Australia, who were at 208. Shigenobu was among six players, including such threats as Tsuneyuki Nakajima, Graham Marsh and Kuramoto at 209.

Shigenobu's par 72 was enough for a two-stroke victory Sunday as strong winds drove up the scores. In Fact, Hideto was two over par for the round after 15 holes, but he birdied the 16th, saved a par after missing the 17th green and opened the two-stroke winning margin when he birdied the par-five 18th for his 281 total. Kuramoto (74) and David Ishii (70) were already finished with 283s and took second place as Ozaki fell into a fifth-place tie with 78 and Inoue plunged even further as he collapsed with an 83.

Now, we must digress. For several weeks, the start of the Japanese Tour runs concurrently with the finish of the Asia Circuit. The Japanese season began in late March traditionally with the Shizuoka Open.

Shizuoka Open—¥30,000,000
Winner: Akiyoshi Omachi

Akiyoshi Omachi, a promising young player not long out of the collegiate ranks, gained his first tour victory at the expense of Teruo Sugihara, the storied veteran who was going after his 50th in the Shizuoka Open at the Hamaoka course of Shizuoka Country Club. But it took four playoff holes for Omachi to accomplish this in the rain-shortened tournament.

The two players entered the final round two strokes off the lead, held after 54 holes by Takashi Kurihara with an even-par 216. Masashi Ozaki was at 217 and Omachi and Sugihara shared third place with Hsieh Min Nan and Seiichi Kanai. When the weather—heavy rains and strong winds—moved in, the final round was reduced to nine holes and Omachi and Sugihara forged their tie with 36s for 254. Kurihara had 41 and Ozaki 44 in the poor conditions as Hsieh finished third at 255 and Kanai fourth at 256. A par on the fourth extra hole gave Omachi the initial victory he had sought without success during his first three pro seasons. Akiyoshi had shared the first-round lead at 71 and went in front Friday with another 71 for 142 before dropping behind Kurihara Saturday.

Kuzuha International—¥15,000,000
Winner: Yoshitaka Yamamoto

It required overtime effort to decide a winner in another early-season standard, the 36-hole Kuzuha International at the Kuzuha public course near Osaka. Yoshitaka Yamamoto captured that playoff to record his 14th career victory on the Japanese circuit after he and Seiichi Kanai tied at 137 over the regulation route. As was the case with Akiyoshi Omachi's victory at Shizuoka, a par won the playoff when Kanai three-putted the par-three 16th, the first extra hole.

Yamamoto led after the first round with his five-under-par 65, but was overtaken in Friday's final round when he shot 72 and Kanai put a 69 with his opening 68. Wayne Riley of Australia finished third with 71–67—138.

Pocari Sweat Open—¥40,000
Winner: Hajime Meshiai

Late-blooming Hajime Meshiai picked up in early 1986 where he had left off at the end of the 1985 Japanese season. Meshiai, 32, had scored his first individual victory in eight years of campaigning in 1985 and jumped from 40th place the previous year to ninth on the season's money list, having a generally-consistent series of finishes to go with the win in the KBC Augusta in early September. He wasted little time at the beginning of the 1986 season, emerging with the title from the 36-hole Sunday finish of the Pocari Sweat Open at Daiwa. Meshiai came from two strokes off the pace with rounds of 73 and 65, his 277 edging Nobumitzu Yuhara and Ian Baker-Finch by a shot.

The 36-hole final day resulted from a storm that washed out Thursday's first round. Baker-Finch and Tateo Ozaki grabbed the lead when the first round was played Friday, but yielded to Ikuo Shirahama and his 69–68—137 Saturday. Shirahama, winless in eight tour seasons, led Hideki Takamiya by one; Ozaki, Meshiai, Kikuo Arai, Brian Jones and Shizuoka winner Akiyoshi Omachi by two. Meshiai was solid in shooting the winning, six-under-par 65 Sunday afternoon. He scored the winning sixth birdie at the par-five 17th hole. Yuhara had 68–69 and Baker-Finch 70–67 Sunday in finishing in the co-runnerup slot.

Bridgestone Aso Open—¥35,000,000
Winner: Brian Jones

Weather continued to plague the Japanese Tour in its early weeks when rain washed out the second round of the Bridgestone Aso Open at Kunamoto and forced a 27-hole final Sunday and a 63-hole tournament. Brian Jones, the Japan-based Australian with two previous victories on the circuit, came from three strokes off the lead Sunday with a 67–34 to take his third win by a shot with his 240 total. Jones, who also has won in his home country and on the Asia Circuit, had eight birdies and a bogey over the final 27 holes.

Namio Takasu made most of the early noise. The veteran Takasu opened with 67, tying for the lead with Yoshitaka Yamamoto, the Kuzuha winner, then moved a stroke in front after the rainout with a 69 for 136 Saturday. Seiji Ebihara and Teruo Sugihara were at 137. Among others, Nobumitsu Yuhara was at 138 and Jones at 139. At the end of 18 holes Sunday, Jones with his 67 and Yuhara with a 68 shared the lead at 206. Three birdies and a bogey brought Jones his 34 and the victory as Yuhara took a 35 and finished second for the second Sunday in a row. Masashi Ozaki, with 69–34, placed third at 243.

At this point, the Japanese and Asia Circuits converged on Ibaraki for the Dunlop International, won, as previously noted, by Hideto Shigenobu.

Chunichi Crowns—¥90,000,000
Winner: David Ishii

For the fifth time in six years, Japan's second richest tournament title—the Chunichi Crowns—wound up in the hands of a fore'gner. In 1986, the champion was David Ishii, the 30-year-old Japanese-American from Hawaii, who has been playing frequently in Japan since 1980 and steadily improving over those years. Ishii, who had won his first Japanese Tour victory in 1985 in the Tohoku Classic, never trailed in the rich tournament at Nagoya Golf Club's Wago course and won going away from the early-season's strongest field. He had rounds of 68, 67, 71 and 68, finishing six under par at 274 and four strokes in front of Japanese powerhouse Tsuneyuki Nakajima. Thus, Ishii joined fellow Americans Gary Hallberg (1982) and Scott Simpson (1984), Graham Marsh of Australia (1981) and Chen Tze Ming of Taiwan (1983) as non-Japanese winners of the Chunichi Crowns, Seiji Ebihara the only interrupter in 1985.

Ishii broke from a four-way, first-place tie at 68 the first day to take sole possession of the lead Friday with 67 for 135. Five birdies and two bogeys produced the 67 and a one-shot lead over Kazuo Yoshikawa. Brian Jones, Naomichi Ozaki and D. A. Weibring were three strokes further back at 139. David maintained his one-shot lead over Yoshikawa Saturday as both shot 71s. Weibring moved into a threatening position with 69 for 208. The winner actually had an easy time of it Sunday. Yoshikawa quickly fell out of contention and Weibring lost ground as Ishii birdied the eighth and 15th holes and parred the rest until taking a meaningless bogey at the final hole. Meanwhile, Nakajima, who had moved within two shots of Ishii on the front nine but got no closer, took over second place with his closing 67. Weibring finished third with his 71 for 279.

Fuji Sankei Classic—¥40,000,000
Winner: Masashi Ozaki

Even though it had been almost three years since he had won a 72-hole tournament, Masashi (Jumbo) Ozaki surprised few with his victory in the Fuji Sankei Classic at the Kawana Hotel Golf Club at Ito. The veteran,

Japan's first current-era star of international repute, had been threatening to win virtually every week of the new season, a co-third round leader one time and just a shot back after 54 holes another. At Kawana, Ozaki took a two-stroke lead into the final round and withstood the challenge of David Ishii and his bid to back up his Chunichi Crowns win.

Jumbo was one of four 65 shooters in Thursday's first round, sharing the lead with Masahiro Kuramoto, Kinpachi Yoshimura and Hiroshi Ishii. He dropped back Friday when he took a one-over-par 72 for 137 as Hiroshi Ishii was putting a 70 with his 65 on a day of generally-high scoring. Ozaki then regained the lead the third day with 71 for 208, standing two in front of the two Ishii's, Hiroshi (65–70–75) and David (67–72–71). Jumbo stayed in front Sunday until he took a double-bogey at the 13th hole and David Ishii birdied the 15th. But David dropped a shot back when he bogied the 17th hole and pars by both at the 18th gave Ozaki the 46th victory of his fine career, every one of them scored in Japan. One was the Fuji-Sankei in 1980.

Japan Match Play Championship—¥40,000,000
Winner: Tsuneyuki Nakajima

Tsuneyuki Nakajima used the Japan Match Play Championship as his launching pad for the 1986 season, scoring his second victory in four years in the event at Mito Golf Club. A top-10 finisher in the three previous events, the top-seeded Nakajima capped his sweep through five opponents with a 6-and-5 victory over lightly-regarded Keiichi Kobayashi in the finals. It was a sharp contrast to his first Match Play win in 1983 when he went two overtime holes before defeating Hideto Shigenobu.

The other name players fell by the wayside in the first two rounds as Nakajima ousted Tadao Nakamura, 4 and 2, and Katsuji Hasegawa, 4 and 3, while Kobayashi was advancing with victories over one of those star pros, Masahiro Kuramoto, 1 up, and Yoshihisa Iwashita, 2 and 1. Niether had it easy in the third round, Nakajima besting Naomichi Ozaki, 2 up, and Kobayashi going 19 holes against Katsunari Takahashi. Tsuneyuki reached the finals with a 3-and-1 win over Koichi Suzuki, Keiichi with a 1-up triumph in 37 holes against Koichi Uehara. Nakajima had the upper hand throughout the final match. He led, 4 up, after the morning round and expanded the margin to seven holes before closing it out at the 31st hole.

Pepsi Ube—¥40,000,000
Winner: Naomichi Ozaki

Naomichi Ozaki followed older brother Masashi into the 1986 win column by two weeks when he captured the Pepsi Ube title at Ube Country Club in Yamaguchi in late May. The 30-year-old Naomichi made a strong finish to exchange places with Fujio Kobayashi and win by a stroke, 276 to 277, in a two-man battle in the final round. Ozaki closed with 68 to the 70 of Kobayashi, who had led by a shot after 54 holes.

Both had lingered just off the pace during the first two rounds. They shot 71s the first day as Tadami Ueno and Koiichi Inoue took the lead with 68s. Seiichi Kanai, who had won earlier in the year at Hong Kong, fired the week's best score Friday, his 66 giving him the lead at 138. The Kobayashis, Fujio and Keiichi, were at 139 and Ozaki among four players at 140, Tsuneyuki Nakajima among them. Fujio Kobayashi's second 68, in a five-birdie, one-bogey round, gave him the 54-hole lead at 207 and Ozaki matched the performance to take over the runnerup slot. He had another five-birdie, one-bogey round Sunday in annexing the victory, his fifth on the professional circuit and all in the last three seasons.

Mitsubishi Galant—¥56,000,000
Winner: Tsuneyuki Nakajima

Tsuneyuki Nakajima's hot streak on the Japanese Tour continued into June. He became the year's first multiple winner when he came off a 36-hole Sunday finish with a one-stroke victory in the Mitsubishi Galant at Oharai Golf Club, two weeks after his triumph in the Japan Match Play and five weeks into an uninterrupted stretch of top-10 finishes.

A Friday rain-out had dictated the double round Sunday and Nakajima made the best of it. He came from four strokes off the pace with rounds of 69 and 70 for his eight-under-par 280 total and a one-shot margin over Chen Tze Ming of Taiwan, two over Australia's Terry Gale. Seiichi Kanai, the second-round leader with 137, had a 77 in the afternoon Sunday and dropped to seventh in the final standings. He had shared the first-round lead with Shigeru Kawamata at 67, then moved in front with 70 for the 137, two ahead of Chen and four in front of Nakajima (73–68) and Isao Aoki (72–69), after the rain-enforced Friday layoff.

Tohoku Classic—¥40,000,000
Winner: Teruo Sugihara

The amazing Teruo Sugihara maintained a rare pattern at the Tohoku Classic. In recent years, Sugihara has been keeping pace with his birthdays. At the Tohoku, just six days before his 49th birthday, Teruo scored his 49th victory. Sugihara, who had also won the Tohoku at Nishi Sendai Country Club at Miyagi in 1981, shot a final-round, one-under-par 71 to score a two-stroke victory over Namio Takasu with his 280 total.

The remarkable veteran didn't move to the fore until the third day. Shinsaku Maeda and Kenji Sogame had first place after the first round with their 68s. Teruo was one behind at the midpoint, his 70–69 putting him on the heels of Taisei Inagaki (69–69) and Koiichi Suzuki (71–67). Sugihara's third-round 70 gave him the lead at 209, but he had Graham Marsh and Tateo Ozaki at 211, Takasu, Inagaki and Kikuo Arai at 212 and Isao Aoki at 213 in close pursuit. However, his 71, which included a meaningless bogey at the last hole, gave him the two-shot win. Marsh and Aoki finished third at 283.

Sapporo Tokyu Open—¥40,000,000
Winner: Isao Aoki

It was surprising that Isao Aoki had not won in Japan in more than two years, but not surprising where the dry spell came to an end. The 43-year-old Aoki, Japan's finest player for the better part of a decade before Tsuneyuki Nakajima assumed the helm, had been in the longest slump of his fine career when he arrived at Sapporo International for the Sapporo Tokyu Open in mid-June, a winless spell going back to the season-ending Japan Series in 1983.

What better place for the victory to come. Aoki had scored three of his earlier 45 wins in the Sapporo Tokyu, including the inaugural in 1973. None were more convincing. Isao led from start to finish, shot a 15-under-par 273 and won by three strokes over Shinsaku Maeda. His opening 65 gave him a two-stroke margin and he widened it to five Friday with 67 for 132. Maeda and Seiichi Kanai, who was to finish third, were at 137. A par round Saturday only cost him two strokes of his lead and he and Maeda matched 69s in the final round. Aoki had five birdies and two bogeys Sunday.

Yomiuri Sapporo Beer Open—¥50,000,000
Winner: Koiichi Suzuki

Eleven years of campaigning finally paid off for Koiichi Suzuki in the Yomiuri Sapporo Beer Open, but it required a rash of birdies to get him his first victory. He was 19 under par for his four rounds over the par-73 Yomiuri Country Club course at Osaka, yet his 273 was no laugher. He finished just two strokes in front of Brian Jones, the Japan-based Australian. Both players had all four rounds in the 60s.

Naomichi Ozaki was the first-round leader with 66 and retained the lead Friday, when he added 70 for 136. Bunched close at that point were Suzuki and Jones at 137 and Isao Aoki, Tsuneyuki Nakajima and Masahiro Kuramoto at 138. Suzuki jumped into first place Saturday with 67 for 204 and Jones' 69 placed him second at 206, a shot ahead of Nakajima. All three players shot 69s Sunday, Suzuki taking a bogey against his five birdies, Jones making four birdies and 14 pars. Teruo Sugihara had a 67 and tied Nakajima for third at 276.

Mizuno Open—¥50,000,000
Winner: Tsuneyuki Nakajima

Virtually every season, Japan is weathered into 63-hole tournaments and 1986 was no exception. Two early-season events lost nine holes off their planned length and it happened a third time in late June, when heavy rains shortened the final round of the Mizuno Open at Tokinodai Country Club to nine holes. It made no difference to Tsuneyuki Nakajima, who pulled away to a six-stroke victory even though shooting a one-over-par 37 in the heavy going Sunday. His score, bringing him his third 1986 victory, was 239, 13 under par.

After starting two strokes off the pace with a 69, Nakajima took charge the second day. He shot 65 for 134 and edged a stroke in front of Seiji Ebihara. The only others really still in contention at that point were Hideto Shigenobu at 137 and Tsukasa Watanabe at 138. Tsuneyuki added a 68 Saturday and widened his margin over Ebihara to three, over Watanabe to six. In the altered situation Sunday, Nakajima had a birdie and two bogeys for the 37, but the gap became six strokes when Ebihara fell back to a 41 and dropped into a third-place tie with Tsutomu Irie at 246.

Kansai PGA Championship—¥20,000,000
Winner: Teruo Sugihara

The setting was so appropriate for Teruo Sugihara's landmark victory. What better spot for the remarkable 49-year-old pro to score the 50th triumph of his fine career than in the Kansai PGA Championship, a tournament in Western Japan which he first won in 1964 and has taken eight more times since then. It is believed that no player has won the same event as many times in modern tour competition. And Teruo may be the first 49-year-old ever to win twice in the same season on a regular national tour.

The victory had just a trace of taint, since the tournament was decided at 54 holes after a round was lost to rain. Sugihara came from a stroke off the pace after 36 holes with a closing 67 for 203, 13 under par at Kibi Country Club, and a two-shot victory. Shinsaku Maeda took the first-round lead with a 66 and shared first place after 36 holes at 135 with Hiroshi Ishii. Sugihara had a pair of 68s for starters and was joined at 136 by Yoshitaka Yamamoto. His six birdies and a bogey Sunday forged the two-stroke victory.

Kanto PGA Championship—¥30,000,000
Winner: Tsuneyuki Nakajima

Tsuneyuki Nakajima put the victories back to back for the first time when he followed his Mizuno Open triumph with a decisive win in the Kanto PGA Championship the first week of July when the tour split its talents for the titles of East and West Japan. Nakajima, an Easterner, staged a strong finish over the week-end, shooting a 65 Saturday and a 67 Sunday to post a three-stroke victory over Naomichi Ozaki. He was 19 under par at 269 at Miyagino Golf Club as he won the Kanto PGA for the second year in a row and registered his fourth victory of the season.

Tateo Ozaki took early charge with successive 67s, matched after two rounds by Akiyoshi Omachi (68–66), but Isao Aoki was just two behind and Nakajima was tied at 137 with Naomichi Ozaki and Nobumitsu Yuhara. Tsuneyuki came up with 65 Saturday and finished the day tied for the lead with Aoki at 202 as Omachi shot 71 and Tateo Ozaki 74. Isao moved in front, at one point by three, in the early going Sunday. Then, Nakajima launched a rally. With four birdies, he caught Aoki at the 13th hole. From there in, it was relatively easy for Tsuneyuki. Isao stumbled with three bogeys in the stretch and dropped to third place behind Naomichi Ozaki, who closed with 68 for 272. Nakajima nailed a final birdie at the 17th for the 67 and 269 in recording his 34th tour victory.

Japan PGA Championship—¥50,000,000
Winner: Isao Aoki

Isao Aoki had let one get away the previous week and wasn't about to let it happen again in the prestigious Japan PGA Championship, which he had won twice in the past. The veteran, going for his 47th victory after ending a 30-month victory drought six weeks earlier, trailed only after the first round enroute to his four-stroke victory at Nihon Line Golf Club's West Course. He posted a 272, 16 under par, easily winning a final-round battle against old nemesis Masashi (Jumbo) Ozaki.

Coming off his victory in the Kansai PGA the last time out, Teruo Sugihara jumped in front Thursday with a seven-under-par 65, but ran out of gas after that, shooting 81 Friday and finishing far down the line. Aoki, who had opened with 66, moved in front with 68 and 134 Friday. Masanobu Kimura and Masaji Kusakabe were at 136. Isao's 69 Saturday widened his margin to three strokes, then over Jumbo Ozaki, who scored 206 with his third-round 67. Little happened on the early holes Sunday. Then, Ozaki birdied the seventh and Aoki countered with one of his own at the eighth. Isao took complete charge on the back nine with birdies at the 10th, 14th and 16th, the final one a tap-in off a fine wedge approach. Ozaki's birdies at the 15th and 17th came too late and he bogeyed the final hole. He had 70 for 276, nipping Toru Nakamura for second by a stroke.

Niigata Open—¥35,000,000
Winner: David Ishii

David Ishii enhanced his growing reputation in Asian golf with his second victory of the Japanese Tour season in the young Niigata Open at Nagaoka Country Club. Ishii stood off the challenge of Tateo Ozaki, making his 12-under-par 276 stand up for the triumph, the third in two seasons for the 30-year-old Japanese-American from Hawaii.

Ishii entered the title picture in the third round. Ikuo Shirahama led after 18 holes and a 64, then turned first place over to Ozaki (68–68) and Seiichi Kanai (69–67). David fired seven birdies and a bogey Saturday for 66 and a two-stroke lead over Kanai, 134 to 136. Ozaki was a shot farther back after a 70. Ishii had to settle uncomfortably with a 72 Sunday with a birdie and a bogey. Ozaki caught him with four birdies and a bogey, but lost his chance for a playoff when he bogeyed the final hole. He had a 70 for 277, finishing two ahead of Shirahama and Joji Furuki.

ACOM Doubles—¥45,000,000
Winners: Hajime Meshiai and Satoshi Higashi

Hajime Meshiai and Satoshi Higashi emerged from a tightly-packed field with the fourth title of the ACOM Doubles, the two-man team championship on the Japanese Tour. They closed with a 65, which gave them a 72-hole score of 257 and a one-stroke victory over four other teams at Shigaraki Country Club in Shiga Prefecture. Among the four runnerup teams was the Australian pairing of Brian Jones and Mike Ferguson, the defending champions.

The Meshiai/Higashi victory came when David Ishii and Hideto Shigenobu were not able to sustain the pace that had produced a 62 and the third-round lead at 191 Saturday. They slipped to 68 Sunday and dropped into a three-way tie for sixth place at 259. Koichi Inoue and Tadami Ueno had done them one better Friday with a tournament-record 61, but it had only lifted them into a four-way tie for the second-round lead. In its three previous appearances, the ACOM Doubles had produced winning teams of Australians, Taiwanese and Japanese.

Nikkei Cup/Torakichi Nakamura Memorial—¥40,000,000
Winner: Masashi Ozaki

Jumbo Ozaki kept the Nikkei Cup in the family in 1986. In the second showing of the Torakichi Nakamura Memorial tournament, he contrived to succeed younger brother Naomichi as the winner and did so in convincing style, rolling to a four-stroke victory at Gamo Golf Club in Shiga Prefecture with a 20-under-par score of 268, the lowest 72-hole total of the season. It was Ozaki's second win in his resurgency, boosting his career total to 47 and putting him dead even with Isao Aoki on the victory list behind only Teruo Sugihara.

Ozaki was never out of the 60s at Gamo, although that really didn't pay off until the final round. He was just one of 20 players in the 60s Thursday, when Koichi Inoue led with 65. A pair of 66s Friday switched the lead to Kinpachi Yoshimura with Ozaki then just two back after a 68–66 start. Ikuo Shirahama shot 65 Saturday to enter a three-way tie at 202 with Ozaki (68) and Yoshimura (70). Kinpachi fell back early Sunday and Ozaki took the lead for good at the 11th hole with a three-foot birdie putt and secured the easy victory with subsequent birdies at the 13th and 14th holes. He shot 66 for the 268 and four-shot win over Shirahama.

Maruman Nihonkai Open—¥50,000,000
Winner: Masashi Ozaki

Jumbo Ozaki never slowed down as the Japanese Tour moved from the site of his Nikkei Cup victory to the Maruman Nihonkai (Japan Sea) Open at Katayamatsu Golf Club at Kaga. He fired his fifth straight score in the 60s—

a brilliant 64—and jumped off to a three-stroke lead. That was his eventual margin Sunday afternoon when he posted his second straight victory and third of the season with a 12-under-par 276.

Despite the blazing start, Ozaki did not lead wire to wire. He yielded first place to Hiroshi Oku, the 182nd man on the 1985 money list, who had 135 after rounds of 67–68. Ozaki took a 72 and trailed by a stroke in the company of brother Naomichi Ozaki (71–65), Katsunari Takahashi (67–69) and Hisao Inoue (69–67). Jumbo regained the lead Saturday with his 70 for 206, heading Oku (73), Naomichi Ozaki (72), Takahashi (72) and Kikuo Arai (68) by two strokes. And he wrapped it up Sunday with 15 pars to go with an eagle, a birdie and a bogey, another 70 and the three-shot win over Naomichi Ozaki and Saburo Fujiki, who leaped into the second-place tie with a closing 65.

KBC Augusta—¥ 42,000,000
Winner: Isao Aoki

It has been years since anybody won three tournaments in a row on the Japanese circuit and nobody has come closer than Jumbo Ozaki, The 39-year-old Ozaki came within a missed birdie putt on the 72nd hole of the KBC Augusta tournament of having that chance in late August. His miss on the 18th green of the Kyushu Shima Country Club course from seven feet gave the KBC Augusta title to Isao Aoki, who came from four strokes off the pace in the final round to nail his third win of the year and 48th of his career. Aoki closed with 67 for 282, six under par and one of the season's highest winning scores.

In fact, only eight scores in the 60s were posted all week at Kyushu Shima, the three lowest all in the final round. Ozaki had one of them—a 69 in the third round—to take the lead at 211. Aoki had started with 74, but followed with 72–69 to move within four strokes of Jumbo, who already had 48 wins on his career record. Aoki made his move on the front nine with four birdies and was then in the midst of the title fight with Ozaki, Masahiro Kuramoto and Nobumitsu Yuhara. Costly bogeys took the latter two players out of the race, leaving it to the two titans of Japanese golf to settle things on the final green. Aoki insured a happy 44th birthday by making his sixth birdie of the round there and watching Ozaki miss his seven-footer for the tie.

Talent was spread all over the country the first week of September. The bulk of the leading players competed in the Kanto and Kansai Opens with the remainder involved in four small-purse, 72-hole events. Picking up those titles were Eitaro Deguchi in the Chubu Open, Kinpachi Yoshimura in the Kyushu Open, Katsunari Takahashi in the Hokkaido Open and Tadami Ueno in the Chu-Shikoku Open. Takahashi, winning the Hokkaido Open for the third time in four years, finished seven shots ahead of runnerup Kazuhiro Takami with 276. Deguchi and Yoshimura each posted 281s, Eitaro to win by three at Chubu and Kinpachi by four at Kyushu, his second straight there. The tightest finish was Ueno's one-shot win over Masahiro Kuramoto, who had won the tournament five years in a row before yielding to Mitoshi

Tomita in 1985. Ueno shot 275, 13 under par at Ube Country Club in Yamaguchi.

Kanto Open—¥30,000,000
Winner: Isao Aoki

Of greatest interest that week was the Kanto Open, where Isao Aoki, Masashi Ozaki and Tsuneyuki Nakajima were competing. Appropriately, the tournament generated one of the year's most exciting finishes and it involved those three leading lights of Japanese golf. Aoki came out with the victory, by one over Ozaki and four over Nakajima. Isao birdied the last three holes to beat off Ozaki's challenge and score his second victory in eight days. He shot 279, 13 under par on the East Course of Central Golf Club in Ibaraki Prefecture.

Nobody could break 70 the first day on the par-73 course, four players shooting that score, but Aoki and Ozaki were among five players who found the 60s Friday. Jumbo shot 68 for 139 and the lead, Isao 69 for 141. They traded places Saturday as Aoki fashioned a 70 and Ozaki slumped to 74, slipping two strokes behind. The two stars battled all the way Sunday. They were tied after the 14th hole, where Ozaki birdied. Jumbo made two more on the way home, but fell one short as Isao birdied those last three holes. Nakajima finished strongly with rounds of 69 and 65, but couldn't overcome the setback of his second-round 77. He placed third at 283, three behind Ozaki.

Kansai Open—¥20,000,000
Winner: Yoshiyuki Isomura

The companion Kansai Open in Western Japan produced one of the year's few first-time winners. Yoshiyuki Isomura, who had campaigned on the Japanese Tour for eight years without a victory, scored a relatively-easy, three-stroke triumph at Rokko Kokusai Golf Club. On a final day of generally-high scoring, his 74 for 284 brought that initial win by three over Shinsaku Maeda, Kazuo Yoshikawa and Yoshio Ichikawa.

Earlier, it appeared that the impressive Teruo Sugihara might put the Kansai Open, which had won eight times in the past, with his ninth Kansai PGA victory in July. Sugihara was tied for the lead after 36 holes with Isomura and Kosaku Shimada at 141. But, Sugihara fell off to 74s the last two days and Isomura took charge with 69 Saturday for 210 and a four-stroke lead. That took off the Sunday pressure and it showed as Yoshiyuki had four birdies and six bogeys in shooting his winning 74.

Suntory International Open—¥60,000,000
Winner: Graham Marsh

Two weeks earlier, Isao Aoki had nipped Jumbo Ozaki's bid for a third victory in a row on the Japanese Tour with a birdie on the 72nd hole. The shoe was on the other foot for Aoki in the Suntory International Open, in which he was going for a third straight win, and he came even closer to making it. Isao shot a final-round 69 to overtake Graham Marsh and throw the decision into a playoff, the first on the circuit since those that settled the first two events of the year back in March. However, Marsh birdied the first playoff hole to snap Aoki's streak and score his 22nd victory over the years on Japanese soil and sole triumph of 1986.

The Australian, by far the most successful foreign player to have competed on the Japanese circuit, had taken the lead at the 54-hole mark with rounds of 67, 69 and 67 and the 203 total, wresting it from Toru Nakamura, who followed a pair of 68 with 76. Graham had a three-shot lead over Aoki, Masashi Ozaki and Hajime Meshiai at that point. Marsh got away fast in Sunday's final round with three birdies on the first six holes, but he gave those strokes back with bogeys at the eighth, 12th and 14th holes. That opened the door for Aoki, who had overcome bogeys on the first and third holes with a run of six birdies on the next 10 holes. Isao had the lead until he bogeyed the 17th hole. They both parred the long 18th at Narashino Country Club in Chiba Prefecture, forcing the overtime effort and bringing about Marsh's win. One of the earlier 21 was 10 years earlier in the same tournament. Much interest during the week focused on Jack Nicklaus, making a rare Japanese appearance. He closed with 67 but still finished 23rd.

Ana Sapporo Open—¥50,000,000
Winner: Masahiro Kuramoto

Masahiro Kuramoto, who had been close several times earlier in the year, finally broke into the victory column in the All Nippon Airways Sapporo Open, one of the tournaments he won in his brilliant rookie season of 1981. The 30-year-old Kuramoto broke from a 54-hole deadlock to score a two-stroke victory with his seven-under-par 281. The runnerup: Isao Aoki, who had two wins and a playoff setback in his three previous starts.

After the early sparring left Hiroshi Ishii in front after 36 holes with 140, Kuramoto and Koichi Suzuki appropriated shares of the lead with 211s, Kuramoto reaching that score with a third-round 66, the best score of the week at Sapporo Golf Club, a par-72, 7,065-yard course. Close behind were Aoki and the Ozakis, Jumbo and Tateo, at 213. Kuramoto's 70 Sunday settled the issue as Suzuki took a 73 and slipped into third place at 284. Aoki took the No. 2 position with a 70 and Jumbo Ozaki trailed Suzuki by a stroke at 285.

Jun Classic—¥56,000,000
Winner: Masashi Ozaki

Jun Classic officials couldn't have asked for a better finish—Jumbo Ozaki, Masahiro Kuramoto and Isao Aoki battling down the stretch and ending one-two-three in that order with just a stroke separating each of the three men. Ozaki, winning his third title in six weeks, came from four shots off the lead in the final round to claim the victory, the 49th of his career. He shot 70 for 279, nine under par for the 7,082 yards of the Jun Classic Country Club course at Ogawa.

Brian Jones had things going his way for two rounds. The Australian shot rounds of 65 and 68 for starters and had a three-stroke lead over Yoshimi Niizeki (69–67) before the top stars established their positions. Kuramoto, going for two in a row, moved within two strokes of Jones, who had a third-round 72 for 205. Kuramoto shot 67, Ozaki had 68 for 209 and Aoki was at 211 after a 70. Jones plunged with a 79 Sunday and Kuramoto, with three bogeys on the back nine, took 73, opening the opportunity for Ozaki, who shot 70 with five birdies and three bogeys for the 279 and his second Jun Classic title. Ozaki also won at Ogawa in 1983. Aoki matched Ozaki's 70 to finish third at 281, a shot behind Kuramoto.

Tokai Classic—¥50,000,000
Winner: Masahiro Kuramoto

The general pattern of the September-October competition continued as Masahiro Kuramoto scored his second victory in three weeks with the wins sandwiched around a second-place finish. Another hot streak by a top pro. Kuramoto's second 1986 victory, the 18th of his six-year pro career, came in the Tokai Classic and he won going away. He was 17 under par at Miyoshi Country Club with his 271 and his nine-stroke margin was the biggest of the season.

Masahiro seized the reins in the third round. He was among five players who opened with 68s and was just a stroke behind leader Toshiharu Kawada (136) when he followed with 69. Then, Kuramoto fired a 65 Saturday and jumped four strokes into the lead as Kawada took a 70. Masahiro wasn't exactly the steadiest Sunday, taking four bogeys against his seven birdies, but the 69 widened the gap to nine as Kawada faltered again with 75 for 281. Shinsaku Maeda jumped into second place with 68 for 280. The other two torrid players of the moment—Isao Aoki and Masashi Ozaki—tied for sixth at 284. Kuramoto has a real affinity for the Tokai, having won it now three times since 1981.

Japan Open Championship—¥60,000,000
Winner: Tsuneyuki Nakajima

Tsuneyuki Nakajima had cooled off through the middle of the Japanese season after scoring four victories in a seven-week stretch, looking on from close range as other members of the country's pro elite were racking up the titles. He picked the prestigious Japan Open for his return to the winner's circle in mid-October, landing the national championship for the second straight year.

Nakajima saved his best round for last, shooting a 69 the final day at Totsuka Country Club's 7,066-yard West course near Yokohama to score a one-stroke victory with his four-under-par 284. The 31-year-old Nakajima had trailed by two shots entering the Sunday round and needed a little negative help from Tateo Ozaki to convert the 69 into the 25th victory of his career. Tateo bogeyed the last two holes after getting to five under par for the day and dropped into a tie for fourth with Yoshiyuki Isomura at 286. Former champions Isao Aoki and Masashi Ozaki finished at 285, Aoki with a closing 71 and Ozaki with 69.

Masahiro Kuramoto, coming off two victories in the previous three weeks, was erratic at Totsuka. He led the first day with 68, then took a 74 and a 78 before finishing with another 68 to tie for seventh. Naomichi Ozaki jumped into a three-stroke lead the second day with 69–68—137 and stayed in front Saturday by a stroke despite a 76. Aoki and Toru Nakamura were then second at 214 and Nakajima was among four men at 215 with his rounds of 70–73–72, ready for his final-round charge to his 35th career victory in Japan.

Polaroid Cup Golf Digest—¥60,000,000
Winner: Tsuneyuki Nakajima

Memories are made of this. Ten years earlier, Tsuneyuki Nakajima signaled future stardom with three victories in his rookie pro season, the most important win of which was in the Golf Digest tournament at Tomei Country Club. Thirty-three victories later, the brilliant Nakajima finished on top again in that same event at that same course, this time doing it with a playoff victory over David Ishii after the two men had tied after 72 holes with nine-under-par 275s. The win followed immediately upon Tsuneyuki's Japan Open championship and was his sixth of the season.

Nakajima seized the lead in the third round after unknown Kenjiro Iwama held it the first day with 65 and Yoshitaka Yamamoto took over in the second round with 67–66—133. Tsuneyuki then trailed by three strokes after posting a pair of 68s, but had only Ishii (at 135 with rounds of 67 and 68) between him and the top. He shot 67 Saturday with six birdies and two bogeys to move two shots in front with his 203 as Yamamoto took a 72 for 205. With 71, Ishii dropped into a three-way tie at 206 with Masahiro Kuramoto and Taisei Inagaki.

Ishii, who had won the rich Chunichi Crowns earlier in the season, forced the playoff when he mustered a 69 to Nakajima's 72 Sunday, the two finishing two strokes ahead of Inagaki and Tsukasa Watanabe. American D. A. Weibring, the defending champion, had a second-round 66 but eventually tied for eighth at 279.

Bridgestone—¥70,000,000
Winner: Tateo Ozaki

Tateo Ozaki joined his brothers in the 1986 winners' circle, consigning one of them, Naomichi, to second place as he captured the Bridgestone tournament at Sodegaura Country Club in Chiba. Oldest brother Masashi already had four victories to his credit in 1986 and Naomichi had won the Pepsi Ube back in May. The two younger Ozakis were neck and neck in the Sunday stretch run of the Bridgestone until Tateo pulled away to a two-stroke victory with birdies on the final two holes. They gave him a 70 and a 12-under-par 276. Naomichi had mounted the strongest charge at his brother, who led by three strokes after 54 holes with rounds of 71, 67 and 68 for 206, but his blazing 65 proved only good enough for clear possession of second place at 278, a shot in front of Scott Verplank, the first-year American pro who won the 1985 Western Open on the U.S. tour while still an amateur.

Tateo Ozaki moved in front Saturday after Katsuji Hasegawa opened in front with 67 and Yoshihisa Iwashita took over Friday with 68–68—136, two ahead of the ultimate winner. In the sibling duel Sunday, Naomichi Ozaki actually surged into the lead by a shot through 16 holes. However, he bogeyed the par-three 17th as Tateo was holing a 33-foot birdie putt to regain first place. Tateo then secured his ninth pro victory when he birdied from seven feet on the final green.

ABC U.S. vs Japan Team Matches—¥65,000,000
Winners: Team—United States; Individual—Curtis Strange

Curtis Strange had a mediocre performance the week before in the Bridgestone tournament at Chiba, but it apparently prepared him for his next golfing labors in Japan. The standout American, leading money-winner on the U.S. tour in 1985, led his countrymen to a come-from-behind victory in the annual Asahi Broadcasting Company matches at Sports Shinko Country Club at Kawanishi. Strange shot a course-record, eight-under-par 64 in the final round that helped the nine-man U.S. team overcome a seven-stroke deficit and nose a victory ahead—8–7–1—in the 16-year-old competition. Strange breezed to a four-stroke triumph in the individual competition, scoring his first victory ever in Japan and his second of the year. The team margin was seven strokes over the Japanese pros.

Koichi Suzuki was Japan's leading light for three rounds. He opened with 65 to take the individual lead by two shots, but the U.S. team grabbed a 566–569 margin (best-eight-of-nine scores count) that first day. The 30-year-old Suzuki kept his cards bogey-free through 36 holes, adding a 66 Friday for 131 and a four-stroke lead over Strange. The team situation was unchanged as both squads posted 554 totals. Despite a 73 Saturday, Suzuki retained the lead by three over Strange and Chip Beck and his compatriots took Japan to the seven-shot lead. Suzuki was at 204, Strange and Beck at 207.

Besides the 64 of Strange Sunday, Mark O'Meara shot 66, Beck and Donnie Hammond 68s and D. A. Weibring and Peter Jacobsen 69s as the major contributions to the U.S. rally. The eight best American scores totalled 544 to 558 for the Japanese to secure the team victory, 2,229 to 2,236. Suzuki's game came apart so badly on the final nine—a double-bogey, three bogeys and a birdie—that his 75 was the discarded score for Japan Sunday. He dropped to sixth place in the individual standings as Strange, with his 271, finished four ahead of Beck and seven in front of third-place co-finishers Tateo Ozaki, Tsuneyuki Nakajima and O'Meara.

On the Friday and Saturday of the ABC event, Toshimitsu Kai won the 36-hole Wakayama Open and Kunikihara Golf Club, shooting 71–65 for 136.

Hiroshima Open—¥40,000,000
Winner: Toru Nakamura

After a big 1984 season that included four victories, Toru Nakamura seemed to have lost the winning touch. Nothing in 1985 nor in 1986 with the season in its final stages. Then, he turned things around with the 22nd victory of his career in the Hiroshima Open, played the same week as the Nissan Cup. The win didn't come easily. He trailed Saburo Fujiki by two strokes going into the final round at Hiroshima Country Club, shot a seven-under-par 65 and still had to go into a playoff as Fujiki shot 67 for his 272. They went four extra holes before Nakamura gained the decision.

Hideki Kase took the first-round lead with 66, one shot in front of Fujiki and two ahead of Nakamura and Seiji Ebihara. Fujiki scored a 68 for 135 Friday, moving a stroke ahead of Nakamura and Teruo Sugihara and two in front of Kase, who slipped with 71 to 137. It was basically a battle between Nakamura and Fujiki the rest of the way.

Nissan Cup—$900,000
Winners: Team—Japan; Individual—Tsuneyuki Nakajima

Japan enjoyed one of its proudest golfing experiences in many years in early November when its six-man team of leading pros, headed by its No. 1 star, Tsuneyuki Nakajima, prevailed against crack teams from the United States, Europe and Australia/New Zealand in the round-robin Nissan Cup competition, staged in 1986 at Yomiuri Country Club near Tokyo. The victory came just a week after the U.S. victory over Japan in the similar ABC Matches.

Japan and Europe emerged as the finalists Sunday after all teams had played each other Thursday, Friday and Saturday. Europe (Bernhard Langer, Nick Faldo, Gordon J. Brand, Howard Clark, Sandy Lyle and Ian Woosnam) won all three of its matches—over Japan, 7–5. Thursday; over the U.S., 8–4, Friday, and over Australia/New Zealand, 7–5, Saturday. After its Thursday setback, Japan (Masashi, Tateo and Naomichi Ozaki, Koichi Suzuki, Nobumitsu Yuhara and Nakajima) took the measure of Australia/New Zealand Friday and the U.S. Saturday by 7–5 scores. The Americans (Bob Tway, Dan Pohl, Payne Stewart, John Mahaffey, Hal Sutton and Calvin Peete) wound up without a victory, losing to Australia/New Zealand, 7–5, Thursday and in the playoff for third and fourth place Sunday, 11–1.

Nakajima and Naomichi and Jumbo Ozaki won their matches, Suzuki fell back into a tie with Faldo on a birdie-bogey swing at the final hole and Yuhara pulled off a tie with Lyle with a sparkling birdie there moments later. Woosnam was the only winner for Europe in the 8–4 loss. Nakajima took the individual lead Saturday when he followed two 68s with a 66 to go two in front of Langer and Tway and he maintained that margin over Langer Sunday as both shot 68s. Tsuneyuki was 18 under par in winning three matches and tying the fourth with Faldo the first day. The Australia/New Zealand team consisted of Greg Norman, Brian Jones, Ian Baker-Finch, Rodger Davis, Graham Marsh and David Graham.

Taiheiyo Club (Pacific) Masters— ¥ 80,000,000
Winner: Yasuhiro Funatogawa

The Taiheiyo Club Masters marks the start of a three-tournament stretch on the Japanese Tour schedule that attracts strong international fields with some of the biggest money of the year. For the third year in a row, though, the Japanese pros stood off the invaders, this time in the person of Yasuhiro Funatogawa, a 31-year-old journeyman on the circuit with just three previous victories on his record. Funatogawa survived a final-round bid by American Larry Nelson, the former U.S. Open and PGA champion, and won by two strokes with his four-under-par 274.

Yasuhiro was in the thick of things from the first round on. He trailed Naomichi Ozaki by a shot the first day, shooting 67. Then, he followed with 68 for 135 that put him into a first-place tie with Masashi Ozaki as Naomichi Ozaki soared to a 73. Two back-nine bogeys forced Funatogawa to settle for a two-under-par 70 Saturday over the 7,071 yards of the Taiheiyo Club's Gotemba course, but he still moved two strokes in front. Ozaki shot 73 and David Graham took over the runnerup spot with his 68 for 209.

Nelson entered the picture with a vengeance Sunday. He made five birdies early and took the lead when Funatogawa bogeyed the 13th and 14th holes. However, Nelson, winless since the 1984 Walt Disney Classic, ran dry in the stretch and Funatogawa regained the lead and established his two-stroke final margin with birdies on three of the last four holes. Graham closed with 70 for 277, finishing third.

Dunlop Phoenix—¥130,000,000
Winner: Bobby Wadkins

Bobby Wadkins has had a most unusual career in professional golf and he added an upbeat twist to it in Japan in late November. Wadkins, long in the shadow of his very successful brother Lanny, is on the verge of passing the million-dollars earning mark on the U.S. tour, but has never won a tournament; yet he has captured Japan's richest event twice now—in 1979 and 1986. The first time, it was more survival as a closing 73 didn't hurt him. This time, he came from three strokes off the pace to win a battle against two of the game's most prominent players—Tsuneyuki Nakajima and Graham Marsh.

Wadkins, who had elected to play in just the Dunlop Phoenix on the trip to Japan, didn't really get into strong contention until the third round of the ¥130,000,000 extravaganza at the resort city of Miyazaki in southern Japan. A tired Nakajima, who had withdrawn from the Pacific Masters the previous Friday because of exhaustion-caused nosebleeds, nonetheless was the dominant figure for three days at Miyazaki. He shared the first-round lead with Marsh, Kikuo Arai and Doug Tewell, then moved a shot in front of Arai with a 70 for 137, shaking off a four-putt double-bogey at the eighth hole.

Tsuneyuki widened his margin to two Saturday with 69 for 206, Marsh rebounding from 73 with a 68 for 208. Enter Wadkins, who shot 67 after earlier rounds of 69 and 73. That put him at 209 with Jumbo Ozaki.

Everything focused on the last threesome—Wadkins, Marsh and Nakajima—Sunday. Nakajima clung to his lead on the front nine Sunday, but he began slipping after the turn. By the 12th hole, all three were tied, Wadkins having birdied the ninth and 11th holes, his first two of five birdies that day. Another tie, this time between Wadkins and Marsh ahead of the fading Nakajima, occurred with another Wadkins birdie at the 16th. All three bogeyed the 17th, Nakajima then trailing the others by two strokes. At the par-five 18th, Wadkins put his third shot from a greenside bunker four feet from the cup and watched as Marsh missed his birdie putt from 22 feet, then dropped his for the ¥23,400,000 victory. He had a final-round score of 68 for 277. Marsh shot 70 for his 278, Nakajima 74 for 280.

Casio World Open—¥85,000,000
Winner: Scott Hoch

Even without a victory, it had been a good year for Scott Hoch. He had played so consistently well throughout the season in America that he had a Vardon Trophy-winning scoring average of 70.08 and earnings well over $200,000. He embellished all that with a runaway victory in the third leg of Japan's late-season series of big-money events—the Casio World Open—and a win with partner Gary Hallberg in the Chrysler Team tournament two weeks later back in America.

It was Hoch's second victory in the Casio, which oddly has not been won by a Japanese player in its six-year history. Scott won it before in 1982, the year he also captured the Taiheiyo Club Masters. He joins Bill Rogers as the only U.S. tour regulars to have won as many as three times in Japan.

Coming off his near-miss the previous Sunday in the Dunlop Phoenix, Graham Marsh jumped off to a big lead in the Casio at Ibusuki Golf Club. The Australian had nine birdies and a bogey as he shot 64 and took a three-stroke lead over Hoch and Namio Takasu. He added a 70 on a showery Friday and the 134 widened his margin to four over Takasu and Jose-Maria Olazabal of Spain. Hoch shot 72 for 139, tied there with Ian Baker-Finch of Australia. Then, the 31-year-old American took over. When Marsh suffered a 74, Scott leaped into the lead with his 68 for 207 on a blustery Saturday. Olazabal shot 70 and was tied for second with Marsh at 208. The winds remained high Sunday and only Hoch among the contenders handled them. He made four birdies and took a bogey for 69 as Olazabal was shooting 74 and Marsh 76, winning by six strokes with his 276. The Spaniard was at 282, the Aussie at 284.

Japan Series—¥30,000,000
Winner: Toru Nakamura

Toru Nakamura had won the exclusive Japan Series two years earlier by leading from start to finish and piling up a seven-stroke victory margin. He went the opposite route in winning it again in 1986. Toru came from one shot off the pace of Isao Aoki in Sunday's final round at Yomiuri Country Club at Inagi in Tokyo, his final round 69 and 275 giving him a two-stroke victory over Aoki.

The tournament, which has just 16 players who qualify by winning certain important non-commercial tournaments or by finishing in the top 10 on the year's money list, has a split venue for its first-week-of-December staging. Masahiro Kuramoto opened a shot in front of Kikuo Arai with a seven-under-par 66 in the first of two rounds played at Osaka's Yomiuri Country Club, a par-73, 7,078-yard course. The two traded places the next day as Arai, making a fruitless try for a 1986 victory, shot 70 for 137 and Kuramoto took a 72 for 138 to share second place with Isao Aoki (69–69).

The lead changed hands yet again when the tournament resumed after an off-day in Tokyo, where par at that Yomiuri Country Club is 72, making par for the tournament 290. Aoki was the new leader Saturday night, having added a 67 to his 138 for 205 and the one-shot lead over Nakamura, who moved into contention with a 66 that day in a sensational finish. He birdied the final three holes and five of the last eight. Aoki also had a three-birdie streak while shooting his 67. Kuramoto was a distant third at 211 after 54 holes and the final round was simply a Nakamura-Aoki duel. Isao was erratic all day, enduring four bogeys and mustering four birdies for a par round. On the other hand, Nakamura was rock steady. He birdied the fourth hole and had 15 pars before wrapping up the victory with a 20-foot birdie putt at the 17th and virtual tap-in off a brilliant two-iron tee shot at the 224-yard 18th. It was Nakamura's second win of 1986 and the 23rd of his career.

Daikyo Open—¥60,000,000
Winner: Tateo Ozaki

Kikuo Arai came closer in the Daikyo Open, but had to resign himself to a winless year as Tateo Ozaki defeated him in a sudden-death playoff in the final event of the Japanese season at Daikyo Country Club in Okinawa. Arai, who was an early leader the previous week in the Japan Series before faltering in the last two rounds, put on a strong finish in the Daikyo, shooting a final-round 67 for the seven-under-par 277 that Ozaki matched with his closing 70. The two men went three extra holes before Kikuo bogeyed and Ozaki won his second title of 1986 and the 10th of his career.

Unfamiliar names topped the standings the first two days. Hiroshi Makino, Yoshinori Kaneko and Yoshiharu Ota led the first day with 67s and Hikaru Emoto took over the second day with a 66 for 134 that included an eagle at the par-five 17th. Isao moved into second place that day with an eight-birdie, two-bogey 65 for 135 and he seized the lead Saturday when he birdied the final hole for a par 71 and 206. Tateo Ozaki shot his third straight 69, advancing into second place at 207, while Arai, with 70 for 210, had seven players between him and the leader. Aoki opened the door for Ozaki and Arai when he double-bogeyed the first hole Sunday. He eventually sot 72 and missed the playoff by a shot with his 278, as did Masahiro Kuramoto, who closed with a 69.

Nine worldwide victories put Greg Norman behind the micro-
phone for much of the year.

Bob Tway was No. 2 on the U.S. money list with four wins including the PGA Championship.

The Doral winner,
Andy Bean, was third
on the money list.

Hal Sutton was a double
winner—at Phoenix
and the Memorial.

Dan Pohl was the Colonial and World Series winner.

A four-man playoff at the Western Open provided Tom Kite's single 1986 victory.

Commissioner Deane Beman presented the TPC trophy to John Mahaffey.

Continuing to beat the odds with his bad back, Fuzzy Zoeller was the winner of the AT&T Pebble Beach Pro-Am, Heritage Classic and Anheuser-Busch Classic.

Ever-accurate Calvin Peete won titles in the Tournament of Champions and USF&G Classic.

Mac O'Grady seemed to spend as much time talking with reporters as he did playing, but by the year's end, controversy was behind him—and he had a win at Hartford.

In addition to the U.S. Open, Raymond Floyd won the late-year Disney tournament.

Another over-40 champion was Bob Murphy in the Canadian Open.

With only one victory between them
were Curtis Strange (above),
the 1985 leading money winner, and
Lanny Wadkins, the 1985
Player of the Year.

Adding to his 1985 British Open title, Sandy Lyle triumphed in the Greater Greensboro Open.

Canadian Dan Halldorson won at Hattiesburg, Mississippi, during Masters week.

West German Bernhard Langer had a great record, but didn't win in America.

Corey Pavin charged to wins in Hawaii and Milwaukee.

Kenny Knox won the Honda Classic.

Arnold Palmer with Dan Forsman, the Hertz Bay Hill Classic winner.

International winner Ken Green, with sister Shelley, his caddy.

Once-maverick Roger Maltbie, now a Policy Board member, earned over $200,000.

It was a surprise that neither Mark O'Meara (above) nor Fred Couples won on the U.S. tour.

Ben Crenshaw won twice—
his first since the 1984 Masters.

It's hard to believe, but Tom Watson
was frustrated again in 1986.

Hale Irwin's pre-season win in the
Bahamas was not an indication of
things to come.

Amateur sensation Scott
Verplank virtually
disappeared after
turning professional.

Davis Love III was the tour's
longest driver.

Many thought Sam Randolph
was the best young prospect.

Betsy King had two LPGA victories.

Highly-touted Juli Inkster won four time

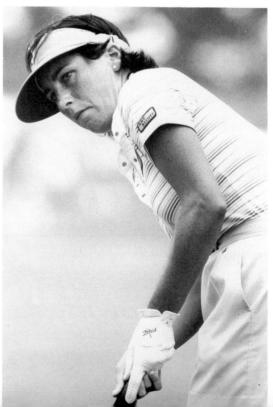

Amy Alcott's two wins
highlighted another steady year.

Pat Bradley virtually owned the LPGA with five victories
including three majors.

Why is this lady smiling? Her husband was Most Valuable Player of baseball's World Series—Nancy Lopez was off most of 1986 to have their second child.

14. The LPGA Tour

Pat Bradley. If we were to use two words to describe the 1986 LPGA season, "Pat Bradley" must be the words. After years of being underrated because she had finished second twice as often as she won, Bradley burned her name into the record books with a performance that will not be forgotten.

She won three of the four Grand Slam events with triumphs at the Nabisco Dinah Shore, LPGA Championship and du Marrier Classic. Only the U.S. Women's Open, won by Jane Geddes in an 18-hole playoff with Sally Little, eluded Bradley.

Bradley shattered the tour's earnings record with $492,021, which was $200,000 more than Betsy King earned in second place. Winning nearly one-half million dollars made Bradley the first LPGA member to pass $2 million in career earnings.

What else? Bradley had the second lowest scoring average (71.1) in LPGA history. She won five titles, also including the S&H Classic and the Nestle World Championship. No other golfer won five times, although Juli Inkster won four titles and Patty Sheehan three.

There's still more. Bradley ran away with the Mazda Series title and the Rolex Player of the Year award. King finished second in the Mazda standings and Inkster was second in the Rolex race. Bradley also led the Tour in Top 10 finishes with 17, one more than King.

Perhaps the only irony of Bradley's season is that she still hasn't met the LPGA's rules for entering its Hall of Fame. A suggestion might be that the LPGA take a close look at those rules, because the rest of the world now knows for sure that the name "Pat Bradley" ranks among the greatest names in golf.

Not all of the honors belonged to Pat. King and Inkster each had seasons good enough to finish No. 1 in most other years. Double winners included King, Geddes, Sheehan, Amy Alcott, Mary Beth Zimmerman and Ayako Okamoto. Jody Rosenthal, who earned $106,523, edged Deb Richard for Rookie of the Year honors.

An indicator of LPGA growth is that Beth Daniel earned $103,547 and finished just 21st in the standings. It was not that long ago that the 10th player in the standings was unable to earn more than $100,000.

Two major names were missing from the scoreboards for most of the season. Nancy Lopez waited until the end of the year to play a few tournaments after the birth of her second child. And JoAnne Carner was plagued all season with physical problems. Hopefully both will be back among the leaders in 1987, which certainly promises to be the most competitive in LPGA history.

Mazda Classic—$200,000
Winner: Val Skinner

Val Skinner opened the 1986 LPGA season in the same way she closed the North American portion of the 1985 campaign—with a champagne victory. Skinner poured the champagne herself after a one-shot triumph in the Mazda Championship. "It's a tradition we started last year in California," Skinner said as she served the press. "Without you guys, there wouldn't be any tour."

Skinner obviously knows the way to a reporter's heart. More important, she now knows how to win. The Konica San Jose Classic, last 1985 event in the United States, was her first triumph in three years on the tour. The Mazda Classic was her second and, although they came five months apart, the two victories were in succession.

Playing for the first time on the new Stonebridge course in Boca Raton, Florida, Skinner needed help from Sandra Palmer and got it. Palmer bogeyed the last hole and watched as Skinner birdied it to shoot a closing 69 and eight-under-par 280.

The leaderboard changed every day. Judy Clark Dickinson and Betsy King shared the opening lead at 68 each with Skinner far back at 74. JoAnn Washam shot 67 in the second round to lead at 138. Then Barb Thomas shot a career round of 66 on Saturday to lead at 208.

Patty Sheehan was an early leader on the final day, but a harsh wind elevated the scores on the backside. Palmer took a two-stroke lead with birdies on Nos. 16 and 17. But she hit a six iron over the final green, chipped back and two-putted from seven feet for the disastrous bogey.

Skinner, playing one group behind, birdied No. 17 to close within a stroke. Then she got a bit of good fortune on No. 18 when her wedge approach hit the front of the green and rolled down a slope to within a foot of the cup for an easy birdie and a pleasing victory.

Defending champion Hollis Stacy and Becky Pearson tied for third at 283, Thomas was fifth at 284, and Sheehan sixth at 285. Alone in seventh place at 286 and barely noticed was Pat Bradley, but the year was young.

Elizabeth Arden Classic—$200,000
Winner: Ayako Okamoto

In one of the strangest cross-cultural duels in LPGA history, Ayako Okamoto's use of acupuncture proved to be one shot superior to Muffin Spencer-Devlin's study of Zen in the Elizabeth Arden Classic at Turnberry Isle in North Miami, Florida.

Okamoto, the Fuzzy Zoeller of the LPGA Tour, used self-administered acupuncture pins to relieve shoulder and back problems before shooting an eight-under-par 280 for her fifth victory in the United States.

Spencer-Devlin, using Zen techniques to remain calm, finished one shot back. "I never had any duels with Okamoto like this one in Japan," Spencer-

Devlin said. "She always was a much better player than I was, but maybe I'm catching up."

Debbie Massey, who finished third at 283, was the first-round leader with a 68, one shot ahead of Okamoto and Spencer-Devlin. Okamoto took the lead with a second-round 67 and held it despite a 73 on the third day. She went into the final day one shot ahead of Beth Daniel, two up on Massey and three ahead of Spencer-Devlin.

"I had confidence all day I could win," she said. "After winning 25 or 26 tournaments in Japan and several in this country, I felt confident."

Okamoto birdied three of the first six holes and appeared to be a runaway winner. But Spencer-Devlin birdied the last four holes on the front, while Okamoto bogeyed No. 10 to cut her lead to a stroke.

The situation hardly changed. Spencer-Devlin bogeyed No. 12, birdied No. 16, then bogeyed No. 18, while Okamoto parred seven consecutive holes then also bogeyed the last one.

Tied for fourth at 285 was Pat Bradley.

Sarasota Classic—$200,000
Winner: Patty Sheehan

Patty Sheehan blasted the LPGA administration then proceeded to blast her opposition by winning what may have been the last Sarasota Classic by three strokes, her second consecutive victory at the final stop on the early Florida portion of the Tour.

Sheehan jumped out front with an opening 68 despite winds gusting to 40 miles an hour. Rain also delayed the third round by a day, but Sheehan won wire-to-wire with successive rounds of 69–71–71 for a nine-under-par 279. Late-charging Pat Bradley and late-fading Juli Inkster tied for second at 282.

Sheehan startled the tour with her pre-tournament comments, charging, "We're in a stagnant period. We need to have more pizzazz. We need some leadership with new ideas."

Her remarks prompted the arrival of LPGA commissioner John Laupheimer on opening day of the tournament. "Our players are individual entrepreneurs," he said. "They have a say which they are free to express."

Laupheimer and Sheehan talked on Thursday. After that she refused to comment again on her remarks, saying she had decided to concentrate on her golf instead.

It paid off, although Sheehan even concentrates in an individualistic manner. On the night before the final round she relaxed by playing tennis.

Inkster had fired a 64 in the delayed third round and closed to within two shots of Sheehan. And Inkster held the lead until Sheehan dropped birdie putts on Nos. 10, 11 and 12. Inkster then bogeyed three of the next four holes to end all doubt about the outcome.

Bradley shot a closing 69 but never got closer to Sheehan than two strokes.

Samaritan Turquoise Classic—$250,000
Winner: Mary Beth Zimmerman

The Samaritan Turquoise Classic in Phoenix, Arizona, has become a breeding ground for first-time winners, and the latest is Mary Beth Zimmerman, who overcame an identity crisis to win by one shot over Donna Caponi and Cathy Kratzert.

"Nobody knew who I was," Zimmerman said about the tournament crowd. "But hopefully someday I'll be a big name. This is my third year, and I know I have the ability."

Everyone else knew it, too, by the time the week was over on the Arizona Biltmore's Adobe Course. Zimmerman, raised in Illinois and an All-America player for Florida International University, shot a progression of 68–69–70–71 for a 10-under-par 278. Caponi and Kratzert finished one shot back.

Juli Inkster was the first-round leader with a 67, but Zimmerman took the midpoint lead at 137 and held a two-shot margin going into the final round.

Zimmerman, Caponi and Kratzert battled all day in the final threesome. Kratzert had tied Zimmerman for the lead with Caponi one back going into the 17th hole, but Zimmerman sank a 40-foot putt there to regain the advantage.

The final hole was bizarre. Zimmerman put her drive far to the right on the 15th fairway, hit a tree with her second and was 10 feet from the cup after three on the par-four hole. Kratzert hit a tree with her drive and found a bunker with her second before blasting to within eight feet.

Caponi was on in two and could have forced a playoff but missed a 12-foot birdie putt. Zimmerman then missed her putt for a bogey and faced a playoff again, but Kratzert missed, too.

"I'm happy. I won," Zimmerman said. "I think I can go on and have a good season."

Four of the six winners in the tournament have made the Samaritan their initial victory. In 1985 Chris Johnson made headlines by winning the next week, too. The idea must have appealed to Zimmerman.

Uniden LPGA Invitational—$330,000
Winner: Mary Beth Zimmerman

Some tournaments cannot help but have bittersweet endings. The finish of the Uniden LPGA Invitational was a sweet thrill for Mary Beth Zimmerman, but a bitter disappointment for Laura Baugh.

After two winless seasons on Tour, Zimmerman earned her second victory in two weeks with steady rounds of 70–70–70–71 for a seven-under-par 281. And the first-place prize of $49,500 placed her atop the money board after five weeks with $92,400.

In her 13th season on tour, Baugh finished second for the eighth time. She has never won a tour tournament and thought this would be the one when she went into the final round with a four-shot lead after rounds of 68–70–68. But a closing 76 deprived her of her biggest goal once again.

"I tried to protect what wasn't mine," Baugh said with tears in her eyes. "I didn't want to play defensively, but knowing it and doing it are two different things."

Meanwhile Zimmerman went into the final round trying to protect her second-place standing. "I figured I didn't have a prayer," she said. But she made a birdie from the fringe on No. 16, again from the fringe on No. 17 and sank a five-foot birdie putt on the par-three final hole to win again.

Baugh shared the first-round lead at 68 with Amy Benz, Patty Sheehan and Cathy Morse, before taking the lead on her own the second day at 138. On the final day Pat Bradley closed with a 69 to tie Baugh for second, although Bradley's days as a professional bridesmaid nearly were over and Baugh may never get a better chance.

Women's Kemper Open—$300,000
Winner: Juli Inkster

The Rogers and Hammerstein musical *South Pacific* was filmed just a few miles from where the Women's Kemper Open was played. This time it was Juli Inkster who had the happy ending and, if anyone makes a movie of her week, she will call it, Patience Pays.

Conquering the sometimes baffling greens at the Princeville Makai Course on Kauai, Hawaii, took all the patience Inkster could command. But the result was well worth it as she earned $45,000 by shooting a 12-under-par 276, one stroke ahead of Amy Alcott.

Inkster shot an opening par 72 despite excellent play from tee to green to start five shots behind first-day leader Marci Bozarth. Inkster three-putted four times before taking the exotic advice of University of Hawaii product Cindy Rarick, who said, "Everything breaks toward Bali Ha'i."

Using that beautiful mountain range as a marker, Inkster set a course record of 64 in the second round. She birdied six straight holes on the way to climb into second place one shot behind Chris Johnson. After a third round of 70 Inkster was tied for the lead with Bozarth at 10 under with Alcott and Johnson two shots back.

Inkster took a two-shot lead during the final round on No. 8 when she birdied and Bozarth bogeyed. She increased her lead to three strokes with birds on Nos. 10 and 12 and still led by two going into the final hole, a double-dogleg par five.

Alcott managed to birdie the final hole to take second, while Inkster played a safe par for the victory. Johnson, who was one week away, tied with Bozarth for third at 278, and JoAnne Carner shot a closing 66 to take fourth at 279.

Mary Beth Zimmerman, who had won the previous two weeks, tied for 29th at 289, and Pat Bradley had her worst finish of the young season, a tie for 36th at 290.

GNA Classic—$250,000
Winner: Chris Johnson

Until someone figures out how to put a dome over golf courses, the sport shall be at the mercy of the elements. And the weather conditions showed no mercy at the GNA Classic until nature finally decided to smile upon Chris Johnson.

The tournament was wrecked by six inches of rain that fell from Thursday through Sunday. On Monday it was decided to finish the last six holes of the third round, placing Johnson in an abbreviated match against Jane Geddes. They were tied for the lead after 48 holes at one under par.

Johnson dropped birdie putts on Nos. 14, 15 and 18 to finish at four-under-par 212 to beat Geddes by two shots. Johnson broke the Oakmont Country Club record with a closing five-under 67 even though it took her three days to finish the round.

Confusion reigned because of the rain all week at the course in Glendale, California. Because rounds were never completed as scheduled, it was difficult to decide who the leaders were.

"This wasn't golf. It was survival of the fittest," Pat Bradley said on Friday after she resumed her first round at 7:15 a.m. and finished her second round at 5:45 p.m., playing 30 holes during the day.

The first round began Thursday and ended Friday. The second round began Friday and ended Saturday. The third round began Saturday and did not finish until Monday because no golf was played on Sunday. The fourth round, of course, was abandoned.

For the record, Shelly Hamlin, Amy Alcott and rookie Kristi Arrington were the first-round leaders at 71. Hamlin and Laurie Rinker led after 36 holes at 141, and if the third round had been washed out, they would have played a one-hole playoff for a reduced first prize. But Johnson sank a 45-foot putt on the last hole she played Saturday to tie Geddes before awaiting Monday's six-hole finish. After Geddes, July Inkster was third at even-par 216. Bradley was tied for 11th at 220.

Circle K—$200,000
Winner: Penny Pulz

Although it did not seem that way at the time, the story of the Circle K championship was a tale of two champions: Penny Pulz, who won the tournament, and Pat Bradley, who made the final adjustments on her game before beginning her conquest of the 1986 LPGA Tour.

Bradley was almost ready. She opened the tournament on the Randolph North course in Tucson, Arizona, with a seven-under-par 65 to lead by three strokes, shot a 68 to lead by six after three rounds, then a 72 to still lead by three going into the final round.

But Pulz was not to be denied. After rounds of 72–71–69, she entered the final day seven shots behind Bradley. And after touring the front side of the final round in just one under, she hardly seemed a candidate for victory.

It's amazing what a seven-under-par 29 on the final nine can do for your standings in a tournament. After sinking birdie putts on five of the backside holes, she made an eagle three on the final hole for a tournament record 64 and 12-under total of 276.

Betsy King had a closing 66 to finish second at 280, four strokes back. And Bradley's game unraveled for a 76 to tie for third with Jerilyn Britz and Myra Blackwelder at 281.

Bradley was a champion in defeat, saying: "Penny has paid her dues out here, and I'm very pleased for her. She's struggled, a lot more than I have."

Despite the loss and despite not winning in the tour's first eight weeks, Bradley was third in earnings. And with the Dinah Shore Classic coming up, it was time to rewrite the record books.

Nabisco Dinah Shore Classic—$500,000
Winner: Pat Bradley

Pat Bradley's rewriting of LPGA history began with a two-stroke victory in the Nabisco Dinah Shore Classic, richest event on the tour and the first of the LPGA's designated major tournaments.

Bradley shot 68–72–69–71 for an eight-under-par 280 on the Mission Hills Country Club "Old Course." The victory was worth $75,000, placing Bradley in range of becoming the first woman to earn $2 million on the tour. Her career earnings were $1,948,421.

Bradley entered the final day with a three-stroke lead on Juli Inkster, invoking memories of the Dinah Shore's final round in 1984 when Bradley led Inkster by two with four holes to play but eventually lost a playoff to Inkster.

Not this year. Inkster shot 76 to fade into a tie for fifth at 288. Bradley, after a bogey on the first hole, birdied No. 4 from six feet and No. 5 from 50 feet. By the turn Bradley had a five-stroke lead and coasted home.

Suddenly the press was reviewing Bradley's "bridesmaid" career. The Dinah Shore, her fourth major victory, was her 17th career triumph in 349 events. And she had finished second 40 times to be known as the steadiest but never the best player on tour.

"People don't care about seconds, people don't care about consistency," Bradley said. "I don't think people realize how difficult it is to be in the hunt and make those top 10 finishes week in and week out. Maybe this will boost my ratings."

The boost had just begun.

Bradley's opening 68 gave her a one-shot lead on Inkster, starting the talk about 1984. The talk continued after the second round when Inkster shot 71 and Bradley 72 to tie for the lead at 140. Laura Baugh, who had finished second nine times but never won, joined the final threesome by totaling 141.

Baugh fell out of the race Saturday with a 77. With one hole to play in the third round Bradley led Inkster by a stroke, and really may have won the tournament on the next hole. Playing into a 40-mile-an-hour wind on the 18th hole, Bradley used a five iron from 125 yards out instead of her usual nine iron, and landed 15 feet short of the cup to insure a par. Inkster used a half four wood for her approach and went 50 feet past the cup, then putted 20 feet beyond it coming downhill. Two more putts by Inkster gave Bradley a three-shot lead for the final round.

Val Skinner birdied the last three holes in the final round to shoot 69 and take second place, worth $40,000, at 282. Mary Beth Zimmerman, the tour's only two-event winner at this point in 1986, shot 70—285 for third and $25,000. Betsy King had 72—287 for fourth. Jan Stephenson shot 68 and Jane Geddes 70 to tie Inkster for fifth at 288.

Kyocera Inamori Classic—$200,000
Winner: Patty Sheehan

No matter who has the hot hand or how hot it may be, somebody is always ready to challenge to be champion for a week. Patty Sheehan rose up to capture the Kyocera Inamori Classic and prevent Pat Bradley from adding that title to her list of conquests in 1986.

Sheehand dropped an 18-foot birdie putt on the final hole to edge Bradley by a stroke. It was Sheehan's third victory in the six-year history of the tournament, last stop on the early Western swing of the LPGA Tour.

Sheehan had rounds of 69–71–68–70 for a 278 total on the Bernardo Heights course in San Diego, California. Bradley shot 69–68–74–68, obviously losing the tournament in the third round.

Mindy Moore, the LPGA vice president, took the opening lead with a 66. Bradley had a two-shot lead after the second round but could not cope with a temperature that dropped into the 40s and winds that gusted up to 30 miles per hour.

Sheehan ignored the elements and shot a superb 68 on Saturday to take a three-shot lead on Bradley and Ayako Okamoto. But a three-putt bogey on No. 15 in the final round by Sheehan allowed Bradley to tie her and set up the finish on No. 18.

"It was Patty's week," Bradley said. "She matched or bettered whatever I did—no matter what I did. A win for me this week was not meant to be."

Bradley would not have to wait long before entering the victory circle once again.

S&H Classic—$200,000
Winner: Pat Bradley

There comes a time in a champion's career when reputation is almost as valuable as skill. It is possible Pat Bradley won the S&H Classic partly because Janet Coles expected her to win.

Coles had played some of the best golf of her life to lead Bradley by three strokes after three rounds at the Pasadena Yacht and Country Club in St. Petersburg, Florida. But Coles revealed her misgivings when she said: "I'm going to have to play as well as I have the last three days. Pat Bradley is a great player who is probably playing the best golf of anybody on tour."

So true. Coles shot a closing 69, but Bradley shot a seven-under-par 65 to win by a stroke. And the winning stroke was a 25-foot birdie putt on the final hole. Coles could have tied by sinking one from eight feet but failed to convert.

It was another match-play finish. Bradley had rounds of 69–67–71–65 for 16-under 272, tying the tournament record. Coles shot 68–69–67–69 for 273. Third place went to Jane Crafter, well back at 279.

Bradley's second victory of the season was worth another $30,000, giving her earnings of $202,724 after just 11 weeks. And she was just $3,079 shy of becoming the first LPGA player to win $2 million over her career.

Cathy Kratzert, sister of PGA Tour player Bill Kratzert, took the opening lead with a 67. But Lori Garbacz equaled the course record of 64 with an eight birdie-no bogey round on the second day to lead by two at 134. Then Coles shot her third-round 67 to take temporary command. "Temporary" is the operative word as Bradley had tied her after three holes of the final round. The two stayed within a stroke of each other the rest of the day until Bradley prevailed on the final hole.

United Virginia Bank Classic—$250,000
Winner: Muffin Spencer-Devlin

Many golfers are students of history and find it inspirational, but Muffin Spencer-Devlin believes she won the United Virginia Bank Classic because she was part of history in that area.

"I know that I have had previous lives, from experiences in my therapy and in my dreams," she explained. "I have had some of my most vivid dreams of fighting in the Civil War—in and around where this course is now."

Spencer-Devlin does not remember whether she was on the winning or losing side in her country's Civil War, but she was the only winner on the Portsmouth Sleepy Hole course in Suffolk, Virginia. Despite an opening 76, she won on two rounds of 69 each, good enough for a two-under-par 214.

Tied for second, one shot back, were veteran Debbie Massey, third-year player Barb Thomas and rookie Jody Rosenthal. Any of the three could have forced Spencer-Devlin into a playoff, but Massey bogeyed No. 17, Thomas had to one-putt to save par on the last two holes, and Rosenthal missed an eight-foot birdie putt on the final hole.

Bonnie Lauer and rookie Deb Richard shared the first-round lead at 69. And despite a 73, Lauer still led by one going into the final round with Spencer-Devlin almost unnoticed three shots back.

Pat Bradley did not play, postponing her bid to become the LPGA's first multimillionaire in career earnings.

Chrysler-Plymouth Classic—$200,000
Winner: Becky Pearson

The 1986 Chrysler-Plymouth Classic will be remembered for two reasons: Becky Pearson won her first LPGA tournament, worth $30,000, and Pat Bradley finished in a tie for 11th to earn $3,425. Why should Bradley's tie for 11th place be memorable? Because the check was just enough to make her the first LPGA player to earn more than $2 million during her career—$2,000,346 to be exact.

Tour Commissioner John Laupheimer was on hand to present Bradley with jewelry to commemorate her accomplishment. "I wanted to do it here," Bradley said, "because I have won here and have a lot of support."

As for Pearson, a victory anywhere has been her dream. And her triumph was exciting as she needed a birdie on the final hole to shoot 71–70–71 for a six-under-par 212, one stroke ahead of rookie Deb Richard and Betsy King.

King and Jane Blalock were first-round leaders with 67 each, but Blalock followed with an 85. King shot 72 and began the final round with a one-shot lead, but as many as six golfers shared the lead during the last day at the Fairmont course in Chatham Township, New Jersey.

Richard had finished at five-under 213 when Pearson and King came to the final hole. Pearson also was five under and King was one shot back. King made a chip and putt for a birdie on the short par five to tie, but Pearson also chipped to within three feet and sank the putt for birdie and her first victory.

Corning Classic—$250,000
Winner: Laurie Rinker

It's often one shot that determines the outcome of a tournament, and that shot is not always the final one. For Laurie Rinker the shot of the year would come on the 68th hole of the Corning Classic.

No. 14 on the Corning (New York) Country Club course is a par five to an elevated green. Rinker's drive and nine iron approach had left her 82 yards to the cup, slightly downwind.

She took out a sand wedge and swung. Then she heard the sound of the crowd, and so did Corning leader Beth Daniel. "Definitely an eagle roar," Daniel told her caddie.

"Unbelievable," said Rinker. "I saw it bounce and then heard everybody go nuts. I kind of trotted up the hill, yelling 'This is it!' "

Indeed it was. Rinker had her eagle and went on to shoot a six-under par 66 to pass Daniel and sensational Pat Bradley for the third victory of her five-year career. Rounds of 72–70–70–66 gave her a 10-under-par 278, three shots better than Daniel, who closed with a 74, and Bradley, who shot 72.

Daniel led for the first three days on rounds of 67, 70 and 70 again. A resurrection of her lost putting skills gave her a two-shot lead on Bradley and five-shot advantage on Rinker going into the final 18 holes.

Bradley dropped out of contention at the turn with bogeys on Nos. 10 and 11. The next great moment of her year was one week away in the LPGA Championship.

Daniel still was three shots ahead of Rinker when the leader bogeyed No. 13 only to hear Rinker's "eagle roar" seconds later from the 14th green. They were briefly tied until Daniel missed an eagle of her own on No. 14 by eight inches but regained the lead with a tap-in birdie.

But disaster struck Daniel on the 125-yard 15th hole. Swirling winds forced her to guess at an eight iron that went over the green. Then she cut under a wedge that left the ball two feet from her feet, leading to a double-bogey five.

Rinker led by one. Then she led by three when she sank a 10-foot birdie putt on No. 17 ad Daniel three-putted for a bogey on No. 16. The tournament was over. In fact it really ended when Rinker swung that sand wedge back on No. 14 and heard the eagle roar.

LPGA Championship—$300,000
Winner: Pat Bradley

If anyone was left in the world of golf who doubted Pat Bradley's place among the great names in the game, the doubt had to vanish after Bradley won the 1986 LPGA Championship to become the first woman to win all four of the LPGA's major events during her career. More than that, after already winning the 1986 Dinah Shore, she was two-for-two in her quest of a one-year Grand Slam, with the U.S. Open and du Maurier Classic still to come.

And it was befitting her growing status that the LPGA Championship was not won easily. First she had to overcome Ayako Okamoto's three-stroke lead on the final round, then she had to match a birdie putt by Patty Sheehan on the final hole to win by a stroke.

"Pat's best simply is the best on Tour," Sheehan said. "We won't roll over and play dead, but we also won't be surprised if she actually wins the grand slam this year."

The LPGA Championship was played on the short Grizzly Course at the Jack Nicklaus Golf Center in King's Island, Ohio. Wide fairways and deep greens made the course difficult for anyone to stage a rally, but both Bradley and Sheehan were up to the task.

Bradley won $45,000 on rounds of 67–72–70–68, totaling an 11-under-par 277. Sheehan, with a progressively improving 72–70–69–67, finished one shot back to earn $27,750.

Okamoto, who faded with a closing 74, and Juli Inkster (69) tied for third at 279, two shots back. Muffin Spencer-Devlin (68) was alone in fifth at 281. And attractive Cindy Mackey (74) became a television celebrity by holding on to sixth place at 282.

Lori Garbacz took the opening lead with a tournament-low 65, but a pair of 74s took her out of contention. Okamoto thrilled the TV audience in Japan by shooting 66–70–69 to take the lead after the second and third rounds. Going into the last day, Okamoto led Mackey by three shots, Bradley by four, and Sheehan by six.

Sheehan immediately posted her intentions with an eagle on the first hole of the final round. Okamoto made 11 regulation pars, then lost the lead for good with a bunkered bogey on No. 12. Bradley and Sheehan shared the lead until Bradley's sand edge pitch-and-run ran into the hole for a one-shot lead going into the dogley par five final hole.

Sheehan went for the green in two and came up just short in the front bunker, 40 feet from the cup. She thrilled the enormous crowd by nearly holing the bunker shot and tapping in for a birdie.

Meanwhile Bradley was 15 feet from the cup in three, and the forgotten Inkster was 25 feet away—on the same line. Inkster made her putt to show the line to Bradley—and you never give a champion that kind of edge. Bradley dropped her birdie putt to avoid a playoff with Sheehan and prove beyond a doubt that her signature has taken its place among the great names in golf.

McDonald's Championship—$450,000
Winner: Juli Inkster

Not every major accomplishment of the year would belong to Pat Bradley. She missed the cut while Juli Inkster cut a swath through the opposition to win the $450,000 McDonald's Championship.

Inkster played so well for three rounds that the final round did not matter. After leading every day on rounds of 68–67–69, Inkster had an eight-shot lead going into the final 18 holes. She shot a disappointing 77—and still won by three strokes over friend Mary Beth Zimmerman.

"I wanted to attack the course, but it attacked me," Inkster said after her closing round. "Actually I was watching the scoreboards and wondering what the others were doing instead of playing the course."

The White Manor course in suburban Philadelphia had been Inkster's plaything for 54 holes. She doubled her lead each day, leading by two strokes after 18 holes, four after 36, and eight after 54. Even with her five-over-par 77 on the final day, she posted a seven-under 281 total and never was in trouble.

Zimmerman shot a final 72 to earn $41,625 for second. Amy Alcott (70) finished one shot back in third at 285, worth $30,375. Three more players— Becky Pearson, Bonnie Lauer and Ok-Hee-Ku—were under par at 287 and made $19,500 each.

After Inkster's romp, the second most startling event was Bradley's failure to make the cut with rounds of 80 and 73. "I'm a little tired and do want to take some time off," Bradley said after playing in 15 of the year's first 16 events.

Inkster, however, was just getting her second wind along with her second win of the year.

Lady Keystone Open—$250,000
Winner: Juli Inkster

Winning the McDonald's Championship was so much fun that Juli Inkster kept her streak going by winning the Lady Keystone Open, too. Of course, it's beginning to seem as if Inkster always will win the Lady Keystone at the Hershey (Pennsylvania) Country Club.

While earning the LPGA Rookie of the Year award in 1984, Inkster finished second in her first appearance at the Keystone. Then she won the event in 1985 and again in 1986. Her prize this time of $37,500 pushed her three-year earnings to more than $560,000, including $90,000 from the Keystone alone.

This time the victory was both difficult and easy. Difficult because her three identical rounds of 70 each for a six-under-par 210 left her in a playoff with Cindy Hill and Debbie Massey. Easy because Inkster won the playoff with a two-putt par from 12 feet after watching Massey take a bogey and Hill a double bogey.

Actually the tournament had been Massey's to win. A 10-year veteran who has not won since 1979, Massey entered the final round with a one-stroke lead after rounds of 72 and 66. And she still was a shot ahead of Inkster and Hill, who had already finished, when she teed up on the final hole. Massey needed to make an eight-foot putt for a winning par but missed, setting up the playoff.

Second-year pro Cindy Rarick led after the opening round with a 68 but shot 77 the second day. A closing 69 left in a tie for 17th at 214. Pat Bradley, after missing the cut the previous week, tied for 11th at 213.

Rochester International—$255,000
Winner: Judy Dickinson

PGA Senior Gardner Dickinson was not with his wife, Judy Dickinson, when she faced the opportunity and emotional threat of contending for the Rochester International title, but the Dickinson was able to reach out and touch his wife's faltering confidence when she needed it the most.

After a history of throwing away opportunities on the final holes of many previous tournaments, Judy Dickinson came through this time with a closing two-under-par 70 to shoot a seven-under 281 and hold off who else but Pat Bradley by a stroke. It was Dickinson's second victory in nine years on Tour.

"Gardner knows I get nervous," Judy said. "The morning before the final round we talked on the telephone, and he said, 'I don't care what you shoot, I love you anyway.' "

But Judy cared. After three rounds at the Locust Hill Country Club in Rochester, New York, she and Val Skinner were tied for the lead, three strokes ahead of four others including Bradley. Judy did not want to give this one away.

On the dreaded back nine, Bradley applied the pressure with a birdie on No. 10 to tie Dickinson for the lead. But Dickinson rallied by hitting a pitching wedge from 87 yards on the par-five 11th that backed into the cup for an eagle and a two-shot lead. Bradley, who shot 68, never caught her again.

Laurie Rinker led the first round with a 69, five shots ahead of Dickinson's

74. Hollis Stacy and Patti Rizzo led midway at two-under 142 each, one shot ahead of Dickinson's 74–69. A third-round 68 set up Dickinson's victory.

Mayflower Classic—$350,000
Winner: Sandra Palmer

On the American tours this was a week for "senior citizens." Dale Douglass, 50, won the U.S. Senior Open, Bob Murphy, 43, won the Canadian Open and popular Sandra Palmer, 45, won the Mayflower Classic to become the LPGA's 13th millionaire in earnings.

Palmer, who had 20 previous tour victories but had not won since 1982, captured a one-hole playoff against Jan Stephenson and Chris Johnson to take the lucrative first prize of $52,500. All three had shot eight-under-par 280s in regulation with Palmer's coming on rounds of 68–68–72–72 at the Indianapolis (Indiana) Country Club.

Johnson and Stephenson each birdied the 72nd hole to a par for Palmer that forced the playoff, which started and ended on No. 14, a par four. Johnson fell out of the hunt when her drive went behind trees to the right, forcing her to scramble to save par. Palmer then watched Stephenson fail to sink a 20-foot birdie putt before calmly sinking a 12-footer of her own.

"It was meant to be," Palmer said. "It was my attitude. I was convinced I was going to win this tournament."

Debbie Massey led the first round with a 67, but Palmer took control with her second round of 68. Stephenson shot 69 in the third round to tie Palmer for the lead, three shots ahead of the field. Johnson caught the two leaders with a closing 68 but, as Palmer said, her victory "was meant to be" on what should have been Veterans' Day.

Mazda Hall of Fame Championship—$300,000
Winner: Amy Alcott

Amy Alcott probably would not mind it being said she has the golfing instincts of a killer shark. Once you have attracted her interest you had better not falter for a moment, a lesson learned by Amy Benz and then Lauren Howe in the Mazda Hall of Fame Championship.

Alcott caught and passed Benz in regulation play, then disposed of Howe with two shots on the first hole of a brief playoff at the LPGA Headquarters and Hall of Fame course in Sugar Land, Texas. She won $45,000 on rounds of 70–70–72–72 for a four-under-par 72, plus the two-shot birdie in the playoff.

Benz held a two-shot lead after both of the first two rounds by shooting 67 and 71. Late in the third round she had moved five shots ahead of Alcott before she went bogey, double-bogey, double bogey on the last three holes. Smelling blood, Alcott played the final three holes in one under to take a one-shot lead into the final round.

Benz did not quit, however. With two holes to play on Sunday she was tied with Alcott at four under. But she bogeyed both holes to fall back, while Howe birdied No. 17 to fashion a 68 and tie Alcott.

Not for long. On the par-three 16th in overtime, Howe missed the green and Alcott used a three-iron to get within 25 feet on the 188-yard hole. Howe chipped to within three feet, but it didn't matter as Alcott sank her putt for the 25th victory of her career.

"I'd played too hard to let this one get away," Alcott said. "I was ready to get it over with."

Pat Bradley finished 10 shots behind the leaders at 294 in a tie for 18th place with the U.S. Open one week away.

United States Open—$350,000
Winner: Jane Geddes

The 1986 United States Open had it all, from a phosphorus fire to thunderstorms and an earthquake. It also had an unexpected and courageous winner in young Jane Geddes, who defeated resurgent Sally Little in an 18-hole playoff, 71 to 73.

What this U.S. Open did not have was a historic ending for Pat Bradley. Having won the first two legs of the LPGA's Grand Slam (the Dinah Shore and LPGA Championship), Bradley was going after the U.S. Open with the du Maurier Classic to follow. But Bradley shot 76 without benefit of a birdie in the opening round to kill her chances. After rounds of 71 and 74, she closed with a 69 to finish at two-over 290, in a tie for fifth and three shots out of the playoff.

Back to what the tournament did have for much of the week, which was chaos for the most part. The "attack" began Tuesday afternoon when a 44-car train derailed near the NCR Country Club course outside of Dayton, Ohio. A tanker spilled white phosphorus, a chemical that can irritate eyes, skin and lungs. Then the tanker caught fire, sending clouds of phosphorus-ridden smoke over the course.

The fire was extinguished Tuesday night but reignited Wednesday morning. More clouds of phosphorus covered the course, which prompted many golfers to give up practice and head for as far as Cincinnati to find safe lodging. Hollis Stacy broke the tension for many by asking: "Is a phosphorus cloud one or two clubs more?"

After the phosphorus cleared, the tournament began on Thursday—and so did the thunderstorms. A rain delay of 83 minutes kept nine golfers from finishing their round but did not prevent Beth Daniel from taking the lead with a two-under 70.

Betsy King and Judy Dickinson, shooting 72–71 each, grabbed the lead on Friday despite two more rain delays. Sportswriter Gary Nuhn wondered in Friday's *Dayton Daily News*: "Saturday, how about an earthquake?"

At 4:20 a.m. Saturday an earthquake registering 4.2 on the Richter Scale knocked folks out of their Dayton beds. Golfers were looking for Nuhn to find out if he knew about any tornadoes or hordes of locusts for later in the day.

All that happened was another thunderstorm and more than a two-hour delay on Saturday. And King shot a 70 to hold a one-shot lead with Geddes three shots back, but King slipped to a 75 Sunday and finished in a tie for third with Ayako Okamoto at even-par 288.

As for Little, she reached one under with a birdie on No. 15 and stayed there, shooting 70 for her 287. Geddes birdied the 17th from 10 feet for a 69 and her matching 287 total.

Reaching the playoff was a solid step forward for Little. Abdominal surgery in 1982 and later knee problems had made her a stranger to most leaderboards. In the playoff she made birdies on Nos. 4, 5 and 6 for a three-shot lead but soon gave the lead back with a bogey on No. 8 and double bogey on No. 9.

Geddes, 26, was seeking her first tour victory in her fourth year on tour. On the back side she stayed even in the match until Little faded with bogeys on the last three holes. And having had the taste of victory, Geddes wanted more with or without earthquakes.

Boston Five Classic—$275,000
Winner: Jane Geddes

Once Jane Geddes got the feel of victory in the U.S. Open, she refused to let go of it and captured the Boston Five Classic despite nearly losing a ball in a man's shirt pocket in the final round. Considering the earthquake that disrupted the Open, Geddes must have felt she was playing in the Twilight Zone.

The bizarre Boston occurrence took place on No. 6 at the Tara Ferncroft layout, actually located in Danvers, Massachusetts. Geddes hit her tee shot into a spectator's shirt pocket—on the fly. A package of cigarettes kept him from being hurt, which is one benefit of smoking that medical science had never considered.

"Just lie down," Geddes told him, "and I'll hit it right from here." The gentleman opted for a free drop instead, Geddes took her only bogey of the day—and the real excitement began.

The final round began with four co-leaders—local favorite Pat Bradley, Cindy Hill and rookies Val Skinner and Deb Richard. Geddes was two shots back.

Richard took the lead on No. 12 when her eight-iron shot on the 150-yard hole took one bounce and found the cup for a hole-in-one. But a bogey and five pars after that would not be quite enough.

Geddes had caught Richard and Bradley going into the 17th and won the tournament there with a 15-foot, downhill birdie putt. After conservative rounds of 71–70–72, she finished with a 68 for a seven-under-par 281. Richard finished second, one shot back, and Bradley tied for third with Ok-Hee-Ku of Seoul at 283. Ku had led the first two rounds with a pair of 68s.

As for Geddes, who had finished second here the year before but had not won anywhere until the week before, she was the third player of the year to win back-to-back events, joining Mary Beth Zimmerman and Juli Inkster. "I was very calm," she said after earning nearly $92,000 in two weeks. "Winning the U.S. Open took a tremendous amount of pressure off me."

du Maurier Classic—$350,000
Winner: Pat Bradley

When Pat Bradley was hailed as the LPGA's most consistent player it was a back-handed compliment, meaning she usually finished near the top but not at the top. But after winning three of the year's four major events, Bradley gave a new meaning to the term "consistency."

The du Maurier Classic in Toronto was the final event of the four majors. Bradley won it in courageous fashion. After shooting 67–66 in the final two rounds, she still had to play one hole of sudden death to defeat Ayako Okamoto, who had shot an amazing 64 in the last round.

Bradley, who had rounds of 73–70–67–66, was nine shots out of the lead at the midway point but rallied for the 20th victory of her career and fourth of the season with a 12-under-par 276 on the hilly and unromantically named Metropolitan Toronto Board of Trade Country Club course.

"Can you believe it?" Bradley asked. "I shoot 66 and it's only good enough to get me into a playoff." The playoff did not last long. Bradley and Okamoto returned to the par-three 16th, where Bradley laced a six iron dead on line and 10 feet short of the cup. Okamoto placed her tee shot 12 feet above the cup and missed the putt. Bradley drilled her birdie putt for victory.

"I never doubt myself and I never count myself out," Bradley said. "It was a great day and I accomplished a lot of things."

Bradley hardly seemed a factor on the tournament's first day after she shot 73 and Chris Johnson led with 67. Probably the most exciting news of the first round was that JoAnne Carner shot 69 despite the yeast infection that hampered her breathing and had kept her out of contention all season. Carner eventually finished in a tie for 14th at 286.

The second round belonged to unknown Nancy Scanton from the first shot. She was the first golfer off the tee and equaled Carner's tournament record of 64 to take the lead at 10-under 134, one shot ahead of Johnson and nine ahead of Bradley.

The rest was history, Bradley's history. She holed an 80-foot chip with an eight iron for an eagle on the first hole of the third round, declaring: "My goodness, we're off to the races." Her 67 elevated her to second place, one shot behind Johnson, who had shot 74. Scranton had shot 78 to fall back.

Okamoto and Bradley had the course to themselves on the final day. Okamoto birdied the last hole of regulation play from one foot while Bradley watched from the fairway. Bradley then hit a bump-and-run approach and sank a six-foot birdie putt to force the overtime before claiming her third du Maurier title.

Scranton, with a closing 69, tied Betsy King for third at 281, five shots back. Johnson and Cathy Morse tied for fifth at 282. But the tournament band was playing "My Irish Eyes Are Smiling" for Bradley, who has made "consistent" synonymous with "best."

LPGA National Pro-Am—$300,000
Winner: Amy Alcott

No matter what kind of season Pat Bradley was having, Amy Alcott had a score to settle in the LPGA National Pro-Am. Revenge can be a strong motivational factor when properly used, and Alcott made the most of it for her second victory in five weeks.

Alcott shot a five-under-par 283 on two courses in the Denver, Colorado area to finish one shot ahead of Bradley, and steady Chris Johnson in the second National Pro-Am, the successor on tour to the old Columbia Classic.

Victory was sweet for Alcott, who led the same event on the final day last year but gave that triumph to Bradley. In 1985 Alcott shot a closing 74 to 68 for Bradley and then lost the title in a two-hole playoff. But not again.

"I am an extremely patient person," Alcott said, meaning that if the victory doesn't come one year, then it can come the next. "I knew exactly what I had to do."

The tournament was a four-person affair, including resurgent Debbie Massey along with Alcott, Bradley and Johnson. Massey, trying to put her game back together after serving three years as an LPGA officer, shot 68 to tie for the first-round lead with Sue Fogleman and Judy Dickinson.

Johnson, on two rounds of 70 each, took the midway lead. Then Massey regained the lead at 211 after three rounds, one shot ahead of Johnson and two ahead of both Alcott and Bradley.

But on Sunday Massey bogeyed three of the last four holes to shoot 74 and finish fourth at 285. Johnson could not make birdie putts on the last two holes to finish one shot behind Alcott. As for Bradley, she birdied No. 10 to tie Massey for the lead, two shots ahead of Alcott and Johnson. But lightning halted play for 66 minutes at that point and seemed to drain the momentum from Bradley.

The tournament turned at No. 12, where Bradley three-putted for a bogey and Alcott dropped a 20-foot birdie putt to tie for the lead. A three-foot birdie on the par-five 14th put Alcott ahead by a shot and it was all she needed as Bradley was unable to pick up a stroke on the last six holes.

Henredon Classic—$230,000
Winner: Betsy King

When you are playing in the final threesome on the final day, you expect to be noticed. But Betsy King had to wait until she won a two-hole playoff before anyone realized that she had defied history and sentiment to win the Henredon Classic, her first victory of the season.

Admittedly sentiment was not on her side in the playoff when she defeated JoAnne Carner, par to bogey, for the title. Carner, called "Medium Momma" after ill health and a diet had caused a 30-pound weight loss, delighted the fans at Willow Creek in High Point, North Carolina, by being competitive again.

But the high point of the tournament was the next-to-last pairing on the final day. There was Carner, along with Kathy Whitworth. And they were joined by Nancy Lopez, making her first start of the year as Henredon's defending champion after a maternity leave of absence.

A crowd estimated at 12,000 followed that threesome around the course, while the final threesome of King, Debbie Massey and Robin Walton played in their shadow.

But King created her own spotlight with three consecutive birdies on Nos. 6, 7 and 8. With two holes to play, she and Carner were tied at 11 under par. Neither could make a bird on the last two holes and settled for the playoff.

King missed a three-foot birdie putt on the first playoff hole, No. 16. On the next hole, Carner drove into rough and then hit a rare flier over the green. She couldn't get up and down, allowing King to two putt from 20 feet for par and victory.

Lopez shot a closing 69 to tie Walton, who shot 74, for third at 279, two shots back. Cathy Krazert moved up with a final 68 to take fifth at 280. A double bogey on the last hole dropped Whitworth into a tie for sixth with Massey at 281.

Pat Bradley skipped the Henredon, but would return to the tour the following week for a superstar showdown with Lopez and King.

Nestle World Championship—$240,000
Winner: Pat Bradley

Despite all she had already done in 1986, Pat Bradley demonstrated once again that she can win from anywhere in the field as long as she's playing in the final round. Don't ever count her out as she proved by making up an eight-shot deficit in the final round of the Nestle World Championship.

After three even-par rounds of 72 each, Bradley shot a tournament record 63 for a nine-under-par 279 over the hilly Stouffer PineIsle Resort course at Lake Lanier Islands, Georgia. The historic round was enough to make up eight shots and pass eight players in the field of a dozen stars. Of her 21 career victories, Bradley has won 17 coming from behind on the final day.

When Bradley's smoke had cleared, Betsy King and Nancy Lopez were tied for second at 281, two shots back. Playing the way Bradley used to play (i.e. always close), Chris Johnson was fourth at 282.

Bradley's fifth victory of the season was worth $78,000, raising her season's total to $482,496. That broke the 1985 record of $416,472 set by Lopez and was nearly twice as much as earned by her closest competitor, Juli Inkster, who had $241,524 at the time.

"It's been a year I'll never forget," Bradley said. "My year has made a statement to me, the public and the fans—that Pat Bradley now is the player people thought she would be. It's just taken me longer."

About that final round:

Bradley began eight strokes behind King and playing four groups ahead. She birdied five of the first eight holes, then had to settle for six consecutive pars. But a birdie at No. 15 ignited her fire once again and led to the par-five 16th hole.

After a solid drive, Bradley hit a 206-yard four wood that came to rest three inches from the cup. She tapped in for the eagle, giving her a share of the lead for the first time during the tournament. She and Johnson were leading at eight under.

On to No. 17, a tricky 172-yard par three. Bradley placed her tee shot 15 feet short of the cup, then drilled the birdie putt to go to nine under for the day and the tournament. That was it as Johnson bogeyed the final two holes, while neither Lopez nor King could mount a charge.

MasterCard International Pro-Am—$200,000
Winner: Cindy Mackey

While Pat Bradley was dazzling the rest of the tour's superstars in the Nestle World Championship, a new star was born in charming Cindy Mackey at the MasterCard International Pro-Am. Mackey did not just win her first LPGA tournament, but she also sent the LPGA to its record books by finishing 14 strokes ahead of the field.

The 14-stroke victory was the widest margin on tour since 1949, when Louise Suggs won the U.S. Open by the same margin. However, Mackey's margin of victory needs an asterisk next to it, because the margin would have been five shots if Colleen Walker had not signed an incorrect scorecard after her final round.

Mackey shot a 12-under-par 276 playing across three courses in Westchester County, New York. She had rounds of 71–70–65–70 and, after Walker's disqualification, was the only player under par. Rookie Jody Rosenthal and Cathy Johnston tied for second at two-over 290.

On the last day Walker took a bogey six on No. 16, but defending champion Muffin Spencer-Devlin scored it as a par five. Walker realized the mistake after the awards ceremony and forfeited second-place money of $18,500.

No other golfer really challenged Mackey. Her strongest competitors were her nerves and the weather, which forced the golfers into splitting the final round over two days.

Sue Ertl had led the first round with a 65, then Walker led at 72–67, 139. But Mackey's 65 in the third round gave her a four-shot lead on Walker. Mackey lost two shots to Walker after nine holes Sunday before rain and lightning postponed the second half of the round until 14 hours later on Monday morning.

Mackey birdied No. 10 on Monday morning but took a double bogey on No. 11, cutting her lead to one shot. However, she bounced back with birdies on Nos. 13, 16 and 17 to pull away from Walker. She already was about a time zone ahead of the rest of the field.

Atlantic City Classic—$225,000
Winner: Juli Inkster

With Pat Bradley taking a short break, Juli Inkster decided to come out and play in the inaugural Atlantic City Classic over the Bay course of the Marriott Seaview Country Club in Galloway Township, New Jersey, three miles from the famous boardwalk.

As it turned out, Inkster nearly had a cakewalk. She had rounds of 67–71–71 for a seven-under-par 209, good enough for a three-shot victory over Patti Rizzo. It was Inkster's fourth victory of the season and eighth of her LPGA career for the three-time U.S. Amateur champion.

The first-place prize of $33,750 placed Inkster in second place for tour earnings at $275,274, still more than $200,000 behind Bradley. "But second place isn't all that bad," Inkster said, "when you consider the kind of year Pat is having."

Inkster led this one all the way with Rizzo serving as her only serious threat. Inkster's opening 67, low round of the 54-hole event, gave her a two-shot lead. But a second-round 71 allowed Rizzo (70–68) to tie at 138.

In the final round both leaders shot par on the front and remained tied. But a four-foot birdie on No. 10 put Inkster ahead by a shot, and a 20-foot birdie on No. 11 gave her another shot on Rizzo. Inkster settled the outcome on No. 12 with a six-foot birdie, her third in a row, while Rizzo missed the green and bogeyed to fall four back.

Inkster was not the only winner. Crowds were good all three days, inspiring backers of the first-year event to commit themselves for at least another three years.

Rail Classic—$200,000
Winner: Betsy King

This was a season when it simply was not safe to be a final-round leader. Betsy King proved it once again in the Rail Classic by shooting a career-low 63 to make up seven shots on the leaders before winning in a playoff with Cathy Kratzert and Alice Ritzman.

The victory was the seventh of King's short career. It also was her second triumph via a playoff in a month as she defeated JoAnne Carner in sudden death to take the Henredon. And it also was King's second consecutive victory at the Rail Golf Club in Springfield, Illinois. She won the tournament in 1985 by the same score of 11-under-par 205.

King's closing 63, after rounds of 70 and 72, was a beautiful nine-birdie, no-bogey effort. She finished more than an hour ahead of the early leaders and patiently waited to see if 205 was enough.

Ritzman was ahead by a stroke with one hole to play but watched in shocked dismay as a five-foot par putt on the final hole of regulation hung on the lip and refused to fall. That dropped her into the playoff, while Kratzert got into it with a scrambling par on the final hole.

The playoff was more long than dramatic. Each parred three holes, before coming to the decisive hole, a par five. King was the only one to reach the green in two shots and two putted from 50 feet for a winning birdie.

Kratzert, sister of PGA Tour player Bill Kratzert, was chasing her first victory in her second year on tour. She led the first round with a 65, then was tied for the second-round lead with Lauri Peterson at 135. King was seven shots back, but it seems today's stars are never too far back.

However, Pat Bradley displayed her first signs of some burn out. She had rounds of 74–73–72 for a three-over 219 and tied for 47th. Her winnings of $653 probably did not match the interest accumulating on her season earnings of $483,149.

Cellular One-Ping Championship—$200,000
Winner: Ayako Okamoto

Japan's Ayako Okamoto says her favorite courses at home have "trees, tight fairways and fast greens." When she discovered those conditions in the Cellular One-Ping Championship, she showed the rest of the LPGA Tour how awesome she can be.

Okamoto tied the course record at the Columbia-Edgewater Country Club in Portland, Oregon, by shooting a six-under-par 66 in the final round to defeat frustrated Nancy Lopez and unfortunate Colleen Walker by six shots each. Okamoto, on rounds of 70–71–66, finished at nine-under 207 for her second victory of the season.

Lopez was disappointed because it was her fourth and final tournament of a season abbreviated by the birth of her second child. With 34 career victories, she needs one more to become the 11th player installed into the LPGA Hall of Fame. She wanted to do it right here.

Walker was hanging tough in a difficult season that included being disqualified twice for signing incorrect scorecards. One of the mistakes cost her $18,500 for finishing second in the MasterCard International Pro-Am.

Veteran M. J. Smith, contemplating retirement at the end of the season, set the course record of 66 in the first round. After a 73 in the second round, Smith led Lopez and Walker by a shot and was two shots ahead of Okamoto going into the last day.

But the last day belonged to Okamoto, who came out firing. She sank birdie putts of 60 and 12 feet on the first two holes to take the lead. For the day she had seven birdies and one bogey.

Smith faded with bogeys on the final five holes to shoot 76 and finish in a tie for sixth at 215. Walker took a double bogey on No. 14, saying "I hit the wall there," to drop out of contention.

Lopez was two shots back with two to play but had to pack her dreams of gaining entrance into the Hall of Fame until next year after she took a bogey and Okamoto sank a five-foot birdie putt on No. 17. Lopez hit her tee shot out of bounds on the final hole, suffering a double bogey to turn Okamoto's victory into a rout.

Safeco Classic—$200,000
Winner: Judy Dickinson

Judy Dickinson discovered the perfect birthday gift to give to the golfing husband who has everything: Victory. She celebrated Gardner Dickinson's 59th birthday by running away with first prize in the Safeco Classic at the Meridian Valley course in Seattle, Washington.

Judy did not think of the gift until halfway through the tournament. After two rounds of 71 and 73, she was tied for 15th place and eight strokes out of the lead. But she almost shot Gardner's age in the third round, firing a nine-under-par 63 to tie Jan Stephenson for the lead. A closing 67 gave her a tournament record, 14-under 274, and her second victory of the season.

The key was changing putters. While young Kris Monaghan took the first-round lead with a 67 and Stephenson grabbed the midway command with rounds of 67–69, Dickinson stayed at even par despite five three-putt greens and a four-putt disaster in her first 32 holes.

But Dickinson did not have a bogey in her last 40 holes. On Saturday she passed one name after another on the scoreboard by sinking birdie putts on six of her last seven holes.

Stephenson faded quickly in the final round, then rallied for a 73 that gave her third place at 280. Dickinson would have had a runaway except for Hollis Stacy, who shot 69 to finish second at 278, four shots back.

Konica San Jose Classic—$275,000
Winner: Patty Sheehan

With "just" two victories, Patty Sheehan had considered 1986 to be an off year until she won a four-way playoff to capture first place in the Konica San Jose Classic, the last event of the season in the United States.

Sheehan's 15-foot birdie putt on the first playoff hole was enough to defeat Amy Alcott, Betsy King and Ayako Okamoto, the Portland-Ping winner two weeks previously. All four shot four-under-par 212 in regulation play with Sheehan's total coming on rounds of 71–70–71.

Okamoto and U.S. Open champion Jane Geddes shared the first-round lead with 69 each. Then Okamoto shared the second-round lead with Alcott and Lauren Howe at 140 with Sheehan a stroke back.

On the final day King appeared to be the winner. She reached seven under after 13 holes, but bogeys on Nos. 14, 15 and 17 dropped her to four under. Then Sheehan, with pars on the last eight holes, came in with the same total.

Playing in the last group, Alcott had to birdie three of the last four holes, including No. 18 with a 12-foot putt, to join the gang at four under. That left Okamoto, who was five under with one hole to play and only needed to two-putt for par to win. But Okamoto missed her second putt from four feet to create the playoff.

The foursome went to the par-four 12th hole, a tricky dogleg left. All hit good drives, and all hit the green with their approach shots.

King barely missed her birdie attempt from 40 feet. Alcott, from 30 feet, left her putt four feet short. Sheehan, from 15 feet, played her putt to break eight inches from left to right and that's exactly what it did. Then Okamoto, from just five feet above the cup, left her putt on the left side to present Sheehan with a "season-saving" victory.

The first-place check for $41,250 raised Sheehan to fifth on the earnings list at $212,981. That meant 1986 was the fifth consecutive year that Sheehan had earned more than $200,000.

Rookie of the year honors went to Jody Rosenthal almost by default. She shot 223 to earn $589, while Deb Richard missed the cut of 149 by a shot. Rosenthal won the title by earning $3,412 more than Richard in their initial seasons.

Mazda Japan Classic—$300,000
Winner: Ai-Yu Tu

Taiwan's Ai-Yu Tu, the queen of the Japan LPGA Tour, wrapped up her fifth consecutive money title on that circuit with her eighth victory of the year in the Mazda Japan Classic. The final LPGA tournament of 1986, held at Lions Country Club near Osaka, featured an international field of 82 golfers, 52 from the United States.

Tu won on the fourth playoff hole over Mary Beth Zimmerman, after Becky Pearson and Cathy Kratzert had dropped from the playoff with bogeys on the first extra hole. Tu sank a 25-foot birdie there, only to be matched by Zimmerman. On the fourth extra hole, Zimmerman missed the green and had a 10-foot putt for bogey. Tu three-putted from 12 feet for a bogey, but won when Zimmerman missed the 10-footer.

After scores of 68 and 69, Tu entered the final round with a three-shot lead, only to shoot 76 on the rainy and cold last day for a 213 total. Zimmerman surged in with a 68, while Pearson shot 70 and Kratzert, 71. Tied at 214 were Japan's Chako Higuichi, Jane Geddes, Debbie Massey and Sandra Palmer.

It looked like a run-away victory for Tu, but a wayward driver and trouble on the greens left her struggling. She missed a three-foot putt to send the tournament to extra holes, but recovered for her 52nd career victory.

APPENDIXES

World Money List

This listing of the 200 leading money winners in the world of professional golf in 1986 was compiled from the results of all tournaments carried in the Appendixes of this edition, along with such other non-tour and international events for which accurate figures could be obtained and in which the players competed for prize money provided by someone other than the players themselves. Skins games are not included.

In the 21 years during which World Money Lists have been compiled, the earnings of the player in the 200th position have risen from a total of $3,326 in 1966 to $86,733 in 1986. The top 200 players in 1966 earned a total of $4,680,287. In 1986, the comparable total was $46,470,840.

Because of the fluctuating values of money throughout the world in 1986, it was necessary to determine an average value of non-American currency to U.S. money to prepare this listing. The conversion rates used were: British pound = US$1.50; South African rand = US40¢; Australian and New Zealand dollars = US65¢; 160 Japanese yen = US$1.

POS.	PLAYER, COUNTRY	TOTAL MONEY
1	Greg Norman, Australia	$1,146,584
2	Tsuneyuki Nakajima, Japan	789,067
3	Bob Tway, U.S.	782,330
4	Bernhard Langer, West Germany	745,878
5	Andy Bean, U.S.	688,438
6	Bob Charles, New Zealand	580,753
7	Mark McNulty, South Africa	565,719
8	Payne Stewart, U.S.	564,809
9	Masashi Ozaki, Japan	552,228
10	Isao Aoki, Japan	542,751
11	Bruce Crampton, Australia	532,515
12	Dan Pohl, U.S.	514,855
13	Chi Chi Rodriguez, U.S.	497,323
14	David Graham, Australia	488,515
15	Lanny Wadkins, U.S.	457,972
16	Don January, U.S.	457,858
17	Gary Player, South Africa	453,879
18	Hal Sutton, U.S.	448,767
19	Severiano Ballesteros, Spain	445,448
20	Ben Crenshaw, U.S.	441,802
21	Tom Kite, U.S.	432,660
22	Tateo Ozaki, Japan	430,565
23	Fuzzy Zoeller, U.S.	424,115
24	Raymond Floyd, U.S.	420,674
25	Curtis Strange, U.S.	419,944
26	Lee Elder, U.S.	419,212
27	John Mahaffey, U.S.	412,493
28	Naomichi Ozaki, Japan	405,217
29	Scott Hoch, U.S.	399,635
30	Dale Douglass, U.S.	394,582
31	Calvin Peete, U.S.	392,253
32	Rodger Davis, Australia	391,621
33	Bobby Wadkins, U.S.	379,267
34	Masahiro Kuramoto, Japan	371,754
35	Joey Sindelar, U.S.	365,248

POS.	PLAYER, COUNTRY	TOTAL MONEY
36	Mike Hulbert, U.S.	360,139
37	David Ishii, U.S.	359,388
38	Mark O'Meara, U.S.	358,847
39	Ian Woosnam, Wales	355,491
40	Doug Tewell, U.S.	352,907
41	Ken Green, U.S.	350,495
42	Larry Mize, U.S.	348,110
43	Jim Thorpe, U.S.	338,887
44	Sandy Lyle, Scotland	337,570
45	Corey Pavin, U.S.	333,622
46	Gene Littler, U.S.	332,621
47	Miller Barber, U.S.	326,080
48	Donnie Hammond, U.S.	318,349
49	Howard Clark, England	315,864
50	Tom Purtzer, U.S.	315,337
51	Tom Watson, U.S.	313,064
52	Paul Azinger, U.S.	312,233
53	Kenny Knox, U.S.	310,476
54	Graham Marsh, Australia	310,370
55	Jose-Maria Olazabal, Spain	290,558
56	Mark Wiebe, U.S.	287,515
57	Don Pooley, U.S.	281,034
58	David Frost, South Africa	273,336
59	Chen Tze Chung, Taiwan	272,341
60	John Cook, U.S.	271,428
61	Chip Beck, U.S.	269,640
62	Mac O'Grady, U.S.	268,195
63	Tim Simpson, U.S.	265,191
64	Koichi Suzuki, Japan	261,639
65	Gordon J. Brand, England	258,029
66	Ian Baker-Finch, Australia	256,684
67	Craig Stadler, U.S.	253,527
68	Jack Nicklaus, U.S.	249,533
69	Nick Price, South Africa	244,733
70	Nobumitsu Yuhara, Japan	242,689
71	Arnold Palmer, U.S.	241,123
72	Billy Casper, U.S.	238,588
73	Harold Henning, South Africa	238,251
74	Charles Owens, U.S.	238,205
75	Jay Haas, U.S.	228,298
76	Jim Ferree, U.S.	227,567
77	D. A. Weibring, U.S.	224,904
78	Toru Nakamura, Japan	223,743
79	David Love III, U.S.	222,682
80	Roger Maltbie, U.S.	222,472
81	Clarence Rose, U.S.	221,029
82	Tony Sills, U.S.	219,431
83	Gary Koch, U.S.	217,442
84	Brian Jones, Australia	209,389
85	Scott Simpson, U.S.	207,694
86	Nick Faldo, England	205,706
87	Jodie Mudd, U.S.	205,550
88	Gene Sauers, U.S.	200,544
89	Dan Forsman, U.S.	199,656
90	Phil Blackmar, U.S.	194,228
91	Bob Murphy, U.S.	193,445
92	Mark Calcavecchia, U.S.	192,192
93	Peter Thomson, Australia	187,218
94	Kikuo Arai, Japan	186,954
95	Bruce Lietzke, U.S.	186,311

POS.	PLAYER. COUNTRY	TOTAL MONEY
96	Steve Pate, U.S.	185,693
97	Teruo Sugihara, Japan	182,872
98	Larry Nelson, U.S.	182,007
99	Peter Jacobsen, U.S.	176,814
100	Jeff Sluman, U.S.	175,337
101	Mike Sullivan, U.S.	174,616
102	Willie Wood, U.S.	174,029
103	Katsunari Takahashi, Japan	170,962
104	Orville Moody, U.S.	166,765
105	Saburo Fujiki, Japan	165,287
106	Seiichi Kanai, Japan	163,858
107	Howard Twitty, U.S.	161,819
108	Gordon Brand Jr., Scotland	161,210
109	Dave Barr, Canada	161,017
110	Wayne Levi, U.S.	158,526
111	Hale Irwin, U.S.	158,509
112	Fred Couples, U.S.	157,520
113	Rick Fehr, U.S.	155,537
114	J. C. Snead, U.S.	151,119
115	Gay Brewer, U.S.	150,109
116	Curt Byrum, U.S.	149,519
117	Ronan Rafferty, Northern Ireland	146,790
118	Mike Reid, U.S.	145,651
119	Terry Gale, Australia	142,821
120	Shinsaku Maeda, Japan	142,778
121	Anders Forsbrand, Sweden	142,735
122	Sam Torrance, Scotland	141,489
123	Yasuhiro Funatogawa, Japan	141,241
124	Danny Edwards, U.S.	140,515
125	Greg Turner, New Zealand	140,389
126	Pat McGowan, U.S.	139,285
127	Lee Trevino, U.S.	137,225
128	Gary Hallberg, U.S.	134,412
129	Ken Brown, England	134,080
130	Hubert Green, U.S.	132,908
131	Mark McCumber, U.S.	132,345
132	Mark Hayes, U.S.	130,054
133	Brian Claar, U.S.	129,043
134	Yoshihisa Iwashita, Japan	127,811
135	Bill Glasson, U.S.	127,771
136	Ernie Gonzalez, U.S.	127,106
137	Mike Donald, U.S.	125,544
138	Hajime Meshiai, Japan	124,533
139	David Edwards, U.S.	123,562
140	Hideto Shigenobu, Japan	123,079
141	Yoshimi Niizeki, Japan	122,879
142	Dan Halldorson, Canada	120,476
143	Des Smyth, Ireland	119,381
144	George Lanning, U.S.	118,315
145	Hugh Biaocchi, South Africa	116,153
146	Lennie Clements, U.S.	115,975
147	David Feherty, Northern Ireland	115,734
148	Brad Faxon, U.S.	115,452
149	Hiroshi Ishii, Japan	115,400
150	Ove Sellberg, Sweden	114,966
151	Lon Hinkle, U.S.	114,646
152	Ben Smith, U.S.	114,519
153	Hsieh Min Nan, Taiwan	113,730
154	Jim Colbert, U.S.	113,726
155	Hiroshi Makino, Japan	112,990

POS.	PLAYER, COUNTRY	TOTAL MONEY
156	Akiyoshi Omachi, Japan	110,540
157	Chen Tze Ming, Taiwan	109,214
158	Fred Wadsworth, U.S.	109,112
159	Morris Hatalsky, U.S.	108,918
160	Keith Clearwater, U.S.	108,737
161	Eitaro Deguchi, Japan	107,734
162	Bobby Cole, South Africa	107,659
163	Charles Sifford, U.S.	107,145
164	Tsukasa Watanabe, Japan	106,792
165	Butch Baird, U.S.	106,411
166	Walter Zembriski, U.S.	105,970
167	Yoshitaka Yamamoto, Japan	105,112
168	John Bland, South Africa	105,039
169	Jose-Maria Canizares, Spain	104,667
170	Bob Gilder, U.S.	103,669
171	Doug Sanders, U.S.	103,665
172	Brett Upper, U.S.	101,721
173	Bobby Nichols, U.S.	99,126
174	Gil Morgan, U.S.	98,770
175	Bobby Clampett,U.S.	98,088
176	Bob Goalby, U.S.	96,052
177	Namio Takasu, Japan	95,056
178	Peter Senior, Australia	94,815
179	Russ Cochran, U.S.	94,794
180	Buddy Gardner, U.S.	94,640
181	Al Balding, U.S.	94,356
182	Bob Lohr, U.S.	93,846
183	Joe Jimenez, U.S.	93,668
184	Seiji Ebihara, Japan	92,732
185	Charles Bolling, U.S.	92,601
186	George Archer, U.S.	91,575
187	Lu Hsi Chuen, Taiwan	91,532
188	Howie Johnson, U.S.	91,298
189	Leonard Thompson, U.S.	90,695
190	Roberto de Vicenzo, Argentina	90,209
191	Tom Byrum, U.S.	89,739
192	Ikuo Shirahama, Japan	89,384
193	Kinpachi Yoshimura, Japan	88,836
194	Blaine McCallister, U.S.	88,732
195	Larry Rinker, U.S.	88,033
196	Denis Watson, South Africa	87,603
197	Dick Mast, U.S.	87,600
198	Bob Eastwood, U.S.	87,260
199	Katsuji Hasegawa, Japan	87,178
200	Mark James, England	86,733

The Sony Ranking

The Sony Ranking is based on a rolling three-year average. There are four grades of tournaments: Grade 1 (major championships), Grade 2 (leading tournaments and championships), Grade 3 (intermediate tournaments and major invitational events), and Grade 4 (other tournaments and invitational events). Current-year points are multiplied by four; previous-year points, by two; and third-year points, by one, to provide more emphasis on current ability.

POS.	PLAYER, COUNTRY	POINTS	POS.	PLAYER, COUNTRY	POINTS
1	Greg Norman, Australia	1507	46	Gordon J. Brand, England	305
2	Bernhard Langer, W. Germany	1181		Sam Torrance, Scotland	305
3	Seve Ballesteros, Spain	1175	48	Nick Faldo, England	302
4	Tsuneyuki Nakajima, Japan	899	49	Gary Koch, U.S.	301
5	Andy Bean, U.S.	694	50	Roger Maltbie, U.S.	285
6	Bob Tway, U.S.	687	51	Bobby Wadkins, U.S.	283
7	Hal Sutton, U.S.	674	52	Don Pooley, U.S.	282
8	Curtis Strange, U.S.	653	53	David Ishii, U.S.	278
9	Payne Stewart, U.S.	652	54	Nick Price, S. Africa	276
10	Mark O'Meara, U.S.	639	55	Scott Simpson, U.S.	275
11	Isao Aoki, Japan	624	56	Peter Jacobsen, U.S.	270
12	Sandy Lyle, Scotland	619	57	Bruce Lietzke, U.S.	247
13	Calvin Peete, U.S.	614	58	Mac O'Grady, U.S.	244
14	Raymond Floyd, U.S.	612	59	Gordon Brand, Scotland	243
15	Lanny Wadkins, U.S.	600	60	Ken Green, U.S.	242
16	Tom Kite, U.S.	579	61	Tim Simpson, U.S.	238
17	Rodger Davis, Australia	572	62	Donnie Hammond, U.S.	234
18	Tom Watson, U.S.	564		Mark Weibe, U.S.	234
19	Corey Pavin, U.S.	539		D. A. Weibring, U.S.	234
20	Fuzzy Zoeller, U.S.	520	65	Jodie Mudd, U.S.	228
21	Mark McNulty, S. Africa	480	66	Chen Tze-Chung, Taiwan	224
22	Craig Stadler, U.S.	476	67	Wayne Levi, U.S.	217
23	Masashi Ozaki, Japan	475		Toru Nakamura, Japan	217
24	John Mahaffey, U.S.	469		Larry Nelson, U.S.	217
25	Jack Nicklaus, U.S.	464	70	Mike Hulbert, U.S.	216
26	Dan Pohl, U.S.	427	71	Jay Haas, U.S.	212
27	Howard Clark, England	414	72	Denis Watson, S. Africa	207
28	Ian Baker-Finch, Australia	404	73	Fred Couples, U.S.	200
	Masahiro Kuramoto, Japan	404	74	Jose-Maria Canizares, Spain	196
30	Ian Woosnam, Wales	402		Willie Wood, U.S.	196
31	Graham Marsh, Australia	396	76	Dan Forsman, U.S.	190
32	Tateo Ozaki, Japan	373		Jose Rivero, Spain	190
33	Scott Hoch, U.S.	369		Teruo Sugihara, Japan	190
34	Jim Thorpe, U.S.	367	79	Mark James, England	189
35	David Graham, Australia	356		Tony Sills, U.S.	189
36	Larry Mize, U.S.	354	81	Paul Azinger, U.S.	186
37	Naomichi Ozaki, Japan	348	82	Terry Gale, Australia	185
38	Ben Crenshaw, U.S.	347	83	Gil Morgan, U.S.	181
39	David Frost, S. Africa	345	84	Ronan Rafferty, N. Ireland	180
	Lee Trevino, U.S.	345	85	Phil Blackmar, U.S.	178
41	Joey Sindelar, U.S.	336	86	Mark McCumber, U.S.	175
42	Doug Tewell, U.S.	330	87	Kenny Knox, U.S.	174
43	Jose-Maria Olazabal, Spain	326	88	Hugh Baiocchi, S. Africa	173
44	Hubert Green, U.S.	308		John Bland, S. Africa	173
45	Chip Beck, U.S.	307	90	John Cook, U.S.	165

POS.	PLAYER, COUNTRY	POINTS	POS.	PLAYER, COUNTRY	POINTS
91	Clarence Rose, U.S.	164	147	Eamonn Darcy, Ireland	88
92	Greg Turner, New Zealand	163		Davis Love III, U.S.	88
93	Kikuo Arai, Japan	162		Mark Lye, U.S.	88
	Hale Irwin, U.S.	162		Yoshitaka Yamamoto, Japan	88
	Shinsaku Maeda, Japan	162	151	Ian Stanley, Australia	86
96	Anders Forsbrand, Sweden	161	152	Ian Mosey, England	85
97	Des Smyth, Ireland	160	153	Saburo Fujiki, Japan	84
98	Andy North, U.S.	158	154	Curt Byrum, U.S.	82
	Manuel Pinero, Spain	158		Hsieh Min Nan, Taiwan	82
100	Jack Renner, U.S.	155		Mike Donald, U.S.	82
	Peter Senior, Australia	155	157	Yoshihisa Iwashita, Japan	81
102	Brian Jones, Australia	154		Gavin Levenson, S. Africa	81
	Johnny Miller, U.S.	154	159	Ed Fiori, U.S.	80
104	Katsunari Takahashi, Japan	153		Hideto Shigenobu, Japan	80
	Tom Purtzer, U.S.	153		Jeff Sluman, U.S.	80
106	Dave Barr, U.S.	152	162	Seiji Ebihara, Japan	79
107	Danny Edwards, U.S.	150		Brian Marchbank, Scotland	79
108	Mike Reid, U.S.	149	164	Masaji Kusakabe, Japan	76
109	Christy O'Connor, Ireland	147		Leonard Thompson, U.S.	76
	Bob Shearer, Australia	147		Brett Upper, U.S.	76
111	George Burns, U.S.	146	167	Ron Streck, U.S.	75
	Gene Sauers, U.S.	146	168	Vaughan Somers, Australia	73
113	Gary Hallberg, U.S.	144		Howard Twitty, U.S.	73
	Fulton Allem, S. Africa	144	170	Lon Hinkle, U.S.	72
115	Ken Brown, Scotland	142	171	Mike Clayton, Australia	70
116	Bob Murphy, U.S.	136		David Ogrin, U.S.	70
117	Robert Lee, England	134		Philip Parkin, Wales	70
	Koichi Suzuki, Japan	134		Kinpachi Yoshimura, Japan	70
119	Wayne Grady, Australia	131	175	Richard Fehr, U.S.	69
120	David Feherty, N. Ireland	129		Rick Hartmann, U.S.	69
	Seiichi Kanai, Japan	129	177	Hiroshi Makino, Japan	68
	Nobumitsu Yuhara, Japan	129	178	Russ Cochran, U.S.	66
123	Vicente Fernandez, Argentina	128		Koichi Inoue, Japan	66
124	Bob Eastwood, U.S.	127	180	Roger Chapman, England	65
125	Chen Tze Ming, Taiwan	126	181	Bob Lohr, U.S.	64
	David Edwards, U.S.	126		Mark Mouland, Wales	64
127	Scott Verplank, U.S.	122		Magnus Persson, Sweden	64
128	Tony Johnstone, S. Africa	120	184	Lu Hsi Chuen, Taiwan	61
129	Bill Glasson, U.S.	119	185	Mark Pheil, U.S.	60
	Ossie Moore, Australia	119		Lyndsay Stephen, Australia	60
131	Larry Rinker, U.S.	115	187	Antonio Garrido, Spain	58
132	Bobby Cole, S. Africa	112	188	Mark Hayes, U.S.	57
	Peter Fowler, Australia	112		Tim Norris, U.S.	57
	Ove Sellberg, Sweden	112	190	Woody Blackburn, U.S.	56
135	Ronnie Black, U.S.	105		Lennie Clements, U.S.	56
	Pat McGowan, U.S.	105		Ernie Gonzalez, U.S.	56
137	Yasuhiro Funatogawa, Japan	103		Hiroshi Ishii, Japan	56
138	J. C. Snead, U.S.	102	194	Rex Caldwell, U.S.	55
	Paul Way, England	102		Katsuji Hasegawa, Japan	55
140	Bill Kratzert, U.S.	100		Teddy Webber, S. Africa	55
141	Mike Calcavecchia, U.S.	97	197	Stewart Ginn, Australia	54
142	Steve Pate, U.S.	96		Koichi Uehara, Japan	54
143	Buddy Gardner, U.S.	94	199	Ross Drummond, Scotland	53
144	Dan Halldorson, U.S.	93		Mike Harwood, Australia	53
145	George Archer, U.S.	92		Lu Chien Soon, Taiwan	53
	Mike Sullivan, U.S.	92		Mike McLean, England	53
				John Morgan, England	53

World Stroke Average List

The World Stroke Averages which follow were compiled from the results of all tournaments carried in this Appendix for the year 1986 with the exception of the match play and team events, regional and senior tournaments and the LPGA Tour. It includes only those players who competed in at least 60 rounds during the year.

POS.	PLAYER, COUNTRY	STROKES	ROUNDS	AVERAGE
1	Severiano Ballesteros, Spain	5,017	72	69.68
2	Mark McNulty, South Africa	9,622	138	69.72
3	Scott Hoch, U.S.	6,860	98	70.00
4	Greg Norman, Australia	7,841	112	70.01
5	Bernhard Langer, West Germany	8,360	119	70.25
6	Tsuneyuki Nakajima, Japan	7,812	111	70.38
7	Calvin Peete, U.S.	6,421	91	70.56
8	Payne Stewart, U.S.	7,555	107	70.60
9	Andy Bean, U.S.	7,626	108	70.61
10	Bob Tway, U.S.	9,463	134	70.62
11	Jose-Maria Olazabal, Spain	5,939	84	70.70
12	Tom Watson, U.S.	4,880	69	70.72
13	Tom Purtzer, U.S.	7,428	105	70.74
14	Raymond Floyd, U.S.	5,732	81	70.76
15	Gordon J. Brand, England	8,210	116	70.77
T16	Dan Pohl, U.S.	6,299	89	70.78
	Masashi Ozaki, Japan	7,821	110.5	70.78
18	D. A. Weibring, U.S.	6,867	97	70.79
19	Paul Azinger, U.S.	7,647	108	70.80
20	Tony Sills, U.S.	7,582	107	70.85
21	Don Pooley, U.S.	6,874	97	70.86
22	Howard Clark, England	5,812	82	70.87
23	Isao Aoki, Japan	8,116	114.5	70.88
24	Bobby Wadkins, U.S.	8,155	115	70.91
T25	David Frost, South Africa	8,369	118	70.92
	Ian Baker-Finch, Australia	9,327	131.5	70.92
T27	Gary Koch, U.S.	6,530	92	70.97
	Donnie Hammond, U.S.	6,175	87	70.97
29	Hal Sutton, U.S.	7,028	99	70.98
30	John Mahaffey, U.S.	7,526	107	71.00
31	Bruce Lietzke, U.S.	5,613	79	71.05
32	Craig Stadler, U.S.	7,037	99	71.08
33	John Cook, U.S.	6,825	96	71.09
T34	Larry Mize, U.S.	7,253	102	71.10
	Chip Beck, U.S.	7,679	108	71.10
36	Jodie Mudd, U.S.	6,045	85	71.11
37	Curtis Strange, U.S.	7,681	108	71.12
38	Tom Kite, U.S.	7,541	106	71.14
39	Sandy Lyle, Scotland	7,756	109	71.15
40	Lanny Wadkins, U.S.	6,903	97	71.16
T41	Corey Pavin, U.S.	7,546	106	71.19
	Chen Tze Chung, Taiwan	8,472	119	71.19
	Rodger Davis, Australia	8,970	126	71.19
	Mark O'Meara, U.S.	7,689	108	71.19
T45	Fuzzy Zoeller, U.S.	5,270	74	71.21
	David Ishii, U.S.	6,338	89	71.21
47	Masahiro Kuramoto, Japan	8,156	114.5	71.23

POS.	PLAYER, COUNTRY	STROKES	ROUNDS	AVERAGE
T48	Jeff Sluman, U.S.	7,767	109	71.26
	Joey Sindelar, U.S.	8,765	123	71.26
50	Naomichi Ozaki, Japan	8,160	114.5	71.27

World's Winners of 1986

U.S. TOUR

Bahamas	Hale Irwin
MONY Tournament of Champions	Calvin Peete
Bob Hope Chrysler Classic	Donnie Hammond
Phoenix Open	Hal Sutton
AT&T Pebble Beach National Pro-Am	Fuzzy Zoeller
Shearson Lehman Brothers Andy Williams Open	Bob Tway
Hawaiian Open	Corey Pavin
Los Angeles Open	Doug Tewell
Honda Classic	Kenny Knox
Doral Eastern Open	Andy Bean
Hertz Bay Hill Classic	Dan Forsman
USF&G Classic	Calvin Peete
Tournament Players Championship	John Mahaffey
Greater Greensboro Open	Sandy Lyle
Masters	Jack Nicklaus
Deposit Guaranty Classic	Dan Halldorson
Sea Pines Heritage Classic	Fuzzy Zoeller
Houston Open	Curtis Strange
Panasonic Las Vegas Invitational	Greg Norman
Byron Nelson Classic	Andy Bean
Colonial National Invitation	Dan Pohl
Memorial Tournament	Hal Sutton
Kemper Open	Greg Norman
Manufacturers Hanover Westchester Classic	Bob Tway
U.S. Open Championship	Ray Floyd
Provident Classic	Brad Faxon
Georgia-Pacific Atlanta Classic	Bob Tway
Canadian Open	Bob Murphy
Canon Sammy Davis Jr-Greater Hartford Open	Mac O'Grady
Anheuser-Busch Classic	Fuzzy Zoeller
Hardee's Classic	Mark Wiebe
Buick Open	Ben Crenshaw
Western Open	Tom Kite
PGA Championship	Bob Tway
International	Ken Green
NEC World Series of Golf	Dan Pohl
Federal Express St. Jude Classic	Mike Hulbert
B. C. Open	Rick Fehr
Bank of Boston Classic	Gene Sauers
Greater Milwaukee Open	Corey Pavin
Southwest Classic	Mark Calcavecchia
Southern Open	Fred Wadsworth
Pensacola Open	Ernie Gonzalez
Walt Disney World/Oldsmobile Classic	Ray Floyd
Vantage Championship	Ben Crenshaw

Seiko-Tucson Match Play Championship	Jim Thorpe
Tallahassee Open	Mark Hayes
Isuzu Kapalua International	Andy Bean
Chrysler Team Championship	Gary Hallberg
	Scott Hoch

EUROPEAN TOUR

Suze (Cannes) Open	John Bland
Cepsa Madrid Open	Howard Clark
Italian Open	David Feherty
Epson Grand Prix of Europe	Ove Sellberg
Peugeot Spanish Open	Howard Clark
Whyte & Mackay PGA Championship	Rodger Davis
London Standard Four Stars Pro-Celebrity	Antonio Garrido
Dunhill British Masters	Severiano Ballesteros
Jersey Open	John Morgan
Carrolls Irish Open	Severiano Ballesteros
Johnnie Walker Monte Carlo Open	Severiano Ballesteros
Peugeot French Open	Severiano Ballesteros
Car Care Plan International	Mark Mouland
British Open Championship	Greg Norman
KLM Dutch Open	Severiano Ballesteros
Scandanavian Enterprise Open	Greg Turner
PLM Open	Peter Senior
Benson and Hedges International Open	Mark James
Bell's Scottish Open	David Feherty
German Open	Bernhard Langer
Ebel European Masters—Swiss Open	Jose-Maria Olazabal
Panasonic European Open	Greg Norman
Lawrence Batley Tournament Players' Championship	Ian Woosnam
Dunhill Cup	Australia
Suntory World Match Play Championship	Greg Norman
Sanyo Open	Jose-Maria Olazabal
Lancome Trophy	Tie—Severiano Ballesteros
	Bernhard Langer
Quinto do Lago Portuguese Open	Mark McNulty

AFRICAN TOURS

ICL International	Gavin Levenson
Lexington PGA Championship	Bobby Cole
Wild Coast Classic	Mark McNulty
Southern Suns South African Open	David Frost
AECI Charity Classic	Fulton Allem
Barclays Bank Classic	Mark McNulty
Palabora Classic	Fulton Allem
Swazi Sun Pro-Am	Mark McNulty
Trust Bank Tournament of Champions	Mark McNulty
Nigerian Open	Gordon J. Brand
Ivory Coast Open	Gordon J. Brand
Kenya Open	Ian Woosnam
Zambian Open	Garry Cullen
Zimbabwe Open	Stephen Bennett
Sun City Challenge	Mark McNulty
Helix Wild Coast Classic (Nov.)	Mark McNulty
Germiston Centenary	Mark McNulty
Safmarine South African Masters	Mark McNulty
Goodyear Classic	Tony Johnstone

AUSTRALASIA TOUR

Nissan-Mobil New Zealand PGA Championship	Frank Nobilo
Foster's Tasmanian Open	Stewart Ginn
Robert Boyd Transport Victorian Open	Ossie Moore
Robert Boyd Transport Match Play Championship	Peter Fowler
Australian Masters	Mark O'Meara
Rich River Classic	Bob Shearer
Halls Head Estates-Nissan Nedlands Masters	Lyndsay Stephen
Fourex Queensland PGA	Ossie Moore
Stefan Queensland Open	Greg Norman
National Panasonic New South Wales Open	Greg Norman
West End Jubilee South Australian Open	Greg Norman
Toshiba Australian PGA Championship	Mike Harwood
Victorian PGA	Wayne Smith
National Panasonic Australian Open	Rodger Davis
National Panasonic Western Australian Open	Greg Norman
Air New Zealand-Shell Open	Rodger Davis
Nissan-Mobil New Zealand Open	Rodger Davis

ASIA/JAPAN TOURS

Cathay Pacific Hong Kong Open	Seiichi Kanai
Benson and Hedges Malaysian Open	Stewart Ginn
Singapore Open	Greg Turner
Indonesian Open	Frankie Minoza
Thailand Open	Ho Ming Chung
Charminar Challenge Indian Open	Lu Hsi Chuen
Republic of China Open	Lu Hsi Chuen
Korean Open	Tsao Chin Teng
Dunlop International	Hideto Shigenobu
Shizuoka Open	Akiyoshi Omachi
Pocari Sweat Open	Hajime Meshiai
Bridgestone Aso Open	Brian Jones
Chunichi Crowns International	David Ishii
Fuji Sankei Classic	Masashi Ozaki
Japan Match Play Championship	Tsuneyuki Nakajima
Pepsi Ube	Naomichi Ozaki
Mitsubishi Galant	Tsuneyuki Nakajima
Tohoku Classic	Teruo Sugihara
Sapporo Tokyu Open	Isao Aoki
Yomiuri Sapporo Beer Open	Koichi Suzuki
Mizuno Open	Tsuneyuki Nakajima
Kansai PGA Championship	Teruo Sugihara
Kanto PGA Championship	Tsuneyuki Nakajima
Japan PGA Championship	Isao Aoki
Niigata Open	David Ishii
Acom Doubles	Hajime Meshiai
	Satoshi Higashi
Nikkei Cup/Torakichi Nakamura Memorial	Masashi Ozaki
Maruman Nihonkai Open	Masashi Ozaki
KBC Augusta	Isao Aoki
Kanto Open	Isao Aoki
Kansai Open	Yoshiyuki Isomura
Hokkaido Open	Katsunari Takahashi
Chu-Shikoku Open	Tadami Ueno

Kyushu Open	Kinpachi Yoshimura
Chubu Open	Eitaro Deguchi
Suntory International Open	Graham Marsh
ANA Sapporo Open	Masahiro Kuramoto
Jun Classic	Masashi Ozaki
Tokai Classic	Masahiro Kuramoto
Japan Open Championship	Tsuneyuki Nakajima
Polaroid Cup Golf Digest	Tsuneyuki Nakajima
Bridgestone	Tateo Ozaki
ABC U.S. vs Japan Team Matches	Team—United States
	Individual—Curtis Strange
Wakayama Open	Toshimitsu Kai
Nissan Cup	Team—Japan
	Individual—Tsuneyuki Nakajima
Hiroshima Open	Toru Nakamura
Taiheiyo Club (Pacific) Masters	Yasuhiro Funatogawa
Dunlop Phoenix	Bobby Wadkins
Casio World Open	Scott Hoch
Japan Series	Toru Nakamura
Daikyo Open	Tateo Ozaki

SENIOR TOUR (*Non-tour event)

MONY Senior Tournament of Champions	Miller Barber
Treasure Coast Classic	Charles Owens
General Foods PGA Seniors Championship	Gary Player
Senior PGA Roundup	Charles Owens
Vintage Invitational	Dale Douglass
Johnny Mathis Classic	Dale Douglass
*Doug Sanders Celebrity Classic	Bruce Crampton
Liberty Mutual Legends of Golf	Don January
	Gene Littler
Sunwest Bank/Charley Pride Classic	Gene Littler
Benson & Hedges Invitational at Dominion	Bruce Crampton
United Hospitals Senior Championship	Gary Player
*Coca Cola Grand Slam Championship	Lee Elder
Denver Post Champions of Golf	Gary Player
Senior Players Reunion Pro-Am	Don January
Senior Tournament Players Championship	Chi Chi Rodriguez
USGA Senior Open	Dale Douglass
Greenbrier American Express Championship	Don January
Grand Rapids Classic	Jim Ferree
MONY Syracuse Classic	Bruce Crampton
The Commemorative	Lee Elder
Digital Classic	Chi Chi Rodriguez
GTE Northwest Classic	Bruce Crampton
Showdown Classic	Bobby Nichols
	Curt Byrum
Bank One Senior Classic	Gene Littler
Chrysler Cup	United States
United Virginia Bank	Chi Chi Rodriguez
PaineWebber World Seniors Invitational	Bruce Crampton
*Unionmutual Classic	Arnold Palmer
Fairfield Barnett Classic	Dale Douglass
Cuyahoga International	Butch Baird
Pepsi Challenge	Bruce Crampton
Seiko-Tucson Senior Match Play	Don January
Las Vegas Classic	Bruce Crampton

Shearson-Lehman Brothers Classic	Bruce Crampton
Mazda Champions	Bob Charles
	Amy Alcott

LPGA TOUR

Mazda Classic	Val Skinner
Elizabeth Arden Classic	Ayako Okamoto
Sarasota Classic	Patty Sheehan
Standard Register/Samaritan Turquoise Classic	Mary Beth Zimmerman
Uniden Invitational	Mary Beth Zimmerman
Women's Kemper Open	Juli Inkster
GNA/Glendale Federal Classic	Chris Johnson
Circle K Tucson Open	Penny Pulz
Nabisco Dinah Shore	Pat Bradley
Kyocera Inamori Classic	Patty Sheehan
S&H Classic	Pat Bradley
United Virginia Bank Classic	Muffin Spencer-Devlin
Chrysler-Plymouth Classic	Becky Pearson
Corning Classic	Laurie Rinker
LPGA Championship	Pat Bradley
McDonald's Championship	Juli Inkster
Lady Keystone Open	Juli Inkster
Rochester International	Judy Dickinson
Mayflower Classic	Sandra Palmer
Mazda Hall of Fame Championship	Amy Alcott
U.S. Women's Open	Jane Geddes
Boston Five Classic	Jane Geddes
Du Maurier Classic	Pat Bradley
LPGA National Pro-Am	Amy Alcott
Henredon Classic	Betsy King
Mastercard International Pro-Am	Cindy Mackey
Nestle World Championship	Pat Bradley
Atlantic City Classic	Juli Inkster
Rail Charity Classic	Betsy King
Cellular One Ping Championship	Ayako Okamoto
Safeco Classic	Judy Dickinson
Konica San Jose Classic	Patty Sheehan
Mazda Japan Classic	Ai Yu Tu
JC Penney Classic	Juli Inkster
	Tom Purtzer

Multiple Winners of 1986

PLAYER	WINS	PLAYER	WINS
Mark McNulty	9	Masashi Ozaki	4
Greg Norman	9	Bob Tway	4
Bruce Crampton	8	Amy Alcott	3
Tsuneyuki Nakajima	7	Andy Bean	3
Severiano Ballesteros	6	Gene Littler	3
Pat Bradley	5	Gary Player	3
Juli Inkster	5	Chi Chi Rodriguez	3
Isao Aoki	4	Patty Sheehan	3
Rodger Davis	4	Fuzzy Zoeller	3
Dale Douglass	4	Fulton Allem	2
Don January	4	Gordon J. Brand	2

PLAYER	WINS	PLAYER	WINS
Howard Clark	2	Ossie Moore	2
Ben Crenshaw	2	Toru Nakamura	2
Judy Dickinson	2	Ayako Okamoto	2
Lee Elder	2	Jose-Maria Olazabal	2
David Feherty	2	Charles Owens	2
Raymond Floyd	2	Tateo Ozaki	2
Jane Geddes	2	Corey Pavin	2
Stewart Ginn	2	Calvin Peete	2
Scott Hoch	2	Dan Pohl	2
David Ishii	2	Curtis Strange	2
Betsy King	2	Teruo Sugihara	2
Masahiro Kuramoto	2	Hal Sutton	2
Bernhard Langer	2	Greg Turner	2
Lu Hsi Chuen	2	Ian Woosnam	2
Hajime Meshiai	2	Mary Beth Zimmerman	2

(NOTE: These totals include victories in two-player team events.)

Career World Money List

The following is a listing of the 50 leading money-winners for their careers through the 1986 season. It includes active and inactive players. The World Money List from this and the 20 previous editions of this annual and a table prepared for a companion book, THE WONDERFUL WORLD OF PROFESSIONAL GOLF (Atheneum, 1973), form the basis for this compilation. Additional figures were taken from official records of major golf associations, although the shortcomings in records-keeping in professional golf outside the United States in the 1950s and 1960s and exclusions from U.S. records in a few cases during those years prevent these figures from being completely accurate and complete. Conversions of foreign currency figures to U.S. dollars are based on average values during the particular year involved.

POS.	PLAYER, COUNTRY	TOTAL MONEY
1	Jack Nicklaus, U.S.	$5,938,309
2	Tom Watson, U.S.	4,910,633
3	Lee Trevino, U.S.	4,621,409
4	Raymond Floyd, U.S.	4,331,858
5	Severiano Ballesteros, Spain	4,116,122
6	Isao Aoki, Japan	3,866,730
7	Lanny Wadkins, U.S.	3,661,095
8	Gary Player, South Africa	3,627,250
9	Miller Barber, U.S.	3,482,485
10	Tom Kite, U.S.	3,474,424
11	Johnny Miller, U.S.	3,441,551
12	Hale Irwin, U.S.	3,391,190
13	Greg Norman, Australia	3,363,017
14	Don January, U.S.	3,341,451
15	Billy Casper, U.S.	3,293,026
16	Gene Littler, U.S.	3,268,645
17	Arnold Palmer, U.S.	3,219,689

POS.	PLAYER, COUNTRY	TOTAL MONEY
18	David Graham, Australia	3,159,418
19	Andy Bean, U.S.	2,981,201
20	Ben Crenshaw, U.S.	2,943,292
21	Tsuneyuki Nakajima, Japan	2,846,007
22	Curtis Strange, U.S.	2,837,219
23	Graham Marsh, Australia	2,779,742
24	Bernhard Langer, West Germany	2,752,394
25	Craig Stadler, U.S.	2,710,868
26	Hubert Green, U.S.	2,688,181
27	Tom Weiskopf, U.S.	2,630,667
28	John Mahaffey, U.S.	2,514,718
29	Fuzzy Zoeller, U.S.	2,333,014
30	Bruce Lietzke, U.S.	2,318,225
31	Calvin Peete, U.S.	2,286,646
32	Lee Elder, U.S.	2,176,958
33	Masashi Ozaki, Japan	2,174,709
34	Gil Morgan, U.S.	2,084,639
35	Larry Nelson, U.S.	2,059,311
36	Bruce Crampton, Australia	2,047,039
37	George Archer, U.S.	2,008,561
38	Bob Charles, New Zealand	1,928,951
39	Jerry Pate, U.S.	1,917,253
40	Sandy Lyle, Scotland	1,897,069
41	Gay Brewer, U.S.	1,894,850
42	Hal Sutton, U.S.	1,884,034
43	Bill Rogers, U.S.	1,863,134
44	Mark O'Meara, U.S.	1,844,609
45	Nick Faldo, England	1,843,271
46	J. C. Snead, U.S.	1,795,610
47	Jim Colbert, U.S.	1,737,084
48	Bob Murphy, U.S.	1,698,712
49	Chi Chi Rodriguez, U.S.	1,673,327
50	Toru Nakamura, Japan	1,664,432

LPGA Money List

POS.	PLAYER	MONEY
1	Pat Bradley	$503,021
2	Amy Alcott	496,710
3	Juli Inkster	358,951
4	Betsy King	302,195
5	Jane Geddes	232,645
6	Mary Beth Zimmerman	227,572
7	Patty Sheehan	223,031
8	Chris Johnson	215,448
9	Ayako Okamoto	212,862
10	Judy Dickinson	207,359
11	Val Skinner	204,493
12	Jan Stephenson	187,648
13	Becky Pearson	169,499
14	Sandra Palmer	151,547
15	Debbie Massey	133,495
16	Hollis Stacy	118,286
17	Laurie Rinker	114,881

POS.	PLAYER	MONEY
18	Muffin Spencer-Devlin	111,034
19	Cathy Kratzert	110,763
20	Jody Rosenthal	108,278
21	Beth Daniel	104,332
22	Debra A. Richard	98,451
23	Alice Ritzman	91,443
24	Lauren Howe	91,326
25	Nancy Lopez	89,350
26	Patti Rizzo	88,936
27	Cathy Morse	86,781
28	JoAnne Carner	82,802
29	Colleen Walker	82,064
30	Jane Crafter	81,051
31	Ku Ok Hee	79,327
32	Penny Pulz	79,272
33	Sally Little	78,172
34	Amy Benz	74,432
35	Rosie Jones	73,154
36	Lori Garbacz	72,160
37	Marta Figueras-Dotti	69,971
38	Janet Coles	65,516
39	Cindy Hill	65,245
40	Bonnie Lauer	64,917
41	Penny Hammel	64,160
42	Sherri Turner	61,148
43	Kathy Postlewait	59,445
44	Cindy Mackey	58,201
45	Myra Blackwelder	57,948
46	Kathy Whitworth	56,394
47	Dale Eggeling	54,709
48	Robin Walton	54,404
49	Dawn Coe	54,332
50	Lisa Young	53,411

Above list includes LPGA official money, J. C. Penney, Mazda Champions and Spalding events.

The U. S. Tour

Bahamas Classic

Paradise Island Golf & Country Club, Nassau   January 2–5
Par 36–36 – 72; 6,976 yards   purse, $300,000

	SCORES				TOTAL	MONEY
Hale Irwin	70	68	64	67	269	$72,000
Donnie Hammond	69	67	73	66	275	42,000
Davis Love	65	68	73	70	276	24,000
Scott Hoch	67	68	67	75	277	16,000
Jeff Sluman	69	68	69	72	278	13,000
Jodie Mudd	72	71	69	67	279	10,375
Bob Tway	67	66	72	74	279	10,375
Mike Donald	70	71	68	71	280	8,125

	SCORES				TOTAL	MONEY
Ed Fiori	67	69	68	76	280	8,125
Mark Hayes	69	69	72	71	281	6,533.34
Jeff Lewis	68	71	70	72	281	6,533.33
Bob Lohr	64	69	74	74	281	6,533.33
Ron Streck	70	73	70	69	282	5,500
Jay Haas	74	67	74	68	283	4,500
Mike Smith	71	71	72	69	283	4,500
Doug Tewell	69	70	74	70	283	4,500
Bill Glasson	72	68	70	73	283	4,500
Mark McCumber	66	71	70	76	283	4,500
Ronan Rafferty	71	71	73	69	284	3,375
Jim Thorpe	68	70	76	70	284	3,375
Morris Hatalsky	73	69	72	70	284	3,375
Bill Kratzert	73	70	69	72	284	3,375
Clarence Rose	70	72	74	69	285	2,700
Howard Twitty	73	71	70	71	285	2,700
Greg Maycock	73	72	74	67	286	2,200
Tommy Valentine	72	68	74	72	286	2,200
Mac O'Grady	71	73	71	71	286	2,200
J. C. Snead	71	74	71	71	287	1,800
Woody Blackburn	71	70	75	72	288	1,550
Paul Azinger	70	73	73	72	288	1,550
Willie Wood	68	69	74	78	289	1,400
Brett Upper	71	70	69	74	290	1,350
Brad Fabel	71	74	73	73	291	1,300
Jimmy Delancey	74	72	75	71	292	1,225
Brad Faxon	72	69	75	76	292	1,225
Joe Inman	72	76	71	74	293	1,162.50
Frank Conner	72	72	76	73	293	1,162.50
Rex Caldwell	77	74	73	71	295	1,087.50
Steve Pate	72	72	74	77	295	1,087.50
Ben Crenshaw	74	69	75	77	295	1,087.50
Anders Forsbrand	72	74	72	77	295	1,087.50
Vance Heafner	75	74	74	74	297	1,025
David Ogrin	81	72	75	76	304	1,000

MONY Tournament of Champions

La Costa Country Club, Carlsbad, California

Par 36–36 – 72; 6,911 yards

January 8–11

purse, $500,000

	SCORES				TOTAL	MONEY
Calvin Peete	68	67	64	68	267	$90,000
Mark O'Meara	70	65	67	71	273	57,000
Philip Blackmar	74	68	66	69	277	37,000
Danny Edwards	70	69	69	71	279	25,000
Bernhard Langer	69	69	71	70	279	25,000
*Scott Verplank	72	67	68	72	279	
Hal Sutton	71	77	66	67	281	19,166.67
Jim Thorpe	70	68	71	72	281	19,166.67
Tim Simpson	72	73	66	70	281	19,166.66
Tom Kite	69	66	73	75	283	16,500
Hale Irwin	72	71	69	72	284	15,000
Mark McCumber	68	73	70	73	284	15,000
Sandy Lyle	70	72	71	72	285	13,000
Roger Maltbie	74	71	69	71	285	13,000

	SCORES				TOTAL	MONEY
George Burns	71	71	73	71	286	10,666.67
Lanny Wadkins	73	73	67	73	286	10,666.67
Bill Glasson	74	70	70	72	286	10,666.66
Dan Forsman	72	69	76	70	287	9,000
Andy North	70	70	73	74	287	9,000
Corey Pavin	71	75	74	67	287	9,000
Ray Floyd	73	72	72	71	288	7,800
Ken Green	76	70	68	74	288	7,800
John Mahaffey	73	75	68	72	288	7,800
Curtis Strange	70	75	71	75	291	7,400
Wayne Levi	70	72	73	77	292	7,200
Fuzzy Zoeller	71	74	69	79	293	7,000
Joey Sindelar	74	70	75	75	294	6,800
Mark Wiebe	72	75	74	75	296	6,600
Bob Eastwood	75	73	70	79	297	6,400
Woody Blackburn	78	74	74	78	304	6,200
Hubert Green	75	73	80	78	306	6,000

Bob Hope Chrysler Classic

Bermuda Dunes Country Club, Bermuda Dunes, California   January 15–19
Par 36–36 – 72; 6,837 yards   purse, $600,000

Indian Wells Country Club, Indian Wells, California
Par 36–36 – 72; 6,478 yards

La Quinta Country Club, La Quinta, California
Par 36–36 – 72; 6,911 yards

El Dorado Country Club, Palm Desert, California
Par 36–36 – 72; 6,708 yards

	SCORES					TOTAL	MONEY
Donnie Hammond	69	64	68	68	66	335	$108,000
John Cook	68	67	65	69	66	335	64,800
(Hammond defeated Cook on first hole of sudden-death playoff)							
Jodie Mudd	72	65	63	68	69	337	40,800
Hal Sutton	65	70	69	65	69	338	28,800
Craig Stadler	67	65	69	70	68	339	21,900
Payne Stewart	72	67	71	64	65	339	21,900
Gary Koch	67	68	68	68	68	339	21,900
David Graham	69	73	63	67	68	340	18,600
Lennie Clements	71	68	72	64	66	341	16,800
Ray Floyd	68	70	65	73	65	341	16,800
Bernhard Langer	70	70	66	68	68	342	13,800
Wayne Levi	69	69	69	68	67	342	13,800
John Mahaffey	69	70	69	67	67	342	13,800
Jack Renner	68	68	72	69	66	343	10,500
Jeff Sluman	66	74	64	69	70	343	10,500
Paul Azinger	66	71	68	68	70	343	10,500
Mark McCumber	69	68	67	68	71	343	10,500
Steve Pate	67	69	69	68	71	344	8,100
Jim Colbert	71	67	70	68	68	344	8,100
Sandy Lyle	71	67	67	70	69	344	8,100
Bob Murphy	70	70	69	68	67	344	8,100
Don Pooley	74	70	64	67	70	345	5,133.34
Mike Reid	70	69	70	67	69	345	5,133.34

		SCORES				TOTAL	MONEY
Bill Kratzert	68	69	74	67	67	345	5,133.34
Curtis Strange	69	71	70	68	67	345	5,133.33
Jim Thorpe	67	69	70	67	72	345	5,133.33
Clarence Rose	69	69	69	71	67	345	5,133.33
Chip Beck	71	68	67	67	72	345	5,133.33
Johnny Miller	70	71	70	66	68	345	5,133.33
Ken Green	71	69	68	69	68	345	5,133.33
Scott Simpson	71	70	70	68	67	346	3,480
Tim Simpson	69	73	70	65	69	346	3,480
Richard Zokol	71	77	64	69	65	346	3,480
Mac O'Grady	71	65	67	74	69	346	3,480
Larry Mize	66	66	71	71	72	346	3,480
Peter Jacobsen	72	68	71	66	69	346	3,480
Tom Purtzer	71	70	69	68	69	347	2,760
Joey Sindelar	69	71	69	69	69	347	2,760
Philip Blackmar	68	71	70	68	70	347	2,760
Pat Lindsey	73	68	69	71	66	347	2,760
Howard Twitty	68	75	67	71	67	348	2,280
Jeff Grygiel	70	69	70	71	68	348	2,280
Jay Haas	70	72	67	71	68	348	2,280
Tom Kite	74	69	65	71	69	348	2,280
Robert Wrenn	68	70	72	68	71	349	1,651.50
Lanny Wadkins	68	71	71	71	68	349	1,651.50
Gary McCord	68	71	69	68	73	349	1,651.50
Fred Couples	69	67	72	69	72	349	1,651.50
Jay Delsing	68	68	70	74	69	349	1,651.50
Dan Halldorson	71	71	70	66	71	349	1,651.50
Scott Hoch	69	73	70	66	71	349	1,651.50
Brian Mogg	69	71	68	72	69	349	1,651.50

Phoenix Open

Phoenix Country Club, Phoenix, Arizona
Par 36–35 – 71; 6,726 yards

January 23–26
purse, $500,000

		SCORES			TOTAL	MONEY
Hal Sutton	64	64	68	71	267	$90,000
Tony Sills	68	68	65	68	269	44,000
Calvin Peete	64	69	68	68	269	44,000
Dan Forsman	70	68	66	66	270	24,000
Don Pooley	74	61	67	69	271	19,000
Greg Norman	64	71	66	70	271	19,000
Larry Mize	64	71	68	70	273	14,041.67
Joey Sindelar	69	64	69	71	273	14,041.67
John Mahaffey	67	65	70	71	273	14,041.67
Andy Bean	66	69	68	70	273	14,041.67
Ronnie Black	66	66	69	72	273	14,041.66
Bernhard Langer	69	68	67	69	273	14,041.66
Doug Tewell	72	66	68	68	274	10,000
Bill Glasson	73	66	65	70	274	10,000
Curtis Strange	69	67	65	74	275	7,500
Scott Simpson	69	68	69	69	275	7,500
John Cook	69	70	65	71	275	7,500
Bill Kratzert	68	69	67	71	275	7,500
Bob Gilder	68	69	65	73	275	7,500
Lon Hinkle	68	67	70	70	275	7,500
Barry Jaeckel	65	70	68	72	275	7,500

	SCORES				TOTAL	MONEY
Johnny Miller	70	66	68	72	276	5,000
Mike Reid	73	68	66	69	276	5,000
Jeff Sluman	65	68	73	70	276	5,000
Howard Twitty	67	63	70	76	276	5,000
Mark Wiebe	68	64	72	73	277	3,700
Tom Sieckmann	66	68	74	69	277	3,700
Bob Tway	67	71	70	69	277	3,700
Donnie Hammond	70	68	67	72	277	3,700
Sandy Lyle	66	69	71	71	277	3,700
Tim Simpson	68	69	70	71	278	3,031.50
Dan Pohl	68	69	71	70	278	3,031.50
Chen Tze Ming	69	69	70	70	278	3,031.50
Scott Hoch	69	69	68	72	278	3,031.50
Steve Pate	75	66	70	68	279	2,258.23
Paul Azinger	67	70	67	75	279	2,258.23
Larry Nelson	71	70	68	70	279	2,258.22
Clarence Rose	71	70	67	71	279	2,258.22
David Peoples	68	72	71	68	279	2,258.22
Corey Pavin	70	69	70	70	279	2,258.22
Lee Trevino	70	69	71	69	279	2,258.22
Jeff Grygiel	66	70	68	75	279	2,258.22
Peter Jacobsen	70	66	70	73	279	2,258.22
Billy Pierot	72	66	68	74	280	1,445
Jerry Pate	69	72	70	69	280	1,445
Miller Barber	72	69	70	69	280	1,445
Ken Brown	72	68	70	70	280	1,445
Chen Tze Chung	66	66	73	75	280	1,445
Jim Gallagher	70	70	71	69	280	1,445
David Lundstrom	72	67	67	74	280	1,445
Mike McCullough	66	70	68	76	280	1,445

AT&T Pebble Beach National Pro-Am

Pebble Beach, California

January 30–February 2
purse, $600,000

Pebble Beach Golf Links
Par 36–36 – 72; 6,799 yards

Cypress Point Golf Club
Par 36–36 – 72; 6,506 yards

(Second round rained out)

Spyglass Hill Golf Club
Par 36–36 –72; 6,810 yards

	SCORES			TOTAL	MONEY
Fuzzy Zoeller	69	66	70	205	$108,000
Payne Stewart	71	69	70	210	64,800
Mark Wiebe	70	69	72	211	31,200
Tom Watson	71	67	73	211	31,200
Tony Sills	72	68	71	211	31,200
Dan Pohl	71	70	72	213	19,425
Mark Pfeil	73	67	73	213	19,425
Ken Brown	74	73	66	213	19,425
Bob Eastwood	70	70	73	213	19,425

	SCORES			TOTAL	MONEY
Chi Chi Rodriguez	72	72	70	214	15,000
Jim Thorpe	72	68	74	214	15,000
Andy Bean	75	71	68	214	15,000
Lanny Wadkins	71	71	73	215	11,250
John McComish	69	72	74	215	11,250
Bernhard Langer	78	69	68	215	11,250
David Edwards	73	68	74	215	11,250
Blaine McCallister	72	76	68	216	7,080
Mark O'Meara	74	69	73	216	7,080
Johnny Miller	77	69	70	216	7,080
John Mahaffey	77	70	69	216	7,080
Bobby Wadkins	77	71	68	216	7,080
Craig Stadler	72	73	71	216	7,080
Kikuo Arai	68	73	75	216	7,080
George Archer	82	66	68	216	7,080
Rex Caldwell	73	70	73	216	7,080
Jay Delsing	73	70	73	216	7,080
Tom Kite	76	69	72	217	3,993.75
Bob Tway	75	73	69	217	3,993.75
Hal Sutton	73	73	71	217	3,993.75
Steve Pate	76	69	72	217	3,993.75
Mark Lye	74	72	71	217	3,993.75
Scott Hoch	71	72	74	217	3,993.75
Bob Gilder	74	71	72	217	3,993.75
David Graham	71	71	75	217	3,993.75
Corey Pavin	76	68	74	218	2,649
Sandy Lyle	76	73	69	218	2,649
Willie Wood	68	74	76	218	2,649
Jeff Sluman	76	72	70	218	2,649
Larry Mize	75	68	75	218	2,649
Richard Zokol	76	69	73	218	2,649
Lennie Clements	73	73	72	218	2,649
Ben Crenshaw	76	74	68	218	2,649
Mark Hayes	73	71	74	218	2,649
Mike Gove	76	71	71	218	2,649
Lee Trevino	77	72	70	219	1,716
Tim Simpson	73	69	77	219	1,716
Jeff Lewis	72	73	74	219	1,716
Frank Conner	78	70	71	219	1,716
Peter Jacobsen	69	71	79	219	1,716
Dan Forsman	74	75	70	219	1,716

Shearson Lehman Brothers Andy Williams Open

Torrey Pines Golf Club, La Jolla, California

February 6–9
purse, $450,000

North Course: Par 36–36 – 72; 6,667 yards
(First two rounds only)
South Course: Par 36–36 – 72; 7,002 yards
(All four rounds)

(Third round rained out.)

	SCORES			TOTAL	MONEY
Bob Tway	67	68	69	204	$81,000
Bernhard Langer	70	66	68	204	48,600

(Tway defeated Langer on second hole of sudden-death playoff)

	SCORES			TOTAL	MONEY
Mike Hulbert	69	69	67	205	23,400
Mark Lye	70	66	69	205	23,400
Paul Azinger	67	69	69	205	23,400
Gary Koch	70	69	67	206	15,075
Larry Rinker	66	72	68	206	15,075
Gary Hallberg	70	69	67	206	15,075
Don Pooley	68	70	69	207	12,600
Danny Edwards	66	69	72	207	12,600
D. A. Weibring	69	68	71	208	8,935.72
Tom Watson	69	69	70	208	8,935.72
Richard Fehr	67	69	72	208	8,935.72
Bill Israelson	70	67	71	208	8,935.71
Mark Wiebe	66	70	72	208	8,935.71
Joey Sindelar	70	68	70	208	8,935.71
John Adams	69	68	71	208	8,935.71
Bruce Lietzke	70	70	69	209	5,670
Steve Pate	70	69	70	209	5,670
Larry Mize	66	68	75	209	5,670
Tony Sills	70	66	73	209	5,670
Bill Sander	71	68	70	209	5,670
Jim Colbert	69	70	70	209	5,670
Robert Wrenn	66	73	71	210	3,836.25
Bobby Wadkins	71	71	68	210	3,836.25
Davis Love	71	71	68	210	3,836.25
John Cook	70	66	74	210	3,836.25
Mac O'Grady	74	68	69	211	2,578.85
Andy Bean	71	71	69	211	2,578.85
Chip Beck	71	71	69	211	2,578.85
Woody Blackburn	66	74	71	211	2,578.85
Chen Tze Chung	71	70	70	211	2,578.85
Lennie Clements	71	70	70	211	2,578.85
Barry Jaeckel	70	71	70	211	2,578.85
Bob Eastwood	70	66	75	211	2,578.85
Johnny Miller	73	70	68	211	2,578.84
Doug Tewell	70	72	69	211	2,578.84
Brian Mogg	67	69	75	211	2,578.84
J. C. Snead	73	68	70	211	2,578.84
Ray Floyd	71	69	71	211	2,578.84
Howard Twitty	71	72	69	212	1,492
Payne Stewart	73	70	69	212	1,492
Pat McGowan	68	70	74	212	1,492
Tom Pernice	72	68	72	212	1,492
Curtis Strange	71	71	70	212	1,492
Dan Pohl	70	72	70	212	1,492
Mark Hayes	69	71	72	212	1,492
Tom Kite	71	70	71	212	1,492
Tom Byrum	71	69	72	212	1,492
Tom Purtzer	68	71	74	213	1,040.25
Gary McCord	76	67	70	213	1,040.25
David Peoples	69	69	75	213	1,040.25
Mike West	70	71	72	213	1,040.25
Mark O'Meara	72	70	71	213	1,040.25
Eduardo Romero	72	69	72	213	1,040.25
Scott Simpson	71	71	71	213	1,040.25
Leonard Thompson	68	74	71	213	1,040.25
Andy Dillard	67	71	75	213	1,040.25
Keith Fergus	69	72	72	213	1,040.25
Bill Glasson	67	70	76	213	1,040.25
Lou Graham	71	71	71	213	1,040.25
*Pat Duncan	72	69	72	213	

Hawaiian Open

Waialae Country Club, Honolulu, Hawaii
Par 36–36 – 72; 6,914 yards

February 13–16
purse, $500,000

	SCORES			TOTAL	MONEY
Corey Pavin	68	68	73 72	271	$90,000
Paul Azinger	70	65	69 70	274	54,000
Bernhard Langer	67	74	67 68	276	29,000
Tom Watson	68	69	66 73	276	29,000
David Ogrin	66	70	74 67	277	18,250
Andy Dillard	69	71	69 68	277	18,250
Hubert Green	71	68	68 70	277	18,250
Jodie Mudd	71	69	66 72	278	15,500
Dave Rummells	68	68	72 71	279	11,571.43
Bob Tway	70	68	68 73	279	11,571.43
Craig Stadler	67	72	67 73	279	11,571.43
Bobby Wadkins	68	70	71 70	279	11,571.43
Isao Aoki	72	69	70 68	279	11,571.43
Jay Haas	68	72	72 67	279	11,571.43
Wayne Levi	67	70	70 72	279	11,571.42
Jack Renner	69	71	67 73	280	7,014.29
John Mahaffey	69	69	71 71	280	7,014.29
Mac O'Grady	64	69	74 73	280	7,014.29
George Burns	63	72	73 72	280	7,014.29
Howard Twitty	68	71	68 73	280	7,014.28
Tony Sills	66	72	71 71	280	7,014.28
Russ Cochran	70	68	71 71	280	7,014.28
Jim Thorpe	70	72	66 73	281	4,016.67
Nick Price	70	70	71 70	281	4,016.67
Chip Beck	66	71	75 69	281	4,016.67
Nick Faldo	70	71	67 73	281	4,016.67
Donnie Hammond	69	68	71 73	281	4,016.67
Scott Hoch	74	67	67 73	281	4,016.67
Tom Purtzer	69	66	72 74	281	4,016.66
Tom Byrum	70	67	72 72	281	4,016.66
Ed Fiori	64	71	75 71	281	4,016.66
Dan Pohl	68	67	73 74	282	2,958.67
Rex Caldwell	69	73	71 69	282	2,958.67
George Archer	68	74	70 70	282	2,958.66
Gene Sauers	70	67	70 76	283	2,518.50
Calvin Peete	69	71	68 75	283	2,518.50
Blaine McCallister	72	69	68 74	283	2,518.50
Jim Gallagher, Jr.	68	74	68 73	283	2,518.50
Greg Norman	71	71	72 70	284	2,050
Jack Nicklaus	70	69	71 74	284	2,050
Lanny Wadkins	70	69	69 76	284	2,050
Jeff Sluman	69	71	76 68	284	2,050
Davis Love	69	69	71 75	284	2,050
Loren Roberts	67	71	71 76	285	1,475.72
Mark Brooks	67	69	74 75	285	1,475.72
Buddy Gardner	70	70	69 76	285	1,475.72
Larry Mize	71	69	70 75	285	1,475.71
Robert Lohr	71	68	71 75	285	1,475.71
Mike Hulbert	69	69	70 77	285	1,475.71
Gary Koch	68	70	72 75	285	1,475.71

Los Angeles Open

Riviera Country Club, Pacific Palisades, California
Par 35–36 – 71; 6,946 yards

February 20–23
purse, $450,000

	SCORES				TOTAL	MONEY
Doug Tewell	69	72	66	63	270	$81,000
Clarence Rose	73	70	66	68	277	48,600
Willie Wood	72	69	67	70	278	30,600
Jay Delsing	66	74	71	68	279	19,800
Jim Gallagher, Jr.	71	71	68	69	279	19,800
Lanny Wadkins	71	70	67	72	280	14,568.75
Corey Pavin	74	68	69	69	280	14,568.75
Antonio Cerda	74	67	69	70	280	14,568.75
Barry Jaeckel	73	70	67	70	280	14,568.75
Dennis Trixler	66	71	71	73	281	10,800
Lennie Clements	69	70	71	71	281	10,800
Mark Lye	72	66	73	70	281	10,800
Masahiro Kuramoto	72	69	70	70	281	10,800
Bob Tway	74	71	69	68	282	8,325
Fred Couples	73	71	66	72	282	8,325
Bobby Wadkins	71	72	70	70	283	6,975
Tony Sills	72	70	70	71	283	6,975
Jim Colbert	73	66	71	73	283	6,975
Keith Fergus	72	71	70	70	283	6,975
Tom Purtzer	71	71	74	68	284	5,058
Mac O'Grady	68	68	75	73	284	5,058
Jim Dent	69	74	72	69	284	5,058
Donnie Hammond	72	73	69	70	284	5,058
Tom Kite	71	69	70	74	284	5,058
Jodie Mudd	70	72	71	72	285	3,290.63
Brett Upper	70	74	68	73	285	3,290.63
Rick Dalpos	73	71	70	71	285	3,290.63
Morris Hatalsky	76	68	70	71	285	3,290.63
Mark Pfeil	72	73	70	70	285	3,290.62
Billy Pierot	73	70	72	70	285	3,290.62
Mike McCullough	74	72	70	69	285	3,290.62
John Cook	74	69	70	72	285	3,290.62
Larry Rinker	70	73	70	73	286	2,377.50
Charles Bolling	73	72	70	71	286	2,377.50
Ben Crenshaw	74	70	68	74	286	2,377.50
Johnny Miller	69	73	69	75	286	2,377.50
Larry Mize	69	76	70	71	286	2,377.50
Peter Jacobsen	70	73	72	71	286	2,377.50
Scott Simpson	73	67	75	72	287	1,665
Calvin Peete	73	71	68	75	287	1,665
Chip Beck	70	74	71	72	287	1,665
Rex Caldwell	72	73	70	72	287	1,665
Frank Conner	73	70	71	73	287	1,665
Gary McCord	73	70	72	72	287	1,665
Mike Donald	75	69	73	70	287	1,665
Pat McGowan	74	70	70	73	287	1,665
Andrew Magee	72	72	71	72	287	1,665
Gene Sauers	71	73	70	74	288	1,108.13
Tom Sieckmann	71	71	72	74	288	1,108.13
Howard Twitty	76	70	72	70	288	1,108.13
Andy Dillard	69	71	75	73	288	1,108.13
Craig Stadler	72	74	70	72	288	1,108.12
Dave Stockton	72	74	72	70	288	1,108.12

	SCORES				TOTAL	MONEY
Buddy Gardner	70	72	76	70	288	1,108.12
Bill Israelson	72	68	76	72	288	1,108.12

Honda Classic

TPC at Eagle Trace, Coral Springs, Florida
Par 36–36 – 72; 7,037 yards

February 27–March 2
purse, $500,000

	SCORES				TOTAL	MONEY
Kenny Knox	66	71	80	70	287	$90,000
Jodie Mudd	70	72	75	71	288	33,000
Clarence Rose	70	73	72	73	288	33,000
John Mahaffey	74	70	76	68	288	33,000
Andy Bean	69	69	77	73	288	33,000
Barry Jaeckel	76	70	74	69	289	18,000
Tom Purtzer	71	71	80	68	290	16,750
Payne Stewart	69	74	73	75	291	15,000
Mike Reid	69	78	72	72	291	15,000
Lance Ten Broeck	74	69	78	71	292	13,000
Bruce Lietzke	72	70	77	73	292	13,000
Pat McGowan	77	71	75	70	293	9,800
George Burns	72	70	80	71	293	9,800
Jim Colbert	73	70	77	73	293	9,800
Steve Jones	73	71	81	68	293	9,800
Gary Koch	70	72	80	71	293	9,800
Tim Simpson	69	74	82	69	294	6,325
Philip Blackmar	70	75	76	73	294	6,325
Tom Kite	75	71	78	70	294	6,325
Russ Cochran	74	71	74	75	294	6,325
Keith Fergus	70	75	76	73	294	6,325
Ed Fiori	69	76	80	69	294	6,325
Ray Floyd	73	69	81	71	294	6,325
Buddy Gardner	72	68	78	76	294	6,325
Roger Maltbie	74	71	79	71	295	3,900
Bill Rogers	72	72	76	75	295	3,900
Curtis Strange	73	70	78	74	295	3,900
Ron Streck	70	72	80	73	295	3,900
Lon Hinkle	75	69	80	71	295	3,900
Mark McCumber	70	72	84	70	296	2,971.43
Steve Pate	81	66	76	73	296	2,971.43
Willie Wood	77	71	79	69	296	2,971.43
Leonard Thompson	74	74	79	69	296	2,971.43
Craig Stadler	72	73	80	71	296	2,971.43
Hale Irwin	71	71	81	73	296	2,971.43
Bill Glasson	68	75	82	71	296	2,971.42
Howard Twitty	77	71	81	68	297	2,250
Billy Pierot	72	73	80	72	297	2,250
Bobby Clampett	76	70	76	75	297	2,250
Frank Conner	75	70	80	72	297	2,250
Davis Love	73	75	75	74	297	2,250
Loren Roberts	74	74	78	72	298	1,800
Tom Weiskopf	71	68	86	73	298	1,800
Mark Brooks	75	72	75	76	298	1,800
Ken Brown	78	70	78	72	298	1,800
Mike Sullivan	72	74	80	73	299	1,417.50
Brad Fabel	70	73	82	74	299	1,417.50
Sandy Lyle	78	67	79	75	299	1,417.50

	SCORES				TOTAL	MONEY
Bill Israelson	74	73	82	70	299	1,417.50
Tim Norris	72	68	85	75	300	1,217.50
Robert Wrenn	74	73	79	74	300	1,217.50
Dave Barr	74	73	80	73	300	1,217.50
Brad Faxon	77	71	78	74	300	1,217.50

Doral Eastern Open

Doral Country Club, Blue Course, Miami, Florida
Par 36–36 – 72; 6,939 yard

March 6–9
purse, $500,000

	SCORES				TOTAL	MONEY
Andy Bean	71	68	68	69	276	$90,000
Hubert Green	70	70	64	72	276	54,000
(Bean defeated Green on fourth hole of sudden-death playoff)						
Mark O'Meara	70	67	74	66	277	29,000
Tom Kite	66	67	73	71	277	29,000
Mac O'Grady	73	67	69	70	279	19,000
Mike Sullivan	71	69	69	70	279	19,000
Tom Purtzer	66	71	73	70	280	16,750
Bobby Wadkins	72	69	69	71	281	13,500
Mark Calcavecchia	65	72	72	72	281	13,500
Ed Fiori	68	68	74	71	281	13,500
David Frost	69	70	73	69	281	13,500
Bill Kratzert	72	70	69	70	281	13,500
D. A. Weibring	69	67	71	75	282	8,571.43
Paul Azinger	74	67	69	72	282	8,571.43
Ken Brown	68	68	73	73	282	8,571.43
Mike Donald	71	70	70	71	282	8,571.43
Ray Floyd	70	70	71	71	282	8,571.43
Bob Gilder	69	72	70	71	282	8,571.43
Doug Tewell	69	69	73	71	282	8,571.43
Jim Thorpe	68	69	70	76	283	5,825
Howard Twitty	70	70	69	74	283	5,825
Greg Ladehoff	68	71	73	71	283	5,825
Danny Edwards	69	69	72	73	283	5,825
Tim Simpson	68	72	70	74	284	4,150
Mark McCumber	71	68	71	74	284	4,150
Hal Sutton	71	71	69	73	284	4,150
Lance Ten Broeck	75	67	69	73	284	4,150
Bruce Lietzke	73	69	71	71	284	4,150
Tom Weiskopf	73	70	70	72	285	3,325
Larry Nelson	69	72	73	71	285	3,325
Dave Barr	70	71	72	72	285	3,325
Ben Crenshaw	73	70	70	72	285	3,325
Tom Watson	69	70	71	76	286	2,477.78
Loren Roberts	72	69	69	76	286	2,477.78
Mike Nicolette	74	69	71	72	286	2,477.78
Tom Sieckmann	66	71	76	73	286	2,477.78
Tony Sills	73	67	70	76	286	2,477.78
Charles Bolling	70	70	74	72	286	2,477.78
Richard Fehr	69	73	73	71	286	2,477.78
Chris Perry	69	72	70	75	286	2,477.77
Morris Hatalsky	71	71	71	73	286	2,477.77
Mike McCullough	71	69	76	71	287	1,750
Roger Maltbie	66	74	72	75	287	1,750

	SCORES				TOTAL	MONEY
David Edwards	75	68	73	71	287	1,750
Mike Hulbert	72	66	75	74	287	1,750
Hale Irwin	69	73	69	76	287	1,750
Gene Sauers	70	73	71	74	288	1,268.75
J. C. Snead	70	73	71	74	288	1,268.75
Denis Watson	71	70	71	76	288	1,268.75
George Archer	68	72	73	75	288	1,268.75
Bobby Clampett	75	65	71	77	288	1,268.75
Jay Delsing	72	69	71	76	288	1,268.75
Jack Nicklaus	70	70	73	75	288	1,268.75
Robert Lohr	71	71	72	74	288	1,268.75

Hertz Bay Hill Classic

Bay Hill Club and Lodge, Orlando, Florida
Par 36–35 – 71; 7,103 yards

March 13–16
purse, $500,000

(Friday, Saturday rounds rained out. Tournament shortened to 54 holes.)

	SCORES			TOTAL	MONEY
Dan Forsman	68	67	67	202	$90,000
Ray Floyd	68	69	66	203	44,000
Mike Hulbert	70	69	64	203	44,000
Wayne Levi	70	67	67	204	24,000
Curtis Strange	70	70	65	205	19,000
Dan Pohl	68	70	67	205	19,000
Bernhard Langer	72	66	68	206	15,583.34
Mark Wiebe	70	70	66	206	15,583.33
Corey Pavin	69	70	67	206	15,583.33
Bob Tway	66	72	69	207	13,500
Mark Lye	74	65	69	208	11,500
Tom Purtzer	74	68	66	208	11,500
Bruce Lietzke	71	70	67	208	11,500
Scott Simpson	69	68	72	209	8,000
Paul Azinger	71	70	68	209	8,000
Joey Sindelar	71	69	69	209	8,000
Nick Price	72	68	69	209	8,000
Bobby Wadkins	73	66	70	209	8,000
Tom Watson	75	65	69	209	8,000
Fuzzy Zoeller	72	68	69	209	8,000
Scott Hoch	72	69	69	210	4,835.72
Tony Cerda	74	64	72	210	4,835.72
Ben Crenshaw	69	71	70	210	4,835.72
Nick Faldo	74	67	69	210	4,835.71
George Burns	71	68	71	210	4,835.71
Gary Koch	73	69	68	210	4,835.71
Mark O'Meara	74	70	66	210	4,835.71
Bob Murphy	73	67	71	211	3,625
Sandy Lyle	71	72	68	211	3,625
Tom Kite	68	71	73	212	2,906.25
Andy Dillard	71	71	70	212	2,906.25
Don Pooley	74	69	69	212	2,906.25
Larry Mize	74	68	70	212	2,906.25
Ken Brown	73	71	68	212	2,906.25
Andy Bean	74	66	72	212	2,906.25
D. A. Weibring	72	70	70	212	2,906.25

	SCORES			TOTAL	MONEY
Keith Fergus	74	67	71	212	2,906.25
Greg Norman	70	73	70	213	2,150
Mac O'Grady	73	70	70	213	2,150
Bill Kratzert	72	70	71	213	2,150
Roger Maltbie	69	74	70	213	2,150
Donnie Hammond	75	71	67	213	2,150
Hal Sutton	73	72	69	214	1,650
Payne Stewart	74	71	69	214	1,650
Charles Bowles	70	69	75	214	1,650
Jack Renner	73	67	74	214	1,650
Bob Eastwood	74	69	71	214	1,650
Ronnie Black	72	73	70	215	1,256.67
Mike Nicolette	73	73	69	215	1,256.67
Gary Hallberg	74	74	67	215	1,256.67
Phil Blackmar	73	68	74	215	1,256.67
Mark McCumber	75	68	72	215	1,256.66
Jodie Mudd	72	71	72	215	1,256.66

USF&G Classic

Lakewood Country Club, New Orleans, Louisiana
Par 36–36 – 72; 7,080 yards

March 20–23
purse, $500,000

	SCORES				TOTAL	MONEY
Calvin Peete	68	67	66	68	269	$90,000
Pat McGowan	69	69	68	68	274	54,000
Greg Ladehoff	75	68	64	70	277	24,000
Tom Sieckmann	73	70	67	67	277	24,000
Doug Tewell	71	69	69	68	277	24,000
Nick Faldo	68	72	68	69	277	24,000
Don Pooley	71	71	70	69	281	14,550
Tom Watson	71	74	66	70	281	14,550
Dick Mast	72	64	71	74	281	14,550
Dave Barr	73	72	67	69	281	14,550
Bill Israelson	73	65	74	69	281	14,550
Lanny Wadkins	71	71	69	71	282	9,500
Tony Sills	72	69	71	70	282	9,500
Andrew Magee	74	71	70	67	282	9,500
Ronnie Black	75	70	70	67	282	9,500
Charles Bollins	72	70	70	70	282	9,500
Steve Elkington	74	68	68	72	282	9,500
Mike Sullivan	71	69	70	73	283	7,500
Kenny Knox	70	68	73	73	284	6,275
Bill Glasson	73	73	68	70	284	6,275
Jay Haas	72	70	66	76	284	6,275
Mike Hulbert	75	70	71	68	284	6,275
Mike Reid	70	71	71	73	285	4,600
Fred Couples	74	69	69	73	285	4,600
Robert Lohr	73	69	72	71	285	4,600
Davis Love	71	73	68	73	285	4,600
Greg Norman	74	72	73	67	286	3,550
George Archer	73	68	71	74	286	3,550
Dan Forsman	73	68	73	72	286	3,550
David Graham	72	70	73	71	286	3,550
Lon Hinkle	70	73	72	71	286	3,550
Chris Perry	70	74	69	74	287	2,958.67
Rod Curl	76	69	70	72	287	2,958.67

	SCORES				TOTAL	MONEY
Dan Halldorson	75	69	72	71	287	2,958.67
Dave Rummells	71	72	75	70	288	2,360.57
Steve Pate	71	74	72	71	288	2,360.57
Nick Price	75	70	71	72	288	2,360.57
David Peoples	76	70	68	74	288	2,360.57
Ken Brown	74	72	73	69	288	2,360.57
Ben Crenshaw	71	75	70	72	288	2,360.57
Mike McCullough	73	73	74	68	288	2,360.57
Tim Norris	73	72	71	73	289	1,850
Mike Nicolette	75	66	71	77	289	1,850
Gil Morgan	74	72	74	69	289	1,850
Robert Wrenn	74	70	72	74	290	1,464
Isao Aoki	74	71	75	70	290	1,464
Woody Blackburn	73	71	72	74	290	1,464
Andy Dillard	72	74	72	72	290	1,464
Gary McCord	73	71	73	73	290	1,464
Ron Streck	71	75	70	75	291	1,245
Blaine McCallister	71	73	73	74	291	1,245

Tournament Players Championship

Tournament Players Club, Ponte Vedra, Florida
Par 36–36 – 72; 6,857 yards

March 27–30
purse, $900,000

	SCORES				TOTAL	MONEY
John Mahaffey	69	70	65	71	275	$162,000
Larry Mize	66	68	66	76	276	97,200
Tim Simpson	72	70	66	72	280	61,200
Jim Thorpe	69	68	74	70	281	37,200
Brett Upper	71	65	73	72	281	37,200
Tom Kite	69	69	71	72	281	37,200
Hal Sutton	71	72	68	71	282	28,050
John Cook	71	73	70	68	282	28,050
Jay Haas	73	68	73	68	282	28,050
Doug Tewell	68	68	74	73	283	21,600
Dave Rummells	70	65	79	69	283	21,600
Bob Tway	66	73	72	72	283	21,600
Payne Stewart	71	67	75	70	283	21,600
Davis Love	71	71	75	67	284	16,200
Bob Murphy	69	65	74	76	284	16,200
Scott Hoch	69	74	71	70	284	16,200
Joey Sindelar	70	70	73	72	285	13,950
Ronnie Black	70	71	74	70	285	13,950
Jim Simons	69	72	70	75	286	12,150
David Edwards	67	69	76	74	286	12,150
Tom Sieckmann	70	69	77	71	287	7,627.50
Larry Rinker	72	70	75	70	287	7,627.50
Lee Trevino	68	73	70	76	287	7,627.50
Dick Mast	69	73	68	77	287	7,627.50
Andy Bean	70	73	72	72	287	7,627.50
Charles Bolling	73	70	73	71	287	7,627.50
Jim Colbert	73	70	73	71	287	7,627.50
Danny Edwards	68	72	74	73	287	7,627.50
Keith Fergus	66	73	73	75	287	7,627.50
Ray Floyd	67	73	75	72	287	7,627.50
Gary Koch	72	70	72	73	287	7,627.50
Kenny Knox	71	73	69	74	287	7,627.50

	SCORES				TOTAL	MONEY
Tony Sills	66	75	70	77	288	4,654.29
Ken Green	66	75	76	71	288	4,654.29
Morris Hatalsky	74	70	69	75	288	4,654.29
Peter Jacobsen	72	69	72	75	288	4,654.29
D. A. Weibring	70	71	74	73	288	4,654.28
Greg Norman	70	71	77	70	288	4,654.28
Mark O'Meara	68	74	74	72	288	4,654.28
David Ogrin	70	74	71	74	289	3,240
Mike Sullivan	72	68	75	74	289	3,240
Lanny Wadkins	67	73	76	73	289	3,240
Loren Roberts	70	73	73	73	289	3,240
Jeff Sluman	70	74	75	70	289	3,240
Mike Donald	73	71	72	73	289	3,240
Bruce Lietzke	70	71	75	73	289	3,240
Bernhard Langer	70	73	73	73	289	3,240
Mark Pfeil	69	74	70	77	290	2,262
Tom Purtzer	72	70	77	71	290	2,262
Dave Stockton	72	72	76	70	290	2,262
Wayne Levi	73	71	76	70	290	2,262
David Frost	70	69	75	76	290	2,262
Roger Maltbie	70	73	79	68	290	2,262

Greater Greensboro Open

Forest Oaks Country Club, Greensboro, North Carolina
Par 36–36 – 72; 6,984 yards

April 3–6
purse, $500,000

	SCORES				TOTAL	MONEY
Sandy Lyle	68	64	73	70	275	$90,000
Andy Bean	68	70	72	67	277	54,000
Leonard Thompson	66	72	72	69	279	29,000
Isao Aoki	73	71	69	66	279	29,000
Lanny Wadkins	75	68	68	69	280	20,000
Tom Purtzer	68	72	68	73	281	15,125
Craig Stadler	69	69	71	72	281	15,125
Payne Stewart	70	70	74	67	281	15,125
Chip Beck	72	69	71	69	281	15,125
David Edwards	67	72	74	68	281	15,125
David Frost	69	72	68	72	281	15,125
Willie Wood	71	72	68	71	282	11,500
Dan Pohl	71	69	70	73	283	9,375
Pat McGowan	73	70	71	69	283	9,375
Mark O'Meara	72	71	69	71	283	9,375
Mike Sullivan	72	72	71	68	283	9,375
Bobby Wadkins	75	69	68	72	284	7,750
Chen Tze Chung	72	70	72	70	284	7,750
Jim Simons	68	69	75	73	285	6,060
Dick Mast	72	68	73	72	285	6,060
Fuzzy Zoeller	71	70	73	71	285	6,060
John Adams	72	69	73	71	285	6,060
Lennie Clements	70	73	73	69	285	6,060
John Cook	72	72	74	68	286	4,262.50
Greg Ladehoff	71	74	74	67	286	4,262.50
Buddy Gardner	70	69	74	73	286	4,262.50
Mike Hulbert	71	72	72	71	286	4,262.50
Tim Norris	70	71	76	70	287	3,400

	SCORES			TOTAL	MONEY
Steve Pate	71	72	72	287	3,400
Wayne Levi	75	69	74 69	287	3,400
Danny Edwards	68	71	74 74	287	3,400
Richard Fehr	73	70	72 72	287	3,400
Brett Upper	69	73	75 71	288	2,425
Mark Wiebe	72	71	71 74	288	2,425
Billy Pierot	74	71	71 72	288	2,425
Joey Sindelar	71	72	73 72	288	2,425
David Thore	69	73	71 75	288	2,425
Dennis Trixler	75	69	71 73	288	2,425
Howard Twitty	69	73	76 70	288	2,425
Bobby Clampett	71	71	80 66	288	2,425
Mark Hayes	70	73	72 73	288	2,425
Vance Heafner	72	71	75 70	288	2,425
Brian Mogg	74	71	73 71	289	1,461
Jack Renner	69	73	71 76	289	1,461
Jim Thorpe	70	71	77 71	289	1,461
Larry Nelson	72	68	71 78	289	1,461
Dave Rummells	75	70	71 73	289	1,461
Charles Bolling	72	73	73 71	289	1,461
Mark Brooks	74	67	74 74	289	1,461
Fred Couples	73	71	67 78	289	1,461
Andy Dillard	69	71	75 74	289	1,461
Nick Faldo	74	68	75 72	289	1,461

The Masters Tournament

Augusta National Golf Club, Augusta, Georgia
Par 36–36 – 72; 6,905 yards

April 10–13
purse, $805,100

	SCORES			TOTAL	MONEY
Jack Nicklaus	74	71	69 65	279	$144,000
Tom Kite	70	74	68 68	280	70,400
Greg Norman	70	72	68 70	280	70,400
Seve Ballesteros	71	68	72 70	281	38,400
Nick Price	79	69	63 71	282	32,000
Tom Watson	70	74	68 71	283	27,800
Jay Haas	76	69	71 67	283	27,800
Payne Stewart	75	71	69 69	284	23,200
Bob Tway	70	73	71 70	284	23,200
Tommy Nakajima	70	71	71 72	284	23,200
Donnie Hammond	73	71	67 74	285	16,960
Sandy Lyle	76	70	68 71	285	16,960
Mark McCumber	76	67	71 71	285	16,960
Corey Pavin	71	72	71 71	285	16,960
Calvin Peete	75	71	69 70	285	16,960
Dave Barr	70	77	71 68	286	12,000
Ben Crenshaw	71	71	74 70	286	12,000
Gary Koch	69	74	71 72	286	12,000
Bernhard Langer	74	68	69 75	286	12,000
Larry Mize	75	74	72 65	286	12,000
Fuzzy Zoeller	73	73	69 72	287	9,300
Curtis Strange	73	74	68 72	287	9,300
Chen Tze Chung	69	73	75 71	288	8,000
Roger Maltbie	71	75	69 73	288	8,000
Scott Simpson	76	72	67 74	289	6,533.34
Bill Glasson	72	74	72 71	289	6,533.33

	SCORES				TOTAL	MONEY
Peter Jacobsen	75	73	68	73	289	6,533.33
David Graham	76	72	74	68	290	5,666.67
Johnny Miller	74	70	77	69	290	5,666.67
Danny Edwards	71	71	72	76	290	5,666.66
Fred Couples	72	77	70	72	291	4,875
Lanny Wadkins	78	71	73	69	291	4,875
Bruce Lietzke	78	70	68	75	291	4,875
Dan Pohl	76	70	72	73	291	4,875
Wayne Levi	73	76	67	76	292	4,300
Larry Nelson	73	73	71	76	293	3,850
Richard Fehr	75	74	69	75	293	3,850
Hubert Green	71	75	73	74	293	3,850
Tony Sills	76	73	73	71	293	3,850
*Sam Randolph	75	73	72	73	293	
Don Pooley	77	72	73	72	294	3,400
Bill Kratzert	68	72	76	79	295	3,200
John Mahaffey	79	69	72	75	295	3,200
Ken Green	68	78	74	76	296	3,000
Philip Blackmar	76	73	73	76	298	2,700
Jim Thorpe	74	74	73	77	298	2,700
Lee Trevino	76	73	73	77	299	2,500
Mark O'Meara	74	73	81	73	301	2,300

Out of Final 36 Holes

			TOTAL	
Craig Stadler		74	76	150
Gary Player		77	73	150
Andy Bean		75	76	151
Bob Eastwood		79	72	151
Ray Floyd		74	77	151
Buddy Gardner		74	77	151
Gary Hallberg		78	73	151
Kenny Knox		75	76	151
Hal Sutton		80	71	151
George Burns		74	78	152
Dan Forsman		78	74	152
*Jay Sigel		74	78	152
Hale Irwin		76	76	152
*Robert Lewis		74	78	152
Joey Sindelar		79	73	152
Mac O'Grady		82	70	152
Gay Brewer		77	76	153
Billy Casper		78	75	153
Charles Coody		76	77	153
*Chip Drury		76	77	153
Jack Renner		76	77	153
*Peter Persons		76	77	153
Larry Rinker		73	81	154
Mark Wiebe		76	78	154
*Jack Kay		80	74	154
Doug Tewell		74	80	154
*Scott Verplank		77	77	154
George Archer		75	80	155
Tommy Aaron		79	77	156
Isao Aoki		79	77	156
Doug Ford		78	78	156
Denis Watson		80	76	156
*Garth McGimpsey		78	78	156
Bill Rogers		80	76	156

	SCORES		TOTAL	MONEY
Arnold Palmer	80	76	156	
*Michael Podolak	82	74	156	
Tim Simpson	78	79	157	
*Randy Sonnier	81	77	158	
Bob Goalby	79	80	159	
Chen Tze Ming	79	81	160	

(All professionals who started but did not survive 36-hole cut received $1,500.)

Deposit Guaranty Classic

Hattiesburg Country Club, Hattiesburg, Mississippi   April 10–13
Par 35–35 – 72; 6,654 yards   purse, $200,000

	SCORES				TOTAL	MONEY
Dan Halldorson	64	67	66	66	263	$36,000
Paul Azinger	64	69	66	66	265	21,600
Scott Hoch	67	69	65	67	268	13,600
John Adams	66	69	71	64	270	9,600
Eduardo Romero	66	70	68	67	271	7,025
Ron Streck	66	69	67	69	271	7,025
Tom Byrum	68	65	70	68	271	7,025
Vance Heafner	67	69	70	65	271	7,025
Richard Zokol	64	71	71	66	272	5,000
Antonio Cerda	67	67	69	69	272	5,000
Gibby Gilbert	68	68	72	64	272	5,000
Gary Martin	67	74	66	65	272	5,000
Rocco Mediate	65	66	70	71	272	5,000
Mike West	70	69	65	69	273	3,300
Steven Bowman	67	70	68	68	273	3,300
Brian Claar	68	68	67	70	273	3,300
Frank Conner	66	70	69	68	273	3,300
Andy Dillard	66	73	66	68	273	3,300
Bruce Fleisher	69	69	68	67	273	3,300
Bobby Cole	67	72	68	67	274	2,413.34
Tom Pernice	67	69	68	70	274	2,413.33
Mike Donald	69	68	66	71	274	2,413.33
Danny Briggs	66	70	69	70	275	1,730
Mark Brooks	75	67	65	68	275	1,730
Russ Cochran	69	67	68	71	275	1,730
Victor Regalado	71	68	72	64	275	1,730
Mike Miles	68	66	72	69	275	1,730
Peter Oosterhuis	64	74	68	69	275	1,730
Greg Twiggs	69	70	69	68	276	1,360
Thomas Gleeton	70	68	68	70	276	1,360
Mike McCullough	66	77	67	66	276	1,360
Kermit Zarley	70	68	68	71	277	1,183.34
DeWitt Weaver	71	69	66	71	277	1,183.33
Anders Forsbrand	67	69	72	69	277	1,183.33
Adrian Stills	68	70	72	68	278	1,080
Steve Elkington	67	72	70	70	279	901.43
Denny Hepler	70	66	70	73	279	901.43
Steve Jones	70	71	69	69	279	901.43
Mike Blackburn	73	69	68	69	279	901.43
Brad Bryant	72	70	70	67	279	901.43
Ed Dougherty	66	72	70	71	279	901.43

	SCORES				TOTAL	MONEY
George Cadle	69	73	73	64	279	901.42
Billy Pierot	68	70	69	73	280	660
Rick Dalpos	72	69	70	69	280	660
Ernie Gonzalez	62	74	74	70	280	660
Kris Moe	73	68	69	70	280	660
Robert Wrenn	67	71	68	74	280	660
Larry Ziegler	70	73	70	68	281	524
Jeff Lewis	69	72	71	69	281	524
Mike Morley	72	70	70	69	281	524

Sea Pines Heritage Classic

Harbour Town Golf Links, Hilton Head Island, South Carolina   April 17–20
Par 36–35 – 71; 6,788 yards   purse, $450,000

	SCORES				TOTAL	MONEY
Fuzzy Zoeller	68	68	69	71	276	$81,000
Roger Maltbie	67	72	69	69	277	33,600
Greg Norman	70	68	69	70	277	33,600
Chip Beck	70	67	70	70	277	33,600
Jay Haas	71	70	66	71	278	18,000
Ray Floyd	69	72	72	66	279	15,075
Ken Green	71	70	71	67	279	15,075
Tom Kite	70	72	70	67	279	15,075
Don Pooley	69	66	75	71	281	12,150
Hal Sutton	71	71	69	70	281	12,150
Danny Edwards	74	70	70	67	281	12,150
Doug Tewell	70	69	73	70	282	9,450
Tim Simpson	72	68	71	71	282	9,450
Andy Bean	69	72	70	71	282	9,450
Bob Tway	72	69	71	71	283	7,425
Mike Sullivan	70	69	71	73	283	7,425
Denis Watson	72	71	71	69	283	7,425
Donnie Hammond	75	69	72	67	283	7,425
Curtis Strange	69	70	74	71	284	5,647.50
Larry Rinker	71	75	67	71	284	5,647.50
Mike Donald	73	68	74	69	284	5,647.50
Scott Hoch	69	72	72	71	284	5,647.50
Bernhard Langer	72	74	64	75	285	4,680
David Ogrin	74	70	71	71	286	3,481.88
Lanny Wadkins	74	72	70	70	286	3,481.88
Dan Halldorson	66	68	76	76	286	3,481.88
Gary Koch	74	71	72	69	286	3,481.88
Howard Twitty	72	70	72	72	286	3,481.87
Clarence Rose	73	71	68	74	286	3,481.87
Jeff Sluman	74	73	66	73	286	3,481.87
Mike Reid	72	72	74	68	286	3,481.87
Chris Perry	70	75	70	72	287	2,490
John Cook	74	71	71	71	287	2,490
Jodie Mudd	73	70	71	73	287	2,490
Hale Irwin	71	73	71	72	287	2,490
Peter Jacobsen	76	68	73	70	287	2,490
Pat Lindsey	69	77	69	72	287	2,490
D. A. Weibring	74	72	69	73	288	2,025
John Adams	74	71	69	74	288	2,025
Vance Heafner	75	70	70	73	288	2,025

	SCORES				TOTAL	MONEY
Dick Mast	76	70	71	72	289	1,665
Bill Glasson	75	68	71	75	289	1,665
Tim Norris	72	70	77	70	289	1,665
Kenny Knox	72	68	75	74	289	1,665
Davis Love	71	76	72	70	289	1,665
Joey Sindelar	69	74	76	71	290	1,224
Paul Azinger	73	71	73	73	290	1,224
Jim Colbert	71	74	73	72	290	1,224
Ben Crenshaw	74	71	71	74	290	1,224
Brad Faxon	74	71	71	74	290	1,224
Billy Pierot	70	74	70	76	290	1,224

Houston Open

TPC at the Woodlands, The Woodlands, Texas
Par 36–36 – 72; 7,042 yards

April 24–27
purse, $500,000

	SCORES				TOTAL	MONEY
Curtis Strange	72	68	68	66	274	$90,000
Calvin Peete	65	70	70	69	274	54,000
(Strange defeated Peete on third hole of sudden-death playoff)						
Tom Watson	69	68	68	71	276	34,000
Bruce Lietzke	68	72	71	68	279	20,666.67
David Edwards	73	71	66	69	279	20,666.67
Jay Haas	68	70	67	74	279	20,666.66
Doug Tewell	71	70	71	68	280	16,125
Payne Stewart	69	73	71	67	280	16,125
Craig Stadler	69	70	71	72	282	12,500
Charles Bolling	73	67	72	70	282	12,500
Brian Claar	74	71	67	70	282	12,500
Lennie Clements	72	69	72	69	282	12,500
Bill Glasson	72	71	70	69	282	12,500
Nick Price	70	72	69	72	283	9,500
Philip Parkin	72	73	70	69	284	8,250
Chip Beck	72	71	73	68	284	8,250
Nick Faldo	68	69	70	77	284	8,250
Wayne Grady	65	72	70	77	284	8,250
Mike Sullivan	75	63	74	73	285	6,060
Steve Pate	70	71	71	70	285	6,060
Mike Donald	73	71	71	70	285	6,060
Donnie Hammond	72	73	70	70	285	6,060
Mike Hulbert	67	72	72	74	285	6,060
Gil Morgan	70	73	71	72	286	4,050
Howard Twitty	70	71	72	73	286	4,050
Mark Brooks	71	71	72	72	286	4,050
Frank Conner	73	71	70	72	286	4,050
David Frost	72	70	72	72	286	4,050
Mark Hayes	72	69	72	73	286	4,050
Mike Reid	71	72	73	71	287	3,250
David Ogrin	70	75	71	71	287	3,250
Willie Wood	72	72	69	74	287	3,250
Mark Lye	69	76	71	72	288	2,825.34
Tim Norris	70	72	72	74	288	2,825.33
Steven Bowman	69	73	72	74	288	2,825.33
Lanny Wadkins	73	70	72	74	289	2,304
Corey Pavin	70	74	70	75	289	2,304

	SCORES				TOTAL	MONEY
Antonio Cerda	72	73	71	73	289	2,304
Bobby Clampett	71	70	73	75	289	2,304
Steve Elkington	71	73	72	73	289	2,304
Brad Faxon	71	73	69	76	289	2,304
John Mahaffey	71	74	74	71	290	1,700
Dave Rummells	74	69	69	78	290	1,700
Leonard Thompson	72	73	73	72	290	1,700
Jack Nicklaus	72	73	72	73	290	1,700
Brett Upper	69	72	73	76	290	1,700
John Adams	71	70	71	78	290	1,700
John McComish	73	70	75	73	291	1,256.67
Gene Sauers	73	69	75	74	291	1,256.67
Rod Curl	68	76	73	74	291	1,256.67
Gary Hallberg	74	69	75	73	291	1,256.67
Don Pooley	72	71	74	74	291	1,256.66
J. C. Snead	79	66	73	73	291	1,256.66

Panasonic Las Vegas Invitational

Las Vegas, Nevada

April 30–May 4
purse, $1,150,000

Las Vegas Country Club
Par 35–36 – 71; 7,077 yards

Desert Inn Country Club
Par 36–36 – 72; 7,088 yards

Spanish Trail Golf and Country Club
Par 36–36 – 72; 7,088 yards

	SCORES					TOTAL	MONEY
Greg Norman	73	63	68	64	65	333	$207,000
Dan Pohl	68	70	67	66	69	340	124,200
Larry Nelson	67	69	67	69	69	341	66,700
Steve Pate	67	73	69	65	67	341	66,700
Don Pooley	70	70	67	68	67	342	43,700
Andy Bean	70	69	66	69	68	342	43,700
Bob Tway	70	71	63	68	71	343	35,843.34
Gil Morgan	67	67	70	71	68	343	35,843.33
John Cook	66	68	70	71	68	343	35,843.33
Wayne Levi	69	69	68	68	70	344	25,491.67
Hal Sutton	67	69	69	73	66	344	25,491.67
John Mahaffey	69	70	65	71	69	344	25,491.67
Tom Watson	73	68	66	69	68	344	25,491.67
Robert Lohr	67	65	70	72	70	344	25,491.66
Jim Colbert	69	71	64	69	71	344	25,491.66
Dave Rummells	66	70	67	69	73	345	18,400
Fred Couples	73	69	65	67	71	345	18,400
Jay Haas	71	70	68	68	68	345	18,400
Bernhard Langer	70	70	71	69	66	346	13,938
Tom Purtzer	70	69	67	69	71	346	13,938
Nick Price	72	67	70	66	71	346	13,938
Chris Perry	69	69	66	71	71	346	13,938
Donnie Hammond	70	66	66	73	71	346	13,938
Joey Sindelar	71	72	67	72	65	347	9,805
David Ogrin	71	66	70	68	72	347	9,805
George Burns	69	70	71	75	62	347	9,805

	SCORES					TOTAL	MONEY
Mike Hulbert	69	65	72	68	73	347	9,805
Bobby Wadkins	72	66	71	70	69	348	7,822
Gary Koch	65	71	74	67	71	348	7,822
Blaine McCallist	71	68	67	72	70	348	7,822
Payne Stewart	69	72	70	68	69	348	7,822
Pat McGowan	71	71	69	70	67	348	7,822
Tony Sills	68	71	70	68	72	349	5,950
Mike Reid	68	72	70	71	68	349	5,950
Mike Sullivan	73	68	70	69	69	349	5,950
Ken Brown	69	71	69	68	72	349	5,950
Chen Tze Chung	67	70	71	69	72	349	5,950
Jim Dent	68	71	70	69	71	349	5,950
Nick Faldo	70	67	72	69	71	349	5,950
Roger Maltbie	66	71	70	73	70	350	4,145
Corey Pavin	69	69	71	75	67	350	4,145
Larry Rinker	68	71	69	71	71	350	4,145
Dave Barr	70	68	72	71	69	350	4,145
Chip Beck	68	67	72	73	70	350	4,145
Ken Green	67	69	74	71	69	350	4,145
Barry Jaeckel	73	66	72	68	71	350	4,145
Pat Lindsey	69	70	67	70	74	350	4,145
Tim Simpson	73	67	68	71	72	351	2,890
Johnny Miller	70	68	72	70	71	351	2,890
Mac O'Grady	69	68	72	71	71	351	2,890
Tim Norris	69	70	70	69	73	351	2,890
Bill Sander	69	70	70	71	71	351	2,890
Curtis Strange	71	69	68	70	73	351	2,890

Byron Nelson Classic

Tournament Players Course at Las Colinas, Irving, Texas   May 8–11
Par 35–35 – 70; 6,767 yards   purse, $600,000

	SCORES				TOTAL	MONEY
Andy Bean	66	68	67	68	269	$108,000
Mark Wiebe	69	66	68	67	270	64,800
Bobby Wadkins	68	69	66	70	273	40,800
Craig Stadler	69	69	65	71	274	23,625
Payne Stewart	70	66	67	71	274	23,625
Gene Sauers	71	68	66	69	274	23,625
Mark Hayes	64	72	68	70	274	23,625
Robert Lohr	70	70	67	68	275	16,800
D. A. Weibring	71	68	68	68	275	16,800
Nick Price	73	66	69	67	275	16,800
Dan Halldorson	72	69	64	70	275	16,800
Andrew Magee	69	68	73	66	276	11,057.15
Bernhard Langer	72	66	66	72	276	11,057.15
Mike McCullough	71	68	70	67	276	11,057.14
Jim Simons	72	68	66	70	276	11,057.14
John Cook	69	69	70	68	276	11,057.14
Ray Floyd	73	69	65	69	276	11,057.14
Lon Hinkle	72	69	67	68	276	11,057.14
Tom Purtzer	74	63	69	71	277	7,020
Billy Pierot	70	71	71	65	277	7,020
Tim Norris	71	71	65	70	277	7,020
Mark Brooks	68	73	69	67	277	7,020
George Burns	68	72	63	74	277	7,020

	SCORES				TOTAL	MONEY
David Graham	72	67	68	70	277	7,020
*Scott Verplank	72	68	67	70	277	
Tony Sills	70	69	69	70	278	4,580
Jodie Mudd	72	70	67	69	278	4,580
Bruce Lietzke	71	70	67	70	278	4,580
Ken Brown	67	76	67	68	278	4,580
Trevor Dodds	68	72	69	69	278	4,580
Danny Edwards	71	69	70	68	278	4,580
Hal Sutton	72	71	69	67	279	3,260
Chris Perry	70	72	68	69	279	3,260
Bill Sander	69	68	70	72	279	3,260
Tom Pernice	70	68	74	67	279	3,260
Lanny Wadkins	76	65	69	69	279	3,260
Steven Bowman	70	67	74	68	279	3,260
Peter Jacobsen	70	70	72	67	279	3,260
Ed Fiori	71	65	72	71	279	3,260
Jim Gallagher	68	67	71	73	279	3,260
Pat McGowan	70	70	70	70	280	2,280
Scott Simpson	70	66	73	71	280	2,280
David Ogrin	71	69	68	72	280	2,280
Russ Cochran	70	71	68	71	280	2,280
Jeff Lewis	69	71	70	70	280	2,280
Greg Ladehoff	74	69	69	68	280	2,280
J. C. Snead	72	68	68	73	281	1,581
Willie Wood	72	71	69	69	281	1,581
Denis Watson	72	68	68	73	281	1,581
Paul Azinger	71	70	73	67	281	1,581
Mark Lye	70	69	72	70	281	1,581
Bobby Clampett	70	70	70	71	281	1,581
Bob Eastwood	71	68	72	70	281	1,581
Wayne Grady	72	70	71	68	281	1,581

Colonial National Invitation

Colonial Country Club, Fort Worth, Texas
Par 35–35 – 70; 7,116 yards

May 15–18
purse, $600,000

(Second round rained out, shortened to 54 holes.)

	SCORES			TOTAL	MONEY
Dan Pohl	68	69	68	205	$108,000
Payne Stewart	72	67	66	205	64,800
(Pohl defeated Stewart on first hole of sudden-death playoff)					
Bill Rogers	67	71	69	207	31,200
Tom Watson	75	68	64	207	31,200
Bernhard Langer	70	70	67	207	31,200
Mike Sullivan	70	69	69	208	20,100
Gene Sauers	66	72	70	208	20,100
David Frost	70	71	67	208	20,100
Bob Tway	69	68	72	209	15,600
Paul Azinger	75	67	67	209	15,600
Ronnie Black	71	68	70	209	15,600
David Edwards	69	67	73	209	15,600
Bobby Wadkins	70	71	69	210	10,920
Lee Trevino	73	68	69	210	10,920
Jim Colbert	72	70	68	210	10,920

	SCORES			TOTAL	MONEY
Bob Gilder	73	65	72	210	10,920
Barry Jaeckel	72	70	68	210	10,920
Nick Price	68	76	67	211	7,302.86
Buddy Gardner	69	71	71	211	7,302.86
Ken Green	74	66	71	211	7,302.86
Bruce Lietzke	70	70	71	211	7,302.86
Steve Pate	72	71	68	211	7,302.86
Tony Sills	72	71	68	211	7,302.85
Howard Twitty	68	68	75	211	7,302.85
Doug Tewell	69	70	73	212	4,387.50
D. A. Weibring	68	70	74	212	4,387.50
Lennie Clements	68	72	72	212	4,387.50
Ben Crenshaw	70	72	70	212	4,387.50
Scott Simpson	68	74	70	212	4,387.50
Jay Haas	70	70	72	212	4,387.50
Corey Pavin	70	68	74	212	4,387.50
Robert Lohr	69	69	74	212	4,387.50
Calvin Peete	71	69	73	213	3,315
Wayne Grady	73	69	71	213	3,315
Curtis Strange	75	68	70	213	3,315
Joey Sindelar	71	71	71	213	3,315
Fuzzy Zoeller	74	68	72	214	2,640
Fred Couples	76	68	70	214	2,640
Keith Fergus	72	70	72	214	2,640
Lon Hinkle	75	68	71	214	2,640
Roger Maltbie	70	70	74	214	2,640
Jim Thorpe	68	73	73	214	2,640
Hal Sutton	70	71	74	215	1,788
Bill Glasson	73	70	72	215	1,788
Tom Kite	72	72	71	215	1,788
Gary Koch	72	72	71	215	1,788
Mark Lye	71	73	71	215	1,788
Denis Watson	73	71	71	215	1,788
Larry Mize	72	73	70	215	1,788
Gil Morgan	76	68	71	215	1,788
Bob Murphy	72	67	76	215	1,788

Memorial Tournament

Muirfield Village Golf Club, Dublin, Ohio
Par 36–36 – 72; 7,106 yards

May 22–25
purse, $607,730

	SCORES				TOTAL	MONEY
Hal Sutton	68	69	66	68	271	$100,000
Don Pooley	69	67	70	69	275	60,000
Johnny Miller	70	69	69	68	276	32,225
Mark O'Meara	68	75	67	66	276	32,225
John Mahaffey	68	71	69	69	277	21,110
Jack Nicklaus	66	70	72	69	277	21,110
Scott Simpson	70	72	68	68	278	17,313.34
Payne Stewart	72	69	69	68	278	17,313.33
Chip Beck	71	66	70	71	278	17,313.33
Craig Stadler	72	69	71	67	279	13,335
Tom Purtzer	68	69	73	69	279	13,335
Doug Tewell	66	70	70	73	279	13,335
Greg Norman	73	67	71	68	279	13,335

	SCORES				TOTAL	MONEY
Ray Floyd	70	74	68	68	280	10,940
Bruce Lietzke	69	72	70	70	281	10,110
Mark McCumber	73	73	69	66	281	10,110
Phil Blackmar	69	74	68	71	282	7,908.34
Jay Haas	70	69	68	75	282	7,908.34
Joey Sindelar	71	68	72	71	282	7,908.33
Andy Bean	72	66	71	73	282	7,908.33
Lennie Clements	69	68	72	73	282	7,908.33
Peter Jacobsen	66	71	72	73	282	7,908.33
Fuzzy Zoeller	71	72	69	71	283	5,723.34
Lanny Wadkins	67	78	71	67	283	5,723.33
Dan Pohl	72	71	71	69	283	5,723.33
Mark Wiebe	75	71	69	69	284	4,666.67
Larry Mize	69	68	73	74	284	4,666.67
Scott Hoch	71	72	70	71	284	4,666.66
Bob Tway	70	73	72	70	285	3,628
Clarence Rose	69	73	65	78	285	3,628
Jim Colbert	75	68	72	70	285	3,628
Danny Edwards	74	71	68	72	285	3,628
Dan Halldorson	65	71	70	79	285	3,628
Kenny Knox	72	69	73	71	285	3,628
Davis Love	72	73	67	73	285	3,628
Gil Morgan	70	74	70	71	285	3,628
Bob Murphy	72	73	71	69	285	3,628
Andy North	72	70	70	73	285	3,628
D. A. Weibring	72	71	75	68	286	2,668
Jim Simons	71	72	74	69	286	2,668
Curtis Strange	76	69	70	71	286	2,668
Mike Sullivan	71	75	69	71	286	2,668
Mac O'Grady	68	77	70	71	286	2,668
George Burns	69	72	72	74	287	2,220
Hale Irwin	75	69	72	71	287	2,220
Mark Lye	75	70	72	70	287	2,220
Tim Simpson	74	71	71	72	288	1,858
Bill Glasson	71	72	70	75	288	1,858
Larry Rinker	74	69	71	74	288	1,858
Pat McGowan	67	71	75	75	288	1,858
Tony Sills	73	73	69	73	288	1,858

Kemper Open

Congressional Country Club, Bethesda, Maryland
Par 36–36 – 72; 7,173 yards

May 29–June 1
purse, $500,000

	SCORES				TOTAL	MONEY
Greg Norman	72	69	70	66	277	$90,000
Larry Mize	67	71	70	69	277	54,000
(Norman defeated Mize on sixth hole of sudden-death playoff)						
Mike Reid	68	70	71	70	279	29,000
John Cook	72	69	71	67	279	29,000
Bobby Wadkins	70	71	73	66	280	20,000
Curtis Strange	73	67	71	71	282	18,000
Bob Gilder	73	71	73	66	283	15,583.34
Chip Beck	74	70	68	71	283	15,583.33
Buddy Gardner	72	70	71	70	283	15,583.33
Craig Stadler	73	68	73	70	284	11,500

	SCORES				TOTAL	MONEY
David Ogrin	68	74	70	72	284	11,500
Gil Morgan	75	71	66	72	284	11,500
Roger Maltbie	71	70	73	70	284	11,500
Donnie Hammond	71	68	75	70	284	11,500
Joey Sindelar	71	73	71	70	285	8,250
Rick Dalpos	70	74	71	70	285	8,250
Dan Forsman	70	69	72	74	285	8,250
Bill Glasson	71	74	70	70	285	8,250
Greg Twiggs	72	71	70	73	286	6,275
Steve Pate	72	70	74	70	286	6,275
Andrew Magee	70	73	72	71	286	6,275
Bobby Clampett	74	64	74	74	286	6,275
Howard Twitty	71	71	73	72	287	3,925
Brett Upper	74	72	71	70	287	3,925
Loren Roberts	74	72	71	70	287	3,925
Willie Wood	71	74	70	72	287	3,925
Mike McCullough	73	70	68	76	287	3,925
Charles Bolling	67	70	77	73	287	3,925
Lennie Clements	72	72	74	69	287	3,925
Russ Cochran	72	72	73	70	287	3,925
Bob Eastwood	69	73	72	73	287	3,925
Kenny Knox	74	72	71	70	287	3,925
Mark O'Meara	71	73	74	70	288	2,641.67
George Archer	74	72	68	74	288	2,641.67
Fred Couples	64	77	73	74	288	2,641.67
Bill Israelson	75	70	70	73	288	2,641.67
Jeff Lewis	72	72	74	70	288	2,641.66
Vance Heafner	69	74	74	71	288	2,641.66
J. C. Snead	70	72	75	72	289	1,802
Chris Perry	72	73	69	75	289	1,802
Leonard Thompson	68	70	79	72	289	1,802
Bob Tway	72	72	72	73	289	1,802
Tim Simpson	73	73	70	73	289	1,802
Brian Claar	71	73	72	73	289	1,802
Charles Coody	72	73	71	73	289	1,802
Andy Dillard	75	68	77	69	289	1,802
John Mahaffey	71	74	76	68	289	1,802
Ernie Gonzalez	71	74	72	72	289	1,802
Tom Sieckmann	67	77	75	71	290	1,280
Gary Hallberg	74	71	72	73	290	1,280

Manufacturers Hanover Westchester Classic

Westchester Country Club, Rye, New York
Par 36–35 – 71; 6,722 yards

June 5–8
purse, $600,000

	SCORES				TOTAL	MONEY
Bob Tway	73	63	69	67	272	$108,000
Willie Wood	71	63	73	66	273	64,800
Scott Simpson	71	67	70	67	275	34,800
Gil Morgan	69	69	70	67	275	34,800
Mike Reid	68	69	68	72	277	24,000
Andrew Magee	72	67	71	70	280	20,850
Mark Wiebe	68	71	73	68	280	20,850
Tom Watson	72	70	70	69	281	16,800
Brett Upper	68	66	74	73	281	16,800

	SCORES				TOTAL	MONEY
Doug Tewell	70	66	74	71	281	16,800
Jay Haas	65	73	73	70	281	16,800
Roger Maltbie	72	72	70	68	282	12,150
Kenny Knox	71	69	72	70	282	12,150
Brad Faxon	71	70	71	70	282	12,150
Ray Floyd	68	67	70	77	282	12,150
D. A. Weibring	73	71	69	70	283	9,900
Mark Pfeil	70	73	70	70	283	9,900
Tom Pernice	70	67	72	75	284	7,302.86
Frank Conner	70	70	74	70	284	7,302.86
Jim Dent	73	72	70	69	284	7,302.86
Mike Hulbert	75	65	70	74	284	7,302.86
Mike Gove	73	72	70	69	284	7,302.86
Lennie Clements	74	67	74	69	284	7,302.85
Hubert Green	72	65	74	73	284	7,302.85
Andy North	69	71	72	73	285	4,387.50
Pat McGowan	71	71	72	71	285	4,387.50
Don Pooley	73	72	73	67	285	4,387.50
Rod Curl	73	71	71	70	285	4,387.50
Joe Inman	72	68	72	73	285	4,387.50
Mike Donald	70	72	72	71	285	4,387.50
David Frost	73	68	75	69	285	4,387.50
Jim Gallagher	70	73	73	69	285	4,387.50
Wayne Levi	74	66	72	74	286	3,390
Tom Sieckmann	65	69	75	77	286	3,390
Gibby Gilbert	72	71	76	67	286	3,390
Mark Lye	74	69	73	71	287	2,826
Chris Perry	73	68	75	71	287	2,826
J. C. Snead	71	73	70	73	287	2,826
Billy Pierot	70	74	74	69	287	2,826
Jim Colbert	70	74	73	70	287	2,826
Jeff Sluman	75	67	76	70	288	2,100
Larry Rinker	70	69	74	75	288	2,100
Bill Rogers	74	69	75	70	288	2,100
Charles Coody	76	68	73	71	288	2,100
Andy Dillard	72	72	71	73	288	2,100
Ed Fiori	68	71	72	77	288	2,100
Bill Israelson	67	75	73	73	288	2,100
Howard Twitty	73	71	76	69	289	1,477.50
Mike Smith	74	71	71	73	289	1,477.50
David Peoples	74	71	77	67	289	1,477.50
George Archer	68	73	79	69	289	1,477.50
Rex Caldwell	75	69	72	73	289	1,477.50
Bobby Clampett	72	71	77	69	289	1,477.50
Lou Graham	73	72	72	72	289	1,477.50
Jeff Grygiel	69	73	73	74	289	1,477.50

U.S. Open Championship

Shinnecock Hills Golf Club, Southampton, New York
Par 35–35 – 70; 6,912 yards

June 12–15
purse, $700,000

	SCORES				TOTAL	MONEY
Ray Floyd	75	68	70	66	279	$115,000
Lanny Wadkins	74	70	72	65	281	47,646
Chip Beck	75	73	68	65	281	47,646

	SCORES			TOTAL	MONEY
Lee Trevino	74	68	69	71	282	26,269
Hal Sutton	75	70	66	71	282	26,269
Payne Stewart	76	68	69	70	283	19,009
Ben Crenshaw	76	69	69	69	283	19,009
Bob Tway	70	73	69	72	284	14,500.75
Bernhard Langer	74	70	70	70	284	14,500.75
Jack Nicklaus	77	72	67	68	284	14,500.75
Mark McCumber	74	71	68	71	284	14,500.75
Denis Watson	72	70	71	72	285	11,870
Greg Norman	71	68	71	75	285	11,870
Mark Calcavecchia	75	75	72	65	287	11,028
Joey Sindelar	81	66	70	71	288	8,884.67
Scott Verplank	75	72	67	74	288	8,884.67
Jodie Mudd	73	75	69	71	288	8,884.67
Bobby Wadkins	75	69	72	72	288	8,884.67
Craig Stadler	74	71	74	69	288	8,884.67
David Frost	72	72	77	67	288	8,884.67
Fuzzy Zoeller	75	74	71	68	288	8,884.66
David Graham	76	71	69	72	288	8,884.66
Gary Koch	73	73	71	71	288	8,884.66
Larry Mize	75	71	73	70	289	6,461.80
Calvin Peete	77	73	70	69	289	6,461.80
Don Pooley	75	71	74	69	289	6,461.80
Larry Rinker	77	71	70	71	289	6,461.80
Tom Watson	72	71	71	75	289	6,461.80
Mike Reid	74	73	66	76	289	6,461.80
Seve Ballesteros	75	73	68	73	289	6,461.80
Andy Bean	76	72	73	68	289	6,461.80
Lennie Clements	75	72	67	75	289	6,461.80
Dave Eichelberger	80	70	72	67	289	6,461.80
Paul Azinger	78	72	70	70	290	5,575
Mark McNulty	75	72	68	76	291	5,170.20
Larry Nelson	75	73	70	73	291	5,170.20
Phil Blackmar	75	75	70	71	291	5,170.20
Tom Kite	74	74	73	70	291	5,170.20
John Cook	75	73	70	73	291	5,170.20
*Sam Randolph	79	71	68	73	291	
Roger Maltbie	76	70	73	73	292	4,566
Mark O'Meara	76	73	71	72	292	4,566
Doug Tewell	74	73	71	74	292	4,566
Bruce Fleisher	76	73	71	72	292	4,566
Johnny Miller	76	72	71	74	293	3,963
Dave Barr	75	73	73	72	293	3,963
Mark Lye	80	70	70	73	293	3,963
Sandy Lyle	78	71	72	72	293	3,963
Kenny Knox	72	76	74	71	293	3,963
Mac O'Grady	75	69	73	77	294	3,427
Barry Jaeckel	75	74	71	74	294	3,427
David Hobby	76	74	71	73	294	3,427
Tommy Nakajima	72	72	78	73	295	3,092
Bill Glasson	76	74	69	76	295	3,092
Greg Powers	80	70	72	74	296	2,914.50
Wayne Levi	77	70	74	75	296	2,914.50
Bill Israelson	79	71	72	74	296	2,914.50
Hubert Green	75	75	75	71	296	2,914.50
Peter Jacobsen	76	72	73	76	297	2,791
Chen Tze Chung	76	72	75	74	297	2,791
Frank Conner	75	73	77	72	297	2,791
Jeff Sluman	75	74	75	74	298	2,761

	SCORES				TOTAL	MONEY
David Ogrin	76	73	74	75	298	2,761
Rick Fehr	72	77	75	74	298	2,761
Dick Mast	76	74	76	74	300	2,761
Howard Twitty	79	71	75	76	301	2,761
Andy North	79	71	77	75	302	2,761
Mike Malaska	74	74	80	75	303	2,761
Peter Oosterhuis	78	70	78	78	304	2,761
Brad Greer	78	72	79	76	305	2,761

Out of Final 36 Holes

			TOTAL	
Tom Pernice		80	71	151
Chris Perry		75	76	151
Don Reese		74	77	151
Dan Pohl		79	72	151
Bill Rogers		75	76	151
Mark Brooks		75	76	151
Bob Lohr		73	78	151
Chen Tze Ming		74	77	151
Thomas Cleaver		77	74	151
Bob Murphy		79	72	151
*Tim Fleming		76	75	151
Donnie Hammond		78	73	151
Joe Inman		79	72	151
Hale Irwin		77	74	151
Tim Simpson		78	74	152
Jim Thorpe		79	73	152
Rafael Alarcon		81	71	152
Ronnie Black		78	74	152
Donald Dubois		74	78	152
Danny Edwards		83	69	152
John Mahaffey		79	73	152
Tracy Nakazaki		82	70	152
David Thore		79	74	153
Adrian Stills		78	75	153
Brett Upper		79	74	153
Bruce Zabriski		77	76	153
Ossie Moore		78	75	153
Bobby Clampett		81	72	153
Brad Fabel		79	74	153
Mark Pfeil		79	74	153
Scott Simpson		78	76	154
Fred Wadsworth		81	73	154
Wayne Smith		77	77	154
Jack Lewis		77	77	154
Tom Byrum		81	73	154
Jeff Maggert		81	73	154
Buddy Gardner		82	72	154
Jerry Haas		80	74	154
Dave Rummells		78	76	154
Curtis Strange		76	79	155
John Adams		79	76	155
Jim Albus		79	76	155
Thomas Lehman		78	77	155
Roy Biancalana		78	77	155
Jeff Lewis		79	76	155
George Burns		83	72	155
Greg Farrow		83	72	155
Mike Gove		78	77	155

	SCORES		TOTAL
Jay Haas	78	77	155
Mike Hulbert	81	74	155
Bobby Pancratz	78	77	155
Kirk Triplett	78	78	156
Evan Schiller	82	74	156
John McGinnis	83	73	156
Mike Colandro	80	76	156
Bob Gilder	76	80	156
Mike Smith	81	75	156
Cary Hungale	79	77	156
*Brian Watts	82	75	157
Miller Barber	80	77	157
Gene George	76	81	157
Tom Sieckmann	77	81	158
Cleve Coldwater	77	81	158
Corey Pavin	80	79	159
Andrew Magee	82	77	159
Ray Cragun	84	75	159
Steve Gotsche	81	78	159
Walt Chapman	82	78	160
Ed Dougherty	82	78	160
Rick Schuller	85	76	161
Scott Williams	83	78	161
Fred Funk	84	77	161
Gary Krueger	84	77	161
William Sakas	86	75	161
Perry Arthur	85	77	162
Doug Campbell	86	76	162
*Bob Lewis Jr.	83	79	162
Barney Thompson	80	83	163
Lee Chill	86	78	164
*John Daly	88	76	164
Jim Smith	86	78	164
Stanley Utley	80	86	166
R. W. Eaks	85	86	171
Ken Green	82	WD	
Jack Renner	85	WD	

(All professionals who did not complete 72 holes received $600.)

Provident Classic

Valleybrook Country Club, Hixson, Tennessee   June 12–15
Par 35–35 – 70; 6,516 yards   purse, $300,000

	SCORES				TOTAL	MONEY
Brad Faxon	67	62	69	63	261	$54,000
Scott Hoch	67	63	66	66	262	32,400
Clarence Rose	65	66	65	69	265	20,400
Loren Roberts	67	68	69	63	267	12,400
Bill Bergin	67	69	65	66	267	12,400
Gary McCord	69	67	63	68	267	12,400
J. C. Snead	69	68	67	64	268	9,675
Tommy Armour	71	62	67	68	268	9,675
Ken Brown	71	66	65	67	269	7,800
Brian Claar	67	69	65	68	269	7,800
Jim Gallagher	64	68	69	68	269	7,800

	SCORES				TOTAL	MONEY
Steve Jones	70	67	64	68	269	7,800
Danny Briggs	66	66	67	71	270	5,800
Antonio Cerda	68	68	65	69	270	5,800
John McComish	68	71	66	65	270	5,800
Leonard Thompson	69	67	68	67	271	4,650
Ernie Gonzalez	65	69	73	64	271	4,650
Denny Hepler	69	64	69	69	271	4,650
David Peoples	69	67	66	69	271	4,650
George Cadle	67	66	69	70	272	3,250
Russ Cochran	67	68	72	65	272	3,250
Lou Graham	70	66	68	68	272	3,250
Morris Hatalsky	66	67	68	71	272	3,250
Gene Sauers	66	68	68	70	272	3,250
Harry Taylor	67	65	70	70	272	3,250
Charles Bolling	67	67	69	70	273	2,265
Steve Bowman	70	66	70	67	273	2,265
David Canipe	66	70	69	68	273	2,265
Gibby Gilbert	68	65	71	69	273	2,265
Greg Twiggs	70	68	68	68	274	1,863
Rod Curl	70	66	69	69	274	1,863
Andy Dillard	68	67	68	71	274	1,863
Mark Hayes	68	68	66	72	274	1,863
David Lundstrom	71	65	70	68	274	1,863
Rocco Mediate	65	71	69	70	275	1,479
Billy Pierot	70	67	67	71	275	1,479
Tim Norris	69	72	68	66	275	1,479
Vance Heafner	70	68	65	72	275	1,479
Blaine McCallister	72	67	69	67	275	1,479
Rick Dalpos	68	69	69	70	276	1,200
Robert Wrenn	71	70	68	67	276	1,200
Tom Gleeton	70	67	65	74	276	1,200
Stu Ingraham	73	65	66	72	276	1,200
Eduardo Romero	70	69	67	71	277	990
Ed Fiori	69	69	69	70	277	990
Brian Mogg	69	69	70	69	277	990
Bobby Cole	67	69	73	69	278	846
Bill Sander	70	69	71	68	278	846
Bob E. Smith	71	68	70	70	279	780
Richard Zokol	69	70	66	75	280	718
Jeff Grygiel	69	72	69	70	280	718
Gary Hallberg	70	70	68	72	280	718
Ron Streck	69	71	68	72	280	718
Kermit Zarley	71	67	70	72	280	718
Greg Ladehoff	71	66	73	70	280	718

Georgia-Pacific Atlanta Classic

Atlanta Country Club, Marietta, Georgia
Par 36–36 – 72; 7,018 yards

June 19–22
purse, $500,000

	SCORES				TOTAL	MONEY
Bob Tway	68	66	71	64	269	$90,000
Hal Sutton	66	68	67	70	271	54,000
Scott Hoch	67	66	70	70	273	24,000
Greg Norman	71	72	66	64	273	24,000
Willie Wood	67	68	70	68	273	24,000
Mark O'Meara	67	67	70	69	273	24,000

	SCORES				TOTAL	MONEY
Gary Koch	72	63	72	67	274	16,750
Tom Purtzer	69	69	66	71	275	15,500
Doug Tewell	68	64	71	73	276	13,500
Rex Caldwell	71	72	65	68	276	13,500
David Graham	71	71	67	67	276	13,500
D. A. Weibring	67	71	68	71	277	9,800
Tom Kite	69	69	67	72	277	9,800
Paul Azinger	68	71	68	70	277	9,800
Andy Bean	70	72	65	70	277	9,800
Bill Bergin	69	66	70	72	277	9,800
Denis Watson	67	71	70	70	278	7,250
Bill Rogers	72	70	69	67	278	7,250
David Frost	71	65	72	70	278	7,250
Morris Hatalsky	72	66	67	73	278	7,250
Jeff Sluman	69	73	69	68	279	5,400
George Archer	69	72	72	66	279	5,400
Chip Beck	69	72	68	70	279	5,400
Danny Edwards	68	69	71	71	279	5,400
Larry Mize	69	73	71	67	280	3,987.50
Jim Simons	73	69	70	68	280	3,987.50
Scott Simpson	72	70	66	72	280	3,987.50
Ray Floyd	70	69	71	70	280	3,987.50
Tim Simpson	72	70	69	70	281	3,325
Larry Nelson	73	69	71	68	281	3,325
Bobby Clampett	72	70	67	72	281	3,325
Gibby Gilbert	69	69	70	73	281	3,325
Clarence Rose	72	71	72	67	282	2,762.50
Howard Twitty	69	70	72	71	282	2,762.50
Dan Pohl	71	70	68	73	282	2,762.50
Phil Blackmar	71	70	72	69	282	2,762.50
Larry Rinker	74	69	69	71	283	2,150
Tim Norris	72	70	70	71	283	2,150
Robert Wrenn	70	73	72	68	283	2,150
David Ogrin	70	73	69	71	283	2,150
Rick Fehr	66	74	73	70	283	2,150
Jim Gallagher	70	72	73	68	283	2,150
Mark Hayes	68	72	73	70	283	2,150
Brian Claar	71	72	71	70	284	1,475.72
Brad Faxon	73	70	71	70	284	1,475.72
Davis Love	68	72	72	72	284	1,475.72
Greg Twiggs	69	69	72	74	284	1,475.71
T. M. Chen	72	71	70	71	284	1,475.71
Jeff Grygiel	69	72	67	76	284	1,475.71
Andrew Magee	67	69	70	78	284	1,475.71

Canadian Open

Glen Abbey Golf Club, Oakville, Ontario, Canada
Par 35-37 – 72; 7,102 yards

June 26–29
purse, $600,000

	SCORES				TOTAL	MONEY
Bob Murphy	71	70	68	71	280	$108,000
Greg Norman	72	76	62	73	283	64,800
Davis Love III	72	68	70	74	284	31,200
Andy Bean	69	69	74	72	284	31,200
Mike Donald	69	73	69	73	284	31,200
Clarence Rose	69	76	70	70	285	20,100

	SCORES				TOTAL	MONEY
Mac O'Grady	73	68	69	75	285	20,100
Brian Claar	73	73	69	70	285	20,100
David Ogrin	73	71	72	70	286	13,885.72
Curtis Strange	73	70	70	73	286	13,885.72
Nick Price	71	71	71	73	286	13,885.72
Jeff Sluman	72	73	70	71	286	13,885.71
Bob Tway	70	71	72	73	286	13,885.71
Bobby Cole	71	72	69	74	286	13,885.71
Jay Delsing	75	69	71	71	286	13,885.71
Jack Nicklaus	74	69	70	74	287	9,000
Paul Azinger	70	69	77	71	287	9,000
Dave Barr	70	71	70	76	287	9,000
Fred Couples	74	71	70	72	287	9,000
Ben Crenshaw	74	72	67	74	287	9,000
Pat McGowan	72	70	70	76	288	6,000
Joey Sindelar	74	72	70	72	288	6,000
Lee Trevino	74	69	69	76	288	6,000
Ernie Gonzalez	71	69	72	76	288	6,000
Dan Halldorson	69	74	69	76	288	6,000
Steve Jones	75	73	66	74	288	6,000
Tom Purtzer	75	69	71	74	289	4,530
Johnny Miller	71	72	71	75	289	4,530
Steve Pate	73	74	72	71	290	3,732.86
John Adams	73	72	71	74	290	3,732.86
Scott Hoch	71	75	69	75	290	3,732.86
Dave Eichelberger	71	75	71	73	290	3,732.86
David Graham	73	72	71	74	290	3,732.86
Mark Wiebe	71	73	70	76	290	3,732.85
Jim Simons	73	73	71	73	290	3,732.85
Sam Randolph	70	73	75	73	291	2,765
Robert Wrenn	76	70	70	75	291	2,765
Jim Colbert	74	71	72	74	291	2,765
Hale Irwin	68	73	73	77	291	2,765
Gary Hallberg	73	74	73	71	291	2,765
Morris Hatalsky	74	69	73	75	291	2,765
Peter Oosterhuis	77	70	71	74	292	2,280
Charles Bolling	71	71	73	77	292	2,280
Jodie Mudd	73	72	75	73	293	1,864.80
Corey Pavin	75	70	74	74	293	1,864.80
Bruce Lietzke	77	70	71	75	293	1,864.80
Brad Fabel	69	76	73	75	293	1,864.80
Wayne Grady	73	72	70	78	293	1,864.80
Greg Twiggs	74	74	74	72	294	1,480.80
Harry Taylor	71	75	70	78	294	1,480.80
John Cook	73	71	76	74	294	1,480.80
Rocco Mediate	74	74	72	74	294	1,480.80
Brad Faxon	71	75	74	74	294	1,480.80

Canon Sammy Davis Jr.—Greater Hartford Open

TPC of Connecticut, Cromwell, Connecticut
Par 36–35 – 71; 6,786 yards

July 3–6
purse, $700,000

	SCORES				TOTAL	MONEY
Mac O'Grady	71	69	67	62	269	$126,000
Roger Maltbie	66	67	70	66	269	75,600
(O'Grady defeated Maltbie on first hole of sudden-death playoff.)						
Mark O'Meara	69	72	64	67	272	36,400

	SCORES				TOTAL	MONEY
Paul Azinger	67	70	66	69	272	36,400
Scott Hoch	71	66	68	67	272	36,400
Curtis Strange	71	69	65	68	273	23,450
Tom Watson	65	67	70	71	273	23,450
Tim Simpson	64	66	74	69	273	23,450
Chip Beck	66	73	65	70	274	18,900
John Cook	68	69	69	68	274	18,900
Mike Donald	69	68	68	69	274	18,900
Denis Watson	65	71	73	66	275	13,300
David Lundstrom	69	70	67	69	275	13,300
John Mahaffey	67	71	69	68	275	13,300
Steve Pate	69	69	72	65	275	13,300
Mark Calcavecchia	70	69	70	66	275	13,300
Dan Forsman	65	68	72	70	275	13,300
Dan Pohl	69	72	67	68	276	8,820
Scott Simpson	68	67	72	69	276	8,820
Clarence Rose	69	71	68	68	276	8,820
Jim Dent	68	69	67	72	276	8,820
Jim Gallagher	71	68	72	65	276	8,820
Gary Hallberg	72	67	67	70	276	8,820
Mike McCullough	67	73	67	70	277	5,810
Kenny Knox	66	69	67	75	277	5,810
David Edwards	69	71	71	66	277	5,810
Mark Hayes	70	68	73	66	277	5,810
Mike Hulbert	69	72	68	68	277	5,810
Loren Roberts	69	72	69	68	278	4,355.15
Ronnie Black	69	69	71	69	278	4,355.15
Lee Trevino	70	70	70	68	278	4,355.14
D. A. Weibring	68	71	70	69	278	4,355.14
John Adams	70	69	69	70	278	4,355.14
Brian Claar	69	72	68	69	278	4,355.14
Tom Kite	68	69	69	72	278	4,355.14
Corey Pavin	69	69	70	71	279	3,154.86
Howard Twitty	72	67	69	71	279	3,154.86
Mark Pfeil	70	70	70	69	279	3,154.86
Peter Jacobsen	73	68	67	71	279	3,154.86
Steve Jones	71	69	70	69	279	3,154.86
Jodie Mudd	71	70	68	70	279	3,154.85
Lennie Clements	71	69	70	69	279	3,154.85
Billy Pierot	73	69	68	70	280	2,045.40
Leonard Thompson	69	73	69	69	280	2,045.40
Fuzzy Zoeller	68	73	74	65	280	2,045.40
Sam Randolph	73	67	70	70	280	2,045.40
Eduardo Romero	74	66	71	69	280	2,045.40
Antonio Cerda	68	73	69	70	280	2,045.40
Russ Cochran	71	70	70	69	280	2,045.40
Wayne Levi	70	69	72	69	280	2,045.40
Dave Eichelberger	69	69	73	69	280	2,045.40
Lon Hinkle	70	71	68	71	280	2,045.40

Anheuser-Busch Classic

Kingsmill Golf Club, Williamsburg, Virginia
Par 36–35 – 71; 6,746 yards

July 10–13
purse, $500,000

	SCORES				TOTAL	MONEY
Fuzzy Zoeller	70	68	72	64	274	$90,000
Jodie Mudd	65	70	72	69	276	54,000

	SCORES				TOTAL	MONEY
Joey Sindelar	70	68	72	67	277	34,000
Scott Hoch	68	69	74	67	278	22,000
Mac O'Grady	69	72	70	67	278	22,000
Clarence Rose	69	71	70	69	279	16,187.50
Chen Tze Chung	71	70	70	68	279	16,187.50
Rick Fehr	71	67	72	69	279	16,187.50
David Frost	68	71	72	68	279	16,187.50
Hale Irwin	70	69	71	70	280	11,500
Tony Sills	70	65	75	70	280	11,500
Jeff Sluman	66	73	74	67	280	11,500
Don Pooley	67	72	72	69	280	11,500
Corey Pavin	70	72	69	69	280	11,500
John Mahaffey	67	71	73	70	281	7,750
Davis Love III	67	72	70	72	281	7,750
Mark O'Meara	73	63	73	72	281	7,750
Harry Taylor	69	73	70	69	281	7,750
Denis Watson	69	69	71	72	281	7,750
Mark Hayes	71	65	80	65	281	7,750
Mark Wiebe	67	71	74	70	282	5,200
Bob Murphy	71	70	70	71	282	5,200
Dick Mast	67	72	76	67	282	5,200
Gary McCord	73	69	73	67	282	5,200
Russ Cochran	69	69	73	71	282	5,200
Scott Simpson	68	72	71	72	283	3,475
Tim Simpson	67	70	72	74	283	3,475
Lanny Wadkins	70	71	73	69	283	3,475
Mike Sullivan	70	71	69	73	283	3,475
Craig Stadler	69	69	75	70	283	3,475
Roger Maltbie	70	67	73	73	283	3,475
Rod Curl	68	74	71	70	283	3,475
Mike Donald	70	72	68	73	283	3,475
Jack Renner	73	68	72	71	284	2,471.43
Hal Sutton	70	67	71	76	284	2,471.43
Willie Wood	69	73	70	72	284	2,471.43
Richard Zokol	72	66	67	79	284	2,471.43
Kenny Knox	71	66	70	77	284	2,471.43
Paul Azinger	72	70	76	66	284	2,471.43
Steve Jones	72	70	71	71	284	2,471.42
Mike McCullough	72	68	70	75	285	1,900
Mark McCumber	72	68	70	75	285	1,900
Lennie Clements	70	72	71	72	285	1,900
Donnie Hammond	67	74	72	72	285	1,900
Robert Wrenn	70	71	72	73	286	1,401.43
Adrian Stills	65	71	73	77	286	1,401.43
Steve Pate	67	73	75	71	286	1,401.43
Bill Bergin	69	69	76	72	286	1,401.43
Tom Byrum	70	71	73	72	286	1,401.43
Tony DeLuca	66	70	79	71	286	1,401.43
Mark Brooks	73	69	75	69	286	1,401.42

Hardee's Classic

Oakwood Country Club, Coal Valley, Illinois
Par 35–35 – 70; 6,514 yards

July 17–20
purse, $400,000

	SCORES				TOTAL	MONEY
Mark Wiebe	69	65	66	68	268	$72,000
Curt Byrum	64	70	64	71	269	43,200

	SCORES			TOTAL	MONEY
Pat Lindsey	73	66	66	66	271	27,200
Bill Glasson	72	68	66	66	272	19,200
Bob Lohr	63	71	69	70	273	14,600
Calvin Peete	68	67	72	66	273	14,600
Morris Hatalsky	72	68	65	68	273	14,600
Brett Upper	71	70	65	68	274	11,200
George Archer	69	67	68	70	274	11,200
Mark Brooks	67	70	66	71	274	11,200
Russ Cochran	66	67	70	71	274	11,200
Blaine McCallister	69	66	69	71	275	7,371.43
Mike Smith	73	63	66	73	275	7,371.43
Dick Mast	66	72	67	70	275	7,371.43
Mark Calcavecchia	68	67	69	71	275	7,371.43
Bob Gilder	70	67	66	72	275	7,371.43
Scott Hoch	68	67	70	70	275	7,371.43
Brian Claar	73	67	66	69	275	7,371.42
Jeff Sluman	66	68	69	73	276	5,200
Jay Delsing	68	72	68	68	276	5,200
Mark Hayes	67	68	72	69	276	5,200
Larry Ziegler	69	67	71	70	277	3,340
David Ogrin	69	71	67	70	277	3,340
Gil Morgan	69	69	66	73	277	3,340
David Peoples	72	69	63	73	277	3,340
Eduardo Romero	67	67	71	72	277	3,340
Dave Rummells	68	69	72	68	277	3,340
John Adams	69	67	70	71	277	3,340
Charles Bolling	69	72	68	68	277	3,340
Jeff Lewis	67	71	71	68	277	3,340
Chen Tze Chung	71	68	66	72	277	3,340
J. C. Snead	71	69	67	71	278	2,075.56
Tony Sills	69	68	73	68	278	2,075.56
Victor Regalado	69	72	67	70	278	2,075.56
Dave Stockton	70	71	71	66	278	2,075.56
Bart Bryant	68	69	67	74	278	2,075.56
Willie Wood	70	70	66	72	278	2,075.55
Gene Sauers	69	69	71	69	278	2,075.55
Tommy Valentine	68	69	71	70	278	2,075.55
Bobby Cole	67	71	68	72	278	2,075.55
Andy North	71	67	71	70	279	1,362
Jim Rutledge	68	70	71	70	279	1,362
Dave Barr	68	72	66	73	279	1,362
Brad Bryant	68	70	69	72	279	1,362
Pat McGowan	72	67	68	72	279	1,362
Tom Gleeton	68	72	67	72	279	1,362
Mike Morley	71	69	70	69	279	1,362
Phil Hancock	70	68	70	71	279	1,362
Mike Sullivan	70	71	68	71	280	955.56
Jack Renner	69	72	70	69	280	955.56
Tommy Aaron	72	68	70	70	280	955.56
Bill Israelson	73	66	66	75	280	955.56
Rick Dalpos	67	71	70	72	280	955.56
Leonard Thompson	71	69	70	70	280	955.55
Adrian Stills	72	69	71	68	280	955.55
Tom Shaw	71	66	71	72	280	955.55
Rod Curl	73	67	71	69	280	955.55

Buick Open

Warwick Hills Golf and Country Club, Grand Blanc, Michigan   July 24–27
Par 36–36 – 72; 7,014 yards   purse, $500,000

	SCORES				TOTAL	MONEY
Ben Crenshaw	69	67	66	68	270	$90,000
J. C. Snead	67	70	68	66	271	44,000
Doug Tewell	70	68	67	66	271	44,000
Ed Fiori	66	69	70	67	272	24,000
Bobby Wadkins	69	66	70	68	273	19,000
Davis Love III	65	67	70	71	273	19,000
Gene Sauers	69	67	67	71	274	16,125
Steve Pate	70	67	65	72	274	16,125
Tom Purtzer	68	68	66	73	275	11,571.43
Scott Hoch	70	69	66	70	275	11,571.43
Kenny Knox	68	68	68	71	275	11,571.43
Wayne Levi	71	67	68	69	275	11,571.43
Lee Trevino	69	68	70	68	275	11,571.43
Brian Claar	68	68	71	68	275	11,571.43
Jeff Sluman	69	67	69	70	275	11,571.42
Jodie Mudd	70	67	69	70	276	7,750
Mike Sullivan	71	69	68	68	276	7,750
T. C. Chen	70	71	64	71	276	7,750
Jim Colbert	67	69	72	68	276	7,750
Bob Lohr	72	65	71	69	277	6,250
Wayne Grady	69	67	69	72	277	6,250
Andrew Magee	71	65	72	70	278	4,800
Mike Hill	70	69	69	70	278	4,800
Bob Eastwood	69	70	69	70	278	4,800
Danny Edwards	71	68	71	68	278	4,800
Morris Hatalsky	70	70	69	69	278	4,800
Gary Pinns	72	68	71	68	279	3,190
Bruce Lietzke	69	67	72	71	279	3,190
Hal Sutton	68	69	70	72	279	3,190
Tony Sills	71	68	68	72	279	3,190
Mike McCullough	71	68	69	71	279	3,190
Leonard Thompson	72	69	69	69	279	3,190
Billy Pierot	65	72	72	70	279	3,190
Lon Hinkle	69	67	73	70	279	3,190
Peter Jacobsen	68	70	70	71	279	3,190
David Graham	68	70	71	70	279	3,190
Dick Mast	71	67	73	69	280	2,050
Bobby Clampett	69	71	69	71	280	2,050
John Cook	69	71	68	72	280	2,050
Rick Cramer	73	68	70	69	280	2,050
Steve Jones	71	70	69	70	280	2,050
Tom Kite	68	68	70	74	280	2,050
Joe Inman	69	69	72	70	280	2,050
Dave Eichelberger	70	66	69	75	280	2,050
Buddy Gardner	69	71	71	69	280	2,050
Scott Verplank	72	68	70	71	281	1,386
Lanny Wadkins	71	68	70	72	281	1,386
D. A. Weibring	71	69	68	73	281	1,386
Howard Twitty	67	72	72	70	281	1,386
Vance Heafner	71	69	73	68	281	1,386

Western Open

Butler National Golf Club, Oak Brook, Illinois
Par 36–36 – 72; 7,097 yards

July 31–August 3
purse, $500,000

	SCORES				TOTAL	MONEY
Tom Kite	70	75	73	68	286	$90,000
Nick Price	71	71	73	71	286	37,333.34
Fred Couples	70	68	73	75	286	37,333.33
David Frost	74	66	71	75	286	37,333.33
(Kite Defeated Price, Couples and Frost on first hole of sudden-death playoff.)						
Greg Norman	71	74	72	70	287	16,950
Bobby Wadkins	69	69	74	75	287	16,950
Leonard Thompson	71	73	69	74	287	16,950
Dick Mast	69	73	72	73	287	16,950
Bruce Lietzke	74	70	73	70	287	16,950
Mark Pfeil	72	71	73	73	289	12,000
George Burns	71	70	71	77	289	12,000
Tom Byrum	70	70	72	77	289	12,000
Danny Edwards	75	72	73	69	289	12,000
Corey Pavin	73	72	76	69	290	9,000
Russ Cochran	78	70	68	74	290	9,000
Gary Hallberg	68	71	79	72	290	9,000
George Archer	74	73	70	74	291	6,766.67
Ronnie Black	70	73	72	76	291	6,766.67
Bobby Clampett	72	70	73	76	291	6,766.67
Mark Hayes	72	73	72	74	291	6,766.67
Isao Aoki	71	73	74	73	291	6,766.66
Ben Crenshaw	72	73	71	75	291	6,766.66
Bill Rogers	73	73	71	75	292	4,214.29
Calvin Peete	69	76	73	74	292	4,214.29
Brian Claar	72	73	69	78	292	4,214.29
Bob Gilder	68	75	76	73	292	4,214.29
Tom Purtzer	69	70	76	77	292	4,214.28
Loren Roberts	68	76	74	74	292	4,214.28
Bill Israelson	75	72	72	73	292	4,214.28
*Billy Andrade	70	78	73	71	292	
Tony Sills	74	71	75	73	293	3,037.67
Brett Upper	79	67	70	77	293	3,037.67
Scott Simpson	69	71	75	78	293	3,037.67
Kenny Knox	76	72	73	72	293	3,037.67
Larry Rinker	76	72	73	72	293	3,037.66
Brad Faxon	75	71	70	77	293	3,037.66
J. C. Snead	74	74	72	74	294	2,304
Jim Simons	71	77	69	77	294	2,304
Hal Sutton	73	73	72	76	294	2,304
Rex Caldwell	76	69	77	72	294	2,304
Trevor Dodds	72	76	73	73	294	2,304
Mike Donald	74	72	76	72	294	2,304
Pat Lindsey	72	75	75	73	295	1,750
Lennie Clements	70	74	78	73	295	1,750
Dave Eichelberger	74	68	77	76	295	1,750
Nick Faldo	73	70	73	79	295	1,750
Lou Graham	74	74	71	76	295	1,750
David Ogrin	71	71	81	73	296	1,301.67
Joey Sindelar	78	69	75	74	296	1,301.67
Mark Brooks	71	76	74	75	296	1,301.67
Bob Lohr	75	73	76	72	296	1,301.67
Gene Sauers	74	72	72	78	296	1,301.66
Andy Dillard	71	76	77	72	296	1,301.66

PGA Championship

Inverness Club, Toledo, Ohio   August 7–11
Par 35–36 – 71; 6,982 yards   purse, $800,000

(Final round postponed Sunday; completed Monday.)

	SCORES				TOTAL	MONEY
Bob Tway	72	70	64	70	276	$140,000
Greg Norman	65	68	69	76	278	80,000
Peter Jacobsen	68	70	70	71	279	60,000
D. A. Weibring	71	72	68	69	280	42,865
Bruce Lietzke	69	71	70	71	281	32,500
Payne Stewart	70	67	72	72	281	32,500
Mike Hulbert	69	68	74	71	282	20,833.34
Jim Thorpe	71	67	73	71	282	20,833.33
David Graham	75	69	71	67	282	20,833.33
Doug Tewell	73	71	68	71	283	15,000
Lonnie Nielsen	73	69	72	70	284	12,000
Lee Trevino	71	74	69	70	284	12,000
Lanny Wadkins	71	75	70	68	284	12,000
Ben Crenshaw	72	73	72	67	284	12,000
Donnie Hammond	70	71	68	75	284	12,000
Jack Nicklaus	70	68	72	75	285	8,500
Don Pooley	71	74	69	71	285	8,500
Tony Sills	71	72	69	73	285	8,500
Tom Watson	72	69	72	72	285	8,500
Chip Beck	71	73	71	70	285	8,500
Corey Pavin	71	72	70	73	286	6,120
Hal Sutton	73	71	70	72	286	6,120
Ronnie Black	68	71	74	73	286	6,120
David Frost	70	73	68	75	286	6,120
Wayne Grady	68	76	71	71	286	6,120
Dan Pohl	71	71	74	71	287	4,900
Ken Green	71	72	71	73	287	4,900
Hale Irwin	76	70	73	68	287	4,900
Tom Kite	72	73	71	71	287	4,900
Calvin Peete	72	73	69	74	288	4,000
Ian Woosnam	72	70	75	71	288	4,000
Jeff Sluman	70	71	76	71	288	4,000
Gene Sauers	69	73	70	76	288	4,000
Craig Stadler	67	74	73	74	288	4,000
Wayne Levi	68	73	71	76	288	4,000
Brett Upper	71	73	72	73	289	3,400
Isao Aoki	73	69	74	73	289	3,400
Mark Lye	72	71	70	76	289	3,400
Fred Couples	69	73	72	75	289	3,400
Buddy Gardner	72	73	71	73	289	3,400
Scott Simpson	70	70	75	75	290	2,850
Jodie Mudd	72	73	73	72	290	2,850
Mike Reid	71	73	70	76	290	2,850
Bobby Wadkins	69	74	70	77	290	2,850
Hubert Green	75	70	74	71	290	2,850
Scott Hoch	72	70	75	73	290	2,850
Mark Wiebe	75	67	72	77	291	2,250
Dave Barr	71	73	73	74	291	2,250
Davis Love III	70	72	72	77	291	2,250
Mike Donald	74	69	73	75	291	2,250
Tommy Nakajima	71	73	71	76	291	2,250

	SCORES				TOTAL	MONEY
Roger Maltbie	73	70	74	74	291	2,250.00
Dave Stockton	70	75	74	73	292	1,740.42
Steve Pate	76	69	71	76	292	1,740.42
Joey Sindelar	74	72	73	73	292	1,740.42
Andy Bean	74	70	72	76	292	1,740.42
John Cook	71	72	75	74	292	1,740.42
Bob Gilder	69	75	73	75	292	1,740.42
Jay Haas	69	77	74	72	292	1,740.42
Mark McCumber	71	74	68	79	292	1,740.42
Mike Sullivan	72	73	74	73	292	1,740.41
Clarence Rose	73	71	72	76	292	1,740.41
Phil Blackmar	67	73	79	73	292	1,740.41
Larry Mize	69	76	75	72	292	1,740.41
James Blair	72	74	72	75	293	1,600
Gary Koch	68	77	74	75	294	1,590
Lennie Clements	71	75	72	77	295	1,580
David Edwards	72	69	76	79	296	1,570
Bob Murphy	73	73	74	77	297	1,560
Ken Brown	73	73	72	80	298	1,550
Denis Watson	71	74	77	77	299	1,550
J. C. Snead	70	76	75	79	300	1,550
Johnny Miller	72	71	73	WD		700

Out of Final 36 Holes

Mark McNulty	75	72	147
Mark O'Meara	73	74	147
Jim Colbert	74	73	147
Nick Faldo	76	71	147
Pat Fitzsimons	73	74	147
Ray Floyd	76	71	147
Larry Rinker	78	69	147
Andrew Magee	74	73	147
Andy North	72	75	147
Mark Hayes	73	74	147
Kevin Morris	74	73	147
Bernhard Langer	73	74	147
Barry Jaeckel	73	74	147
Fuzzy Zoeller	73	75	148
Howard Twitty	72	76	148
Bob Ackerman	76	72	148
Larry Nelson	74	74	148
Tom Purtzer	73	75	148
Ray Freeman	75	73	148
Dan Halldorson	75	73	148
Mike Schleuter	74	74	148
Mac O'Grady	72	76	148
Masahiro Kuramoto	73	75	148
Scott Bess	74	75	149
Manuel Pinero	76	73	149
Curtis Strange	74	75	149
George Burns	73	76	149
Chen Tze Ming	75	74	149
Howard Clark	72	77	149
Peter Oakley	72	77	149
David Duschane	75	74	149
Brad Faxon	77	72	149
Larry Gilbert	73	76	149
John Mahaffey	71	78	149

	SCORES		TOTAL	MONEY
Gil Morgan	77	72	149	
Larry Webb	76	74	150	
Jim White	75	75	150	
Seve Ballesteros	74	76	150	
Tim Simpson	73	77	150	
Pat McGowan	76	74	150	
Bob Lohr	74	76	150	
Gary Hardin	77	73	150	
Lynn Janson	74	76	150	
Kenny Knox	74	76	150	
Ken Allard	75	76	151	
Paul Azinger	72	79	151	
Rick Vershure	75	76	151	
Bill Schumaker	74	77	151	
Leonard Thompson	79	73	152	
Arnold Palmer	75	77	152	
Ed Dougherty	74	78	152	
Danny Edwards	72	80	152	
Ossie Moore	76	76	152	
Bill Glasson	79	73	152	
Jay Overton	72	80	152	
Wheeler Stewart	76	76	152	
Jose-Maria Canizares	72	81	153	
Nick Price	75	78	153	
Jeff Foxx	78	75	153	
Steve Veriato	72	81	153	
Willie Wood	76	78	154	
Robert Hoyt	77	77	154	
Charlie Epps	77	78	155	
Dan Forsman	79	76	155	
Rives McBee	77	78	155	
Mike San Filippo	71	85	156	
Paul Wise	84	72	156	
Roy Vucinich	76	80	156	
Dwight Nevil	79	77	156	
Rick Acton	80	78	158	
Gary Robinson	83	75	158	
Larry Babica	79	82	161	
Gary Ostrega	77	84	161	
Bob Leaver	78	83	161	
Gregg Jones	79	83	162	
Ron Wells	84	79	163	
Paul Way	82	84	166	

(All contestants who did not complete 72 holes received $1,000)

The International

Castle Pines Golf Club, Castle Rock, Colorado
Par 36–36 – 72; 7,503 yards

August 13–17
purse, $1,002,300

FIRST-ROUND LOSERS

STABLEFORD SCORE	WEDNESDAY
+2	Gary McCord, Dave Barr, Leonard Thompson, Buddy Gardner, Loren Roberts, George Burns, Payne Stewart, Bob Lohr.

+ 1	Dave Stockton, Bobby Clampett, Dale Douglass, Bobby Wadkins, Ernesto Perez Acosta.
0	Charles Bolling, Len Clements, Jim Colbert, Bobby Cole, Brad Fabel, Clarence Rose, Denis Watson.
− 1	Joe Inman, Dick Mast, John McComish, Tommy Nakajima.
− 2	John Adams, Larry Nelson, Mark Pfeil.
− 3	Frank Conner, Barry Jaeckel, Steve Jones, Scott Verplank.
− 4	Lou Graham, Arnold Palmer.
− 5	Dan Pohl.
− 6	Wayne Grady.
− 7	Gibby Gilbert.
− 8	Greg Norman, Craig Stadler.
− 9	Gary Hallberg.
− 10	Wayne Levi.
− 11	Bob Eastwood.
DQ	Mark Calcavecchia.

THURSDAY

+ 1	Mike Nicolette, Dennis Trixler, Bob Gilder.
0	Dan Halldorson, Larry Rinker, Chip Beck, Jay Delsing, Andy North, Ben Crenshaw, George Archer, Jeff Grygiel.
− 1	Bobby Wrenn, Brian Claar, Bill Israelson, Blaine McCallister, Chen Tze Ming, Ossie Moore.
− 2	David Graham, Jim Thorpe, Johnny Miller, Curt Byrum, Jet Ozaki.
− 3	Tommy Valentine, Andrew Magee, Larry Wise, Masahiro Kuramoto.
− 4	Woody Blackburn, Pat Lindsey, Ed Sneed, Antonio Cerda.
− 5	Jack Renner.
− 6	Tom Sieckmann, Ed Fiori, Brett Upper.
− 7	David Jones.
− 8	Phil Blackmar, Greg Ladehoff.
− 9	Mike Donald, Pat McGowan, Gil Morgan, David Ogrin.
DQ	Calvin Peete.

(Each first-round loser received $700.)

SECOND-ROUND LOSERS

FRIDAY

+ 2	Willie Wood, Tim Simpson, Bob Murphy, Paul Azinger.
+ 1	Mark O'Meara, D. A. Weibring, Mike McCullough, Tim Norris, Scott Hoch, Doug Tewell.
0	Hale Irwin, Dave Eichelberger, Rick Fehr, Roger Maltbie.
− 1	Jeff Sluman, Mike Sullivan, Bill Glasson, Don Pooley, Steve Pate.
− 2	Russ Cochran, Peter Oosterhuis.
− 3	Scott Simpson, Chris Perry, Lanny Wadkins, Davis Love III.
− 4	Danny Edwards, Bill Rogers, Tom Byrum, Mike Hulbert, Ray Floyd.
− 5	Gene Sauers.
− 6	Rodger Davis.
− 7	Mark Lye, Mike Smith, Mark Wiebe.
− 14	Rex Caldwell.
DQ	Tom Purtzer.
WD	Dave Rummells, Dan Forsman.

(Each second-round loser received $2,000.)

SEMI-FINAL LOSERS

SATURDAY

+ 4	Jay Haas, Brett Ogle.
+ 3	Mark Hayes, John Cook, Jim Gallagher.

+2	Corey Pavin, Morris Hatalsky, David Frost, Lon Hinkle, Billy Pierot.	
+1	Jack Nicklaus, Ken Brown.	
0	Bob Tway, Sam Randolph, Jim Simons.	
−1	Keith Fergus, Bill Kratzert.	
−2	Tom Watson, Mike Reid, Mark McCumber, Manuel Pinero.	
−3	Ronnie Black.	
−5	David Edwards, Hal Sutton, John Mahaffey.	
−7	Richard Zokol.	
−8	Brad Faxon.	

(Each semi-final loser received $6,000.)

FINALS

SUNDAY

+12	Ken Green	$180,000
+9	Bernhard Langer	113,000
+8	J. C. Snead	63,000
	Joey Sindelar	63,000
+6	Nick Price	45,000
+5	Howard Twitty	41,000
+4	Ken Knox	37,250
	Bruce Lietzke	37,250
+1	Andy Dillard	34,000
0	Tom Kite	31,000
	Donnie Hammond	31,000
−1	Chen Tze Chung	28,000

(POINT SYSTEM: Double eagle—10; eagle—5; birdie—2; par—0; bogey— −1;
double bogey or worse— −3.)

NEC World Series of Golf

Firestone Country Club, South Course, Akron, Ohio
Par 35–35 – 70; 7,173 yards

August 21–24
purse, $700,000

	SCORES				TOTAL	MONEY
Dan Pohl	69	66	71	71	277	$126,000
Lanny Wadkins	68	68	70	72	278	75,600
Bobby Cole	74	67	68	70	279	47,600
John Mahaffey	71	66	72	71	280	33,600
Andy Bean	72	74	69	66	281	24,550
Rodger Davis	72	69	69	71	281	24,550
Donnie Hammond	66	68	73	74	281	24,550
Tim Simpson	71	73	72	65	281	24,550
David Ishii	67	71	73	71	282	16,800
Tom Kite	71	69	71	71	282	16,800
Jack Nicklaus	71	69	69	73	282	16,800
Calvin Peete	72	70	71	69	282	16,800
Jim Thorpe	70	72	68	72	282	16,800
Bob Tway	74	72	66	70	282	16,800
Ken Green	68	75	69	71	283	12,600
Bernhard Langer	67	71	71	75	284	11,200
Corey Pavin	70	69	70	75	284	11,200
Joey Sindelar	71	66	73	74	284	11,200
Ed Dougherty	72	73	73	67	285	9,800
Danny Edwards	70	70	72	74	286	8,566.67
David Frost	72	69	72	73	286	8,566.67

Greg Norman	68	71	72	75	286	8,566.66
Masahiro Kuramoto	68	70	77	72	287	8,000
Ben Crenshaw	68	74	75	71	288	7,600
Ray Floyd	66	74	74	74	288	7,600
Fuzzy Zoeller	77	69	71	71	288	7,600
Roger Maltbie	74	70	73	72	289	7,100
Craig Stadler	71	70	77	71	289	7,100
Kenny Knox	72	69	70	79	290	6,700
Mac O'Grady	77	74	68	71	290	6,700
Doug Tewell	76	70	71	73	290	6,700
Tommy Nakajima	77	72	69	73	291	6,400
Tateo Ozaki	70	71	77	73	291	6,400
Mark Wiebe	66	75	71	79	291	6,400
Curtis Strange	69	71	80	72	292	6,200
George Burns	70	71	74	78	293	6,100
Dan Forsman	69	80	73	74	296	6,000
Bob Murphy	76	74	74	73	297	5,900
Greg Turner	72	73	77	79	301	5,800
Seiichi Kanai	73	76	73	80	302	5,650
Hal Sutton	71	72	79	80	302	5,650
Ove Sellberg	80	73	74	76	303	5,500
Hubert Green	77	75	79	74	305	5,400

Federal Express St. Jude Classic

Colonial Country Club, Cordova, Tennessee   August 28–31
Par 36–36 – 72; 7,282 yards

	SCORES				TOTAL	MONEY
Mike Hulbert	71	72	68	69	280	$109,064
Joey Sindelar	71	71	71	68	281	65,438
Payne Stewart	71	70	71	70	282	41,202
Larry Nelson	76	70	67	70	283	29,084
Larry Mize	73	70	68	73	284	23,024.50
Gary Koch	73	69	69	73	284	23,024.50
Tony Sills	74	70	69	72	285	17,632
Jeff Sluman	74	70	70	71	285	17,632
Howard Twitty	71	67	73	74	285	17,632
Fuzzy Zoeller	70	74	71	70	285	17,632
Eugene Elliott	76	72	68	69	285	17,632
Greg Twiggs	76	73	68	69	286	12,724
Clarence Rose	74	72	68	72	286	12,724
Fred Couples	77	69	70	70	286	12,724
Tom Purtzer	73	71	72	71	287	9,694.80
Mike West	74	73	69	71	287	9,694.80
Bobby Wadkins	72	73	69	73	287	9,694.80
Charles Bolling	74	74	72	67	287	9,694.80
Bob Gilder	75	70	69	73	287	9,694.80
Bob Tway	76	71	69	72	288	7,311.34
Steve Jones	77	72	71	68	288	7,311.33
Bill Israelson	75	74	71	68	288	7,311.33
Jack Renner	75	72	73	69	289	5,107
Mark O'Meara	74	69	73	73	289	5,107
Peter Jacobsen	73	74	72	70	289	5,107
Mark McCumber	74	72	72	71	289	5,107
Andy Bean	75	72	74	68	289	5,107
Dave Eichelberger	74	74	68	73	289	5,107

	SCORES				TOTAL	MONEY
Ernie Gonzalez	73	72	71	73	289	5,107
Tom Pernice Jr.	78	70	74	68	290	4,120
Dave Rummells	73	74	71	73	291	3,593.40
Lennie Clements	78	72	71	70	291	3,593.40
Keith Fergus	77	70	72	72	291	3,593.40
Bill Glasson	74	69	74	74	291	3,593.40
Lon Hinkle	72	76	74	69	291	3,593.40
Tim Norris	76	72	71	73	292	2,426.09
Bill Sander	77	71	75	69	292	2,426.09
Gibby Gilbert	73	73	72	74	292	2,426.09
Phil Hancock	74	71	74	73	292	2,426.09
Curtis Strange	74	73	72	73	292	2,426.08
Chris Perry	73	72	77	70	292	2,426.08
Willie Wood	75	73	73	71	292	2,426.08
Larry Ziegler	73	75	70	74	292	2,426.08
George Archer	72	74	75	71	292	2,426.08
Bill Kratzert	80	69	74	69	292	2,426.08
Tom Byrum	79	71	71	71	292	2,426.08
Brad Fabel	78	71	68	75	292	2,426.08
Robert Wrenn	77	72	75	69	293	1,563.25
Steve Bowman	76	72	71	74	293	1,563.25
Ed Fiori	79	70	71	73	293	1,563.25
Mark Hayes	77	73	72	71	293	1,563.25

B. C. Open

En-Joie Golf Club, Endicott, New York
Par 37–34 – 71; 6,966 yards

September 4–7
purse, $400,000

	SCORES				TOTAL	MONEY
Rick Fehr	65	66	67	69	267	$72,000
Larry Mize	64	67	70	68	269	43,200
Howard Twitty	69	68	68	66	271	27,200
Bobby Wadkins	66	68	73	65	272	19,200
Calvin Peete	71	67	70	66	274	15,200
Bill Glasson	66	70	71	67	274	15,200
Jack Renner	72	68	67	68	275	12,900
Jay Haas	70	69	69	67	275	12,900
Tom Purtzer	69	68	70	69	276	11,600
Dick Mast	68	69	68	72	277	10,000
Tony Sills	71	67	70	69	277	10,000
Jeff Sluman	69	68	71	69	277	10,000
D. A. Weibring	72	70	67	69	278	7,733.34
Chip Beck	68	70	68	72	278	7,733.33
Hale Irwin	70	69	68	71	278	7,733.33
Larry Rinker	70	66	69	74	279	5,611.43
Harry Taylor	67	74	67	71	279	5,611.43
Tom Pernice Jr.	71	69	71	68	279	5,611.43
Chris Perry	73	67	71	68	279	5,611.43
Payne Stewart	71	69	68	71	279	5,611.43
Bill Israelson	70	71	71	67	279	5,611.43
Richard Zokol	69	70	72	68	279	5,611.42
Rocco Mediate	69	68	71	72	280	3,840
David Peoples	68	71	73	68	280	3,840
Bobby Cole	67	72	71	70	280	3,840
Lonnie Nielsen	69	70	69	73	281	2,722.23
Mark Hayes	67	71	72	71	281	2,722.23

	SCORES				TOTAL	MONEY
Mike Reid	71	70	71	69	281	2,722.22
Don Pooley	71	69	72	69	281	2,722.22
Greg Twiggs	71	67	71	72	281	2,722.22
Mike Smith	66	69	71	75	281	2,722.22
Jay Delsing	69	72	70	70	281	2,722.22
Vance Heafner	73	63	72	73	281	2,722.22
Denny Hepler	72	67	74	68	281	2,722.22
Blaine McCallister	71	69	72	70	282	2,110
Bob Eastwood	74	66	73	69	282	2,110
Bill Sander	71	71	71	70	283	1,840
Scott Verplank	70	69	72	72	283	1,840
Rick Dalpos	70	70	73	70	283	1,840
Brad Faxon	70	71	67	75	283	1,840
Tim Norris	70	70	72	72	284	1,440
Brian Claar	67	71	74	72	284	1,440
Mike Donald	72	70	71	71	284	1,440
John McComish	71	70	69	74	284	1,440
Steve Hart	72	70	68	74	284	1,440
Mark Lye	72	69	72	71	284	1,440
Charles Bolling	69	72	71	73	285	1,041.34
Ed Dougherty	71	70	75	69	285	1,041.34
Loren Roberts	69	72	74	70	285	1,041.33
Jeff Grygiel	71	68	72	74	285	1,041.33
Pat McGowan	69	69	74	73	285	1,041.33
Mike Hulbert	69	71	72	73	285	1,041.33

Bank of Boston Classic

Pleasant Valley Country Club, Sutton, Massachusetts
Par 36–35 – 71; 7,012 yards

September 11–14
purse, $450,000

	SCORES				TOTAL	MONEY
Gene Sauers	70	71	64	69	274	$81,000
Blaine McCallister	72	68	69	68	274	48,600
(Sauers defeated McCallister on third hole of sudden-death playoff.)						
Curt Byrum	71	68	69	68	276	30,600
Jack Renner	73	70	68	66	277	19,800
Wayne Levi	68	71	70	68	277	19,800
Paul Azinger	71	71	69	67	278	16,200
Curtis Strange	73	65	68	73	279	14,512.50
Mark Calcavecchia	70	69	68	72	279	14,512.50
Larry Rinker	68	74	66	73	281	13,050
Ernie Gonzalez	71	71	66	74	282	11,700
Wayne Grady	66	73	71	72	282	11,700
Larry Ziegler	71	70	69	73	283	8,820
Mark O'Meara	71	67	69	76	283	8,820
D. A. Weibring	72	68	70	73	283	8,820
Phil Blackmar	74	67	73	69	283	8,820
Antonio Cerda	69	71	73	70	283	8,820
John Mahaffey	72	70	73	69	284	5,888.58
Joey Sindelar	75	70	69	70	284	5,888.57
Tom Pernice Jr.	73	71	70	70	284	5,888.57
Mike Reid	73	72	69	70	284	5,888.57
George Archer	74	69	66	75	284	5,888.57
Brian Claar	66	74	72	72	284	5,888.57
Gary Hallberg	73	71	70	70	284	5,888.57
Richard Zokol	71	73	69	72	285	3,836.25

	SCORES				TOTAL	MONEY
Mike McCullough	70	74	71	70	285	3,836.25
Rick Fehr	72	70	68	75	285	3,836.25
Donnie Hammond	69	73	73	70	285	3,836.25
*Billy Andrade	72	69	72	72	285	
J. C. Snead	69	74	72	71	286	3,060
Bobby Cole	71	71	71	73	286	3,060
Fred Couples	75	69	68	74	286	3,060
Ray Floyd	76	69	72	69	286	3,060
Kenny Knox	71	70	73	72	286	3,060
Chris Perry	75	70	70	72	287	2,377.50
Vance Heafner	73	70	68	76	287	2,377.50
Bob Eastwood	71	74	71	71	287	2,377.50
Al Geiberger	69	72	72	74	287	2,377.50
Lon Hinkle	75	68	71	73	287	2,377.50
Jay Haas	73	69	72	73	287	2,377.50
Steve Pate	73	72	68	75	288	1,800
Rocco Mediate	71	72	68	77	288	1,800
Jim Simons	72	71	71	74	288	1,800
Mark Brooks	72	73	72	71	288	1,800
Mark Carnevale	71	73	70	74	288	1,800
Bill Glasson	68	72	73	75	288	1,800
Calvin Peete	73	70	65	81	289	1,354
Mike Nicolette	74	69	72	74	289	1,354
Tom Kite	73	70	71	75	289	1,354
Jay Delsing	72	73	72	72	289	1,354
Tom Shaw	72	72	72	74	290	1,137
George Burns	74	70	69	77	290	1,137
Peter Jacobsen	74	71	74	71	290	1,137

Greater Milwaukee Open

Tuckaway Country Club, Franklin, Wisconsin
Par 36–36 – 72; 7,010 yards

September 18–21
purse, $400,000

	SCORES				TOTAL	MONEY
Corey Pavin	66	72	67	67	272	$72,000
Dave Barr	69	64	69	70	272	43,200
(Pavin defeated Barr on fourth hole of sudden-death playoff.)						
David Frost	69	66	68	70	273	27,200
Tom Purtzer	66	71	68	69	274	16,533.34
Roger Maltbie	72	68	67	67	274	16,533.33
Buddy Gardner	69	68	67	70	274	16,533.33
Joey Sindelar	70	67	67	71	275	12,900
Ronnie Black	68	69	68	70	275	12,900
Mark Calcavecchia	73	70	63	70	276	10,800
Rick Fehr	68	70	68	70	276	10,800
Morris Hatalsky	68	67	70	71	276	10,800
Bob Tway	69	70	67	71	277	8,400
John Adams	67	73	67	70	277	8,400
Andy Bean	70	66	71	70	277	8,400
Bobby Clampett	68	69	70	71	278	7,200
Greg Twiggs	70	68	69	72	279	6,200
Chris Perry	68	68	72	71	279	6,200
Tom Pernice Jr.	68	71	69	71	279	6,200
Bobby Cole	70	70	71	68	279	6,200
Doug Tewell	71	70	70	69	280	4,171.43
John McComish	70	67	71	72	280	4,171.43

	SCORES				TOTAL	MONEY
Peter Oosterhuis	74	66	70	70	280	4,171.43
Phil Blackmar	68	72	69	71	280	4,171.43
Brian Claar	70	71	70	69	280	4,171.43
Jay Delsing	65	73	72	70	280	4,171.43
David Peoples	71	70	67	72	280	4,171.42
Dean Prange	74	68	69	70	281	2,780
Nick Price	71	69	69	72	281	2,780
Eduardo Romero	68	73	74	66	281	2,780
Pat McGowan	71	71	70	69	281	2,780
Curt Byrum	69	70	69	73	281	2,780
Hubert Green	69	67	71	74	281	2,780
Loren Roberts	68	70	71	73	282	2,160
Ron Streck	73	70	70	69	282	2,160
Andrew Magee	72	70	72	68	282	2,160
Jim Gallagher Jr.	69	70	70	73	282	2,160
Gary Hallberg	70	71	71	70	282	2,160
Calvin Peete	69	70	71	73	283	1,600
Clarence Rose	74	68	66	75	283	1,600
Tommy Valentine	71	70	72	70	283	1,600
Larry Mize	69	74	69	71	283	1,600
Tim Simpson	70	70	71	72	283	1,600
Antonio Cerda	69	72	71	71	283	1,600
Frank Conner	66	74	72	71	283	1,600
Dick Mast	73	70	72	68	283	1,600
Mike West	70	72	69	73	284	1,054
Bill Sander	70	73	71	70	284	1,054
Danny Briggs	71	70	73	70	284	1,054
Keith Fergus	75	68	67	74	284	1,054
Al Geiberger	72	71	68	73	284	1,054
Ernie Gonzalez	69	71	74	70	284	1,054
Mark Hayes	71	72	69	72	284	1,054
Vance Heafner	70	70	75	69	284	1,054

Southwest Classic

Fairway Oaks Golf & Racquet Club, Abilene, Texas
Par 36–36 – 72; 7,166 yards

September 25–28
purse, $400,000

	SCORES				TOTAL	MONEY
Mark Calcavecchia	68	70	66	71	275	$72,000
Tom Byrum	68	74	67	69	278	43,200
Craig Stadler	72	72	72	63	279	20,800
D. A. Weibring	66	76	68	69	279	20,800
Morris Hatalsky	66	74	71	68	279	20,800
Ronnie Black	69	74	69	69	281	14,400
Jeff Maggert	68	73	70	71	282	13,400
Corey Pavin	70	74	69	70	283	11,600
Doug Tewell	69	74	69	71	283	11,600
Ben Crenshaw	73	72	71	67	283	11,600
Mark Pfeil	72	72	69	71	284	8,480
Dan Pohl	66	80	69	69	284	8,480
Paul Azinger	68	70	74	72	284	8,480
Bob Eastwood	68	73	71	72	284	8,480
Gary Hallberg	70	77	69	68	284	8,480
Pat McGowan	71	71	72	71	285	5,430
Tony Sills	69	73	71	72	285	5,430
Bob Tway	72	73	68	72	285	5,430

	SCORES				TOTAL	MONEY
Jack Renner	71	69	74	71	285	5,430
Andy Bean	70	73	70	72	285	5,430
Russ Cochran	70	73	70	72	285	5,430
Bobby Cole	71	77	66	71	285	5,430
Ed Fiori	72	70	71	72	285	5,430
Mike McCullough	68	74	74	70	286	3,320
Gene Sauers	70	72	72	72	286	3,320
Gary Koch	71	74	67	74	286	3,320
Charles Bolling	68	75	69	74	286	3,320
David Frost	67	79	67	73	286	3,320
Tim Norris	71	73	74	69	287	2,720
Wayne Levi	72	75	69	71	287	2,720
Andrew Magee	71	76	71	69	287	2,720
Bill Sander	68	75	71	74	288	2,315
Blaine McCallister	74	70	71	73	288	2,315
Mike Hulbert	73	71	69	75	288	2,315
Stu Ingraham	72	76	71	69	288	2,315
Chris Perry	69	77	69	74	289	1,925
Robert Wrenn	74	73	72	70	289	1,925
Kenny Knox	70	74	73	72	289	1,925
Davis Love III	71	77	67	74	289	1,925
Ron Streck	68	80	71	71	290	1,480
Greg Twiggs	67	77	68	78	290	1,480
Frank Conner	70	77	72	71	290	1,480
Trevor Dodds	72	74	72	72	290	1,480
Bill Glasson	72	76	71	71	290	1,480
Tom Gleeton	69	72	74	75	290	1,480
Greg Ladehoff	70	73	73	74	290	1,480
J. C. Snead	71	74	71	75	291	995.20
Harry Taylor	73	75	71	72	291	995.20
George Archer	75	72	73	71	291	995.20
Rex Caldwell	70	75	71	75	291	995.20
Charles Coody	73	75	72	71	291	995.20
Dave Eichelberger	67	77	74	73	291	995.20
Brad Fabel	72	75	71	73	291	995.20
Vance Heafner	72	75	73	71	291	995.20
Danny Mijovic	69	78	71	73	291	995.20
Tom Jenkins	68	77	71	75	291	995.20

Southern Open

Green Island Country Club, Columbus, Georgia
Par 35–35 – 70; 6,791 yards

October 2–5
purse, $350,000

	SCORES				TOTAL	MONEY
Fred Wadsworth	67	67	68	67	269	$63,000
Tim Simpson	68	67	70	66	271	23,100
Jim Thorpe	65	71	64	71	271	23,100
George Archer	69	66	67	69	271	23,100
John Cook	70	71	65	65	271	23,100
Jack Renner	70	69	65	68	272	11,725
Joey Sindelar	70	70	67	65	272	11,725
Payne Stewart	66	67	68	71	272	11,725
Brad Fabel	70	65	69	69	273	10,150
Kenny Knox	67	69	68	70	274	8,050
Larry Nelson	69	67	68	70	274	8,050

	SCORES				TOTAL	MONEY
Mike McCullough	69	65	70	70	274	8,050
Bob Gilder	72	65	70	67	274	8,050
Joe Inman	71	70	65	68	274	8,050
Corey Pavin	70	66	69	70	275	5,775
Andy Bean	68	65	74	68	275	5,775
Lennie Clements	69	69	69	68	275	5,775
Hubert Green	68	70	66	71	275	5,775
Bob Tway	68	70	69	69	276	3,298.08
Gene Sauers	68	68	70	70	276	3,298.08
Larry Mize	68	72	67	69	276	3,298.08
Greg Twiggs	69	68	70	69	276	3,298.08
Chris Perry	69	67	68	72	276	3,298.08
Willie Wood	71	69	66	70	276	3,298.08
Ken Brown	69	72	69	66	276	3,298.08
Charles Coody	68	69	72	67	276	3,298.08
Mike Donald	66	69	67	74	276	3,298.08
Larry Rinker	68	69	68	71	276	3,298.07
Charles Bolling	68	71	66	71	276	3,298.07
Mike Hulbert	72	65	68	71	276	3,298.07
Gary Koch	74	63	70	69	276	3,298.07
Scott Hoch	72	68	69	68	277	1,895
Barry Jaeckel	73	68	72	64	277	1,895
Mark Brooks	72	69	68	68	277	1,895
Frank Conner	68	70	68	71	277	1,895
Rod Curl	70	61	71	75	277	1,895
Jim Dent	71	67	67	72	277	1,895
Wayne Grady	67	69	67	74	277	1,895
Bobby Wadkins	67	72	69	70	278	1,505
Davis Love III	69	70	71	68	278	1,505
Buddy Gardner	67	72	70	69	278	1,505
Tom Sieckmann	67	66	74	72	279	1,260
Paul Azinger	69	69	71	70	279	1,260
Keith Fergus	67	71	70	71	279	1,260
Vance Heafner	71	70	70	68	279	1,260
Don Pooley	67	68	73	72	280	910
Tom Purtzer	69	67	73	71	280	910
Tommy Valentine	72	64	73	71	280	910
Dave Rummells	66	72	71	71	280	910
J. C. Snead	66	72	69	73	280	910
Tony Sills	69	69	71	71	280	910
Rick Dalpos	71	69	67	73	280	910
Ed Fiori	70	70	71	69	280	910
John McComish	71	70	69	70	280	910

Pensacola Open

Perdido Bay Inn and Country Club, Pensacola, Florida
Par 35–36 – 71; 7,093 yards

October 9–11
purse, $225,000

(Tournament shortened to 36 holes, rain. Purse reduced by $75,000.)

	SCORES		TOTAL	MONEY
Ernie Gonzalez	65	63	128	$40,500
Joey Sindelar	67	62	129	24,300
Leonard Thompson	66	65	131	15,300
Mike Hulbert	68	65	133	9,900

	SCORES		TOTAL	MONEY
Kenny Knox	66	67	133	9,900
Fred Wadsworth	69	65	134	6,342.19
Tim Simpson	68	66	134	6,342.19
Jeff Sluman	65	69	134	6,342.19
Tom Byrum	66	68	134	6,342.19
Rick Fehr	68	66	134	6,342.19
Bob Gilder	68	66	134	6,342.19
Bob Murphy	66	68	134	6,342.18
Paul Azinger	67	67	134	6,342.18
Mike Reid	69	66	135	4,050
Phil Blackmar	64	71	135	4,050
Stu Ingraham	68	67	135	4,050
Jeff Lewis	67	69	136	3,045
Larry Rinker	69	67	136	3,045
David Lundstrom	67	69	136	3,045
John Cook	65	71	136	3,045
Buddy Gardner	68	68	136	3,045
Wayne Grady	66	70	136	3,045
Dan Pohl	68	69	137	1,616.79
Mark McCumber	69	68	137	1,616.79
Rocco Mediate	67	70	137	1,616.79
Steve Pate	68	69	137	1,616.79
Tim Norris	67	70	137	1,616.79
Dave Eichelberger	69	68	137	1,616.79
Keith Fergus	69	68	137	1,616.79
Scott Hoch	67	70	137	1,616.79
Pat Lindsey	70	67	137	1,616.78
Loren Roberts	69	68	137	1,616.78
Willie Wood	68	69	137	1,616.78
Peter Jacobsen	66	71	137	1,616.78
Brad Bryant	69	68	137	1,616.78
Nick Faldo	68	69	137	1,616.78
Mike McCullough	70	68	138	900
Payne Stewart	69	69	138	900
John Mahaffey	70	68	138	900
Calvin Peete	68	70	138	900
David Peoples	70	68	138	900
Doug Tewell	70	68	138	900
Chip Beck	67	71	138	900
Danny Briggs	69	69	138	900
Frank Conner	67	71	138	900
Steve Jones	67	71	138	900
Tommy Valentine	73	66	139	536.35
Dennis Trixler	70	69	139	536.35
Bobby Pancratz	69	70	139	536.35
Bob Tway	69	70	139	536.35
Bruce Lietzke	69	70	139	536.35
Joe Inman	68	71	139	536.35
Mike West	69	70	139	536.34
Corey Pavin	70	69	139	536.34
Bill Sander	68	71	139	536.34
Chris Perry	68	71	139	536.34
Bill Rogers	68	71	139	536.34
Mike Smith	70	69	139	536.34
Ken Brown	67	72	139	536.34
Curt Byrum	65	74	139	536.34
Wren Lum	70	69	139	536.34
Trevor Dodds	68	71	139	536.34

Walt Disney World/Oldsmobile Classic

Walt Disney World, Lake Buena Vista, Florida
Magnolia Course: Par 36–36 – 72; 7,150 yards
Palm Course: Par 36–36 – 72; 6,917 yards
Lake Buena Vista Course: Par 36–36 – 72; 6,655 yards

October 16–19
purse, $500,000

	SCORES				TOTAL	MONEY
Ray Floyd	68	66	70	71	275	$90,000
Mike Sullivan	65	69	70	71	275	44,000
Lon Hinkle	67	69	68	71	275	44,000
(Floyd defeated Sullivan and Hinkle on first hole of sudden-death playoff.)						
Pat McGowan	69	70	69	68	276	20,666.67
Payne Stewart	65	66	71	74	276	20,666.67
Gary Koch	66	73	68	69	276	20,666.66
Andy North	71	69	69	69	278	16,125
Phil Blackmar	67	73	68	70	278	16,125
Bob Murphy	68	72	69	70	279	14,500
Chris Perry	72	70	68	70	280	13,000
Tom Purtzer	69	71	67	73	280	13,000
Tim Simpson	67	73	68	73	281	11,000
Dave Rummells	72	70	68	71	281	11,000
David Peoples	67	71	71	73	282	8,500
Dave Barr	70	70	70	72	282	8,500
Brian Claar	69	69	68	76	282	8,500
Buddy Gardner	71	70	66	75	282	8,500
Tom Kite	73	71	69	69	282	8,500
Mike Hulbert	69	72	67	75	283	5,261.12
Bill Sander	76	70	65	72	283	5,261.11
Dan Pohl	72	70	70	71	283	5,261.11
Mark McCumber	69	70	74	70	283	5,261.11
Andy Bean	68	72	71	72	283	5,261.11
Charles Bolling	67	72	69	75	283	5,261.11
Antonio Cerda	76	67	69	71	283	5,261.11
Rick Fehr	70	68	74	71	283	5,261.11
Morris Hatalsky	68	71	68	76	283	5,261.11
Howard Twitty	68	74	70	72	284	3,325
Calvin Peete	68	73	69	74	284	3,325
Bobby Wadkins	70	66	73	75	284	3,325
John Mahaffey	73	70	67	74	284	3,325
Russ Cochran	67	70	72	75	284	3,325
Mark Hayes	72	71	72	69	284	3,325
Jeff Sluman	72	69	73	71	285	2,418.75
J. C. Snead	74	73	67	71	285	2,418.75
Clarence Rose	73	72	69	71	285	2,418.75
Fred Couples	72	68	75	70	285	2,418.75
Jay Delsing	77	68	68	72	285	2,418.75
Danny Edwards	72	69	72	72	285	2,418.75
Dan Halldorson	72	75	67	71	285	2,418.75
Kenny Knox	75	71	69	70	285	2,418.75
Hal Sutton	71	75	69	71	286	1,536
Gene Sauers	70	71	73	72	286	1,536
Eduardo Romero	71	70	71	74	286	1,536
Larry Rinker	74	70	68	74	286	1,536
Wayne Levi	68	70	77	71	286	1,536
Brad Bryant	71	73	71	71	286	1,536
Rod Curl	69	76	69	72	286	1,536
Ken Green	74	69	67	76	286	1,536
Jeff Grygiel	71	69	72	74	286	1,536
Scott Hoch	70	72	73	71	286	1,536

Vantage Championship

Oak Hills Country Club, San Antonio, Texas

Par 35–35 – 70; 6,576 yards

October 24–26

purse, $1,000,000

(Thursday round rained out; 36-hole Sunday schedule shortened to 18 because of mid-day thunderstorm.)

	SCORES			TOTAL	MONEY
Ben Crenshaw	65	67	64	196	$180,000
Payne Stewart	67	65	65	197	108,000
Ronnie Black	68	66	67	201	48,000
Phil Blackmar	66	67	68	201	48,000
Bobby Clampett	67	68	66	201	48,000
Ernie Gonzalez	68	67	66	201	48,000
Jeff Sluman	67	67	68	202	27,071.43
Don Pooley	70	65	67	202	27,071.43
Tom Kite	68	67	67	202	27,071.43
Kenny Knox	66	67	69	202	27,071.43
Mac O'Grady	70	64	68	202	27,071.43
Larry Mize	67	66	69	202	27,071.43
Nick Price	67	68	67	202	27,071.42
Jim Thorpe	68	67	68	203	14,560
Dennis Trixler	68	67	68	203	14,560
Gene Sauers	68	69	66	203	14,560
Tony Sills	67	68	68	203	14,560
Chip Beck	65	70	68	203	14,560
Scott Hoch	68	68	67	203	14,560
Brian Claar	67	69	67	203	14,560
Bob Eastwood	66	68	69	203	14,560
Ray Floyd	69	67	67	203	14,560
Buddy Gardner	69	67	67	203	14,560
Wayne Levi	66	71	67	204	7,914.29
D. A. Weibring	67	66	71	204	7,914.29
Ken Brown	65	68	71	204	7,914.29
Morris Hatalsky	69	66	69	204	7,914.29
Mark O'Meara	68	67	69	204	7,924.28
Danny Briggs	67	71	66	204	7,914.28
Barry Jaeckel	68	69	67	204	7,914.28
Bill Sander	67	67	71	205	5,209.10
Mike Reid	72	64	69	205	5,209.09
Brian Tennyson	67	67	71	205	5,209.09
John Mahaffey	68	69	68	205	5,209.09
Dan Pohl	70	64	71	205	5,209.09
Tom Purtzer	70	66	69	205	5,209.09
Charles Bolling	68	67	70	205	5,209.09
Bernhard Langer	65	70	70	205	5,209.09
Ken Green	70	67	68	205	5,209.09
Gary Hallberg	68	66	71	205	5,209.09
Dan Halldorson	72	65	68	205	5,209.09
Willie Wood	67	69	70	206	3,600
Tom Sieckmann	68	68	70	206	3,600
Bob Gilder	72	65	69	206	3,600
Bill Glasson	67	70	69	206	3,600
Loren Roberts	70	67	70	207	2,772
Richard Zokol	68	68	71	207	2,772
Greg Ladehoff	69	67	71	207	2,772
David Edwards	68	69	70	207	2,772
Bruce Lietzke	68	70	69	207	2,772

Seiko-Tucson Match Play Championship

Randolph Park Golf Course, Tucson, Arizona
Par 35–35 – 70; 6,860 yards

October 30–November 2
purse, $700,000

FIRST ROUND

Jim Thorpe defeated Brad Faxon, 68–70.
Dan Forsman defeated Ronnie Black, 70–71.
Ben Crenshaw defeated Fred Couples, 66–73.
Hubert Green defeated Mike Hulbert, 68–69.
Lennie Clements defeated John Mahaffey, 65–70.
Roger Maltbie defeated Mike Sullivan, 70–73.
Morris Hatalsky defeated Tony Sills, 64–71.
Tim Simpson defeated J. C. Snead, 67–67, fourth extra hole.
Bob Gilder defeated Bernhard Langer, 66–68.
Phil Blackmar defeated Willie Wood, 68–69.
Dave Barr defeated David Frost, 67–67, first extra hole.
Mac O'Grady defeated Ernie Gonzalez, 68–69.
Tom Purtzer defeated Bobby Clampett, 66–72.
Howard Twitty defeated Bob Murphy, 68–69.
Davis Love III defeated John Cook, 69–69, third extra hole.
Don Pooley defeated Mike Reid, 65–71.
Bob Tway defeated Brett Upper, 68–75.
Steve Pate defeated Craig Stadler, 65–68.
Brian Claar defeated Buddy Gardner, 66–67.
Ken Green defeated Bill Glasson, 69–71.
David Edwards defeated Tom Watson, 66–72.
Gene Sauers defeated Rick Fehr, 64–64, first extra hole.
Mike Donald defeated Scott Hoch, 65–68.
Mark Calcavecchia defeated Nick Price, 67–69.
Lon Hinkle defeated Joey Sindelar, 70–71.
Gary Koch defeated Jeff Sluman, 66–71.
Scott Simpson defeated Dan Pohl, 72–72, first extra hole.
Danny Edwards defeated Mark Wiebe, 70–71.
Jim Colbert defeated Paul Azinger, 69–69, third extra hole.
Wayne Levi defeated Clarence Rose, 65–67.
Mark McCumber defeated Jay Haas, 73–74.
Lanny Wadkins defeated Pat McGowan, 67–72.
(Each losing player received $2,500.)

SECOND ROUND

Thorpe defeated Forsman, 70–70, second extra hole.
Crenshaw defeated Hubert Green, 72–75.
Clements defeated Maltbie, 70–73.
Tim Simpson defeated Hatalsky, 71–72.
Blackmar defeated Gilder, 69–69, fourth extra hole.
Barr defeated O'Grady, 71–73.
Purtzer defeated Twitty, 70–70, second extra hole.
Pooley defeated Love, 67–70.
Pate defeated Tway, 69–73.
Ken Green defeated Claar, 71–73.
David Edwards defeated Sauers, 70–72.
Calcavecchia defeated Donald, 73–73, second extra hole.
Koch defeated Hinkle, 71–72.
Scott Simpson defeated Danny Edwards, 70–74.
Colbert defeated Levi, 72–72, fourth extra hole.
Wadkins defeated McCumber, 69–74.
(Each losing player received $5,000.)

THIRD ROUND

Thorpe defeated Crenshaw, 65–67.
Tim Simpson defeated Clements, 66–67.
Blackmar defeated Barr, 65–69.
Pooley defeated Purtzer, 69–70.
Ken Green defeated Pate, 69–70.
David Edwards defeated Calcavecchia, 67–69.
Scott Simpson defeated Koch, 66–73.
Wadkins defeated Colbert, 70–71.
(Each losing player received $12,500.)

QUARTER-FINALS

Thorpe defeated Tim Simpson, 69–71.
Blackmar defeated Pooley, 71–75.
Ken Green defeated David Edwards, 70–71.
Scott Simpson defeated Wadkins, 65–68.
(Each losing player received $25,000.)

SEMI-FINALS

Thorpe defeated Blackmar, 68–71.
Scott Simpson defeated Ken Green, 69–70.

THIRD-FOURTH PLACE PLAYOFF

Ken Green defeated Blackmar, 67–74.
(Green received $60,000, Blackmar $40,000.)

FINALS

Thorpe defeated Scott Simpson, 67–71.
(Thorpe received $150,000, Simpson $90,000.)

Tallahassee Open

Killearn Golf and Country Club, Tallahassee, Florida   October 30–November 2
Par 36–36 – 72; 7,124 yards   purse, $200,000

	SCORES				TOTAL	MONEY
Mark Hayes	68	67	68	70	273	$36,000
Russ Cochran	66	72	66	70	274	21,600
Danny Briggs	67	69	70	69	275	10,400
Jim Gallagher	73	69	68	65	275	10,400
Tom Sieckmann	68	70	71	66	275	10,400
Scott Verplank	68	70	68	70	276	6,950
Steve Jones	68	70	69	69	276	6,950
Kenny Knox	71	68	68	70	277	6,200
John Adams	70	70	68	71	279	5,800
Charles Bolling	74	67	71	68	280	4,800
Jeff Grygiel	70	68	72	70	280	4,800
Dennis Trixler	68	66	70	76	280	4,800
Loren Roberts	72	67	70	71	280	4,800

	SCORES				TOTAL	MONEY
Ed Fiori	69	67	75	70	281	3,600
David Jackson	72	73	69	67	281	3,600
Fred Wadsworth	69	73	70	69	281	3,600
Brad Bryant	72	72	70	68	282	2,900
Denis Watson	71	68	73	70	282	2,900
Rick Pearson	69	71	72	70	282	2,900
Bill Sander	72	70	71	69	282	2,900
Mark Brooks	69	73	72	69	283	2,080
Marco Dawson	73	75	66	69	283	2,080
Forrest Fezler	74	71	69	69	283	2,080
Tommy Valentine	70	72	70	71	283	2,080
Rocco Mediate	72	67	71	73	283	2,080
Rick Dalpos	72	71	69	72	284	1,450
Pat Lindsey	68	69	73	74	284	1,450
Tim Norris	70	72	72	70	284	1,450
Mark Pfeil	69	73	69	73	284	1,450
Larry Rinker	73	74	67	70	284	1,450
Curt Byrum	70	71	71	72	284	1,450
Antonio Cerda	69	72	71	73	285	1,132
Bobby Cole	69	72	74	70	285	1,132
Brad Fabel	70	68	71	76	285	1,132
Wayne Grady	70	69	70	76	285	1,132
Dick Mast	74	73	67	71	285	1,132
Grant Turner	71	77	70	68	286	940
Bob Eastwood	72	71	72	71	286	940
Victor Regalado	69	72	72	73	286	940
*Nolan Henke	72	72	71	71	286	
Brian Mogg	70	71	75	71	287	840
Bobby Pancratz	73	75	71	68	287	840
Greg Twiggs	75	70	70	73	288	700
Robert Wrenn	69	77	68	74	288	700
Andy Dillard	74	71	68	75	288	700
Doug Johnson	68	74	74	72	288	700
Eduardo Romero	72	74	70	72	288	700
Trevor Dodds	74	70	73	72	289	538
Bill Israelson	73	73	71	72	289	538
Brian Kamm	70	71	72	76	289	538
Andrew Magee	68	74	74	73	289	538

Isuzu Kapalua International

Kapalua Golf Club, Bay Course, Kapalua, Maui, Hawaii
Par 36–36 – 72; 6,879 yards

November 12–15
purse, $600,000

	SCORES				TOTAL	MONEY
Andy Bean	72	68	68	70	278	$150,000
Davis Love III	68	69	70	73	280	84,000
Paul Azinger	70	65	75	73	283	53,000
Dan Pohl	70	73	73	70	286	30,333.34
Ben Crenshaw	76	65	71	74	286	30,333.33
Tom Purtzer	71	68	73	74	286	30,333.33
Joey Sindelar	72	71	74	70	287	14,750
David Ishii	74	69	71	73	287	14,750
Howard Clark	72	70	72	73	287	14,750
Nick Faldo	68	71	75	73	287	14,750
Payne Stewart	76	68	73	71	288	9,666.67
Lee Trevino	76	72	66	74	288	9,666.67

	SCORES				TOTAL	MONEY
Mike Hulbert	73	68	72	75	288	9,666.66
Bob Tway	74	76	70	69	289	8,250
Don Pooley	73	69	73	74	289	8,250
John Cook	74	72	74	70	290	6,937.50
Hale Irwin	75	69	75	71	290	6,937.50
Mark Wiebe	79	70	70	71	290	6,937.50
Bobby Wadkins	71	74	73	72	290	6,937.50
Corey Pavin	74	71	74	72	291	5,875
Jodie Mudd	74	71	74	72	291	5,875
Craig Stadler	74	68	74	75	291	5,875
Scott Verplank	73	70	72	76	291	5,875
Lanny Wadkins	74	76	71	71	292	5,125
Jay Haas	78	70	73	71	292	5,125
John Mahaffey	72	71	77	73	293	4,500
Nick Price	75	74	71	73	293	4,500
Anders Forsbrand	76	71	78	68	293	4,500
Chip Beck	79	73	70	73	295	3,875
Peter Jacobsen	76	73	74	72	295	3,875
Mac O'Grady	76	72	74	74	296	3,375
Larry Mize	77	71	75	73	296	3,375
Lance Suzuki	73	74	73	77	297	2,550
Mark O'Meara	77	73	71	76	297	2,550
Tony Sills	76	73	72	76	297	2,550
Roger Maltbie	75	69	77	76	297	2,550
Bruce Lietzke	77	76	71	72	297	2,550
Chi Chi Rodriguez	77	74	74	72	297	2,550
Steve Pate	77	70	76	75	298	2,250
Sandy Lyle	76	73	73	77	299	2,200
Neil Finch	77	76	75	72	301	2,150
Doug Tewell	78	70	78	78	304	2,075
Mark Rolfing	79	76	74	76	305	2,025
Warren Chancellor	77	80	77	77	311	2,000

J. C. Penney Classic

Bardmoor Country Club, Largo, Florida
Par 36–36 – 72; 6,957 yards

December 4–7
purse, $600,000

	SCORES				TOTAL	MONEY(Each
Juli Inkster/Tom Purtzer	61	69	66	69	265	$65,000
Val Skinner/Mike Hulbert	65	66	71	65	267	38,000
Nancy Lopez/Curtis Strange	65	69	70	66	270	21,650
Sally Little/Mike Sullivan	67	68	68	67	270	21,650
Hollis Stacy/Jay Haas	69	69	65	68	271	14,000
Lori Garbacz/Craig Stadler	69	63	68	72	272	11,000
Debbie Massey/Mark McCumber	68	65	68	71	272	11,000
Martha Nause/Larry Mize	68	72	69	64	273	8,750
Colleen Walker/Ron Streck	66	68	71	68	273	8,750
Beth Daniel/Tom Kite	67	72	65	70	274	7,000
Jan Stephenson/Fred Couples	68	69	66	71	274	7,000
Donna Caponi/Andy North	70	69	68	67	274	7,000
Muffin Spencer-Devlin/Denis Watson	68	69	69	68	274	7,000
Alice Ritzman/Jim Thorpe	68	70	67	69	274	7,000
Betsy King/Doug Tewell	72	63	69	71	275	5,500
Cathy Morse/Jeff Sluman	70	72	69	66	277	4,375
Lauri Peterson/Joey Sindelar	71	66	73	67	277	4,375

Seve Ballesteros had six European Tour victories including the
French Open.

Despite eight wins between
them, Bernhard Langer
(left) and Seve Ballesteros
could not take No. 1
in the world.

Greg Norman had good reason to smile—he won nine times and was No. 1 on the Sony Ranking.

Off to a great start, Howard Clark won two of the first five European events.

Ian Woosnam won early and late—in Kenya before the European Tour and in the Lawrence Batley TPC event.

Jose-Maria Olazabal followed his great amateur success with
two victories in his first professional season.

Ove Sellberg provided
Sweden's first pro golf
triumph in the
Epson Grand Prix.

Countryman Anders
Forsbrand ranked No. 8
on the European Tour.

Irishman David Feherty was a surprise winner of two European titles.

South African John Bland opened the European circuit by winning the Cannes Open.

New Zealand's talented young Greg Turner won the Scandinavian Open.

Veteran Mark James had a victory in the Benson & Hedges International.

Nick Faldo was winless, and fell to 15th on the European money list.

Sam Torrance also had a disappointing year and was 17th in earnings.

The No. 3 Spaniard, Jose-Maria Canizares, held 14th place in Europe.

Australian Rodger Davis came to prominence in the Wythe & Mackay PGA Championship, and later had three Australia/New Zealand victories.

South African Mark McNulty was seldom in difficulty, winning eight events on his home circuit and one in Europe.

Gavin Levinson took one of the few South African tournaments not won by McNulty.

American Mark O'Meara
won the Australian Masters,
which also featured the
defending U.S. Masters
champion, Bernhard
Langer.

The greats of Australian golf—Greg Norman shares a joke with David Graham (above) and takes some advice from Peter Thomson.

Japan's Seiichi Kanai won
the Hong Kong Open.

Despite his success in
America, the best
Chen Tze-Chung could
place in Asia was fourth
in Malaysia.

Tsuneyuki Nakajima remained Japan's
No. 1 international golfer, with
seven victories.

Masahiro Kuramoto won the Tokai
Classic and the All-Nippon
Airways Sapporo Open.

Tateo "Jet" Ozaki was the winner
of the Bridgestone and Daikyo events.
Brothers Masashi "Jumbo"
won four times and
Naomichi "Joe" won once.

Bruce Crampton

Chi Chi Rodriguez

Gary Player

Bob Charles

Dale Douglass

USA TODAY

THE NATION'S NEWSPAPER

50 CENTS

THURSDAY

By Patrick Harbron, Sygma
SYDNEY BIDDLE BARROWS: Madam, 1D

NO. 1 IN THE USA . . . 4,792,000 READERS EVERY DAY

FALL FUN:
MUSIC HITS
2-PAGE REPORT, 4, 5D
FRIDAY: BEST READING

FLY CHEAPER, BUY COUPONS
TRAVEL SAVVY, 6D

'MAYFLOWER MADAM' TELLS HER STORY 1D

- **Palmer tips for older golfers, 2C**
- **His lucky 13 holes in one, 2C**
- **New tourney for seniors, 6C**

Arnie's daily magic: Same hole in one

By Steve Hershey
USA TODAY

POTOMAC, Md. — Arnold Palmer on Wednesday hit a hole in one on the same hole for the second straight day — something no other professional golfer ever has done.

Palmer — who used the same five iron both days — said he "couldn't believe it. I was awed by the whole thing. I thought about it all day."

Golf pro Chi Chi Rodriguez, who saw it, said: "I always thought Arnold walked on water. Now I know he does."

The feats came on the third hole at the new Tournament Players Club at Avenel, just outside Washington, D.C., during pro-am events. Palmer, 56, today plays in the inaugural Chrysler Cup for pro golfers over age 50.

Palmer said while walking to the tee, "A little guy told me, 'I came out to see you make another hole in one.' It never entered my mind that I would.

The third hole "was 187 yards yesterday and 182 today. I hit it the same way. Tuesday, it hit five yards short and bounced in and today it went in on the fly.

"I couldn't believe it. You go for years and years and hit shots you think should go in and they don't. Then this happens. Two in two days. It's unbelievable."

Oakley Bayless, 84, of Orlando, Fla., is a veteran of "Arnie's Army" of fans. When he saw the shot, he turned to a friend and said, "Oh no, not again."

Arnold Palmer's two aces in the Chrysler Cup were front-page news across America

	SCORES				TOTAL	MONEY
Sherri Turner/Curt Byrum	70	68	68	71	277	4,375
Janet Coles/Rick Fehr	71	69	68	69	277	4,375
Vicki Tabor/Mike Donald	71	69	67	70	277	4,375
Lauren Howe/Brian Claar	71	69	70	67	277	4,375
Laurie Rinker/Larry Rinker	68	69	74	67	278	3,125
Cathy Kratzert/Bill Kratzert	70	70	69	69	278	3,125
Kathy Postlewait/Dave Barr	70	69	70	69	278	3,125
Sandra Palmer/Mark Hayes	68	69	67	74	278	3,125
Beverly Klass/Calvin Peete	67	69	75	68	279	2,300
Myra Blackwelder/Paul Azinger	68	69	70	72	279	2,300
Chris Johnson/Bruce Crampton	69	68	72	70	279	2,300
Amy Alcott/Bob Gilder	65	69	72	73	279	2,300
Dale Eggeling/Wayne Levi	68	74	72	66	280	2,025
Penny Hammel/Lee Elder	71	68	72	69	280	2,025
Judy Dickinson/Gary Koch	68	66	74	72	280	2,025
Amy Benz/Ken Green	70	70	70	70	280	2,025
Jane Geddes/Ken Knox	68	71	74	68	281	1,890
Marlene Hagge/Jim Simons	65	73	73	70	281	1,890
Marta Figueras-Dotti/Ed Fiori	73	71	70	67	281	1,890
Laura Baugh/Bobby Cole	72	69	72	69	282	1,830
Jody Rosenthal/Brad Faxon	69	74	69	71	283	1,755
Jerilyn Britz/Gay Brewer	69	71	72	71	283	1,755
Becky Pearson/Mark Wiebe	70	74	68	71	283	1,755
Rosie Jones/Bill Glasson	68	73	72	70	283	1,755
Penny Pulz/Brett Upper	69	67	74	74	284	1,620
Kathy Whitworth/Miller Barber	72	70	74	68	284	1,620
Cindy Mackey/Woody Blackburn	69	71	73	71	284	1,620
Jane Crafter/Pat McGowan	72	71	70	71	284	1,620
Robin Walton/Mark Calcavecchia	73	72	71	68	284	1,620
Cindy Hill/Steve Pate	71	69	70	75	285	1,530
Mary Beth Zimmerman/Dan Forsman	73	68	73	72	286	1,500
Bonnie Lauer/Gene Sauers	72	70	75	70	287	1,500
Vicki Fergon/Bob Eastwood	71	75	78	70	294	1,500

Chrysler Team Championship

Boca West Resort & Club, Boca Raton, Florida   December 11–14
Course #1—Par 36–36 – 72; 7,233 yards
Course #2—Par 36–36 – 72; 6,778 yards   purse, $600,000

Broken Sound Country Club, Boca Raton, Florida
Par 36–36 – 72; 6,510 yards

	SCORES				TOTAL	MONEY
						(Each)
Gary Hallberg/Scott Hoch	61	63	64	63	251	$65,932.50
Mike Hulbert/Bob Tway	59	62	64	67	252	35,784.50
Brad Faxon/Denny Hepler	68	63	61	69	255	19,755.50
Jack Nicklaus/Jack Nicklaus II	65	63	63	65	256	13,654.50
Clarence Rose/Tim Simpson	64	65	60	67	256	13,654.50
Dan Forsman/Andy North	65	64	62	66	257	8,710.50
Dave Barr/Bob Eastwood	63	64	65	65	257	8,710.50
Pat Lindsey/Mark McCumber	62	65	63	68	258	6,403.50
Rick Cramer/Steve Jones	63	65	65	65	258	6,403.50
Danny Briggs/Larry Rinker	62	61	68	69	260	4,273
Fred Couples/Mike Donald	68	62	66	64	260	4,273

	SCORES				TOTAL	MONEY
Charlie Bolling/Brad Fabel	65	63	65	67	260	4,273
Dick Mast/David Peoples	60	69	64	67	260	4,273
Russ Cochran/Ernie Gonzalez	61	66	68	66	261	2,558.17
Jeff Lewis/Dave Rummells	66	64	66	65	261	2,558.17
Jodie Mudd/Mac O'Grady	65	65	63	68	261	2,558.17
John Adams/Brad Bryant	69	63	60	69	261	2,558.17
Mark Hayes/Mike Sullivan	63	68	63	67	261	2,558.16
Bob Gilder/Joe Inman	64	64	64	69	261	2,558.16
Steve Bowman/David Ogrin	65	65	63	69	262	1,723.50
Gary Koch/Tom Purtzer	62	62	71	67	262	1,723.50
George Burns/Wayne Levi	64	66	66	66	262	1,723.50
Buddy Gardner/Roger Maltbie	69	66	60	67	262	1,723.50
Mark Brooks/Andrew Magee	65	64	65	68	262	1,723.50
Danny Edwards/David Edwards	71	62	61	69	263	1,483
Bob Murphy/Mike Reid	63	62	67	71	263	1,483
Tom Pernice/Tom Sieckmann	66	64	65	68	263	1,483
Lennie Clements/Bobby Cole	66	64	64	69	263	1,483
Davis Love/J. C. Snead	64	68	64	68	264	1,437
Paul Azinger/Bob Lohr	64	68	64	69	265	1,364
Frank Conner/David Lundstrom	64	66	66	69	265	1,364
John Cook/Joey Sindelar	64	66	65	71	266	1,291.50
Bill Kratzert/Ernie Rodriguez	65	62	68	72	267	1,242.50

The U.S. Senior Tour

MONY Senior Tournament of Champions

La Costa Country Club, Carlsbad, California
Par 36–36 – 72; 6,911 yards

January 8–11
purse, $100,000

	SCORES				TOTAL	MONEY
Miller Barber	70	70	70	72	282	$30,000
Arnold Palmer	72	73	70	72	287	21,000
Lee Elder	69	74	73	72	288	16,000
Don January	76	72	76	69	293	11,500
Harold Henning	73	76	71	75	295	9,000
Peter Thomson	74	73	74	77	298	7,000
Mike Fetchick	83	79	75	81	318	5,500

Treasure Coast Classic

Tournament Players Club at Monte Carlo, Fort Pierce, Florida
Par 36–36 – 72; 6,649 yards

February 6–9
purse, $225,000

	SCORES			TOTAL	MONEY
Charles Owens	65	69	68	202	$33,750
Lee Elder	70	71	64	205	18,562.50
Don January	72	66	67	205	18,562.50
Chi Chi Rodriguez	71	69	66	206	14,062.50

	SCORES			TOTAL	MONEY
Gay Brewer	68	71	70	209	9,187.50
Gary Player	74	70	65	209	9,187.50
Walter Zembriski	67	69	73	209	9,187.50
Harold Henning	66	73	71	210	6,482.82
Billy Casper	68	70	72	210	6,482.81
Paul Harney	66	70	74	210	6,482.81
Bob Brue	76	68	66	210	6,482.81
Jim Ferree	72	69	70	211	5,231.25
Bruce Crampton	71	70	72	213	4,725
Orville Moody	71	72	70	213	4,725
Miller Barber	73	72	69	214	4,275
Gordon Jones	68	74	73	215	3,712.50
Gene Littler	70	74	71	215	3,712.50
Billy Maxwell	71	71	73	215	3,712.50
Arnold Palmer	74	71	70	215	3,712.50
George Lanning	72	70	75	217	2,962.50
Ben Smith	69	72	76	217	2,962.50
Ken Still	71	74	72	217	2,962.50
Joe Jimenez	71	70	77	218	2,700
Art Silvestrone	70	73	76	219	2,587.50
John Brodie	75	71	74	220	2,475
George Bellino	72	74	75	221	2,306.25
Dick King	75	69	77	221	2,306.25
Al Balding	73	76	73	222	1,968.75
Jerry Barber	76	73	73	222	1,968.75
Bill Collins	76	74	72	222	1,968.75
Mike Souchak	70	78	74	222	1,968.75
Al Chandler	71	75	77	223	1,659.38
Dan Sikes	75	75	73	223	1,659.37
Buck Adams	78	75	71	224	1,462.50
Dow Finsterwald	74	77	73	224	1,462.50
Doug Ford	73	76	75	224	1,462.50
Howie Johnson	74	78	72	224	1,462.50
Sam Snead	74	73	77	224	1,462.50
Julius Boros	75	77	73	225	1,265.63
Pete Brown	77	74	74	225	1,265.62

General Foods PGA Seniors Championship

PGA National Golf Club, Champions Course, Palm Beach Gardens, Florida
Par 36–36 – 72; 6,520 yards

February 13–16
purse, $250,000

	SCORES				TOTAL	MONEY
Gary Player	68	68	73	73	281	$45,000
Lee Elder	70	73	69	71	283	28,500
Charles Owens	72	72	74	72	290	15,250
Jim King	74	73	70	73	290	15,250
Chi Chi Rodriguez	73	76	69	73	291	10,500
Billy Casper	75	70	72	74	291	10,500
Gay Brewer	76	75	71	70	292	8,500
Billy Maxwell	74	70	75	73	292	8,500
Orville Moody	74	72	73	75	294	7,000
Doug Sanders	74	74	72	75	295	6,250
Bruce Crampton	72	73	75	75	295	6,250
Miller Barber	68	77	80	71	296	5,500

	SCORES				TOTAL	MONEY
George Lanning	74	72	79	72	297	5,000
Tom Nieporte	77	74	73	74	298	4,500
Al Chandler	73	77	76	73	299	3,900
Don January	78	72	72	77	299	3,900
Stan Thirsk	74	75	77	74	300	3,600
Ken Still	75	74	75	77	301	3,000
Al Balding	78	75	74	74	301	3,000
Mal McMullen	72	81	75	73	301	3,000
Bob Bruno	76	74	73	78	301	3,000
Jim Ferree	75	75	74	77	301	3,000
Billy Farrell	76	74	77	75	302	2,200
Harold Henning	77	73	77	75	302	2,200
Dick Howell	78	75	76	73	302	2,200
Al Mengert	75	76	75	77	303	1,800
Gardner Dickinson	76	75	79	73	303	1,800
Dick Hendrickson	79	74	72	78	303	1,800
Bill Collins	76	73	77	78	304	1,462.50
Jack Fleck	75	76	80	73	304	1,462.50
Joe Jimenez	75	71	81	77	304	1,462.50
Al Kelley	79	76	74	75	304	1,462.50
Pete Hessemer	80	77	74	74	305	1,300
Ralph Terry	77	77	73	79	306	1,150
Ray Montgomery	73	76	84	73	306	1,150
Dow Finsterwald	73	77	78	78	306	1,150
Bob Ross	79	78	76	73	306	1,150
Gene Littler	76	74	80	76	306	1,150
Mack Briggs	81	76	76	74	307	950
Howie Johnson	79	78	72	78	307	950
George Kallish	77	74	79	77	307	950

Senior PGA Roundup

Hillcrest Golf Club, Sun City West, Arizona
Par 36–36 – 72; 6,672 yards

March 14–16
purse, $200,000

	SCORES			TOTAL	MONEY
Charles Owens	71	64	67	202	$30,000
Dale Douglass	67	67	68	202	18,000
(Owens defeated Douglass on second hole of sudden-death playoff.)					
Doug Sanders	67	68	68	203	15,000
Chi Chi Rodriguez	69	67	68	204	12,500
Peter Thomson	66	69	70	205	10,000
Gay Brewer	68	70	68	206	7,250
Billy Casper	71	68	67	206	7,250
Lee Elder	74	67	66	207	6,250
Joe Jimenez	66	71	70	207	6,250
Bruce Crampton	67	70	71	208	5,500
Miller Barber	67	72	71	210	4,850
George Lanning	70	73	67	210	4,850
Charles Sifford	71	69	71	211	4,200
Walter Zembriski	69	73	69	211	4,200
Bob Brue	70	71	71	212	3,400
Paul Harney	72	70	70	212	3,400
Fred Hawkins	70	71	71	212	3,400
Bob Rosburg	74	70	68	212	3,400
Dan Sikes	72	72	68	212	3,400

	SCORES			TOTAL	MONEY
Orville Moody	71	70	72	213	2,633.34
Harold Henning	73	67	73	213	2,633.34
Art Wall	71	70	72	213	2,633.34
Jerry Barber	67	75	72	214	2,300
Jim Ferree	71	74	69	214	2,300
Don January	72	72	70	214	2,300
Stan Dudas	69	71	75	215	2,050
Fred Haas	75	69	71	215	2,050
Al Balding	72	74	70	216	1,750
Hulen Coker	72	72	72	216	1,750
Gordon Jones	69	74	73	216	1,750
Ken Still	75	69	72	216	1,750
Al Chandler	73	72	72	217	1,425
Doug Ford	75	72	70	217	1,425
Lionel Hebert	71	71	75	217	1,425
Ted Kroll	73	70	74	217	1,425
Jack Fleck	74	75	68	218	1,250
Howie Johnson	71	73	74	218	1,250
Jim King	73	73	72	218	1,250
Bob Erickson	75	73	71	219	1,075
Mike Fetchick	73	73	73	219	1,075
Dow Finsterwald	70	76	73	219	1,075
Tommy Jacobs	73	74	72	219	1,075

Vintage Invitational

The Vintage Club, Indian Wells, California
Mountain Course: Par 36–36 – 72; 6,911 yards
Desert Course: Par 35–36 – 71; 6,213 yards

March 20–23
purse, $300,000

	SCORES				TOTAL	MONEY
Dale Douglass	67	70	69	66	272	$40,500
Gary Player	71	69	68	68	276	24,300
Jim Ferree	70	68	69	71	278	18,562.50
Chi Chi Rodriguez	69	71	70	68	278	18,562.50
Lee Elder	69	70	70	70	279	13,500
Billy Casper	73	66	68	73	280	9,787.50
Arnold Palmer	68	71	68	73	280	9,787.50
Dan Sikes	69	69	73	71	282	8,775
Bob Charles	71	73	72	67	283	8,100
Harold Henning	72	74	71	67	284	7,121.25
Howie Johnson	69	68	71	76	284	7,121.25
Bruce Crampton	72	77	69	67	285	6,277.50
Mike Souchak	76	70	67	74	287	5,872.50
Gay Brewer	75	74	70	69	288	4,873.50
Bob Goalby	72	73	71	72	288	4,873.50
Orville Moody	71	74	68	75	288	4,873.50
Charles Owens	73	72	73	70	288	4,873.50
Ben Smith	72	72	76	68	288	4,873.50
Miller Barber	73	75	69	72	289	3,780
Paul Harney	77	67	71	74	289	3,780
Christy O'Connor	76	72	70	71	289	3,780
George Lanning	68	73	74	75	290	3,375
Tommy Bolt	74	77	68	72	291	2,985
Don January	71	75	68	77	291	2,985
Bill Johnston	78	68	70	75	291	2,985

	SCORES				TOTAL	MONEY
Gene Littler	74	72	71	74	291	2,985
Harvie Ward	72	76	74	69	291	2,985
Bob Rosburg	73	69	74	76	292	2,590
Roberto de Vicenzo	74	71	73	75	293	2,320
Gordon Jones	75	68	76	74	293	2,320
Al Mengert	72	69	75	77	293	2,320
Al Balding	77	70	75	73	295	1,982.50
Jerry Barber	75	74	74	72	295	1,982.50
Kel Nagle	73	75	75	72	295	1,982.50
Mike Fetchick	73	71	74	78	296	1,847.50
Bill Collins	73	77	72	75	297	1,678.75
Doug Ford	76	74	72	75	297	1,678.75
Charles Sifford	76	77	74	70	297	1,678.75
Art Wall	75	74	73	75	297	1,678.75
Doug Sanders	77	73	72	76	298	1,476.25
Peter Thomson	75	74	74	75	298	1,476.25

Johnny Mathis Seniors Classic

MountainGate Country Club, Los Angeles, California
Par 36–36 – 72; 6,407 yards

March 27–30
purse, $251,250

	SCORES			TOTAL	MONEY
Dale Douglass	67	69	66	202	$37,500
Chi Chi Rodriguez	70	69	66	205	22,500
Bruce Crampton	69	69	69	207	18,750
Peter Thomson	69	72	67	208	15,625
Bob Charles	71	69	70	210	10,208.34
Bob Brue	71	70	69	210	10,208.33
Mike Fetchick	70	69	71	210	10,208.33
Charles Owens	71	70	70	211	8,125
Ben Smith	68	71	73	212	5,964.29
Roberto de Vicenzo	71	73	68	212	5,964.29
Gay Brewer	73	69	70	212	5,964.29
Ken Still	71	72	69	212	5,964.29
Lee Elder	70	71	71	212	5,964.28
Harold Henning	70	70	72	212	5,964.28
Al Chandler	71	71	70	212	5,964.28
Charles Sifford	73	69	71	213	4,500
Al Balding	75	69	70	214	4,125
Ted Kroll	70	72	72	214	4,125
Orville Moody	72	73	70	215	3,406.25
Billy Maxwell	73	72	70	215	3,406.25
Art Wall	71	69	75	215	3,406.25
Bob Rosburg	71	74	70	215	3,406.25
Miller Barber	71	71	74	216	2,875
Mike Souchak	68	76	72	216	2,875
Fred Hawkins	75	73	68	216	2,875
Paul Harney	70	73	74	217	2,625
Billy Casper	74	73	71	218	2,375
Bob Goalby	71	73	74	218	2,375
John Brodie	70	71	77	218	2,375
Jim Ferree	74	75	70	219	1,953.13
George Lanning	74	72	73	219	1,953.13
Jimmy Powell	75	71	73	219	1,953.12
Joe Jimenez	74	74	71	219	1,953.12

	SCORES			TOTAL	MONEY
Fred Haas	74	72	74	220	1,656.25
Don January	75	68	77	220	1,656.25
Gene Littler	74	74	72	220	1,656.25
Howie Johnson	77	73	70	220	1,656.25
Walter Zembriski	70	73	78	221	1,468.75
Art Silvestrone	75	73	73	221	1,468.75
Jack Fleck	73	77	72	222	1,375

Doug Sanders Celebrity Classic

Memorial Park Golf Course, Houston, Texas
Par 36–36 – 72; 6,490 yards

April 18–20
purse, $140,000

	SCORES			TOTAL	MONEY
Bruce Crampton	66	67	69	202	$25,000
Howie Johnson	67	68	68	203	13,167
Charles Owens	67	67	69	203	13,167
Peter Thomson	68	65	70	203	13,167
Miller Barber	70	65	69	204	7,667
Lee Elder	69	68	67	204	7,667
Doug Sanders	67	69	68	204	7,667
Orville Moody	65	70	70	205	5,500
Dale Douglass	67	67	72	206	4,250
Harold Henning	67	68	71	206	4,250
Bob Charles	68	69	70	207	3,500
Billy Casper	68	70	71	209	2,500
Arnold Palmer	69	68	72	209	2,500
Chi Chi Rodriguez	69	66	74	209	2,500
Mike Fetchick	70	67	74	211	1,700
Roberto de Vicenzo	70	70	72	212	1,400
Jim Ferree	68	71	73	212	1,400
Bob Goalby	68	69	75	212	1,400
Al Besselink	70	72	72	214	1,200
Billy Maxwell	71	68	75	214	1,200
Bobby Nichols	70	72	72	214	1,200
Christy O'Connor	73	71	70	214	1,200
Gay Brewer	66	75	74	215	1,200
Doug Ford	72	71	72	215	1,200
Bill Johnston	70	71	74	215	1,200
Dan Sikes	73	74	69	216	1,200
Al Balding	73	69	76	218	1,200
Bill Collins	70	76	73	219	1,200
George Bayer	71	78	73	222	1,200
Sam Snead	73	73	76	222	1,200
Charles Sifford	72	74	76	222	1,200
Julius Boros	77	68	78	224	1,200
Fred Hawkins	69	75	80	224	1,200
Mike Souchak	73	76	76	225	1,200
Dow Finsterwald	77	71	79	227	1,200
Lionel Hebert	78	73	76	227	1,200

Liberty Mutual Legends of Golf

Onion Creek Country Club, Austin, Texas
Par 35–35 – 70; 6,584 yards

April 24–27
purse, $500,000

	SCORES				TOTAL	MONEY
						(Each)
Don January/Gene Littler	65	61	65	64	255	$50,000
Charlie Sifford/Jim Ferree	66	64	65	62	257	27,000
Lee Elder/Chi Chi Rodriguez	65	63	67	63	258	15,000
Peter Thomson/Harold Henning	67	64	64	66	261	11,166.67
Arnold Palmer/Gary Player	70	64	64	63	261	11,166.67
Bob Toski/Mike Fetchick	66	64	65	66	261	11,166.66
Christy O'Connor/Doug Sanders	64	66	66	66	262	8,500
Orville Moody/Bruce Crampton	63	66	67	67	263	8,000
Dow Finsterwald/Dale Douglass	67	65	66	66	264	6,666.67
Miller Barber/Bob Goalby	65	64	68	67	264	6,666.67
Gay Brewer/Billy Casper	66	63	70	66	265	6,666.66
Fred Hawkins/Jack Fleck	64	69	66	66	265	5,500
Billy Maxwell/Howie Johnson	69	67	64	65	265	5,500
Jack Burke/Paul Harney	61	70	67	67	265	5,500
Julius Boros/Bobby Nichols	66	67	68	66	267	5,500
Jerry Barber/Doug Ford	68	68	67	64	267	5,500
Mike Souchak/Ken Venturi	66	68	65	69	268	5,166.67
Art Wall/Al Balding	66	64	70	68	268	5,166.67
Sam Snead/Tommy Bolt	66	68	66	68	268	5,166.66
Roberto de Vicenzo/Ken Still	68	67	70	64	269	5,000
Kel Nagle/Bob Charles	65	65	72	69	271	5,000
George Bayer/Tom Nieporte	68	67	68	72	275	5,000
Lionel Hebert/Jay Hebert	69	71	67	69	276	5,000
Tommy Jacobs/Dave Marr	70	68	71	68	277	5,000
Bob Rosburg/Gardner Dickinson	71	68	69	72	280	5,000
Chick Harbert/Fred Haas	71	69	71	71	282	5,000
Dan Sikes/Bill Collins	68	68	72	74	282	5,000
Bob Hamilton/Paul Runyan	76	73	73	73	295	5,000

Sunwest Bank/Charley Pride Senior Classic

Four Hills Country Club, Albuquerque, New Mexico
Par 36–36 – 72; 6,722 yards

May 2–4
purse, $250,000

	SCORES			TOTAL	MONEY
Gene Littler	65	66	71	202	$37,500
Don January	69	67	68	204	22,500
Bob Charles	69	68	71	208	18,750
Harold Henning	69	72	68	209	14,062.50
Chi Chi Rodriguez	68	69	72	209	14,062.50
Al Balding	67	73	71	211	9,062.50
George Lanning	70	69	72	211	9,062.50
Charles Sifford	71	70	71	212	8,125
Miller Barber	71	71	71	213	7,187.50
Lee Elder	74	69	70	213	7,187.50
Ken Still	69	73	72	214	6,312.50
Dale Douglass	71	71	73	215	5,265.63
Jim Ferree	72	72	71	215	5,265.63
Charles Owens	74	69	72	215	5,265.62

	SCORES			TOTAL	MONEY
Bob Toski	72	69	74	215	5,265.62
Jack Fleck	72	74	70	216	4,125
Gary Player	69	70	77	216	4,125
Peter Thomson	71	74	71	216	4,125
Walter Zembriski	73	73	70	216	4,125
Bruce Crampton	74	71	72	217	3,218.75
Mike Fetchick	69	75	73	217	3,218.75
Jim King	72	73	72	217	3,218.75
Orville Moody	72	73	72	217	3,218.75
Howie Johnson	71	75	72	218	2,750
Bill Johnston	71	73	74	218	2,750
Doug Sanders	76	69	73	218	2,750
Paul Harney	74	72	74	220	2,375
Joe Jimenez	73	72	75	220	2,375
Jimmy Powell	78	69	73	220	2,375
Dave Marr	74	74	73	221	1,953.13
Bobby Nichols	72	75	74	221	1,953.13
Billy Casper	75	75	71	221	1,953.12
Fred Hawkins	70	72	79	221	1,953.12
Fred Haas	71	77	74	222	1,718.75
Art Wall	75	72	75	222	1,718.75
Jerry Barber	70	78	75	223	1,500
Bob Brue	76	77	70	223	1,500
Gordon Jones	73	78	72	223	1,500
Art Silvestrone	76	78	69	223	1,500
Ben Smith	74	74	75	223	1,500

Benson & Hedges Invitational at the Dominion

The Dominion Country Club, San Antonio, Texas   May 9–11
Par 36–36 – 72; 6,667 yards   purse, $225,000

	SCORES			TOTAL	MONEY
Bruce Crampton	67	67	68	202	$37,500
Bob Charles	67	65	72	204	22,500
Dale Douglass	66	69	72	207	15,625
Gary Player	70	67	70	207	15,625
Doug Sanders	69	68	70	207	15,625
Billy Casper	68	71	69	208	9,375
Chi Chi Rodriguez	69	71	69	209	8,750
Ben Smith	71	68	71	210	8,125
Don January	70	72	70	212	7,187.50
Charles Owens	70	72	70	212	7,187.50
Mike Fetchick	73	72	68	213	5,854.17
Bob Toski	69	73	71	213	5,854.17
Peter Thomson	69	71	73	213	5,854.16
Lee Elder	71	72	71	214	5,062.50
Gay Brewer	70	73	72	215	4,500
Harold Henning	74	69	72	215	4,500
George Lanning	72	68	75	215	4,500
Gordon Jones	72	72	72	216	3,750
Orville Moody	72	71	73	216	3,750
Art Silvestrone	72	69	75	216	3,750
Miller Barber	74	71	72	217	3,062.50
Joe Jimenez	71	72	74	217	3,062.50
Kel Nagle	73	72	72	217	3,062.50

	SCORES			TOTAL	MONEY
Walter Zembriski	73	73	71	217	3,062.50
Jerry Barber	74	70	74	218	2,562.50
Bob Erickson	70	72	76	218	2,562.50
James Hatfield	74	73	71	218	2,562.50
Gene Littler	72	78	68	218	2,562.50
Bill Johnston	73	72	74	219	2,062.50
Bobby Nichols	71	74	74	219	2,062.50
Jimmy Powell	73	74	72	219	2,062.50
Art Wall	70	75	74	219	2,062.50
Al Balding	74	76	70	220	1,625
Jim Cochran	74	72	74	220	1,625
Jack Fleck	74	74	72	220	1,625
Doug Ford	72	75	73	220	1,625
Bob Goalby	73	71	76	220	1,625
Fred Hawkins	77	70	73	220	1,625
Arnold Palmer	74	69	77	220	1,625
Buck Adams	72	69	80	221	1,281.25
Jim Ferree	74	74	73	221	1,281.25
Lionel Hebert	76	73	72	221	1,281.25
Howie Johnson	69	77	75	221	1,281.25

United Hospitals Senior Championship

Chester Valley Country Club, Malvern, Pennsylvania   May 16–18
Par 35–35 – 70; 6,406 yards   purse, $200,000

	SCORES			TOTAL	MONEY
Gary Player	66	70	70	206	$30,000
Lee Elder	71	69	67	207	16,500
Bob Charles	69	71	67	207	16,500
Bruce Crampton	72	65	71	208	12,500
Arnold Palmer	74	66	69	209	10,000
Dale Douglass	70	69	72	211	7,500
Miller Barber	69	75	69	213	7,000
Orville Moody	73	70	71	214	6,250
Don January	74	68	72	214	6,250
Harold Henning	75	70	70	215	5,066.67
Paul Harney	72	72	71	215	5,066.67
Charles Owens	71	73	71	215	5,066.66
Walter Zembriski	69	73	74	216	3,733.34
Gardner Dickinson	69	76	71	216	3,733.34
Mike Fetchick	70	75	71	216	3,733.33
Gay Brewer	72	72	72	216	3,733.33
Jerry Barber	70	73	73	216	3,733.33
Bob Ross	70	75	71	216	3,733.33
Billy Maxwell	76	71	70	217	2,800
Gene Littler	72	75	70	217	2,800
Billy Casper	77	71	69	217	2,800
Al Chandler	72	76	70	218	2,450
Joe Jimenez	76	70	72	218	2,450
Ken Still	77	74	68	219	2,050
Gordon Jones	68	74	77	219	2,050
Dick Hendrickson	77	72	70	219	2,050
Pete Brown	71	72	76	219	2,050
Jack Fleck	73	72	74	219	2,050
Doug Sanders	75	73	71	219	2,050
Charles Sifford	73	74	73	220	1,600

	SCORES			TOTAL	MONEY
Bobby Nichols	76	76	68	220	1,600
George Bayer	71	77	72	220	1,600
Buck Adams	79	68	74	221	1,375
Lionel Hebert	75	76	70	221	1,375
Peter Thomson	75	73	73	221	1,375
Ben Smith	71	75	75	221	1,375
Howie Johnson	75	75	72	222	1,250
Art Wall	78	73	72	223	1,125
Jim Cochran	73	74	76	223	1,125
Bill Collins	73	79	71	223	1,125
Jim King	75	76	72	223	1,125

Coca-Cola Grand Slam Championship

Oak Hills Country Club, Narita, Japan
Par 36–36 – 72; 6,660 yards

May 22–25
purse, $230,000

	SCORES				TOTAL	MONEY
Lee Elder	65	66	71	71	273	$50,000
Miller Barber	71	67	71	70	279	32,000
Don January	71	70	71	69	281	20,250
Gene Littler	72	67	72	70	281	20,250
Billy Casper	74	71	70	68	283	12,500
Bob Charles	72	68	70	73	283	12,500
Masao Hara	68	71	76	71	286	9,000
Orville Moody	76	70	71	71	288	7,500
Gay Brewer	74	71	75	71	291	6,000
Seiha Ching	71	73	78	70	292	4,500
Toshiaki Sekimizu	75	71	74	72	292	4,500
Al Chandler	74	72	72	74	292	4,500
Ikuo Isomura	71	73	80	69	293	3,833.33
Bob Toski	74	76	72	71	293	3,833.33
Ken Still	73	74	74	72	293	3,833.33
George Bayer	80	72	72	70	294	3,500
George Lanning	67	73	79	75	294	3,500
Tom Nieporte	73	73	73	76	295	3,000
Doug Sanders	73	68	74	80	295	3,000
Mike Fetchick	69	70	81	76	296	3,000
Tadashi Kitsuta	81	74	76	69	300	3,000
John Brodie	77	71	81	74	303	2,500
Shiro Matsuda	75	74	86	69	304	2,500
Dave Marr	75	79	78	72	304	2,500
Torakichi Nakamura	78	80	74	74	306	2,250
Toshiro Yamamoto	77	74	74	81	306	2,250
Keinosuke Imada	79	77	83	76	315	2,000
Masanori Miura	79	81	74	81	315	2,000

Denver Post Champions of Golf

TPC at Plum Creek, Castle Rock, Colorado
Par 36–36 – 72; 6,700 yards

May 30–June 1
purse, $250,000

	SCORES			TOTAL	MONEY
Gary Player	70	67	71	208	$37,500
Roberto de Vicenzo	66	71	71	208	22,500

(Player defeated de Vicenzo on fourth hole of sudden-death playoff.)

	SCORES			TOTAL	MONEY
Bruce Crampton	70	70	71	211	17,187.50
Dale Douglass	75	67	69	211	17,187.50
Charles Owens	72	68	72	212	12,500
Bob Charles	73	69	71	213	9,375
Lee Elder	74	72	68	214	8,750
Ken Still	73	71	71	215	8,125
Miller Barber	74	71	71	216	7,500
Chi Chi Rodriguez	69	67	81	217	6,875
Mike Fetchick	69	74	75	218	6,312.50
Al Balding	73	74	72	219	5,265.63
Peter Thomson	73	73	73	219	5,265.63
Ben Smith	75	73	71	219	5,265.62
Walter Zembriski	72	77	70	219	5,265.62
Gay Brewer	71	73	76	220	4,500
Bob Erickson	69	84	68	221	4,125
Joe Jimenez	75	70	76	221	4,125
Bob Goalby	75	73	74	222	3,406.25
Paul Harney	74	72	76	222	3,406.25
George Lanning	74	72	76	222	3,406.25
Gene Littler	73	72	77	222	3,406.25
Bob Brue	73	72	78	223	2,875
Bill Collins	71	78	74	223	2,875
Art Silvestrone	77	73	73	223	2,875
Buck Adams	71	75	78	224	2,437.50
James Barber	72	74	78	224	2,437.50
John Brodie	71	80	73	224	2,437.50
Jim Ferree	80	73	71	224	2,437.50
Jim Cochran	75	74	76	225	2,062.50
Bobby Nichols	72	78	75	225	2,062.50
Doug Ford	80	75	71	226	1,843.75
Bob Stone	75	74	77	226	1,843.75
Al Chandler	76	74	77	227	1,718.75
Gardner Dickinson	77	72	78	227	1,718.75
James Hatfield	82	72	74	228	1,593.75
Charles Sifford	75	72	81	228	1,593.75
Ralph Haddad	75	76	78	229	1,437.50
Howie Johnson	79	76	74	229	1,437.50
Bill Johnston	78	77	74	229	1,437.50

Senior Players Reunion Pro-Am

Bent Tree Country Club, Dallas, Texas   June 6–8
Par 36–36 – 72; 6,804 yards   purse, $200,000

	SCORES			TOTAL	MONEY
Don January	66	68	69	203	$26,250
Chi Chi Rodriguez	66	69	70	205	15,750
Walter Zembriski	69	69	68	206	13,125
Peter Thomson	72	65	72	209	10,937.50
Charles Owens	71	69	70	210	8,750
Billy Casper	68	69	74	211	5,906.25
Bob Charles	71	71	69	211	5,906.25
Bruce Crampton	68	71	72	211	5,906.25
Dale Douglass	74	66	71	211	5,906.25
Bobby Nichols	68	70	74	212	4,812.50
Bob Goalby	75	68	70	213	4,097.92

	SCORES			TOTAL	MONEY
Gene Littler	71	71	71	213	4,097.92
Gary Player	70	72	71	213	4,097.91
Gay Brewer	71	74	69	214	3,434.38
Orville Moody	73	72	69	214	3,434.37
Miller Barber	73	69	73	215	2,712.50
Al Chandler	67	70	78	215	2,712.50
Harold Henning	75	70	70	215	2,712.50
Joe Jimenez	71	72	72	215	2,712.50
Ben Smith	75	69	71	215	2,712.50
Ken Still	73	69	73	215	2,712.50
Jim Cochran	73	70	73	216	2,143.75
Gardner Dickinson	72	71	73	216	2,143.75
Buck Adams	71	75	71	217	1,837.50
Tommy Bolt	75	69	73	217	1,837.50
Pete Brown	73	73	71	217	1,837.50
Doug Ford	76	69	72	217	1,837.50
Charles Sifford	73	71	73	217	1,837.50
Bill Johnston	72	73	73	218	1,408.75
George Lanning	74	72	72	218	1,408.75
Arnold Palmer	71	72	75	218	1,408.75
Doug Sanders	73	71	74	218	1,408.75
Art Silvestrone	75	72	71	218	1,408.75
Mike Fetchick	73	75	71	219	1,225
Paul Harney	71	75	74	220	1,159.38
George Bayer	74	73	73	220	1,159.37
Jack Fleck	69	71	81	221	1,093.75
Billy Maxwell	75	74	73	222	1,050
John Brodie	71	77	75	223	962.50
Bill Collins	74	73	76	223	962.50
Howie Johnson	77	73	73	223	962.50
Al Balding	72	78	74	224	875

Senior Tournament Players Championship

Canterbury Golf Club, Cleveland, Ohio　　　　　　　　June 20–23
Par 36–36 – 72; 6,615 yards　　　　　　　　　　　　purse, $300,000

	SCORES			TOTAL	MONEY
Chi Chi Rodriguez	69	67	70	206	$45,000
Bruce Crampton	72	69	67	208	27,000
Lee Elder	69	71	70	210	18,750
Don January	73	67	70	210	18,750
Arnold Palmer	72	71	67	210	18,750
Gay Brewer	68	71	72	211	10,500
Howie Johnson	69	73	69	211	10,500
Charles Owens	70	72	69	211	10,500
Bob Toski	71	71	70	212	9,000
Dale Douglass	71	71	71	213	7,331.25
Gene Littler	72	71	70	213	7,331.25
Charles Sifford	72	70	71	213	7,331.25
Peter Thomson	71	69	73	213	7,331.25
Jim Ferree	73	71	70	214	5,887.50
Gary Player	68	74	72	214	5,887.50
Bob Charles	74	71	70	215	5,400
Harold Henning	74	71	71	216	4,800
Ken Still	74	71	71	216	4,800

	SCORES			TOTAL	MONEY
Walter Zembriski	74	73	69	216	4,800
Bob Brue	71	71	75	217	4,050
Bob Erickson	73	71	73	217	4,050
George Lanning	72	72	74	218	3,750
Miller Barber	74	70	75	219	3,600
Al Balding	74	75	71	220	3,375
Doug Sanders	71	75	74	220	3,375
Gordon Jones	72	74	75	221	3,075
Art Wall	75	71	75	221	3,075
Mike Fetchick	76	72	74	222	2,625
Jack Fleck	75	73	74	222	2,625
Bob Goalby	75	73	74	222	2,625
Orville Moody	73	73	76	222	2,625
Al Chandler	74	69	80	223	2,137.50
Bill Collins	74	74	75	223	2,137.50
Billy Maxwell	79	74	70	223	2,137.50
Art Silvestrone	74	75	74	223	2,137.50
Fred Hawkins	75	77	72	224	1,912.50
Joe Jimenez	79	74	71	224	1,912.50
Jim Cochran	77	75	73	225	1,725
Bobby Nichols	72	77	76	225	1,725
Ben Smith	74	76	75	225	1,725

USGA Senior Open

Scioto Country Club, Columbus, Ohio
Par 36–35 – 71; 6,709 yards

June 26–29
purse, $275,000

	SCORES				TOTAL	MONEY
Dale Douglass	66	72	68	73	279	$42,500
Gary Player	71	73	66	70	280	22,000
Harold Henning	70	72	70	69	281	15,592
Bruce Crampton	70	72	73	68	283	10,165
Peter Thomson	71	73	70	69	283	10,165
Jim Ferree	69	72	71	72	284	7,778
Miller Barber	72	72	73	68	285	6,934
Gene Littler	72	76	69	69	286	6,336
Orville Moody	73	75	71	68	287	5,765
Billy Casper	71	76	71	70	288	4,759.60
Bob Charles	72	75	70	71	288	4,759.60
Bob Toski	70	73	73	72	288	4,759.60
Jack Fleck	71	74	71	72	288	4,759.60
Chi Chi Rodriguez	74	72	70	72	288	4,759.60
Lee Elder	68	75	74	73	290	4,060
Walker Inman, Jr.	75	67	77	72	291	3,786
Doug Sanders	73	73	73	72	291	3,786
Al Chandler	78	70	71	73	292	3,392
James King	71	79	69	73	292	3,392
Ken Still	69	72	76	75	292	3,392
Buck Adams	70	74	76	73	293	3,045
Quinton Gray	73	73	73	74	293	3,045
Chuck Workman	70	72	73	78	293	3,045
Charles Sifford	72	75	72	75	294	2,842
Bob Bruno	72	78	75	70	295	2,602.20
Arnold Palmer	78	74	73	70	295	2,602.20
Gay Brewer	72	72	78	73	295	2,602.20

	SCORES				TOTAL	MONEY
Art Silvestrone	72	75	73	75	295	2,602.20
Joe Campbell	73	72	74	76	295	2,602.20
Joe Jimenez	73	76	77	70	296	2,289
Art Wall	75	76	72	73	296	2,289
Howie Johnson	75	77	71	73	296	2,289
Ken Mast	75	73	73	75	296	2,289
Billy Maxwell	73	76	73	75	297	2,158
El Collins	72	78	75	73	298	2,079
Stan Dudas	74	76	73	75	298	2,079
Jerry Barber	73	79	75	72	299	2,001
*Robert Hoff	76	75	71	77	299	
*John Cain	75	76	76	73	300	
Hulen Coker	71	77	77	75	300	1,922
Gordon Jones	73	73	75	79	300	1,922
Bobby Nichols	71	79	76	75	301	1,688.58
Ralph Montoya	78	75	73	75	301	1,688.57
Chuck Green	75	78	73	75	301	1,688.57
Al Balding	76	76	73	76	301	1,688.57
*Bob Lowry	75	77	73	76	301	
George Lanning	75	73	76	77	301	1,688.57
Dean Lind	75	73	76	77	301	1,688.57
Bob Goalby	78	75	71	77	301	1,688.57
James Hatfield	69	77	79	77	302	1,455
Dick Plummer	74	74	76	78	302	1,455
*John Harbottle	73	80	77	73	303	
*Morris Beecroft	75	76	76	76	303	
Walter Zembriski	76	75	75	77	303	1,377
Bill Ezinicki	76	76	78	75	305	1,300
Dow Finsterwald	77	75	76	77	305	1,300

Greenbrier American Express Championship

The Greenbrier, White Sulphur Springs, West Virginia
Par 36–36 – 72; 6,709 yards

July 11–13
purse, $200,000

	SCORES			TOTAL	MONEY
Don January	70	66	71	207	$30,000
Jim Ferree	74	67	66	207	18,000
January defeated Ferree on first hole of sudden-death playoff.)					
Miller Barber	70	72	67	209	13,750
Lee Elder	70	69	70	209	13,750
Chi Chi Rodriguez	70	72	68	210	10,000
Bruce Crampton	68	70	73	211	7,250
Dale Douglass	70	70	71	211	7,250
Bob Toski	70	72	70	212	6,500
Harold Henning	73	71	69	213	6,000
Mike Souchak	71	72	72	215	5,500
James Barber	75	73	68	216	4,850
Gay Brewer	74	70	72	216	4,850
Walter Zembriski	76	72	69	217	4,350
Charles Sifford	72	74	72	218	4,050
Buck Adams	73	75	72	220	3,500
Jack Fleck	74	73	73	220	3,500
Joe Jimenez	74	73	73	220	3,500
Arnold Palmer	71	75	74	220	3,500
Pete Brown	75	77	69	221	2,542.86

	SCORES			TOTAL	MONEY
Al Chandler	74	71	76	221	2,542.86
Billy Maxwell	69	74	78	221	2,542.86
Orville Moody	71	76	74	221	2,542.86
Art Wall	73	75	73	221	2,542.86
George Lanning	74	76	71	221	2,542.85
Charles Owens	68	78	75	221	2,542.85
James Hatfield	73	72	77	222	1,900
Howie Johnson	73	73	76	222	1,900
Jim King	77	72	73	222	1,900
Bob Ross	74	73	75	222	1,900
Ben Smith	74	73	75	222	1,900
Jerry Barber	77	75	71	223	1,550
Bill Johnston	74	76	73	223	1,550
Julius Boros	73	77	74	224	1,400
Gene Littler	78	74	72	224	1,400
Jimmy Powell	70	77	77	224	1,400
Bill Collins	74	73	78	225	1,250
Art Silvestrone	72	78	75	225	1,250
Peter Thomson	75	76	74	225	1,250
Gardner Dickinson	76	77	73	226	1,125
Ted Kroll	78	73	75	226	1,125

Grand Rapids Classic

Elks Country Club, Grand Rapids, Michigan
Par 36–35 – 71; 6,453 yards

July 17–20
purse, $251,250

	SCORES			TOTAL	MONEY
Jim Ferree	68	66	70	204	$37,500
Gene Littler	68	67	69	204	20,625
Chi Chi Rodriguez	68	68	68	204	20,625
(Ferree defeated Littler and Rodriguez on first hole of sudden-death playoff.)					
Ben Smith	68	69	68	205	15,625
Harold Henning	73	67	66	206	10,208.34
Charles Owens	67	68	71	206	10,208.33
Bob Toski	74	68	64	206	10,208.33
Bruce Crampton	68	67	72	207	7,500
Dale Douglass	71	69	67	207	7,500
Orville Moody	72	68	67	207	7,500
Billy Casper	72	70	66	208	6,312.50
Miller Barber	72	69	68	209	5,437.50
Gardner Dickinson	69	67	73	209	5,437.50
Lee Elder	72	69	68	209	5,437.50
Al Balding	71	69	70	210	4,625
Bob Brue	69	70	71	210	4,625
Gay Brewer	69	67	75	211	3,875
Jim King	72	70	69	211	3,875
Dan Sikes	72	71	68	211	3,875
Peter Thomson	73	69	69	211	3,875
Al Chandler	73	72	67	212	3,062.50
Jack Fleck	69	71	72	212	3,062.50
Gordon Jones	71	70	71	212	3,062.50
Art Silvestrone	72	69	71	212	3,062.50
James Barber	69	73	71	213	2,687.50
John Brodie	74	66	73	213	2,687.50
Bob Erickson	72	71	71	214	2,312.50

	SCORES			TOTAL	MONEY
Quinton Gray	71	70	73	214	2,312.50
George Lanning	74	72	68	214	2,312.50
Billy Maxwell	73	71	70	214	2,312.50
Joe Jimenez	72	69	74	215	1,791.67
Charles Sifford	74	71	70	215	1,791.67
Gordon Waldespuhl	72	73	70	215	1,791.67
Walter Zembriski	73	71	71	215	1,791.67
Doug Ford	75	71	69	215	1,791.66
Bob Goalby	70	76	69	215	1,791.66
Ted Kroll	74	69	73	216	1,531.25
Bobby Nichols	71	69	76	216	1,531.25
Jerry Barber	69	73	75	217	1,437.50
Bill Collins	73	73	72	218	1,312.50
Howie Johnson	72	70	76	218	1,312.50
Doug Sanders	76	70	72	218	1,312.50

MONY Syracuse Classic

Lafayette Country Club, Jamesville, New York
Par 36–35 – 71; 6,530 yards

July 25–27
purse, $200,000

	SCORES			TOTAL	MONEY
Bruce Crampton	70	65	71	206	$30,000
Roberto de Vicenzo	69	71	67	207	15,166.67
Orville Moody	68	68	71	207	15,166.67
Chi Chi Rodriguez	68	73	66	207	15,166.66
Butch Baird	70	68	70	208	8,166.67
Billy Casper	70	70	68	208	8,166.67
Bob Charles	70	70	68	208	8,166.66
Gene Littler	69	71	69	209	8,166.66
Miller Barber	70	73	67	210	5,750
Ben Smith	69	69	72	210	5,750
Jack Fleck	72	71	68	211	5,050
Dale Douglass	72	67	73	212	4,090
Bob Erickson	67	71	74	212	4,090
Harold Henning	71	71	70	212	4,090
Charles Owens	72	72	68	212	4,090
Art Silvestrone	69	71	72	212	4,090
Al Balding	73	70	71	214	3,300
Joe Jimenez	72	69	73	214	3,300
James Barber	69	74	72	215	2,487.50
Gay Brewer	73	74	68	215	2,487.50
Pete Brown	70	72	73	215	2,487.50
Jim Ferree	75	67	73	215	2,487.50
Doug Ford	73	70	72	215	2,487.50
Casmere Jawor	75	68	72	215	2,487.50
Howie Johnson	71	72	72	215	2,487.50
Peter Thomson	72	72	71	215	2,487.50
Buck Adams	71	75	70	216	1,950
Quinton Gray	72	70	74	216	1,950
Bill Collins	70	75	72	217	1,650
Mike Fetchick	74	71	72	217	1,650
Bill Johnston	73	71	73	217	1,650
George Lanning	76	71	70	217	1,650
Jim Cochran	74	74	70	218	1,450
Howard Brown	73	72	74	219	1,325

	SCORES			TOTAL	MONEY
Al Chandler	74	73	72	219	1,325
Lionel Hebert	75	74	70	219	1,325
Billy Maxwell	71	72	76	219	1,325
Don Hoenig	72	71	77	220	1,150
Jimmy Powell	71	74	75	220	1,150
Walter Zembriski	72	75	73	220	1,150

The Commemorative

Sleepy Hollow Country Club, Scarborough, New York
Par 35–35 – 70; 6,545 yards

August 1–3
purse, $200,000

	SCORES			TOTAL	MONEY
Lee Elder	67	64	68	199	$37,500
Chi Chi Rodriguez	64	71	66	201	22,500
Gene Littler	67	68	67	202	18,750
Bob Charles	67	70	67	204	15,625
Dale Douglass	66	70	69	205	12,500
Buck Adams	73	69	64	206	8,750
Harold Henning	70	68	68	206	8,750
Charles Owens	74	66	66	206	8,750
Gay Brewer	68	69	70	207	6,387.50
Bruce Crampton	71	69	67	207	6,387.50
Roberto de Vicenzo	69	68	70	207	6,387.50
Bob Goalby	68	70	69	207	6,387.50
Orville Moody	69	71	67	207	6,387.50
Miller Barber	68	69	71	208	4,906.25
George Lanning	68	73	67	208	4,906.25
Howie Johnson	70	71	69	210	4,250
Bobby Nichols	68	70	72	210	4,250
Peter Thomson	68	71	71	210	4,250
Billy Casper	72	70	69	211	3,500
Al Chandler	70	72	69	211	3,500
Ben Smith	70	70	71	211	3,500
Bob Brue	68	76	68	212	3,062.50
Arnold Palmer	67	72	73	212	3,062.50
Jim Cochran	72	66	75	213	2,687.50
Gordon Jones	71	70	72	213	2,687.50
Charles Sifford	72	72	69	213	2,687.50
Art Silvestrone	70	67	76	213	2,687.50
Gardner Dickinson	73	71	70	214	1,984.38
Jim Ferree	72	67	75	214	1,984.38
Dan Morgan	72	72	70	214	1,984.38
Bob Toski	69	73	72	214	1,984.38
Butch Baird	70	75	69	214	1,984.37
Jack Fleck	71	76	67	214	1,984.37
Billy Maxwell	70	73	71	214	1,984.37
Doug Sanders	73	69	72	214	1,984.37
Al Balding	70	72	73	215	1,562.50
Bill Johnston	75	69	71	215	1,562.50
Walter Zembriski	69	73	73	215	1,562.50
Jerry Barber	73	71	73	217	1,406.25
Bill Collins	67	73	77	217	1,406.25

Digital Classic

Nashawtuc Country Club, Concord, Massachusetts   August 8–10
Par 36–36 – 72; 6,600 yards   purse, $200,000

	SCORES			TOTAL	MONEY
Chi Chi Rodriguez	70	67	66	203	$30,000
Gary Player	71	65	68	204	18,000
Bob Charles	65	69	71	205	15,000
Bruce Crampton	72	64	70	206	10,000
Harold Henning	72	68	66	206	10,000
Peter Thomson	68	71	67	206	10,000
Bob Erickson	68	71	69	208	7,000
Miller Barber	69	71	70	210	6,250
Lee Elder	72	72	66	210	6,250
Jim Ferree	72	71	68	211	5,066.67
Charles Owens	75	66	70	211	5,066.67
Joe Jimenez	75	70	66	211	5,066.66
Buck Adams	70	76	66	212	4,200
Dale Douglass	73	67	72	212	4,200
Butch Baird	68	73	72	213	3,600
Gay Brewer	65	73	75	213	3,600
Casmere Jawor	72	69	72	213	3,600
Al Balding	71	71	72	214	3,100
Orville Moody	73	70	71	214	3,100
Bobby Nichols	72	73	70	215	2,700
Ben Smith	72	72	71	215	2,700
George Lanning	74	74	68	216	2,400
Charles Sifford	72	73	71	216	2,400
Walter Zembriski	73	73	70	216	2,400
Jack Fleck	72	73	72	217	2,200
James Barber	72	70	76	218	2,050
Pete Brown	69	72	77	218	2,050
Bob Goalby	74	72	73	219	1,750
Fred Haas	74	73	72	219	1,750
Bill Johnston	75	74	70	219	1,750
Gordon Jones	72	75	72	219	1,750
Jerry Barber	74	72	74	220	1,425
Bob Brue	71	71	78	220	1,425
Howie Johnson	72	72	76	220	1,425
Jimmy Powell	73	74	73	220	1,425
John Brodie	79	72	70	221	1,175
Al Chandler	69	82	70	221	1,175
Mike Fetchick	75	73	73	221	1,175
Doug Ford	76	74	71	221	1,175
Jerry Mackedon	74	71	76	221	1,175
Art Silvestrone	72	76	73	221	1,175

GTE Northwest Classic

Sahalee Country Club, Redmond, Washington   August 15–17
Par 36–36 – 72; 6,696 yards   purse, $250,000

	SCORES			TOTAL	MONEY
Bruce Crampton	67	71	72	210	$37,500
Don January	71	67	74	212	20,625
George Lanning	69	73	70	212	20,625

	SCORES			TOTAL	MONEY
Miller Barber	68	72	73	213	14,062.50
Gary Player	70	74	69	213	14,062.50
Butch Baird	73	69	72	214	8,437.50
Billy Casper	70	71	73	214	8,437.50
Harold Henning	69	74	71	214	8,437.50
Gene Littler	69	73	72	214	8,437.50
Gay Brewer	71	74	70	215	5,900
Joe Jimenez	75	70	70	215	5,900
Bill Johnston	73	73	69	215	5,900
Art Silvestrone	70	74	71	215	5,900
Art Wall	70	74	71	215	5,900
Bob Brue	72	69	75	216	4,500
Jim King	74	71	71	216	4,500
Walter Zembriski	67	72	77	216	4,500
John Brodie	72	76	69	217	3,875
Charles Sifford	69	73	75	217	3,875
Al Balding	74	72	73	219	3,500
Al Chandler	72	76	72	220	3,062.50
Jack Fleck	69	74	77	220	3,062.50
Gordon Jones	69	76	75	220	3,062.50
Bobby Nichols	73	75	72	220	3,062.50
Bob Charles	77	74	70	221	2,687.50
Howie Johnson	73	78	70	221	2,687.50
Tommy Atchison	72	78	72	222	2,437.50
Gordon Waldespuhl	74	72	76	222	2,437.50
Jerry Barber	75	76	72	223	2,125
Jim Cochran	73	78	72	223	2,125
Orville Moody	77	77	69	223	2,125
Peter Thomson	73	76	75	224	1,875
Pete Brown	71	82	72	225	1,750
Mike Fetchick	73	78	74	225	1,750
Doug Sanders	76	78	71	225	1,750
Buck Adams	72	78	77	227	1,500
Billy Derickson	79	76	72	227	1,500
Bob Erickson	77	78	72	227	1,500
Fred Haas	75	80	72	227	1,500
Bob Rosburg	73	73	81	227	1,500

The Showdown Classic

Jerermy Ranch Golf Club, Park City, Utah
Par 36–36 – 72; 6,947 yards

August 21–24
purse, $700,000

	SCORES				TOTAL	MONEY
	(Each)					
Bobby Nichols/Curt Byrum	61	65	61	62	249	$33,750
Harold Henning/Denis Watson	67	63	60	61	251	20,550
Gary Player/Wayne Player	62	64	66	60	252	15,468.75
Bob Goalby/Jay Haas	64	62	63	63	252	15,468.75
Orville Moody/Jay Delsing	67	62	63	62	254	11,250
Gene Littler/Andy North	65	65	62	63	255	8,156.25
Ben Smith/Mike Smith	68	63	62	62	255	8,156.25
Don January/Brian Claar	64	60	64	68	256	7,312.50
Miller Barber/Fred Couples	66	61	64	66	257	6,468.75
Bruce Crampton/Lon Hinkle	63	68	64	62	257	6,468.75
Howie Johnson/Howie Johnson Jr.	65	66	62	65	258	5,456.25

	SCORES				TOTAL	MONEY
Chi Chi Rodriguez/Bill Kratzert	63	65	66	64	258	5,456.25
Quinton Gray/Steve Pate	64	65	63	67	259	4,725
Butch Baird/Ed Fiori	65	64	64	66	259	4,725
Lionel Hebert/Leonard Thompson	66	69	59	67	261	4,275
Al Chandler/Dick Mast	67	66	66	63	262	3,937.50
Tom Nieporte/Mike McCullough	63	67	64	68	262	3,937.50
Dale Douglass/Charles Coody	66	63	70	64	263	3,375
Pete Brown/Greg Hickman	67	67	68	61	263	3,375
Jim Cochran/Mark Calcavecchia	67	64	65	67	263	3,375
Gordon Waldespuhl/Larry Ziegler	67	62	66	69	264	2,868.75
Lanny Nielsen/Jimmy Blair	66	66	64	68	264	2,868.75
Gordon Jones/Steve Liebler	65	70	64	66	265	2,418.75
Walter Zembriski/Russ Cochran	65	66	66	68	265	2,418.75
George Bayer/Tim Norris	66	66	65	68	265	2,418.75
George Lanning/Bill Sander	69	66	68	62	265	2,418.75
Billy Casper/Bobby Casper	68	68	64	65	265	2,418.75
George Schneider/Dennis Trixler	66	66	63	70	265	2,418.75
Mike Fetchick/John Adams	67	66	68	65	266	1,912.50
Dick King/Phil Hancock	66	64	66	70	266	1,912.50
Jimmy Powell/Greg Powers	68	66	67	65	266	1,912.50
Jack Fleck/Victor Regalado	67	66	66	68	267	1,687.50
John Brodie/Frank Connor	67	66	67	68	268	1,575
Pat Rea/Mark Brooks	66	71	64	67	268	1,575
John Geersten Jr./Mike Reid	71	63	67	67	268	1,575
Don Fairfield/Jim Fairfield	68	69	66	67	270	1,378.13
Bob McCallister/Rod Curl	65	64	66	75	270	1,378.13
Bob Brue/Bob Menne	67	62	69	72	270	1,378.12
Fred Haas/Richard Zokol	68	69	66	67	270	1,378.12
Joe Jimenez/Jim Colbert	66	67	68	70	271	1,209.38
Tommy Williams/Bob Betley	69	67	68	67	271	1,209.37

Bank One Senior Classic

Griffin Gate Golf Club, Lexington, Kentucky
Par 36–35 – 71; 6,640 yards

August 29–31
purse, $200,000

	SCORES			TOTAL	MONEY
Gene Littler	71	63	67	201	$30,000
Miller Barber	70	63	68	201	16,500
Bob Goalby	67	67	67	201	16,500
(Littler won sudden-death playoff, defeating Goalby on first hole, Barber on third hole.)					
Bob Charles	67	65	71	203	12,500
Charles Sifford	69	67	70	206	10,000
Bruce Crampton	70	68	69	207	6,500
Bob Erickson	65	72	70	207	6,500
Jim King	68	70	69	207	6,500
Jimmy Powell	65	69	73	207	6,500
Art Wall	71	71	65	207	6,500
George Lanning	72	69	67	208	5,050
Gay Brewer	70	69	70	209	4,090
Billy Casper	73	70	66	209	4,090
Dale Douglass	70	68	71	209	4,090
Bobby Nichols	69	71	69	209	4,090
Ben Smith	75	67	67	209	4,090
Howie Johnson	71	71	68	210	3,400

	SCORES			TOTAL	MONEY
Butch Baird	71	71	69	211	3,000
Jim Barber	73	68	70	211	3,000
Walter Zembriski	71	69	71	211	3,000
Buck Adams	71	69	72	212	2,450
John Brodie	70	70	72	212	2,450
Jack Fleck	73	68	71	212	2,450
Orville Moody	69	70	73	212	2,450
Jerry Barber	73	69	71	213	1,850
Pete Brown	71	72	70	213	1,850
Mike Fetchick	73	70	70	213	1,850
Doug Ford	70	69	74	213	1,850
Bill Johnston	72	72	69	213	1,850
Charles Owens	74	67	72	213	1,850
Chi Chi Rodriguez	76	67	70	213	1,850
Bob Stone	69	70	74	213	1,850
Gordon Jones	70	73	71	214	1,425
Art Silvestrone	70	73	71	214	1,425
Al Chandler	75	72	68	215	1,300
Gordon Leishman	72	75	68	215	1,300
Billy Maxwell	70	71	74	215	1,300
Al Balding	72	72	72	216	1,150
George Bayer	73	70	73	216	1,150
Jim Ferree	70	69	77	216	1,150

Chrysler Cup

Tournament Players Club at Avenel, Potomac, Maryland
Par 36-35 – 71; 6,377 yards

September 4–7
purse, $600,000

FINAL RESULT: United States, 68½; International 31½

FIRST ROUND
FOUR-BALL

Harold Henning-Peter Thomson (Int.) defeated Chi Chi Rodriguez-Dale Douglass, 1 up.
Lee Elder-Billy Casper (U.S.) defeated Bruce Crampton-Roberto de Vicenzo, 2 and 1.
Don January-Miller Barber (U.S.) halved with Christy O'Connor-Al Balding.
Arnold Palmer-Gene Littler (US.) defeated Gary Player-Bob Charles, 1 up.
STANDINGS: United States 10, International 6.

SECOND ROUND
SINGLES MATCHES

Thomson (Int.) defeated Elder, 2 and 1.
Rodriguez (U.S.) defeated Charles, 3 and 2.
Douglas (U.S.) defeated O'Connor, 5 and 4.
Crampton (Int.) defeated Casper, 6 and 5.
Littler (U.S.) defeated Player, 1 up.
Barber (U.S.) defeated de Vicenzo, 4 and 3.
Palmer (U.S.) defeated Henning, 1 up.
January (U.S.) defeated Balding, 6 and 4.
STANDINGS: United States 28, International 12.

THIRD ROUND
MEDAL MATCHES

Casper (U.S.) defeated Player, 70–72.
Rodriguez (U.S.) defeated Henning, 69–74.

Littler (U.S.) halves with Charles.
Crampton (Int.) defeated Elder, 68–73.
Palmer (U.S.) defeated Thomson, 71–73.
Douglass (U.S.) defeated Balding, 74–79.
January (U.S.) defeated de Vicenzo, 74–77.
O'Connor (Int.) defeated Barber, 73–75.
STANDINGS: United States 44½; International 19½.

FOURTH ROUND
STROKE PLAY

	SCORE			POINTS
Palmer	35	34	69	7½
Littler	37	32	69	7½
Charles	34	36	70	5½
Rodriguez	36	34	70	5½
January	34	38	72	3
Player	36	36	72	3
Crampton	37	35	72	3
Balding	37	36	73	½
Casper	35	38	73	½
de Vicenzo	37	37	74	
Douglass	35	39	74	
Elder	36	38	74	
Barber	39	36	75	
Henning	40	37	77	
O'Connor	41	36	77	
Thomson	41	40	81	

United Virginia Bank Seniors

Hermitage Country Club, Manakin-Sabot, Virginia
Par 36–36 – 72; 6,640 yards

September 12–14
purse, $300,000

	SCORES			TOTAL	MONEY
Chi Chi Rodriguez	69	67	66	202	$45,000
Don January	71	68	66	205	27,000
Gary Player	69	68	69	206	22,500
Bruce Crampton	70	69	68	207	18,750
Bob Charles	67	73	70	210	12,250
Jimmy Powell	69	69	72	210	12,250
Peter Thomson	69	70	71	210	12,250
Orville Moody	69	71	72	212	9,375
Charles Owens	71	70	71	212	9,375
Harold Henning	72	69	72	213	8,250
Butch Baird	72	75	67	214	7,025
Billy Casper	68	74	72	214	7,025
Lee Elder	74	70	70	214	7,025
Buck Adams	70	73	72	215	5,725
Arnold Palmer	69	73	73	215	5,725
Art Silvestrone	74	73	68	215	5,725
Jim King	73	69	74	216	4,950
Mike Souchak	72	74	70	216	4,950
Jim Ferree	70	73	74	217	4,200
Dow Finsterwald	72	74	71	217	4,200
Walter Zembriski	75	70	72	217	4,200
Roberto de Vicenzo	72	73	73	218	3,450

	SCORES			TOTAL	MONEY
Bob Goalby	70	72	76	218	3,450
Bobby Nichols	70	72	76	218	3,450
Doug Sanders	69	77	72	218	3,450
Ben Smith	72	72	74	218	3,450
Al Chandler	74	72	73	219	2,850
Gene Littler	75	72	72	219	2,850
Art Wall	71	74	74	219	2,850
Jim Cochran	74	76	70	220	2,550
James Barber	75	73	73	221	2,275
Jack Fleck	69	83	69	221	2,275
Howie Johnson	73	75	73	221	2,275
John Brodie	73	73	76	222	2,025
Bob Brue	76	73	73	222	2,025
Mike Fetchick	72	73	77	222	2,025
Jerry Barber	76	74	73	223	1,762.50
Gay Brewer	77	75	71	223	1,762.50
Pete Brown	76	75	72	223	1,762.50
Ted Kroll	73	77	73	223	1,762.50

Paine Webber World Seniors Invitational

Quail Hollow Country Club, Charlotte, North Carolina   September 18–21
Par 36–36 – 72; 6,894 yards   purse, $200,000

	SCORES				TOTAL	MONEY
Bruce Crampton	68	69	72	70	279	$30,021
Lee Elder	70	74	65	71	280	16,521
Chi Chi Rodriguez	70	71	71	68	280	16,521
Peter Thomson	65	72	72	73	282	12,521
Jim Ferree	70	72	71	70	283	10,021
Billy Casper	71	73	72	70	286	6,279.34
Jimmy Powell	69	74	71	72	286	6,279.34
Miller Barber	71	71	70	74	286	6,279.33
John Brodie	70	73	74	69	286	6,279.33
Joe Jimenez	70	73	72	71	286	6,279.33
Gary Player	70	72	73	71	286	6,279.33
Bob Goalby	71	72	70	74	287	4,521
Doug Sanders	77	71	70	69	287	4,521
Bob Charles	71	73	70	74	288	3,946
Gene Littler	71	76	68	73	288	3,946
Jim King	71	71	73	75	290	3,421
Orville Moody	72	74	70	74	290	3,421
Christy O'Connor	71	75	74	70	290	3,421
Roberto de Vicenzo	75	76	68	72	291	3,021
Don January	73	73	71	75	292	2,541
Charles Owens	74	70	75	73	292	2,541
Arnold Palmer	72	76	71	73	292	2,541
Ben Smith	75	74	70	73	292	2,541
Bob Toski	72	74	75	71	292	2,541
Mike Fetchick	70	73	74	76	293	2,171
Art Wall	72	76	72	73	293	2,171
Gay Brewer	71	72	77	74	294	2,012
Dale Douglass	71	73	75	76	295	1,871
Harvie Ward	72	76	71	76	295	1,871
Buck Adams	76	73	73	75	297	1,671
George Lanning	74	81	72	70	297	1,671
Bob Erickson	71	76	77	75	299	1,496

	SCORES			TOTAL	MONEY
Dow Finsterwald	78	72	75 74	299	1,496
Jerry Barber	73	75	74 78	300	1,346
Howie Johnson	76	74	75 75	300	1,346
Bobby Nichols	78	77	22 73	300	1,346
Art Silvestrone	74	73	78 75	300	1,346
Al Balding	75	76	74 77	302	1,146
Al Chandler	75	73	77 77	302	1,146
Charles Sifford	73	74	77 78	302	1,146
Walter Zembriski	73	81	73 75	302	1,146

Unionmutual Classic

Purpoodock Club, Cape Elizabeth, Maine
Par 35–36 – 71; 6,401 yards

September 26–28
purse, $165,000

	SCORES			TOTAL	MONEY
Arnold Palmer	65	67	68	200	$38,000
Don January	70	67	66	203	24,000
Billy Casper	67	67	73	207	17,000
Dale Douglass	72	66	70	208	10,500
Gary Player	68	68	72	208	10,500
Miller Barber	69	74	66	209	5,875
Charles Owens	72	72	65	209	5,875
Lee Elder	68	73	69	209	5,875
Bob Toski	69	69	71	209	5,875
Harold Henning	68	71	71	210	4,250
Peter Thomson	73	67	70	210	4,250
Bob Goalby	72	69	70	211	3,500
George Lanning	70	70	72	212	3,000
Gene Littler	68	72	74	214	2,250
Orville Moody	71	72	71	214	2,250
John Brodie	72	71	72	215	2,000
Al Chandler	71	70	74	215	2,000
Tom Nieporte	70	73	73	216	2,000
Bobby Nichols	75	68	73	216	2,000
Billy Maxwell	73	75	73	221	2,000
Dow Finsterwald	74	74	74	222	2,000

Fairfield Barnett Classic

Suntree Country Club, Melbourne, Florida
Par 36–36 – 72; 6,533 yards

October 10–12
purse, $175,000

	SCORES			TOTAL	MONEY
Dale Douglass	68	67	68	203	$26,250
Miller Barber	68	68	68	204	15,750
Chi Chi Rodriguez	68	69	71	208	13,125
James Barber	70	69	70	209	10,937.50
Bob Charles	71	69	70	210	6,197.92
Bruce Crampton	70	71	69	210	6,197.92
Gordon Jones	71	68	71	210	6,197.92
Bobby Nichols	71	70	69	210	6,197.92
J. C. Goosie	72	69	69	210	6,197.91
Joe Jimenez	70	72	68	210	6,197.91
Butch Baird	71	69	71	211	4,097.92

	SCORES			TOTAL	MONEY
Jim Ferree	69	71	71	211	4,097.92
Charles Owens	70	70	71	211	4,097.91
Mike Fetchick	71	72	70	213	3,339.59
Billy Casper	69	76	68	213	3,339.58
Bob Erickson	68	72	73	213	3,339.58
Bob Goalby	74	72	68	214	2,887.50
Charles Sifford	70	72	72	214	2,887.50
Al Chandler	71	70	74	215	2,537.50
Harold Henning	74	72	69	215	2,537.50
Gene Littler	74	73	69	216	2,231.25
Bob Stone	71	70	75	216	2,231.25
Jim Cochran	74	71	72	217	2,056.25
Harvie Ward	72	72	73	217	2,056.25
Howie Johnson	71	72	75	218	1,793.75
George Lanning	77	71	70	218	1,793.75
Billy Maxwell	70	73	75	218	1,793.75
Orville Moody	73	74	71	218	1,793.75
Al Balding	74	69	76	219	1,487.50
Art Silvestrone	76	73	70	219	1,487.50
Bob Toski	76	73	70	219	1,487.50
Walter Zembriski	72	74	74	220	1,312.50
Peter Thomson	75	72	74	221	1,246.88
Doug Sanders	75	75	71	221	1,246.87
Jerry Barber	78	72	72	222	1,159.38
Dow Finsterwald	70	76	76	222	1,159.37
Gay Brewer	74	73	76	223	1,093.75
Buck Adams	77	71	76	224	1,028.13
Ben Smith	72	74	78	224	1,028.12
Fred Hawkins	73	77	75	225	940.63

Cuyahoga Seniors International

Harbour Town Golf Links, Hilton Head Island, South Carolina   October 17–19
Par 36–35 – 71; 6,435 yards   purse, $200,000

	SCORES			TOTAL	MONEY
Butch Baird	70	71	69	210	$30,000
Chi Chi Rodriguez	72	75	67	214	18,000
Joe Jimenez	71	76	70	217	15,000
Miller Barber	74	70	74	218	8,700
Gay Brewer	72	74	72	218	8,700
Lee Elder	71	75	72	218	8,700
Orville Moody	73	73	72	218	8,700
Walter Zembriski	70	72	76	218	8,700
Harold Henning	73	73	73	219	5,516.67
Arnold Palmer	70	75	74	219	5,516.67
Charles Owens	71	77	71	219	5,516.66
Bob Brue	76	72	73	221	4,212.50
Bruce Crampton	72	74	75	221	4,212.50
Jim Ferree	74	73	74	221	4,212.50
Bobby Nichols	73	78	70	221	4,212.50
Bob Charles	77	69	76	222	3,600
Billy Casper	72	75	76	223	3,300
Jack Fleck	73	76	74	223	3,300
Dale Douglass	72	78	75	225	2,800
Gene Littler	71	75	79	225	2,800

	SCORES			TOTAL	MONEY
Charles Sifford	74	75	76	225	2,800
Al Balding	74	74	79	227	2,450
George Lanning	74	75	78	227	2,450
Gordon Jones	75	74	79	228	2,250
Doug Sanders	77	75	76	228	2,250
George Bayer	77	76	76	229	2,050
Jim Cochran	73	81	75	229	2,050
Dow Finsterwald	74	81	75	230	1,800
Lionel Hebert	72	84	74	230	1,800
Ken Still	76	77	77	230	1,800
Bill Collins	81	74	76	231	1,516.67
Mike Fetchick	74	79	78	231	1,516.67
Mike Souchak	81	76	74	231	1,516.66
Gardner Dickinson	76	82	74	232	1,350
Fred Hawkins	73	87	72	232	1,350
Howie Johnson	75	79	78	232	1,350
Ben Smith	73	79	81	233	1,250
Al Chandler	78	80	76	234	1,125
Bob Goalby	77	77	80	234	1,125
Art Silvestrone	78	76	80	234	1,125
Peter Thomson	81	79	74	234	1,125

Pepsi Senior Challenge

Horseshoe Bend Country Club, Roswell, Georgia   October 24–26 Par 36–36–72;
6,760 yards   purse, $250,000

(Saturday round rained out; tournament shortened to 36 holes.)

	SCORES		TOTAL	MONEY
Bruce Crampton	65	71	136	$37,500
Gary Player	67	70	137	22,500
Jim Ferree	68	70	138	18,750
Butch Baird	70	71	141	12,500
Bob Charles	71	70	141	12,500
Art Wall	71	70	141	12,500
Don January	72	70	142	8,750
Billy Casper	71	72	143	7,500
George Lanning	70	73	143	7,500
Gene Littler	71	72	143	7,500
Gay Brewer	74	70	144	5,656.25
John Brodie	72	72	144	5,656.25
Charles Owens	71	73	144	5,656.25
Walter Zembriski	73	71	144	5,656.25
Harold Henning	73	72	145	4,500
Billy Maxwell	73	72	145	4,500
Jimmy Powell	74	71	145	4,500
Miller Barber	70	76	146	3,437.50
Bill Johnston	73	73	146	3,437.50
Orville Moody	73	73	146	3,437.50
Arnold Palmer	73	73	146	3,437.50
Charles Sifford	73	73	146	3,437.50
Ben Smith	73	73	146	3,437.50
Jim Cochran	74	73	147	2,687.50
Lee Elder	72	75	147	2,687.50
Howie Johnson	75	72	147	2,687.50
Art Silvestrone	75	72	147	2,687.50

	SCORES		TOTAL	MONEY
Chi Chi Rodriguez	78	70	148	2,375
Jerry Barber	76	73	149	2,125
Gardner Dickinson	73	76	149	2,125
Dow Finsterwald	75	74	149	2,125
Bill Byars	74	76	150	1,812.50
Al Chandler	75	75	150	1,812.50
Joe Jimenez	74	76	150	1,812.50
Al Balding	78	73	151	1,593.75
George Bayer	74	77	151	1,593.75
Dale Douglass	76	75	151	1,593.75
Bob Toski	73	78	151	1,593.75
Mike Fetchick	74	78	152	1,375
Bob Goalby	75	77	152	1,375
Ken Still	80	72	152	1,375

Seiko-Tucson Senior Match Play Championship

Randolph Park Golf Course, Tucson, Arizona
Par 35-35 – 70; 6,860 yards

October 30–November 2
purse, $300,000

FIRST ROUND

Harold Henning defeated Al Chandler, 69–75.
George Lanning defeated Orville Moody, 68–73.
Bob Brue defeated Bob Goalby, 70–76.
Bob Charles defeated Mike Fetchick, 74–78.
Jim King defeated Gary Player, 70–71.
Ben Smith defeated Peter Thomson, 73–76.
Dale Douglass defeated Bobby Nichols, 71–75.
Jim Ferree defeated Butch Baird, 69–74.
Chi Chi Rodriguez defeated Art Silvestrone, 72–73.
Gay Brewer defeated Walt Zembriski, 69–73.
Don January defeated Howie Johnson, 70–73.
Miller Barber defeated Doug Sanders, 69–74.
Bruce Crampton defeated Art Wall, 72–77.
Billy Casper defeated Joe Jimenez, 72–75.
Lee Elder defeated Al Balding, 71–76.
Gene Littler defeated Charles Sifford, 69–73.
(Each losing player received $1,687.50.)

SECOND ROUND

Henning defeated Lanning, 71–74.
Charles defeated Brue, 74–75.
Smith defeated King, 69–71.
Douglass defeated Ferree, 73–73, second extra hole.
Brewer defeated Rodriguez, 70–74.
January defeated Barber, 66–70.
Crampton defeated Casper, 70–79.
Elder defeated Littler, 70–74.
(Each losing player received $6,000.)

QUARTER-FINALS

Charles defeated Henning, 70–73.
Smith defeated Douglass, 73–75.
January defeated Brewer, 69–73.
Crampton defeated Elder, 68–69.
(Each losing player received $12,500.)

SEMI-FINALS

Charles defeated Smith, 71–74.
January defeated Crampton, 71–73.

THIRD-FOURTH PLACE PLAYOFF

Crampton defeated Smith, 70–72.
(Crampton received $30,000, Smith $20,000.)

FINALS

January defeated Charles, 70–71.
(January received $75,000, Charles $50,000.)

Las Vegas Senior Classic

Desert Inn and Country Club, Las Vegas, Nevada
Par 36–36 – 72; 6,700 yards

November 7–9
purse, $250,000

	SCORES			TOTAL	MONEY
Bruce Crampton	71	67	68	206	$37,500
Dale Douglass	68	71	69	208	22,500
Bob Charles	66	71	72	209	17,187.50
Lee Elder	69	72	68	209	17,187.50
Don January	71	65	74	210	10,937.50
Chi Chi Rodriguez	73	69	68	210	10,937.50
Jack Fleck	69	73	69	211	8,437.50
Gary Player	70	71	70	211	8,437.50
Miller Barber	69	75	70	214	6,387.50
Harold Henning	71	71	72	214	6,387.50
Orville Moody	73	71	70	214	6,387.50
Arnold Palmer	70	74	70	214	6,387.50
Art Wall	75	70	69	214	6,387.50
George Lanning	70	73	72	215	5,062.50
Walter Zembriski	73	72	71	216	4,750
Bob Goalby	73	73	71	217	4,500
Mike Fetchick	75	72	71	218	4,250
Joe Jimenez	69	71	79	219	3,750
Bill Johnston	74	71	74	219	3,750
Charles Owens	72	75	72	219	3,750
Butch Baird	73	75	72	220	3,187.50
Bobby Nichols	72	72	76	220	3,187.50
Jim Ferree	75	73	73	221	3,000
Billy Casper	77	72	73	222	2,562.50
Don Finsterwald	77	71	74	222	2,562.50
Howie Johnson	76	71	75	222	2,562.50
Larry Mowry	78	75	69	222	2,562.50
Doug Sanders	74	72	76	222	2,562.50
Charles Sifford	72	75	75	222	2,562.50
Gene Littler	73	76	74	223	2,062.50
Ben Smith	76	76	71	223	2,062.50
Tommy Bolt	72	73	79	224	1,843.75
Al Chandler	76	74	74	224	1,843.75
Mike Souchak	76	77	72	225	1,718.75
Ken Still	73	75	77	225	1,718.75
George Bayer	73	77	76	226	1,500
John Brodie	78	72	76	226	1,500

	SCORES			TOTAL	MONEY
Fred Hawkins	74	80	72	226	1,500
Lionel Hebert	75	74	77	226	1,500
Bob Rosburg	75	74	77	226	1,500

Shearson-Lehman Brothers Classic

Gleneagles Country Club, Delray Beach, Florida
Par 36–36 – 72; 6,750 yards

November 20–23
purse, $250,000

	SCORES			TOTAL	MONEY
Bruce Crampton	65	67	68	200	$30,000
Butch Baird	68	68	68	204	18,000
Jim Ferree	69	70	67	206	13,750
Chi Chi Rodriguez	70	68	68	206	13,750
Doug Sanders	68	72	68	208	10,000
Lee Elder	71	71	67	209	7,000
Orville Moody	72	68	69	209	7,000
Walter Zembriski	71	70	68	209	7,000
Gay Brewer	70	73	67	210	5,300
Billy Casper	70	68	72	210	5,300
Dale Douglass	66	74	70	210	5,300
Bob Erickson	68	71	71	210	5,300
Bob Toski	71	67	73	211	4,350
Harold Henning	68	71	73	212	3,925
Joe Jimenez	72	72	68	212	3,925
Al Chandler	69	73	71	213	3,100
Gardner Dickinson	70	74	69	213	3,100
Don January	73	72	68	213	3,100
Howie Johnson	71	70	72	213	3,100
Bobby Nichols	73	73	67	213	3,100
Charles Owens	71	71	71	213	3,100
Miller Barber	74	73	67	214	2,350
Bob Goalby	69	74	71	214	2,350
Dan Sikes	72	72	70	214	2,350
Art Silvestrone	71	70	73	214	2,350
Gene Littler	77	70	68	215	2,050
Ken Still	73	68	74	215	2,050
Buck Adams	69	76	71	216	1,800
Don Finsterwald	69	75	72	216	1,800
Charles Sifford	71	69	76	216	1,800
Jim Cochran	72	74	71	217	1,516.67
Billy Maxwell	72	72	73	217	1,516.67
Bob Brue	72	73	72	217	1,516.66
Lionel Hebert	74	70	74	218	1,375
Ben Smith	75	70	73	218	1,375
George Lanning	74	72	73	219	1,300
Jack Fleck	73	74	73	220	1,225
Gordon Jones	74	75	71	220	1,225
Fred Hawkins	72	75	74	221	1,125
Ted Kroll	73	72	76	221	1,125

Mazda Champions

Tryall Golf and Beach Club, Sandy Bay Jamaica
Par 36–35 – 71; 6,407 yards

December 19–21
purse, $720,000

	SCORES			TOTAL	MONEY
					(each)
Bob Charles/Amy Alcott	64	65	64	193	$250,000
(Charles/Alcott won on first hole of sudden-death playoff.)					
Jim Ferree/Ayako Okamoto	65	63	65	193	14,500
Billy Casper/Jan Stephenson	65	62	66	193	14,500
Gene Littler/Becky Pearson	64	64	66	194	12,500
Arnold Palmer/Chris Johnson	65	64	65	194	12,500
Bruce Crampton/Pat Bradley	63	65	67	195	11,000
Charles Owens/Jane Geddes	67	61	68	196	9,500
Miller Barber/Judy Dickinson	63	67	66	196	9,500
Dale Douglass/Juli Inkster	65	67	68	200	8,000
Don January/Patty Sheehan	67	67	67	201	7,000
Chi Chi Rodriguez/Betsy King	67	68	67	202	6,000
Lee Elder/Mary Beth Zimmerman	69	68	66	203	5,000

The European Tour

Suze (Cannes) Open

Cannes Mougins Country Club, Cannes, France
Par 36–36 – 72; 6,786 yards

April 17–20
purse, £102,040

	SCORES				TOTAL	MONEY
John Bland	68	71	70	67	276	£17,003.71
Severiano Ballesteros	70	69	68	73	280	11,326.53
Neil Hansen	73	68	69	72	282	6,391.47
Des Smyth	70	71	70	72	283	5,102.04
Manuel Pinero	74	71	73	66	284	3,947.12
Ian Woosnam	70	72	69	73	284	3,947.12
Mark Mouland	75	73	67	70	285	2,806.12
Gordon Brand Jr.	74	70	70	71	285	2,806.12
Howard Clark	75	71	72	68	286	2,065.55
Anders Forsbrand	72	76	67	71	286	2,065.55
Mark Roe	70	74	70	72	286	2,065.55
Brian Marchbank	71	75	67	74	287	1,762.52
John O'Leary	71	76	70	71	288	1,539.89
Luis Carbonetti	74	72	71	71	288	1,539.89
Miguel Martin	71	74	72	71	288	1,539.89
Magnus Persson	67	74	72	75	288	1,539.89
Chris Moody	75	73	73	68	289	1,345.08
David J. Russell	70	71	72	76	289	1,345.08
Neil Coles	75	74	74	67	290	1,244.59
Stephen Bennett	76	72	70	72	290	1,244.59
David Llewellyn	73	72	71	74	290	1,244.59
Michael McLean	73	77	73	68	291	1,096.94
Michael Wolseley	73	76	72	70	291	1,096.94

	SCORES				TOTAL	MONEY
Brian Waites	76	74	70	71	291	1,096.94
Andrew Chandler	68	75	76	72	291	1,096.94
Ronan Rafferty	71	74	73	73	291	1,096.94
Jack Ferenz	73	74	69	75	291	1,096.91
Andrew Murray	76	72	77	67	292	887.89
Edward Webber	77	73	70	72	292	887.89
Jeff Hall	75	71	74	72	292	887.89
Antonio Garrido	79	69	71	73	292	887.89
Rick Hartmann	80	69	70	73	292	887.89
Jose-Maria Olazabal	74	75	70	73	292	887.89
Maurice Bembridge	73	74	71	74	292	887.89
Jose Rivero	73	77	73	70	293	714.29
Paul Thomas	74	74	73	72	293	714.29
Tommy Horton	73	75	72	73	293	714.29
Malcolm Mackenzie	76	69	75	73	293	714.29
Gerard Taylor	73	75	71	74	293	714.29
Michel Tapia	74	71	74	74	293	714.29
Eamonn Darcy	74	72	71	76	293	714.29
David Feherty	75	73	76	70	294	565.86
Tony Charnley	75	75	73	71	294	565.86
Frederic Martin	75	74	74	71	294	565.86
Armando Saavedra	75	74	73	72	294	565.86
Manuel Calero	73	75	73	73	294	565.86
Nathaniel Crosby	75	73	73	73	294	565.86
Robert Lee	74	72	73	75	294	565.86
Derrick Cooper	72	75	70	77	294	565.86
Ross Drummond	75	74	67	78	294	565.86

Cepsa Madrid Open

Real Club de la Puerta de Hierro, Madrid, Spain
Par 36–36 – 72; 6,943 yards

April 24–27
purse, £120,000

	SCORES				TOTAL	MONEY
Howard Clark	70	68	67	69	274	£20,000
Severiano Ballesteros	69	67	69	70	275	13,320
Ian Woosnam	69	69	70	71	279	7,520
Jose-Maria Olazabal	72	68	71	69	280	6,000
Ove Sellberg	67	70	72	72	281	5,080
Brian Waites	71	69	69	73	282	3,370
Ronan Rafferty	70	70	71	71	282	3,370
Ross Drummond	71	73	71	67	282	3,370
Glenn Ralph	73	71	68	70	282	3,370
Gordon Brand Jr.	69	70	71	73	283	2,160
Sam Torrance	70	71	73	69	283	2,160
Michael King	70	67	73	73	283	2,160
Andrew Chandler	73	70	70	70	283	2,160
Carl Mason	69	73	70	72	284	1,860
Jimmy Heggarty	70	69	72	74	285	1,760
Armando Saavedra	70	76	69	71	286	1,546.67
John O'Leary	70	71	72	73	286	1,546.67
Miguel Martin	71	73	70	72	286	1,546.67
Jose Rivero	74	69	73	70	286	1,546.67
Gordon Brand	72	71	73	70	286	1,546.67
Mark McNulty	72	69	74	71	286	1,546.67

	SCORES			TOTAL	MONEY
Paul Thomas'	73	70	73	71	287	1,360
Robert Lee	70	72	74	71	287	1,360
Ian Mosey	69	72	72	74	287	1,360
Manuel Sanchez	74	70	72	72	288	1,220
Eamonn Darcy	72	70	76	70	288	1,220
Manuel Calero	71	73	73	71	288	1,220
Michael McLean	72	71	75	70	288	1,220
Jose-Maria Canizares	72	72	72	73	289	1,060
Brian Marchbank	70	76	70	73	289	1,060
John Bland	71	72	74	72	289	1,060
Juan Anglada	73	73	70	73	289	1,060
Rick Hartmann	70	70	72	78	290	846.67
John Slaughter	71	72	71	76	290	846.67
Gavin Levenson	72	71	73	74	290	846.67
Lee Jones	73	73	70	74	290	846.67
David A. Russell	68	71	78	73	290	846.67
Jose Davila	77	68	74	71	290	846.67
Stephen Bennett	74	70	75	71	290	846.67
Paul Curry	76	70	73	71	290	846.67
Tom Lamore	73	72	71	74	290	846.67
Mark Mouland	73	72	73	74	292	690
Santiago Luna	74	72	72	74	292	690
Mark Wiltshire	69	76	74	73	292	690
Ewen Murray	72	73	74	73	292	690
Edward Webber	70	74	74	74	292	690
Adan Sowa	71	74	73	74	292	690
Michel Tapia	69	74	75	75	293	590
Steve Cipa	75	71	73	74	293	590
Gerry Taylor	74	70	73	76	293	590
Des Smyth	72	71	73	77	293	590

Italian Open

Isola de Albarella, Venice, Italy
Par 35–35 — 70; 6,643 yards

May 1–4
purse, £99,535

	SCORES			TOTAL	MONEY
David Feherty	69	67	66	68	270	£16,587.69
Ronan Rafferty	69	69	68	64	270	11,048.36
(Feherty defeated Rafferty on second hold of sudden-death playoff.)					
Andrew Chandler	72	69	65	66	272	6,236.07
Eamonn Darcy	73	67	69	64	273	4,595.91
Severiano Ballesteros	70	67	65	71	273	4,595.91
John Slaughter	67	72	71	64	274	2,634.64
Mike Harwood	68	70	68	68	274	2,634.64
Robert Lee	72	66	71	65	274	2,634.64
Mark James	65	71	67	71	274	2,634.64
Adan Sowa	67	69	68	70	274	2,634.64
Barry Lane	68	72	70	65	275	1,676.95
Sam Torrance	70	69	70	66	275	1,676.95
Jose-Maria Canizares	67	73	71	64	275	1,676.95
Ray Stewart	71	69	68	67	275	1,676.95
Armando Saavedra	70	68	71	67	276	1,346.75
Ronald Stelten	70	66	70	70	276	1,346.75
Gordon Brand Jr.	68	69	68	71	276	1,346.75
Mark McNulty	71	68	66	71	276	1,346.75

	SCORES				TOTAL	MONEY
John Morgan	68	70	68	70	276	1,346.75
Mark Roe	72	69	67	69	277	1,171.70
Santiago Luna	71	71	69	66	277	1,171.70
John O'Leary	70	68	70	69	277	1,171.70
Ove Sellberg	70	68	69	70	277	1,171.70
Bruce Zabriski	70	69	67	72	278	993.18
Mats Lanner	68	69	70	71	278	993.18
Roger Gunn	68	73	70	67	278	993.18
Philip Harrison	72	71	69	66	278	993.18
Roger Chapman	69	74	70	65	278	993.18
Tom Lamore	72	69	69	68	278	993.18
John Bland	70	69	71	68	278	993.18
Wayne Riley	70	67	73	69	279	816.29
Manuel Pinero	70	71	69	69	279	816.29
David A. Russell	71	72	71	65	279	816.29
Stephen Bennett	71	70	74	67	279	816.29
Grant Turner	69	70	74	67	280	696.75
Miguel Martin	68	72	69	71	280	696.75
Costantino Rocca	72	71	70	67	280	696.75
Nathaniel Crosby	70	73	68	69	280	696.75
Manuel Calero	68	71	68	73	280	696.75
Warren Humphreys	72	71	70	67	280	696.75
Derrick Cooper	70	69	72	70	281	575.57
Baldovino Dassu	68	75	65	73	281	575.57
Tony Johnstone	73	67	69	72	281	575.57
Vicente Fernandez	71	72	69	69	281	575.57
Luis Carbonetti	71	69	71	70	281	575.57
Paul Curry	70	70	72	69	281	575.57
Paul Thomas	70	70	70	71	281	575.57
David Williams	65	75	70	71	281	575.57
Magnus Persson	71	72	70	69	282	445.74
Philip Walton	72	71	71	68	282	445.74
Joe Higgins	73	69	72	68	282	445.74
Michael Few	70	72	72	68	282	445.74
Juan Anglada	69	72	73	68	282	445.74
Robin Mann	72	67	73	70	282	445.74
Jack Ferenz	69	72	70	71	282	445.74

Whyte & Mackay PGA Championship

Wentworth Club, West Course, Virginia Water, England
Par 35–37 – 72; 6,945 yards

May 23–26
purse, £210,000

	SCORES				TOTAL	MONEY
Rodger Davis	73	70	68	70	281	£34,990
Des Smyth	70	72	71	68	281	23,310
(Davis defeated Smyth on third hole of sudden-death playoff.)						
Nick Faldo	68	74	74	68	284	13,150
Sam Torrance	74	71	71	69	285	9,700
Philip Walton	71	72	77	65	285	9,700
Gordon Brand	74	74	70	68	286	6,825
Gerard Taylor	71	71	74	70	286	6,825
Michael McLean	72	71	73	71	287	4,716.67
Ian Woosnam	74	70	72	71	287	4,716.67
Sandy Lyle	69	78	72	68	287	4,716.67
Ross Drummond	77	70	72	69	288	3,280.71
Howard Clark	71	71	73	73	288	3,280.71

	SCORES			TOTAL	MONEY
Greg Turner	73	68	74	73	288	3,280.71
Keith Waters	71	71	75	71	288	3,280.71
Ronan Rafferty	69	72	76	71	288	3,280.71
Hugh Baiocchi	72	74	70	72	288	3,280.71
Richard Boxall	72	72	73	71	288	3,280.71
Carl Mason	72	75	73	69	289	2,450
John Morgan	72	74	73	70	289	2,450
Jose-Maria Canizares	72	71	75	71	289	2,450
Andrew Chandler	73	73	72	71	289	2,450
Ian Mosey	75	70	74	70	289	2,450
Bernard Gallacher	74	70	71	74	289	2,450
John Bland	71	72	71	75	289	2,450
Warren Humphreys	71	76	72	70	289	2,450
Mark James	71	70	75	74	290	2,085
Bob E. Smith	72	69	75	74	290	2,085
Adan Sowa	73	73	74	70	290	2,085
Miguel Martin	73	72	74	72	291	1,922.50
Philip Parkin	76	71	73	71	291	1,922.50
Manuel Calero	74	74	69	75	292	1,644.38
Malcolm Mackenzie	72	74	77	69	292	1,644.38
Michael Clayton	72	73	73	74	292	1,644.38
Mark McNulty	72	73	73	74	292	1,644.38
Eamonn Darcy	70	75	74	73	292	1,644.38
Christy O'Connor Jr.	75	71	71	75	292	1,644.38
Manuel Pinero	69	77	76	70	292	1,644.38
Gary Weir	73	75	72	72	292	1,644.38
Tony Johnstone	73	73	71	76	293	1,370
John O'Leary	77	70	73	73	293	1,370
Ian Baker-Finch	70	77	72	74	293	1,370
Glenn Ralph	76	72	72	73	293	1,370
Vicente Fernandez	72	76	74	71	293	1,370
Denis Durnian	75	71	74	74	294	1,170
Jose-Maria Olazabal	75	73	73	73	294	1,170
Rick Hartmann	70	75	75	74	294	1,170
Martin Poxon	76	73	74	71	294	1,170
David Feherty	71	71	75	77	294	1,170
Wayne Riley	76	71	70	78	295	1,010
Andrew Oldcorn	75	74	75	71	295	1,010
Antonio Garrido	73	74	76	72	295	1,010

Epson Grand Prix of Europe

St. Pierre Golf and Country Club, Chepstow, England
Par 35–36 – 71; 6,700 yards

May 9–11
purse, £127,000

FIRST ROUND

Sandy Lyle defeated Christy O'Connor Jr., 1 up.
Rodger Davis defeated Ian Baker-Finch, 5 and 4.
Philip Parkin defeated John O'Leary, 3 and 2.
Eamonn Darcy defeated Paul Way, 5 and 3.
Roger Chapman defeated Manuel Pinero, 1 up, 20 holes.
David Feherty defeated Des Smyth, 4 and 2.
Bernard Gallacher defeated Michael McLean, 2 and 1.
Howard Clark defeated Jose Rivero, 1 up, 20 holes.
Stephen Bennett defeated Sam Torrance, 1 up.
Ove Sellberg defeated Nick Faldo, 1 up.
David J. Russell defeated Gordon Brand, 2 and 1.

Ronan Rafferty defeated Jose-Maria Canizares, 1 up.
Gordon Brand Jr. defeated Rick Hartmann, 5 and 4.
Robert Lee defeated Mark James, 1 up.
Anders Forsbrand defeated Carl Mason, 2 and 1.
Ian Woosnam defeated Hugh Baiocchi, 1 up, 21 holes.
(Each defeated player received £1,350.)

SECOND ROUND

Lyle defeated Davis, 2 and 1.
Parkin defeated Darcy, 1 up.
Feherty defeated Chapman, 3 and 1.
Clark defeated Gallacher, 2 and 1.
Sellberg defeated Bennett, 2 and 1.
Russell defeated Rafferty, 1 up.
Brand Jr. defeated Lee, 4 and 3.
Forsbrand defeated Woosnam, 2 and 1.
(Each defeated player received £2,850.)

QUARTER-FINALS

Lyle defeated Parkin, 2 and 1.
Clark defeated Feherty, 1 up.
Sellberg defeated Russell, 1 up, 19 holes.
Forsbrand defeated Brand Jr., 1 up.
(Each defeated player received £5,000.)

SEMI-FINALS

Clark defeated Lyle, 1 up.
Sellberg defeated Forsbrand, 3 and 2.

PLAYOFF—THIRD AND FOURTH PLACES

Forsbrand defeated Lyle, 1 up, 19 holes.
(Forsbrand received £11,250; Lyle £8,850.)

FINAL

Sellberg defeated Clark, 3 and 2.
(Sellberg received £25,000; Clark £17,500.)

Peugeot Spanish Open

Campo de Golf la Moraleja, Madrid, Spain
Par 36–36 – 72; 6,633 yards

May 15–18
purse, £150,000

	SCORES				TOTAL	MONEY
Howard Clark	68	71	66	67	272	£25,000
Ian Baker-Finch	69	68	68	68	273	16,670
Severiano Ballesteros	74	66	68	68	276	9,380
Robert Lee	72	70	65	71	278	7,500
Ross Drummond	68	72	72	68	280	5,805
Manuel Pinero	73	69	70	68	280	5,805
Jose Rivero	72	68	67	74	281	4,500
Rodger Davis	75	71	72	64	282	3,557.50
Ian Mosey	74	70	68	70	282	3,557.50
Philip Parkin	72	70	71	70	283	2,890
Mark McNulty	73	71	68	71	283	2,890
Jodie Mudd	73	69	73	69	284	2,620
Vicente Fernandez	74	68	76	67	285	2,363.33

	SCORES				TOTAL	MONEY
Mariano Aparacio	68	74	71	72	285	2,363.33
Jose-Maria Olazabal	69	71	72	73	285	2,363.33
Anders Forsbrand	74	68	76	68	286	1,925
Greg Turner	72	71	74	69	286	1,925
Gordon Brand	77	68	72	69	286	1,925
Sam Torrance	77	69	71	69	286	1,925
Antonio Garrido	71	69	75	71	286	1,925
Mike Harwood	74	74	67	71	286	1,925
Mats Lanner	77	69	72	69	287	1,660
John Bland	71	71	73	72	287	1,660
Rick Hartmann	73	74	70	71	288	1,560
Ron Commans	72	75	69	72	288	1,560
Michael McLean	73	74	67	74	288	1,560
Peter Teravainen	72	76	72	69	289	1,440
Ronald Stelten	73	73	73	70	289	1,440
Edward Webber	73	73	68	75	289	1,440
John O'Leary	71	75	77	67	290	1,260
Tony Johnstone	71	77	72	70	290	1,260
Paul Way	72	76	72	70	290	1,260
Gordon Brand Jr.	73	72	74	71	290	1,260
Dillard Pruitt	74	71	70	75	290	1,260
Mark Mouland	73	70	71	76	290	1,260
Baldovino Dassu	74	73	72	72	291	1,002.14
Mark James	76	70	73	72	291	1,002.14
Lee Jones	71	71	76	73	291	1,002.14
Richard Boxall	75	73	70	73	291	1,002.14
Juan Anglada	72	72	70	77	291	1,002.14
Ian Young	71	72	69	79	291	1,002.14
Valentin Barrios	77	71	70	73	291	1,002.14
Hugh Baiocchi	76	72	75	69	292	806
Jose Davila	76	68	78	70	292	806
Ian Woosnam	76	70	74	72	292	806
Des Smyth	73	71	75	73	292	806
Manuel Montes	72	74	76	70	292	806
David Feherty	71	75	78	69	293	690
Adan Sowa	74	74	74	71	293	690
Stuart Reese	73	74	75	71	293	690
David Llewellyn	75	73	74	71	293	690
Paul Hoad	73	74	74	72	293	690
John Morgan	76	71	72	74	293	690

London Standard Four Stars National Pro-Celebrity

Moor Park, Rickmansworth, England
Par 37–35 – 72; 6,817 yards

May 29–June 1
purse, £138,500

	SCORES				TOTAL	MONEY
Antonio Garrido	69	67	71	68	275	£21,660
Ronan Rafferty	71	67	68	70	276	11,290
Jose-Maria Olazabal	68	68	72	68	276	11,290
Mike Clayton	69	72	67	69	277	6,500
Hugh Baiocchi	71	65	74	69	279	5,510
Mark McNulty	70	70	71	69	280	4,225
Philip Parkin	73	68	69	70	280	4,225
Brian Marchbank	70	72	69	70	281	2,788.75
Howard Clark	71	69	74	67	281	2,788.75

	SCORES				TOTAL	MONEY
Tony Johnstone	72	72	69	68	281	2,788.75
Ian Woosnam	68	71	74	68	281	2,788.75
Miguel Martin	70	70	72	70	282	2,200
Rick Hartmann	73	71	71	67	282	2,200
Vaughan Somers	74	71	69	69	283	2,030
John Morgan	74	73	69	68	284	1,920
Chris Moody	74	67	70	74	285	1,743.33
Carl Mason	73	66	77	69	285	1,743.33
Gordon Brand Jr.	72	74	69	70	285	1,743.33
Emmanuel Dussart	67	76	72	71	286	1,501.43
Roger Chapman	72	71	71	72	286	1,501.43
Ken Brown	71	74	71	70	286	1,501.43
David Feherty	70	71	70	75	286	1,501.43
Keith Waters	68	74	76	68	286	1,501.43
Stephen Bennett	75	70	72	69	286	1,501.43
John O'Leary	70	73	74	69	286	1,501.43
Anders Forsbrand	69	69	78	71	287	1,200
Michel Tapia	72	73	72	70	287	1,200
Vicente Fernandez	73	73	73	68	287	1,200
Christy O'Connor Jr.	74	72	71	70	287	1,200
Paul Thomas	70	70	74	73	287	1,200
Ian Baker-Finch	73	71	72	71	287	1,200
Glenn Ralph	71	71	73	72	287	1,200
Sam Torrance	76	71	70	70	287	1,200
Paul Curry	72	73	74	69	288	952
Jose-Maria Canizares	69	77	73	69	288	952
Brian Waites	73	73	71	71	288	952
Derrick Cooper	73	71	74	70	288	952
Michael McLean	76	71	73	68	288	952
Mark Mouland	74	67	74	74	289	795.83
Des Smyth	75	70	74	70	289	795.83
Ross Drummond	75	71	73	70	289	795.83
Magnus Persson	72	78	72	67	289	795.83
Nick Faldo	73	72	76	68	289	795.83
Rodger Davis	74	67	75	73	289	795.83
Neil Coles	75	70	74	71	290	680
Manuel Pinero	77	72	71	70	290	680
Robert Lee	75	76	70	69	290	680
John Bland	70	70	77	73	290	680
Jose Rivero	71	77	68	74	290	680
Grant Turner	75	75	74	67	291	590
Paul Carrigill	75	70	74	72	291	590
Gordon Brand	77	71	72	71	291	590
Paul Way	79	63	72	77	291	590

Dunhill British Masters

Woburn Golf and Country Club, Bow Brickhill, England   June 5–8
Par 34–38 – 72; 6,908 yards   purse, £200,000

	SCORES				TOTAL	MONEY
Severiano Ballesteros	67	68	70	70	275	£33,333
Gordon Brand Jr.	70	71	69	67	277	21,117
Bernhard Langer	68	68	72	70	278	10,960
Robert Lee	69	65	73	71	278	10,960
Brian Marchbank	73	70	68	70	281	6,810

	SCORES				TOTAL	MONEY
Christy O'Connor Jr.	68	73	69	71	281	6,810
Rick Hartsann	66	72	70	73	281	6,810
Andrew Chandler	72	70	69	71	282	4,750
Sam Torrance	70	73	68	72	283	3,728.75
Nick Faldo	73	70	72	68	283	3,728.75
Mark McNulty	71	70	73	69	283	3,728.75
Jose Rivero	70	73	74	66	283	3,728.75
Ove Sellberg	71	73	70	70	284	3,065
David Feherty	74	69	70	71	284	3,065
Wayne Westner	74	74	65	72	285	2,609
Hugh Baiocchi	72	70	74	69	285	2,609
Jerry Anderson	72	72	71	70	285	2,609
Vicente Fernandez	70	67	74	74	285	2,609
Eamonn Darcy	71	70	68	76	285	2,609
Rodger Davis	72	69	71	74	286	2,135
Ian Baker-Finch	74	72	69	71	286	2,135
John Bland	74	73	71	68	286	2,135
Sandy Lyle	70	70	73	73	286	2,135
Bill McColl	75	68	72	71	286	2,135
Gordon Brand	73	72	72	70	287	1,920
Peter Senior	76	71	70	70	287	1,920
Lee Trevino	75	72	71	69	287	1,920
Anders Forsbrand	75	72	72	69	288	1,695
Mark James	70	73	70	75	288	1,695
Ronan Rafferty	76	70	73	69	288	1,695
Des Smyth	73	73	73	69	288	1,695
Brian Waites	73	69	70	76	288	1,695
Tony Johnstone	71	73	72	72	288	1,695
Neil Coles	70	69	71	79	289	1,470
Magnus Persson	77	70	74	68	289	1,470
David Llewellyn	71	74	72	72	289	1,470
Chris Moody	78	67	70	75	290	1,271
John O'Leary	75	73	70	72	290	1,271
Martin Poxon	72	70	72	76	290	1,271
David Williams	74	72	73	71	290	1,271
Bernard Gallacher	75	72	70	73	290	1,271
Michael Clayton	71	70	73	77	291	1,037.50
Jose-Maria Canizares	69	78	70	74	291	1,037.50
David Jones	75	71	76	69	291	1,037.50
Miguel Martin	71	71	74	75	291	1,037.50
Vaughan Somers	74	70	75	72	291	1,037.50
Jeff Hawkes	72	75	74	70	291	1,037.50
Philip Parkin	76	70	71	75	292	897.50
Keith Waters	71	75	69	77	292	897.50
Simon Bishop	70	75	79	68	292	897.50
Warren Humphreys	74	73	70	75	292	897.50

Jersey Open

La Moye Golf Club, St. Brelade, Jersey   June 12–15
Par 36–36 – 72; 6,759 yards   purse, £80,000

	SCORES				TOTAL	MONEY
John Morgan	65	68	71	71	275	£13,330
Peter Fowler	65	71	70	69	275	8,890

(Morgan defeated Fowler on first hole of sudden-death playoff.)

	SCORES				TOTAL	MONEY
Howard Clark	68	68	75	66	277	4,500
Gordon Brand Jr.	62	70	75	70	277	4,500
Ian Mosey	72	70	69	67	278	2,866.67
Rodger Davis	64	73	69	72	278	2,866.67
Hugh Baiocchi	72	64	69	73	278	2,866.67
Brian Marchbank	73	68	69	69	279	2,000
Neil Hansen	67	70	74	69	280	1,700
Chris Moody	69	70	72	69	280	1,700
Carl Mason	68	71	72	70	281	1,440
Andrew Stubbs	70	68	70	73	281	1,440
David Llewellyn	73	71	70	68	282	1,186.67
Vaughan Somers	69	70	74	69	282	1,186.67
Jerry Anderson	67	74	71	70	282	1,186.67
Peter Senior	69	71	72	70	282	1,186.67
Grant Turner	70	69	71	72	282	1,186.67
Paul Thomas	70	70	69	73	282	1,186.67
Michael McLean	70	70	71	72	283	985
Stephen Bennett	67	68	71	77	283	985
Tony Charnley	69	72	75	68	284	851.67
Martin Poxon	73	70	72	69	284	851.67
David Feherty	70	68	76	70	284	851.67
Richard Cromwell	71	71	72	70	284	851.67
Bernard Gallacher	73	69	72	70	284	851.67
Bill Malley	72	70	68	74	284	851.67
Robert Lee	69	72	75	69	285	740
Mark James	69	72	74	70	285	740
David Jones	71	72	71	71	285	740
Paul Curry	73	72	68	72	285	740
Roger Chapman	73	69	70	73	285	740
David Williams	73	69	73	71	286	660
Ronald Stelten	69	71	71	72	286	660
Barry Lane	70	75	66	75	286	660
Frank Nobilo	69	73	77	68	287	600
Richard Boxall	71	71	74	71	287	600
Wayne Riley	74	69	71	73	287	600
Kelly Clair	68	72	75	73	288	540
Ronan Rafferty	72	71	72	73	288	540
Mark Johnson	69	75	68	76	288	540
Malcolm Mackenzie	73	70	75	71	289	480
Philip Walton	68	74	73	74	289	480
Warren Humphreys	70	69	75	75	289	480
Jeff Hawkes	74	71	74	71	290	406.67
Greg Turner	68	70	79	73	290	406.67
David A. Russell	68	71	77	74	290	406.67
Mark Mouland	70	74	71	75	290	406.67
Derrick Cooper	71	68	74	77	290	406.67
Gavin Levenson	73	68	72	77	290	406.67
Jaime Gonzalez	71	73	76	71	291	355
Ian Young	75	69	75	72	291	355
Paul Carrigill	76	68	75	72	291	355
David Ray	70	73	71	77	291	355

Carrolls Irish Open

Portmarnock Golf Club, Dublin, Ireland
Par 36–36 – 72; 7,147 yards

June 19–22
purse, £190,275

	SCORES			TOTAL	MONEY
Severiano Ballesteros	68	75	68	74	285	£31,699.82
Mark McNulty	74	72	71	70	287	16,515.88
Rodger Davis	74	73	71	69	287	16,515.88
Wayne Riley	67	78	71	74	290	8,080.35
Jose-Maria Olazabal	68	78	73	71	290	8,080.35
Howard Clark	74	75	70	71	290	8,080.35
Robert Lee	66	79	73	73	291	4,406.77
Greg Turner	71	76	72	72	291	4,406.77
Gordon Brand	71	78	72	70	291	4,406.77
Roger Chapman	72	79	70	70	291	4,406.77
David Jones	74	73	73	71	291	4,406.77
Ian Woosnam	73	79	71	70	293	3,272.73
Peter Senior	68	79	77	70	294	2,923.89
Bernhard Langer	74	76	70	74	294	2,923.89
Hugh Baiocchi	69	76	75	74	294	2,923.89
Mark Roe	73	76	72	74	295	2,516.39
Ronan Rafferty	70	76	74	75	295	2,516.39
Vaughan Somers	73	77	72	73	295	2,516.39
Andrew Murray	71	78	74	72	295	2,516.39
Manuel Pinero	72	79	71	74	296	2,283.30
Bill McColl	73	77	71	76	297	2,197.68
Carl Mason	71	75	76	75	297	2,197.68
Bob E. Smith	76	71	81	70	298	2,026.43
Jose-Maria Canizares	71	76	76	75	298	2,026.43
Frank Nobilo	74	75	74	75	298	2,026.43
Richard Boxall	72	75	78	73	298	2,026.43
Mark Mouland	75	76	74	74	299	1,826.64
Jeff Hawkes	69	79	78	73	299	1,826.64
Ewen Murray	71	78	72	78	299	1,826.64
Tony Johnstone	70	82	77	71	300	1,528.54
Philip Walton	75	75	71	79	300	1,528.54
Adan Sowa	76	78	75	71	300	1,528.54
Sam Torrance	75	77	75	73	300	1,528.54
Sandy Lyle	72	82	75	71	300	1,528.54
Gerry Taylor	75	79	73	73	300	1,528.54
Stephen Bennett	76	75	75	74	300	1,528.54
David Feherty	75	79	77	69	300	1,528.54
Neil Hansen	76	76	78	70	300	1,528.54
Keith Waters	74	79	77	71	301	1,255.82
Brian Marchbank	72	77	79	73	301	1,255.82
Jose Rivero	72	80	75	74	301	1,255.82
Mark James	74	76	75	76	301	1,255.82
Ron Commans	75	76	76	74	301	1,255.82
Barry Lane	73	79	74	76	302	1,065.54
Mike Harwood	74	79	74	75	302	1,065.54
Grant Turner	73	77	76	76	302	1,065.54
Liam Higgins	72	75	75	80	302	1,065.54
Christy O'Connor	75	79	74	74	302	1,065.54
Kelly Clair	71	80	75	77	303	837.21
Ronald Stelten	70	78	75	80	303	837.21
Gordon Brand Jr.	73	80	76	74	303	837.21
Jimmy Heggarty	72	80	74	77	303	837.21

	SCORES				TOTAL	MONEY
John Morgan	74	78	75	76	303	837.21
Wayne Westner	71	77	80	75	303	837.21
Mike Clayton	72	77	75	79	303	837.21

Johnnie Walker Monte Carlo Open

Mont Agel Golf Club, Monte Carlo
Par 34–35 – 69; 6,198 yards

June 25–28
purse, £158,215

	SCORES				TOTAL	MONEY
Severiano Ballesteros	66	71	64	64	265	£26,365.75
Mark McNulty	68	69	63	67	267	17,561.66
John Bland	66	68	65	69	268	7,515.13
Antonio Garrido	67	66	65	70	268	7,515.13
Michael McLean	67	64	67	70	268	7,515.13
Peter Senior	66	67	66	69	268	7,515.13
Giuseppe Cali	70	67	63	69	269	3,850.63
Jose Rivero	68	68	66	67	269	3,850.63
Miguel Martin	72	63	66	68	269	3,850.63
Steve Elkington	67	66	66	70	269	3,850.63
Ron Commans	66	63	67	74	270	2,819.92
Fulton Allem	71	67	66	66	270	2,819.92
Gordon J. Brand	73	66	65	67	271	2,508.15
Jose Maria Canizares	71	67	70	63	271	2,508.15
Chris Moody	65	69	70	68	272	2,177.76
Mark Roe	70	68	67	67	272	2,177.76
Ove Sellberg	69	65	70	68	272	2,177.76
Sandy Lyle	65	67	71	69	272	2,177.76
Ronald Stelten	66	67	68	72	273	1,911.35
Gordon Brand Jr.	71	69	66	67	273	1,911.35
Ross Drummond	69	69	66	69	273	1,911.35
Bob E. Smith	65	70	68	70	273	1,911.35
Grant Turner	69	67	67	71	274	1,705.44
Neil Hansen	68	68	68	70	274	1,705.44
Gavin Levenson	69	70	66	69	274	1,705.44
Frank Nobilo	70	68	67	69	274	1,705.44
Simon Bishop	68	71	67	69	275	1,500.70
Malcolm Mackenzie	70	68	67	70	275	1,500.70
Des Smyth	68	67	68	72	275	1,500.70
Luis Carbonetti	65	75	64	71	275	1,500.70
Peter Teravainen	70	68	68	70	276	1,275.94
Jose-Maria Olazabal	69	71	69	67	276	1,275.94
Jack Ferenz	72	68	70	66	276	1,275.94
Manuel Calero	69	71	68	68	276	1,275.94
Tony Johnstone	69	69	69	69	276	1,275.94
Rick Hartmann	68	70	69	70	277	1,070.27
Mark Mouland	73	66	68	70	277	1,070.27
Bernard Gallacher	68	68	71	70	277	1,070.27
Paul Thomas	69	68	74	66	277	1,070.27
Ronan Rafferty	72	68	67	70	277	1,070.27
Hugh Baiocchi	67	72	66	72	277	1,070.27
Peter Fowler	69	71	63	74	277	1,070.27
Glenn Ralph	71	67	72	68	278	902.75
David Llewellyn	72	67	69	70	278	902.75
Michel Tapia	72	68	67	71	278	902.75
Warren Humphreys	67	70	69	72	278	902.75

	SCORES				TOTAL	MONEY
Gerry Taylor	68	69	67	74	278	902.75
Brian Marchbank	74	65	74	66	279	763.15
Roger Chapman	69	71	72	67	279	763.15
David Williams	68	69	72	70	279	763.15
Mauro Bianco	69	70	70	70	279	763.15
Michael Few	70	70	69	70	279	763.15

Peugeot French Open Championship

Racing Club de France, Golf La Boulie, Paris, France — July 3–7
Par 36–36 – 72; 6,531 yards — purse, £121,600

	SCORES				TOTAL	MONEY
Severiano Ballesteros	65	66	69	69	269	£20,181.69
Vicente Fernandez	69	65	69	68	271	13,454.46
Bernhard Langer	71	65	68	68	272	7,584.44
Nick Faldo	66	70	68	70	274	6,056.37
Rick Hartmann	71	69	67	68	275	4,686.70
Armando Saavedra	71	68	66	70	275	4,686.70
Ray Stewart	68	66	77	65	276	3,122.91
Mark Roe	70	68	70	68	276	3,122.91
Robert Lee	68	70	66	72	276	3,122.91
Wayne Westner	69	69	67	72	277	2,422.55
Mark Mouland	71	68	71	68	278	2,056.84
Ossie Moore	71	70	68	69	278	2,056.84
Ian Baker-Finch	71	69	67	71	278	2,056.84
Gavin Levenson	71	64	71	72	278	2,056.84
Barry Lane	71	71	71	66	279	1,636.15
Vaughan Somers	71	67	71	70	279	1,636.15
Roger Chapman	72	70	66	71	279	1,636.15
Ronan Rafferty	71	69	68	71	279	1,636.15
Sam Torrance	71	71	66	71	279	1,636.15
Bob E. Smith	67	73	70	70	280	1,434.89
Ross Drummond	72	70	68	70	280	1,434.89
Edward Webber	69	70	69	72	280	1,434.89
Jose Davila	71	72	70	68	281	1,304.44
Paul Curry	72	70	68	71	281	1,304.41
Grant Turner	70	71	68	72	281	1,304.44
Adan Sowa	69	70	70	72	281	1,304.44
Peter Carsbo	69	74	73	66	282	1,155.37
Andrew Chandler	70	69	73	70	282	1,155.37
Lee Fickling	74	69	69	70	282	1,155.37
Phillip Simmons	70	70	72	70	282	1,155.37
Brad Bell	72	71	70	70	283	954.37
Nathaniel Crosby	70	73	69	71	283	954.37
Richard Boxall	69	73	70	71	283	954.37
Tom Lamore	71	72	68	72	283	954.37
Ron Commans	73	68	69	73	283	954.37
Mark Wiltshire	66	69	74	74	283	954.37
Jeff Hall	73	66	70	74	283	954.37
Jose-Maria Olazabal	71	72	72	69	284	776.15
Ronald Stelten	75	68	71	70	284	776.15
Mark James	75	66	71	72	284	776.15
Emmanuel Dussart	73	68	69	74	284	776.15
Neil Hansen	67	72	71	74	284	776.15
Malcolm Mackenzie	71	70	77	67	285	624.27

	SCORES				TOTAL	MONEY
Rick Gibson	75	68	73	69	285	624.27
Giuseppe Cali	69	69	75	72	285	624.27
Juan Quiros	69	71	73	72	285	624.27
Ove Sellberg	68	72	73	72	285	624.27
Costantino Rocca	67	71	74	73	285	624.27
Andrew Sherborne	73	70	69	73	285	624.27
Bradley Sherfy	71	68	72	74	285	624.27
Roger Gunn	70	72	69	74	285	624.27
Anders Forsbrand	73	69	68	75	285	624.27

Car Care Plan International

Moortown Golf Club, Leeds, England
Par 34–35 – 69; 6,507 yards

July 9–12
purse, £110,000

	SCORES				TOTAL	MONEY
Mark Mouland	72	71	65	64	272	£18,330
Anders Forsbrand	69	70	68	66	273	12,210
Sam Torrance	68	72	67	67	274	6,890
Vaughan Somers	70	67	69	69	275	5,500
Jose-Maria Canizares	69	68	70	69	276	4,660
Carl Mason	70	71	67	69	277	3,300
Juan Quiros	68	71	73	65	277	3,300
Hugh Baiocchi	72	70	69	66	277	3,300
Danny Edwards	69	71	69	69	278	2,073
Mark James	69	72	67	70	278	2,073
Mike Clayton	70	71	67	70	278	2,073
Lyndsay Stephen	65	67	76	70	278	2,073
Vicente Fernandez	70	68	72	68	278	2,073
Bill Malley	70	67	69	73	279	1,551
Nick Faldo	71	68	67	73	279	1,551
John Morgan	67	70	75	67	279	1,551
John Bland	69	70	72	68	279	1,551
Mark McNulty	71	67	72	69	279	1,551
Maurice Banbridge	71	71	67	71	280	1,323.75
Malcolm Mackenzie	71	69	70	70	280	1,323.75
Denis Durnian	69	68	72	71	280	1,323.75
Gordon J. Brand	73	68	67	72	280	1,323.75
Gavin Levenson	71	65	74	71	281	1,200
Ian Young	70	71	69	71	281	1,200
Graham Marsh	70	70	66	75	281	1,200
Ossie Moore	71	71	71	69	282	1,060
David Llewellyn	70	69	71	72	282	1,060
Emmanuel Dussart	74	70	69	69	282	1,060
Greg Turner	69	75	71	67	282	1,060
Ian Baker-Finch	68	75	73	66	282	1,060
Bob E. Smith	70	73	70	70	283	921.67
Bill Longauir	75	68	71	69	283	921.67
Tony Charnley	70	72	69	72	283	921.67
Antonio Garrido	70	69	72	73	284	845
Garry Cullen	70	71	73	70	284	845
Neil Hansen	72	71	73	69	285	770
Peter Senior	69	68	73	75	285	770
Grant Turner	75	69	69	72	285	770
Ove Sellberg	70	74	73	68	285	770
David J. Russell	77	66	75	67	285	770

	SCORES				TOTAL	MONEY
Art Russell	71	72	68	75	286	650
Ray Stewart	73	70	72	71	286	650
Stephen Bennett	71	72	71	72	286	650
Andrew Chandler	74	68	72	72	286	650
Derrick Cooper	72	68	74	72	286	650
Richard Boxall	70	71	73	72	286	650
Howard Clark	75	68	75	68	286	650
Miguel Martin	74	69	73	71	287	530
Jaime Gonzalez	73	70	71	73	287	530
Neil Coles	73	69	70	75	287	530
Andrew Stubbs	69	73	70	75	287	530
Tony Johnstone	71	73	72	71	287	530

British Open Championship

Turnberry Hotel, Ailsa Course, Turnberry, Scotland
Par 35–35 – 70; 6,957 yards

July 17–20
purse, £606,850

	SCORES				TOTAL	MONEY
Greg Norman	74	63	74	69	280	£70,000
Gordon J. Brand	71	68	75	71	285	50,000
Bernhard Langer	72	70	76	68	286	35,000
Ian Woosnam	70	74	70	72	286	35,000
Nick Faldo	71	70	76	70	287	25,000
Severiano Ballesteros	76	75	73	64	288	22,000
Gary Koch	73	72	72	71	288	22,000
Brian Marchbank	78	70	72	69	289	17,333.33
Tommy Nakajima	74	67	71	77	289	17,333.33
Fuzzy Zoeller	75	73	72	69	289	17,333.33
Christy O'Connor Jr.	75	71	75	69	290	14,000
David Graham	75	73	70	72	290	14,000
Jose-Maria Canizares	76	68	73	73	290	14,000
Andy Bean	74	73	73	71	291	11,500
Curtis Strange	79	69	74	69	291	11,500
Jose-Maria Olazabal	78	69	72	73	292	9,000
Raymond Floyd	78	67	73	74	292	9,000
Anders Forsbrand	71	73	77	71	292	9,000
Bob Charles	76	72	73	72	293	7,250
Manuel Pinero	78	71	70	74	293	7,250
Vicente Fernandez	78	70	71	75	294	5,022.22
Derrick Cooper	72	79	72	71	294	5,022.22
Ronan Rafferty	75	74	75	70	294	5,022.22
Ben Crenshaw	77	69	75	73	294	5,022.22
Philip Parkin	78	70	72	74	294	5,022.22
Robert Lee	71	75	75	73	294	5,022.22
Sam Torrance	78	69	71	76	294	5,022.22
Vaughan Somers	73	77	72	72	294	5,022.22
Danny Edwards	77	73	70	74	294	5,022.22
John Mahaffey	75	73	75	72	295	3,800
D. A. Weibring	75	70	76	74	295	3,800
Sandy Lyle	78	73	70	74	295	3,800
Ian Stanley	72	74	78	71	295	3,800
Masahiro Kuramoto	77	73	73	72	295	3,800
Gary Player	75	72	73	76	296	3,168.75
Payne Stewart	76	69	75	76	296	3,168.75
Andrew Brooks	72	73	77	74	296	3,168.75

424 / THE EUROPEAN TOUR

	SCORES				TOTAL	MONEY
Roger Chapman	74	71	78	73	296	3,168.75
Ron Commans	72	77	73	74	296	3,168.75
Mark James	76	73	73	75	296	3,168.75
Tom Watson	77	71	77	71	296	3,168.75
Greg Turner	73	71	75	77	296	3,168.75
Mark O'Meara	80	69	74	74	297	2,800
Roger Maltbie	78	71	76	72	297	2,800
Ho Ming Chung	77	74	69	77	297	2,800
Larry Mize	79	69	75	75	298	2,475
Jack Nicklaus	78	73	76	71	298	2,457
Lu Hsi Chuen	80	69	73	76	298	2,475
Mike Clayton	76	74	75	73	298	2,475
Jeff Hawkes	78	73	72	75	298	2,475
Bob Tway	74	71	76	77	298	2,475
Tommy Armour III	76	70	75	77	298	2,475
Tony Charnley	77	73	76	72	298	2,475
Fred Couples	78	73	75	72	298	2,475
Mac O'Grady	76	75	77	70	298	2,475
Graham Marsh	79	71	75	75	300	2,150
Carl Mason	76	73	73	78	300	2,150
Sam Randolph	72	76	77	75	300	2,150
Lee Trevino	80	71	75	75	301	1,925
Malcolm Mackenzie	79	70	77	75	301	1,925
Tom Lamore	76	71	77	77	301	1,925
Frank Nobilo	76	75	71	79	301	1,925
Mark McNulty	80	71	79	71	301	1,925
Eamonn Darcy	76	75	75	75	301	1,925
Martin Gray	75	76	76	75	302	1,650
Andrew Chandler	78	72	78	74	302	1,650
Scott Simpson	78	71	75	78	302	1,650
Donnie Hammond	74	71	79	78	302	1,650
Jimmy Heggarty	75	72	80	75	302	1,650
Ossie Moore	76	74	79	74	303	1,500
Peter Fowler	80	71	77	75	303	1,500
David Jones	75	76	79	75	305	1,500
Ross Drummond	76	74	77	78	305	1,500
Tommy Horton	77	73	82	74	306	1,500
Gary Weir	78	69	80	80	307	1,500
Kristen Moe	76	74	82	82	314	1,500
Hubert Green	77	73	81	WD		1,500

Out of Final 36 Holes

Bill Rogers			80	72	152	
Scott Verplank			77	75	152	
David Frost			78	74	152	
Simon Bishop			79	73	152	
Philip Walton			75	77	152	
Peter Jacobsen			77	75	152	
Neil Hansen			77	75	152	
Tom Kite Jr.			78	74	152	
Ove Sellberg			76	76	152	
Johnny Miller			75	77	152	
Edward Webber			77	76	153	
Mark Mouland			77	76	153	
Dan Pohl			75	78	153	
Joey Sindelar			80	73	153	
Des Smyth			80	73	153	
Martin Poxon			79	74	153	
Deane Beman			75	78	153	

	SCORES		TOTAL	MONEY
Denis Watson	78	75	153	
Andrew Oldcorn	80	73	153	
David Williams	81	72	153	
Antonio Garrido	77	76	153	
Jerry Anderson	81	73	154	
David A. Russell	81	73	154	
Peter Senior	81	73	154	
Peter Allan	83	71	154	
Emmanuel Dussart	78	76	154	
Maurice Bembridge	76	78	154	
Richard Masters	73	81	154	
Richard Boxall	78	76	154	
Peter Teravainen	75	79	154	
Howard Clark	81	73	154	
Rodger Davis	81	74	155	
Adam Hunter	78	77	155	
Ian Baker-Finch	86	69	155	
Hugh Baiocchi	81	74	155	
Mike Harwood	77	78	155	
Terry Gale	81	74	155	
David Llewellyn	82	73	155	
Paul Way	79	77	156	
John Bland	82	74	156	
Bruce Zabriski	77	79	156	
Denis Durnian	78	78	156	
*Mark Davis	78	78	156	
Fulton Allem	82	74	156	
Larry Nelson	81	75	156	
Jim Thorpe	77	79	156	
Michel Tapia	78	78	156	
Jose Rivero	81	75	156	
Eddie Polland	79	77	156	
Wayne Weatner	78	78	156	
Corey Pavin	81	76	157	
Jeff Hall	80	77	157	
Michael Cahill	83	74	157	
*Andrew Cotton	79	79	158	
Seiichi Kanai	87	71	158	
Gordon Brand Jr.	80	79	159	
Bill Longmuir	83	76	159	
Glenn Ralph	81	79	160	
Tony Johnstone	87	73	160	
Ken Brown	81	80	161	
*Garth McGimpsey	85	76	161	
David Feherty	81	80	161	
Andrew Murray	83	78	161	
Adan Sowa	86	75	161	
Paul Carrigill	85	76	161	
*J.G.S. Robinson	83	79	162	
Robert Richardson	85	77	162	
Ray Stewart	85	79	164	
*David Curry	85	80	165	
Jaime Gonzalez	85	82	167	
Howard Francis	85	82	167	
Mark Wiltshire	85	84	169	
George Ritchie	87	84	171	
Guy McQuitty	95	87	182	
Craig Stadler	82	WD		
Andrew Broadway	WD			

(All professionals who missed 36-hole cut received £400.)

KLM Dutch Open

Noordwijkse Golf Club, Noordwijkse, Holland
Par 36–36 – 72; 6,901 yards

July 24–27
purse, £140,000

	SCORES				TOTAL	MONEY
Severiano Ballesteros	69	63	71	68	271	£23,330
Jose Rivero	72	66	69	72	279	15,550
Vicente Fernandez	68	69	71	72	280	7,880
Philip Parkin	71	64	73	72	280	7,880
Ian Baker-Finch	72	66	71	72	281	4,336
Gordon Brand Jr.	71	67	69	74	281	4,336
Brian Marchbank	73	66	72	70	281	4,336
Manuel Pinero	70	66	71	74	281	4,336
Des Smyth	75	63	73	70	281	4,336
Graham Marsh	72	66	75	69	282	2,800
Michael Allen	70	64	74	75	283	2,440
Grant Turner	74	66	72	71	283	2,440
Ian Woosnam	73	64	76	70	283	2,440
Stephen Bennett	71	66	72	75	284	2,047.50
Terry Gale	73	67	73	71	284	2,047.50
Christy O'Connor Jr.	74	69	69	72	284	2,047.50
Jose-Maria Olazabal	70	66	76	72	284	2,047.50
Nick Faldo	74	69	71	71	285	1,770
Antonio Garrido	72	68	70	75	285	1,770
Chris Moody	71	65	75	74	285	1,770
Mark McNulty	75	68	71	72	286	1,583.33
Mark Roe	76	66	71	73	286	1,583.33
Peter Senior	73	66	75	72	286	1,583.33
Peter Fowler	72	69	70	76	287	1,440
Jimmy Heggarty	70	68	75	74	287	1,440
Barry Lane	79	62	73	73	287	1,440
Ronan Rafferty	77	63	76	71	287	1,440
Bernard Gallacher	75	69	72	72	288	1,300
Bill Longmuir	72	67	74	75	288	1,300
David Williams	73	66	73	76	288	1,300
Rodger Davis	74	69	76	70	289	1,160
Santiago Luna	72	69	74	74	289	1,160
Ossie Moore	73	67	74	75	289	1,160
Mark Mouland	75	68	70	76	289	1,160
Manuel Calero	72	68	82	68	290	970
David Feherty	75	65	72	78	290	970
Peter Harrison	75	65	75	75	290	970
Tony Johnstone	74	67	77	72	290	970
John Morgan	74	69	72	75	290	970
Andrew Murray	71	68	73	78	290	970
David Ray	74	70	72	74	290	970
Jerry Anderson	75	66	75	75	291	746.67
Eamonn Darcy	76	67	72	76	291	746.67
Neil Hansen	77	66	76	72	291	746.67
Lee Jones	76	63	74	78	291	746.67
David Llewellyn	74	65	75	77	291	746.67
Carl Mason	77	67	70	77	291	746.67
Ian Mosey	71	67	77	76	291	746.67
Vaughan Somers	71	70	76	74	291	746.67
John Woof	78	63	76	74	291	746.67

Scandinavian Enterprise Open

Ullma Golf Club, Stockholm, Sweden
Par 36–36 – 72; 6,724 yards

July 31–August 3
purse, £153,250

	SCORES				TOTAL	MONEY
Greg Turner	69	62	69	70	270	£25,536.40
Craig Stadler	66	66	66	72	270	17,030.65
(Turner defeated Stadler on first hole of sudden-death playoff.)						
Ian Baker-Finch	65	67	71	71	274	9,578.54
Jose Rivero	70	67	67	72	276	7,088.12
Ronan Rafferty	67	66	68	75	276	7,088.12
Howard Clark	72	70	66	70	278	5,363.98
Mark James	66	71	71	72	280	4,597.70
Ove Sellberg	71	72	72	66	281	3,065.14
Ray Stewart	71	70	71	69	281	3,065.14
Mats Lanner	69	73	70	69	281	3,065.14
Mike Clayton	71	71	69	70	281	3,065.14
Terry Gale	70	67	72	72	281	3,065.14
Rodger Davis	73	65	71	72	281	3,065.14
Christy O'Connor Jr.	68	75	71	68	282	2,078.55
Anders Forsbrand	72	70	71	69	282	2,078.55
Derrick Cooper	71	68	73	70	282	2,078.55
Mark Roe	71	71	70	70	282	2,078.55
Des Smyth	73	69	69	71	282	2,078.55
Sandy Lyle	67	71	72	72	282	2,078.55
Philip Walton	71	70	70	71	282	2,078.55
Sam Torrance	69	69	70	74	282	2,078.55
Rick Hartmann	72	69	73	69	283	1,628.35
Peter Senior	70	72	70	71	283	1,628.35
Brian Marchbank	71	71	70	71	283	1,628.35
Edward Webber	70	70	68	75	283	1,628.35
Vicente Fernandez	69	73	78	64	284	1,436.78
Denis Durnian	74	66	75	69	284	1,436.78
Malcolm Mackenzie	71	71	73	69	284	1,436.78
Paul Thomas	74	70	70	70	284	1,436.78
Ossie Moore	73	70	70	71	284	1,436.78
Carl Mason	73	71	68	72	284	1,436.78
Ross Drummond	73	70	73	69	285	1,226.05
Bruce Zabriski	72	69	74	70	285	1,226.05
Ian Mosey	69	73	73	70	285	1,226.05
John O'Leary	70	74	71	70	285	1,226.05
Michael McLean	73	70	69	73	285	1,226.05
*Christian Hardin	74	69	71	71	285	
Brad Bell	68	71	78	69	286	1,053.64
Jay Townsend	72	72	73	69	286	1,053.64
Graham Marsh	74	70	72	70	286	1,053.64
David A. Russell	71	67	75	73	286	1,053.64
John Slaughter	69	75	73	70	287	900.38
David Williams	69	74	72	72	287	900.38
Vaughan Somers	70	73	71	73	287	900.38
Chris Moody	71	70	72	74	287	900.38
Robert Lee	72	71	77	68	288	766.28
Eamonn Darcy	73	70	75	70	288	766.28
Mark Mouland	69	74	74	71	288	766.28
Grant Turner	75	69	73	71	288	766.28
Frank Nobilo	73	71	71	73	288	766.28
Bill Malley	68	71	73	77	288	680.08

	SCORES				TOTAL	MONEY
Bill McCall	72	71	76	70	289	680.08
John Morgan	73	68	72	76	289	680.08
Philip Parkin	73	71	69	76	289	680.08

PLM Open

Falsterbo Golf Club, Malmo, Sweden
Par 34-37 – 71; 6,738 yards

August 7–10
purse, £117,075

	SCORES				TOTAL	MONEY
Peter Senior	69	72	64	68	273	£19,512.20
Mats Lanner	73	70	65	67	275	12,995.12
Ove Sellberg	76	66	68	66	276	7,336.59
Tommy Armour III	70	68	70	69	277	5,853.66
Magnus Persson	71	70	71	66	278	3,873.17
Gordon J. Brand	69	70	70	69	278	3,873.17
David A. Russell	71	65	70	72	278	3,873.17
Greg Turner	68	66	72	72	278	3,873.17
Eamonn Darcy	76	70	65	68	279	2,367.48
Ray Stewart	74	68	69	68	279	2,367.48
Ronan Rafferty	72	68	73	66	279	2,367.48
Graham Marsh	70	75	66	69	280	1,709.76
Mark Mouland	72	72	71	65	280	1,709.76
Sam Torrance	73	68	69	70	280	1,709.76
Ian Baker-Finch	73	67	72	68	280	1,709.76
Tom Lamore	75	65	69	71	280	1,709.76
Mikael Högberg	73	67	68	72	280	1,709.76
Denis Durnian	73	66	67	74	280	1,709.76
Rick Hartmann	68	69	73	70	280	1,709.76
David Feherty	73	70	73	65	281	1,346.34
Chris Moody	71	72	66	72	281	1,346.34
Michael McLean	71	70	70	70	281	1,346.34
Brian Marchbank	71	67	72	71	281	1,346.34
Barry Lane	65	73	69	74	281	1,346.34
Bob E. Smith	68	69	73	71	281	1,346.34
Richard Boxall	75	69	69	69	282	1,170.73
Richard Cromwell	75	65	73	69	282	1,170.73
Andrew Murray	70	70	72	70	282	1,170.73
Mark Roe	75	70	68	70	283	1,073.17
Tony Johnstone	72	70	68	73	283	1,073.17
John Morgan	71	71	73	69	284	956.10
Edward Webber	73	67	74	70	284	956.10
Paul Hoad	72	68	73	71	284	956.10
Jose Rivero	72	68	70	74	284	956.10
Anders Forsbrand	76	70	71	68	285	809.76
Des Smyth	75	69	68	73	285	809.76
David Ray	74	69	74	68	285	809.76
John O'Leary	75	67	73	70	285	809.76
Keith Waters	72	70	67	76	285	809.76
Grant Turner	69	71	76	69	285	809.76
Vicente Fernandez	76	69	75	66	286	673.17
Michael Clayton	76	69	73	68	286	673.17
Miguel Martin	74	71	66	75	286	673.17
Mike Harwood	73	70	74	69	286	673.17
Gordon Brand Jr.	74	68	73	71	286	673.17
Peter Teravainen	70	70	76	70	286	673.17

	SCORES				TOTAL	MONEY
Jaime Gonzalez	73	67	73	73	286	673.17
Philip Parkin	74	71	70	71	286	673.17
Lyndsay Stephen	71	73	70	73	287	565.85
Mark James	70	72	76	69	287	565.85
Steve Elkington	73	68	74	72	287	565.85

Benson and Hedges International Open

Fulford Golf Club, York, England
Par 36–36 – 72; 6,809 yards

August 14–17
purse, £180,000

	SCORES				TOTAL	MONEY
Mark James	65	70	69	70	274	£30,000
Hugh Baiocchi	66	70	70	68	274	15,650
Lee Trevino	66	67	73	68	274	15,650
(James defeated Baiocchi and Trevino on first hole of sudden-death playoff.)						
Gordon Brand Jr.	65	67	72	71	275	9,000
Mark McNulty	68	69	72	67	276	6,466.67
John O'Leary	66	69	72	69	276	6,466.67
Ian Woosnam	71	68	70	67	276	6,466.67
Christy O'Connor Jr.	72	65	72	68	277	4,130
Jose-Maria Olazabal	67	71	67	72	277	4,130
Robert Lee	68	69	71	70	278	3,400
Jose-Maria Canizares	68	72	68	70	278	3,400
Nick Faldo	71	70	71	67	279	3,100
Ian Baker-Finch	70	72	70	68	280	2,860
Mark Roe	67	72	72	69	280	2,860
Vicente Fernandez	67	74	72	68	281	2,600
Brian Waites	72	69	71	69	281	2,600
Graham Marsh	69	71	71	70	281	2,600
Tommy Armour III	68	73	70	71	282	2,320
Howard Clark	66	73	71	72	282	2,320
Jimmy Heggarty	69	69	70	74	282	2,320
Jeff Hawkes	69	72	74	67	282	2,320
Philip Walton	70	71	71	71	283	1,920
Terry Gale	68	76	71	68	283	1,920
Ove Sellberg	68	73	72	70	283	1,920
Armando Saavedra	71	73	72	67	283	1,920
Jerry Anderson	74	68	72	69	283	1,920
Anders Forsbrand	73	70	73	67	283	1,920
Neil Hansen	67	69	75	73	284	1,620
Jaime Gonzalez	66	71	76	71	284	1,620
Jay Townsend	69	75	71	69	284	1,620
Dillard Pruitt	69	74	73	68	284	1,620
Jeff Hall	69	74	73	69	285	1,420
David Llewellyn	69	72	73	71	285	1,420
John Morgan	71	71	70	73	285	1,420
Roger Chapman	73	71	74	67	285	1,420
Peter Senior	71	70	74	70	285	1,420
Bernard Gallacher	72	69	76	68	285	1,420
Keith Waters	70	74	69	73	286	1,140
Mike Harwood	70	74	74	68	286	1,140
Barry Lane	70	71	72	73	286	1,140
Miguel Martin	69	71	72	74	286	1,140
Antonio Garrido	68	72	76	70	286	1,140
Gordon J. Brand	69	73	72	72	286	1,140

	SCORES				TOTAL	MONEY
David Ray	68	72	75	71	286	1,140
David A. Russell	73	69	73	71	286	1,140
John Slaughter	67	75	74	71	287	920
David Feherty	72	72	70	73	287	920
Edward Webber	70	73	76	68	287	920
Carl Mason	72	72	72	72	288	785
Ronan Rafferty	69	73	72	74	288	785
Vaughan Somers	72	72	75	69	288	785
Paul Way	71	71	77	69	288	785

Bell's Scottish Open

Haggs Castle, Glasgow, Scotland
Par 36–35 – 71; 6,605 yards

August 21–24
purse, £130,000

	SCORES				TOTAL	MONEY
David Feherty	69	68	66	67	270	$21,660
Christy O'Connor Jr.	67	66	69	68	270	11,290
Ian Baker-Finch	66	66	66	72	270	11,290

(Feherty won sudden-death playoff, defeating Baker-Finch on first hole, O'Connor on second.)

	SCORES				TOTAL	MONEY
Ross Drummond	71	71	65	65	272	6,500
Hugh Baiocchi	68	68	67	70	273	5,510
Paul Thomas	72	66	68	68	274	4,550
Sandy Lyle	70	69	66	71	276	3,575
Brian Waites	67	69	72	68	276	3,575
Mark Roe	73	68	71	65	277	2,752.50
Gordon Brand Jr.	69	70	71	67	277	2,752.50
John Bland	70	70	68	70	278	2,266.67
Roger Chapman	66	74	70	68	278	2,266.67
Grant Turner	73	67	69	69	278	2,266.67
Des Smyth	72	67	69	71	279	1,801.67
Gavin Levenson	74	67	71	67	279	1,801.67
Frank Nobilo	65	76	68	70	279	1,801.67
Mark McNulty	72	70	68	69	279	1,801.67
Adan Sowa	69	74	69	67	279	1,801.67
Philip Harrison	71	73	68	67	279	1,801.67
Derrick Cooper	67	67	75	71	280	1,500
Ossie Moore	69	75	65	71	280	1,500
Carl Mason	69	72	70	69	280	1,500
Peter Senior	71	69	70	70	280	1,500
Chris Moody	69	74	67	70	280	1,500
Andrew Oldcorn	74	70	72	65	281	1,340
Tommy Armour III	71	71	72	67	281	1,340
Sam Torrance	69	70	70	72	281	1,340
Noel Ratcliffe	68	72	75	67	282	1,200
Graham Marsh	69	71	72	70	282	1,200
Ian Woosnam	70	74	68	70	282	1,200
Stephen Bennett	72	71	67	72	282	1,200
Robert Lee	69	71	72	71	283	1,040
Steve Elkington	73	73	67	70	283	1,040
Costantino Rocca	69	73	69	72	283	1,040
Paul Carrigill	70	73	70	70	283	1,040
David Ray	72	68	72	72	284	890
Howard Clark	71	74	69	70	284	890
Warren Humphreys	72	72	69	71	284	890

	SCORES				TOTAL	MONEY
Philip Walton	68	72	72	72	284	890
Ray Stewart	69	76	70	69	284	890
Michael McLean	71	70	71	73	285	740.71
Bill McColl	75	70	70	70	285	740.71
Dillard Pruitt	75	71	70	69	285	740.71
Santiago Luna	71	73	73	68	285	740.71
Jimmy Heggarty	68	76	73	68	285	740.71
Jose-Maria Canizares	72	73	71	69	285	740.71
Tony Charnley	76	68	69	72	285	740.71
Peter Baker	71	73	71	71	286	630
Lee Jones	72	71	71	72	286	630
Wayne Westner	75	70	67	74	286	630
Ian Mosey	74	72	69	71	286	630
*David Curry	71	75	72	68	286	

German Open

Hubbelrath Golf Club, Dusseldorf, West Germany
Par 36–36 – 72; 6,754 yards

August 28–31
purse, £164,750

	SCORES				TOTAL	MONEY
Bernhard Langer	75	65	66	67	273	£27,446.46
Rodger Davis	68	73	68	64	273	18,286.66
(Langer defeated Davis on fifth hole of sudden-death playoff.)						
Sandy Lyle	70	71	68	66	275	9,275.12
Mark McNulty	67	72	69	67	275	9,257.12
Mark Mouland	68	73	66	69	276	6,375.62
Ian Woosnam	74	68	68	66	276	6,375.62
Ian Baker-Finch	68	68	70	72	278	4,250.62
Gordon Brand Jr.	71	71	66	70	278	4,250.41
Des Smyth	73	67	70	68	278	4,250.41
Peter Baker	67	70	70	72	279	3,053.27
Severiano Ballesteros	69	69	73	68	279	3,053.27
Ian Mosey	72	67	70	70	279	3,053.27
David Feherty	68	71	68	73	280	2,586.49
Ray Stewart	68	73	71	68	280	2,586.49
Tony Johnstone	70	70	72	69	281	2,372.33
Carl Mason	68	74	70	69	281	2,372.33
Mats Lanner	70	75	67	70	282	2,174.63
David Williams	73	69	70	70	282	2,174.63
Nathaniel Crosby	70	69	72	72	283	2,009.88
Jose Rivero	72	74	68	69	283	2,009.88
Roger Chapman	74	66	73	71	284	1,902.80
Edward Webber	75	72	69	68	284	1,902.80
Robert Lee	72	74	68	71	285	1,803.96
Sam Torrance	70	73	67	75	285	1,803.96
Hugh Baiocchi	72	74	72	68	286	1,581.55
Eamonn Darcy	73	72	71	70	286	1,581.55
Denis Durnian	67	75	72	72	286	1,581.55
Vicente Fernandez	74	69	72	71	286	1,581.55
Philip Harrison	74	69	76	67	286	1,581.55
Christy O'Connor Jr.	73	70	70	73	286	1,581.55
Wayne Riley	71	74	71	70	286	1,581.55
Giuseppe Cali	74	72	70	71	287	1,334.43
Paul Curry	72	71	71	73	287	1,334.43
Lee Jones	68	75	73	71	287	1,334.43

	SCORES				TOTAL	MONEY
Ossie Moore	72	69	73	73	287	1,334.43
Tony Charnley	69	67	78	75	289	1,219.11
David Llewellyn	72	69	75	73	289	1,219.11
Sam Randolph	76	69	73	71	289	1,219.11
Maurice Bembridge	72	72	72	74	290	1,103.79
John Bland	72	74	75	69	290	1,103.79
Mark Roe	73	74	73	70	290	1,103.79
Bruce Zabriski	74	73	71	72	290	1,103.79
Bill McColl	68	73	76	74	291	1,004.95
Bob E. Smith	71	74	74	72	291	1,004.95
Chris Moody	74	70	72	76	292	955.52
Jaime Gonzalez	73	69	77	74	293	922.57
Derrick Cooper	73	74	73	74	294	823.72
Rick Hartmann	70	74	78	72	294	823.72
John Morgan	72	74	77	71	294	823.72
Vaughan Somers	75	72	74	73	294	823.72
Heinz P. Thuel	72	72	75	75	294	823.72

Ebel European Masters—Swiss Open

Crans-Sur-Sierre Golf Club, Switzerland
Par 36–36 – 72; 6,811 yards

September 4–7
purse, £263,160

	SCORES				TOTAL	MONEY
Jose-Maria Olazabal	64	66	66	66	262	£43,846.15
Anders Forsbrand	69	68	63	65	265	29,230.77
Gordon J. Brand	68	65	63	71	267	14,817.81
Ian Baker-Finch	70	63	65	69	267	14,817.81
Ronan Rafferty	64	66	68	70	268	10,182.19
Hugh Baiocchi	65	68	68	67	268	10,182.19
Mark McNulty	69	66	68	66	269	6,097.17
Jose-Maria Canizares	71	68	69	61	269	6,097.17
Sam Torrance	66	70	69	64	269	6,097.17
Tommy Armour III	71	69	64	65	269	6,097.17
Craig Stadler	67	67	65	70	269	6,097.17
David Williams	66	69	67	69	271	4,574.90
Ron Commans	70	69	68	65	272	3,902.83
Des Smyth	71	69	67	65	272	3,902.83
Sandy Lyle	69	69	68	66	272	3,902.83
Bill Longmuir	66	71	65	70	272	3,902.83
Manuel Pinero	65	67	68	72	272	3,902.83
Philip Parkin	68	67	69	69	273	3,299.60
Gordon Brand Jr.	72	64	65	72	273	3,299.60
Sam Randolph	68	69	67	69	273	3,299.60
Lyndsay Stephen	71	67	70	66	274	3,036.44
Howard Clark	68	71	67	68	274	3,036.44
Paul Thomas	66	70	69	69	274	3,036.44
John Bland	66	73	70	66	275	2,834.01
Art Russell	69	71	69	66	275	2,834.01
Carl Mason	69	70	70	67	276	2,591.10
Ove Sellberg	69	70	67	70	276	2,591.10
Rodger Davis	68	67	70	71	276	2,591.10
Donnie Hammond	70	69	71	66	276	2,591.10
Brian Marchbank	69	70	74	64	277	2,078.27
Miguel Martin	71	70	71	65	277	2,078.27
John Morgan	69	71	71	66	277	2,078.27

	SCORES				TOTAL	MONEY
Antonio Garrido	70	68	71	68	277	2,078.27
Gavin Levenson	66	68	74	69	277	2,078.27
Eddie Polland	71	67	70	69	277	2,078.27
Philip Harrison	70	71	67	69	277	2,078.27
Andrew Murray	68	73	66	70	277	2,078.27
Eamonn Darcy	70	71	66	70	277	2,078.27
Robert Lee	70	71	68	69	278	1,631.58
Mike Clayton	73	66	69	70	278	1,631.58
Peter Teravainen	70	70	68	70	278	1,631.58
Derrick Cooper	64	71	72	71	278	1,631.58
Magnus Persson	70	70	64	74	278	1,631.58
Ian Woosnam	70	71	71	67	279	1,477.74
Keith Waters	70	68	73	68	279	1,477.74
Emmanuel Dussart	66	73	71	70	280	1,336
Nathaniel Crosby	68	71	71	70	280	1,336
Jeff Hawkes	68	69	72	71	280	1,336
Peter Fowler	66	70	71	73	280	1,336
Rick Hartmann	65	71	70	74	280	1,336

Panasonic European Open

Sunningdale Golf Club, Old Course, Berkshire, England   September 11–14
Par 35–35 – 70; 6,580 yards   purse, £210,000

	SCORES				TOTAL	MONEY
Greg Norman	67	67	69	66	269	£35,000
Ken Brown	67	67	68	67	269	23,310
(Norman defeated Brown on first hole of sudden-death playoff.)						
Bernhard Langer	69	68	66	68	271	13,150
Severiano Ballesteros	64	72	72	65	273	8,916.67
Nick Faldo	62	72	71	68	273	8,916.67
Jose-Maria Olazabal	68	67	72	66	273	8,916.67
Rodger Davis	71	67	69	67	274	5,775
Peter Fowler	65	68	73	68	274	5,775
John Bland	68	72	67	68	275	4,253.33
Bernard Gallacher	65	68	73	69	275	4,253.33
Miguel Martin	67	73	67	68	275	4,253.33
Bill Longmuir	71	70	69	66	276	3,413.33
Ian Mosey	70	65	70	71	276	3,413.33
Emilio Rodriguez	68	71	70	67	276	3,413.33
Jeff Hawkes	70	70	68	69	277	3,020
Sandy Lyle	66	72	71	68	277	3,020
Hugh Baiocchi	69	71	72	66	278	2,635
Howard Clark	67	68	67	76	278	2,635
Vicente Fernandez	69	70	71	68	278	2,635
Ronan Rafferty	67	73	72	66	278	2,635
Anthony Stevens	69	69	68	72	278	2,635
Gordon Brand Jr.	68	70	68	73	279	2,345
Ross Drummond	70	73	70	66	279	2,345
Mark McNulty	71	69	71	68	279	2,345
Jose-Maria Canizares	70	70	68	72	280	2,117.50
Neil Coles	68	72	70	70	280	2,117.50
Christy O'Connor Jr.	69	67	73	71	280	2,117.50
Ronald Stelten	71	71	72	66	280	2,117.50
Tommy Armour III	70	71	70	70	281	1,746.25
Peter Baker	71	69	71	70	281	1,746.25

	SCORES			TOTAL	MONEY
Stephen Bennett	69 71 70 71			281	1,746.25
Gordon J. Brand	69 67 70 75			281	1,746.25
Mark Roe	69 73 71 68			281	1,746.25
Des Smyth	69 73 71 68			281	1,746.25
Adan Sowa	69 69 70 73			281	1,746.25
Sam Torrance	71 71 71 68			281	1,746.25
Jimmy Heggarty	69 73 67 73			282	1,470
Dillard Pruitt	67 70 77 68			282	1,470
Jose Rivero	68 66 78 70			282	1,470
Greg Turner	73 69 70 70			282	1,470
Neil Hansen	73 69 71 70			283	1,310
Barry Lane	70 72 70 71			283	1,310
Magnus Persson	68 72 73 70			283	1,310
Martin Poxon	68 75 70 70			283	1,310
Gavin Levenson	74 68 75 67			284	1,190
Andrew Oldcorn	67 74 69 74			284	1,190
Maurice Bembridge	70 72 75 68			285	1,050
Antonio Garrido	72 71 73 69			285	1,050
Peter Harrison	70 65 75 75			285	1,050
David Jones	72 69 73 71			285	1,050
Philip Parkin	67 72 74 72			285	1,050

Lawrence Batley Tournament Players' Championship

The Belfry, Brabazon Course, Sutton Coldfield, England
Par 36–36 – 72; 7,191 yards

September 18–21
purse, £130,000

	SCORES			TOTAL	MONEY
Ian Woosnam	71 71 66 69			277	£21,660
Ken Brown	73 70 72 69			284	11,290
Jose-Maria Canizares	70 72 71 71			284	11,290
Michael Allen	70 72 72 72			286	4,742
Ross Drummond	76 67 70 73			286	4,742
Neil Hansen	73 71 71 71			286	4,742
Jeff Hawkes	69 71 73 73			286	4,742
Jose Rivero	70 71 70 75			286	4,742
Anders Forsbrand	75 68 70 74			287	2,905
Stephen Bennett	71 71 73 73			288	2,286
Christy O'Connor Jr.	79 72 73 68			288	2,286
Manuel Pinero	73 72 71 72			288	2,286
Greg Powers	72 72 72 72			288	2,286
Ronald Stelten	71 69 74 74			288	2,286
Carl Mason	71 75 71 72			289	1,700
Jose-Maria Olazabal	74 72 71 72			289	1,700
Magnus Persson	75 70 69 75			289	1,700
Ronan Rafferty	73 67 73 76			289	1,700
Noel Ratcliffe	75 73 71 70			289	1,700
Greg Turner	69 74 74 72			289	1,700
Ian Young	73 70 71 75			289	1,700
Andrew Chandler	77 68 73 72			290	1,420
Vicente Fernandez	74 69 71 76			290	1,420
Tony Johnstone	73 70 74 73			290	1,420
Bill Malley	75 70 73 72			290	1,420
Brian Marchbank	74 70 73 73			290	1,420
Peter Allan	76 69 70 76			291	1,240
Eamonn Darcy	73 70 72 76			291	1,240

	SCORES				TOTAL	MONEY
Lee Jones	73	75	70	73	291	1,240
Robert Lee	76	68	75	72	291	1,240
Bernard Gallacher	75	71	73	73	292	1,041.67
Mark McNulty	75	70	75	72	292	1,041.67
Greg Olson	74	73	72	73	292	1,041.67
Philip Parkin	74	67	69	82	292	1,041.67
David A. Russell	72	75	74	71	292	1,041.67
Sam Torrance	79	69	71	73	292	1,041.67
Tony Charnley	74	72	70	77	293	823.12
Howard Clark	75	72	74	72	293	823.12
Neil Coles	74	73	72	74	293	823.12
Paul Curry	74	70	75	74	293	823.12
Mats Lanner	74	69	77	73	293	823.12
Ian Mosey	77	71	70	75	293	823.12
Andrew Oldcorn	74	74	72	73	293	823.12
Ray Stewart	78	68	73	74	293	823.12
Tommy Armour III	75	71	70	78	294	680
Hugh Biocchi	73	71	77	73	294	680
John Bland	74	69	75	76	294	680
Peter Carsbo	77	70	72	75	294	680
Brian Waites	72	75	72	75	294	680
Jaime Gonzalez	78	70	76	71	295	580
Mark James	73	73	74	75	295	580
Miguel Martin	77	70	74	74	295	580
Frank Nobilo	74	74	74	73	295	580
David Williams	76	72	75	72	295	580

Dunhill Cup

Old Course, St. Andrews, Scotland   September 25–28
Par 36–36 – 72; 6,933 yards   purse, US$1,000,000

FIRST ROUND

WALES DEFEATED NEW ZEALAND, 3–0
Mark Mouland (W) defeated Greg Turner, 69–77; Ian Woosnam (W) defeated Frank Nobilo, 66–71; Philip Parkin defeated Bob Charles, 69–73.

JAPAN DEFEATED SOUTH KOREA, 3–0
Tsuneyuki Nakajima (J) defeated Choi Youn Soo, 68–78; Tateo Ozaki (J) defeated Choi Sang Ho, 71–79; Naomichi Ozaki (J) defeated Cho Ho Sang, 67–74.

CANADA DEFEATED SWEDEN, 2–1
Dave Barr (C) defeated Mats Lanner, 69–74; Ove Sellberg (S) defeated Richard Zokol, 72–75; Dan Halldorson (C) defeated Anders Forsbrand, 69–71.

UNITED STATES DEFEATED ZAMBIA, 3–0
Raymond Floyd (US) defeated Peter Sinyama, 72–81; Mark O'Meara (US) defeated Samiel Mwanza, 70–83; Lanny Wadkins (US) defeated Paul Tembo, 70–79.

SCOTLAND DEFEATED INDONESIA, 3–0
Sam Torrance (S) defeated Sumarno, 68–76; Gordon Brand Jr. (S) defeated Maan Naasim, 71–83; Sandy Lyle (S) defeated Engkun Tachyana, 69–83.

ARGENTINA DEFEATED ENGLAND, 2–1
Vicente Fernandez (A) defeated Howard Clark, 67–70; Adan Sowa (A) defeated Gordon J. Brand, 69–70 Nick Faldo (E) defeated Armando Saavedra, 69–72.

AUSTRALIA DEFEATED ITALY, 3–0
Rodger Davis (A) defeated Costantino Rocca, 65–70; Greg Norman (A) defeated
Giuseppe Cali, 67–77; David Graham (A) defeated Baldovino Dassu, 68–69.

IRELAND DEFEATED SPAIN, 2–1
Ronan Rafferty (I) defeated Severiano Ballesteros, 67–74; Jose Rivero (S) defeated
David Feherty, 71–73; Des Smyth (I) defeated Jose-Maria Olazabal, 71–73.

(Each member of each losing team received US$7,500.)

SECOND ROUND

UNITED STATES DEFEATED CANADA, 2–1
O'Meara (US) defeated Zokol, 74–76; Barr (C) defeated Wadkins, 66–68; Floyd
(US) defeated Halldorson, 69–70.

JAPAN DEFEATED ARGENTINA, 2–1
Nakajima (J) defeated Fernandez, 67–68; Naomichi Ozaki (J) defeated Sowa,
69–71; Saavedra (A) defeated Tateo Ozaki, 69–72.

AUSTRALIA DEFEATED WALES, 3–0
Davis (A) defeated Mouland, 71–73; Norman (A) defeated Woosnam, 67–71;
Graham (A) defeated Parkin, 68–69.

SCOTLAND DEFEATED IRELAND, 3–0
Brand (S) defeated Rafferty, 68–70; Torrance (S) defeated Smyth, 70–72; Lyle (S)
defeated Feherty, 70–72.

(Each member of each losing team received US$15,000.)

SEMI-FINALS

JAPAN DEFEATED UNITED STATES, 2–1
O'Meara (US) defeated Tateo Ozaki, 70–77; Naomichi Ozaki (J) defeated Wadkins,
69–74; Nakajima (J) defeated Floyd, 69–76.

AUSTRALIA DEFEATED SCOTLAND, 2–1
Davis (A) defeated Brand, 72–74; Lyle (S) defeated Graham, 68–70; Norman (A)
defeated Torrance, 70–72.

PLAYOFF—THIRD-FOURTH PLACES

SCOTLAND DEFEATED UNITED STATES, 2–1
Brand (S) defeated O'Meara, 75–78; Floyd (US) defeated Torrance, 73–78; Lyle (S)
defeated Wadkins, 73–78.

(Each Scottish player received US$36,666; each U.S. player received US$26,666.)

FINALS

AUSTRALIA DEFEATED JAPAN, 3–0
Davis (A) defeated Tateo Ozaki, 76–81; Graham (A) defeated Naomichi Ozaki,
81–82; Norman (A) defeated Nakajima, 73–76.

(Each Australian player received US$100,000; each Japanese player received
US$50,000.)

Suntory World Match Play Championship

Wentworth Club,
West Course, Virginia Water, Surrey, England
Par 434 534 444 – 35; 345 434 455 – 37 – 72;
6,945 yards

October 2–5, 1986
purse, £180,000

FIRST ROUND

Rodger Davis defeated Nick Price 2 and 1

Davis	435	534	444	36	334	533	354	33	69
Price	435	433	443	33	344	325	454	34	67

Price leads, 2 up

Davis	424	434	444	33	333	434	54
Price	536	444	444	38	334	443	34

Sandy Lyle defeated Howard Clark, 1 hole

Lyle	434	434	554	36	354	535	444	37	73
Clark	434	534	445	36	245	535	354	36	72

Clark leads, 1 up

Lyle	424	434	54W	X	334	333	454	32	X
Clark	444	524	44C	X	344	345	344	34	X

Jose-Maria Olazabal defeated Lanny Wadkins 2 and 1

Wadkins	535	434	454	37	334	433	454	33	70
Olazabal	434	535	344	35	244	433	443	31	66

Olazabal leads, 4 up

Wadkins	424	644	354	36	343	434	34
Olazabal	435	434	444	35	344	534	34

Joe Ozaki defeated Ben Crenshaw 7 and 6

Crenshaw	434	433	444	33	344	435	554	37	70
Ozaki	425	534	344	34	345	324	444	33	67

Ozaki leads, 3 up

Crenshaw	535	633	544	38	W44
Ozaki	335	323	454	32	C33

SECOND ROUND

Rodger Davis defeated Severiano Ballesteros 7 and 6

Ballesteros	435	434	545	37	344	423	444	32	69
Davis	535	423	444	34	344	424	354	33	67

Davis leads, 2 up

Ballesteros	434	635	454	38	344
Davis	434	424	434	32	334

Sandy Lyle defeated Tommy Nakajima at 38th hole

Nakajima	533	324	444	32	343	434	444	33	65
Lyle	424	433	444	32	344	334	354	33	65

Match all-square

Nakajima	444	424	343	32	234	424	454	32	64
Lyle	423	323	355	30	344	534	443	34	64

Match all-square

Nakajima	46
Lyle	45

Jack Nicklaus defeated Jose-Maria Olazabal 5 and 4

Nicklaus	435	423	443	32	344	434	444	34	66
Olazabal	435	434	454	36	334	434	456	36	72

Nicklaus leads, 5 up

Nicklaus	435	434	344	34	343	53	
Olazabal	534	434	343	33	354	33	

Greg Norman defeated Joe Ozaki 4 and 2

Norman	434	434	354	34	444	444	354	36	70
Ozaki	435	544	455	39	334	334	455	34	73

Norman leads, 3 up

Norman	33C	534	544	X	433	435	4
Ozaki	423	635	444	35	344	434	5

SEMI-FINALS

Sandy Lyle defeated Rodger Davis 2 and 1

Davis	434	534	344	34	345	525	454	37	71
Lyle	424	433	444	32	344	435	354	35	67

Lyle leads, 4 up

Davis	434	C44	444	X	334	325	44
Lyle	534	W24	444	X	344	435	44

Greg Norman defeated Jack Nicklaus, 1 hole

Nicklaus	534	434	444	35	344	534	344	34	69
Norman	434	434	444	34	335	435	444	35	69

Match all-square

Nicklaus	434	544	444	36	33W	335	444	X
Norman	424	544	344	34	34C	434	434	X

FINAL

Greg Norman defeated Sandy Lyle 2 and 1

Lyle	436	444	545	39	344	334	445	34	73
Norman	425	434	444	34	334	425	555	36	70

Norman leads, 3 up

Lyle	434	433	445	34	344	433	3C
Norman	335	434	354	34	344	434	4W

THIRD PLACE

Jack Nicklaus defeated Rodger Davis 2 and 1

Davis	534	444	434	35	344	434	43
Nicklaus	433	544	443	34	343	334	53

PRIZE MONEY: Norman £50,000; Lyle £25,000; Nicklaus £20,000; Davis £15,000; Ballesteros, Nakajima, Olazabal, Ozaki £10,000 each; Price, Clark, Wadkins, Crenshaw £7,500 each.

LEGEND: C—conceded hole to opponent; W—won hole by concession without holding out; X—no total score.

Sanyo Open

Real Club de Golf El Prat, Barcelona, Spain
Par 35–37 – 72; 6,503 yards

October 9–12
purse, £175,000

	SCORES				TOTAL	MONEY
Jose-Maria Olazabal	69	68	69	67	273	£29,150
Howard Clark	72	68	69	67	276	19,440
Ian Mosey	73	67	68	69	277	10,950
Severiano Ballesteros	67	67	73	71	278	7,433.33
Ove Sellberg	70	71	65	72	278	7,433.33
Ian Woosnam	71	68	69	70	278	7,433.33
Juan Anglada	67	74	67	71	279	4,056
Gordon Brand Jr.	69	70	68	72	279	4,056
Eamonn Darcy	71	70	70	68	279	4,056
Andrew Oldcorn	73	67	71	68	279	4,056
Ronan Rafferty	69	71	70	69	279	4,056
Gordon J. Brand	72	69	69	70	280	2,940
Manuel Pinero	71	68	70	71	280	2,940
Mariano Aparicio	72	69	68	72	281	2,595
Tony Johnstone	71	72	71	67	281	2,595
Magnus Persson	72	69	70	70	281	2,595
Roger Chapman	69	71	71	71	282	2,273.33
Rafael Gallardo	72	67	74	69	282	2,273.33
Robert Lee	73	66	72	71	282	2,273.33
Jose-Maria Canizares	71	72	68	72	283	1,908.12
David Feherty	73	70	69	71	283	1,908.12
Philip Harrison	73	67	71	72	283	1,908.12
Jimmy Heggarty	70	69	74	70	283	1,908.12
Warren Humphreys	70	69	70	74	283	1,908.12
Christy O'Connor Jr.	71	67	78	72	283	1,908.12
Art Russell	74	67	67	75	283	1,908.12
David Williams	70	71	68	74	283	1,908.12
Manuel Calero	73	71	72	68	284	1,556.67
Emmanuel Dussart	75	67	71	71	284	1,556.67
Malcolm Mackenzie	74	70	65	75	284	1,556.67
Carl Mason	72	70	69	73	284	1,556.67
Manuel Montes	70	69	71	74	284	1,556.67
Peter Teravainen	72	70	70	72	284	1,556.67
Andrew Chandler	75	69	71	70	285	1,360
Santiago Luna	71	71	72	71	285	1,360
Mark Roe	73	71	70	71	285	1,360
Peter Carsbo	73	70	75	68	286	1,200
Neil Hansen	71	70	69	76	286	1,200
Mark James	71	73	67	75	286	1,200
Michel Tapia	72	70	74	70	286	1,200
Mark Wiltshire	71	70	73	72	286	1,200
Steve Cipa	71	71	72	73	287	968.75
Jose Davila	73	70	70	74	287	968.75
Joe Higgins	73	70	72	72	287	968.75
Mark Johnson	69	72	72	74	287	968.75
Emilio Rodriguez	73	67	72	75	287	968.75
Armando Saavedra	71	72	72	72	287	968.75
Sandy Stephen	75	69	70	73	287	968.75
Brian Waites	72	71	70	74	287	968.75
Stephen Bennett	71	73	70	74	288	785
Tony Charnley	67	70	75	76	288	785
Robin Mann	72	71	75	70	288	785
Michael McLean	72	70	71	75	288	785

Lancome Trophy

St. Nom la Breteche Golf Club, Paris, France
Par 36–36 – 72; 6,713 yards

October 16–19
purse, £165,775

(Co-champions declared when darkness halted playoff after four holes.)

	SCORES				TOTAL	MONEY
Severiano Ballesteros	67	69	68	70	274	£27,272.73
Bernhard Langer	73	66	66	69	274	27,272.73
Des Smyth	72	69	68	66	275	12,834.22
Sam Torrance	71	64	74	67	276	9,625.67
Sandy Lyle	70	66	70	70	276	9,625.67
John Bland	72	71	68	66	277	5,811.05
Gordon J. Brand	69	69	68	71	277	5,811.05
Jose-Maria Olazabal	71	69	66	71	277	5,811.05
Curtis Strange	69	67	70	72	278	4,705.88
Hugh Baiocchi	69	70	73	67	279	4,278.07
Anders Forsbrand	72	67	68	73	280	3,957.22
Ronan Rafferty	73	69	71	69	282	3,556.15
Mark James	70	67	72	73	282	3,556.15
Ian Woosnam	70	69	75	70	284	3,121.66
Mark McNulty	70	72	70	72	284	3,121.66
Ove Sellberg	72	71	68	73	284	3,121.66
Gordon Brand Jr.	72	70	64	78	284	3,121.66
Jose-Maria Canizares	73	70	73	71	287	2,780.74
Antonio Garrido	71	74	67	75	287	2,780.74
Warren Humphreys	73	71	71	73	288	2,620.32
Robert Lee	78	72	71	70	291	2,406.42
Howard Clark	72	74	70	75	291	2,406.42
Nick Price	75	69	75	72	291	2,406.42
Michel Tapia	76	72	70	74	292	2,094.47
John Morgan	74	74	70	74	292	2,094.47
Emmanuel Dussart	72	73	72	75	292	2,094.47
Mark Mouland	74	69	80	73	296	1,951.87
Jack Nicklaus Jr.	74	77	79	78	308	1,898.40
David Feherty	75	73	71	WD		1,818.18
Jim Thorpe	70	72	WD			1,818.18

Quinta Do Lago Portuguese Open

Quinta do Lago Golf Club, Algarve, Portugal
Par 36–36 – 72; 5,933 yards

October 23–26
purse, £100,000

	SCORES				TOTAL	MONEY
Mark McNulty	66	69	69	66	270	£16,660
Ian Mosey	69	69	69	67	274	11,100
John Bland	67	66	71	72	276	5,630
Jose-Maria Canizares	68	70	72	66	276	5,630
Anders Forsbrand	72	66	71	68	277	3,580
Tony Johnstone	69	71	66	71	277	3,580
Sandy Lyle	66	67	71	73	277	3,580
Gordon J. Brand	68	70	72	69	279	2,246.67
Roger Chapman	73	71	69	66	279	2,246.67
Joe Higgins	72	67	68	72	279	2,246.67
Michael Allen	70	70	69	71	280	1,596.67

	SCORES				TOTAL	MONEY
Giuseppe Cali	70	71	72	67	280	1,596.67
Roger Gunn	71	74	66	69	280	1,596.67
Manuel Pinero	71	72	64	73	280	1,596.67
Des Smyth	74	68	68	70	280	1,596.67
Grant Turner	70	73	68	69	280	1,596.67
Gordon Brand Jr.	73	66	73	69	281	1,293.33
Mats Lanner	75	66	69	71	281	1,293.33
David Llewellyn	71	67	71	72	281	1,293.33
Hugh Baiocchi	72	71	70	69	282	1,140
Antonio Garrido	72	69	69	72	282	1,140
Paul Hoad	70	68	71	73	282	1,140
Andrew Oldcorn	70	67	70	75	282	1,140
Philip Parkin	69	70	70	73	282	1,140
Tony Charnley	71	74	67	71	283	990
Mark Johnson	67	74	69	73	283	990
Christy O'Connor Jr.	70	70	75	68	283	990
Alfonso Pinero	69	71	73	70	283	990
Mark Roe	74	71	68	70	283	990
Ross Drummond	72	72	70	70	284	846
Peter Harrison	73	68	73	70	284	846
John Morgan	73	72	67	72	284	846
Juan Quiros	73	70	74	67	284	846
Ronald Stelten	71	74	70	69	284	846
Mariano Aparicio	70	72	73	70	285	730
Eamonn Darcy	73	71	71	70	285	730
Barry Lane	73	71	70	71	285	730
Miguel Martin	69	72	73	71	285	730
Carl Mason	71	73	71	70	285	730
Ronan Rafferty	70	74	69	72	285	730
Paul Curry	73	69	74	70	286	630
Michael King	72	73	71	70	286	630
Bill Longmuir	69	70	75	72	286	630
Sam Torrance	70	69	73	74	286	630
Peter Baker	69	72	74	72	287	530
Derrick Cooper	72	72	71	72	287	530
Emmanuel Dussart	72	67	71	77	287	530
Alan Evans	72	71	72	72	287	530
David Gilford	73	71	71	72	287	530
David Ray	76	69	74	68	287	530

The African Tours

ICL International

Zwartkops Country Club, Pretoria

January 15–18
purse, R100,000

	SCORES				TOTAL	MONEY
Gavin Levenson	71	65	67	67	270	R16,000
David Frost	66	69	68	68	271	11,500
Fulton Allem	69	69	68	68	274	6,000
Mark McNulty	66	67	69	72	274	6,000
Tienie Britz	72	69	67	67	275	4,200
John Bland	69	73	67	67	276	3,300

	SCORES	TOTAL	MONEY
Tertius Claassens	66 70 67 73	276	3,300
Robert Richardson	69 69 70 69	277	2,350
Simon Hobday	65 69 71 72	277	2,350
Bobby Cole	68 70 70 70	278	1,900
Warren Humphreys	72 65 70 71	278	1,900
Tony Johnstone	70 74 67 68	279	1,700
Trevor Dodds	70 71 72 67	280	1,600
Wilhelm Winsnes	71 71 72 67	281	1,425
Rick Hartman	71 71 71 68	281	1,425
Don Robertson	67 68 73 73	281	1,425
Teddy Webber	70 71 67 73	281	1,425
Chris Williams	69 71 70 72	282	1,300
Alan Henning	68 74 72 69	283	1,225
Wayne Westner	71 69 69 74	283	1,225
John Fourie	71 70 72 71	284	1,160
Ian Young	75 72 70 68	285	1,100
Stewart Smith	76 70 70 69	285	1,100
Hugh Biaocchi	68 72 73 72	285	1,100
Wayne Player	73 71 70 72	286	1,040
Don Levin	73 71 72 71	287	995
Phil Simmons	69 76 68 74	287	995
Kevin Klier	71 75 73 69	288	905
David O'Kelly	70 74 72 72	288	905
Bob E. Smith	74 72 70 72	288	905
Joe Dlamini	71 71 72 74	288	905
Brian Evans	72 72 72 73	289	840

Lexington PGA Championship

Wanderers Golf Club, Johannesburg
Par 36–36 – 72; 6,906 yards

January 22–25
purse, R110,000

	SCORES	TOTAL	MONEY
Bobby Cole	66 65 66 68	265	R17,600
David Frost	68 70 63 69	270	10,175
Teddy Webber	66 70 64 70	270	10,175
Mark McNulty	66 68 69 68	271	5,500
Alan Henning	68 69 68 70	275	4,620
Ian Mosey	66 71 70 70	277	3,960
Kevin Klier	69 71 71 67	278	2,823.33
Bobby Lincoln	69 71 70 68	278	2,823.33
Joe Dlamini	67 71 70 70	278	2,823.33
David Feherty	71 70 67 71	279	1,952.50
Hugh Baiocchi	66 67 72 74	279	1,952.50
Tony Johnstone	68 67 71 73	279	1,952.50
Gavin Levenson	70 67 68 74	279	1,952.50
Don Levin	70 74 66 70	280	1,622.50
John Bland	69 70 70 71	280	1,622.50
Bill Brask	70 72 70 69	281	1,512.50
Wayne Westner	70 72 69 70	281	1,512.50
Tienie Britz	68 72 70 72	282	1,430
Don Robertson	71 72 70 70	283	1,375
Harold Henning	75 71 71 67	284	1,279.67
Rick Hartman	68 76 70 70	284	1,279.67
Nigel Burch	68 70 73 73	284	1,279.67
David O'Kelly	71 73 72 69	285	1,094.50

	SCORES				TOTAL	MONEY
Fulton Allem	75	70	70	70	285	1,094.50
Graham Henning	73	68	72	72	285	1,094.50
Solly Sepeng	71	70	71	73	285	1,094.50
Jon Mannie	69	71	71	74	285	1,094.50
Robert Richardson	71	72	68	74	285	1,094.50
Jack Ferenz	68	70	72	75	285	1,094.50
Trevor Dodds	73	71	67	74	285	1,094.50

Wild Coast Classic

Wild Coast Country Club   January 29–February 1
purse, R100,000

	SCORES				TOTAL	MONEY
Mark McNulty	66	66	71	64	267	R16,000
David Frost	70	66	69	68	273	11,500
Tony Johnstone	71	64	75	66	276	7,000
Rick Hartman	69	66	72	71	278	4,600
David Feherty	73	67	68	70	278	4,600
Ian Palmer	72	69	72	66	279	3,300
Bobby Cole	74	69	68	68	279	3,300
Simon Hobday	70	70	73	67	280	2,500
Wayne Player	73	70	71	67	281	2,000
Warren Humphreys	70	69	73	69	281	2,000
Bob E. Smith	68	70	73	70	281	2,000
Bobby Lincoln	70	69	74	69	282	1,600
Dale Hayes	70	68	72	72	282	1,600
Jack Ferenz	72	70	68	72	282	1,600
Jay Townsend	73	70	74	66	283	1,375
Hugh Baiocchi	74	69	72	68	283	1,375
Hendrik Buhrmann	71	67	75	70	283	1,375
Vin Baker	73	70	69	71	283	1,375
Bobby Verwey	69	70	75	70	284	1,151.67
Manuel Calero	68	69	77	70	284	1,151.67
Don Robertson	72	70	72	70	284	1,151.67
Phil Harrison	72	72	69	71	284	1,151.67
Joe Dlamini	73	68	70	73	284	1,151.67
Jon Mannie	70	69	70	75	284	1,151.67
David O'Kelly	74	68	74	69	285	1,025
Fulton Allem	69	68	76	72	285	1,025
John Bland	72	73	74	67	286	935
Ian Young	74	72	72	68	286	935
Trevor Dodds	72	69	74	71	286	935
Teddy Webber	73	70	70	73	286	935

Southern Suns South African Open Championship

Royal Johannesburg Golf Club, Johannesburg   February 5–8
Par 36–36 – 72   purse, R100,000

	SCORES				TOTAL	MONEY
David Frost	72	70	66	67	275	R16,306
Tony Johnstone	68	67	74	69	278	11,698
Trevor Dodds	70	69	71	70	280	7,123

	SCORES			TOTAL	MONEY
Bobby Cole	70	69	71	71	281	5,089
Mark Harkness	73	71	70	68	282	3,970.50
Teddy Webber	71	69	73	69	282	3,970.50
Manuel Calero	69	70	73	71	283	2,801
John Bland	72	68	71	72	283	2,801
Bobby Lincoln	72	73	70	69	284	2,140.50
Mark McNulty	70	71	70	73	284	2,140.50
Brian Evans	74	72	69	70	285	1,733.67
Warren Humphreys	74	66	73	72	285	1,733.67
Simon Hobday	72	72	67	74	285	1,733.66
Tienie Britz	70	73	70	73	286	1,479.34
Gavin Levenson	72	72	69	73	286	1,479.33
David Feherty	69	72	71	74	286	1,479.33
Mark Wiltshire	75	71	72	69	287	1,327.67
Fulton Allem	73	73	73	68	287	1,327.67
John Fourie	70	72	72	73	287	1,327.66
Ian Palmer	71	71	74	72	288	1,188.66
Alan Henning	76	67	72	73	288	1,188.66
David O'Kelly	71	69	74	74	288	1,188.67
Justin Hobday	75	72	71	71	289	1,063.20
Jay Townsend	74	71	72	72	289	1,063.20
Tertius Claassens	70	70	73	76	289	1,063.20
Ian Mosey	74	72	69	74	289	1,063.20
Bob E. Smith	71	70	74	74	289	1,063.20
Pietro Molteni	73	70	74	73	290	956.50
Mark Jordan	73	72	69	76	290	956.50

AECI Charity Classic

Rand Park Golf Club, Johannesburg
Par 36–36 – 72; 7,067 yards

February 12–15
purse, R100,000

	SCORES			TOTAL	MONEY
Fulton Allem	70	63	66	67	266	R16,000
Mark McNulty	69	67	64	67	267	11,500
Mark Hartness	69	69	70	67	275	7,000
Ian Mosey	66	69	73	68	276	4,600
Alan Henning	68	69	71	68	276	4,600
Tony Johnstone	73	67	71	66	277	2,825
Bob E. Smith	67	70	71	69	277	2,825
Trevor Dodds	69	67	70	71	277	2,825
Bobby Cole	71	68	66	72	277	2,825
John Bland	67	69	73	69	278	2,000
Gavin Levenson	67	69	72	71	279	1,750
Hugh Biaocchi	68	68	71	72	279	1,750
John Mashego	70	73	67	70	280	1,550
Jack Ferenz	69	68	72	71	280	1,550
Jay Townsend	70	71	73	67	281	1,400
Hendrik Buhrmann	73	69	68	71	281	1,400
Frank Edmonds	74	66	69	72	281	1,400
Don Levin	72	72	71	67	282	1,250
Dale Hayes	70	71	73	68	282	1,250
John Fourie	69	67	73	73	282	1,250
Don Robertson	72	71	71	69	283	1,100
Robert Richardson	68	72	73	70	283	1,100
Wayne Westner	64	75	74	70	283	1,100
Phil Harrison	71	69	73	70	283	1,100

	SCORES	TOTAL	MONEY
Kevin Klier	69 67 75 72	283	1,100
Wilhelm Winsnes	73 70 72 69	284	965
Mark Bright	71 69 74 70	284	965
Phil Simmons	68 71 74 71	284	965
Bobby Lincoln	71 71 71 71	284	965
Ian Young	70 75 73 68	286	875
Brian Jacobs	75 70 71 70	286	875

Barclays Bank Classic

Gary Player Country Club, Sun City, Bophuthatswana
Par 36–36 – 72; 7,665 yards

February 20–23
purse, R100,000

	SCORES	TOTAL	MONEY
Mark McNulty	73 66 71 69	279	R16,000
Fulton Allem	69 70 73 73	285	11,500
David Feherty	73 70 71 72	286	7,000
Wayne Westner	74 76 67 70	287	4,600
Mark Wiltshire	73 74 66 74	287	4,600
Warren Humphreys	72 74 70 72	288	3,600
Lee Rinker	77 70 74 68	289	2,425
Hugh Biaocchi	74 70 73 72	289	2,425
Tony Johnstone	69 73 74 73	289	2,425
Phil Simmons	71 73 71 74	289	2,425
Gavin Levenson	74 74 72 70	290	1,650
Simon Hobday	71 75 74 70	290	1,650
Brian Evans	74 69 74 73	290	1,650
Rick Hartman	70 72 73 75	290	1,650
Trevor Dodds	75 66 76 74	291	1,450
Ian Young	70 77 74 71	292	1,350
Bobby Lincoln	68 75 76 73	292	1,350
Mark Hartness	75 73 72 72	292	1,350
Jack Ferenz	73 75 70 75	293	1,250
John Bland	74 73 77 70	294	1,163.33
Robert Richardson	74 74 74 72	294	1,163.33
Teddy Webber	71 75 73 75	294	1,163.33
Bobby Verwey	70 76 74 75	295	1,085
Len O'Kennedy	72 75 72 76	295	1,085
John Fourie	75 77 74 70	296	995
Bobby Cole	72 73 75 76	296	995
Derek James	76 72 70 78	296	995
Joe Dlamini	72 73 73 78	296	995
Bob Molt	76 78 72 71	297	890
Peter Mkata	71 72 81 73	297	890
Tienie Britz	71 74 76 76	297	890
David O'Kelly	71 78 77 72	298	810

Palabora Classic

Hans Merensky Golf Club, Phalaborwa

February 26–March 1
purse, R120,000

	SCORES	TOTAL	MONEY
Fulton Allem	69 67 69 65	270	R19,200
Hugh Baiocchi	68 67 70 68	273	13,800

	SCORES				TOTAL	MONEY
Jay Townsend	68	68	67	71	274	8,400
Chris Williams	69	67	69	70	275	5,520
Alan Henning	66	69	69	71	275	5,520
Warren Humphreys	71	69	69	67	276	3,960
Trevor Dodds	72	69	68	67	276	3,960
Phil Simmons	65	70	70	72	277	3,000
Bobby Cole	73	67	71	67	278	2,400
John Bland	68	73	71	66	278	2,400
Tony Johnstone	72	68	70	68	278	2,400
Ian Mosey	69	70	69	71	279	2,040
Derek James	67	73	72	68	280	1,657.50
Ian Palmer	69	69	73	69	280	1,657.50
Mark Bright	72	69	70	69	280	1,657.50
Mark Hartness	68	71	71	70	280	1,657.50
Mark Jordan	73	69	67	71	280	1,657.50
Bobby Verwey	70	71	68	71	280	1,657.50
Ian Young	68	71	68	73	280	1,657.50
Don Robertson	67	67	70	76	280	1,657.50
Robbie Stewart	72	72	69	68	281	1,392
Justin Hobday	70	72	71	69	282	1,338
Bobby Lincoln	73	68	72	69	282	1,338
John Fourie	72	70	75	66	283	1,230
Hendrik Buhrmann	68	73	73	69	283	1,230
Frank Edmonds	70	72	72	69	283	1,230
Gavin Levenson	72	67	71	73	283	1,230
Mike White	74	71	70	69	284	1,086
Andries Oosthuizen	74	68	72	70	284	1,086
Mark McNulty	75	70	69	70	284	1,086
Lee Rinker	71	74	65	74	284	1,086

Swazi Sun Pro-Am

Royal Swazi Sun Golf Course, Mbabane, Swaziland   March 6–9
Par 36–36 – 72; 7,152 yards   purse, R100,000

	SCORES				TOTAL	MONEY
Mark McNulty	64	66	68	65	263	R16,000
Fulton Allem	67	63	67	66	263	11,500
Gavin Levenson	65	69	68	64	266	7,000
Hugh Baiocchi	68	67	69	67	271	4,266.67
Warren Humphreys	70	65	67	69	271	4,266.67
John Bland	70	71	63	67	271	4,266.67
Mark Bright	69	66	67	70	272	3,000
Robert Lendzion	68	68	69	68	273	2,500
Jack Ferenz	70	69	65	70	274	2,200
Bobby Cole	67	70	71	67	275	1,833.33
Bobby Lincoln	68	69	70	68	275	1,833.33
Stuart Smith	69	69	67	70	275	1,833.33
Alan Henning	68	68	72	68	276	1,550
Tony Johnstone	70	66	71	69	276	1,550
Hendrik Buhrmann	66	70	73	68	277	1,350
Phil Simmons	69	71	69	68	277	1,350
Don Robertson	71	68	70	68	277	1,350
Ian Mosey	71	72	65	69	277	1,350
Teddy Webber	70	67	67	73	277	1,350
Dale Hayes	72	68	72	66	278	1,180
Jon Mannie	69	72	66	71	278	1,180

	SCORES				TOTAL	MONEY
David O'Kelly	73	70	68	68	279	1,040
Justin Hobday	71	72	68	68	279	1,040
Derek James	69	72	68	70	279	1,040
Tertius Claasens	75	65	68	71	279	1,040
Lee Rinker	70	67	70	72	279	1,040
Joe Dlamini	69	72	66	72	279	1,040
Ian Palmer	73	71	69	67	280	920
David Feherty	69	72	72	68	281	863.33
Phil Harrison	68	76	68	69	281	863.33
Trevor Dodds	69	70	71	71	281	863.33

Trust Bank Tournament of Champions

Kensington Golf Club, Johannesburg   March 12–15
Par 36–35 – 71; 6,774 yards   purse, R115,000

	SCORES				TOTAL	MONEY
Mark McNulty	70	68	68	66	272	R20,000
Jack Ferenz	70	71	70	67	278	10,489.50
Tony Johnstone	69	70	70	69	278	10,489.50
John Bland	71	72	66	70	279	5,216.40
Warren Humphreys	69	70	70	70	279	5,216.40
Justin Hobday	68	70	73	69	280	3,742.20
Bobby Cole	66	72	72	70	280	3,742.20
Bobby Lincoln	64	76	73	68	281	2,313.36
Simon Hobday	70	72	69	70	281	2,313.36
Robert Lendzion	70	67	72	72	281	2,313.36
Brian Evans	70	69	69	73	281	2,313.36
David O'Kelly	69	72	66	74	281	2,313.36
Ian Mosey	72	74	69	67	282	1,719.90
Gavin Levenson	69	75	69	69	282	1,719.90
Hugh Baiocchi	70	70	71	71	282	1,719.90
Robert Richardson	71	73	68	71	283	1,587.60
Trevor Dodds	68	72	73	71	284	1,474.20
Ross Palmer	73	69	70	72	284	1,474.20
Andrew Chandler	68	68	74	74	284	1,474.20
Ian Young	73	70	71	71	285	1,338.12
Alan Henning	72	71	69	73	285	1,338.12
Mark Wiltshire	68	79	71	68	286	1,196.37
Don Robertson	73	75	67	71	286	1,196.37
Robbie Stewart	73	72	70	71	286	1,196.37
Wayne Westner	74	69	72	71	286	1,196.37
Teddy Webber	68	73	72	73	286	1,196.37
Fulton Allem	73	72	67	74	286	1,196.37
Mark Bright	72	70	72	73	287	1,043.28
Paul Campher	71	72	71	73	287	1,043.28
Chris Williams	69	73	71	74	287	1,043.28

Nigerian Open

Ikoyi Club, Lagos, Nigeria   February 13–16
Par 36–35 – 71; 6,389 yards   purse, £100,650

	SCORES				TOTAL	MONEY
Gordon Brand	71	67	66	69	273	£9,737.10
Brian Marchbank	68	67	68	72	275	6,484.91

	SCORES				TOTAL	MONEY
Andrew Murray	72	67	70	67	276	3,661.15
Bill Longmuir	72	67	68	72	279	2,921.13
Garry Cullen	73	68	66	73	280	2,473.22
John Morgan	72	71	70	68	281	1,640.70
Joe Higgins	73	74	70	64	281	1,640.70
Peter Cowen	73	71	67	70	281	1,640.70
Stephen Bennett	70	70	69	72	281	1,640.70
David Ray	71	70	74	67	282	1,084.06
Emmanuel Dussart	69	70	74	69	282	1,084.06
Paul Thomas	69	75	68	70	282	1,084.06
Mark Mouland	72	68	72	71	283	929.90
Peter Barber	71	69	72	71	283	929.90
Neil Hansen	75	71	70	68	284	767.84
Anders Sorensen	72	74	67	71	284	767.84
Richard Boxall	71	67	73	73	284	767.84
David Llewellyn	69	71	71	73	284	767.84
Grant Turner	74	71	72	67	284	767.84
Mark Roe	72	69	70	73	284	767.84
Tony Charnley	70	68	71	75	284	767.84
David Williams	75	70	70	70	285	652.39
Bobby Mitchell	70	76	68	71	285	652.39
Mike Miller	71	76	65	73	285	652.39
Gary Smith	71	70	70	74	285	652.39
Paul Kent	73	72	69	72	286	555.02
Pavel Jirsa	70	76	68	72	286	555.02
Peter Harrison	73	74	72	67	286	555.02
Martin Poxon	72	68	72	74	286	555.02
Paul Carrigill	72	74	66	74	286	555.02
Bill McColl	71	72	75	68	286	555.02

Ivory Coast Open

President Golf Club, Yamoussoukro, Ivory Coast
Par 36–36 – 72; 6,691 yards

February 20–23
purse, £58,425

	SCORES				TOTAL	MONEY
Gordon Brand	70	67	65	70	272	£16,581.38
Malcolm Mackenzie	70	70	70	70	280	11,051.88
Neil Hansen	67	75	73	68	283	5,140.96
Gary Smith	70	75	69	69	283	5,140.96
Paul Kent	68	70	71	74	283	5,140.96
Paul Carrigill	72	72	70	71	285	2,780.73
Andrew Murray	70	70	74	71	285	2,780.73
David Jones	74	72	66	73	285	2,780.73
Jacob Omoruah	69	71	70	75	285	2,780.73
Joe Higgins	72	68	72	74	286	1,890.55
Brian Marchbank	72	69	70	75	286	1,890.55
Mark Johnson	73	72	74	68	287	1,467.66
David Jagger	77	69	71	70	287	1,467.66
Peter Akakasiaka	72	73	72	70	287	1,467.66
David Ray	71	74	71	71	287	1,467.66
David J. Russell	74	71	69	73	287	1,467.66
Grant Turner	71	70	72	74	287	1,467.66
Carl Mason	72	68	73	74	287	1,467.66
David Williams	69	72	71	75	287	1,467.66
Garry Cullen	67	75	76	70	288	1,217.13

	SCORES				TOTAL	MONEY
Bill Longmuir	69	79	68	72	288	1,217.13
Mark Roe	74	74	73	68	289	1,099.86
James Lebbie	70	72	74	73	289	1,099.86
Keith Waters	68	75	72	74	289	1,099.86
Laurie Turner	69	71	75	74	289	1,099.86
Paul Thomas	77	70	75	68	290	967.78
Bello Seibidor	71	72	77	70	290	967.78
Jerry Mulubah	76	71	71	72	290	967.78
Ole Eskildsen	71	72	78	70	291	864.25
Mike Inglis	72	72	74	73	291	864.25
Martin Poxon	73	72	72	74	291	864.25
Lee Jones	69	74	74	74	291	864.25
Glenn Ralph	72	70	75	74	291	864.25

Kenya Open

Muthaiga Golf Club, Kenya   March 6–9
Par 36–35 – 71; 6,765 yards   purse, £56,750

	SCORES				TOTAL	MONEY
Ian Woosnam	70	64	67	72	273	£9,455.25
Bill Longmuir	68	70	69	66	273	6,304.50
(Woosnam defeated Longmuir on third hole of sudden-death playoff.)
Jose-Maria Canizares	68	66	72	70	276	3,552.46
Jose-Maria Olazabal	73	70	66	68	277	2,626.77
Gordon Brand Jr.	69	70	68	70	277	2,626.77
Garry Cullen	69	73	72	64	278	1,471.95
Gordon Brand	70	69	71	68	278	1,471.95
Bobby Mitchell	72	68	69	69	278	1,471.95
Paul Kent	70	71	66	71	278	1,471.95
Bernard Gallacher	68	71	73	71	278	1,471.95
Emmanuel Dussart	70	69	73	67	279	1,001.29
Mats Lanner	68	74	67	70	279	1,001.29
Paul Carrigill	70	72	69	69	280	847.54
David Llewellyn	72	68	70	70	280	847.54
Glenn Ralph	71	67	72	70	280	847.54
Roger Chapman	72	65	73	70	280	847.54
Jose Rivero	69	68	72	71	280	847.54
Mark Roe	72	73	71	65	281	735.76
Peter Harrison	67	72	70	72	281	735.76
John Morgan	71	71	72	68	282	661.16
Tommy Horton	72	72	69	69	282	661.16
Ross Drummond	69	74	70	69	282	661.16
Barry Lane	73	68	72	69	282	661.16
Bruce Zabriski	71	69	73	69	282	661.16
Anthony Edwards	72	70	71	70	283	582.44
Bill McColl	67	71	72	73	283	582.44
Andrew Sherborne	67	68	75	73	283	582.44
Ronan Rafferty	72	74	71	67	284	481.42
Grant Turner	74	72	69	69	284	481.42
Tim Price	65	79	71	69	284	481.42
Neil Hansen	70	72	73	69	284	481.42
David Ray	72	72	70	70	284	481.42
Simon Bishop	70	70	74	70	284	481.42
Mark Mouland	71	72	69	72	284	481.42
Sandy Stephen	71	71	70	72	284	481.42

Zambian Open

Lusaka Golf Club, Zambia
Par 35–38 – 73; 7,259 yards

March 13–16
purse, £55,000

	SCORES				TOTAL	MONEY
Garry Cullen	70	69	75	69	283	£9,160
Eamonn Darcy	73	68	73	69	283	6,110
(Cullen defeated Darcy on first hole of sudden-death playoff.)						
Bill Longmuir	71	73	69	71	284	3,220
Gordon Brand	72	74	66	72	284	3,220
Ian Woosnam	71	67	74	73	285	2,600
Paul Thomas	70	68	76	72	286	2,050
Bill McColl	77	71	67	71	286	2,050
Glenn Ralph	71	73	69	74	287	1,250
John Morgan	72	73	69	73	287	1,250
Tommy Horton	74	69	74	70	287	1,250
Gordon Brand Jr.	71	69	76	71	287	1,250
Jose-Maria Olazabal	71	74	72	71	288	812
Carl Mason	75	72	68	73	288	812
Mats Lanner	71	72	71	74	288	812
Roger Chapman	72	70	73	73	288	812
Richard Boxall	69	75	72	72	288	812
Stuart Reese	74	71	70	75	290	671.66
Craig Maltman	81	68	72	69	290	671.66
John Fowler	73	75	76	66	290	671.66
Martin Poxon	76	72	69	74	291	601.66
David Jones	73	76	70	72	291	601.66
Michael Ingham	74	73	74	70	291	601.66
Keith Waters	75	77	71	69	292	540
Philip Walton	74	74	71	73	292	540
Brian Waites	73	75	73	71	292	540
Brian Marchbank	75	74	70	73	292	540
Malcolm Mackenzie	73	76	70	73	292	540
Mark Mouland	74	78	70	71	293	472.50
Miguel Martin	73	77	74	69	293	472.50
David Llewellyn	74	73	72	74	293	472.50
Paul Hoad	72	75	74	72	293	472.50

Zimbabwe Open

Chapman Golf Club, Harare, Zimbabwe
Par 36–36 – 72; 7,173 yards

March 20–23
purse, £54,585.14

	SCORES				TOTAL	MONEY
Stephen Bennett	68	69	71	69	277	£9,096.07
Stuart Reese	69	72	66	72	279	6,061.14
Simon Bishop	69	73	71	67	280	3,074.24
Ronan Rafferty	73	70	69	68	280	3,074.24
Keith Waters	69	70	71	71	281	2,312.23
Bill McColl	70	70	71	71	283	1,910.48
Sandy Stephen	70	73	72	68	283	1,328.60
Ross Drummond	74	69	68	72	283	1,328.60
Peter Brown	71	71	67	74	283	1,328.60
Glenn Ralph	72	69	72	70	283	1,328.60
Philip Walton	68	70	73	73	284	975.98
Roger Chapman	72	72	74	66	284	975.98

	SCORES				TOTAL	MONEY
Tommy Horton	72	71	72	70	285	807.86
David Llewellyn	69	69	73	74	285	807.86
Malcolm Mackenzie	70	71	72	72	285	807.86
Carl Mason	73	70	68	74	285	807.86
John Morgan	70	75	71	69	285	807.86
Tom Lamore	73	73	70	70	286	669.43
Mark Roe	73	71	73	69	286	669.43
Brian Waites	71	73	69	73	286	669.43
Steve Cipa	71	72	73	70	286	669.43
David Jones	70	73	71	72	286	669.43
Barry Lane	72	69	73	73	287	598.25
Mats Lanner	71	71	72	73	287	598.25
Paul Carrigill	73	70	73	71	287	598.25
Peter Cowen	72	69	72	75	288	528.38
Gordon Brand	73	73	73	69	288	528.38
Grant Turner	70	72	72	74	288	528.38
Jeffrey Pinsent	75	67	71	75	288	528.38
Joe Higgins	72	71	71	74	288	528.38

Safmarine South African Masters

December 10–13

Stellenbosch Golf Club

purse, R110,000

	SCORES				TOTAL	MONEY
Mark McNulty	70	65	67	68	270	R17,600
Fulton Allem	67	67	68	72	274	12,650
Teddy Webber	69	68	67	71	275	7,700
David Frost	69	69	70	69	277	5,500
John Bland	69	72	74	64	279	4,620
Simon Hobday	65	69	72	74	280	3,960
Warren Humphreys	71	69	72	70	282	3,300
Wayne Westner	69	72	71	71	283	2,585
Chris Williams	67	71	72	73	283	2,585
Steve Van Vuuren	72	70	72	70	284	2,200
Bobby Lincoln	71	73	71	70	285	1,900
Andrew Chandler	72	72	71	71	286	1,815
Schlak V. D. Merwe	68	78	67	73	286	1,815
Robert Richardson	73	74	73	67	287	1,622.50
Hendrik Buhrmann	69	76	69	73	287	1,622.50
Don Robertson	73	74	72	69	288	1,485
Gavin Levenson	74	72	71	71	288	1,485
Wilhelm Winsnes	75	71	69	73	288	1,485
Robbie Stewart	72	74	73	70	289	1,284.80
Richard Mogoerane	74	73	71	71	289	1,284.80
Peter Mkata	71	74	72	72	289	1,284.80
Phil Simmons	75	70	71	73	289	1,284.80
Mark Wiltshire	73	73	69	74	289	1,284.80
Derek James	74	72	74	70	290	1,111
David Russell	73	71	76	70	290	1,111
Richard Kaplan	76	70	73	71	290	1,111
Bob E. Smith	76	74	70	70	290	1,111
Roger Wessels	69	73	76	72	290	1,111
Rick Hartman	73	75	74	69	291	965.25
Bobby Verwey	76	73	73	69	291	965.25
Michael Bullock	72	76	71	72	291	965.25
Peter V. D. Riet	74	71	72	74	291	965.25

Goodyear Classic

December 18–21

Humewood Golf Club, Port Elizabeth

purse, R100,000

	SCORES				TOTAL	MONEY
Tony Johnstone	69	67	70	69	275	R16,000
Fulton Allem	68	66	73	69	276	11,500
Bobby Lincoln	65	66	71	76	278	6,000
Joe Dlamini	65	66	73	74	278	6,000
Denis Watson	67	69	66	77	279	4,200
Justin Hobday	68	69	69	74	280	3,600
Warren Humphreys	73	69	74	66	282	2,566.67
Mark McNulty	66	71	71	74	282	2,566.67
Ian Mosey	68	68	74	72	282	2,566.66
David Russell	67	69	72	76	284	2,000
Rick Hartman	68	67	78	72	285	1,750
Trevor Dodds	71	71	69	74	285	1,750
Hugh Baiocchi	68	72	71	74	285	1,750
Gavin Levenson	75	70	72	69	286	1,500
Bob E. Smith	69	70	73	74	286	1,500
Hendrik Buhrmann	71	73	73	70	287	1,300
John Bland	69	72	74	72	287	1,300
Don Robertson	66	76	72	73	287	1,300
Andre Cruse	71	70	72	74	287	1,300
Ian Palmer	67	76	70	74	287	1,300
Wilhelm Winsnes	70	72	70	75	287	1,200
Phil Harrison	74	74	73	67	288	1,200
Teddy Webber	72	71	71	74	288	1,025
Mark Wiltshire	72	69	78	70	289	1,025
Phil Simmons	73	67	77	72	289	1,025
Roger Wessels	67	73	76	73	289	1,025
Robbie Stewart	69	73	74	73	289	1,025
Mark Hartness	72	69	78	71	290	920
Robert Richardson	75	69	74	72	290	920
Bobby Verwey	73	73	75	70	291	850
Daddy Naidoo	75	75	71	70	291	850
Phil Jonas	73	70	72	76	291	850
Tertius Claassens	72	72	69	78	291	850

Sun City Challenge

Gary Player Country Club, Sun City, Bophuthatswana
Par 36–36 – 72; 7,665 yards

December 4–7
purse, US$1,000,000

	SCORES				TOTAL	MONEY
Mark McNulty	74	70	70	68	282	$350,000
Lanny Wadkins	69	72	74	70	285	150,000
Bernhard Langer	70	68	74	74	286	105,000
Chen Tze Chung	75	68	75	69	287	81,000
Ian Woosnam	75	70	71	71	287	81,000
Howard Clark	69	69	74	76	288	65,000
David Frost	71	75	71	72	289	60,000
David Graham	73	74	72	71	290	56,000
Gary Player	75	74	71	73	293	52,000

Helix Wild Coast Classic

Wild Coast Country Club

November 20–23
purse, R100,000

	SCORES				TOTAL	MONEY
Mark McNulty	66	74	75	64	279	R16,000
John Bland	70	67	74	70	281	11,500
Hendrik Buhrmann	70	72	75	65	282	6,000
Hugh Baiocchi	68	73	74	57	282	6,000
Fulton Allem	68	77	72	67	284	3,900
Ian Palmer	70	68	76	70	284	3,900
Tony Johnstone	69	74	75	68	286	3,000
Bob Byman	68	78	79	66	291	2,350
Tertius Claassens	76	78	70	67	291	2,350
Bobby Lincoln	76	74	76	66	292	1,900
Teddy Webber	69	79	76	69	292	1,900
Alan Henning	71	78	81	63	293	1,562.50
Gavin Levenson	70	78	78	67	293	1,562.50
Bobby Verwey, Jr.	72	75	78	68	293	1,562.50
Len O'Kennedy	69	78	74	72	293	1,562.50
Wilhelm Winsnes	69	78	78	69	294	1,325
Mark Hartness	74	75	78	67	294	1,325
Joe Dlamini	72	72	80	70	294	1,325
Don Robertson	70	72	79	73	294	1,325
Wayne Westner	72	77	79	67	295	1,163.34
John Fourie	72	77	77	69	295	1,163.33
Mark Wiltshire	70	80	75	70	295	1,163.33
Vincent Tshabalala	65	77	82	72	296	1,100
Phil Simmons	72	78	80	67	297	1,025
Warren Humphreys	73	74	80	70	297	1,025
Simon Hobday	72	73	82	70	297	1,025
Daddy Naidoo	72	71	81	73	297	1,025
Peter V. D. Riet	76	75	79	68	298	920
Andries Oosthuizen	71	78	78	71	298	920
Ian Mosey	71	78	78	71	298	920

Germiston Centenary

Germiston Golf Course

November 26–29

purse, R100,000

	SCORES				TOTAL	MONEY
Mark McNulty	64	69	65	68	266	R16,000
Fulton Allem	70	67	63	67	267	11,500
David Frost	66	68	68	68	270	7,000
Hugh Baiocchi	64	72	68	69	273	5,000
Bobby Lincoln	67	71	69	68	275	4,200
Tony Johnstone	70	71	69	66	276	2,825
John Bland	67	71	70	68	276	2,825
Wayne Westner	71	67	65	73	276	2,825
Phil Simmons	68	70	65	73	276	2,825
Gavin Levenson	70	69	70	69	278	2,000
Mark Wiltshire	71	69	70	69	279	1,750
Don Robertson	72	68	71	68	279	1,750
Michael Burnhope	68	71	72	70	281	1,516.67

	SCORES				TOTAL	MONEY
Jimmy Johnson	70	75	65	71	281	1,516.67
Ian Mosey	65	69	72	75	281	1,516.67
Dean Van Staden	70	72	69	71	282	1,400
Garth Person	71	71	72	69	283	1,275
Andre Cruse	72	68	73	70	283	1,275
Warren Humphreys	73	70	71	69	283	1,275
David Russell	71	71	71	70	283	1,275
Roger Wessels	74	71	70	69	284	1,130
Simon Hobday	73	74	68	69	284	1,130
Teddy Webber	67	72	74	71	284	1,130
Schalk V. D. Merwe	72	69	74	70	285	1,025
Mark Hartness	73	69	71	72	285	1,025
Michael Bullock	69	72	72	72	285	1,025
Len O'Kennedy	70	71	71	73	285	1,025
Karl Williams	72	74	70	70	286	935
Steve Van Vuuren	73	71	71	71	286	935
John Fourie	72	75	70	70	287	875
Tertius Claassens	71	72	72	72	287	875

The Australasian Tour

Nissan-Mobil New Zealand PGA Championship

Mount Maunganui Golf Club, Tauranga
Par 36–36 – 72; 6,664 yards

December 28–31, 1985
purse, NZ$75,000

	SCORES				TOTAL	MONEY
Frank Nobilo	72	67	70	71	280	NZ$13,500
Brett Ogle	70	70	73	69	282	8,100
Bob Charles	67	70	74	72	283	5,175
Mike Harwood	69	71	70	74	284	3,735
Peter Fowler	73	69	70	73	285	3,120
Wayne Riley	70	74	68	74	286	2,865
Tommy Jansson	72	69	74	72	287	2,400
Simon Owen	70	72	73	72	287	2,400
Greg Turner	75	68	73	72	288	1,668.75
Peter Hamblett	72	72	73	71	288	1,668.75
Anthony Gilligan	71	75	68	74	288	1,668.75
David Hartshorne	70	74	69	75	288	1,668.75
John Lister	71	77	70	71	289	1,130
Peter Jones	71	69	75	74	289	1,130
Stuart Reese	72	72	70	75	289	1,130
Brett Griffiths	73	70	72	75	290	990
Wayne Davies	73	71	75	73	292	954
Michael Loughland	71	73	76	73	293	877.50
Richard Coombes	70	76	74	73	293	877.50
Peter Stoddart	76	71	75	72	294	780
Mike Moynihan	72	74	75	73	294	780
Arun Kumar	74	74	72	74	294	780
Geoff Smart	72	76	72	74	294	780
Tony Maloney	74	70	74	77	295	705
Barry Vivian	73	76	72	75	296	660
Greg Alexander	74	72	74	76	296	660
Mike Dodd	71	74	76	76	297	600

	SCORES				TOTAL	MONEY
Ian Roberts	71	77	75	74	297	600
Barry Jamieson	75	78	69	76	298	530
Brandon Perry	78	73	72	75	298	530
Kelly Murray	73	73	74	78	298	530

Foster's Tasmanian Open

Royal Hobart Golf Club, Hobart, Tasmania
Par 36–36 – 72; 6,636 yards

January 30–February 2
purse, A$50,000

	SCORES				TOTAL	MONEY
Stewart Ginn	70	71	69	71	281	A$9,000
Magnus Persson	73	69	65	74	281	5,500
(Ginn defeated Persson on the second hole of sudden-death playoff.)						
Terry Gale	73	69	71	70	283	3,535
Steve Elkington	71	73	69	71	284	2,020
Peter Fowler	69	72	71	72	284	2,020
Jeff Senior	68	71	71	74	284	2,020
Vaughan Somers	72	77	69	66	284	2,020
Greg Turner	74	72	69	69	284	2,020
Ian Baker-Finch	76	69	68	72	285	1,500
Mike Harwood	74	70	71	71	286	1,300
Mats Lanner	76	69	71	70	286	1,300
Brett Ogle	73	75	67	71	286	1,300
John Clifford	73	72	68	74	287	1,050
Rodger Davis	76	72	68	71	287	1,050
Peter Croker	72	70	71	75	288	900
Ossie Moore	73	71	70	75	289	775
George Serhan	72	74	69	74	289	775
Lyndsay Stephen	70	71	74	75	290	650
Peter Jones	71	74	68	77	290	650
Robert Stephens	72	70	72	76	290	650
Kelly Murray	75	71	73	72	291	512.50
Rick Vershure	76	70	69	76	291	512.50
Frank Nobilo	73	74	67	77	291	512.50
Wayne Riley	69	74	70	78	291	512.50
Jamie Crow	73	72	71	76	292	450
Mark Nash	73	75	73	72	293	420
Greg Hohnen	76	73	69	75	293	420
Craig Parry	74	75	73	72	294	361
Frank Conallin	72	71	77	74	294	361
Gerry Taylor	74	74	71	75	294	361
Noel Ratcliffe	74	74	71	75	294	361
Brian Jones	75	71	72	76	294	361

Robert Boyd Transport Victorian Open

Yarra Yarra Golf Club, Melbourne, Victoria
Par 36–36 – 72; 6,627 yards

February 6–9
purse, A$100,000

	SCORES				TOTAL	MONEY
Ossie Moore	71	67	70	72	280	A$18,000
Greg Turner	73	70	72	66	281	8,850
Vaughan Somers	68	66	72	75	281	8,850

	SCORES			TOTAL	MONEY
Peter Fowler	71	71	69	72	283	4,980
Mike Colandro	71	71	73	69	284	3,990
Bob Shearer	70	71	73	70	284	3,990
Bill Dunk	71	74	68	73	286	3,200
Craig Parry	66	73	73	74	286	3,200
Terry Gale	71	71	73	72	287	2,700
Ian Baker-Finch	75	68	72	73	288	2,066.66
Stewart Ginn	71	74	75	68	288	2,066.66
Brett Ogle	68	76	74	70	288	2,066.66
Paul Foley	72	71	75	72	290	1,640
David Merriman	75	69	76	71	291	1,400
Roger Stephens	70	73	75	73	291	1,400
Steve Montgomerie	69	71	73	78	291	1,400
Gerry Taylor	74	72	71	75	292	1,130
Mike Clayton	70	75	71	76	292	1,130
Peter McWhinney	78	71	74	69	292	1,130
Greg Alexander	73	73	76	70	292	1,130
Robert Stephens	70	75	74	73	292	1,130
Rodger Davis	74	71	75	72	292	1,130
Magnus Persson	67	72	77	77	293	860
Peter Hamblett	75	68	76	74	293	860
Wayne Smith	74	75	70	74	293	860
Mike Harwood	76	72	70	75	293	860
Steve Elkington	77	68	78	70	293	860
Simon Owen	72	72	78	71	293	860
Peter Croker	70	71	79	73	293	860
Jeff Senior	68	73	73	80	294	690
Lucien Tinkler	71	72	73	78	294	690

Robert Boyd Transport Australian Match Play

Kingston Heath Golf Club, Melbourne, Victoria
Par 36–36 – 72; 6,827 yards

February 15–16
purse, A$60,000

FIRST ROUND

Ossie Moore defeated *Brad King, 3 and 2
Anders Forsbrand defeated Wayne Riley, 5 and 3
Peter Fowler defeated Graham Marsh, 2 and 1
Stewart Ginn defeated Ian Stanley, 5 and 4
Bob Shearer defeated Ian Baker-Finch, 5 and 4
Rodger Davis defeated Frank Nobilo, 4 and 3
Mike Clayton defeated Terry Gale, 4 and 2
Brian Jones defeated Gerry Taylor, 2 and 1

SECOND ROUND

Anders Forsbrand defeated Ossie Moore, 2 and 1
Mike Clayton defeated Brian Jones, 2 and 1
Bob Shearer defeated Rodger Davis, 2 up
Peter Fowler defeated Stewart Ginn, 1 up, 20 holes

SEMI-FINALS

Peter Fowler defeated Anders Forsbrand, 3 and 2
Bob Shearer defeated Mike Clayton, 1 up at 19th

THIRD-FOURTH PLACE PLAYOFF

Anders Forsbrand defeated Mike Clayton, 3 and 2

FINAL

Peter Fowler defeated Bob Shearer, 6 and 5

PRIZE MONEY:

Fowler A$16,000; Shearer A$10,000; Forsbrand A$7,000; Clayton A$5,000.

Australian Masters

Huntingdale Golf Club, Melbourne, Victoria
Par 37–36 – 73; 6,955 yards

February 20–23
purse, A$275,000

	SCORES				TOTAL	MONEY
Mark O'Meara	74	66	71	73	284	A$49,500
David Graham	69	71	71	74	285	29,700
Ian Stanley	70	70	71	75	286	18,975
Bernhard Langer	72	73	71	71	287	12,567.50
Ian Baker-Finch	70	72	72	73	287	12,567.50
Terry Gale	73	69	71	75	288	10,505
Chen Tze Chung	72	69	74	74	289	9,405
Greg Norman	74	71	74	72	291	6,930
Mike Clayton	73	73	73	72	291	6,930
Michael McLean	74	72	76	69	291	6,930
Magnus Persson	78	71	72	70	291	6,930
Greg Turner	69	76	70	77	292	4,510
Wayne Riley	70	72	72	78	292	4,510
Philip Parkin	70	72	76	74	292	4,510
Gerry Taylor	75	74	72	72	293	3,476
Brian Jones	76	72	73	72	293	3,476
Mike Harwood	74	76	67	76	293	3,476
Brett Ogle	71	74	72	76	293	3,476
Sandy Harper	74	70	74	75	293	3,476
Manuel Pinero	74	74	73	73	294	2,860
Noel Ratcliffe	69	76	73	76	294	2,860
Ossie Moore	75	75	74	70	294	2,860
Rodger Davis	71	71	77	75	294	2,860
*David Smith	75	73	74	73	295	
Bob Shearer	73	76	73	73	295	2,475
Ian Woosnam	71	73	74	77	295	2,475
Stewart Ginn	74	72	77	72	295	2,475
Paul Foley	71	72	75	78	296	2,145
Peter McWhinney	78	72	71	75	296	2,145
Robert Stephens	74	72	80	70	296	2,145
Anders Forsbrand	76	71	77	73	297	1,842.50
Larry Canning	74	70	78	75	297	1,842.50
Rob McNaughton	72	72	78	75	297	1,842.50
Lyndsay Stephen	72	77	73	75	297	1,842.50
George Serhan	72	77	71	78	298	1,650
Katsunari Takahashi	75	74	75	74	298	1,650
Mats Lanner	76	74	78	70	298	1,650
Frank Nobilo	77	70	78	74	299	1,540
*John Lindsay	76	74	75	74	299	
Graham Marsh	75	74	74	77	300	1,402.50
Peter Fowler	70	74	78	78	300	1,402.50
Ken Dukes	72	74	78	76	300	1,402.50
Ove Sellberg	73	73	80	74	300	1,402.50
Akira Yabe	72	76	79	74	301	1,182.50

	SCORES				TOTAL	MONEY
Peter Croker	73	76	75	77	301	1,182.50
Lucien Tinkler	74	73	76	78	301	1,182.50
Sam Torrance	75	66	78	82	301	1,182.50
Anthony Gilligan	78	68	75	81	302	1,017.50
Simon Owen	75	75	76	76	302	1,017.50
John Clifford	72	77	76	78	303	880
Michael Loughland	73	73	78	79	303	880
*Peter Baker	74	75	80	74	303	
Vaughan Somers	74	76	79	74	303	880

Rich River Classic

Rich River Golf Club, Moama, New South Wales
Par 35–36 – 71; 6,524 yards

February 27–March 2
purse, A$70,000

	SCORES				TOTAL	MONEY
Bob Shearer	64	68	66	69	267	A$12,600
Ian Stanley	70	74	66	65	275	7,560
Mike Colandro	70	67	68	71	276	4,830
Rob McNaughton	68	70	69	70	277	3,024
Rodger Davis	70	65	70	72	277	3,024
Mike Clayton	69	66	71	71	277	3,024
Trevor McDonald	68	70	68	72	278	2,394
Anthony Painter	68	71	70	71	280	1,764
Steve Elkington	67	69	72	72	280	1,764
Mike Harwood	68	71	69	72	280	1,764
John Clifford	70	68	70	72	280	1,764
Ossie Moore	70	72	70	69	281	1,106
Jamie Crow	71	69	71	70	281	1,106
Vaughan Somers	67	73	68	73	281	1,106
Peter Jones	68	71	68	74	281	1,106
Jeff Senior	73	71	71	67	282	842.80
Ken Dukes	69	69	70	74	282	842.80
Robert Stephens	73	65	70	74	282	842.80
Darrell Brown	67	71	69	75	282	842.80
Mark Nash	67	72	68	75	282	842.80
Frank Nobilo	71	69	72	71	283	728
Ken Trimble	69	74	70	70	283	728
Jason Deep	71	71	71	71	284	644
Bill Dunk	70	72	71	71	284	644
Max Stevens	74	64	73	73	284	644
Rick Vershure	71	71	67	75	284	644
Peter Hamblett	69	70	74	72	285	546
Sandy Harper	72	72	69	72	285	546
Anthony Gilligan	75	65	72	73	285	546

Halls Head Estates-Nissan Nedlands Masters

Nedlands Golf Club, Perth, Western Australia
Par 36–36 – 72; 6,289 yards

May 15–18
purse, A$50,000

	SCORES				TOTAL	MONEY
Lyndsay Stephen	70	70	66	66	272	A$9,000
Ian Stanley	69	71	72	69	281	5,500

	SCORES				TOTAL	MONEY
Peter Jones	68	67	70	77	282	3,535
Mike Cahill	72	69	74	68	283	2,500
Brett Ogle	71	71	74	68	284	1,820
John Clifford	72	73	70	69	284	1,820
Stewart Ginn	71	70	72	71	284	1,820
Robert Stephens	71	69	70	74	284	1,820
Terry Gale	72	71	68	73	284	1,820
Ken Dukes	71	75	70	69	285	1,200
Jason Deep	76	69	70	70	285	1,200
David Smith	72	72	70	71	285	1,200
Graham Marsh	70	69	72	74	285	1,200
Bob Shearer	73	66	70	76	285	1,200
Roger Mackay	70	72	71	73	286	850
Roger Stephens	71	71	71	73	286	850
*Jon Evans	69	74	71	72	286	
Craig Parry	75	73	70	69	287	675
Anthony Painter	71	70	74	72	287	675
Gerry Merrick	71	70	73	73	287	675
Charles Henderson	71	73	70	73	287	675
Ross Metherell	73	72	68	75	288	550
Ian Roberts	72	73	74	70	289	525
Vaughan Somers	76	70	73	71	290	475
Mark Nash	74	71	72	73	290	475
Colin Hunt	74	71	72	73	290	475
Bruce Sorrenson	76	71	74	70	291	420
Paul Foley	74	73	69	75	291	420
Gary Hopkins	75	73	75	69	292	390
*Glenn Carbon	73	72	74	73	292	

Fourex Queensland PGA

Indooroopilly Golf Club, Brisbane, Queensland
Par 35-37 – 72; 6,875 yards

October 2–5
purse, A$100,000

	SCORES				TOTAL	MONEY
Ossie Moore	69	70	66	72	277	A$18,000
Brett Ogle	68	71	73	75	287	8,850
Peter Senior	73	73	69	72	287	8,850
Paul Foley	74	70	72	72	288	4,570
Wayne Riley	68	72	75	73	288	4,570
John Clifford	71	74	71	73	289	3,820
Mike Ferguson	73	73	74	70	290	3,200
Mike Clayton	71	72	70	77	290	3,200
Richard Gilkey	73	77	70	71	291	2,530
Peter Fowler	77	70	71	73	291	2,530
Gerry Taylor	73	73	77	69	292	1,672
Mike Cahill	73	73	75	71	292	1,672
Bob Shearer	71	74	75	72	292	1,672
Peter Jones	72	74	74	72	292	1,672
Anthony Painter	73	73	73	73	292	1,672
Craig Parry	75	71	72	75	293	1,290
Mark Nash	76	71	71	75	293	1,290
Mark K. Nash	74	71	75	74	294	1,170
Wayne Smith	68	78	71	77	294	1,170
Stewart Ginn	75	75	74	71	295	1,040
Ken Trimble	73	78	73	71	295	1,040
Michael Loughland	70	76	74	75	295	1,040

	SCORES				TOTAL	MONEY
Jeff Woodland	73	72	74	76	295	1,040
Jamie Crow	72	71	78	75	296	840
Carl Johnsen	69	75	77	75	296	840
Kelly Murphy	71	74	76	75	296	840
Brett Griffiths	76	70	74	76	296	840
Greg Smith	74	71	74	77	296	840
Peter McWhinney	71	70	73	82	296	840
Bob Weir	77	74	73	73	297	680
John Victorsen	72	75	74	76	297	680
Darrell Brown	71	74	76	76	297	680

Stefan Queensland Open

Coolangatta-Tweed Heads Golf Club, Coolangatta, Queensland   October 9–12
Par 36–36 – 72; 6,745 yards   purse, A$100,000

	SCORES				TOTAL	MONEY
Greg Norman	67	70	70	70	277	A$18,000
Peter Senior	71	68	73	71	283	8,850
Jeff Woodland	64	73	68	78	283	8,850
Brett Ogle	69	66	73	76	284	4,980
Steve Elkington	71	73	71	71	286	4,160
Roger Mackay	70	71	72	74	287	3,406.67
Peter Fowler	70	69	71	77	287	3,406.67
Bruce Soulsby	65	72	73	77	287	3,406.67
Bob Shearer	70	72	72	74	288	2,700
Lyndsay Stephen	71	72	71	75	289	2,200
George Serhan	69	71	73	76	289	2,200
Greg Hohnen	73	72	72	73	290	1,720
David Graham	73	71	71	75	290	1,720
*Peter O'Malley	68	73	73	76	290	
Mike Ferguson	70	76	73	72	291	1,400
David Smith	72	72	73	74	291	1,400
Peter McWhinney	69	74	73	75	291	1,400
Kyi Hla Han	72	73	75	72	292	1,175
Frank Nobilo	70	73	76	73	292	1,175
Wayne Smith	73	69	73	77	292	1,175
Robert Stephens	64	74	75	79	292	1,175
Tony Maloney	70	71	75	77	293	1,040
Paul Foley	69	72	71	81	293	1,040
Craig Warren	73	73	76	72	294	960
Mike Colandro	74	72	70	78	294	960
Anthony Painter	72	76	73	74	295	820
Ian Roberts	73	74	73	75	295	820
Lu Chien Soon	73	72	73	77	295	820
Andrew Gutteridge	71	73	75	76	295	820
Ossie Moore	72	71	71	81	295	820

National Panasonic New South Wales Open

Concord Golf Club, Sydney, New South Wales
Par 35–36 – 71; 6,660 yards

October 16–19
purse, A$125,000

	SCORES				TOTAL	MONEY
Greg Norman	65	70	67	73	275	A$22,500
Lyndsay Stephen	72	67	69	72	280	13,500
Steve Elkington	69	73	70	69	281	8,625
Ian Stanley	75	68	69	70	282	6,225
Roger Mackay	70	72	70	71	283	4,493.75
Gerry Taylor	71	73	67	72	283	4,493.75
Frank Nobilo	69	69	69	76	283	4,493.75
Ossie Moore	69	69	71	74	283	4,493.75
Peter Jones	69	72	71	72	284	3,162.50
David Graham	69	73	70	72	284	3,162.50
Maurice Bembridge	72	74	66	73	285	2,550
Ian Baker-Finch	74	68	73	71	286	2,250
Peter Senior	68	68	77	74	287	1,950
Vaughan Somers	68	72	74	73	287	1,950
Mike Harwood	69	71	73	75	288	1,700
Peter Teravainen	73	71	66	78	288	1,700
Craig Parry	70	73	72	74	289	1,500
Mike Clayton	74	70	70	75	289	1,500
Rob McNaughton	72	72	70	75	289	1,500
*Lester Peterson	72	72	73	72	289	
Peter McWhinney	74	69	74	73	290	1,300
Brett Ogle	73	74	70	73	290	1,300
Bob Shearer	72	74	70	74	290	1,300
Robert Stephens	71	71	73	75	290	1,300
Peter Fowler	74	71	76	70	291	1,100
Chris Tickner	68	74	75	74	291	1,100
Jeff Woodland	70	73	73	75	291	1,100
Jeff Senior	71	75	69	76	291	1,100
David Sheather	73	75	75	69	292	875
John Clifford	71	77	71	73	292	875
Bruce Soulsby	73	74	71	74	292	875
Greg Hohnen	74	69	74	75	292	875
Wayne Smith	72	74	71	75	292	875
Wayne Case	70	69	75	78	292	875

West End Jubilee South Australian Open

Kooyonga Golf Club, Adelaide, South Australia
Par 37–35–72; 6,731 yards

October 22–25
purse, A$100,000

	SCORES				TOTAL	MONEY
Greg Norman	75	68	75	65	283	A$18,000
David Graham	72	69	74	71	286	10,800
Peter Senior	73	70	75	70	288	5,940
Bob Shearer	72	69	77	70	288	5,940
Ian Baker-Finch	70	74	73	72	289	4,160
Vaughan Somers	71	72	74	73	290	3,820
Wayne Riley	73	75	76	67	291	3,033.33
Mike Harwood	77	72	75	67	291	3,033.33
Ossie Moore	77	72	73	69	291	3,033.33

	SCORES				TOTAL	MONEY
Bruce Soulsby	72	77	74	69	292	2,066.66
Ian Stanley	74	73	73	72	292	2,066.66
Steve Elkington	72	74	72	74	292	2,066.66
Robert Stephens	72	71	76	74	293	1,640
Peter McWhinney	71	76	74	73	294	1,400
Jeff Senior	75	74	74	71	294	1,400
Lyndsay Stephen	75	72	68	79	294	1,400
Ken Trimble	77	74	73	71	295	1,230
Wayne Smith	76	73	74	72	295	1,230
Brett Ogle	77	77	73	69	296	1,140
Craig Warren	70	76	77	74	297	1,080
Stewart Ginn	76	72	72	77	297	1,080
Greg Alexander	76	74	74	74	298	1,000
Kyi Hla Han	79	73	72	74	298	1,000
Peter Jones	74	78	78	69	299	880
Tim Elliott	77	76	73	73	299	880
Roger Stephens	77	75	75	72	299	880
*Glenn Joyner	75	72	71	81	299	
Colin Hunt	76	76	73	74	299	880
Greg Hohnen	75	74	78	73	300	740
Roger Mackay	78	71	78	73	300	740
John Clifford	75	77	76	72	300	740

Toshiba Australian PGA Championship

Castle Hill Country Club, Sydney, New South Wales
Par 36–36 – 72; 6,830 yards

October 30–November 2
purse, A$180,000

	SCORES				TOTAL	MONEY
Mike Harwood	69	69	73	64	275	A$32,400
Greg Norman	69	69	66	73	277	19,440
Graham Marsh	68	69	70	71	278	12,420
Greg Turner	76	68	65	70	279	8,964
Ian Baker-Finch	68	71	71	70	280	7,488
Brett Ogle	73	67	72	69	281	5,814
Peter Senior	68	70	73	70	281	5,814
Rodger Davis	71	68	67	75	281	5,814
Peter McWhinney	72	69	67	73	281	5,814
Peter Fowler	67	72	73	70	282	3,216
Gerry Taylor	68	71	73	70	282	3,216
Wayne Riley	69	71	71	71	282	3,216
Ken Dukes	68	69	73	72	282	3,216
Mike Colandro	66	72	71	73	282	3,216
John Clifford	70	69	70	73	282	3,216
Lyndsay Stephen	69	73	72	70	284	2,322
Dan Talbot	69	68	75	72	284	2,322
Bob Shearer	70	68	74	73	285	2,160
Ian Stanley	75	70	72	69	286	1,980
Steen Tinning	71	73	72	70	286	1,980
Peter Jones	67	75	71	73	286	1,980
Ian Roberts	71	70	78	68	287	1,692
Russell Swanson	74	72	71	70	287	1,692
Shizuo Mori	69	71	76	71	287	1,692
Wayne Smith	74	70	70	73	287	1,692
Rob McNaughton	73	66	72	76	287	1,692
Mike Cahill	74	71	73	70	288	1,404
Bruce Soulsby	73	73	70	72	288	1,404

	SCORES				TOTAL	MONEY
Terry Gale	71	74	71	72	288	1,404
George Serhan	70	73	76	70	289	1,260

Victorian PGA

Warrnambool Golf Club, Warrnambool, Victoria   November 6–9
Par 35–37 – 72; 6,175 yards   purse, A$100,000

	SCORES				TOTAL	MONEY
Wayne Smith	67	68	70	70	275	A$18,000
Terry Gale	72	69	67	69	277	10,800
Ossie Moore	65	73	71	70	279	6,900
Ian Stanley	70	70	71	69	280	4,980
Greg Turner	70	72	69	70	281	4,160
Russell Swanson	72	74	68	68	282	3,620
Mike Cahill	72	70	67	73	282	3,620
Bob Shearer	75	69	69	70	283	2,680
Wayne Riley	70	68	73	72	283	2,680
Mike Clayton	75	68	67	73	283	2,680
Jamie Crow	73	74	69	68	284	1,740
Peter Teravainen	70	72	72	70	284	1,740
Craig Parry	70	70	72	72	284	1,740
Mark Spencer	71	70	71	72	284	1,740
Shizuo Mori	69	73	71	72	285	1,326.66
Greg Hohnen	68	70	74	73	285	1,326.66
George Serhan	74	69	69	73	285	1,326.66
Peter Fowler	76	70	71	69	286	1,104
Paul Foley	75	70	71	70	286	1,104
Steen Tinning	70	70	75	71	286	1,104
Steve Bann	68	75	71	72	286	1,104
Rob McNaughton	69	75	68	74	286	1,104
Wayne Case	73	71	75	68	287	860
Vaughan Somers	72	70	74	71	287	860
Sandy Harper	70	73	73	71	287	860
Greg Alexander	68	74	73	72	287	860
Doug Murray	71	70	73	73	287	860
Stewart Ginn	74	73	68	72	287	860
Jean-Louis Lamarre	76	68	71	72	287	860
Brett Ogle	71	74	75	68	288	630
Mike Ferguson	74	71	72	71	288	630
Jeff Senior	76	70	72	70	288	630
Robert Stephens	72	68	76	72	288	630
Mike Harwood	70	73	72	73	288	630
David Smith	71	73	71	73	288	630
Roger Stephens	69	73	70	76	288	630
Brett Officer	72	74	73	69	288	630

National Panasonic Australian Open Championship

Metropolitan Golf Club, Melbourne, Victoria   November 13–16
Par 37–35 – 72; 7,000 yards   purse, A$275,000

	SCORES				TOTAL	MONEY
Rodger Davis	67	71	72	68	278	A$49,500
Graham Marsh	70	71	69	69	279	20,790

	SCORES				TOTAL	MONEY
Ian Baker-Finch	66	69	72	72	279	20,790
Bob Shearer	69	71	70	69	279	20,790
Magnus Persson	67	71	72	70	280	11,440
Roger Mackay	71	70	71	69	281	10,505
Greg Norman	70	72	72	68	282	8,341.66
Bernhard Langer	69	70	72	71	282	8,341.66
Vaughan Somers	71	70	71	70	282	8,341.66
Mark Nash	74	70	70	71	285	6,490
Terry Gale	72	72	70	72	286	5,280
Greg Turner	76	72	74	74	286	5,280
Brett Ogle	71	73	72	71	287	4,290
Wayne Grady	72	74	74	67	287	4,290
Ian Stanley	72	76	70	70	288	3,740
Mike Clayton	70	73	74	71	288	3,740
Jeff Senior	69	72	72	76	289	3,168
Lyndsay Stephen	72	70	73	74	289	3,168
Sandy Harper	74	72	72	71	289	3,168
Steen Tinning	74	73	71	71	289	3,168
Jamie Crow	67	74	77	71	289	3,168
Mike Harwood	76	73	70	71	290	2,640
Peter Croker	75	74	72	69	290	2,640
John Clifford	72	74	74	70	290	2,640
Rob McNaughton	73	72	72	73	290	2,640
Mike Ferguson	74	72	76	69	291	2,365
Frank Nobilo	73	71	73	75	292	2,090
Ken Dukes	73	74	73	72	292	2,090
Peter McWhinney	76	72	72	72	292	2,090
Peter Teravainen	71	75	75	71	292	2,090
Dan Talbot	70	75	75	73	293	1,870
*David Ecob	75	75	72	71	293	
David Armstrong	75	75	69	75	294	1,760
Ken Trimble	72	70	79	73	294	1,760
*Brad King	76	74	75	69	294	
Peter Senior	69	74	77	74	294	1,760
Maurice Bembridge	73	77	70	75	295	1,540
Mike Colandro	72	73	76	74	295	1,540
Peter Dahlberg	74	72	77	72	295	1,540
Peter Jones	75	72	74	74	295	1,540
Stewart Ginn	73	75	79	68	295	1,540
Brandon Coleman	78	70	72	76	296	1,347.50
Larry Canning	74	73	78	71	296	1,347.50
Carl Johnsen	79	71	77	70	297	1,127.50
Ian Roberts	76	71	77	73	297	1,127.50
Steve Bann	69	80	73	75	297	1,127.50
Michael Barry	74	76	72	75	297	1,127.50
Kyi Hla Han	78	72	75	72	297	1,127.50
Simon Owen	72	78	75	72	297	1,127.50
Shizuo Mori	72	78	75	73	298	880
Mark Spencer	74	73	75	76	298	880
Trevor McDonald	73	73	77	75	298	880

National Panasonic Western Australian Open

Lake Karrinyup Country Club, Perth, Western Australia
Par 36–36 – 72; 6,650 yards

November 20–23
purse, A$100,000

	SCORES				TOTAL	MONEY
Greg Norman	72	70	66	68	276	A$18,000
Terry Gale	68	70	68	71	277	10,800
Peter Senior	64	75	70	74	283	6,900
Mark O'Meara	75	71	73	66	285	4,570
Lyndsay Stephen	76	71	69	69	285	4,570
Ossie Moore	69	70	77	71	287	3,620
David Smith	70	70	73	74	287	3,620
Jamie Crow	69	72	75	73	289	2,980
Peter Jones	70	77	73	70	290	2,366.66
Jeff Senior	72	73	74	71	290	2,366.66
Trevor Downing	72	73	72	73	290	2,366.66
Dan Talbot	67	79	70	75	291	1,720
Rodger Davis	68	74	73	76	291	1,720
Richard Gilkey	74	74	72	72	292	1,400
Noel Ratcliffe	71	75	72	74	292	1,400
Mike Cahill	67	76	68	81	292	1,400
John Clifford	72	75	76	70	293	1,108.57
George Serhan	72	75	75	71	293	1,108.57
Magnus Persson	72	76	73	72	293	1,108.57
Vaughan Somers	75	76	71	71	293	1,108.57
Ian Stanley	76	73	71	73	293	1,108.57
Bob Shearer	70	76	73	74	293	1,108.57
Matthew Cole	73	74	72	74	293	1,108.57
Greg Alexander	73	74	76	71	294	920
Roger Mackay	72	72	72	78	294	920
*Jon Evans	74	77	72	71	294	
Mike Clayton	75	76	73	71	295	820
Kyi Hla Han	75	76	73	71	295	820
Gerry Taylor	71	78	70	76	295	820
Sandy Harper	73	76	75	72	296	706.66
Robert Stephens	77	71	77	71	296	706.66
Wayne Smith	76	77	73	70	296	706.66

Air New Zealand-Shell Open

Titirangi Golf Club, Auckland
Par 35–35 – 70; 6,286 yards

November 27–30
purse, NZ$150,000

	SCORES				TOTAL	MONEY
Rodger Davis	64	65	67	72	267	NZ$27,000
Bob Shearer	69	70	65	66	270	13,275
Curtis Strange	67	67	63	73	270	13,275
Peter Senior	65	67	73	68	273	6,855
D. A. Weibring	66	68	65	74	273	6,855
Vaughan Somers	71	64	68	71	274	5,430
Simon Owen	67	70	66	71	274	5,430
Jeff Senior	69	72	67	67	275	4,260
Noel Ratcliffe	65	71	69	70	275	4,260
Greg Alexander	72	68	68	68	276	3,300

	SCORES				TOTAL	MONEY
Mike Clayton	67	68	71	70	276	3,300
Terry Gale	69	72	69	67	277	2,700
Gerry Taylor	71	70	68	69	278	2,260
Marc Girouard	73	69	66	70	278	2,260
Ian Stanley	68	65	74	71	278	2,260
Dan Talbot	69	73	69	68	279	1,845
Mike Colandro	72	68	69	70	279	1,845
Craig Parry	64	74	70	71	279	1,845
Maurice Bembridge	65	71	66	77	279	1,845
Brett Officer	74	67	71	68	280	1,560
Bob Charles	69	66	74	71	280	1,560
Richard Gilkey	69	71	68	72	280	1,560
Paul Minifie	67	71	70	72	280	1,560
Craig Warren	72	68	71	70	281	1,410
Michael Loughland	68	70	71	73	282	1,350
Anthony Gilligan	67	71	76	69	283	1,102.50
Frank Nobilo	68	72	73	70	283	1,102.50
Matthew Cole	74	67	72	70	283	1,102.50
Carl Johnsen	72	70	71	70	283	1,102.50
Anthony Painter	67	70	74	72	283	1,102.50
Barry Vivian	70	73	69	71	283	1,102.50
Ken Trimble	75	67	68	73	283	1,102.50
Lyndsay Stephen	67	72	68	76	283	1,102.50

Nissan-Mobil New Zealand Open

Grange Golf Club, Auckland
Par 35–35 – 70; 6,599 yards

December 4–7
purse, NZ$120,000

	SCORES				TOTAL	MONEY
Rodger Davis	67	62	65	68	262	NZ$21,600
Bob Shearer	68	65	69	68	270	12,960
Ian Baker-Finch	66	70	69	70	275	8,280
Vaughan Somers	67	65	74	71	277	5,184
Jeff Senior	67	67	72	71	277	5,184
Frank Nobilo	73	66	66	72	277	5,184
Jose-Maria Olazabal	66	70	69	73	278	4,104
Ian Stanley	70	68	74	68	280	3,024
Bob Charles	72	72	69	67	280	3,024
Brett Officer	71	71	69	69	280	3,024
Corey Pavin	72	69	69	70	280	3,024
Peter Senior	66	67	72	76	281	2,160
Kyi Hla Han	72	65	74	71	282	1,808
Lucien Tinkler	74	66	72	70	282	1,808
Mike Colandro	72	67	70	73	282	1,808
Maurice Bembridge	71	71	72	70	284	1,444.80
*Glen Goldfinch	71	70	73	70	284	
Terry Gale	71	69	73	71	284	1,444.80
Wayne Riley	72	68	70	74	284	1,444.80
*Michael Barltrop	65	67	78	74	284	
Ian Roberts	71	68	70	75	284	1,444.80
Ove Sellberg	71	71	68	74	284	1,444.80
Simon Owen	72	72	71	70	285	1,248
Peter Fowler	73	71	71	70	285	1,248
Barry Vivian	71	74	71	70	286	1,128
Tom Sutter	71	73	70	72	286	1,128
Stewart Ginn	74	70	65	77	286	1,128

	SCORES				TOTAL	MONEY
Steve Andersen-Chapman	72	71	72	72	287	1,008
Dan Talbot	73	73	68	73	287	1,008
*Peter O'Malley	71	71	72	73	287	

The Asia/Japan Tours

Cathay Pacific Hong Kong Open

Royal Hong Kong Golf Club, Composite Course, Fanling   February 27–March 2
Par 36–35 – 71; 6,722 yards   purse, US$150,000

	SCORES				TOTAL	MONEY
Seiichi Kanai	72	73	70	70	285	US$25,000
Ian Baker-Finch	76	68	71	71	286	16,600
Hsieh Yu Shu	69	71	75	72	287	9,390
Greg Turner	68	72	77	72	289	6,370
Brian Jones	73	71	74	71	289	6,370
Jim Rutledge	68	72	75	74	289	6,370
Liao Kuo Chih	78	69	73	70	290	4,125
Manuel Pinero	72	74	73	71	290	4,125
Ho Ming Chung	70	73	74	75	292	3,360
Art Russell	75	70	78	70	293	2,895
Choi Sang Ho	72	73	77	71	293	2,895
Tsao Chien Teng	72	74	77	71	294	2,113
Ray Stewart	74	73	76	71	294	2,113
Sam Torrance	74	75	73	72	294	2,113
Bill Barrett	74	74	73	73	294	2,113
Ronan Rafferty	73	73	74	74	294	2,113
Doug Black	69	74	76	75	294	2,113
Chen Tze Chung	73	73	73	75	294	2,113
Katsunari Takahashi	74	69	76	75	294	2,113
Li Wen Shen	74	73	72	75	294	2,113
Chen Tze Ming	73	74	71	76	294	2,113
Peter Teravainen	70	78	73	74	295	1,670
Chris Cookson	72	72	76	75	295	1,670
Junji Hashizoe	69	77	74	75	295	1,670
Park Shi Wan	71	72	80	73	296	1,547
Mitch Adcock	76	73	73	74	296	1,547
Terry Gale	72	75	72	77	296	1,547
Kuo Chi Hsiung	72	74	78	73	297	1,390
Lu Hsi Chuen	75	72	75	75	297	1,390
Tony Grimes	72	75	74	76	297	1,390
Lin Chia	76	71	75	75	297	1,390

Benson and Hedges Malaysian Open

Royal Selangor Golf Club, Kuala Lumpur, Malaysia   March 6–9
Par 35–36 – 71; 6,935 yards   purse, US$150,000

	SCORES				TOTAL	MONEY
Stewart Ginn	70	69	67	70	276	US$25,000
Brian Jones	68	71	67	71	277	16,600
Lu Hsi Chuen	69	68	73	68	278	9,390

	SCORES				TOTAL	MONEY
Chen Tze Chung	69	69	68	73	279	6,930
Sam Torrance	67	71	72	69	279	6,930
Choi Sang-Hi	70	68	73	69	280	5,250
Mario Siodina	71	74	69	67	281	4,500
Lu Chien Soon	68	71	73	70	282	3,370
Greg Turner	71	68	72	71	282	3,370
Mike Cunning	72	73	69	69	283	3,370
Terry Gale	72	73	69	69	283	2,561
Chen Tze Ming	74	69	70	70	283	2,561
Liao Kuo Chin	73	67	68	75	283	2,561
Frankie Minoza	74	67	73	69	283	2,561
Peter Fowler	73	70	70	71	284	2,167
Stewart Ray	69	68	73	74	284	2,167
Jim Rutledge	72	70	74	69	285	1,896
Rudy Lavares	70	73	71	71	285	1,896
Jim Hallet	73	71	74	67	285	1,896
Duffy Waldorf	69	72	73	71	285	1,896
Kyi Hla Han	72	72	74	68	286	1,628
Ho Ming Chung	69	72	73	72	286	1,628
Lee Myung Ha	74	69	72	71	286	1,628
Curt Byrum	72	72	68	74	286	1,628
Naza Yusof	72	69	72	73	286	1,628
Noel Radcliffe	72	72	73	69	286	1,628
Ian Baker-Finch	71	72	72	71	286	1,628
Adan Sowa	70	73	72	72	287	1,391
Katsuyoshi Tomori	72	73	72	70	287	1,391
Mitch Adcock	71	72	69	75	287	1,391
John Burckle	72	73	71	71	287	1,391

Singapore Open

Royal Singapore Golf Club, Bukit Course
Par 35–36 – 71; 6,674 yards

March 13–16
purse, US$125,000

	SCORES				TOTAL	MONEY
Greg Turner	65	70	65	71	271	US$20,825
Duffy Waldorf	69	70	69	67	275	10,857
Tony Grimes	69	66	70	70	275	10,857
Chen Tze Chung	71	69	68	69	277	6,250
Curt Byrum	68	68	71	71	278	5,300
Hsieh Yu Shu	72	67	70	70	279	4,063
Tsao Chien Teng	70	68	70	71	279	4,063
Bryan Norton	72	69	69	70	280	2,688
Wayne Smith	71	71	69	69	280	2,688
Roger Antonio	73	65	70	72	280	2,688
Ray Stewart	71	66	69	74	280	2,688
Kuo Chi Hsiung	70	68	71	72	281	2,071
Gary Webb	70	70	71	70	281	2,071
Bob E. Smith	69	68	75	69	281	2,071
Steve Anderson-Chapman	69	70	67	76	282	1,759
Mario Siodina	72	71	68	71	282	1,759
Park Shi Whan	71	71	70	70	282	1,759
Michael McLean	71	71	69	72	283	1,490
Rudy Lavares	70	73	73	67	283	1,490
Lin Chia	73	69	69	72	283	1,490
Katsuyoshi Tomori	74	69	70	70	283	1,490

	SCORES			TOTAL	MONEY
Jim Roberts	71	71	73	68	283	1,490
Craig McClellan	74	69	72	68	283	1,490
Eleuterio Nival	71	70	73	70	284	1,179
Choi Yoon Soo	70	70	74	70	284	1,179
Peter Fowler	72	71	71	70	284	1,179
Lee Myung Ha	70	70	73	71	284	1,179
Lu Chien Soon	67	73	71	73	284	1,179
Kelly Clair	72	69	70	73	284	1,179
Choi Dang Hoe	73	67	71	73	284	1,179
Lu Hsi Chuen	70	69	71	74	284	1,179
Ron Commans	74	69	73	68	284	1,179
Rodger Davis	72	68	79	65	284	1,179

Indonesian Open

Jakarta Golf Club, Rawamangun Course, Jakarta, Indonesia   March 20–23
Par 35–35 – 70; 6,466 yards   purse, US$100,000

	SCORES				TOTAL	MONEY
Frankie Minoza	69	68	67	66	270	US$13,334
Hsieh Yu Shu	65	67	69	70	271	9,217
Stewart Ginn	69	67	65	71	272	4,392
Ho Ming Chung	65	71	65	71	272	4,392
Lin Chia	68	68	66	70	272	4,392
Wayne Smith	68	71	68	68	275	2,975
*Buari	69	68	70	69	276	
Rudy Lavares	69	68	69	71	277	2,338
Yu Chin Han	67	70	72	68	277	2,338
Jim Rutledge	66	71	70	71	278	1,728
Lu Hsi Chuen	70	68	72	68	278	1,728
Ray Stewart	71	68	68	71	278	1,728
Peter Fowler	65	70	68	76	279	1,479
Mitch Adcock	70	69	69	73	280	1,300
Don Klenk	68	69	72	71	280	1,300
Robert Meir	71	71	69	71	282	1,059
Kim Young II	65	71	72	74	282	1,059
Shen Chung Shyan	69	69	70	74	282	1,059
Tsao Chien Teng	70	67	70	75	282	1,059
Tony Grimes	67	72	72	71	282	1,059
Greg Conley	70	71	70	72	283	898
Per Arne Broested	70	73	68	72	283	898
Mario Siodina	71	72	73	67	283	898
Tracy Nakazaki	66	74	70	73	283	898
Hsu Chi San	72	70	72	69	283	898
Yasuo Sone	69	71	73	70	283	898
Steve Schroeder	72	68	72	71	283	898
Eleuterio Nival	68	71	72	73	284	702
Paterno Braza	71	68	70	78	284	702
Hung Weng Neng	72	71	71	70	284	702
Ron Commans	73	68	72	71	284	702
Kelly Clair	75	67	71	71	284	702
Jim Hallet	73	69	70	72	284	702
Yurio Akitomi	72	70	70	72	284	702
Bill Barrett	70	72	70	72	284	702
Bob E. Smith	69	71	72	72	284	702

Thailand Open

Bangphra Golf Club, Bangphra, Thailand
Par 36-36 – 72; 7,070 yards

March 27–30
purse, US$100,000

	SCORES				TOTAL	MONEY
Ho Ming Chung	72	72	72	72	288	US$16,660
Lu Chien Soon	74	73	71	71	289	11,110
Peter Fowler	71	72	75	72	290	5,166
Ray Stewart	73	73	75	69	290	5,166
Lu Hsi Chuen	75	71	71	73	290	5,166
Stewart Ginn	73	76	71	71	291	2,810
Kyi Hla Han	76	71	73	71	291	2,810
Frankie Minoza	74	72	74	71	291	2,810
Saneh Saengsui	70	73	74	74	291	2,810
Kuo Chi Hsiung	72	73	73	74	292	2,000
Wayne Smith	73	73	75	72	293	1,664
Hung Wen Neng	74	75	71	73	293	1,664
Robert Michael	75	69	74	75	293	1,664
Kampol Sinsuebpol	72	78	75	68	293	1,664
Suthep Meesawadi	72	75	73	73	293	1,664
Rick Gibson	76	75	75	68	294	1,315
Yau Sui Ming	74	72	76	72	294	1,315
Park Shi Hwan	74	73	75	72	294	1,315
Bob E. Smith	75	75	72	72	294	1,315
Kim Young II	69	76	76	74	295	1,218
Kin Chia	74	74	76	71	295	1,218
Yu Chin Han	72	73	76	74	295	1,218
Mike Allen	75	75	74	71	295	1,218
Bryan Gathright	75	75	75	70	295	1,218
Don Klenk	71	74	75	75	295	1,218
Mario Manubay	72	75	79	70	296	985
Shen Chung Shyan	74	76	72	74	296	985
John Jacobs	73	76	74	73	296	985
Prasarn Rueyruen	74	75	73	74	296	985
Craig Parry	72	79	72	74	297	813
Steve Anderson-Chapman	73	77	75	72	297	813
Mario Siodina	74	75	76	72	297	813
Lim Kian Tiong	77	71	75	74	297	813
Lai Chung Jen	70	73	80	74	297	813
Tsao Chien Teng	74	74	74	75	297	813
Jim Carter	71	77	75	74	297	813
Kurt Cox	75	76	71	75	297	813

Charminar Challenge Indian Open

Royal Calcutta Golf Club, Calcutta, India
Par 36-37 – 73; 7,190 yards

April 3–6
purse, US$100,000

	SCORES				TOTAL	MONEY
Lu Hsi Chuen	69	68	70	72	279	US$16,660
Lu Chien Soon	67	72	67	75	281	11,110
Somsak Sri-Sanga	69	72	67	75	285	6,260
Jim Carter	71	72	71	73	287	5,000
Basad Ali	69	72	75	72	288	4,240
Stewart Ginn	72	75	68	74	289	3,500

	SCORES				TOTAL	MONEY
Mitch Adcock	70	72	71	77	290	2,580
Per Arne Brostedt	72	73	68	77	290	2,580
John Burckle	69	75	73	73	290	2,580
Hung Wen Neng	71	74	69	77	291	1,930
Sukree Onsham	74	70	74	73	291	1,930
Scott Taylor	71	76	72	73	292	1,657
Jim Hallet	73	75	70	74	292	1,657
Wayne Smith	69	76	75	72	292	1,657
Craig Parry	70	75	76	72	293	1,445
Pat Horgan	73	72	71	77	293	1,445
Duffy Waldorf	72	73	71	78	294	1,265
Tony Grimes	75	73	73	73	294	1,265
Mike Cunning	77	73	71	73	294	1,265
Robert Meyer	73	73	75	73	294	1,265
Tommy Armour III	72	71	72	80	295	1,170
Mike Harwood	73	74	75	74	296	1,086
Rodolfo Rodriguez	74	73	75	74	296	1,086
Steve Cook	72	74	75	75	296	1,086
Alan Pate	78	71	75	72	296	1,086
Sinsubol Kampol	74	70	75	77	296	1,086
Rick Gibson	76	75	73	73	297	955
Hideyo Nishigai	77	74	72	74	297	955
Feroz	77	72	75	73	297	955
Curt Byrum	75	74	73	75	297	955

Republic of China Open

Chang Gung Country Club, Taipeh, Taipei, Taiwan April 10–13
Par 36–36 – 72; 7,015 yards purse, US$120,000
(Rain washed out Friday round;
tournament shortened to 54 holes)

	SCORES			TOTAL	MONEY
Lu Hsi Chuen	67	76	69	212	US$17,000
John Jacobs	70	76	67	213	8,335
Curt Byrum	70	71	72	213	8,335
Sheng Chung Shyan	70	75	69	214	4,712
Lu Chien Soon	69	73	72	214	4,712
Hsu Sheng San	71	72	72	215	3,060
Kuo Chi Hsiung	71	72	72	215	3,060
Yu Chin Han	67	72	76	215	3,060
Hsieh Min Nan	70	74	72	216	2,074
Wayne Smith	68	74	74	216	1,952
Lai Chung Hui	70	73	73	216	2,074
Tsao Chien Teng	70	77	71	218	1,734
Mike Allen	70	74	74	218	1,632
Hsieh Yu Shu	70	78	71	219	1,476
Hsu Tien Lai	72	74	73	219	1,476
Katsuyoshi Tomori	72	73	74	219	1,476
Mark Aebli	71	75	74	220	1,160
Kazuo Kanayama	73	72	75	220	1,160
Per Arne Brostedt	71	74	75	220	1,160
Wong Teh Chong	69	75	76	220	1,233
Mike Cunning	68	75	77	220	1,160
Alan Pate	74	75	72	221	1,030
Art Russell	69	77	75	221	1,030

	SCORES			TOTAL	MONEY
Duffy Waldorf	73	78	70	221	1,030
Ho Ming Chung	72	79	70	221	1,094
Lin Kuo Chen	72	77	73	222	974
Ted Lehmann	72	77	73	222	917
John Clifford	72	75	75	222	917
Lai Chung Jen	71	73	78	222	974

Korean Open

Nam Seoul Country Club, Seoul, South Korea　　　　　　　　　April 17–20
Par 36–36 – 72; 6,861 yards　　　　　　　　　　　　　　purse, US$130,000

	SCORES				TOTAL	MONEY
Tsao Chin Teng	71	67	71	71	280	US$21,500
Hsieh Yu Shu	68	73	69	71	281	14,400
Oh Jong Man	73	71	71	67	282	8,120
Peter Fowler	73	66	73	73	285	6,500
Lu Hsi Chuen	71	71	71	75	288	4,275
Chen Tze Chung	72	70	71	75	288	4,275
Koichi Suzuki	75	76	68	69	288	4,275
Cho Chul Sang	73	72	69	74	288	4,275
Lee Myung Ha	70	74	73	72	289	2,900
Ho Ming Chung	75	73	71	71	290	2,200
Jim Rutledge	78	71	73	68	290	2,200
Ossie Moore	72	71	77	70	290	2,200
Wayne Smith	74	73	69	74	290	2,200
Rodger Davis	71	76	71	72	290	2,200
Gi lai Hwa	78	70	70	72	290	2,200
Mark Aebli	75	74	72	70	291	1,700
Tommy Armour III	73	76	71	71	291	1,700
Choi Sang Ho	74	72	72	73	291	1,700
Kim Young II	71	73	74	73	291	1,700
Shen Chung Shyan	72	70	75	75	292	1,520
John Clifford	75	73	70	74	292	1,520
Hsieh Yung Yo	74	72	74	72	292	1,520
Li Wen Shen	72	72	75	74	293	1,351
K. Miyata	74	70	74	75	293	1,351
Jim Hallet	77	73	70	73	293	1,351
Alan Pate	74	70	72	77	293	1,351
Kwak Heung Soo	72	74	77	70	293	1,351
Choi Yoon Soo	75	75	72	71	293	1,351
Kuo Chi Hsiung	70	76	75	73	294	1,108
Lin Chia	78	70	73	73	294	1,108
Shimon Takamatsu	70	77	69	78	294	1,108
Motomasa Aoki	72	76	74	72	294	1,108
Mitch Thomas	79	70	70	54	294	1,108
Hahn Chang Sang	72	75	75	72	294	1,108
Kim II Soon	78	73	71	72	294	1,108

Dunlop International

Ibaraki Golf Club, Ina, Japan
Par 36–36 – 72; 7,163 yards

April 24–27
purse, ¥50,000,000

	SCORES			TOTAL	MONEY
Hideto Shigenobu	74	67	68	72	281	¥9,000,000
David Ishii	69	72	72	70	283	4,200,000
Masahiro Kuramoto	64	70	75	74	283	4,200,000
Wayne Smith	72	68	68	76	284	2,400,000
Eitaro Deguchi	67	74	74	70	285	1,630,000
Yoshikazu Yokoshima	72	72	67	74	285	1,630,000
Graham Marsh	69	72	68	76	285	1,630,000
Noboru Sugai	67	70	71	77	285	1,630,000
Masashi Ozaki	70	67	70	78	285	1,630,000
Naomichi Ozaki	70	68	75	73	286	1,125,000
Katsuji Hasegawa	71	69	69	77	286	1,125,000
Tony Grimes	68	71	73	75	287	815,000
Lin Chia	72	69	72	74	287	815,000
Curt Byrum	70	72	70	75	287	815,000
Tsuneyuki Nakajima	70	69	70	78	287	815,000
Brian Jones	71	75	71	71	288	585,000
Toru Nakamura	70	75	72	71	288	585,000
Masaji Kusakabe	73	72	71	72	288	585,000
Peter Fowler	73	72	68	75	288	585,000
Art Russell	72	68	76	73	289	470,000
Jim Hallet	72	73	70	74	289	470,000
John Clifford	77	67	71	74	289	470,000
Koichi Suzuki	72	71	68	78	289	470,000
Tracy Nakazaki	72	72	74	72	290	420,000
Pat Horgan	68	73	73	76	290	420,000
Hisao Inoue	66	72	69	83	290	420,000
Soiichi Sato	73	73	71	74	291	370,285
Gary Webb	69	73	75	74	291	370,285
John Burckle	74	68	74	75	291	370,285
Kazuo Kanayama	75	69	72	75	291	370,285
Pete Izumikawa	75	69	71	76	291	370,285
Lyao Kuo Chih	70	69	75	77	291	370,285
Tommy Armour III	73	65	71	82	291	370,285

Shizuoka Open

Shizuoka Country Club, Hamaoka Course, Shizuoka
Par 72; 6,912 yards

March 20–23
purse, ¥30,000,000

	SCORES			TOTAL	MONEY
Yoshiaki Omachi	71	71	76	36	254	¥6,300,000
Teruo Sugihara	76	71	71	36	254	3,500,000
Hsieh Min Nan	76	69	73	37	255	2,380,000
Seiichi Kanai	74	73	71	38	256	1,446,666
Murakami Takashi	74	73	72	37	256	1,446,666
Yamamoto Yoshitaka	77	69	73	37	256	1,446,666
Kurihara Takashi	75	69	72	41	257	1,067,500
Niizeki Yoshimi	75	71	75	36	257	1,067,500
Takahashi Katsunari	76	70	77	39	258	729,400
Eitaro Deguchi	75	69	75	39	298	729,400

	SCORES				TOTAL	MONEY
Katsuji Hasegawa	74	77	70	37	258	729,400
Maruyama Tomohiro	81	68	72	37	258	729,400
Yasuhiro Miyamoto	77	74	74	33	258	729,400
Teruo Suzuki	78	71	73	37	259	504,000
Saburo Fujiki	80	73	71	35	259	504,000
Shinsaku Maeda	77	72	72	38	259	504,000
Naomichi Ozaki	83	70	69	38	260	372,400
Toshiharu Kawada	79	74	74	37	260	372,400
Seiji Kusakabe	75	70	76	39	260	372,400
Yutaka Hagawa	77	73	71	39	260	372,400
Nobumitsu Yuhara	77	71	73	39	260	372,400
Motomasa Aoki	77	74	70	40	261	302,400
Futoshi Irino	74	72	76	39	261	302,400
Koiichi Uehara	73	74	75	39	261	302,400
Masashi Ozaki	74	70	73	44	261	302,400
Haruo Yasuda	74	77	73	37	261	302,400
Tsutomu Irie	80	69	78	39	262	276,500
Mitoshi Tomita	77	75	70	40	262	276,500
Koiichi Inoue	76	73	76	38	263	259,000
Yoshihiko Nakada	81	71	75	36	263	259,000
Akira Yabe	78	73	74	38	263	259,000

Pocari Sweat Open

Hakuryuko Country Club, Hiroshima Prefecture
Par 71; 6,769 yards

April 10–13
purse, ¥40,000,000

	SCORES				TOTAL	MONEY
Hajime Meshiai	71	68	73	65	277	¥7,200,000
Nobumitsu Yuhara	73	68	68	69	278	3,360,000
Ian Baker-Finch	67	74	70	67	278	3,360,000
Mike Ferguson	76	66	68	69	279	1,760,000
Ossie Moore	72	72	71	64	279	1,760,000
Akiyoshi Omachi	71	68	69	72	280	1,168,000
Yoshitaka Yamamoto	70	72	67	71	280	1,168,000
Yoshimi Niizeki	71	73	68	68	280	1,168,000
Ikuo Shirahama	69	68	73	70	280	1,168,000
Tateo Ozaki	67	72	71	70	280	1,168,000
Seiichi Kanai	73	70	69	69	281	768,000
Toru Nakamura	70	72	68	71	281	768,000
Haruo Yasuda	73	72	67	70	282	554,666
Tsutomu Irie	70	72	69	71	282	554,666
Namio Takasu	73	70	68	71	282	554,666
Koiichi Suzuki	71	72	72	67	282	554,666
Norio Mikami	70	71	68	73	282	554,666
Hiroshi Makino	72	68	72	70	282	554,666
Teruo Sugihara	74	70	72	67	283	384,000
Yasuhiro Miyamoto	70	72	71	70	283	384,000
Yasuhiro Funatogawa	70	71	72	70	283	384,000
Toyotake Nakao	72	71	67	73	283	384,000
Brian Jones	72	67	74	70	283	384,000
Masashi Ozaki	73	69	69	73	284	336,000
Koiichi Inoue	75	70	70	69	284	336,000
Masahiro Kuramoto	72	72	69	71	284	336,000
Katsunari Takahashi	71	72	71	71	285	304,000
Akira Ishihara	70	72	68	75	285	304,000

	SCORES				TOTAL	MONEY
Joji Furuki	73	67	73	72	285	304,000
Keiichi Kobayashi	69	72	73	71	285	304,000
Nobuhiro Yoshino	72	72	70	71	285	304,000

Bridgestone Aso Open

Aso Golf Club, Kunamoto   April 17–20
Par 72; 7,036 yards   purse, ¥35,000,000

	SCORES				TOTAL	MONEY
Brian Jones	70	69	67	34	240	¥6,300,000
Nobumitsu Yuhara	69	69	68	35	241	3,500,000
Masashi Ozaki	70	70	69	34	243	2,380,000
Namio Takasu	67	69	72	36	244	1,540,000
Naomichi Ozaki	68	70	70	36	244	1,540,000
Tomohiro Maruyama	73	69	67	36	245	968,333
Seiji Ebihara	70	67	74	34	245	968,333
Joji Furuki	72	68	71	34	245	968,333
David Ishii	70	73	67	35	245	968,333
Toshimitsu Kai	72	69	70	34	245	968,333
Haruhito Yamamoto	72	73	67	33	245	968,333
Eitaro Deguchi	70	71	72	34	247	616,000
Tadami Ueno	73	67	74	33	247	616,000
Teruo Shugihara	69	68	74	37	248	504,000
Koiichi Uemura	71	72	68	37	248	504,000
Hisao Inoue	74	72	67	35	248	504,000
Hsieh Min Nan	75	69	71	34	249	372,400
Ikuo Shirahama	71	73	71	34	249	372,400
Masaji Kusakabe	72	71	71	35	249	372,400
Isao Isozaki	69	74	72	34	249	372,400
Graham Marsh	70	72	69	38	249	372,400
Hiroshi Makino	71	69	71	39	250	310,333
Pete Izumikawa	72	72	71	35	250	310,333
Yoshino Mizumaki	70	71	72	37	250	310,333
Koiichi Inoue	74	71	71	35	251	287,000
Yurio Akitomi	72	73	70	36	251	287,000
Kazuhiro Takami	71	72	71	37	251	287,000
Akiyoshi Omachi	73	72	69	38	252	266,000
Katsuji Hasegawa	71	72	71	38	252	266,000
Masami Itoh	73	67	74	38	252	266,000
Yasuhiro Miyamoto	71	70	74	38	253	236,833
Yasuhiro Funatogawa	75	71	71	36	253	236,833
Satoshi Higashi	73	70	73	37	253	236,833
Noboru Sugai	69	72	72	40	253	236,833
Noriichi Kawakami	75	71	73	34	253	236,833
Hiroshi Ishii	73	67	73	40	253	236,833
Yoshitaka Yamamoto	67	72	77	38	254	203,000
Shinsaku Maeda	71	75	74	34	254	203,000
Akira Ishihara	71	73	73	37	254	203,000
Kinpachi Yoshimura	71	74	74	35	254	203,000
Hisashi Kaji	73	73	74	34	254	203,000
Toshiya Shibuya	68	74	76	36	254	203,000
*Tsunehisa Yamamoto	72	75	72	35	254	
Tateo Ozaki	70	69	76	40	255	175,000
Toyotake Nakao	74	72	74	35	255	175,000
Kikuo Arai	71	71	76	37	255	175,000

		SCORES			TOTAL	MONEY
Masanobu Kimura	72	73	73	37	255	175,000
Futoshi Irie	73	72	75	36	256	161,000
Ian Baker-Finch	76	66	75	40	257	154,280
Yoshihisa Iwashita	73	70	79	35	257	154,280
Takafumi Ogawa	71	74	74	38	257	154,280
Susumu Hano	71	75	72	39	257	154,280
Shiro Yoshinari	73	73	76	35	257	154,280

Chunichi Crowns International

Nagoya Golf Club, Wago Course, Nagoya
Par 70; 6,492 yards

May 1–4
purse, ¥80,000,000

		SCORES			TOTAL	MONEY
David Ishii	68	67	71	68	274	¥16,200,000
Tsuneyuki Nakajima	72	68	71	67	278	9,000,000
D. A. Weibring	70	69	69	71	279	6,120,000
Naomichi Ozaki	71	68	73	68	280	3,720,000
Koichi Suzuki	73	70	73	64	280	3,720,000
Terry Gale	69	73	72	66	280	3,720,000
Brian Jones	71	68	73	69	281	2,226,000
Masashi Ozaki	69	73	71	68	281	2,226,000
Noboru Sugai	70	70	69	72	281	2,226,000
Koiichi Inoue	75	67	67	72	281	2,226,000
Katsunari Takahashi	77	66	72	66	281	2,226,000
Pete Izumikawa	74	71	69	67	281	2,226,000
Saburo Fujiki	71	71	71	69	282	1,404,000
Kazuo Yoshikawa	69	67	71	75	282	1,404,000
Doug Tewell	71	69	70	72	282	1,404,000
Ian Baker-Finch	70	77	67	69	283	1,022,400
Namio Takasu	68	72	73	70	283	1,022,400
Yoshimi Niizeki	71	70	75	67	283	1,022,400
Koiichi Uehara	73	72	71	67	283	1,022,400
Tom Kite	72	74	74	63	283	1,022,400
*Takahiro Nakagawa	71	69	71	72	283	
Hideto Shigenobu	73	72	69	70	284	781,714
Eitaro Deguchi	72	75	70	67	284	781,714
Yasuhiro Miyamoto	71	71	72	70	284	781,714
Toru Nakamura	76	66	71	71	284	781,714
Tateo Ozaki	70	71	73	70	284	781,714
Hiroshi Ishii	71	72	73	68	284	781,714
Satsuki Takahashi	72	71	70	71	284	781,714
Masahiro Kuramoto	70	72	73	70	285	675,000
Motomasa Aoki	70	71	72	72	285	675,000
Choi Yoon Soon	69	75	70	71	285	675,000
Akimitsu Tokita	74	68	74	69	285	675,000
Teruo Sugihara	71	71	70	74	286	615,600
Shinsaku Maeda	74	69	74	69	286	615,600
Kinpachi Yoshimura	72	70	72	72	286	615,600
Akiyoshi Omachi	74	73	68	72	287	543,600
Yoshihisa Iwashita	70	71	74	72	287	543,600
Toyotake Nakao	72	75	73	67	287	543,600
Futoshi Irino	72	73	72	70	287	543,600
Fujio Kobayashi	75	70	70	72	287	543,600
Hsu Sheng San	70	70	75	72	287	543,600
Clarence Rose	68	73	73	73	287	543,600
Masaji Kusakabe	74	69	69	76	288	471,600

	SCORES				TOTAL	MONEY
Seiiji Ebihara	71	73	72	72	288	471,600
Mamoru Kondo	72	73	75	68	288	471,600
Ikuo Shirahama	74	69	74	72	289	423,000
Yutaka Suzuki	71	73	74	71	289	423,000
Hsieh Yung Yo	71	71	74	73	289	423,000
Shigeru Uchida	74	72	72	71	289	423,000
Hsieh Min Nan	73	73	73	71	290	396,000
Yoshitaka Yamamoto	74	71	71	74	290	396,000
Graham Marsh	77	70	74	69	290	396,000

Fuji Sankei Classic

Kawana Hotel Golf Club, Ito
Par 71; 6,694 yards

May 8–11
purse, ¥40,000,000

	SCORES				TOTAL	MONEY
Masashi Ozaki	65	72	71	72	279	¥7,200,000
David Ishii	67	72	71	70	280	4,000,000
Masahiro Kuramoto	65	75	73	69	282	2,320,000
Hiroshi Ishii	65	70	75	72	282	2,320,000
Terry Gale	69	71	73	70	283	1,600,000
Tsuneyuki Nakajima	68	74	73	69	284	1,440,000
Nobumitsu Yuhara	71	71	74	69	285	1,220,000
Haruo Yasuda	69	73	73	70	285	1,220,000
Yasuhiro Funatogawa	75	70	71	71	287	920,000
Yoshimi Niizeki	67	74	75	71	287	920,000
Kazuhiro Kono	68	74	69	76	287	920,000
Shinsaku Maeda	69	74	74	71	288	708,000
Kikuo Arai	68	74	70	76	288	708,000
Yoshitaka Yamamoto	70	71	72	76	289	600,000
Tateo Ozaki	68	73	72	76	289	600,000
Yoshihisa Iwashita	72	74	72	72	290	528,000
Koiichi Suzuki	73	70	78	70	291	448,000
Namio Takasu	71	75	71	74	291	448,000
Toyotake Nakao	72	76	74	69	291	448,000
Teruo Suzumura	72	72	72	76	292	344,800
Naomichi Ozaki	71	73	73	75	292	344,800
Tsutomu Irie	69	74	75	74	292	344,800
Motomasa Aoki	72	75	76	69	292	344,800
Hsieh Min Nan	74	73	73	72	292	344,800
Kinpachi Yoshimura	65	73	76	78	292	344,800
Kenji Sogame	77	71	69	75	292	344,800
Saburo Fujiki	71	73	77	71	292	344,800
Tsukasa Watanabe	73	73	75	71	292	344,800
Isao Isozaki	71	75	71	75	292	344,800
Kazuo Yoshikawa	67	74	77	75	293	284,400
Toru Nakamura	69	70	80	74	293	284,400
Tomohiro Maruyama	70	70	75	78	293	284,400
Toshiharu Kawada	71	76	75	71	293	284,400

Japan Match Play Championship

Mito Golf Club, Ibaraki Prefecture
Par 72; 6,687 yards

May 15–18
purse, ¥40,000,000

FIRST ROUND

Tsuneyuki Nakajima defeated Tadao Nakamura, 4 and 2.
Katsuji Hasegawa defeated Akira Yabe, 6 and 4.
Naomichi Ozaki defeated Eitaro Deguchi, 3 and 1.
Horoshi Makino defeated Masashi Ozaki, 4 and 3.
Seiichi Kanai defeated Teruo Suzuki, 3 and 2.
Motomasa Aoki defeated Yoshitaka Yamamoto, 2 and 1.
Teruo Sugihara defeated Hideto Shigenobu, 5 and 4.
Koichi Suzuki defeated Kikuo Arai, 3 and 2.
Keiichi Kobayashi defeated Masahiro Kuramoto, 1 up.
Yoshihisa Iwashita defeated Seijii Ebihara, 1 up, 24 holes.
Katsunari Takahashi defeated Ysauhiro Funatogawa, 1 up.
Toru Nakamura defeated Koichi Inoue, 5 and 4.
Tateo Ozaki defeated Shinsaku Maeda, 3 and 1.
Hsieh Min Nan defeated Hajime Meshiai, 1 up.
Isao Aoki defeated Tsutomu Irie, 4 and 3.
Koichi Uehara defeated Nobumitsu Yuhara, 2 and 1.
(Each losing player received ¥200,000.)

SECOND ROUND

Nakajima defeated Hasegawa, 4 and 3.
Naomichi Ozaki defeated Makino, 5 and 3.
Kanai defeated Motomasa Aoki, 1 up.
Suzuki defeated Sugihara, 2 up.
Kobayashi defeated Iwashita, 2 and 1.
Takahashi defeated Nakamura, 2 up.
Tateo Ozaki defeated Hsieh, 2 and 1.
Uehara defeated Isao Aoki, 2 and 1.
(Each losing player received ¥400,000.)

THIRD ROUND

Nakajima defeated Naomichi Ozaki, 2 up.
Suzuki defeated Kanai, 1 up, 20 holes.
Kobayashi defeated Takahashi, 1 up, 19 holes.
Uehara defeated Tateo Ozaki, 2 and 1.
(Each losing player received ¥800,000.)

SEMI-FINALS

Nakajima defeated Suzuki, 3 and 1.
Kobayashi defeated Uehara, 1 up, 37 holes.

PLAYOFF FOR THIRD/FOURTH PLACES

Uehara defeated Suzuki, 2 up.
(Uehara received ¥3,000,000; Suzuki ¥2,000,000.)

FINALS

Nakajima defeated Kobayashi, 6 and 5.
(Nakajima received ¥10,000,000; Kobayashi ¥5,000,000.)

Pepsi Ube

Ube Country Club, North Course, Yamaguchi
Par 72; 7,049 yards

May 22–25
purse, ¥40,000,000

	SCORES				TOTAL	MONEY
Naomichi Ozaki	71	69	68	68	276	¥7,200,000
Fujio Kobayashi	71	68	68	70	277	4,000,000
Hsieh Min Nan	72	74	65	69	280	2,720,000
Seiichi Kanai	72	66	73	70	281	1,920,000
Hiroshi Makino	71	72	70	70	283	1,440,000
Satoshi Higashi	71	75	68	69	283	1,440,000
Yurio Akitomi	75	70	68	70	283	1,440,000
Yoshimi Niizeki	73	71	71	69	284	1,040,000
Shinsaku Maeda	70	73	69	72	284	1,040,000
Joji Furuki	72	72	68	72	284	1,040,000
David Ishii	72	70	73	70	285	656,000
Tsuneyuki Nakajima	70	70	75	70	285	656,000
Katsunari Takahashi	74	71	70	70	285	656,000
Tadami Ueno	68	73	74	70	285	656,000
Norio Mikami	71	73	71	70	285	656,000
Yasushi Katayama	70	74	72	69	285	656,000
Nobumitsu Yuhara	73	70	73	70	286	464,000
Tadao Nakamura	72	70	73	71	286	464,000
Yoshitaka Yamamoto	73	74	71	69	287	384,000
Hiroshi Ishii	73	69	72	73	287	384,000
Kikuo Arai	71	69	79	68	287	384,000
Seiki Okuda	73	72	70	72	287	384,000
Chen Tze Ming	75	71	71	70	287	384,000
Keiichi Kobayashi	69	70	76	73	288	332,000
Koiichi Inoue	68	74	72	74	288	332,000
Satsuki Takahashi	72	74	71	71	288	332,000
Ian Stanley	69	74	73	72	288	332,000
Motomasa Aoki	74	72	72	71	289	300,000
Futoshi Irino	72	75	72	70	289	300,000
Yoshinori Ichioka	71	74	71	73	289	300,000
Stewart Ginn	70	71	75	73	289	300,000

Mitsubishi Galant

Oharai Golf Club, Ibaraki Prefecture
Par 72; 7,190 yards

May 29–June 1
purse, ¥56,000,000

	SCORES				TOTAL	MONEY
Tsuneyuki Nakajima	73	68	69	70	280	¥10,080,000
Chen Tze Ming	70	69	76	66	281	5,600,000
Terry Gale	71	72	67	72	282	3,808,000
Masashi Ozaki	72	73	69	69	283	2,688,000
Kikuo Arai	75	73	69	67	284	2,128,000
Isao Aoki	72	69	73	70	284	2,128,000
Seiichi Kanai	67	70	71	77	285	1,792,000
Masahiro Kuramoto	73	74	69	70	286	1,540,000
Saburo Fujiki	74	71	75	66	286	1,540,000
Kazushije Kono	73	70	72	72	287	1,288,000
Koiichi Suzuki	77	72	71	68	288	883,085
Yoshimi Niizeki	72	72	70	74	288	883,085

	SCORES				TOTAL	MONEY
Yoshihisa Iwashita	74	72	70	72	288	883,085
Mamoru Kondo	73	73	71	71	288	885,085
Toshiharu Kawada	72	70	73	73	288	885,085
Lu Hsi Chuen	74	69	71	74	288	885,085
Teruo Nakamura	72	75	70	71	288	885,085
David Ishii	77	72	71	69	289	576,800
Yasuhiro Miyamoto	73	73	71	72	289	576,800
Seuiji Ebihara	72	72	74	71	289	576,800
Yutaka Suzuki	74	72	72	71	289	576,800
Hiroshi Makino	76	70	70	74	290	496,533
Hisao Inoue	71	75	71	73	290	496,533
Masami Morishita	76	79	75	69	290	496,533
Hideto Shigenobu	76	70	76	69	291	431,200
Brian Jones	72	71	72	76	291	431,200
Noboru Sugai	72	72	74	73	291	431,200
Katsunari Takahashi	74	72	75	70	291	431,200
Koichi Inoue	74	72	77	68	291	431,200
Akira Yabe	73	74	73	71	291	431,200
Masahiro Shioda	71	72	78	70	291	431,200
Norio Adachi	74	74	68	75	291	431,200

Tohoku Classic

Nishi Sendai Country Club, Miyagi
Par 72; 6,993 yards

June 5–8
purse, ¥40,000,000

	SCORES				TOTAL	MONEY
Teruo Sugihara	70	69	70	71	280	¥7,200,000
Namio Takasu	73	73	66	70	282	4,000,000
Graham Marsh	71	70	70	72	283	2,320,000
Isao Aoki	73	71	69	70	283	2,320,000
Kikuo Arai	69	71	72	72	284	1,440,000
Tateo Ozaki	72	68	71	73	284	1,440,000
Taisei Inagaki	69	69	74	72	284	1,440,000
Brian Jones	70	71	72	72	285	1,100,000
Hiroshi Ishii	71	73	72	69	285	1,100,000
Shinsaku Maeda	68	74	72	72	286	782,000
Yasuhiro Miyamoto	72	73	69	72	286	782,000
Satsuki Takahashi	69	74	72	71	286	782,000
Kenji Mori	73	74	71	68	286	782,000
Ian Stanley	73	74	72	68	287	600,000
Stewart Ginn	77	68	74	68	287	600,000
Nobumitsu Yuhara	73	73	73	69	288	485,333
Suzuki Koiichi	71	67	78	72	288	485,333
Mitoshi Tomita	73	73	73	69	288	485,333
Akiyoshi Omachi	72	71	72	74	289	366,000
Noboru Sugai	72	73	71	73	289	366,000
Yoshitaka Yamamoto	71	73	70	75	289	366,000
Masaji Kusakabe	73	73	71	72	289	366,000
Takashi Murakami	71	69	72	77	289	366,000
Akira Yabe	71	71	72	75	289	366,000
Masahiro Shioda	70	74	73	72	289	366,000
Kazuhiro Takami	72	70	69	78	289	366,000
Yoshimi Niizeki	72	72	73	73	290	289,000
Koiichi Inoue	70	75	72	73	290	289,000
Eitaro Deguchi	75	72	73	70	290	289,000
Hiroshi Makino	73	73	73	71	290	289,000

	SCORES				TOTAL	MONEY
Pete Izumikawa	75	69	73	73	290	289,000
Kazushige Kono	73	72	72	73	290	289,000
Tsutomu Irie	73	73	74	70	290	289,000
Lu Hsi Chuen	76	69	72	73	290	289,000
Norio Suzuki	73	74	73	70	290	289,000

Sapporo Tokyu Open

Sapporo Kokusai Country Club, Hokkaido
Par 72; 6,949 yards

June 12–15
purse, ¥40,000,000

	SCORES				TOTAL	MONEY
Isao Aoki	65	67	72	69	273	¥7,200,000
Shinsaku Maeda	69	68	70	69	276	4,000,000
Seiichi Kanai	67	70	73	67	277	2,720,000
Masaji Kusakabe	67	71	70	70	278	1,920,000
Teruo Sugihara	68	71	71	70	280	1,520,000
Kazushige Kono	76	70	68	66	280	1,520,000
David Ishii	75	73	67	67	282	1,160,000
Namio Takasu	72	72	69	69	282	1,160,000
Yurio Akitomi	71	70	73	68	282	1,160,000
Saburo Fujiki	71	71	73	69	284	920,000
Masahiro Kuramoto	70	69	76	70	285	768,000
Teruo Suzuki	71	76	67	71	285	768,000
Masashi Ozaki	71	69	75	71	286	624,000
Hiroshi Ishii	73	72	71	70	286	624,000
Toru Nakamura	73	71	71	71	286	624,000
Yoshikazu Yokoshima	73	72	70	72	287	504,000
Norio Suzuki	71	71	73	72	287	504,000
Brian Jones	74	73	70	71	288	394,667
Koichi Inoue	72	75	69	72	288	394,667
Hiroshi Makino	69	71	72	76	288	394,667
Yasuhiro Miyamoto	72	71	71	74	288	394,667
Yasuhiro Funatogawa	69	72	76	71	288	394,667
Tsukasa Watanabe	74	74	69	71	288	394,667
Koichi Suzuki	74	72	73	70	289	340,000
Mitoshi Tomita	72	75	69	73	289	340,000
Hideto Shigenobu	72	70	74	74	200	320,000
Graham Marsh	69	74	75	72	290	320,000
Pete Izimikawa	69	75	72	74	290	320,000
Hsieh Min Nan	74	72	73	72	291	296,000
Tateo Ozaki	70	76	72	73	291	296,000
Kazuo Yoshikawa	69	72	73	77	291	296,000

Yomiuri Sapporo Beer Open

Yomiuri Country Club, Osaka, Hyogo Prefecture
Par 73; 7,063 yards

June 19–22
purse, ¥50,000,000

	SCORES				TOTAL	MONEY
Koichi Suzuki	68	69	67	69	273	¥9,000,000
Brian Jones	69	68	69	69	275	5,000,000
Tsuneyuki Nakajima	71	67	69	69	276	2,900,000
Teruo Sugihara	71	69	69	67	276	2,900,000

	SCORES				TOTAL	MONEY
Yoshimi Niizeki	69	71	68	69	277	2,000,000
Masahiro Kuramoto	70	68	71	69	278	1,700,000
Satoshi Higashi	67	74	70	67	278	1,700,000
Naomichi Ozaki	66	70	76	68	279	1,300,000
Isao Aoki	69	69	73	68	279	1,300,000
Saburo Fujiki	70	71	73	65	279	1,300,000
Katsunari Takahashi	71	72	70	67	280	885,000
Toru Nakamura	70	69	70	71	280	885,000
Pete Izumikawa	70	70	69	71	280	885,000
Futoshi Irino	73	71	68	68	280	885,000
Akiyoshi Omachi	72	67	72	70	281	660,000
Graham Marsh	71	73	68	69	281	660,000
Haruo Yasuda	73	69	69	70	281	660,000
David Ishii	73	68	72	69	282	515,000
Terry Gale	70	67	72	73	282	515,000
Hsieh Yung Yo	73	70	70	69	282	515,000
Osamu Machino	70	74	72	66	282	515,000
Satsuki Takahashi	71	71	71	70	283	450,000
Nobuo Serizawa	76	68	69	70	283	450,000
Seiichi Kanai	70	72	69	73	284	415,000
Kikuo Arai	73	67	71	73	284	415,000
Hiroshi Makino	70	67	71	76	284	415,000
Hisao Inoue	69	71	70	74	284	415,000
Masashi Ozaki	70	72	71	72	285	370,000
Hideto Shigenobu	71	71	74	69	285	370,000
Namio Takasu	73	71	71	70	285	370,000
Kazuo Yoshikawa	70	71	71	73	285	370,000
Yoshinori Shikota	74	70	67	74	285	370,000

Mizuno Open

Tokinodai Country Club, Ishikawa Prefecture

Par 72; 6,874 yards

June 26–29

purse, ¥50,000,000

	SCORES				TOTAL	MONEY
Tsuneyuki Nakajima	69	65	68	37	239	¥9,000,000
Tsukasa Watanabe	67	71	70	37	245	5,000,000
Tsutomu Irie	70	71	69	36	246	2,900,000
Seiji Ebihara	68	67	70	41	246	2,900,000
Hiroshi Makino	71	76	66	34	247	1,800,000
Brian Jones	74	68	69	36	247	1,800,000
Hideto Shigenobu	71	66	71	39	247	1,800,000
Yoichi Yamamoto	75	70	70	33	248	1,164,000
David Ishii	72	71	69	36	248	1,164,000
Motomasa Aoki	70	71	71	36	248	1,164,000
Hiroshi Ishii	69	72	71	36	248	1,164,000
Yoshihisa Iwashita	71	71	68	38	248	1,164,000
Akiyoshi Omachi	73	71	70	35	249	780,000
Naomichi Ozaki	73	68	70	38	249	780,000
Toru Nakamura	74	70	68	37	249	780,000
Toshimitsu Kai	75	70	68	37	250	585,000
Yusuke Sugita	71	72	69	38	250	585,000
Nobumitsu Yuhara	72	71	71	36	250	585,000
Isao Aoki	74	70	69	37	250	585,000
Pete Izumikawa	74	69	74	35	252	470,000
Masashi Ozaki	70	76	68	38	252	470,000

	SCORES				TOTAL	MONEY
Yasuhiro Miyamoto	71	75	71	35	252	470,000
Namio Takasu	73	71	71	37	252	470,000
Tomohiro Maruyama	74	70	72	37	253	415,000
Toyotake Nakao	74	71	71	37	253	415,000
Teruo Sugihara	73	68	73	39	253	415,000
Saburo Fujiki	70	73	73	37	253	415,000
Yoshitaka Yamamoto	75	69	74	36	254	375,000
Tateo Ozaki	72	71	73	38	254	375,000
Shinsaku Maeda	78	69	72	35	254	375,000
Isao Isozaki	74	72	71	37	254	375,000

Kansai PGA Championship

Kibi Country Club, Okayama Prefecture
Par 72
(Shortened to 54 holes because of rain.)

July 3–6
purse, ¥20,000,000

	SCORES			TOTAL	MONEY
Teruo Sugihara	68	68	67	203	¥3,600,000
Kinpachi Yoshimura	70	68	67	205	1,680,000
Hiroshi Ishii	67	68	70	205	1,680,000
Masahiro Kuramoto	68	70	68	206	880,000
Shinsaku Maeda	66	69	71	206	880,000
Akio Toyota	71	69	67	207	720,000
Tadao Nakamura	71	68	69	208	640,000
Toshimitsu Kai	71	69	69	209	520,000
Masahiro Shioda	68	71	70	209	520,000
Misao Yamamoto	69	69	71	209	520,000
Yoshitaka Yamamoto	70	66	74	210	400,000
Kenji Sokame	68	73	70	211	368,000
Eitaro Deguchi	67	76	69	212	312,000
Toshiharu Kusaka	69	73	70	212	312,000
Atsushi Ikehara	70	70	72	212	312,000
Yasuhiro Miyamoto	71	72	70	213	252,000
Hisashi Kaji	71	72	70	213	252,000
Akimitsu Tokita	73	72	69	214	210,667
Takayoshi Nishikawa	70	71	73	214	210,667
Yoshinori Ichioka	72	69	73	214	210,666
Nobuhiro Yoshino	69	76	70	215	184,000
Hisao Inoue	72	73	70	215	184,000
Tsutomu Irie	72	71	72	215	184,000
Masamitsu Oguri	73	73	70	216	170,000
Shigeru Uchida	71	71	74	216	170,000
Hiroshi Oku	73	72	72	217	146,600
Hideto Shigenobu	73	71	73	217	146,600
Katsumi Hirai	71	73	73	217	146,600
Chen Chien Chin	72	71	74	217	146,600
Katsuyoshi Tomori	73	70	74	217	146,600
Masanori Imakura	72	71	74	217	146,600
Tatsuya Shiraishi	71	72	74	217	146,600
Toshihiro Matsuda	74	73	70	217	146,600
Kiyoshi Nomura	69	73	75	217	146,600
Hatsutoshi Sakai	70	72	75	217	146,600

Kanto PGA Championship

Miyagino Golf Club, Miyagi Prefecture
Par 72

July 3–6
purse, ¥30,000,000

	SCORES				TOTAL	MONEY
Tsuneyuki Nakajima	68	69	65	67	269	¥5,400,000
Naomichi Ozaki	69	68	67	68	272	3,000,000
Isao Aoki	68	68	66	71	273	2,040,000
Akiyoshi Omachi	68	66	71	69	274	1,440,000
Saburo Fujiki	71	68	65	71	275	1,200,000
Nobumitsu Yuhara	69	68	69	70	276	1,080,000
Haruo Yasuda	71	68	73	65	277	960,000
Noboru Sugai	68	73	69	68	278	735,000
Motomasa Aoki	74	66	70	68	278	735,000
Tateo Ozaki	67	67	74	70	278	735,000
Yoshihisa Iwashita	71	69	69	69	278	735,000
Hidenori Nakajima	68	70	70	71	279	528,000
Hsieh Min Nan	70	69	70	70	279	528,000
Seiichi Kanai	71	70	71	68	280	468,000
Seiji Ebihara	68	71	69	73	281	432,000
Toshiharu Kawada	73	70	69	70	282	351,000
Masaji Kusakabe	70	70	70	72	282	351,000
Koji Nakajima	71	68	72	71	282	351,000
Katsunari Takahashi	68	71	75	68	282	351,000
Satsuki Takahashi	70	72	69	72	283	288,000
Yoshikazu Yokoshima	70	69	73	71	283	288,000
Toru Nakayama	75	69	69	70	283	288,000
Hajime Meshiai	71	70	72	71	284	252,000
Nobuo Serizawa	74	70	70	70	284	252,000
Akira Yabe	72	70	70	72	284	252,000
Koichi Suzuki	72	70	71	71	284	252,000
Takashi Murakami	71	72	68	73	284	252,000
Satoshi Higashi	71	70	71	73	285	231,000
Satoshi Ogawa	74	71	70	71	286	216,000
Isao Isozaki	72	70	73	71	286	216,000
Shoji Kikuchi	68	75	72	71	286	216,000

Japan PGA Championship

Nihon Line Golf Club, West Course, Gifu Prefecture
Par 72

July 24–27
purse, ¥50,000,000

	SCORES				TOTAL	MONEY
Isao Aoki	66	68	69	69	272	¥9,000,000
Masashi Ozaki	71	68	67	70	276	5,000,000
Toru Nakamura	74	68	70	65	277	3,400,000
Masaji Kusakabe	66	70	72	70	278	2,400,000
Tsuneyuki Nakajima	69	72	73	66	280	1,900,000
Masanobu Kimura	66	70	75	69	280	1,900,000
Joji Furuki	71	71	70	70	282	1,450,000
Futoshi Irino	70	67	71	74	282	1,450,000
Taisei Inagaki	68	71	73	70	282	1,450,000
Nobumitsu Yuhara	70	68	72	73	283	1,023,334
Katsuji Hasegawa	71	72	69	71	283	1,023,333
Masahiro Shioda	71	71	71	70	283	1,023,333

	SCORES				TOTAL	MONEY
Hiroshi Oku	69	68	73	74	284	750,000
Mamoru Kondo	71	74	68	71	284	750,000
Katsunari Takahashi	68	74	75	67	284	750,000
Isao Isozaki	69	72	70	73	284	750,000
Hajime Meshiai	72	70	72	71	285	482,000
Satoshi Higashi	67	73	76	69	285	482,000
Kazushige Kono	68	74	73	70	285	482,000
Norihiko Matsumoto	75	71	70	69	285	482,000
Shinsaku Maeda	70	75	71	69	285	482,000
Hisao Inoue	69	72	71	73	285	482,000
Naomichi Ozaki	73	71	73	68	285	482,000
Yoshihisa Iwashita	74	69	68	74	285	482,000
Nobuo Serizawa	69	73	72	71	285	482,000
Saburo Fujiki	73	73	67	72	285	482,000
Hisashi Suzumura	71	73	73	69	286	395,000
Seiji Ebihara	69	68	78	71	286	395,000
Toshimitsu Kai	74	69	73	71	287	360,000
Noboru Sugai	70	73	72	72	287	360,400
Teruo Sugihara	65	81	72	69	287	360,400
Masahiro Kuramoto	69	72	73	73	287	360,400
Yoshitaka Yamamoto	73	68	73	73	287	360,400
Tadashige Kusano	74	72	72	70	288	326,000
Koki Idoki	69	71	72	76	288	326,000
Minoru Kumabe	70	74	74	70	288	326,000
Tatsuya Shiraishi	72	74	75	68	289	298,000
Koji Nakajima	72	70	74	73	289	298,000
Misao Yamamoto	69	72	74	74	289	298,000
Yoichi Yamamoto	70	73	75	71	289	298,000
Hideto Shigenobu	70	74	72	74	290	266,000
Koichi Uehara	71	73	76	70	290	266,000
Hikaru Enomoto	73	67	74	76	290	266,000
Mitoshi Tomita	71	71	74	74	290	266,000
Yasuhiro Funatogawa	73	71	74	73	291	242,000
Takeshi Matsukawa	71	70	74	76	291	242,000
Shozo Miyamoto	73	68	76	75	292	223,200
Shigeru Kawamata	74	70	74	74	292	223,200
Keiichi Kobayashi	73	72	75	72	292	223,200
Kiyokuni Kimoto	70	73	74	75	292	223,200
Hiroshi Ishii	69	74	74	75	292	223,200

Niigata Open

Nagaoka Country Club, Nagaoka
Par 72, 6,917 yards

July 31–August 3
purse, ¥35,000,000

	SCORES				TOTAL	MONEY
David Ishii	68	70	66	72	276	¥6,300,000
Tateo Ozaki	68	68	71	70	277	3,500,000
Joji Furuki	71	72	65	71	279	2,030,000
Ikuo Shirahama	64	74	69	72	279	2,030,000
Aikyoshi Omachi	70	75	68	67	280	1,198,750
Seiichi Kanai	69	67	70	74	280	1,198,750
Masanobu Kimura	70	71	70	69	280	1,198,750
Koji Nakajima	70	68	71	71	280	1,198,750
Nobumitsu Yuhara	70	68	73	70	281	805,000
Seiji Ebihara	75	69	68	69	281	805,000

	SCORES				TOTAL	MONEY
Nobuhiro Yoshino	71	70	73	67	281	805,000
Toyotake Nakao	68	71	72	71	282	644,000
Teruo Sugihara	69	71	69	74	283	546,000
Kinpachi Yoshimura	69	68	71	75	283	546,000
Isao Isozaki	69	74	68	72	283	546,000
Brian Jones	69	72	70	73	284	387,333
Mamoru Kondo	70	71	68	75	284	387,333
Toshimitsu Kai	69	72	71	72	284	387,333
Tatsuya Shiraishi	69	71	72	72	284	387,333
Takashi Iwai	72	70	70	72	284	387,333
Kyokuni Kimoto	70	71	71	72	284	387,333
Saburo Fujiki	70	69	71	75	285	306,250
Yoshimi Niizeki	70	70	71	74	285	306,250
Pete Izumikawa	72	72	68	73	285	306,250
Katsuyoshi Tomori	72	70	70	73	285	306,250
Katsuji Hasegawa	72	71	72	71	286	283,500
Hideki Kikugawa	70	71	69	76	286	283,500
Toru Nakamura	72	70	71	74	287	255,733
Katsunari Takahashi	73	69	74	71	287	255,733
Yoshitaka Yamamoto	69	73	74	71	287	255,733
Motomasa Aoki	70	72	75	70	287	255,733
Takashi Murakami	70	74	73	70	287	255,733
Minoru Kawakami	71	74	71	71	287	255,733

Acom Doubles

Shigaraki Country Club, Shiga Prefecture
Par 72; 6,918 yards

August 7–10
purse, ¥45,000,000

	SCORES				TOTAL	MONEY (Team)
Hajime Meshiai/Satoshi Higashi	62	66	64	65	257	¥10,000,000
Brian Jones/Mike Ferguson	65	65	65	63	258	3,375,000
Kazushige Kono/Futoshi Irino	63	66	65	64	258	3,375,000
Saburo Fujiki/Yoshimi Niizeki	65	66	61	66	258	3,375,000
Kunio Hihama/Kenjiro Iwama	65	65	64	64	258	3,375,000
Namio Takasu/Seiji Ebihara	63	66	65	65	259	1,633,333
Isao Isozaki/Kosaku Shimada	64	64	64	67	259	1,633,333
Hideto Shigenobu/David Ishii	65	64	62	68	259	1,633,333
Lu Liang Huan/Lu Hsi Chuen	65	64	64	67	260	1,400,000
Koichi Inoue/Tadayoshi Ueno	67	61	68	65	261	1,114,000
Hisao Inoue/Shunichi Yamaguchi	63	65	67	66	261	1,114,000
Akio Kanemoto/Norio Mikami	63	68	64	66	261	1,114,000
Satsuki Takahashi/Yoshikazu Yokoshima	64	67	62	68	261	1,114,000
Kinpachi Yoshimura/Nobuhiro Yoshino	64	67	63	67	261	1,114,000
Nobuo Serizawa/Tomohiro Maruyama	64	67	65	66	262	806,666
Kiyokuni Kimoto/Shozo Miyamoto	64	66	65	67	262	806,666
Tatsuya Shiraishi/Masuaki Nakamura	65	65	64	68	262	806,666
Toru Nakamura/Toshiaki Nakagawa	65	63	68	67	263	700,000
Yoshihisa Iwashita/Shoji Kikuchi	63	66	65	67	263	700,000
Koichi Uehara/Noboru Sugai	67	64	67	66	264	620,000
Mitoshi Tomita/Noriichi Kawakami	65	67	64	68	264	620,000

	SCORES				TOTAL	MONEY
Akiyoshi Omachi/Pete Izumikawa	66	65	68	66	265	540,000
Eitaro Deguchi/Teruo Nakamura	64	65	67	69	265	540,000
Shinsaku Maeda/Kazuo Yoshikawa	63	68	67	69	267	480,000
Masahiro Shioda/Hiroaki Uenishi	64	67	67	68	268	440,000
Takashi Kurihara/Joji Furuki	64	67	69	69	269	400,000
Tsutomu Irie/Yurio Akitomi	66	66	65	73	270	370,000
Yoichi Yamamoto/Koki Idoki	66	66	70	68	270	370,000

Nikkei Cup/Torakichi Nakamura Memorial

Gamo Golf Club, Shiga Prefecture
Par 72

August 14–17
purse, ¥40,000,000

	SCORES				TOTAL	MONEY
Masashi Ozaki	68	66	68	66	268	¥7,200,000
Ikuo Shirahama	68	69	65	70	272	4,000,000
Hiroshi Makino	67	69	69	68	273	2,720,000
Kinpachi Yoshimura	66	66	70	72	274	1,920,000
Katsuji Hasegawa	67	67	73	68	275	1,600,000
Katsuyoshi Tomori	69	69	72	66	276	1,293,333
Masahiro Shioda	67	68	72	69	276	1,293,333
Nobuo Serizawa	71	68	68	69	276	1,293,333
Naomichi Ozaki	67	71	72	67	277	980,000
Yoshimi Niizeki	69	68	71	69	277	980,000
Masami Kawamura	73	69	67	69	278	708,000
Koichi Inoue	65	74	72	67	278	708,000
Satsuki Takahashi	69	67	71	71	278	708,000
Yoshinori Mizumaki	70	67	71	70	278	708,000
Koichi Suzuki	69	70	70	70	279	528,000
Taiichi Nakagawa	72	71	67	69	279	528,000
Yoshikazu Yokoshima	73	67	71	68	279	528,000
Akira Yabe	70	68	70	72	280	403,200
Koichi Uehara	70	72	72	67	280	403,200
Motomasa Aoki	70	68	70	72	280	403,200
Teruo Sugihara	69	71	70	70	280	403,200
Haruo Yasuda	68	71	71	70	280	403,200
Hisashi Suzumura	71	66	73	71	281	336,000
Takashi Murakami	72	70	68	71	281	336,000
Noboru Sugai	70	70	68	73	281	336,000
Toru Nakamura	68	67	71	75	281	336,000
Yoshihiko Nakata	71	71	71	68	281	336,000
Akiyoshi Omachi	75	68	71	68	282	308,000
Tadao Nakamura	71	71	70	70	282	308,000
Katsunari Takahashi	69	69	74	71	283	292,000
Tomishige Ikeda	72	66	71	74	283	292,000

Maruman Nihonkai Open

Katayamatsu Golf Club,
Par 72; 6,984 yards

August 21–24
purse, ¥50,000,000

	SCORES				TOTAL	MONEY
Masashi Ozaki	64	72	70	70	276	¥9,000,000
Saburo Fujiki	72	71	71	65	279	4,200,000

	SCORES				TOTAL	MONEY
Naomichi Ozaki	71	65	72	71	279	4,200,000
Lu Liang Huan	72	67	72	69	280	2,200,000
Hsieh Min Nan	71	71	72	66	280	2,200,000
Kikuo Arai	69	71	68	73	281	1,700,000
Futoshi Irino	67	72	70	72	281	1,700,000
Katsunari Takahashi	67	69	72	74	282	1,375,000
Hiroshi Oku	67	68	73	74	282	1,375,000
Hung Wen Neng	73	72	69	70	284	1,023,333
Yoshihisa Iwashita	67	76	72	69	284	1,023,333
Haruo Yasuda	70	70	76	68	284	1,023,333
Hajime Meshiai	72	68	70	75	285	750,000
Satsuki Takahashi	70	69	72	74	285	750,000
Hideto Shigenobu	69	72	72	72	285	750,000
Tsukasa Watanabe	72	72	67	74	285	750,000
Shigeru Uchida	69	74	72	71	286	580,000
Yasuhiro Funatogawa	70	70	71	75	286	580,000
Taiichi Nakagawa	71	70	72	74	287	457,500
Hisao Inoue	69	67	75	76	287	457,500
Nobuo Serizawa	72	73	72	70	287	457,500
Teruo Sugihara	70	69	75	73	287	457,500
Yoshinori Sasayama	71	72	69	75	287	457,500
Nobuhiro Yoshino	71	74	71	71	287	457,500
Chen Tze Ming	71	74	68	74	287	457,500
Katsuyoshi Tomori	70	74	72	71	287	457,500
Kazushige Kono	70	72	76	70	288	380,000
Koichi Suzuki	69	70	73	76	288	380,000
Nobumitsu Yuhara	73	70	70	75	288	380,000
Toshimitsu Kai	74	71	72	71	288	380,000
Toshiyuki Tsuchiyama	70	73	69	76	288	380,000

KBC Augusta

Kyushu Shima Country Club, Fukuoka
Par 72; 7,125 yards

August 18–31
purse, ¥42,000,000

	SCORES				TOTAL	MONEY
Isao Aoki	74	72	69	67	282	¥8,000,000
Masashi Ozaki	70	72	69	72	283	3,350,000
Masahiro Kuramoto	72	71	70	70	283	3,350,000
Nobumitsu Yuhara	70	68	76	71	285	1,366,000
Masaji Kusakabe	73	72	70	70	285	1,366,000
Chen Tze Ming	73	73	72	67	285	1,366,000
Kikuo Arai	74	73	71	70	288	1,000,000
Keiichi Kobayashi	74	73	70	71	288	1,000,000
Akira Yabe	74	70	74	70	288	1,000,000
Hsieh Min Nan	76	70	73	70	289	800,000
Yoshimi Niizeki	75	68	73	73	289	800,000
Katsunari Takahashi	73	73	73	70	289	800,000
Katsuji Hasegawa	73	76	70	70	289	800,000
Yoshikazu Yokoshima	72	75	76	66	289	800,000
Hajime Meshiai	72	76	70	72	290	606,000
Hiroshi Makino	75	75	73	67	290	606,000
John Mahaffey	74	71	73	72	290	606,000
Teruo Sugihara	71	73	75	72	291	525,000
Namio Takasu	79	71	71	70	291	525,000
Saburo Fujiki	70	71	79	72	292	438,000
Shinsaku Maeda	74	76	70	72	292	438,000

	SCORES				TOTAL	MONEY
Kinpachi Yoshimura	75	69	74	74	292	438,000
Koji Nakajima	76	72	72	72	292	438,000
Yoshinori Kaneko	76	70	71	75	292	438,000
Koichi Inoue	76	74	71	70	293	385,000
Graham Marsh	74	72	71	76	293	385,000
Satsuki Takahashi	75	75	72	71	293	385,000
Tomohiro Maruyama	70	77	74	72	293	385,000
Katsuyoshi Tomori	77	72	72	73	294	350,000
Akira Ishihara	72	79	71	72	294	350,000
Shigeru Noguchi	77	73	71	73	294	350,000

Kanto Open

Central Golf Club, East Course, Ibaraki Prefecture
Par 73; 7,262 yards

September 4–7
purse, ¥30,000,000

	SCORES				TOTAL	MONEY
Isao Aoki	72	69	70	68	279	¥6,000,000
Masashi Ozaki	71	68	74	67	280	3,000,000
Tsuneyuki Nakajima	72	77	69	65	283	1,800,000
Tateo Ozaki	70	74	73	69	286	1,200,000
Satoshi Higashi	72	75	72	68	287	1,000,000
*Koichi Nogami	73	71	71	72	287	
Koichi Suzuki	75	73	71	69	288	850,000
Shigeru Kawamata	72	70	74	72	288	850,000
Yoshihisa Iwashita	70	72	74	73	289	725,000
Kazushige Kono	72	74	71	72	289	725,000
Saburo Fujiki	76	72	67	75	290	590,000
Hsieh Min Nan	72	73	75	70	290	590,000
Motomasa Aoki	74	72	73	71	290	590,000
Pete Izumikawa	72	72	71	75	290	590,000
Naomichi Ozaki	73	70	74	74	291	456,000
Kikuo Arai	72	70	74	73	291	456,000
Takashi Murakami	70	70	75	76	291	456,000
Tsukasa Watanabe	73	72	74	72	291	456,000
Masami Kawamura	73	73	69	76	291	456,000
Nobumitsu Yuhara	73	70	75	74	292	370,000
Taisei Inagaki	74	75	74	69	292	370,000
Takashi Kurihara	75	74	72	71	292	370,000
Toru Nakayama	73	67	76	76	292	370,000
Tomishige Ikeda	75	74	72	71	292	370,000
Akiyoshi Omachi	74	71	72	76	293	335,000
Yoshimi Niizeki	73	76	70	74	293	335,000
Hajime Meshiai	72	76	76	70	294	310,000
Toshiharu Kawada	72	75	71	76	294	310,000
Takashi Iwai	75	68	72	79	294	310,000
*Tetsuo Sakata	71	74	77	72	294	
*Daisuke Serizawa	74	72	72	76	294	

Kansai Open

Rokko Kokusai Golf Club, Kobe
Par 72

September 4–7
purse, ¥20,000,000

	SOCRES			TOTAL	MONEY
Yoshiyuki Isomura	69	72	69	74	284	¥5,000,000
Shinsaku Maeda	73	70	71	73	287	1,633,333
Kazuo Yoshikawa	70	73	70	74	287	1,633,333
Yoshio Ichikawa	73	69	72	73	287	1,633,333
Hisai Inoue	72	71	71	74	288	900,000
Teruo Sugihara	69	72	74	74	289	750,000
Kazuo Kanayama	67	75	74	73	289	750,000
Toshimitsu Kai	71	75	70	75	291	525,000
Toshiharu Kusaka	74	72	74	71	291	525,000
Yoshiharu Harato	71	75	69	76	291	525,000
Keiichi Nagata	69	77	76	69	291	525,000
Akio Kanemoto	74	75	72	71	292	375,000
Tsuneo Uchida	74	70	70	78	292	375,000
Yoichi Yamamoto	72	76	71	74	293	237,500
Kosaku Shimada	73	68	74	78	293	237,500
Masakatsu Sano	76	70	77	70	293	237,500
Yukihiro Yamamoto	76	75	71	71	293	237,500
*Takahiro Nakagawa	74	75	69	75	293	
Hideo Hashimoto	74	72	73	75	294	200,000
Hisashi Terada	74	74	72	74	294	200,000
Kenji Tokuyama	73	73	70	78	294	200,000
Yasuo Sone	72	72	74	77	295	160,000
Akio Teramoto	70	79	75	72	296	160,000
Toshiharu Morimoto	74	76	70	76	296	160,000
Takeshi Kitadai	75	73	75	73	296	160,000
Koji Kobayashi	74	77	72	74	297	137,500
Ryozo Ishizu	74	76	75	72	297	137,500
Hiromitsu Yamane	74	74	72	77	297	137,500
Kiyotaka Okamoto	76	74	74	73	297	137,500
Yoshinori Sasayama	75	71	75	77	298	123,333
Takeshi Matsukawa	78	73	74	73	298	123,333
Hisashi Nakase	73	75	74	76	298	123,333

Hokkaido Open

Ishikarigawa Ebetsu Golf Club
Par 72

September 4–7
purse, ¥10,000,000

	SCORES			TOTAL	MONEY
Katsunari Takahashi	72	69	65	70	276	¥3,000,000
Kazuhiro Takami	74	68	71	70	283	1,500,000
Ryoichi Takamoto	72	74	72	68	286	1,000,000
Kesahiko Uchida	73	74	71	69	287	600,000
Mitsuyoshi Goto	70	69	77	72	288	450,000
Masaaki Fujii	73	72	77	67	289	400,000
Masanori Yoshimizu	76	75	69	71	291	
Satoshi Sudo	73	71	72	75	291	235,000
Koichi Uehara	70	75	72	74	291	235,000
Masakazu Sato	75	74	74	69	292	200,000
Toshiaki Nakamura	74	75	73	72	294	155,000

	SCORES				TOTAL	MONEY
Akihiko Kojima	77	73	70	74	294	155,000
*Kuniaki Kigawa	80	73	72	71	296	
Masaru Sato	74	74	73	76	297	130,000
Yoshiharu Takai	77	72	72	76	297	130,000
Mamoru Takahashi	79	73	78	67	297	130,000
Yoshitaka Igawa	77	75	70	75	297	130,000
*Seiji Takahashi	76	72	79	72	299	
*Mikio Komon	74	75	77	73	299	
Masaru Mori	72	78	75	74	299	100,000

Chu-Shikoku Open

Ube Country Club, Yamaguchi
Par 72; 6,847 yards

September 4–7
purse, ¥15,000,000

	SCORES				TOTAL	MONEY
Tadami Ueno	67	71	68	69	275	¥4,000,000
Masahiro Kuramoto	70	70	68	68	276	2,000,000
Nobuhiro Yoshino	70	67	73	71	281	708,000
Takashi Nakaya	70	69	73	69	281	708,000
Hideto Shigenobu	70	70	69	72	281	708,000
Mitoshi Tomita	64	76	71	70	281	708,000
Hironori Kato	71	71	70	69	281	708,000
Atsuo Suemura	73	69	69	70	281	708,000
Katsumi Hara	68	68	77	69	282	375,000
Hiroshi Tokunaga	68	71	73	70	282	375,000
*Toshihiro Matsumoto	71	71	69	73	284	
Kenji Sokame	69	72	72	71	285	300,000
Shigeru Yamada	72	71	71	71	285	300,000
Yoshikazu Sakamoto	72	71	71	71	285	300,000
Mitsuru Hara	70	71	70	74	285	300,000
Tsuyoshi Sato	75	70	73	69	287	180,000
Katsumasa Iwao	67	70	75	76	288	165,000
*Yukio Ozaki	70	69	77	72	288	
Koji Inaba	72	71	69	76	288	165,000
Yoshihiro Miyanaka	69	72	75	73	289	135,000
Mitsuhiko Masuda	73	71	73	72	289	135,000
Yasumi Okuda	69	77	70	73	289	135,000
Takamasa Miyata	75	74	67	73	289	135,000

Kyushu Open

Kagoshima Airport 36 Golf Club, Kagoshima Prefecture
Par 72

September 4–7
purse, ¥15,000,000

	SCORES				TOTAL	MONEY
Kinpachi Yoshimura	68	73	70	70	281	¥4,000,000
*Kiyotaka Oie	68	70	78	69	285	
Katsuyoshi Tomori	73	73	70	69	285	1,350,000
Noriichi Kawakami	69	70	74	72	285	1,350,000
Keiji Tejima	73	66	75	73	287	650,000
Tadashige Kusano	74	70	77	68	289	550,000
Tsugiomi Takita	74	73	70	73	290	425,000
Kazutaka Nagata	71	73	72	74	290	425,000

	SCORES				TOTAL	MONEY
Yusuke Sugitā	77	71	74	69	291	277,500
Kunio Koike	73	73	74	71	291	277,500
Yurio Akitomi	68	71	79	73	291	277,500
Chikara Nagata	73	71	75	72	291	277,500
Takamasa Sakai	74	73	74	71	292	185,000
Toshiya Shibutani	70	75	75	72	292	185,000
Yojiro Horiuchi	77	69	76	71	293	160,000
Atsushi Ikehara	72	74	76	71	293	160,000
*Toshihide Sonoda	72	71	76	74	293	
*Takehisa Shinozuka	73	75	77	69	294	
Tatsuya Shiraishi	72	76	73	73	294	135,000
Masuaki Nakamura	72	73	76	74	295	110,000
Norio Suzuki	74	72	74	75	295	110,000

Chubu Open

Nanzan Country Club, Aichi Prefecture
Par 72

September 4–7
purse, ¥15,000,000

	SCORES				TOTAL	MONEY
Eitaro Deguchi	71	68	71	71	281	¥4,000,000
Kakuji Matsui	71	71	71	71	284	2,000,000
Masami Ito	72	70	75	68	285	1,200,000
Masafumi Fujisaka	77	71	70	68	286	750,000
Takeshi Shibata	68	71	75	72	286	750,000
Toshihiko Kikuichi	75	71	69	72	287	550,000
Kazuaki Niwa	72	71	72	73	288	450,000
Toshiki Matsui	73	71	78	67	289	350,000
Akio Toyota	70	78	71	70	289	350,000
Tadao Nakamura	75	73	68	73	289	350,000
Teruo Nakamura	78	69	74	69	290	230,000
Hideaki Yamashita	77	71	70	72	290	230,000
Teruo Suzumura	70	76	74	71	291	185,000
Yutaka Suzuki	71	71	76	73	291	185,000
Tatsuo Ukai	73	77	71	71	292	155,000
Yoshihiro Nakamura	71	76	73	72	292	155,000
Masahiro Shioda	73	71	75	73	292	155,000
Katsuhiko Urata	70	73	75	74	292	155,000
*Yoshiaki Ono	72	73	73	74	292	
*Katsuji Miyamoto	73	74	76	70	293	
Masamitsu Oguri	74	73	75	71	293	120,000
Takuo Terashima	71	75	74	73	293	120,000
Hisashi Suzumura	70	72	77	74	293	120,000

Suntory International Open

Narashino Country Club, Chiba Prefecture
Par 72; 7,102 yards

September 11–14
purse, ¥60,000,000

	SCORES				TOTAL	MONEY
Graham Marsh	67	69	67	72	275	¥10,800,000
Isai Aoki	70	67	69	69	275	6,000,000
(Marsh defeated Aoki on first hole of sudden-death playoff.)						
Masashi Ozaki	66	71	69	70	276	3,480,000
Katsunari Takahashi	68	70	69	69	276	3,480,000

	SCORES				TOTAL	MONEY
Shigeru Noguchi	68	72	72	66	278	2,400,000
Tsuneyuki Nakajima	71	69	70	69	279	1,845,000
David Ishii	68	73	71	67	279	1,845,000
Saburo Fujiki	70	70	70	69	279	1,845,000
Terry Gale	66	72	73	68	279	1,845,000
Tateo Ozaki	68	74	73	65	280	1,228,000
Hajime Meshiai	68	70	68	74	280	1,228,000
Kinpachi Yoshimura	67	73	69	71	280	1,228,000
Satoshi Higashi	72	69	73	67	281	972,000
Motomasa Aoki	73	71	68	69	281	972,000
Masahiro Kuramoto	70	71	71	70	282	734,400
Hideto Shigenobu	71	72	69	70	282	734,400
Yoshimi Niizeki	70	72	70	70	282	734,400
Kazushige Kono	68	72	71	71	282	734,400
Masahiro Shioda	69	74	68	71	282	734,400
Nobumitsu Yuhara	68	71	70	74	283	576,000
Norio Suzuki	72	72	69	70	283	576,000
Atsushi Ikehara	70	73	71	69	283	576,000
Akiyoshi Omachi	70	73	73	68	284	504,000
Seiichi Kanai	71	71	69	73	284	504,000
Yoshihisa Iwashita	66	73	74	71	284	504,000
Toshiyuki Tsuchiyama	69	72	73	70	284	504,000
Jack Nicklaus	71	74	72	67	284	504,000
Koichi Suzuki	68	69	75	73	285	450,000
Koichi Uehara	73	71	70	71	285	450,000
Yoshiyuki Isomura	71	69	70	75	285	450,000
Tomohiro Maruyama	69	75	73	68	285	450,000

Ana Sapporo Open

Sapporo Golf Club, Sapporo
Par 72; 7,065 yards

September 18–21
purse, ¥50,000,000

	SCORES				TOTAL	MONEY
Masahiro Kuramoto	73	72	66	70	281	¥9,000,000
Isao Aoki	71	72	70	70	283	5,000,000
Koichi Suzuki	72	69	70	73	284	3,400,000
Masashi Ozaki	75	69	69	72	285	2,400,000
Yoshihisa Iwashita	73	73	72	68	286	2,000,000
Tateo Ozaki	73	70	70	74	287	1,800,000
Eitaro Deguchi	72	74	72	70	288	1,375,000
Seiji Ebihara	72	72	73	71	288	1,375,000
Shigeru Uchida	70	72	72	74	288	1,375,000
Terry Gale	73	73	69	73	288	1,375,000
Toru Nakamura	72	72	71	74	289	960,000
Hisataka Fujii	71	71	72	75	289	960,000
David Ishii	72	72	75	71	290	720,000
Hajime Meshiai	74	69	75	72	290	720,000
Kazushige Kono	75	72	73	70	290	720,000
Katsuji Hasegawa	75	71	72	72	290	720,000
Taisei Inagaki	72	71	77	70	290	720,000
Tsuneyuki Nakajima	71	74	72	74	291	560,000
Kuichi Tahira	75	71	74	72	292	520,000
Brian Jones	73	72	73	75	293	470,000
Yoshikazu Yokoshima	73	73	72	75	293	470,000
Chen Tze Ming	73	72	72	76	293	470,000
Norio Suzuki	77	72	71	73	293	470,000

	SCORES				TOTAL	MONEY
Akiyoshi Omachi	76	70	72	76	294	395,000
Hiroshi Ishii	71	69	78	76	294	395,000
Tsukasa Watanabe	71	73	72	78	294	395,000
Hiroshi Makino	73	76	70	75	294	395,000
Motomasa Aoki	72	72	72	78	294	395,000
Masahiro Shioda	75	73	73	73	294	395,000
Fujio Kobayashi	74	73	73	74	294	395,000
Kazuo Yoshikawa	72	69	80	73	294	395,000

Jun Classic

Jun Classic Country Club, Ogawa
Par 72; 7,082 yards

September 25–28
purse, ¥56,000,000

	SCORES				TOTAL	MONEY
Masashi Ozaki	69	72	68	70	279	¥10,080,000
Masahiro Kuramoto	70	70	67	73	280	5,600,000
Isao Aoki	70	71	70	70	281	3,808,000
Yoshimi Niizeki	69	67	76	71	283	2,688,000
David Ishii	71	73	72	68	284	1,648,000
Brian Jones	65	68	72	79	284	1,648,000
Nobumitsu Yuhara	71	73	71	69	284	1,648,000
Katsuji Hasegawa	72	73	69	70	284	1,648,000
Motomasa Aoki	69	70	73	72	284	1,648,000
Tsutomu Irie	69	69	74	72	284	1,648,000
Chen Tze Chung	72	70	72	70	284	1,648,000
Toru Nakamura	75	68	72	71	286	1,030,400
Hsieh Min Nan	75	71	68	73	287	873,333
Masahiro Shioda	73	73	71	70	287	873,333
Isao Isozaki	69	70	75	73	287	873,333
Koichi Suzuki	69	70	73	76	288	739,200
Hiroshi Makino	69	73	74	73	289	595,840
Yoshihisa Iwashita	73	70	73	73	289	595,840
Seiji Ebihara	71	71	74	73	289	595,840
Tsukasa Watanabe	66	73	72	74	289	595,840
Tatsuya Shiraishi	68	70	72	79	289	595,840
Yoshitaka Yamamoto	71	73	73	73	290	490,000
Taisei Inagaki	69	73	75	73	290	490,000
Norihiko Matsumoto	73	71	71	75	290	490,000
Takaaki Fukuzawa	73	74	69	74	290	490,000
Hideto Shigenobu	74	69	73	75	291	453,600
Seiichi Kanai	71	72	70	78	291	453,600
Teruo Sugihara	72	75	73	72	292	414,400
Kikuo Arai	73	73	74	72	292	414,400
Yoshikazu Yokoshima	70	73	71	78	292	414,400
Toyotake Nakao	73	71	74	74	292	414,400
Koji Ueda	74	73	71	74	292	414,400

Tokai Classic

Miyoshi Country Club, Miyoshi
Par 72, 7,102 yards

October 2–5
purse, ¥50,000,000

	SCORES				TOTAL	MONEY
Masahiro Kuramoto	68	69	65	69	271	¥9,000,000
Shinsaku Maeda	71	73	68	68	280	5,000,000

	SCORES				TOTAL	MONEY
Toshiharu Kawada	69	67	70	75	281	3,400,000
Graham Marsh	68	71	71	72	282	2,400,000
Nobumitsu Yuhara	72	71	71	69	283	2,000,000
Isao Aoki	73	68	74	69	284	1,616,666
Toshihisa Iwashita	73	70	72	69	284	1,616,666
Masashi Ozaki	75	63	73	73	284	1,616,666
Bernahrd Langer	72	72	74	67	285	1,150,000
Eitaro Deguchi	74	70	73	68	285	1,150,000
Hiroshi Makino	72	72	72	69	285	1,150,000
Chen Tze Chung	69	74	72	71	286	846,666
Dan Pohl	72	69	72	73	286	846,666
David Ishii	72	71	69	74	286	846,666
Tsutomu Irie	72	74	73	68	286	846,666
Hiroshi Ishii	74	71	73	69	287	635,000
Koichi Inoue	68	71	76	72	287	635,000
Ho Ming Chung	76	70	69	72	287	635,000
Motomasa Aoki	69	72	76	71	288	500,000
Teruo Nakamura	74	70	71	73	288	500,000
Teruo Sugihara	71	71	72	74	288	500,000
Toru Nakamura	76	70	71	72	289	426,666
Yoichi Yamamoto	71	70	76	72	289	426,666
Hideto Shigenobu	70	71	75	73	289	426,666
Hisao Inoue	73	72	70	74	289	426,666
Koichi Suzuki	68	75	71	75	289	426,666
Taisei Inagaki	73	73	74	69	289	426,666
Seiichi Kanai	75	68	74	73	290	352,222
Terry Gale	73	66	77	74	290	352,222
Katsunari Takahashi	72	70	74	74	290	352,222
Yoshitaka Yamamoto	72	71	73	74	290	352,222
Nobuhiro Yoshino	72	70	71	77	290	352,222
Katsuji Hasegawa	72	72	70	76	290	352,222
Tsukasa Watanabe	72	71	76	71	290	352,222
Yoshiyuki Isomura	72	73	75	70	290	352,222
Toshimitsu Kai	71	73	76	70	290	352,222

Japan Open Championship

Totsuka Country Club, West Course, Yokohama
Par 72; 7,066 yards

October 9–12
purse, ¥60,000,000

	SCORES				TOTAL	MONEY
Tsuneyuki Nakajima	70	73	72	69	284	¥10,000,000
Masashi Ozaki	71	71	74	69	285	5,000,000
Isao Aoki	74	68	72	71	285	5,000,000
Tateo Ozaki	73	73	71	69	286	2,750,000
Yoshiyuki Isomura	70	72	75	69	286	2,750,000
Hiroshi Ishii	69	71	75	72	287	2,200,000
Masahiro Kuramoto	68	74	78	68	288	1,800,000
Naomichi Ozaki	69	68	76	75	288	1,800,000
Nobumitsu Yuhara	72	70	73	73	288	1,800,000
Toru Nakamura	70	70	74	75	289	1,400,000
Yoshitaka Yamamoto	76	72	72	69	289	1,400,000
Chen Tze Chung	72	70	73	74	289	1,400,000
Chen Tze Ming	74	72	70	74	290	1,260,000
David Ishii	72	76	74	70	292	900,000
Shinsaku Maeda	73	71	74	74	292	900,000
Eitaro Deguchi	75	69	74	74	292	900,000

	SCORES				TOTAL	MONEY
Tsukasa Watanabe	73	72	75	72	292	900,000
Rodger Davis	73	76	74	69	292	900,000
Brian Jones	74	68	77	74	293	597,500
Katsunari Takahashi	73	73	73	74	293	597,500
Terry Gale	75	72	76	70	293	597,500
Pete Izumikawa	73	73	70	77	293	597,500
Hajime Meshiai	76	71	72	75	294	500,000
Kinpachi Yoshimura	70	75	74	75	294	500,000
Namio Takasu	74	71	76	73	294	500,000
Ikuo Shirahama	73	74	72	75	294	500,000
Tadao Nakamura	77	70	74	73	294	500,000
Kazuo Kanayama	72	75	76	71	294	500,000
Masami Kawamura	73	72	76	74	295	455,000
Stewart Ginn	73	73	76	73	295	455,000
Graham Marsh	71	75	76	74	296	415,000
Kazuo Yoshikawa	74	72	73	77	296	415,000
Shigeru Uchida	70	74	75	77	296	415,000
Yoichi Yamamoto	76	71	76	73	296	415,000
Teruo Nakamura	74	74	76	72	296	415,000
Taiichi Nakagawa	71	76	77	72	296	415,000
*Tsuyoshi Yoneyama	76	73	77	70	296	
Nobuhiro Yoshino	76	73	77	71	297	365,000
Masanobu Kimura	76	73	76	72	297	365,000
Lu Hsi Chuen	73	74	75	75	297	365,000
Takuo Tejima	72	73	81	71	297	365,000
Saburo Fujiki	74	72	77	75	298	325,000
Tsutomu Irie	71	75	79	73	298	325,000
Koichi Uehara	73	75	75	75	298	325,000
Lu Liang Huan	73	76	75	74	298	325,000
*Yoshihiro Itoh	75	74	77	72	298	
Hideto Shigenobu	72	75	79	73	299	280,000
Seiichi Kanai	73	71	77	78	299	280,000
Hiroshi Makino	77	72	78	72	299	280,000
Kikuo Arai	74	75	75	75	299	280,000
Shoji Kikuchi	76	70	80	73	299	280,000
Tadaaki Uehara	73	74	76	76	299	280,000

Polaroid Cup Golf Digest

Tomei Country Club, Susono
Par 71, 6,752 yards

October 16–19
purse, ¥60,000,000

	SCORES				TOTAL	MONEY
Tsuneyuki Nakajima	68	68	67	72	275	¥10,800,000
David Ishii	67	68	71	69	275	6,000,000
(Nakajima defeated Ishii in sudden-death playoff.)						
Tsukasa Watanabe	68	72	70	67	277	3,480,000
Taisei Inagaki	68	69	69	71	277	3,480,000
Akiyoshi Omachi	72	69	66	71	278	2,160,000
Yoshitaka Yamamoto	67	66	72	73	278	2,160,000
Futoshi Irino	69	69	69	71	278	2,160,000
Kikuo Arai	71	66	71	71	279	1,560,000
D. A. Weibring	71	66	70	72	279	1,560,000
Chen Tze Chung	72	66	73	68	279	1,560,000
Yoshimi Niizeki	70	67	70	73	280	1,200,000
Isao Aoki	69	70	73	69	281	978,000
Masahiro Kuramoto	71	68	67	75	281	978,000

	SCORES				TOTAL	MONEY
Graham Marsh	71	70	69	71	281	978,000
Namio Takasu	67	73	71	70	281	978,000
Eitaro Deguchi	70	70	71	71	282	702,000
Chen Tze Ming	70	72	69	71	282	702,000
Ikuo Shirahama	72	69	71	70	282	702,000
Tadao Sakashita	70	71	70	71	282	702,000
Saburo Fujiki	72	69	69	73	283	564,000
Hideto Shigenobu	68	69	72	74	283	564,000
Hajime Meshiai	70	69	70	74	283	564,000
Masahiro Shiota	71	73	69	70	283	564,000
Brian Jones	71	69	70	74	284	492,000
Yoshihisa Iwashita	70	69	75	70	284	492,000
Tadao Nakamura	67	70	72	75	284	492,000
Shigeru Uchida	69	73	72	70	284	492,000
Takenori Hiraishi	69	73	72	70	284	492,000
Nobumitsu Yuhara	71	71	74	69	285	427,200
Terry Gale	71	71	70	73	285	427,200
Seiichi Kanai	74	69	71	71	285	427,200
Katsuji Hasegawa	72	72	71	70	285	427,200
Pete Izumikawa	69	73	70	73	285	427,200
Taiichi Nakagawa	70	72	72	71	285	427,200

Bridgestone

Sodegaura Country Club, Chiba
Par 36-36 – 72; 7,121 yards

October 23–26
purse, ¥70,000,000

	SCORES				TOTAL	MONEY
Tateo Ozaki	71	67	68	70	276	¥12,600,000
Naomichi Ozaki	69	72	72	65	278	7,000,000
Scott Verplank	71	70	68	70	279	4,760,000
Shinsaku Maeda	77	67	67	69	280	3,080,000
Kikuo Arai	70	69	72	69	280	3,080,000
Tsuneyuki Nakajima	71	71	71	68	281	2,520,000
Kazushige Kohno	72	72	70	68	282	2,240,000
Brian Jones	73	70	71	69	283	1,925,000
Chen Tze Chung	70	70	75	68	283	1,925,000
Nobumitsu Yuhara	75	69	68	72	284	1,262,333
Saburo Fujiki	68	71	73	72	284	1,262,333
Katsunari Takahashi	75	69	72	68	284	1,262,333
Voshihisa Iwashita	68	68	74	74	284	1,262,333
Seiji Ebihara	75	70	72	67	284	1,262,333
Clarence Rose	72	70	72	70	284	1,262,333
Hajime Meshiai	73	66	70	77	286	819,000
Chen Tze Ming	72	75	69	70	286	819,000
Shigeru Uchida	74	69	74	69	286	819,000
Curtis Strange	73	70	71	72	286	819,000
Masashi Ozaki	77	70	71	69	287	658,000
Hiroshi Ishii	72	72	74	69	287	658,000
Isao Isozaki	74	70	67	76	287	658,000
Yurio Akitomi	72	73	71	71	287	658,000
Isao Aoki	70	74	72	72	288	581,000
Tsutomu Irie	74	72	68	74	288	581,000
Noboru Sugai	73	71	73	71	288	581,000
Kazuaki Yamamoto	76	70	73	69	288	581,000
Eitaro Deguchi	76	70	73	70	289	481,345
Hsieh Min Nan	71	72	73	73	289	481,345

	SCORES				TOTAL	MONEY
Yoshitaka Yamamoto	74	73	72	70	289	481,345
Pete Izumikawa	73	69	75	72	289	481,345
Yoshikazu Yokoshima	72	69	76	72	289	481,345
Kazuo Yoshikawa	73	71	72	73	289	481,345
Satsuki Takahashi	69	72	75	73	289	481,345
Tadao Nakamura	72	75	71	71	289	481,345
Shigeru Noguchi	71	76	74	68	289	481,345
Koji Nakajima	75	71	71	72	289	481,345
Yoshimi Watanabe	69	75	73	72	289	481,345
Teruo Sugihara	72	70	72	76	290	378,000
Hiroshi Makino	74	69	74	73	290	378,000
Namio Takasu	75	70	71	74	290	378,000
Masaji Kusakabe	74	73	70	73	290	378,000
Satoshi Higashi	74	72	69	75	290	378,000
Mitoshi Tomita	75	69	72	74	290	378,000
Nick Faldo	73	73	72	72	290	378,000
David Ishii	76	71	72	72	291	323,866
Masanobu Kimura	73	71	73	74	291	323,866
Hideyoshi Kikukawa	74	70	77	70	291	323,866
Masahiro Kuramoto	71	75	70	76	292	309,400
Hideki Kase	73	74	73	72	292	309,400

ABC U.S. vs Japan Team Matches

Sports Shinko Country Club, Kawanishi
Par 72; 6,822 yards

October 30–November
purse, ¥65,000,000

	SCORES				TOTAL	MONEY
Curtis Strange	67	68	72	64	271	¥13,000,000
Chip Beck	70	66	71	68	275	6,500,000
Tateo Ozaki	68	70	70	70	278	2,633,333
Mark O'Meara	70	73	69	66	278	2,633,333
Tsuneyuki Nakajima	71	70	68	69	278	2,633,333
Koichi Suzuki	65	66	73	75	279	1,900,000
Katsunari Takahashi	72	70	68	70	280	1,700,000
Corey Pavin	74	65	71	70	280	1,700,000
D. A. Weibring	71	68	72	69	280	1,700,000
Peter Jacobsen	70	71	71	69	281	1,500,000
Nobumitsu Yuhara	74	70	68	70	282	1,400,000
Naomichi Ozaki	73	67	73	70	283	1,250,000
Toru Nakamura	72	73	71	67	283	1,250,000
Seiichi Kanai	74	71	68	71	284	1,100,000
Hale Irwin	72	72	71	70	285	950,000
Bill Rogers	72	73	69	71	285	950,000
Donnie Hammond	77	71	71	68	287	800,000
Masahiro Kuramoto	79	70	69	71	289	700,000

TEAM RESULTS

U.S. 2,229 (566–554–565–544); JAPAN 2,236 (569–554–555–558). Best eight scores counted for each team each day.

Each U.S. player received ¥1,600,000, each Japanese player ¥800,000 in team competition.

Hiroshima Open

Hiroshima Country Club, Hiroshima
Par 72; 6,865 yards

November 6–9
purse, ¥40,000,000

	SCORES				TOTAL	MONEY
Toru Nakamura	68	68	71	65	272	¥7,200,000
Saburo Fujiki	67	68	70	67	272	4,000,000
(Nakamura defeated Fujiki on fourth hole of sudden-death playoff.)						
Tadami Ueno	73	66	69	69	277	2,720,000
Hideki Kase	66	71	72	70	279	1,920,000
Ikuo Shirahama	71	71	69	69	280	1,600,000
Seiji Ebihara	68	73	71	69	281	1,440,000
Yasuhiro Funatogawa	72	71	70	69	282	1,280,000
Masahiro Shiota	70	70	73	70	283	1,040,000
Nobuo Serizawa	71	71	71	70	283	1,040,000
Eiichi Itai	71	73	70	69	283	1,040,000
Noboru Sugai	73	71	68	72	284	736,000
Toshiharu Kawata	70	70	73	71	284	736,000
Yasuo Nukaga	69	70	73	72	284	736,000
Hideto Shigenobu	72	71	70	72	285	576,000
Chen Tze Ming	70	71	69	75	285	576,000
Fujio Kobayashi	70	73	73	69	285	576,000
Teruo Sugihara	69	67	72	78	286	448,000
Kakuji Matsui	71	73	70	72	286	448,000
Yutaka Suzuki	71	72	71	72	286	448,000
Yoshihisa Iwashita	69	74	71	74	288	369,000
Hiroshi Makino	71	73	73	71	288	369,000
Koichi Inoue	71	72	72	73	288	369,000
Yoshikazu Yokoshima	70	70	73	75	288	369,000
Mamoru Kondo	76	69	70	73	288	369,000
Yoshimi Niizeki	72	70	76	71	289	300,000
Kikuo Arai	70	74	71	74	289	300,000
Tsutomu Irie	76	70	71	72	289	300,000
Tadao Nakamura	72	72	72	73	289	300,000
Takashi Kurihara	69	73	72	75	289	300,000
Hiroshi Oku	75	70	71	73	289	300,000
Masami Kawamura	75	71	70	73	289	300,000
Takeshi Shibata	72	72	76	69	289	300,000
Kosaku Shimada	71	71	75	72	289	300,000
Seiichi Numazawa	72	69	71	77	289	300,000

Nissan Cup

Yomiuri Country Club, Tokyo, Japan
Par 36–36 – 72; 7,017 yards

November 6–9
purse, US$900,000
(¥144,000,000)

TEAM

THURSDAY

AUSTRALIA/NEW ZEALAND defeated UNITED STATES, 7–5.
Brian Jones tied with Payne Stewart, 69–69.
Ian Baker-Finch defeated Bob Tway, 67–69.
Hal Sutton defeated Rodger Davis, 67–70.

Graham Marsh defeated Dan Pohl, 67–70.
John Mahaffey defeated David Graham, 68–73.
Greg Norman defeated Calvin Peete, 68–72.

EUROPE defeated JAPAN, 7–5.
Ian Woosnam defeated Masashi Ozaki, 69–71.
Sandy Lyle defeated Nobumitsu Yuhara, 68–72.
Bernhard Langer defeated Tateo Ozaki, 68–74.
Nick Faldo tied with Tsuneyuki Nakajima, 68–68.
Naomichi Ozaki defeated Gordon J. Brand, 72–69.
Koichi Suzuki defeated Howard Clark, 67–70.

FRIDAY

EUROPE defeated UNITED STATES, 8–4.
Gordon J. Brand defeated Payne Stewart, 70–74.
Bob Tway defeated Ian Woosnam, 65–71.
Howard Clark defeated Dan Pohl, 67–69.
John Mahaffey defeated Nick Faldo, 68–72.
Sandy Lyle defeated Calvin Peete, 70–72.
Bernhard Langer defeated Hal Sutton, 66–69.

JAPAN defeated AUSTRALIA/NEW ZEALAND, 7–5
Naomichi Ozaki defeated Brian Jones, 68–74.
Nobumitsu Ozaki tied with Ian Baker-Finch, 69–69.
Koichi Suzuki defeated Rodger Davis, 69–72.
David Graham defeated Masashi Ozaki, 71–73.
Tsuneyuki Nakajima defeated Graham Marsh, 68–70.
Greg Norman defeated Tateo Ozaki, 69–70.

SATURDAY

EUROPE defeated AUSTRALIA/NEW ZEALAND, 7–5.
Bernhard Langer defeated Ian Baker-Finch, 70–72.
Nick Faldo defeated Graham Marsh, 71–73.
Rodger Davis defeated Gordon J. Brand, 69–71.
Howard Clark tied with Brian Jones, 72–72.
Sandy Lyle defeated David Graham, 68–69.
Greg Norman defeated Ian Woosnam, 71–74.

JAPAN defeated UNITED STATES, 7–5.
Masashi Ozaki defeated Dan Pohl, 69–71.
Payne Stewart defeated Koichi Suzuki, 68–71.
John Mahaffey defeated Tateo Ozaki, 69–73.
Nobumitsu Yuhara defeated Calvin Peete, 70–72.
Hal Sutton tied with Naomichi Ozaki, 70–70.
Tsuneyuki Nakajima defeated Bob Tway, 66–70.

  THREE-DAY POINT TOTALS: Europe 22, Japan 19, Australia/New Zealand 17, United States 14.

PLAYOFF FOR THIRD/FOURTH PLACES

AUSTRALIA/NEW ZEALAND defeated UNITED STATES, 11–1.
Rodger Davis defeated Bob Tway, 70–71.
Ian Baker-Finch defeated Dan Pohl, 67–71.
Brian Jones defeated Payne Stewart, 68–76.
Graham Marsh defeated John Mahaffey, 69–73.
Greg Norman defeated Hal Sutton, 68–72.
David Graham tied with Calvin Peete, 71–71.

FINAL

JAPAN defeated EUROPE, 8–4.
Naomichi Ozaki defeated Bernhard Langer, 67–68.
Ian Woosnam defeated Tateo Ozaki, 70–76.
Nick Faldo tied with Koichi Suzuki, 69–69.
Tsuneyuki Nakajima defeated Howard Clark, 68–70.
Masashi Ozaki defeated Gordon J. Brand, 72–73.
Sandy Lyle tied Nobumitsu Yuhara, 72–72.

TEAM PRIZE MONEY: JAPAN—$50,000 each; EUROPE—$30,000 each; AUS-TRALIA/NEW ZEALAND—$20,000 each; UNITED STATES—$15,000 each.

INDIVIDUAL

	SCORES				TOTAL	MONEY
Tsuneyuki Nakajima	68	68	66	68	270	$25,000
Bernhard Langer	68	66	70	68	272	18,000
Naomichi Ozaki	69	68	70	67	274	13,000
Ian Baker-Finch	67	69	72	67	275	9,000
Bob Tway	69	65	70	71	275	9,000
Koichi Suzuki	67	69	71	69	276	6,500
Greg Norman	68	69	71	68	276	6,500
John Mahaffey	68	68	69	73	278	4,333.34
Hal Sutton	67	69	70	72	278	4,333.33
Sandy Lyle	68	70	68	72	278	4,333.33
Graham Marsh	67	70	73	69	279	
Howard Clark	70	67	72	70	279	
Nick Faldo	68	72	71	69	280	
Rodger Davis	70	72	69	70	281	
Dan Pohl	70	69	71	71	281	
Nobumitsu Yuhara	72	69	70	72	283	
Brian Jones	69	74	72	68	283	
Ian Woosnam	69	71	74	70	284	
David Graham	73	71	69	71	284	
Masashi Ozaki	71	73	69	72	285	
Gordon J. Brand	72	70	71	73	286	
Payne Stewart	69	74	68	76	287	
Calvin Peete	72	72	72	71	287	
Tateo Ozaki	74	70	73	76	293	

Taiheiyo Club (Pacific) Masters

Taiheiyo Club, Gotemba Course
Par 72; 7,071 yards

November 13–16
purse, ¥80,000,000

	SCORES				TOTAL	MONEY
Yasuhiro Funatogawa	67	68	70	69	274	¥14,400,000
Larry Nelson	72	69	68	67	276	8,000,000
David Graham	69	70	68	70	277	5,440,000
Kenny Knox	72	65	71	70	278	3,520,000
Ian Woosnam	68	74	67	69	278	3,520,000
Yoshitaka Yamamoto	70	69	72	68	279	2,880,000
Chen Tze Chung	69	69	70	72	280	2,560,000
Gordon Brand	71	67	70	73	281	2,200,000

		SCORES			TOTAL	MONEY
Hiroshi Makino	74	67	70	70	281	2,200,000
Masashi Ozaki	67	68	73	74	282	1,500,000
Naomichi Ozaki	66	73	71	72	282	1,500,000
Yoshimi Niizeki	70	74	68	70	282	1,500,000
Hajime Meshiai	67	74	69	72	282	1,500,000
Toru Nakamura	69	71	75	67	282	1,500,000
Isao Aoki	71	67	71	74	283	1,104,000
Kazushige Kono	74	67	70	72	283	1,104,000
Tateo Ozaki	69	71	70	74	284	832,000
Nobumitsu Yuhara	71	74	71	68	284	832,000
Kikuo Arai	72	68	74	70	284	832,000
Hiroshi Ishii	71	71	72	70	284	832,000
Mike Reid	70	71	72	71	284	832,000
Jim Thorpe	73	70	70	71	284	832,000
Masaji Kusakabe	72	74	67	72	285	696,000
Futoshi Irino	71	72	70	72	285	696,000
Tsukasa Watanabe	73	72	71	70	286	664,000
Chen Tze Ming	73	72	71	70	286	664,000
Eitaro Deguchi	74	71	72	70	287	616,000
Ikuo Shirahama	72	70	68	77	287	616,000
Ove Sellberg	70	74	74	69	287	616,000
Ken Green	73	72	71	71	287	616,000
Seiichi Kanai	72	71	72	73	288	541,000
Yoshihisa Iwashita	72	69	70	77	288	541,000
Kinpachi Yoshimura	68	72	76	72	288	541,000
Koichi Inoue	70	75	71	72	288	541,000
Haruo Yasuda	73	71	70	74	288	541,000
Tom Kite	73	68	74	73	288	541,000
Masahiro Kuramoto	79	68	72	70	289	451,000
Katsuji Hasegawa	72	71	74	72	289	451,000
Motomasa Aoki	76	68	71	74	289	451,000
Tsutomu Irie	75	70	68	76	289	451,000
Yoshiyuki Isomura	72	70	74	73	289	451,000
Noboru Sugai	73	71	73	72	289	451,000
Toshiharu Kawada	72	71	75	71	289	451,000
Masanobu Kimura	73	72	72	72	289	451,000
Jose-Maria Olazabal	71	73	74	72	290	393,000
Teruo Sugihara	74	68	76	73	291	366,000
Koichi Suzuki	74	72	74	71	291	366,000
Hideto Shigenobu	71	75	70	75	291	366,000
Akira Yabe	72	68	75	76	291	366,000
Katsunari Takahashi	72	71	76	73	292	350,000
Tadami Ueno	70	76	71	75	292	350,000

Dunlop Phoenix

Phoenix Country Club, Miyazaki
Par 72; 6,993 yards

November 20–23
purse, ¥130,000,000

		SCORES			TOTAL	MONEY
Bobby Wadkins	69	73	67	68	277	¥23,400,000
Graham Marsh	67	73	68	70	278	13,000,000
Tsuneyuki Nakajima	67	70	69	74	280	8,840,000
Isao Aoki	72	69	71	69	281	6,240,000
Masashi Ozaki	69	71	69	74	283	5,200,000
Andy Bean	69	71	72	72	284	4,680,000
Ken Green	73	71	72	69	285	4,160,000

	SCORES				TOTAL	MONEY
Kikuo Arai	67	71	73	75	286	3,770,000
Tom Kite	75	71	71	70	287	3,380,000
Doug Tewell	67	73	74	74	288	2,795,000
Bob Tway	73	72	68	75	288	2,795,000
Seve Ballesteros	70	73	72	74	289	2,201,333
Larry Mize	72	72	71	74	289	2,201,333
Hiroshi Ishii	71	74	69	75	289	2,201,333
Yasuhiro Funatogawa	72	74	72	72	290	1,872,000
Tateo Ozaki	71	74	72	74	291	1,404,000
David Ishii	71	72	74	74	291	1,404,000
Tim Simpson	71	70	75	75	291	1,404,000
Ian Woosnam	72	74	73	72	291	1,404,000
Nobumitsu Yuhara	71	72	74	74	291	1,404,000
Naomichi Ozaki	70	75	73	73	291	1,404,000
Kenny Knox	69	74	74	74	291	1,404,000
Larry Nelson	74	74	70	74	292	1,131,000
Bob Murphy	71	75	72	74	292	1,131,000
Hideto Shigenobu	72	74	75	72	293	1,079,000
Brian Jones	74	75	73	71	293	1,079,000
Toshiharu Kawada	69	73	75	77	294	1,040,000
Tsukasa Watanabe	74	68	78	75	295	975,000
Motomasa Aoki	69	75	75	76	295	975,000
Ikuo Shirahama	71	74	76	74	295	975,000
Saburo Fujiki	72	77	74	72	295	975,000
Hiroshi Makino	71	68	78	79	296	889,200
Norio Suzuki	74	71	73	78	296	889,200
Koichi Suzuki	73	73	74	76	296	889,200
Hajime Meshiai	74	73	72	78	297	795,600
Seiji Ebihara	76	71	74	76	297	795,600
Tom Watson	73	76	76	72	297	795,600
Noboru Sugai	73	73	74	77	297	795,600
Namio Takasu	72	73	75	77	297	795,600
Tadami Ueno	69	74	79	75	297	795,600
Katsunari Takahashi	77	69	76	76	298	670,800
Katsuji Hasegawa	72	77	74	75	298	670,800
Sandy Lyle	71	74	77	76	298	670,800
Johnny Miller	70	77	74	77	298	670,800
Koichi Inoue	74	73	76	75	298	670,800
Yoshihisa Iwashita	74	75	71	78	298	670,800
Keiichi Kobayashi	74	75	74	76	299	580,320
Koichi Uehara	73	73	75	78	299	580,320
Akiyoshi Omachi	68	75	78	79	300	548,600
Ben Crenshaw	71	76	75	78	300	548,600
Yoshitaka Yamamoto	71	76	78	75	300	548,600
Joji Furuki	75	73	72	80	300	548,600
Kazushige Kono	73	71	78	78	300	548,600
Fujio Kobayashi	70	77	74	79	300	548,600

Casio World Open

Ibusuki Golf Club, Ibusuki
Par 72, 6,985 yards

November 27–30
purse, ¥85,000,000

	SCORES				TOTAL	MONEY
Scott Hoch	67	72	68	69	276	¥15,300,000
Jose-Maria Olazabal	69	69	70	74	282	8,500,000
Graham Marsh	64	70	74	76	284	5,780,000

	SCORES				TOTAL	MONEY
Ian Baker-Finch	70	69	72	74	285	3,513,333
Yoshihisa Iwashita	72	69	72	72	285	3,513,333
Bob Tway	70	71	77	67	285	3,513,333
Kenny Knox	71	70	73	72	286	2,592,500
David Ishii	74	71	71	70	286	2,592,500
Teruo Sugihara	75	73	70	69	287	1,697,166
Namio Takasu	67	71	76	73	287	1,697,166
Craig Stadler	72	68	76	71	287	1,697,166
Masashi Ozaki	70	72	71	74	287	1,697,166
Hubert Green	74	70	73	70	287	1,697,166
Tateo Ozaki	72	72	71	72	287	1,697,166
Sandy Lyle	69	72	76	71	288	1,008,666
Ian Woosnam	73	69	76	70	288	1,008,666
Shigeru Noguchi	71	71	74	72	288	1,008,666
Katsuji Hasegawa	73	70	72	73	288	1,008,666
Seiichi Kanai	74	72	72	70	288	1,008,666
Hiroshi Ishii	69	71	74	74	288	1,008,666
Masahiro Kuramoto	73	74	67	75	289	769,250
Yoshitaka Yamamoto	73	71	71	74	289	769,250
Isao Isozaki	69	72	76	72	289	769,250
Chen Tze Ming	73	67	76	73	289	769,250
Larry Mize	74	71	71	74	290	714,000
Naomichi Ozaki	71	72	75	73	291	688,500
Doug Tewell	74	71	73	73	291	688,500
Yasuo Nukaga	70	71	75	76	292	629,000
Kikuo Arai	71	71	75	75	292	629,000
Yoshimi Niizeki	70	71	75	76	292	629,000
Masaji Kusakabe	71	76	72	73	292	629,000
Chen Tze Chung	74	70	72	76	292	629,000
Fujio Kobayashi	72	75	74	72	293	561,000
Nobumitsu Yuhara	74	70	77	72	293	561,000
Isao Aoki	73	72	76	72	293	561,000
Noboru Sugai	72	71	75	75	293	561,000
Nobuo Serizawa	71	72	76	75	294	527,000
Tsukasa Watanabe	71	72	79	73	295	479,400
Tsuneyuki Nakajima	77	71	76	71	295	479,400
Hiroshi Makino	76	72	73	74	295	479,400
Scott Simpson	73	69	77	76	295	479,400
Hajime Meshiai	75	71	76	73	295	479,400
Masahiro Shioda	74	74	75	72	295	479,400
Kinpachi Yoshimura	72	71	81	72	296	405,960
Hsieh Min Nan	73	75	75	73	296	405,960
Yasuhiro Funatogawa	75	73	78	70	296	405,960
Toru Nakamura	73	72	75	76	296	405,960
Brian Jones	68	73	76	79	296	405,960

Japan Series

Yomiuri Country Club, Osaka (first 2 rounds)   December 3–7
Par 73; 7,078 yards

Yomiuri Country Club, Tokyo (final 2 rounds)   purse, ¥30,000,000
Par 72; 7,017 yards

	SCORES				TOTAL	MONEY
Toru Nakamura	70	70	66	69	275	¥8,000,000
Isao Aoki	69	69	67	72	277	5,000,000

	SCORES			TOTAL	MONEY
Masahiro Kuramoto	66	72	73	69	280	3,000,000
Masashi Ozaki	74	72	70	68	284	2,400,000
Tateo Ozaki	74	72	70	69	285	1,633,333
Saburo Fujiki	70	71	71	73	285	1,633,333
Katsunari Takahashi	72	77	70	66	285	1,633,333
Kikuo Arai	67	70	76	74	287	1,100,000
Shinsaku Maeda	73	72	72	72	289	950,000
Tsuneyuki Nakajima	75	72	73	71	291	850,000
Koichi Suzuki	76	74	68	74	292	750,000
Teruo Sugihara	71	74	75	73	293	675,000
Naomichi Ozaki	71	71	74	77	293	675,000
Nobumitsu Yuhara	77	75	70	72	294	600,000
Yasuhiro Funatogawa	74	80	68	74	296	550,000
Yoshiyuki Isomura	72	79	72	74	297	550,000

Daikyo Open

Daikyo Country Club, Onnason, Okinawa
Par 36–35 – 71; 6,445 yards

December 11–14
purse, ¥60,000,000

	SCORES				TOTAL	MONEY
Tateo Ozaki	69	69	69	70	277	¥10,800,000
Kikuo Arai	68	72	70	67	277	6,000,000
(Ozaki defeated Arai on third hole of sudden-death playoff.)						
Masahiro Kuramoto	74	66	69	69	278	3,480,000
Isao Aoki	70	65	71	72	278	3,480,000
Seiichi Kanai	69	69	72	69	279	2,280,000
Hsieh Min Nan	69	73	69	68	279	2,280,000
Eitaro Deguchi	72	66	75	67	280	1,920,000
Hajime Meshiai	68	73	68	72	281	1,560,000
Yoshikazu Yokoshima	71	67	72	71	281	1,560,000
Katsunari Takahashi	70	73	70	68	281	1,560,000
Toru Nakamura	69	70	72	71	282	1,062,000
Chen Tze Ming	72	69	69	72	282	1,062,000
Koichi Suzuki	72	69	72	69	282	1,062,000
Yurio Akitomi	71	70	69	72	282	1,062,000
Naomichi Ozaki	71	69	69	74	283	792,000
Hikaru Emoto	68	66	74	75	283	792,000
Yoshitaka Yamamoto	68	72	73	70	283	792,000
Nobumitsu Yuhara	71	70	74	69	284	648,000
Haruo Yasuda	74	68	69	73	284	648,000
Tadao Nakamura	68	70	73	74	285	600,000
Atsushi Ikehara	72	71	71	72	286	535,200
Tatsuya Shiraishi	70	70	72	74	286	535,200
Seiji Ebihara	68	68	72	78	286	535,200
Yoshimi Niizeki	68	73	72	73	286	535,200
Tsukasa Watanabe	73	69	74	70	286	535,200
Kazuo Yoshikawa	75	67	73	72	287	462,000
Katsuji Hasegawa	72	68	74	73	287	462,000
Yoshiyuki Isomura	71	72	70	74	287	462,000
Mamoru Kondo	73	70	69	75	287	462,000
Motomasa Aoki	68	71	75	73	287	462,000
Norikazu Kawakami	71	69	76	71	287	462,000